THE Building Christian English SERIES

Building

Christian English

Communicating Effectively

Grades 9 and 10

Book Two

Teacher's Manual

Rod and Staff Publishers, Inc.
P.O. Box 3, Hwy. 172
Crockett, Kentucky 41413

Telephone: (606) 522-4348

Acknowledgments

We are indebted first and most of all to God, whose blessing made possible the writing and publishing of this book.

We express gratitude to each one who was involved in this work. Bruce Good wrote the text. Samuel Hoover and Lester Miller illustrated the book. Marvin Eicher and Ernest Wine were the editors, and various other brethren were reviewers. We are also indebted to the teachers who used the material on a laboratory basis in their classrooms, as well as to numerous people who assisted along the way by providing finances, by encouraging those directly involved in the work, and by interceding in prayer for the work.

Various reference books were consulted in accomplishing this task, such as English handbooks, other English textbooks, encyclopedias, and dictionaries. For these too we are grateful. We have chosen to favor the more conservative schools of thought that are considered authoritative in correct English usage.

—The Publishers

Copyright 2001

by

Rod and Staff Publishers, Inc.
Crockett, Kentucky 41413

Printed in U.S.A.

ISBN 978-07399-0537-1
Catalog no. 12992.3

3   4   5   6   7   —   22   21   20   19   18   17   16   15   14   13

Table of Contents

(Stars indicate lessons on editing skills, writing style, or speaking style.)

Introduction 9

Chapter 1 Mechanics

1. Capitalization and End Punctuation 10
2. Commas..14
★ **3. Improving Your Writing Style, Part 1: Originality** 19
4. Colons, Semicolons, and Ellipsis Points 23
5. Quotation Marks and Italics 27
6. Dashes, Parentheses, Brackets, Apostrophes, and Hyphens....................31
★ **7. Improving Your Editing Skills, Part 1** 36
8. Chapter 1 Review 39

Chapter 2 Study Skills

9. Preparing to Study 42
10. Using the SQ3R Method 47
11. Developing the Art of Skimming 52
12. Taking Notes and Summarizing 56
★ **13. Improving Your Editing Skills, Part 2** 61
14. Outlining Written Material 64
15. Outlining the Life Story of a Bible Character: Finding the Main Ideas..........71
16. Outlining the Life Story of a Bible Character: Filling In the Details..................73
★ **17. Improving Your Speaking Style, Part 1: Eye Contact** 76
18. Chapter 2 Review 78

Chapter 3 Sentence Grammar

19. Complete Sentences and Sentence Skeletons...80
20. Sentence Complements 83
21. Retained Objects and Objective Complements 88
★ **22. Improving Your Writing Style, Part 2: Active Verbs** 92
23. Phrases and Clauses 96
24. Appositives and Independent Elements..100
25. Classes of Sentences 104
★ **26. Improving Your Editing Skills, Part 3** 108
27. Chapter 3 Review 111

Chapter 4 Writing an Expository Essay

28. Understanding an Expository Essay 114
29. Choosing a Limited Topic 119
30. Taking Notes for an Expository Essay 122
31. Organizing Your Material 125
32. Writing an Expository Essay ....12(

★ 33. Improving Your Editing Skills, Part 4 131
34. Proofreading an Expository Essay...133
35. Writing the Final Draft 134
36. Chapter 4 Review 141

Chapter 5 Glossary of Usage

37. Correct Word Usage, Part 1 144
38. Correct Word Usage, Part 2 148
★ 39. Improving Your Writing Style, Part 3: Active Voice 152
40. Correct Word Usage, Part 3 155
41. Correct Word Usage, Part 4 159
42. Correct Word Usage, Part 5 164
43. Correct Word Usage, Part 6 168
★ 44. Improving Your Editing Skills, Part 5 172
45. Correct Word Usage, Part 7 175
46. Correct Word Usage, Part 8 179
47. Chapter 5 Review 183

Chapter 6 Writing a Short Story

48. The Writer of a Story 186
49. The Message of a Story 189
★ 50. Improving Your Editing Skills, Part 6 198
51. The Structure and Elements of a Story 201
52. Characterization in a Story 206
53. The Point of View and Plot of a Story 210
54. Developing a General Plan for a Story 219
55. Planning the Details of a Story 221
56. Writing a Story 224
★ 57. Improving Your Speaking Style, Part 2: Voice Control 226
58. Chapter 6 Review 228

Chapter 7 Substantives

59. Identifying Nouns..232
60. Verbals and Clauses as Nouns 235
61. Plural and Possessive Nouns 241
62. Personal and Compound Personal Pronouns 246
63. Other Pronoun Classes 252
★ 64. Improving Your Writing Style, Part 4: Poetic Devices..257
65. Identifying Substantives 260
66. Chapter 7 Review 264

Chapter 8 Improving the Style of a Story

67. Make a Story Live 266
68. Keep the Action Flowing...272
69. Paint Descriptive Details 279
★ 70. Improving Your Editing Skills, Part 7 282
71. Proofreading and Rewriting a Story 285
72. Chapter 8 Review 287

Chapter 9 Verbs

73. Verbs and the Principal Parts of Verbs 290
74. Simple and Perfect Tenses..293
75. Moods of Verbs...298
76. Transitive and Intransitive Verbs 304
77. Forms of Verbs 308
78. Subject–Verb Agreement...312
★ **79. Improving Your Editing Skills, Part 8** 317
80. Chapter 9 Review 320

Chapter 10 Writing Description

81. Employing Descriptive Language 322
82. Selecting and Arranging the Details 325
83. Writing Description Within Other Compositions....................................328
84. Planning a Descriptive Essay 331
85. Writing a Descriptive Essay 334
★ **86. Improving Your Editing Skills, Part 9** 336
87. Proofreading and Rewriting a Descriptive Essay 339
88. Chapter 10 Review 340

Chapter 11 Modifiers

89. Recognizing Adjectives 342
90. Adjective Phrases and Clauses 346
91. Recognizing Adverbs..351
92. Recognizing Other Adverbs 355
93. Adverb Phrases and Clauses..359
★ **94. Improving Your Writing Style, Part 5: Sentence Rhythm**...........................364
95. Forms of Comparison for Modifiers 367
96. Chapter 11 Review 370

Chapter 12 General Reference Sources

97. Using a Dictionary 374
98. Using a Thesaurus 378
99. Using Reference Books of General Information.....................................384
★ **100. Improving Your Speaking Style, Part 3: Enthusiasm** 387
101. Using the Public Library 390
102. Understanding the Library Filing System 392
103. Using the Indexes of a Library 397
104. Chapter 12 Review 401

Chapter 13 Connecting Words, Interjections, and Idioms

105. Prepositions and Prepositional Phrases...404
106. Coordinating Conjunctions 408
107. Subordinating Conjunctions and Interjections 412
108. Idioms...416
★ **109. Improving Your Writing Style, Part 6: Review** 419
110. Chapter 13 Review 422

Chapter 14 Parliamentary Procedure

111. Introduction to Parliamentary Procedure 424
112. Fundamentals of Parliamentary Procedure 429
★ **113. Improving Your Editing Skills, Part 10**..435
114. Parliamentary Motions 438
115. Chapter 14 Review 443

Year-end Reviews

116. Final Review 1 446
117. Final Review 2 451
118. Final Review 3 454

Editing Sheet Answers

Lesson 7 ....T–458
Lesson 8, Parts A–E T–460
Lesson 13 ....T–462
Lesson 26 ....T–464
Lesson 33 ....T–466
Lesson 44 ....T–468
Lesson 50 ....T–470
Lesson 70 ....T–472
Lesson 79 ....T–474
Lesson 86 ....T–476
Lesson 113..T–478

Miscellaneous

Lesson 11, Part D T–480
Lesson 77, Part D T–482

Test Answers

Chapter   1 ....T–483
Chapter   2 ....T–486
Chapter   3 ....T–490
Chapter   4 ....T–494
Chapter   5 ....T–496
Chapter   6 ....T–498
Chapter   7 ....T–501
Chapter   8 ....T–504
Chapter   9 ....T–507
Chapter 10 ....T–509
Chapter 11 ....T–511
Chapter 12 ....T–513
Chapter 13 ....T–515
Chapter 14 ....T–517
Final..T–519

Index

Index..T–532

Introduction

New Features in Grades 9 and 10 of *Building Christian English*

Welcome to a new level in the study of English. In previous years of the *Building Christian English* series, you focused mainly on grammar—things like sentence structure and parts of speech. Now in Books One and Two, you will find several things that are different from the earlier books in the series.

One difference is that Books One and Two place a stronger emphasis on composition than the earlier books did. Instead of studying several lessons on grammar and then one on composition, you will have entire chapters on composition (alternating with chapters on grammar). The lessons in these chapters will give you practical help in effective listening, speaking, reading, and writing.

Another difference is that Books One and Two are parallel rather than consecutive. That is, Book Two does not build on Book One. Instead, each book reviews grammar concepts from grade 8 and previous years, and each book deals with different kinds of composition. For this reason, you may study either Book One or Book Two first, and grades 9 and 10 can be in the same English class.

A third difference is the three new kinds of lessons distributed throughout Books One and Two. They are called "Improving Your Writing Style," "Improving Your Speaking Style," and "Improving Your Editing Skills." These lessons will give you regular practice with writing, public speaking, and proofreading. In the writing and speaking lessons, the focus is on the style rather than the mechanics of a written or an oral presentation. That is, instead of teaching you how to gather and organize information, these lessons will teach you how to make your oral and written compositions more interesting and effective.

May God bless your study of English this year.

To the Teacher

English grammar is an objective, study-skills subject. In this *Building Christian English* series, the main emphasis through grade 8 is on grammar, and the book for each grade builds directly on the previous book.

In contrast to grammar, English composition is a more subjective study. The two books for grades 9 and 10 place a stronger emphasis on composition than the earlier books do. Moreover, the grammar lessons in these two books primarily review concepts from the previous books in the series. Therefore, the books for grades 9 and 10 are deliberately designed to be interchangeable. This also allows the combining of grades 9 and 10 for English class in a multigrade classroom.

The Pupil's Book

In these two books, many of the lessons on grammar and mechanics teach no new concepts; they merely review important facts in order to rivet them in the students' minds. These lessons often include little explanatory text. Some are written in a handbook style, and others have brief explanations with a few examples. Lessons that review more difficult concepts (introduced only in grade 7 or 8) do include detailed explanations and illustrations.

In the lessons on grammar and mechanics, most of the exercises include sufficient material for classwork and for written assignments. You can divide each set of exercises into equal parts by using the odd- or even-numbered exercises in class and assigning the others as written work. Both halves give complete coverage of the concepts in the lesson. For those exercises that do not divide in this way, a note in the teacher's guide alerts the teacher to that fact.

The composition lessons include detailed explanations and illustrations. The exercises in these lessons rarely divide as do those in the grammar and mechanics lessons.

Interspersed throughout this text are three new kinds of lessons: "Improving Your Writing Style," "Improving Your Speaking Style," and "Improving Your Editing Skills." These lessons are designed to give students regular practice in writing, public speaking, and proofreading. Generally, the writing and speaking lessons do not require much preparation time for the students. Their focus is on the style rather than the mechanics of a written or an oral presentation.

Each chapter ends with a review lesson covering the material taught in that chapter. The test booklet has a test for each chapter and includes the exercises for the lessons on "Improving Your Editing Skills." The proofreading exercises may be photocopied as needed.

The Teacher's Guide

Each lesson in the teacher's guide begins by stating the **Purpose** of the lesson. If the lesson introduces a concept that is new in this English series, that concept is marked with a star.

After the Purpose, most lessons have a part called **Teaching Suggestions.** This section includes additional information and comments about items that need special attention.

Each lesson ends with a section of **Answers** to the exercises in the pupil's book.

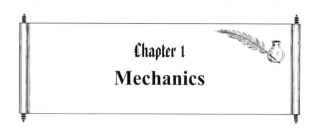

Chapter 1
Mechanics

1. Capitalization and End Punctuation

The mechanics of English relate primarily to the rules of capitalization and punctuation. Like road signs, these rules help a reader to understand where the road of thought turns, pauses, or stops.

Capitalization

1. *Capitalize the first word of every sentence, direct quotation, and line of poetry.*

   <u>M</u>y father says, "<u>D</u>on't count the minutes; just make the minutes count."

   <u>H</u>ave more than thou showest,
   <u>S</u>peak less than thou knowest.

2. *Capitalize all proper nouns.*
   a. Names of persons, including titles, abbreviations, and initials. Capitalize a title only if it is used as part of the name or in place of a name. Capitalize the word *president* when it refers to the current president of the United States.

   <u>D</u>r. <u>L</u>loyds
   <u>B</u>rother <u>R</u>obert; a faithful <u>b</u>rother
   <u>D</u>aniel <u>J</u>. <u>H</u>oover, <u>S</u>r.
   the <u>P</u>resident; former <u>p</u>residents

   b. Names that refer to God, and words that refer to the Bible or to parts of it. Also capitalize personal pronouns that refer to God.

   our <u>S</u>hepherd; the <u>s</u>hepherds of Palestine
   <u>P</u>salm 23; a beloved <u>p</u>salm
   the <u>P</u>entateuch
   the <u>M</u>ajor <u>P</u>rophets
   the <u>E</u>pistle of <u>J</u>ames; an <u>e</u>pistle

   c. Names of geographical features, such as rivers, lakes, and mountains; and of political units, such as cities, states, provinces, and nations. Capitalize words like *north* and *southwest* only when they name specific geographical regions, not when they name directions.

   <u>M</u>ount <u>R</u>obson; a high <u>m</u>ountain   <u>O</u>ntario
   came from the <u>S</u>outh; <u>s</u>outh of the equator   <u>B</u>razil

Lesson 1

Purpose: To review capitalization rules and the use of periods, question marks, and exclamation points.

Teaching Suggestions:

This lesson should require little teaching time or effort. Quite likely, your effort should be concentrated on the following points: *2a* (the use of *president*), *2c* (words like *north*), and *2h* (brand names and trademarks). In relation to Rule *2f*, you may want to remind students that underlining (italics) is used for the names of specific vehicles. This rule is taught in Lesson 5.

Remember that in grammar lessons, you can use the odd- or even-numbered exercises in class and assign the others as written work. Both halves give complete coverage of the concepts in the lesson.

d. Titles of stories, poems, songs, and publications. Capitalize the first and last words and other important words. Do not capitalize articles, coordinating conjunctions, and prepositions of fewer than four letters.

"Bring the Seekers In" (story)   *A Home for Grandma* (book)

e. Names of specific organizations, businesses, institutions, groups, races, and languages.

Glendale Mennonite Church   the United States Supreme Court
American Cancer Society   Africans and Europeans
Harris Plumbing and Heating   an Italian family

f. Names of specific ships, airplanes, trains, buildings, monuments, natural phenomena, and heavenly bodies.

the *Orient Express*   Saturn
the Washington Monument   Jupiter
Old Faithful (geyser)   Earth

Note: Capitalize *earth* only if you use it as a proper noun to name the planet on which we live. Omit the article *the* in such a case.

The next planet beyond Earth is Mars. (proper noun)
The surface features of Mars can be seen from the earth. (common noun)

g. Names of parks, historic sites, events, eras, and documents.

Sequoia National Park   the Reformation
the Flood   the Treaty of Versailles

h. Brand names and registered trademarks. Do not capitalize a common noun that follows the brand name or trademark, even if it is capitalized in a label.

Vicks cough drops   Toyota car
Holsum bread   Rockwell table saw

i. Names of school subjects derived from proper nouns or followed by numbers.

Canadian geography   Typing II   bookkeeping class

j. Calendar items, but not the names of seasons.

September   Ascension Day
Thursday   spring

3. *Capitalize most words derived from proper nouns.* A word may become so common that it is no longer capitalized. Check a dictionary if you are not sure.

Jewish customs   Alaskan winter   macadam road

4. *Capitalize the pronoun* I *and the interjection* O. The word *O* occurs mainly in poetry and in archaic English, such as that in the King James Bible. In modern prose,

it signifies a solemn appeal and always precedes a noun of direct address. Do not confuse *O* with the interjection *oh.*

> "Unto thee, <u>O</u> L<small>ORD</small>, will <u>I</u> sing."
> Stand firm for the right, <u>O</u> youth; <u>oh</u>, how the church needs faithful young people!

5. *Capitalize the greeting, closing, and signature of a letter.*

> <u>D</u>ear <u>S</u>irs:
>
> . . . .
>   <u>S</u>incerely,
>   <u>L</u>ouella <u>U</u>nruh

6. *Capitalize abbreviations of proper nouns and of many other common terms.* Check a dictionary or an English handbook when you are not sure.

> 9:15 <u>A</u>.<u>M</u>.   650 <u>B</u>.<u>C</u>.

End Punctuation

7. *Use a period after a declarative sentence, an indirect question, and an imperative sentence.*

> The Bible is God's unchanging Word<u>.</u>
> Some people actually question whether the Bible is true<u>.</u>
> Hold the Bible in highest reverence<u>.</u>

8. *Use periods with initials and with many abbreviations.* Common exceptions include the two-letter abbreviations for states and provinces and the abbreviations for organizations and government agencies. Check a dictionary or an English handbook when you are not sure. Avoid most abbreviations in formal writing.

> Mrs<u>.</u> Donna A<u>.</u> West   BC (British Columbia)
> 6 yd<u>.</u>   FDA (Food and Drug Administration)
> 8 bu<u>.</u>

9. *Use a question mark after an interrogative sentence or quotation.* For emphasis, you may use question marks between items in a series within an interrogative sentence.

> "Is it time for lunch already<u>?</u>" asked Warren.
> Have you read the entire lesson<u>?</u> answered all the questions<u>?</u> learned the memory verse<u>?</u>

10. *Use a question mark within parentheses to indicate uncertainty about the preceding information.*

> Abram Martin moved from the Jura Mountains <u>(?)</u> to Lancaster in 1725.

11. *Use an exclamation point after a strong interjection and after an exclamatory sentence or quotation.*

> "Behold<u>!</u> What a wonderful Saviour is Jesus<u>!</u>" declared Brother Amos.

Applying the Lesson

A. Write correctly each word or abbreviation that has a capitalization error.
1. our heavenly father tenderly cares for his children.
2. the lord has preserved the bible unto our generation.
3. Because the canaanites served false Gods, israel was commanded to destroy them.
4. Even in the days of the Apostles, many false Christs were trying to undermine the gospel.
5. For many years, New York city depended heavily on Ferries.
6. A dutchman named cornelis dircksen started the first ferry line between manhattan and brooklyn in 1638.
7. Cornelis lived on Manhattan island and ferried people across the east river to Brooklyn, where a fast-growing dutch settlement was located.
8. During the 1800s, the City swelled with european immigrants.
9. According to the october 1959 *american heritage,* scores of ferries served the Region by 1910.
10. Yes, i enjoyed the story "apple on my conscience" in aunt Norma's book *short stories and illustrations.*
11. A nabisco shredded wheat biscuit soaked in hot milk makes a delicious Breakfast on a chilly Winter morning.
12. Our neighbor bought a honda riding mower at White Corner equipment last saturday.
13. Yesterday i attended ascension day services at Mount Dillborn Mennonite church.
14. In closing, Brother Harvey said, "consider well, o Youth, that your present choices will deeply influence your future character."
15. In Science class, we discussed some recent discoveries about jupiter, as reported in the *daily times of Lockesburg.*
16. We had our first snow before thanksgiving day; by christmas, the snow was here to stay until Spring.
17. Yesterday the president announced that the head of the epa had resigned.
18. In our History class on monday, we learned about the treaty of ghent.
19. On our trip to visit my Grandparents in the south, we met a swiss family.
20. The president toured the northeast to see the damage inflicted by hurricane edna.
21. We saw a picture of the *allegheny climber* in *reminiscences of early trains.*
22. The Doctor gave father an informative pamphlet from the aha.
23. When grandfather prayed, he said, "help us to remember, o Lord, that our Christian Heritage is a priceless blessing."
24. Carlton's country market is running a special on mueller's noodles the Week of the nineteenth.

B. Copy each word that should be followed by end punctuation, and add the correct mark.
1. What a privilege it is to know a heavenly Father's care

Lesson 1 Answers

Applying the Lesson

A. 1. Our, Father, His
2. The, Lord, Bible
3. Canaanites, gods, Israel
4. apostles, christs, Gospel
5. City, ferries
6. Dutchman, Cornelis Dircksen, Manhattan, Brooklyn
7. Island, East River, Dutch
8. city, European
9. October, <u>American Heritage</u>, region
10. I, Apple, My, Conscience, Aunt, <u>Short, Stories, Illustrations</u>
11. Nabisco, breakfast, winter
12. Honda, Equipment, Saturday
13. I, Ascension Day, Church
14. Consider, O, youth
15. science, Jupiter, <u>Daily</u>, <u>Times</u>
16. Thanksgiving Day, Christmas, spring
17. President, EPA
18. history, Monday, Treaty, Ghent
19. grandparents, South, Swiss
20. President, Northeast, Hurricane Edna
21. <u>Allegheny Climber</u>, <u>Reminiscences, Early, Trains</u>
22. doctor, Father, AHA
23. Grandfather, Help, O, heritage
24. Country Market, Mueller's, week

B. 1. care!

2. Do you truly trust His care when peace rests on your life's sea when storms of trouble threaten to sink your ship of faith when undercurrents of temptations pull you toward the rocks of sin

3. "How thankful we can be that God will never forsake His children" declared Father

4. Curtis wondered why we often tend to worry rather than trust

5. "Do you suppose it's because we tend to look at ourselves too much and at God too little" Carol asked

6. "If only we could readily see the folly of trusting in ourselves" she mused

7. Can you name examples of self-confident people from the Old Testament from the New Testament from recent times

8. Gerald asked if King Asa was one such example

C. Write a correct abbreviation for each word or phrase.
1. United Parcel Service
2. before midday *(ante meridiem)*
3. page
4. Company
5. Monday
6. ounce
7. Pacific Standard Time
8. northeast
9. Alaska
10. miles per hour

Review Exercises

Copy each numbered word, and write the abbreviation for the part of speech that it is.

noun—n.	adjective—adj.	conjunction—conj.
pronoun—pron.	adverb—adv.	interjection—interj.
verb—v.	preposition—prep.	

Is the Sea of Galilee a sea [1]or a [2]lake? [3]Well, [4]since [5]this body of water is not part [6]of an ocean, geographers [7]actually classify [8]it as a lake. It is also [9]known as the Lake of Gennesaret and the Sea of Tiberias. [10]With its clear, [11]sparkling waters and its soft, balmy [12]breezes, [13]this is one of the [14]most beautiful lakes in the world. [15]Jewish [16]rabbis wrote long ago, "The Lord [17]created [18]seven seas, [19]but the Sea of Gennesaret is His [20]delight."

---

2. sea? faith? sin?
3. children! Father.
4. trust.
5. little? asked.
6. ourselves! mused.
7. Testament? Testament? times?
8. example.

C. (Answers will vary according to dictionaries used.)
1. UPS
2. A.M., a.m.
3. p.
4. Co.
5. Mon.
6. oz.
7. P.S.T., PST
8. NE
9. Alas., AK
10. m.p.h., mph

Review Exercises

1. or—conj.
2. lake—n.
3. Well—interj.
4. since—conj.
5. this—adj.
6. of—prep.
7. actually—adv.
8. it—pron.
9. known—v.
10. With—prep.
11. sparkling—adj.
12. breezes—n.
13. this—pron.
14. most—adv.
15. Jewish—adj.
16. rabbis—n.
17. created—v.
18. seven—adj.
19. but—conj.
20. delight—n.

2. Commas

1. *Use a comma before the coordinating conjunction that joins the clauses of a compound sentence.* (The common coordinating conjunctions are *and, but, or, for, nor, yet,* and *so.*) If the clauses are very short and closely related, you may omit the comma. If one or both of the clauses are long and already contain several commas, the comma between the clauses is often changed to a semicolon to make the division between the clauses more clear.

Youth is a time of great energy, but that energy must be directed properly.

Lesson 2

Purpose: To review rules for using commas.

Teaching Suggestions:

As with Lesson 1, this material should require little teaching. Be prepared, however, to clarify the following points.

(2*b*) You may want to emphasize more strongly the three tests given in the seventh and eighth grade books.

1. Do you pause between the adjectives as you read them?
2. Does it sound right to use *and* between the adjectives?
3. Does it sound right to change the order of the adjectives?

(4*a*) Previous books in this series taught only that nonrestrictive adjective *clauses* are set off with commas. This lesson broadens the principle to phrases and words as well. For both 4*a* and 4*b*, be sure the students can discern the difference between restrictive and nonrestrictive items.

Seek the Lord and He will direct you.
Three important virtues are faith, hope, and love; and of these three, love is
the greatest.

2. *Use commas to separate items in a series.*
    a. A series of words, phrases, or clauses. If a pair within the series is joined
by a conjunction (as *chicken and rice* in the second example below), no comma
is used between those two items. If a writer wishes to emphasize the number and
variety of the things listed, he may connect all the items with conjunctions and
omit the commas.

> Stephen mowed the lawn, trimmed the hedge, and washed the car.
> Mother suggested that Kathryn could make baked beans, chicken and rice,
> or pizza for lunch.
> Bethany cooed and squealed and laughed and waved as the children played
> with her.

    b. A series of descriptive adjectives that have equal rank. When two adjec-
tives have equal rank, (1) you generally pause as you read them, (2) you could
place *and* between them, and (3) you generally could switch their order. Sometimes
the adjective immediately before the noun is closely related to the noun (almost
like a compound noun) and should not be preceded by a comma.

> A crooked, gnarled apple tree stood forlornly beside the deserted shack.
>   (*Crooked* and *gnarled* have equal rank, but *apple* is closely related to
>   *tree*.)

3. *Use commas to set off certain introductory material.*
    a. Words of response and mild interjections.

> No, I did not know the answer.
> Oh, Velma has the dictionary now.

    b. Verbal phrases.

> Painted in large letters, the Gospel sign catches many people's attention.

    c. Long prepositional phrases or a series of prepositional phrases. Do not use
a comma, however, if a sentence has inverted word order.

> To the salt lick beside the brook, many deer come regularly.
> To the salt lick beside the brook come many deer.
>   (inverted word order—no comma)

    d. Adverb clauses.

> If we sit quietly behind these bushes, we should see a number of deer within
> an hour.

4. *Use commas to set off nonrestrictive and parenthetical elements.*
    a. Nonrestrictive words, phrases, and clauses used as adjectives. Whereas a
restrictive adjective limits the meaning of a substantive by telling *which one,* a

nonrestrictive adjective merely gives additional information. Because it is not needed to make the meaning of the sentence clear, it is set off with commas.

> Harlan and Wilmer, tired and thirsty, deserve a break.
>   (words are nonrestrictive—set off with commas)
> The boys <u>inside</u> are resting from their hard work.
>   (word is restrictive—no comma)

> Mabel, humming softly to herself, snapped the green beans.
>   (phrase is nonrestrictive—set off with commas)
> The girl humming softly to herself is Mabel.
>   (phrase is restrictive—no commas)

   b. Nonrestrictive appositives. Like an adjective phrase, an appositive is nonrestrictive if it merely gives additional information about the substantive it follows. It is restrictive if it is necessary to the meaning of a sentence and restricts that substantive. A restrictive appositive generally consists of only one or two words and is closely related to the substantive it follows.

> Paul, the apostle to the Gentiles, wrote many New Testament epistles.
>   (appositive is nonrestrictive—set off with commas)
> The apostle Paul wrote many New Testament epistles.
>   (appositive is restrictive—no commas)

   In the phrase "the apostle Paul," you may think *apostle* should be capitalized because it is a title. But consider that *the* does not normally come before a title of respect; "the Brother Paul" would not be correct. So "the apostle Paul" must be a phrase in which the noun *apostle* is followed by the appositive *Paul*.

   c. Titles of family relationship or of professional rank that follow names.

> Lloyd Smith, Jr., lives next door to us.
> Our family physician is Dr. George Wampler, M.D.

   d. Nouns of direct address.

> Clara, this pie is delicious!   Your answer, Lyle, makes a good point.

   e. Parenthetical expressions such as explanatory words, transitional expressions, and contrasting ideas.

> The truth of the matter, no doubt, will become known eventually.
> Furthermore, we know that God will settle all accounts.
> God's will, not public opinion, should govern our decisions.

5. *Use commas in certain conventional situations.*
   a. To separate the parts of addresses and dates.

> Route 4, Box 113
> Souderton, PA 18924
> September 9, 20—

On July 15, 2000, the Witmers moved to 5245 Snow Avenue, Akron, Ohio, to help with the church work there.

b. To separate large numerals into periods of thousands, millions, and so forth.

186,000 miles per second   4,122 people

c. To follow the greeting of a friendly letter and the closing of any letter.

Dear Aunt Lucy,   Sincerely yours,

d. To separate a direct quotation from the rest of the sentence unless some other punctuation is used.

"Gertie is quite a mischievous little goat," commented Sandra.
"It seems that every time we turn around," continued Alice, "she is finding a new kind of mischief."

6. *Use a comma if it is needed to prevent misunderstanding.* Only rarely should you use a comma that is not clearly required by one of the basic rules. Using too many commas is just as undesirable as omitting necessary commas.

This spring, housecleaning the church will be quite a task.
(comma needed to prevent reading *This spring housecleaning* as a phrase)

Applying the Lesson

A. Write the number and letter of the rule illustrated by each comma. If two commas have the same letter, one rule applies to that pair.
1. Hear us,[a] heavenly Father,[a] and grant us Thy blessing,[b] free and abundant.
2. Because we trust our heavenly Father's care,[a] our hearts are not filled with anxious,[b] unsettled thoughts.
3. Standing on the promises of God's Word,[a] we are truly secure,[b] for God's Word never changes.
4. Jesus Christ,[a] who endured strong temptations Himself,[a] is well able to understand,[b] comfort,[b] and strengthen those who are tempted today.
5. Francisco Gomez,[a] Juan's uncle,[a] was a gentle,[b] respectable man.
6. He was not,[a] however,[a] a Christian,[b] so we prayed daily for his salvation.
7. "After we helped him rebuild his fire-damaged house,[a] he started coming to church,"[b] Ramon recalled.
8. "Well,[a] sometimes God does use adversity to lead men to repentance,"[b] stated Aunt Dora.
9. In any event,[a] we all rejoice to see him serving the Lord,[b] desiring to be baptized,[b] and taking his place as a Christian father.
10. Around the outside of the cottage,[a] several flower beds,[b] Mrs. Stutzman's handiwork,[b] flaunt their rich colors and fragrances.
11. Inside,[a] the windowsills are loaded with flowers that are planted in the unique boxes built by Abraham M. Stutzman,[b] Sr.

12. Having admired his handiwork before,[a] I wonder,[b] Mrs. Stutzman,[b] how your husband did such good work despite his handicap.
13. On Uncle Laban's farm in Maryland,[a] migrant workers harvested 50,000[b] pounds of watermelons by August 1,[c] 20—.
14. Above,[a] the dark clouds rolled in threateningly as we entered the office of Malcolm S. Gruber,[b] M.D.,[b] of Fairview,[c] Alberta.

B. Copy each word or number with which a comma should be used, and put the comma where it belongs.
1. Yes God has blessed us abundantly but we are too often ungrateful.
2. From the Bible principles can be applied to every temptation every trial and every task.
3. By the power of the Gospel you can surely live consistently O youth.
4. If we cultivate a respectful outlook we can experience contrary to the ideas of many a truly satisfying relationship with those in authority.
5. Flourishing in the cooler ocean waters several species of Laminariales better known as kelp serve as a significant resource for man.
6. Growing as long as two hundred feet the giant kelp which grows only in the Pacific Ocean is the largest of the kelps.
7. Because the ocean waves and currents are constantly moving God has designed these large kelps with holdfasts rootlike structures that attach the kelp to the ocean floor.
8. The Japanese have gathered kelp for food for centuries and various kinds of kelp important resources yet today are still harvested in large quantities.
9. Kelp is used for example in manufacturing ice cream mayonnaise aspirin and skin lotions.
10. Well Cindy kelp is also used extensively as fertilizer and as a valuable concentrated source of iodine.
11. At our barn yards of concrete were poured on July 15 20— to make a smooth spacious holding area.
12. After five hours of driving we finally arrived at Uncle Glen's farm near Markham Illinois.

Review Exercises

Write correctly each word that should be capitalized. If no capital letter is needed, write *correct*. [1] (Turn to the lesson number in brackets if you need help.)
1. at rocky springs country store
2. a letter from aunt susan
3. for thy service, o lord
4. a french family from the west
5. a lutheran family at church
6. a large river of sandy valley
7. between spring and autumn
8. both spanish and typing II
9. my uncle's book, *in all things*
10. the edict of milan

12. a. 3b   b. 4d
13. a. 3c   b. 5b   c. 5a
14. a. 6   b. 4c   c. 5a

B. 1. Yes, abundantly,
   2. Bible, temptation, trial,
   3. Gospel, consistently,
   4. outlook, experience, many,
   5. waters, Laminariales, kelp,
   6. feet, kelp, Ocean,
   7. moving, holdfasts,
   8. centuries, kelp, today,
   9. used, example, (ice) cream, mayonnaise, aspirin,
   10. Well, Cindy, valuable,
   11. barn, 15, 20—, smooth,
   12. driving, Markham,

Review Exercises
1. Rocky Springs Country Store
2. Aunt Susan
3. Thy, O, Lord
4. French, West
5. Lutheran
6. Sandy Valley
7. correct
8. Spanish, Typing
9. In All Things
10. Edict, Milan

3. Improving Your Writing Style, Part 1: Originality

Originality
Active Verbs
Active Voice
Poetic Devices
Rhythm

You have had many lessons on writing with good content and organization. This is important, for writing must say something meaningful and say it logically if readers are to understand it.

But content and organization alone do not produce effective writing. How many times have you started to read something, decided it was not interesting, and laid it aside without finishing it? You can be assured that people will do the same thing with your writing if it fails to capture their interest. The challenge is to write in a way that gets and keeps the reader's attention.

How can we accomplish this? These lessons on writing style will give a number of helps for making our writing more interesting and enjoyable to read.

A major element of an effective and forceful style is ***originality.*** Do not always settle for the first thing that comes to your mind. Seek rather to be creative, to express your ideas in a way that is fresh, a way that the reader will enjoy. For example, in describing some unusually warm weather, you could write the following sentence.

> On July 15 the temperature reached 101 degrees, breaking a 75-year record.

This sentence expresses its thought clearly. Anyone who knows English should be able to understand it. But stop and think. Can you say this in a more appealing way, a way deliberately designed to be interesting? One writer stated it like this:

> On July 15 the temperature reached 101 degrees, melting a 75-year record.

To speak of *melting a record* is a surprising twist that we can hardly fail to notice—and enjoy. As a matter of fact, heat does generally melt things rather than break them! And whether a record is *broken* or *melted,* it no longer stands. By the skillful choice of one unusual word, the writer has stated his point in a way that sparks our interest.

Here is another example to consider.

> By the end of the hike, my knees were aching terribly.

Most of us have experienced something like this. If our knees were not aching, then our feet or ankles were. We understand the sentence clearly. Now compare the following way of saying the same thing.

> By the end of the hike, my knees were begging for relief.

Which way of writing carries more force? Most people will agree that the second example is more interesting. To say that knees are begging for relief clearly conveys the agony felt by the writer. His knees did not beg with words, of course, but they did beg with cries of pain. We enjoy this kind of writing because the writer has given careful thought to expressing himself creatively.

In your effort to be creative, be careful that you do not merely use descriptive phrases that most people have heard before. The following sentence has a phrase like that.

> I felt uncomfortable because he was watching me like a hawk.

Lesson 3

Purpose: To introduce *the lessons on writing style, and to emphasize *originality as an element of creative writing.

Teaching Suggestions:

Of the elements of effective writing style selected for these lessons, originality is the most abstract. Matters like active verbs, active voice, and so forth can be pinpointed specifically. "Here is a verb that shows no action." "Here is a verb in the passive voice." Deciding when an expression is worn out with use is harder. Determining what is merely a normal, everyday expression is harder yet.

Part of the reason is that originality hinges not so much on certain words or phrases as on the general tone of an entire composition. Perhaps it is also partly because originality cannot be forced; as stated in the lesson, it must flow "from an active, imaginative mind."

Take ample time to discuss the original expressions in the lesson, and compare them with their less appealing counterparts. Also explain the evaluation chart and exactly how you intend to grade the students' work in these lessons.

Hawks have extremely keen eyesight, and to speak of *watching like a hawk* is quite descriptive. However, we have heard this phrase so many times before that it now lacks the force that it once had. A phrase like this is a ***cliché*** (klē·shā′). You have heard many such expressions.

> <u>After all is said and done</u>, Jeremy usually accomplishes more than Curvin does.
> With diligent application, my scores improved <u>by leaps and bounds</u>.
> Your hands are <u>as cold as ice</u>.
> Eleanor proved quite <u>equal to the occasion</u>.

Clichés are common in speech, when people have little time to think of original expressions. But in writing you usually have plenty of time to express yourself creatively. Put that time to good use, and let your readers enjoy the results.

In striving for originality, you need to beware of two pitfalls. One of these is the temptation to step over the bounds of propriety. You must never stoop to using slangy expressions or expressions that treat sacred subjects lightly or irreverently. This kind of originality cheapens your work and weakens its power to convey a worthwhile message.

The other pitfall is to try so hard to be original that your writing sounds strained. If a student writes expressions that he would consider too pretentious for speech, he has probably fallen into this trap. You do not need to write something unusual in every other sentence. Originality is truly effective only when it flows from an active, imaginative mind.

No originality:
> The June sun shone brightly through the hazy sky as we slowly picked strawberries. In the heat we sweated profusely.

Strained:
> The June sun blazed relentlessly through the hazy gases that surrounded us and the strawberry beds. As we slowly advanced down the extensive rows, our faces were drowned in oceans of perspiration. The salty substance caused burning sensations as it poured down our faces and necks.

Creative:
> The June sun beat us mercilessly as we inched down the long strawberry rows. With rivers of sweat coursing down our necks, we writhed along under its lashes.

For these lessons on writing style, you will write various compositions that your teacher will likely evaluate by using the chart below. The element introduced in this first lesson is *Originality,* so this assignment will be evaluated only for that point of emphasis. The element introduced in the next writing style lesson will be *Active Verbs,* and then you will be evaluated on both originality and active verbs.

Each of the third through fifth writing style lessons will introduce another point of emphasis, and each will add one more item to the number of points on which your writing is evaluated. The last lesson is a review of the five elements of effective writing style.

Evaluation of Writing Style

Part		Points of Emphasis			
	Originality	*Active Verbs*	*Active Voice*	*Poetic Devices*	*Sentence Rhythm*
1.	———	....	....	....	....
2.	———	———	....	....	....
3.	———	———	———	....	....
4.	———	———	———	———	....
5.	———	———	———	———	———
6.	———	———	———	———	———

G = Good   **F** = Fair   **P** = Poor

Now read the following sample compositions. Especially compare the underlined words in the first one with the way the same thought is expressed in the second one. Can you appreciate the originality that is evident in the second composition? Do you see how a writer's thought and effort can greatly improve the style of his composition?

Perils Among the Poles

Lacks originality:

Our pole lima beans were <u>bearing a very heavy crop</u>. Father was away for a meeting in another state. Mother was caring for baby Brian, and the older boys were busy in the fields. That meant that I, the only girl in the family, <u>had to pick those beans all alone</u>! Even before nine o'clock, the air was shimmering with heat waves. I sighed as I glanced at all those <u>big bean tepees standing around me in the garden</u>.

Already <u>tired of the boring job</u>, I reached down to pick some fat beans near the ground. A warty toad, <u>disturbed from its position</u> under the leaves, hopped across my hand. I jumped but sighed with relief as it hopped out of sight.

<u>After picking from a few more stalks</u>, I reached into a spider web, nearly touching a big black spider. The spider <u>disappeared</u>.

Illustrates originality:

Our pole lima beans were <u>bearing quite well—too well, it seemed to me</u>. Father was away for a meeting in another state. Mother was caring for baby Brian, and the older boys were busy in the fields. That meant that I, the only girl in the family, <u>was stuck in the bean patch by myself</u>! Even before nine o'clock, the air was shimmering with heat waves. I sighed as I glanced at all those <u>bean tepees standing like green giants around me</u>.

Already <u>aching with the monotony of the job</u>, I reached down to pick some fat beans near the ground. A warty toad, <u>surprised from its hideout</u> under the leaves, hopped across my hand. I jumped but sighed with relief as it hopped out of sight.

<u>A few stalks later</u>, I reached into a spider web, nearly touching a big black spider. The spider <u>quickly retreated</u>. I shuddered

(Lacks originality)

I shuddered and stifled a scream. <u>I did not pick any more beans on that part of the stalk!</u>

I had barely <u>moved away</u> from that spider when I felt something land on my shoulder. Turning my head, <u>I saw a big grasshopper</u>. My bucket flew out of my hand as I swatted the ugly thing away.

For a while I picked beans in peace. The sun bore down hotter and hotter. My back <u>ached</u>. The shade of the big oak tree <u>was a very inviting sight</u>. Then I spotted a praying mantis, almost invisible on a green stalk. Fascinated, I watched it slowly swivel its triangular head. But the beans were waiting to be picked, so I reluctantly left the praying mantis <u>behind</u>.

My job was almost finished when I had the worst fright of all. I thrust my head into a tepee to <u>see if any beans were in there</u>. Suddenly I <u>saw a beady-eyed garter snake</u>! With a terrified screech, I jumped back, landing right on top of my bucket. <u>I did not pick any more beans on that stalk either!</u>

After I had finally circled the last tepee, I pulled the wagonload of beans over to the back yard. What a relief to <u>sit down under that old oak</u>!

(Illustrates originality)

and stifled a scream. <u>The beans on that part of the stalk stayed right there for the spider!</u>

I had barely <u>escaped</u> from that spider when I felt something land on my shoulder. Turning my head, <u>I found myself eye to eye with a great green grasshopper</u>. My bucket flew out of my hand as I swatted the ugly thing away.

For a while I picked beans in peace. The sun bore down hotter and hotter. My back <u>cried for relief</u>. The shade of the big oak tree <u>beckoned invitingly</u>. Then I spotted a praying mantis, almost invisible on a green stalk. Fascinated, I watched it slowly swivel its triangular head. But the beans were waiting to be picked, so I reluctantly left the praying mantis <u>to guard that tepee</u>.

My job was almost finished when I had the worst fright of all. I thrust my head into a tepee to <u>find any beans hiding there</u>. Suddenly I <u>was peering into the beady eyes of a garter snake</u>! With a terrified screech, I jumped back, landing right on top of my bucket. <u>The beans still on that stalk ripened some more too!</u>

After I had finally circled the last tepee, I pulled the wagonload of beans over to the back yard. What a relief to <u>gain the safety of that old oak</u>!

Applying the Lesson

Write a composition of 150–200 words, telling about an interesting experience you had this past summer. Can you incorporate originality and creativity that will make your writing interesting to read? Do your best!

Lesson 3 Answers
(Individual work.)

4. Colons, Semicolons, and Ellipsis Points

Colons

1. *Use a colon to separate the numbers in Scripture references and in expressions of time.*

> Ecclesiastes 12:1   3:45 P.M.

2. *Use a colon after the salutation of a business letter.*

> Dear Sir: Gentlemen: Dear Mr. Irvington:

3. *Use a colon to introduce something that is to follow.* What follows may be a list, an explanation, a question, an appositive, or a formal quotation. In this use, the colon is a literary arrow: it points to the information that follows, directing the reader's attention there.

> Our congregation has scheduled street meetings on the following dates: June 3, July 1, and August 5.
> Our street meetings serve one basic purpose: spreading the Gospel.

If a complete sentence follows a colon, that sentence may begin with a capital letter, especially if it is long.

> Many ask a simple but profound question: Who are you people, and why do you dress as you do?

A formal quotation is a notable statement made by a respected or high-ranking person. If it is introduced by a colon, it must be written with quotation marks and proper capitalization.

> Calvin Coolidge made this worthwhile statement: "There is no dignity quite so impressive and no independence quite so satisfying as living within your means."

The words before a colon must express a complete thought. Therefore, a colon should never separate a verb from its complement or a preposition from its object.

> **Incorrect:**
> The electric eel lives in rivers of: Peru, Colombia, Brazil, and Venezuela.
> **Correct:**
> The electric eel lives in rivers of Peru, Colombia, Brazil, and Venezuela.
> **Correct:**
> The electric eel lives in rivers of the following countries: Peru, Colombia, Brazil, and Venezuela.

Semicolons

4. *Use a semicolon to join independent clauses in certain cases.*
   a. When no conjunction is used.

> More than half of an electric eel's body contains organs that produce electricity; the snakelike creature can deliver a powerful charge.

Lesson 4

Purpose: To review the uses of colons, semicolons, and ellipsis points.

Teaching Suggestions:

The breaks marked by colons and semicolons are greater than those for commas but smaller than those for periods. These marks occur mostly in formal writing of a technical or scholarly nature; they are not very common in informal writing or in a free, easily readable writing style. For that reason, some of the sentences used as examples and exercises may strike you as somewhat stiff, unnatural, or hard to follow. On the other hand, our students should know how to use these marks; they do fill an important place in writing.

b. When a conjunctive adverb is used.

> No other fish can deliver a greater electric shock; indeed, it produces enough electricity to turn on eleven 100-watt light bulbs.

c. When commas are already used in one or more of the clauses. Sometimes either a comma or a semicolon is correct, depending on the degree of separation intended by the writer.

> With a discharge of over six hundred volts, the electric eel can paralyze humans; [*or* humans,] yet neither the eel itself nor other eels suffer any apparent effects.

5. *Use a semicolon to separate items in a series when individual items contain commas.*

> On our trip we visited Uncle Seth Krahn, Mother's oldest brother; Calvin Witmer's family; and Wayne Nolt's family.

Ellipsis Points

6. *Use ellipsis points to show an omission within a quotation.* Such an omission may be desirable when space is limited or when the omitted words do not apply specifically to the subject under discussion. But you need to guard against changing the meaning of a quotation by a careless omission. And you must *never* change the meaning deliberately by omitting certain words.

Original:
> And be not conformed to this world: but be ye transformed by the renewing of your mind, that ye may prove what is that good, and acceptable, and perfect, will of God. [Romans 12:2]

Unacceptable quotation:
> "And be not conformed to this world: . . . that ye may prove what is that good, and acceptable, and perfect, will of God."
> (May suggest that merely being different from the world, without an inner change, is God's will.)

Acceptable quotation:
> "And be not conformed to this world: but be ye transformed, . . . that ye may prove what is that good, and acceptable, and perfect, will of God."

When omitting words within a sentence, you may choose to retain or omit the punctuation immediately before or after the omission. If you retain punctuation, place it directly after the first part (before the ellipsis points). Study the following example, which shows three possible ways to punctuate the same quotation.

Original:
> Do violence to no man, neither accuse any falsely; and be content with your wages. [Luke 3:14]

Quotations:

"Do violence to no man,... and be content with your wages."
(comma retained)

"Do violence to no man;... and be content with your wages."
(semicolon retained)

"Do violence to no man... and be content with your wages."
(no punctuation retained)

When you quote two sentences and omit the ending of the first sentence, place the appropriate end punctuation directly after the first part if it makes a complete sentence. Then use ellipsis points to show the omission, and continue with the quotation.

Original:

Wherefore the king said unto me, Why is thy countenance sad, seeing thou
art not sick? this is nothing else but sorrow of heart. Then I was very
sore afraid. [Nehemiah 2:2]

Quotation:

"Wherefore the king said unto me, Why is thy countenance sad?... Then
I was very sore afraid."

Do not use ellipsis points at the beginning or end of a quotation. Remember: Ellipsis points indicate an omission *within* a quotation. They are not necessary at the beginning or the end.

Incorrect quotations:

"Wherefore the king said unto me, Why is thy countenance sad...?"
"... Why is thy countenance sad...?"

Correct quotations:

"Wherefore the king said unto me, Why is thy countenance sad?"
"Why is thy countenance sad?"
(No ellipsis points are needed even though the beginning and ending of
the verse are omitted.)

7. *Use ellipsis points to indicate that a sentence trails off without a proper ending.* Do not use any end punctuation with these ellipsis points.

Well, the kitchen floor still needs to be mopped, but...

Applying the Lesson

A. Write the number and letter of the rule illustrated by each colon, semicolon, or set of ellipsis points. If two marks have the same letter, one rule applies to that pair.
1. "Lay up...[a] treasures in heaven," our permanent home;[b] but while you sojourn on this earth, be a good steward of material possessions.
2. After giving His model prayer, Jesus emphasized one point: forgiveness.
3. The Lord's Prayer, as we commonly call it, gives us an important pattern for prayer; Jesus surely did not intend that it be repeated meaninglessly.

Lesson 4 Answers

Applying the Lesson

A. 1. a. 6   b. 4c
   2. 3
   3. 4a

4. "Not every one that saith . . .ᵃ Lord, Lord, shall enter into the kingdom of heaven";ᵇ indeed, many in our day profess to know the Lord but deny Him by their lives.
5. Grandmother must take these pills at the following times:ᵃ before breakfast, at 2:00ᵇ P.M., and at bedtime.
6. On Sunday we had visitors from the following places:ᵃ West Liberty, Kentucky;ᵇ Versailles, Missouri;ᵇ and Columbiana, Ohio.
7. Someone must have left the gate open, and now . . .
8. After being off for over four hours, our electricity came on at 5:20 P.M.
9. The teachers at our school are Sister Ada Mae Hoover, grades 1–3; Sister Betty Zehr, grades 4–6; and Brother Alvin Yoder, grades 7–10.
10. The snow is falling very thickly now;ᵃ Father must have . . .ᵇ

B. Copy each word or number with which there is a punctuation error. Place the correct mark where it belongs, or omit the unnecessary mark.
   1. The doldrums, vast areas of the ocean near the equator, have little wind, so early sailors, who depended on wind power, feared these regions.
   2. Sometimes ships drifted aimlessly in the doldrums for weeks until
   3. Man conquered the doldrums when ocean travel was changed by one major invention, the steam engine.
   4. The doldrums form where the trade winds on the two sides of the equator meet, the winds are forced upward, leaving the area below calm.
   5. The sun shone brightly, however, a brisk north wind kept the temperature cool.
   6. Heavy snow fell during the morning hours, moreover, by 200 P.M. a strong wind began to blow.
   7. We had expected Grandpa's to arrive by 430 P.M., but since it's 600 now, we
   8. Mr. Lawson has orders for chairs on: Monday, June 16, Wednesday, July 16, and Friday, August 15.
   9. The only people named in the Bible as lifelong Nazarites were: Samson, a judge of Israel, Samuel, another judge, and John the Baptist, the forerunner of Christ.
   10. Because God is all-wise, He can best choose the way for us, and because He is all-gracious, He can choose the best way for us.

C. Copy these quotations, using ellipsis points correctly to indicate omissions.
   1. "But he that is an hireling seeth the wolf coming, and leaveth the sheep" (John 10:12).
   2. "Looking unto Jesus; who for the joy that was set before him endured the cross" (Hebrews 12:2).
   3. "And the LORD said unto Cain, Why art thou wroth? If thou doest well, shalt thou not be accepted?" (Genesis 4:6, 7).
   4. "His name shall endure for ever: all nations shall call him blessed" (Psalm 72:17).

4. a. 6   b. 4b
5. a. 3   b. 1
6. a. 3   b. 5
7. 7
8. 1
9. 5
10. a. 4a   b. 7

B. 1. wind;
   2. until . . .
   3. invention:
   4. meet;
   5. brightly;
   6. hours;   2:00
   7. 4:30 P.M.;   6:00   we . . .
   8. on   16;   16;
   9. were   Israel;   judge;
   10. us;

C. 1. "But he that is an hireling . . . seeth the wolf coming, and leaveth the sheep" (John 10:12).
   2. "Looking unto Jesus; . . . who for the joy that was set before him endured the cross" (Hebrews 12:2).
   3. "And the LORD said unto Cain, Why art thou wroth? . . . If thou doest well, shalt thou not be accepted?" (Genesis 4:6, 7).
   4. "His name shall endure for ever: . . . all nations shall call him blessed" (Psalm 72:17).

Review Exercises

For each underlined word, write *yes* or *no* to tell whether it should be followed by a comma. [2]

1. Our <u>thoughts</u> the source of our conduct, must be guarded with <u>strict</u> constant care.
2. In your <u>mind</u> set patterns of thinking become <u>entrenched</u> and strongly affect your entire life.
3. "Consider carefully, dear <u>friend</u> what the quality of your thoughts reveals about your <u>character</u>" Brother Fred exhorted.
4. If we fill our minds with good <u>thoughts</u> we can develop the noble <u>character</u> that pleases God.
5. <u>Lo</u> God provides for us through His Word, His <u>Spirit</u> and His people.

————————————

5. Quotation Marks and Italics

Quotation Marks

1. *Enclose a direct quotation in quotation marks.* In a divided quotation, capitalize the second part only if it begins a new sentence.

> "Standing firmly for what you know is right," observed Father, "is not always the easiest thing to do."
> "But it is always the right thing to do," added Mother. "And God will surely bless you if you have a good purpose of heart."

In a quotation of more than one paragraph, place quotation marks at the beginning of each paragraph. Do not place quotation marks at the end of a paragraph, except the last one.

2. *Enclose a quotation from a printed source in quotation marks.*

> In *Doctrines of the Bible,* Daniel Kauffman writes, "The tempter has hard work making inroads into the lives of those who habitually wrestle with God in prayer."

If a quotation is long, it may be printed in smaller type as an indented block without quotation marks.

3. *Enclose the title of a minor work in quotation marks.* Minor works include songs, short stories, sections of books, and poems less than book length. Generally, a comma is unnecessary before such a title.

> In the book *Selections for Oral Reading,* I especially enjoyed the story "Strange Tracks on the Hill" and the poem "Winter Winds."

4. *Use single quotation marks for a quotation within a quotation.* For the rare

Review Exercises

1. yes, yes
2. yes, no
3. yes, yes
4. yes, no
5. yes, yes

Lesson 5

Purpose: To review the use of quotation marks and italics.

Teaching Suggestions:

Rule 5 is new as well as a bit arbitrary. What one writer calls into question, another may not. Be sure to emphasize the note following number 5. For this use, it is better to omit some quotation marks that might be permissible than to use quotation marks too freely.

occasion when another quotation occurs within the inner quotation, use another set of double quotation marks.

> "The apostle Paul could declare, 'I have learned, in whatsoever state I am, therewith to be content,'" commented Brendon.
> "I think I heard Wanda say, 'I like the other tune of "Jesus, Lover of My Soul" better,'" said Dorothy.

5. *You may use quotation marks to enclose an expression you wish to call into question.* If you use *so-called,* however, do not also use quotation marks.

> Apostate churches often try to cover up their disobedience to the Scriptures with "spiritual" activities.
> Apostate churches often try to cover up their disobedience to the Scriptures with so-called spiritual activities.

Be careful not to overuse quotation marks for this purpose. They tend to make writing look cluttered.

Other Punctuation With Quotation Marks

6. *If a quotation is followed by a comma or period, place that mark inside the quotation marks.*

> "For reading class on Monday," said Brother James, "practice reading the poem 'A Fence or an Ambulance.'"

Note this exception to the rule above: If a reference follows a quotation from a written source, place the reference in parentheses after the quotation marks, and place the comma or period after the parentheses.

> "The Lord is risen indeed" (Luke 24:34), and we rejoice in the salvation that He has wrought.

7. *If a quotation is followed by a colon or semicolon, place that mark outside the quotation marks.*

> When life goes smoothly, we can easily pray, "Thy will be done"; when life is full of difficulty, however, that prayer becomes much more difficult.

8. *If a quotation is followed by a dash, a question mark, or an exclamation point, place that mark inside the quotation marks if it applies to the quotation, and outside the quotation marks if it applies to the whole sentence.*

> Suddenly James shouted, "Watch those top bales!"
> (The exclamation point applies to the quotation.)
> Did Fanny Crosby write the words to "Safe in the Arms of Jesus"?
> (The question mark applies to the whole sentence, not to the quotation.)
> Jesus said, "Blessed are the poor in spirit"—a direct contrast to human philosophy. (The dash applies to the whole sentence, not to the quotation.)

9. *If a sentence contains a quotation within a quotation, place the question mark or exclamation point with the part of the sentence that is a question or an exclamation.*

> "Was Mother saying, 'Dinner is ready'?" asked Elton.
>> (The inner quotation is not a question, so the question mark is outside the single quotation mark. But Elton's words are a question, so the question mark is inside the double quotation marks.)
> "Was Mother asking, 'Are you ready for dinner?'" asked Elton.
>> (Both the inner quotation and Elton's words are questions, so the mark is inside both the single and the double quotation marks.)

Italics

Italics are not actually punctuation marks. But since they help us to communicate clearly, they are part of the mechanics of English just as capitalization and punctuation are. In handwritten or typewritten material, italics are indicated by underlining.

10. *Use italics for the title of a major work.* Major works include books, newspapers, pamphlets, book-length poems, and periodicals such as church papers, magazines, and newsletters. Italicize and capitalize an article (*a, an, the*) when it begins a book title, but not when it begins the title of a newspaper or periodical.

> For my birthday, Grandfather gave the book *The Valley Between*.
> I was inspired by the article "Lord, Teach Us to Pray" in the *Christian Contender*.
>> (not *The Christian Contender,* even though that is the actual title of this periodical)

11. *Use italics for the specific name of a ship, an airplane, a train, or another vehicle.*

> Our veterinarian, Dr. Jansen, calls his van the *Vet Express*.
>> (*The* is usually not part of the specific name.)

12. *Use italics for a word, phrase, letter, number, or symbol that is the subject of discussion.* Such an item is not being used in its normal sense, but is being discussed as a word, phrase, letter, or other symbol.

> Your *e* is so tall that this word looks more like *quilt* than *quiet*.
> When you use *for example* as a parenthetical element, set it off with commas.
> The *#* symbol can mean "pounds."

13. *Italicize foreign words that have not been adopted into the English language.*

> The common abbreviation *e.g.* comes from the Latin words *exempli gratia*.

14. *You may occasionally use italics for emphasis.* Use italics sparingly for this purpose; otherwise, they will lose their effectiveness.

> You must *learn to study* before you can *study to learn*.

Applying the Lesson

A. If the underlined part of the sentence has a punctuation error, write it correctly. If it is correct, write *correct.*

1. "Have you considered Jesus' words, 'Out of the abundance of the heart the mouth speaketh?'" asked Brother Dale.
2. "How wonderful that we can say, 'The Lord is my helper!'" declared Mother.
3. Brother Lavern said, "Let's practice the slurs in 'All Hail, Immanuel!'"
4. "Plutarch said, 'Nothing is cheap which is superfluous, for what one does not need, is dear at a penny,'" quoted Father.
5. Many things are promised to "him that overcometh:" hidden manna, a white stone with a new name, and other rewards.
6. Jesus plainly taught, "Swear not at all"; therefore, we refuse to give a legal oath.
7. Charles Wesley, who wrote thousands of hymns, wrote "A Charge to Keep I Have".
8. "Did Mr. Griggs ask, 'Will you folks come back to sing for us again'?" asked Mae.
9. William exclaimed, "What a shock to hear the man shout, 'Get out of here!'"
10. "I want you to read the story 'Is That All'?" said Martha.
11. "Jeremy Taylor wrote to be proud of learning is the greatest ignorance,'" said Sister Arlene.
12. You should meditate on the words of "Love and Help Each Other."

B. Copy the words with which there are errors in the use of punctuation or italics (underlining), and put the missing marks where they belong. Do not punctuate words as a direct quotation unless the sentence has explanatory words.

1. Have you read the chapter The Bible in Doctrines of the Bible? asked Mark.
2. This Christian nation is actually notorious for its evil.
3. The Christianity preached by many is a disgrace to the Name of Christ.
4. Did you think about it, Aaron, asked Brother Stoltzfus that you repeated the word and four times in this sentence?
5. The motto of Arizona is ditat Deus, meaning "God enriches."
6. The Bible clearly teaches that God created the world ex nihilo (out of nothing).
7. The second syllable in respite rhymes with fit.
8. The book I am reading, Insect Parables, has an intriguing chapter titled The Maker of Ping-Pong Balls.
9. The first Mennonite immigrants to the Lancaster area noted Grandfather arrived in Philadelphia on September 22, 1710, aboard the Maria Hope.
10. My cousins named their rowboat the Cocalico Cruiser.

Review Exercises

Write correctly each word that should be capitalized. If no capital letter is needed, write *correct.* [1]

1. to the gateway arch last summer
2. saw the president in washington

Lesson 5 Answers
Applying the Lesson

A. 1. speaketh'?"
   2. helper'!"
   3. correct
   4. correct
   5. overcometh":
   6. correct
   7. Have."
   8. again?'"
   9. correct
   10. All?'"
   11. wrote, 'To
   12. correct

B. 1. "Have   'The Bible' Doctrines of the Bible?"
   2. "Christian"
   3. "Christianity"
   4. "Did Aaron," Stoltzfus, "that and sentence?"
   5. ditat Deus
   6. ex nihilo
   7. respite   fit
   8. Insect Parables "The Maker of Ping-Pong Balls."
   9. "The area," Grandfather, "arrived Maria Hope."
   10. Cocalico Cruiser

Review Exercises
1. Gateway Arch
2. President, Washington

3. the poem "an answer to the cry"
4. saw chinese foods in wan's grocery
5. with father and my uncle
6. bought knapp shoes and some stanley tools
7. went west to the living desert state park
8. mr. watt of memphis, tenn.
9. visited a province farther east
10. science in the dark ages

3. An, Answer, Cry
4. Chinese, Wan's Grocery
5. Father
6. Knapp, Stanley
7. Living Desert State Park
8. Mr. Watt, Memphis, Tenn.
9. correct
10. Dark Ages

---

6. Dashes, Parentheses, Brackets, Apostrophes, and Hyphens

Dashes

1. *Use a dash to show a sudden interruption or change in thought.*
   a. A sudden break in thought.

   "What do you think—well, I sure didn't expect that!" exclaimed Brent.

   b. Parenthetical matter that is abrupt or that has commas within it.

   I like to use *The Treasury of Scripture Knowledge*—a thorough cross-reference resource—when studying Scripture verses.
   If you want to know the original meaning of a Bible word, check *Strong's Exhaustive Concordance*—widely recognized as a thorough, dependable reference book.

   c. Interrupted speech. Ellipsis points can also indicate interrupted speech. Ellipsis points suggest hesitancy or uncertainty; a dash shows abruptness.

   "Did you hear what—" Galen stopped, remembering his resolve to avoid gossip.

Parentheses

2. *Use parentheses to enclose a parenthetical element that is relatively unimportant.*

   My parents lived near Mercersburg (James Buchanan's birthplace) for several years.

Note: Commas, dashes, and parentheses are all used to set off parenthetical elements. You must choose which to use according to the meaning you want to convey.
   a. Commas make the parenthetical element a part of the sentence. Therefore, they cannot set off elements that are complete sentences or that have other punctuation. Of these three marks, commas are by far the most common in normal writing.

   Amigo, our mixed-breed dog, certainly earns his keep around our farm.

Lesson 6

Purpose: To review the use of dashes, parentheses, brackets, apostrophes, and hyphens.

Teaching Suggestions:

Most of the rules in this lesson are simple to understand and should be familiar to your students. Be prepared, however, to spend sufficient time discussing the differences between commas, dashes, and parentheses for setting off parenthetical elements.

Note on Rule 11f: In printed material, an en dash is used instead of a hyphen when a prefix is added to an open compound. For example, *anti-Biblical* requires a hyphen, but *pre–Civil War* requires an en dash.

b. Dashes sharply emphasize the parenthetical element. Sometimes they set off an exclamation or a question.

> Amigo—an outstanding cattle dog—certainly earns his keep around our farm.
> Amigo—what an outstanding cattle dog he is!—certainly earns his keep around our farm.

c. Parentheses minimize the importance of the parenthetical element, making it somewhat beside the point of the sentence.

> Amigo (someone dropped him off here when he was a puppy) certainly earns his keep around our farm.

3. *Use parentheses to enclose supplementary or illustrative matter, such as a Scripture reference or a short explanation.*

> "Can two walk together, except they be agreed?" (Amos 3:3).
> We looked in the Franklin County (Georgia) Courthouse for information.
> This issue of the *Christian Pathway* (June 15, 1997) has a story that challenges us to be kind to mentally handicapped people.

4. *Use parentheses to enclose figures or letters used for enumeration within a sentence.* If letters are used for this purpose, they should be italicized.

> We had these writing assignments during the past six weeks: (1) a story for English class, (2) a report for history class, and (3) a report on a book from the required reading list.

Brackets

5. *Use brackets to enclose a comment or correction within a quotation.*

> On the need for growth, Edward Gibbon wrote, "All that is human must retrograde [go backward] if it do not advance."

6. *Use brackets as parentheses in material already enclosed by parentheses.*

> Thailand (formerly known as Siam [sī·am′]) covers an area of 198,247 square miles.

7. *Learn the correct use of other punctuation marks with dashes, parentheses, and brackets.*

a. If a dash ends a sentence fragment, omit any end punctuation.

> "What was—" Father dashed out the door as Jonathan screamed in pain.

b. Place other punctuation marks inside these marks if they apply to the enclosed matter, and outside if they apply to the whole sentence.

> We certainly enjoyed the picnic (it was your father's idea, wasn't it?) that we had beside the pond. (question mark inside parentheses because the enclosed matter is a question)

What do you plan to do about the situation (if the report is really true)?
(question mark outside parentheses because the whole sentence is a question)

Apostrophes

8. *Use an apostrophe to form the possessive case of a noun or an indefinite pronoun.* For specific rules and examples, see Lessons 61 and 63.

9. *Use an apostrophe to show an omission in a contraction or other shortened form.* Contractions are acceptable for informal writing, such as friendly letters and the dialogue in stories. You should generally avoid them in formal writing.

isn't   we're   o'clock   a '96 yearbook

10. *Use an apostrophe to form the plural of a letter, a figure, an abbreviation followed by a period, or a word used as the subject of discussion.* No apostrophe is needed in the plural form of a number with several digits or of an abbreviation with several capital letters (1900s, POWs). Remember to italicize (underline) such an item when it is the subject of discussion, but do not italicize the *'s.*

Change the *&*'s to *and*'s and remove the *etc.*'s.
Your essay has too many *then*'s and *so*'s.
The COs had no Th.D.'s, but they knew the Bible well.

Hyphens

11. *Use a hyphen to join some compound words.* Pay special attention to the following groups of compound words.

a. Compound number words from twenty-one through ninety-nine.

forty-two   three hundred ninety-nine

b. A fraction written in words. (A hyphen joins the numerator and denominator unless either one already has a hyphen.)

one-fifth   twenty-one hundredths   two and two-thirds cups

c. Words ending with *-in-law.*

mother-in-law   brother-in-law

d. Compound words beginning with *great-* that refer to relatives, those beginning with *self-*, and many beginning with *all-*.

great-uncle   self-contained   all-knowing God

e. Many compound adjectives, in which two or more words form a unit that modifies a substantive.

a four-lane highway   a bad-tempered dog

f. A proper noun or adjective with a prefix.

inter-Caribbean trade   anti-Biblical

12. *In a series of hyphenated adjective–noun combinations, with the noun included in only the last one, use a hyphen after each adjective.*

    fifty- or sixty-hour weeks   two-, five-, and ten-pound bags

13. *Use a hyphen to divide a word between syllables at the end of a line.* Observe these three rules: (1) divide only between syllables, (2) never leave a single letter at the beginning or end of a line, and (3) divide a hyphenated word only at the existing hyphen. The following words illustrate permissible divisions.

    def-i-ni-tion   iden-ti-cal   cu-rio

14. *Use a hyphen to show a series of connected numbers, as in Scripture references or dates.*

    Romans 12:1–3, 9–16   1921–1987

Applying the Lesson

A. Copy enough words to show where commas, dashes, parentheses, and brackets are needed, and add the missing marks. Some sentences have notes telling you how to treat the parenthetical elements.
1. The Ten Commandments God Himself gave them to man express timeless principles. (sharp emphasis)
2. The principles of the Ten Commandments which are not directly binding today have been restated in the New Testament. (part of the sentence)
3. The Ten Commandments found in Exodus 20 reveal God's standard for man's faithfulness to Him and for man's relationships with others. (somewhat beside the point)
4. Jesus' Sermon on the Mount here are high standards indeed! sets the spiritual tone for the New Testament church. (sharp emphasis)
5. "And this your heave offering shall be reckoned unto you, as though it were the corn grain of the threshingfloor" Numbers 18:27.
6. "In my Father's house are many mansions dwellings: if it were not so, I would have told you" John 14:2.
7. "Let's get out to oh, the telephone is ringing," said Father.
8. We shall plan to have Mrs. Wilson's vanilla pies did you know she had stopped in? for dessert. (somewhat beside the point)
9. These loaves of bread which Karen just baked look and smell delicious. (part of the sentence)
10. "I believe that's yes, it is Uncle Mahlon's!" exclaimed Fern.

B. Write correctly the items that have errors in the use of apostrophes or hyphens. If an item needs to be italicized, show it by underlining.
1. When Lamech, Noahs father, was born, his great grandfather Jared had not yet lived one half his total life span.
2. Although Noahs great grandfather Enoch lived only three hundred sixty five years, his grandfather Methuselah lived nine hundred sixty nine years.
3. The world promotes its self expression philosophies, but the Bible teaches the humanly unpopular but soul satisfying doctrine of humility.

Lesson 6 Answers

Applying the Lesson

A. 1. Commandments—God man—express
2. Commandments, which today, have
3. Commandments (found   20) reveal
4. Mount—here   indeed!—sets
5. [grain]   (Numbers 18:27).
6. [dwellings]:   (John 14:2).
7. to—oh
8. pies (did   in?) for
9. bread, which   baked, look
10. that's—yes

B. 1. Noah's   great-grandfather   one-half
2. Noah's   great-grandfather sixty-five   sixty-nine
3. self-expression   soul-satisfying

4. Weve a tremendous privilege to trust in Gods all sufficient grace.
5. Today Im making four, six, and eight foot stakes.
6. The post World War II era saw a marked increase in anti God attitudes.
7. My neighbors father in law still drives his original car, a 45 Buick.
8. People with Ph.D.s are not necessarily wiser than self taught people.
9. For art class, we made large scale maps of the area around the school.
10. My sister in law makes beautiful three dimensional bulletin boards for several teachers.
11. The pre Reformation years are often called the Dark Ages.
12. Mr. Garvers speech is freely punctuated with yes, wells.
13. Mrs. Steffy puts an extra line in her 7s, and they look almost like backward capital Fs.
14. In Spanish, js are pronounced like English hs.
15. As Sister Rose revealed the long awaited surprise, the younger students responded with ohs and ahs of pleasure.
16. Martha makes jelly, cream, and custard filled doughnuts to sell.
17. A two thirds majority is required for this proposal to pass.
18. We picked two and one half bushels of green beans.
19. Six, eight, and ten legged creatures are included in the group known as arthropods.
20. A lop eared rabbit stood on its hind legs and watched us.

4. We've God's all-sufficient
5. I'm four-, six-, and eight-foot
6. post–World anti-God
7. neighbor's father-in-law '45
8. Ph.D.'s self-taught
9. large-scale
10. sister-in-law three-dimensional
11. pre-Reformation
12. Garver's <u>yes, well</u>'s
13. <u>7</u>'s <u>F</u>'s
14. <u>j</u>'s <u>h</u>'s
15. long-awaited <u>oh</u>'s <u>ah</u>'s
16. jelly-, cream-, and custard-filled
17. two-thirds
18. one-half
19. Six-, eight-, and ten-legged
20. lop-eared

Review Exercises

A. Write whether each underlined word should be followed by a *colon,* a *semicolon,* or *ellipsis points.* If none of these marks are needed, write *none.* [4]
1. "Mind not high <u>things</u>" (Romans 12:16).
2. Haman's character is well summarized by one <u>word</u> conceited.
3. Haman fully expected to receive the king's honor <u>himself</u> therefore, he was rudely shocked at the king's command to honor Mordecai.
4. Either wittingly or unwittingly, Haman was fighting <u>against</u> Mordecai, Esther, the Jewish nation, and God Himself.
5. "The day of the LORD of hosts shall be upon every one that is proud and <u>lofty,</u> and he shall be brought low" (Isaiah 2:12).

Review Exercises

A. 1. none
   2. colon
   3. semicolon
   4. none
   5. ellipsis points

B. Write the letter of the sentence in which the boldface part is correct. [5]
1. a. "Was Leona talking about the poem 'Seek Him **Still'?"** asked Barbara.
   b. "Was Leona talking about the poem 'Seek Him **Still?'"** asked Barbara.
2. a. We wanted to sing "Glory Be to **God;"** however, we had no good bass.
   b. We wanted to sing "Glory Be to **God";** however, we had no good bass.
3. a. "The man on the bridge is shouting, 'Come **quick'!"** Keith exclaimed.
   b. "The man on the bridge is shouting, 'Come **quick!'"** Keith exclaimed.
4. a. I read **"Palestine Before the Conquest"** in *Baker's Bible Atlas*.
   b. I read ***Palestine Before the Conquest*** in Baker's Bible Atlas.
5. a. We crossed the lake on the **"Lake Cruiser."**
   b. We crossed the lake on the ***Lake Cruiser.***

B. 1. a
   2. b
   3. b
   4. a
   5. b

7. Improving Your Editing Skills, Part 1

When you have completed the first writing of an essay or a story, is it ready to be printed? No, you have learned in previous years that revising is an essential part of the writing process. As you revise and proofread, you can mark your changes clearly and simply by using the standard symbols that most publishers use.

Throughout this textbook, you will find a series of lessons entitled "Improving Your Editing Skills." These lesson exercises are printed both in this textbook and in a separate booklet of tests and editing sheets, on which you can easily make your proofreading marks. The editing lessons have the following three general purposes.

1. To stimulate critical reading so that you will be able to catch errors in grammar, mechanics, and spelling.
2. To give practice in correct usage of grammar and mechanics.
3. To give practice in the use of proofreading marks.

Study the following table of proofreading marks. The sample manuscript below the table shows how the marks are used.

Marks Used in Editing and Proofreading

˅ or ˄ insert (caret)	ꝯ delete	.... stet (let it stand)
¶ begin new paragraph	*lc* change to lowercase (small letter)	*uc* change to uppercase (capital letter)

Explanations	Sample Manuscript
Delete symbol has loop so that deletion is not overlooked.	Suppose you were a customer of a
Caret shows exact point of insertion.	bank that credited your acount with
Comma after *used* is unnecessary.	$1,440 every day, and every night it
Loop of delete symbol may curve down, especially if deleted item is replaced by item above.	canceled any amount you had not used,
	that day. What would you do? You weed would
Any inserted punctuation is marked by a caret. Question mark or exclamation point is inserted above the caret.	make sure you used every dollar, of
	course! Who would do otherwise? Well,
Time is to be capitalized because it is used as a name.	you do have such a bank, and its name
	is time. Every morning bank credits you this

Lesson 7

Purpose: To introduce the purpose of the "Improving Your Editing Skills" lessons, and to introduce a number of proofreading marks.

Teaching Suggestions:

Generally, these "Improving Your Editing Skills" lessons should require very little teaching time. Take sufficient time, however, to introduce the first several of them.

Emphasize the importance of these marks, and then insist on using them precisely and neatly. You should not need to guess, for example, exactly where a missing letter or punctuation mark is to be inserted or exactly how many letters are to be deleted.

The proofreading exercises in the textbook may be reproduced as needed in teaching this course. They are also available in a separate booklet of tests and editing sheets. In contrast to the exercises in most of the grammar and mechanics lessons, these exercises are not divided into equal parts by taking only the odd or the even numbers.

Comma or period is inserted below the caret.

The word *stet* and the dots mean deleted item is to be retained.

Apostrophe or quotation marks are inserted above inverted caret.

Caret helps to assure that inserted hyphen is not overlooked.

Time is a common noun here.

Parentheses are inserted above carets.

with 1440 minutes, and every evening it cancels any amount ~~that~~ you failed to ~~to~~ invest for a good purpose. It is no ones loss but your own, for you must say good-bye forever to lost Time. Moses wrote, "So teach us to number our days, that we may apply our hearts unto wisdom" (Psalm 90:12).

Observe carefully how the proofreading marks are made, and pattern your marks after them. In this way, both you and others can easily tell what changes you intended.

Editing Practice

A. Use the proper proofreading marks to correct the errors in the sentences below. Each sentence needs one insertion and one deletion or replacement.

1. The fear of the Lord is the begining of wisdome.

2. If you want be wise, fear God, obey the Bible, and respect the your parents.

3. Who would ever regret, any effort put forth in developing noble Christian ideals

4. When Josephs brothers sold him, they did not no that they would meet him in Egypt many years later.

5. The many plants in Grandmothers house reveal her love for growing thengs.

6. "How many busshels of apples did you pick? asked Kevin.

B. Use the proper proofreading marks to correct the errors in capitalization. In each sentence, one letter should be changed to uppercase and one to lowercase.

1. The Lord chose Paul to be the Apostle to the gentiles.

2. How many Sufferings he would need to endure as a christian!

3. Paul traveled through Asia minor and Parts of Europe, spreading the Gospel.

4. Do you know how many Missionary journeys are recorded in the Book of acts?

Lesson 7 Answers

Editing Practice
(Answers are on pages 458–459.)

5. Just as I finished reading "Dreams of no Value," my Mother
   called.

C. Now try your editing skills on the selection below. You will need to do the following things.
   a. Make five insertions.
   b. Make five deletions or replacements. (Be sure to read the note following the selection.)
   c. Make five corrections in capitalization.
   d. Mark two places where a new paragraph should begin.
   e. Show that one word already deleted should be retained.

This means that eighteen corrections are needed. Can you find them all?

1.   Solar eclipses have long struk fear in the hearts of
2. men and have given rise too many myths and superstitions.
3. For example, the ancient chinese thought a dragon was
4. swallowing the sun. They held ~~noisy~~ ceremonies to make
5. the Dragon sick and cause him to spew the sun out again.
6. Chinese astronomers were responsible to to predict coming
7. eclipses so that the people would be ready to rescue the
8. sun. The same kind of ignorance still exists today. Before
9. a total eclipse occurred over south America on July 11
10. 1991, warnings were circulated that looking any part of
11. the sky during the eclipse could cause the blindness.
12. Therefore, all people and livestock—especially horses—
13. were suposed to stay inside ~~all~~ during the whole event.
14. Another report indicated that rocks and dirt mite fall
15. from the sky if the son and the moon rubbed against
16. each other. How much better is knowledge than Ignorance!
17. When a solar eclipse occurs, those living in ignorance
18. prepare to protect themselves from imaginary dangers.
19. But those who know the truth can appreciate the event
20. as one the most awesome examples of God's Handiwork.

Note: In the editing lessons, you will proofread a number of paragraphs on the subject of astronomy. You will not be expected to check the spelling of proper nouns or to verify technical information, such as the distance to a star.

———————

8. Chapter 1 Review

A. Use proofreading marks to correct the errors in capitalization and end punctuation.

1. the theme for our Bible School studies this Summer is "Lessons from Bible youth"

2. "are you developing, o youth," asked brother Seth, "The qualities that god can use to build his kingdom"

3. in Math class we calculated the approximate distance that the israelites traveled from egypt to canaan.

4. What a surprise i had when grandfather invited me to go along to the writers' meeting at Glendale Mennonite church.

5. Although king Solomon gave much good advice in proverbs and ecclesiastes, he apparently did not follow it all himself.

B. Use proofreading marks to add the missing commas.

1. "Do we my brethren have the faith, fortitude and fidelity" asked Brother Amos "to face any persecution that may come?"

2. Knowing the perils of these end times we must stay close to God's Word which is our source of spiritual direction.

3. At our church services are held on the third Sunday evening of each month and we have a song service whenever there is a fifth Sunday.

4. Mr. Alton F. Young Jr. paid $450000 for a productive well-maintained farm near Harrisonburg Virginia.

5. In the vicinity of Clarkdale a cloudburst it is reported dumped over five inches of rain.

Lesson 8 Answers
(Parts A–E are on pages 460–461.)

Lesson 8

Purpose: To review the concepts taught in Chapter 1.

Teaching Suggestions:
Note that some of the written work in this lesson is set up as proofreading exercises. These exercises are included in the separate booklet of tests and editing sheets.

C. Use proofreading marks to correct the errors in the use of colons, semicolons, and ellipsis points. Place ellipsis points below the caret, and colons and semicolons above the caret.

1. "This wisdom descendeth not from above, but is earthly, sensual, devilish. But the wisdom that is from above is first pure . . ." (James 3:15-17).

2. When we feel a lack of wisdom, we should remember one important fact, God gives His wisdom freely to those who sincerely ask.

3. "Surely God is good to man, but how often" Grandfather sighed.

4. Since God has blessed us richly, we should serve Him faithfully, but too many people, proud and selfish by nature, ignore God.

5. Examples of ingratitude in the Scriptures include: the children of Israel, who murmured frequently in the wilderness, Solomon, who turned to idolatry after God had enriched him supernaturally, and Jonah, who complained bitterly because God spared Nineveh.

D. Use proofreading marks to correct the errors in capitalization, punctuation, and italics.

1. Did you expect to hear Mother say, We are having vanilla pie and ice cream for dessert?

2. Get the book The Christian Short Story, and read Chapter 4, entitled Style suggested Brother Weber.

3. Mr. Reed quoted the saying, God helps them who help themselves; however, Father pointed out that this statement does not apply to salvation.

4. Uncle Ben wonders if we would like a ride on his sleigh, Queen of the Snow, which he has restored, announced Galen.

5. Before you leave, would you folks sing Footprints of
   Jesus? asked Mrs. Lee.

E. Use proofreading marks to add the missing dashes, parentheses, and brackets.

1. "When tribulation or persecution ariseth because of the
   word, by and by immediately he is offended" Matthew
   13:21.

2. "I don't quite oh, now I see what you mean!" exclaimed
   Donna.

3. Our strawberries they surely produced abundantly this
   year! have sold well. (give sharp emphasis)

4. Aunt Regina she really isn't related to us spends much
   time knitting. (minimize the importance)

5. "Well, I certainly would not" Timothy gasped as a bolt of
   lightning struck the tree behind the barn.

F. Copy each phrase, using apostrophes and hyphens correctly. If a word needs to be
   italicized, show it by underlining.
   1. twenty one nows in his story
   2. three, five, and ten speed bikes
   3. broke an all time record
   4. isnt a sharp tongued person
   5. wont be here before two oclock
   6. our great grandfather Newswanger
   7. my self confident sister in law
   8. a mid March snowstorm

F. 1. twenty-one <u>now</u>'s in his story
   2. three-, five-, and ten-speed bikes
   3. broke an all-time record
   4. isn't a sharp-tongued person
   5. won't be here before two o'clock
   6. our great-grandfather Newswanger
   7. my self-confident sister-in-law
   8. a mid-March snowstorm

G. Write the correct word for each blank.
   1. A good writing style helps to capture and hold the reader's ———.
   2. If writing has originality, it contains creative expressions that come from an
      ——— mind.
   3. A——— is a descriptive phrase that lacks its original force because it has been
      used so often.
   4. In striving for originality, one pitfall is the temptation to use slang or expres-
      sions that treat ——— subjects lightly.
   5. A second pitfall is to try so hard to be original that the writing sounds ———.
   6. You should generally avoid an expression in writing if you would not consider
      using it in ———.

G. 1. interest *or* attention
   2. active *or* imaginative
   3. cliché
   4. sacred
   5. strained
   6. speech (speaking)

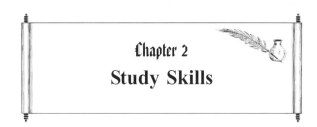

Chapter 2
Study Skills

9. Preparing to Study

You have spent thousands of hours studying in school. Certainly you know how to study. But do you know how to study effectively? Do you work merely to finish your assignments, or are you striving to *learn*? Do you view your school lessons as so many tasks to toil through, or do you see them as building blocks of a productive life?

In your earliest school years, your teachers closely guided your studying. As you developed in your capacity to know and in your ability to pursue knowledge, you became more and more responsible to study on your own. You have learned much about study skills, both directly (as your teachers gave specific pointers) and indirectly (as you observed your teachers' methods and as you learned by trial and error). Now, as you stand near the end of your formal schooling, a closer look at these study skills can benefit you greatly. Although you may soon leave the formal school setting, you will never graduate from study and learning.

Proper Attitudes

Proper attitudes are the foundation of effective study skills. You cannot hope to do your best in studying if you do not think properly about it. What attitudes will a good student have toward study and learning?

1. *Interest.* This is the one most important attitude you must have. If you are interested in your work, you will apply yourself to it. If you are not interested, you simply will not do as well.

Some students will say, "I'm not really interested in this subject, but I do my lessons carefully. I don't see how I could possibly do any better than I am doing now." We might compare this with eating at the table. A well-mannered person will eat the food he is given, even when it is not his favorite dish. But will he take as much as the person who really enjoys it? Will he chew it as thoroughly? Will he ask for a second helping? No, of course not. Just as surely, the uninterested student will never dig into a subject as effectively as the interested one.

Now you may ask, "But what if I don't like a subject? I can't *make* myself like it, can I?" The answer is "Yes." But you must want to be interested.

So what can you do to spark an interest in a subject? Ask yourself, "What would I do if this were really interesting?" Of course, you would dig in with enthusiasm. You would enjoy the challenge of finding the treasures in the lesson. So do that very thing. Dig in just as you would if this were your favorite subject. You may be

Lesson 9

Purpose: To teach *good study skills for effective study.

Teaching Suggestions:

You might begin the class by asking your students what they think is the most important thing they learn in school. Although this is a rhetorical question, it is fair to say that the single most important lesson is *how to study.* Mastering study skills constitutes one of the most important preparations for a fruitful Christian life.

Do not present this lesson in a vague, theoretical manner. Make it practical to your classroom experience. For example, if you know that some of your students have a poor appreciation for a certain subject, give special encouragement to value it. Point out some specific purposes for studying that material.

Generally speaking, our students need encouragement to esteem study skills and learning. On the other hand, there is the danger of esteeming study and education for its own sake. Emphasize the basic principle that whatever we do, including study, must be done to God's glory.

The exercises throughout this chapter are not divided in the normal odd–even pattern.

surprised at how quickly your attitude changes. We find meaning and satisfaction in the things we do with our might.

2. *Self-discipline.* Probably all students (and older people too) depend to some degree on outside influences for motivation to do their work. As a person matures, however, he depends less upon external motivation and more upon the internal motivation of personal self-discipline.

In what areas must you exercise self-discipline in your study? First of all, set to work immediately. Refuse to dawdle with your pen, a library book, or even your textbook. (Did you ever waste five minutes looking at future lessons?) Also, be prepared to work hard. Real studying is not easy. You simply must buckle down and work. Unless you are ready to give yourself to your studies without resentment and without fear of difficulty, you will not learn much. Finally, stick to your work. If you find your mind wandering, rein it in! If surrounding activities or noises distract you, force your mind to concentrate. Without self-discipline, very little learning can occur.

3. *Purpose.* Any undertaking in life becomes easier when we sense a wholesome purpose. What is the true reason for your study? Is it to please your teacher and your parents? to use your time wisely at school? to complete all your assignments promptly and correctly? These are not bad reasons, but true studying has more noble ends. As you study, adopt for yourself the following purposes.

a. *To master the material.* Yes, you want to obey and please your teacher. You do want to use your time well and receive good grades. But beyond that, determine that you will *learn* what you are studying. To go to all the effort of study and fail to learn is a great waste of time!

b. *To develop your mind.* As you study, you are training your mind to think logically. Appreciate this benefit, especially when the work seems unnecessary and difficult. Logical thinking is essential to "rightly dividing the word of truth," to understanding other studies, and to facing many of life's experiences.

c. *To glorify God.* "Whether therefore ye eat, or drink, or whatsoever ye do, do all to the glory of God" (1 Corinthians 10:31). Is God glorified by lazy students? by students who do only as much as necessary to get by? Obviously not. Remember this; and when your studies press you down, rise up to honor God by doing your best. "Study [give diligence] to shew thyself approved unto God."

These purposes should provide you with a strong motivation to develop good study skills.

Study Schedule

A definite study schedule contributes to effective studying. To be a good student, you must make good use of your time. Here are several suggestions to help you manage your time well.

1. *Do your lessons as soon as possible after class.* The rate at which you forget is highest immediately after you have studied something. Later, you forget more slowly, so that the things you remember an hour after class, you will probably remember the next day. By doing a lesson right after class, you review what you have learned and

reinforce it in your mind. This helps to keep you from forgetting in those first critical minutes.

2. *Have a regular time to study.* By maintaining a scheduled study time, you can prevent a very common problem: forgetfulness. If the time after supper, before bedtime, or after breakfast is regularly devoted to study, you will be far less likely to forget to do your lessons than if you try to study whenever it suits.

A regular study schedule is also important because of the time-habit it establishes. When lunchtime nears, your body begins to get hungry. When your regular bedtime arrives, your body begins to shut down for sleep. And when your regular study hour approaches, your mind is conditioned to study at that time.

3. *Be mindful of deadlines.* Tackle first what is due first. This is especially important if your time is limited. It is helpful to list your work in three different groups at the beginning of a day or a study period: the things that you *must do,* those that you *should do,* and some that you *could do* if you have time. Include in the last group a few things you would especially enjoy doing. Then do first what must be done. As time allows, work on your "should do" things. Usually, the "could do" things are more enjoyable, so try to get some of them done too.

4. *Start with the hardest and least enjoyable assignments.* If you have a list of physical chores, do you save the worst and hardest ones for last? Probably not, if you can help it. You want to get them out of the way and off your mind. Treat a list of study chores the same way. Do the hardest and least enjoyable ones while your mind is fresh. This enables you to give your best mental energy to these tasks. Save something enjoyable and easy for last, when you are more tired. In addition to having something easy when your energy is least, you will have something to look forward to throughout your entire study period.

5. *Take occasional breaks.* Study is work, and you can keep your mind functioning at its best by periodically relaxing the brain, exercising the muscles, and recharging your body with fresh oxygen. A five-to-ten-minute break after an hour of study will probably allow you to study more effectively when you return to your work.

Suitable Environment

A suitable environment definitely contributes to effective study. What are some qualities of such an environment? First, have a regular place to study. If you have a definite *time* to study and a definite *place* to study, you have habits of both time and place to aid you. Just as your mind turns to food when you enter the dining room at mealtime (even if no food is in sight), so your mind will turn to study when you go to your desk at study time.

The place of study should be as quiet and free from distractions as practical. The more you can shut out family noise and activity, the better. At the same time, you need to free yourself from distractions of your own making. Remove any pictures, magazines, or hobby items that may divert your attention from your work.

Be sure to have your study tools near at hand. You should not need to interrupt your work to look for basic items like a pencil or pen, a dictionary, or a Bible. Also provide good lighting and ventilation. Such physical comfort is not a mere luxury; it aids your ability to concentrate.

Finally, keep your work station organized. Clutter kills motivation and wastes time.

Good Posture

Good posture plays an important role in effective study. Sit erect on a firm, straight-backed chair that allows your feet to rest comfortably on the floor and your arms on the table. In contrast to a slouching posture, this allows natural breathing that supplies the brain with plenty of oxygen for clear thinking.

In addition to its physical benefits, good posture has the subconscious effect of telling your mind and body that you truly intend to study. Imagine the difference if you should allow yourself to slouch down in a soft, padded chair. Ahh. How relaxing. And relaxing is just what you would tend to do rather than studying diligently.

Good study skills involve a number of attitudes and practices. Although some people are more inclined to study than others, no one performs at his best without diligent cultivation of these skills. And no one is such a poor scholar that he cannot develop these skills and benefit from them.

Applying the Lesson
A. Write *true* or *false*.
1. If a student is interested in a subject, he tends to work hard at it.
2. Taking interest in something helps to make it more appealing.
3. If you truly enjoy your work, it will be easy.
4. You are better able to study at the beginning of a study period than near the end.
5. You should avoid doing your hardest work first because that will tire you out right at the beginning of your study period.
6. A good student needs no external motivation to get his work done.
7. It is best to leave the easier studies for last.
8. Studying for God's glory applies only to Bible study.
9. The primary value of a suitable environment is to make study more pleasant.
10. Slouching has negative effects on your body and your mind.

B. Write the letter of the best answer.
1. If you are not interested in a certain subject, you probably
   a. will never be interested in it.
   b. cannot do anything to become interested.
   c. will not study it as well as you could.
   d. have a good reason for not being interested.
2. By studying like an interested student even if you are not really interested, you are likely to
   a. satisfy your teacher.
   b. actually become interested.
   c. lose what interest you do have.
   d. fool your teacher.

Lesson 9 Answers
Applying the Lesson
A. 1. true
   2. true
   3. false
   4. true
   5. false
   6. false
   7. true
   8. false
   9. false
   10. true

B. 1. c
   2. b

3. Of the following things, the best purpose for studying is
   a. to get a good report card grade.
   b. to meet the expectations of teachers and parents.
   c. to make good use of your time at school.
   d. to learn the material and remember it.
4. You forget the most rapidly
   a. immediately after studying something.
   b. one hour after studying something.
   c. the next day after studying something.
   d. in none of these periods; there is little difference.
5. The best time for you to study is
   a. when you feel like studying.
   b. when you find time to study.
   c. at the same time each day.
   d. early in the morning.
6. When you make a list of things you have to do,
   a. list only the most important things.
   b. decide which of the things are most important.
   c. list only the things you can do that day.
   d. list the things in the order you will do them.

3. d
4. a
5. c
6. b

C. Do these exercises.
   1. Make three lists of your school-related work that is now waiting to be done. Use these headings: *Must Do, Should Do,* and *Could Do.*
   2. Describe the time and the place where you did your homework most recently. Underline any details that should be improved.

C. (Individual work.)

Review Exercises

For each underlined word, write *yes* or *no* to tell whether it should be followed by a comma. [2]

1. The Gila (hē′·lə) monster, which lives in the <u>southwestern</u> United <u>States</u> is a poisonous lizard.
2. This <u>colorful</u> <u>scaly</u> creature grows to a length of about twenty inches.
3. Although it often appears <u>slow</u> and <u>awkward</u> the Gila monster can move rapidly.
4. Its diet consists largely of small <u>animals</u> bird <u>eggs</u> and reptile eggs.
5. The Gila <u>monster</u> and its close relative, the beaded <u>lizard</u> are the only venomous lizards in the world.
6. Produced in glands in the lower <u>jaw</u> the poison travels up the fanglike <u>teeth</u> when the Gila monster bites a victim.
7. Its poison is <u>fatal</u> to small <u>animals</u> but it rarely kills humans.
8. <u>Carla</u> please see if this publisher in <u>Chicago</u> <u>Illinois</u> has a book about desert animals.

Review Exercises

1. no, yes
2. yes, no
3. no, yes
4. yes, yes
5. no, yes
6. yes, no
7. no, yes
8. yes, yes, yes

10. Using the SQ3R Method

Which person is more efficient at doing his tasks—the one who develops a system or the one who works haphazardly? Obviously, the systematic worker is much more efficient than the haphazard one.

The same principle applies to study. By having a definite system, our study will be much more fruitful than if we have no system. This lesson presents a particular system of study known as the *SQ3R method.* The letters in this name stand for five steps that a good student should follow: **S**—Survey, **Q**—Question, **R**—Read, **R**—Recite, **R**—Review.

Survey

Suppose your father gives you the responsibility of painting all the woodwork on the front porch. How will you approach your job? Will you immediately open a paint can and start painting in one corner? Hardly. You will probably look over the whole porch first to gain a good idea of what the job involves. Then you will be ready to start the actual painting.

Apply the same principle to studying a lesson in history, science, or your Sunday school quarterly. The first step is to *survey* the material. Get a bird's-eye view of it. A survey of the lesson helps you to gain a sense of direction that will guide you as you read. It helps you to see the various parts of the lesson in relation to the whole. It also helps you to understand the logical connection between the present lesson and adjoining lessons.

How can you gain such an overall picture? First, consider the lesson title, which usually states the main point of the lesson. Then look at all the boldface headings. They will help you see the various main parts of the lesson. If there are any pictures, graphs, maps, or charts, look at them briefly and read the captions.

Be sure to keep this survey brief. Look for the main points of the lesson, and ignore the smaller details for now.

The study of a new book, a new unit, or a new chapter should also begin with a brief survey. See how the book is organized; read the unit and chapter titles. If a book has a preface, read it to discover the author's purpose for writing. All of this will help you get a general picture of the material you will study. This might be compared to mapping the general route for a trip before beginning to plan the specific details along the way.

Question

The second step in this study method is to *question.* That is, ask questions for which you expect to find answers in the material you will be reading. Many times you can do this by turning each heading into one or more questions. For example, suppose one of the headings in a science lesson is "Pollination by Insects." You would ask, "What insects help with pollination? How do insects help with pollination?" In history, the heading "Christianity Begins to Spread Rapidly" gives rise to several questions: "Why did it begin to spread rapidly? How rapidly did it spread? How far did it spread? To what regions did it spread?"

Lesson 10

Purpose: To teach *the SQ3R method of studying.

Teaching Suggestions:

Your students should have learned how to study years ago. There is definite value, however, in presenting a specific method of study to students at this level.

You will accomplish two things at once if you thoroughly teach the SQ3R method and then have students put it to practice in other classes. Remind them frequently to use this method, and occasionally require them to write down their questions and answers as they study a history or science lesson so that you can see how well they actually perform. As an ideal, students should eventually use the SQ3R method as a matter of habit. Challenge yourself to reach that goal.

You may want to do half of Part C in class and assign the remaining half. You could also do Part D in class and assign the students to follow the directions in Part E to study a specified lesson in science, history, or geography.

What is the value of forming these questions? By asking questions, you stimulate your mind to seek answers. You will have something to look for as you read, and you will be able to recognize the important points as you encounter them.

Read

The third step is the part that you usually do anyway: *read* the material. "Simple enough," you might say. But this is not a mere going through the sentences and paragraphs to "get these pages done." Rather, you are looking for answers to your questions. You are reading to find something specific. This is active reading—something that requires careful thought and attention. It is the heart of meaningful study.

As you read, make sure that you are comprehending the material. Reread a paragraph if you do not understand what it is saying. Look up unfamiliar words. Study the pictures, graphs, maps, and charts. They have been included to clarify the text. Take notes on significant points. Remember, you are reading so you will learn, not just so you can say you have completed your assignment.

Recite

After you have read each section, you should stop and *recite* the main points of the section. You can do this by answering the questions you asked before beginning to read. This tests whether you have read with comprehension. If you cannot state the main points, you have not learned the material. And if you have failed to learn, you must go back and find those answers. You have truly mastered a lesson only when you can repeat the main points in the lesson.

In most of your school studies, recitation also involves completing written assignments. Ideally, you should be able to do much of the written work without turning back to the lesson text. Whenever you must look back, put special effort into remembering that detail. Remember, the whole point of studying a lesson is to master the material.

Review

After you have worked through a lesson, completing the previous four steps, you are ready to *review.* Mentally go back over what you have read and recall the main points. Answer again the questions you asked before reading the lesson. This is the final check, the proof that you have really learned the material.

Do this review actively. Do not merely look at the lesson or your notes and think, "Yes, I remember that." Rather, recall the main points without looking at the text or your notes. Use those helps only if you cannot remember something. You will master the details much more effectively in this way.

Review as soon as possible after the learning experience. Do you remember from Lesson 9 that the rate of forgetting is greatest in the first several minutes after you have studied something? Your most effective review, therefore, is immediately after you have worked through a lesson.

Reviewing is not something that you can do once and then leave. Before class discussion, review the lesson again. Can you still answer your questions? Can you still recite the main points of the lesson? And, of course, you should review before test time. If you have studied the lessons effectively, this final review will not prove burdensome. And it will produce much better results than if you cram for a test.

True study is hard work. The SQ3R method does not make it easy, but it does help to make your study effective and beneficial.

Applying the Lesson

A. Write *true* or *false.*
1. To study a lesson most effectively, you should first read it carefully.
2. When surveying a lesson, you should study each map and chart in detail.
3. One good way to make questions is to transform main headings into questions.
4. The most effective review is done right after you have studied a lesson.
5. If you have used the SQ3R method faithfully, you should not need to review before taking a test.

B. Write the letter of the best answer.
1. Surveying a lesson can help you
   a. to understand how the individual sections of a lesson fit into the whole lesson.
   b. to sense where you are going as you read.
   c. to understand the connection between the present lesson and adjoining lessons.
   d. in all the ways given above.
2. You should ask questions before you read a lesson
   a. so that you can read the lesson with less effort.
   b. so that you have specific goals as you read.
   c. so that you will be encouraged to spend more time with the lesson.
   d. for all the reasons above.
3. Active reading
   a. means that you read to find something.
   b. allows you to think about other things as you read.
   c. is what you naturally do when studying a lesson.
   d. includes all the things above.
4. A good way to determine whether you have read with comprehension is to
   a. see if you can recall the main ideas of the lesson.
   b. answer by memory the questions you raised before reading.
   c. do much of the written assignment without looking back at the lesson.
   d. do all the things above.

C. Write two questions that each of these headings could suggest.
1. American Colonies Build Prosperous Trade
2. Inventions Fuel Industrial Growth
3. Creating a Partial Vacuum
4. The Conduction of Heat
5. The Hindu Caste System
6. Migratory Patterns in Birds

Lesson 10 Answers
Applying the Lesson

A. 1. false
   2. false
   3. true
   4. true
   5. false

B. 1. d
   2. b
   3. a
   4. d

C. (Sample answers.)
1. How did the American colonies build prosperous trade? What was the prosperous trade they built? With whom did they build prosperous trade?
2. What inventions fueled industrial growth? How did they fuel growth? What was the result of the growth?
3. What is a partial vacuum? How is a partial vacuum created? What are the purposes of partial vacuums?
4. What is conduction of heat? How is heat conducted? What is important about the conduction of heat?
5. What is the Hindu caste system? When was it in effect? What are the results of such a system?
6. What are migratory patterns in birds? What birds have such patterns? Why do they have these patterns?

D. Study the following selection, using the SQ3R method. First, *survey* the selection. Next, turn every heading into at least one *question;* and write those questions on your paper, leaving enough room to fill in your answers. Then *read* through each section, *recite* the answers to your questions, and write them on your paper. Finally, *review* by writing from memory on another paper the main points you have learned.

D. (Individual work.)

Modern Times
By Robert Darrow

"The thing that hath been, it is that which shall be; and that which is done is that which shall be done: and there is no new thing under the sun. Is there any thing whereof it may be said, See, this is new? it hath been already of old time, which was before us" (Ecclesiastes 1:9, 10).

We are all aware that the times are changing; things are not the same as they used to be. Each year that goes by brings new events and developments in man's condition on earth. But sometimes, looking backward, we seem to discern a period marked by changes more significant and more profound than those preceding or following—a watershed division between the "old days" and the "new times."

Events That Ushered in Modern Times

History writers recognize such a division in the change from the Middle Ages to modern times, which occurred about five hundred years ago. At that time, a number of events took place—related to each other in many complex ways, and all together making remarkable changes in the course of history. Let us examine some of these events that mark the end of the Middle Ages and the beginning of modern times.

In 1453, the Hundred Years' War between France and England came to a close. After that, France and England began to develop into modern nations with strong central governments, with fairly definite boundaries, and with citizens who thought of themselves as being French or English. Portugal and Spain, meanwhile, were also developing. In a lengthy struggle called the *Reconquista,* they drove the Moors (Arabs) out of Europe and back into Africa. This *Reconquista* was completed in 1492.

Something else happened in 1453: the fierce, hostile Ottoman Turks finally conquered Constantinople after decades of fighting. This city is now Istanbul in modern Turkey. The emperor Constantine had made Constantinople the eastern capital of the Roman Empire in A.D. 330, so its fall actually represented the end of the Roman Empire in the East. (The fall of Rome in A.D. 476 marked the end of the empire in the West.) But more important, the fall of Constantinople shifted the focus of Europe westward to the newly developing nations.

Long before the city fell, thousands of refugees from Greece and Asia Minor had been coming to western Europe to escape the Turks. They brought with them various books and manuscripts containing knowledge long since forgotten or neglected in the West. The influx of this knowledge contributed to an upsurge of learning called the Renaissance (rebirth). People in western lands took a new interest in art, science, and learning in general.

In 1454, Johann Gutenberg printed a Bible on a press with movable type, the first known book printed in this way. Equally important was the development of good-quality paper and ink. The Gutenberg Bible marked the beginning of a new access to literature; before this, books had to be laboriously written out by hand. Such materials contributed to the explosion of knowledge so necessary in modern times.

The hostility of the Turks in the eastern Mediterranean cut off Europe from a highly desirable trade with India and China. The main products of this trade were spices, silk, cotton, and sugar. Spain and Portugal began searching for new routes around Africa or directly west across the Atlantic. The great explorations of Christopher Columbus (1492), Vasco da Gama (1498), and Ferdinand Magellan (1519) opened up new worlds and provided new things for the people of Europe.

Beginning in 1517, the Protestant Reformation resulted in the establishment of national Protestant churches. These churches undid the monopoly of the pope and the Roman Catholic Church, but they did not establish freedom of religion or Scripturally sound, New Testament churches. At the same time, however, the Swiss Brethren and related Anabaptist churches sprang up. The first recorded rebaptism took place in Zurich in 1525. God's guiding hand is seen in the chain of events leading to the rise of His Holy Word and His people, the church!

Results of These Events

The result of all these events was a period of extensive growth. The population increased. The ancient cities began to grow again, and new towns and cities sprang up. Commerce and industry prospered, stimulated by new explorations and new products. More land in Europe was brought under cultivation, and the production per acre increased. Some people accumulated enormous private fortunes.

By 1600, there seemed no end to the things that man could do. Every passing day brought news of fantastic discoveries. People were gazing out into the universe with telescopes, and with microscopes they were discovering the secret worlds hidden in a drop of water. They looked forward with great expectation to the time when all of man's problems would be solved by man himself!

Well, now we know otherwise. We know that this world was corrupted by sinful man, and it will not be saved by him. The more that things change, the more they stay the same! A proper understanding of history teaches us to see both the differences and the constants of all ages.

E. Use the SQ3R method to study your next lesson in science, history, or geography. Do not stop with that, but try to develop the habit of using this method in all your studies.

11. Developing the Art of Skimming

Generally, when you want to gain something from a lesson or an article, you expect to read and study it carefully. Depending on circumstances, however, detailed study may be unwise, unnecessary, or even impossible. Then you may wish to employ the art of skimming.

Have you ever skipped a stone across a still pool of water? One, two, three, and possibly more times the stone came down, briefly touched the water, bounced upward, and again hit the water. That is a picture of skimming—spot reading or briefly glancing over the material for specific ideas.

Purposes and Methods of Skimming

1. *Skimming to gain a bird's-eye view of a book or an article.* You wonder what a new book contains, so you pick up a copy and skim it. You check the table of contents and then page through the book quickly, noticing the information given on the beginning pages. As you proceed through the book, you stop here and there to read a paragraph or two. You pay particular attention to how the book begins and how it ends. When you lay the book down a few minutes later, you will have gained a fairly accurate impression of the kind of book it is and the kind of material it contains.

The following illustration gives a good picture of the pattern you should follow in skimming, especially with an item such as a magazine article.

You should usually read the whole first paragraph (and sometimes the second one) at normal speed. These opening paragraphs often contain an introduction or overview of the material you will skim. You probably do not need to read the whole third paragraph. . . . . Read the first sentence of each paragraph. . . . . However, main ideas occur in various parts of paragraphs. . . . . sometimes in the middle . . . . Sometimes the main idea comes in the last sentence of a paragraph.	Besides the first sentences, try to pick up other details in the middle of the paragraphs. . . . . names . . . . dates . . . . Try to keep up a very fast rate . . . . don't forget yourself. . . . . don't start to read everything . . . . Sometimes the first sentence does not give the main idea. Then you must read the whole paragraph more slowly. You can omit much of the next paragraph. . . . . make up time. . . . .

Lesson 11

Purpose: To teach *the purposes and methods of skimming.

Teaching Suggestions:

The ability to find information quickly in a book or a library is a timesaving and valuable skill. Indeed, in the life of an average person, the accumulated time saved by appropriate skimming must equal many days.

Be sure to emphasize that the art of skimming, though valuable and worthwhile, has a relatively narrow range of proper application. Some students may actually be skimming more than they realize. Remind them to use the SQ3R method when studying lessons for school, for Sunday school, for Bible school, and so forth.

> Don't worry that you don't get anything from many of the paragraphs. . . .
> . . . .
> . . . .
> . . . .
> Some paragraphs merely repeat ideas. . . . .
> . . . .
> . . . . restated points
> . . . .
> This paragraph has nothing important. . . . .
> . . . .
> . . . . . minor details. . . . .
> . . . .
>
> Skimming takes definite effort. . . . .
> . . . .
> . . . . worthwhile skill . . . .
> . . . .
> . . . .
> . . . . easier with practice. . . . . .
> . . . .
> For the last two or three paragraphs, again read at normal speed. These paragraphs often contain a summary of the composition.
> Remember, when you skim to gain an overall view, you need to find the main ideas.

2. *Skimming to find information.* Suppose you have an assignment to write an essay on the migratory habits of North American birds. You have several books about birds. Do you read each book from cover to cover? No. First, you check the table of contents and the index to see if there is any entry on your subject. Then you turn to the page or pages indicated and let your eyes skim each page quickly as illustrated under Point 1 above. You read each heading and subheading. Your eyes may catch something that seems to be on the subject, possibly a word or a phrase, and you read a sentence or a paragraph. In a short time, you can decide whether the book has the information you want.

Or perhaps you have heard a friend mention some information that he read in a gardening magazine that you also subscribe to. You do not begin reading from the beginning of the magazine until you find the information he mentioned. First, you check the table of contents. If this gives you no clues, you quickly leaf through the magazine, page by page, looking at the headings and titles. When you come to an article that you think might contain the information you are looking for, you let your eyes run quickly down the page, reading headings and subheadings (if there are any), reading the beginning and ending sentences of paragraphs, and moving from page to page until you either know you have found the right article or are sure you need to look further.

This is the type of skimming you do to find information. Indexes, titles, headings, and beginning and ending sentences of paragraphs are all clues in finding the needed information quickly.

3. *Skimming to evaluate a book or an article.* Is the material worth reading? A quick skim can often give you a good idea. Again, as with skimming to gain a bird's-eye view of the book, check the beginning pages. Who is the author? Is his purpose for writing the book found in a preface or an introduction? What is that purpose?

Suppose you have a storybook to evaluate. Notice how the story begins. Does the main character appear to be an upright person? Skip back through the book, spot

Part D (Continued)

Thanksgiving Vows

Thanksgiving is the natural response of the child of God. Singing and spoken testimony, two of the most common expressions of thankfulness, are certainly comely and appropriate. However, saying "thank you" with the lips is easier than proving it with the life. "Offer unto God thanksgiving; and pay thy vows unto the most High" (Psalm 50:14). . . .

1. What is the main theme of this article? (We should express our thanksgiving to God.)
2. What are two of the most common expressions of thanksgiving? (singing and spoken testimony)
3. What should counting our blessings move us to? (thanksgiving and commitment)
4. The article lists eight specific points for which we should be thankful. List as many of them as you can. (bountiful harvest, stable government, freedom of the press, religious heritage, spiritual shepherds, the church, the Bible, Jesus Christ)
5. As we enjoy life's spiritual and natural abundance, what promise should we make? (to be faithful stewards)
6. What will be the reward for those who respond properly to their many blessings? (They will someday join the angels in eternal thanksgiving.)

reading here and there. Is the language free of slang and coarse expressions? Do the characters—especially the main character—express hatred, anger, dishonesty, or other ungodly traits? If the book presents unchristian attitudes and conduct, you can reject it without wasting much of your time and without absorbing the wrong influence of the book.

Do you have a nonfiction book or an article to evaluate? Many nonfiction books have a preface or an introduction that indicates the main purpose of the book. The table of contents of a book or the headings in an article often indicate whether the material develops a subject from a worthwhile perspective. From this, you can usually tell whether the material is worth reading.

4. *Skimming to review material you have previously studied.* Are you refreshing in your mind the points of a lesson before class time? Are you reviewing for a test? Skim through the material page by page. Note the headings and the beginning sentences of paragraphs. This skimming will reinforce what you already know and bring it to your active consciousness. It also will reveal if there is something you should read more fully to rivet important information that you have not yet mastered.

Skimming fills a definite place in study. But you must not merely skim a lesson to find answers to the exercises when you have not actually studied the lesson. That is not the way to master facts and concepts. Neither should you use skimming to cram for a quiz or a test when you failed to diligently study the material earlier. Learn to use this study tool, but keep it in its proper place.

Summary of Skimming Skills

You cannot skim lazily if you expect to accomplish anything worthwhile. You must keep your mind alert and observant. You must be quick to sort out and evaluate what you read. The following list summarizes the techniques to use in skimming.
1. Check the table of contents and the index of a book.
2. Read the headings and subheadings.
3. Read the beginning and ending sentences of paragraphs.
4. Read a sentence or two here and there, or even a full paragraph occasionally.
5. With a quick eye, pick out significant words and phrases.

Applying the Lesson

A. Write *true* or *false*.
1. Skimming is the art of looking material over briefly for specific ideas.
2. When you skim to gain a bird's-eye view, you should pay closer attention to the beginning and ending paragraphs than to the middle paragraphs.
3. You should avoid reading any whole paragraphs as you skim.
4. To skim a book for information, you should first page through it to check the chapter titles.
5. When you skim a book to evaluate it, you need not consider the author's preface or introduction.
6. One reason for evaluating a book by skimming it is to avoid absorbing errors that the book may contain.

Lesson 11 Answers
Applying the Lesson
A. 1. true
   2. true
   3. false
   4. false
   5. false
   6. true

Should We Enter Sweepstakes?

There is a growing number of giveaway offers and sweepstakes that promise big dividends to the person who has the lucky number or whose name is selected in a random drawing. The advertisements offer huge cash prizes, trips to distant resorts, sports cars, color TVs, and other items; you simply send in the entry form before the deadline. State laws that regulate gambling forbid the advertisers to require those entering to buy their products or send money. . . .

1. What is the main theme of this article? (Entering sweepstakes is contrary to Scriptural principles.)

2. What are some types of prizes that sweepstakes commonly offer? (huge cash prizes, trips to distant resorts, sports cars, color TVs)
3. What is the basic appeal of sweepstakes? (the lure of receiving something for nothing)
4. According to the Scriptures, how should we supply our own needs? (by working)
5. Why are parents' and God's free gifts acceptable if sweepstakes are not? (Parents' and God's free gifts provide what a person cannot provide for himself.)
6. How does God's distribution of His rewards differ from the distribution of the gifts in a sweepstakes? (Sweepstakes winners are few; God rewards everyone according to his works.)

7. When you review by skimming, information that you had mastered earlier is brought to your active consciousness.
8. By perfecting the art of skimming, you may be able to master your school lessons without reading them closely.

B. Answer these questions by using the table of contents and the index of this English book.
   1. In which lesson will you study note-taking for writing an expository essay?
   2. In which lesson will you study methods of portraying characters in a story?
   3. On which pages would you look for the rules of italicizing words?
   4. On which pages would you look for information about conflict in stories?
   5. On which pages would you look for information about the mood of verbs?

C. Use a Bible with page headings for this exercise. Skim the headings in the Bible, and write the numbers of the chapters in which the following information is found.
   1. The chapter in Matthew that tells of Jesus' death.
   2. The chapters in Acts concerning Stephen's trial.
   3. The chapter in Revelation describing the heavenly Jerusalem.
   4. The chapters in Genesis that tell about Joseph's life in Egypt.
   5. The chapters in Judges that tell about Gideon.

D. Be prepared for a class drill in skimming.

Review Exercises

A. Name the punctuation that should follow each underlined word: *colon, semicolon, ellipsis points,* or *none.* [4]
   1. Especially large amounts of snow fall at Marquette, Michigan; Sault Ste. Marie, Michigan and Buffalo, New York.
   2. Marquette, Michigan, can expect an annual snowfall of over 171 inches that is more than 14 feet!
   3. The amounts of snowfall expected at Sault Ste. Marie and at Buffalo are 160 inches and 115 inches.
   4. People living in these areas had better enjoy one thing snow.
   5. "Well," Nevin said, "I like snow, but"

B. Write the letter of the sentence in which the boldface part is correct. [5, 6]
   1. a. "If we seek God's will," Father stated, **"The** Lord will direct our way."
      b. "If we seek God's will," Father stated, **"the** Lord will direct our way."
   2. a. I read the book **"Bernese Anabaptists"** for my report.
      b. I read the book *Bernese Anabaptists* for my report.
   3. a. Jesus said, "I am the light of the **world";** however, He also said, "Ye are the light of the world."
      b. Jesus said, "I am the light of the **world;"** however, He also said, "Ye are the light of the world."
   4. a. "Which disciple boldly declared, 'Though I should die with thee, yet will I not deny **thee?'"** asked Lisa.
      b. "Which disciple boldly declared, 'Though I should die with thee, yet will I not deny **thee'?"** asked Lisa.

7. true
8. false

B. 1. Lesson 30
   2. Lesson 52
   3. page 29
   4. pages 203–204, 222, 224–225
   5. pages 298–302

C. 1. chapter 27   4. chapters 39–50
   2. chapters 6, 7   5. chapters 6–8
   3. chapter 21

D. (Give the students one or both skimming selections on pages 25–26 of *Tests and Editing Sheets*. If you do not have this booklet, you may duplicate those selections on pages 480–481. The beginning of each selection is shown on pages 53 and 54. Give orally the questions below after the students have skimmed the articles. "Thanksgiving Vows" is an expository essay. This article is the easier of the two to skim because the main points in the body are consistently found at the beginning of the paragraphs. "Should We Enter Sweepstakes?" is an argumentative essay and is a bit more complex than the other.

If you prefer, you may select an article of your own choosing or use a lesson from one of your other textbooks for this exercise.)

Review Exercises

A. 1. semicolon   4. colon
   2. semicolon   5. ellipsis points
   3. none

B. 1. b
   2. b
   3. a
   4. b

7. What often happens to a person who wins a large cash prize? (He wastes it in a short time.)
8. What sin often accompanies the desire to get something for nothing? (dishonesty)
9. Why is it appropriate to accept an advertisement gift or the refreshments served by a business that we regularly patronize? (This is an understood way of promoting the business and thanking customers for their patronage.)
10. How could a person show a covetous spirit in relation to such gifts and refreshments? (by going from place to place in search of free food and gifts)

5. a. The word *adult* may be accented on the first or second syllable.
   b. The word **"adult"** may be accented on the first or second syllable.
6. a. We sang for Sister Laura—how cheerful she **is!**—**on** her ninetieth birthday.
   b. We sang for Sister Laura—how cheerful she **is! on** her ninetieth birthday.
7. a. "We are ready to leave **if" The** rest of the sentence was lost in a thunderous crash.
   b. "We are ready to leave **if—" the** rest of the sentence was lost in a thunderous crash.
8. a. Several students' descriptions contained too many ***and*'s.**
   b. Several students' descriptions contained too many **"ands."**
9. a. Thessalonica (also known as **Salonika, sə•lon′•i•kə**) is a seaport of Greece.
   b. Thessalonica (also known as **Salonika [sə•lon′•i•kə]**) is a seaport of Greece.
10. a. My father is a **self employed** mechanic, who works at home.
    b. My father is a **self-employed** mechanic, who works at home.

5. a
6. a
7. b
8. a
9. b
10. b

---

12. Taking Notes and Summarizing

Study is primarily an activity of the mind. However, there are things we do with our hands which contribute to our study. Note-taking and summarizing are two valuable study skills that involve such physical activity.

Note-taking and summarizing are somewhat similar study skills. Both involve identifying main ideas, and both have several important values.

Values of Note-Taking and Summarizing

Note-taking and summarizing are valuable because they promote concentration. The discipline of taking notes from what you read or hear helps to keep your mind active. Furthermore, the discipline of being alert for the next main point to write in your notes helps you to grasp those points more firmly than a casual listening or reading would do. Likewise, the discipline of reducing a lesson or an article to a summary forces you to concentrate closely on what you are reading.

In the second place, these skills promote logical thinking. You cannot take meaningful notes on a lecture, a sermon, or an article in a haphazard manner. If the notes are to be an accurate representation, they must reflect the logical development followed by the speaker or writer. Similarly, to write an accurate summary, you must grasp well the logic of the original article.

Both of these skills are also valuable because they provide a good source of review material. In fact, this likely would be the primary reason for taking notes or summarizing specifically as a study skill. The brevity of notes and summaries makes them useful for quickly reviewing the main points of what you have studied.

Lesson 12

Purpose: To review the skills of note-taking and summarizing.

Guidelines for Note-Taking

1. *Write down main ideas, not minor details.* Unless you are skilled at shorthand, you cannot possibly write down every detail in a lecture or sermon. And unless you plan to write an article based on the presentation, there is no good reason to do so. To realize the three values suggested above, you must write down only the main points.

2. *Write down significant subpoints.* Sometimes a listing of only the main points is hardly satisfactory. Other details may be essential to explain the main idea. How can you tell when details are significant enough to write down? The following three points will help to answer that.

3. *Write down things the speaker emphasizes.* Sometimes your teacher may say, "This will be on the test." Be sure to write it down, for it is something you must remember. Or he may say, "Be sure to remember this." Again, you can tell it is important. Write it down. Be especially alert whenever your teacher writes something on the chalkboard. That is another sign that he considers a point important.

Speakers use various other means to emphasize important points. They may use transitional words to signal the movement from one point to another. They may speak in a more emphatic tone than usual, and they may repeat a point several times. Whenever a speaker emphasizes a point, however he does it, be sure to get it in your notes.

4. *Write down important definitions, figures, dates, names, and so forth.* For example, a science lesson titled "Sanitary Living" includes these italicized terms: *sanitation, sterile, antiseptics, germicides, disinfectants, quarantine.* The same lesson includes figures such as boiling an object for *20 minutes* to sterilize it and heating milk to *144°F for 30 minutes* to pasteurize it. Your notes would include the italicized terms and their definitions, along with the figures given.

A history lesson, of course, would include more dates and names for your notes. An English lesson may have rules, and an arithmetic lesson may have formulas that you should write in your notes. Whatever the subject, note the types of information that you should definitely remember and that you can expect to find on a test.

5. *Be especially alert for information that is new to you.* Writing down such information will reinforce it in your mind right away. You remember much more of what you write than of what you simply hear. You also will need to review more frequently those things that you have never learned before. Sometimes that new information is material that your teacher brings in from outside your normal text material. Those details, of course, you cannot review from your book; you must rely on your notes for help to remember them.

6. *Keep your notes neat and orderly.* Because you must write rapidly, you must often sacrifice neatness as you take notes. It is therefore a good idea to organize and rewrite your notes soon after class. Do not be satisfied with scribbled notes, for you will find it discouraging to decipher your scribbles later. At a certain point, disorganized and illegible notes become totally useless.

Steps for Writing a Summary

A summary is a condensed review of the main points of an article or other composition. Writing a good summary requires that you be thoroughly familiar with the original writing. Follow these steps to write a summary.

1. *Skim the composition.* Put to practice the points in Lesson 11.

2. *Read the composition carefully for a thorough understanding.* Read as you were taught to read in Lesson 10. Reread a paragraph if necessary to understand it fully. Reread the whole composition if that is necessary.

3. *Write down the main points of the composition.* This list of main points will serve as a guide for your actual writing.

4. *Write the summary.* Use an appropriate heading, stating the title of the original piece and the author's name. If you are summarizing an article from a periodical, include the name and date of the periodical.

Use your own wording as much as possible. Copy from the original only if you want to preserve some unique style or wording of the author. Remember to enclose any exact quotations in quotation marks.

Include all the main points in their original order. Since you are merely summarizing another person's writing, you should not include your own thoughts and opinions. And stick to the *main* points. Include an example or illustration only if it is essential to explaining a point.

Make the summary of an appropriate length. A summary may range from less than one hundred words to about one-third the length of the original composition. Its length is affected by the length of the original composition, the number of main points, and the thoroughness of the summary.

Check the summary for accuracy and clarity. Be sure your summary conveys the same meaning and gives the same slant to the subject as the original does. Review the main points of the original. Does your summary include them in the correct order? Make sure you have properly credited all quotations. And consider whether your summary reads smoothly. Do the thoughts flow well from paragraph to paragraph? Or should you add some transitional expressions to improve it?

Read the following summary of the article that appears in Lesson 10. The original article contains 853 words; this summary contains 280 words, which is about one-third the length of the original.

A Summary of "Modern Times"
By Robert Darrow

Although times constantly change, certain eras bring dramatic changes that mark definite boundaries in history. Beginning in the middle 1400s, various events that were "related to each other in many complex ways" so altered the world that historians call this the beginning of modern times.

The Hundred Years' War between France and England ended in 1453. Soon these two nations were taking on the characteristics of modern nations. Spain and Portugal also were becoming distinct nations. By 1492, these nations had pushed the Arab Moors back into Africa.

In 1453, the Ottoman Turks overthrew Constantinople, the Roman Empire's eastern capital. A flood of refugees from Greece and Asia Minor poured into western Europe, bringing writings and knowledge that helped to spark the Renaissance.

Johann Gutenberg developed a movable-type printing press and printed a Bible in 1454. Because of Gutenberg's invention, it became much cheaper and easier to spread knowledge by the printed page.

Because the Turks controlled the eastern Mediterranean, Europeans could not trade directly with India and China. This spurred an interest in finding other routes to the East. The resulting explorations brought Europe into contact with new worlds and new products.

The Protestant Reformation, which began in 1517, greatly weakened the power of the Roman Catholic Church. Although this movement itself did not bring a revival of true Christianity, the Swiss Brethren of the same era did establish Scriptural churches.

These events produced extensive growth in population, commerce, industry, and agriculture. By 1600, men were daily discovering new things. And they imagined that man would be able to solve all his own problems. But the world remains corrupted by the sin of man; he can never save himself.

Applying the Lesson

A. Write *true* or *false*.
  1. Taking notes promotes concentration because it keeps your mind active.
  2. You should be able to write a good summary of an article after you have skimmed it.
  3. A good rule for note-taking is "The more, the better."
  4. When the teacher writes something on the chalkboard, it is impressed on your mind well enough that you should not need to write it in your notes.
  5. Taking notes on facts that are new to you helps you to learn them better.
  6. A good summary should preserve the author's original wording as much as practical.
  7. Most summaries have two hundred to three hundred words.

B. Write the correct word or phrase for each sentence.
  1. Good notes should mirror the (logical order, supporting details) used by a speaker or writer.
  2. Notes and summaries are useful for review because they are (brief, detailed).
  3. Good notes should include (some, all) of the main points and some of the (interesting, significant) details.
  4. For best results, organizing and rewriting of notes should be done (promptly after class, at the end of each week).
  5. A summary should *not* include your own (opinions, wording).

C. Take notes on one of the next sermons you hear or on a devotional in school.

Lesson 12 Answers

Applying the Lesson

A. 1. true
  2. false
  3. false
  4. false
  5. true
  6. false
  7. false

B. 1. logical order
  2. brief
  3. all, significant
  4. promptly after class
  5. opinions

C. (Individual work.)

D. Summarize the following composition in 200–250 words.

The First Transatlantic Cable (about 600 words)

Cyrus W. Field was a wealthy American merchant who devoted himself to the dream of laying a telegraph cable across the Atlantic Ocean. He probably never imagined how difficult the task would be or how much ridicule and disapproval he would endure because of it.

One great problem was to raise the $1.75 million needed to finance the project. For this purpose, Field went to England and organized the Atlantic Telegraph Company in 1856. Another problem was to design a suitable cable. The planners tried many experiments and saw many failures before a four-inch, brass-bound, insulated copper cable was completed. This cable contained 340,000 miles of wire woven into strands.

The first attempt. The great enterprise was launched in 1857, the same year that the first telegraph was completed across the American continent. In August, the *Niagara* and the *Agamemnon* left Valentia, an island just off the west coast of Ireland. Laying cable and relaying messages to shore went well for more than 300 miles.

Suddenly the messages ceased, but 2½ hours later they resumed. However, the next morning the cable snapped and hope was lost. The ships had to retrace their route.

The second attempt. In June 1858, the *Niagara* and the *Agamemnon* met in the mid-Atlantic, each carrying half of a new cable. Upon successfully splicing the cable, the ships sailed toward opposite shores. But after only 250 miles of cable were laid, it snapped at one ship and then the other. The men returned to England to hear some even more disheartening news. Some of the directors of the Atlantic Telegraph Company were planning to dissolve the company.

The third attempt. Because of the persistence and influence of Cyrus Field, the company continued; and one month later, things were ready for another try. Again the ships met in mid-ocean, and again the men spliced the two cables. But ships were passing too near the sinking cable. Floating icebergs and a passing whale added to the anxiety. Would this attempt also end in failure?

Finally on August 5, 1858, each ship arrived at its harbor with the cable still intact. The transatlantic cable spanned 1,950 miles, and it did transmit electrical signals. But the signals were so weak that when Queen Victoria sent official congratulations to President James Buchanan, it took 67 minutes to transmit her 90-word message.

It soon became evident that the cable's insulation was defective. The signals became more and more feeble, and by October 20 the cable was dead. For over six years, the transatlantic project received little further support or attention.

The fourth attempt. Early in 1865, Field was on the *Great Eastern*—the world's largest steamship at the time—as it left Valentia Island with a new cable. This one measured 3,000 miles long and weighed 7,000 tons. But

D. (Sample summary.)

A Summary of "The First Transatlantic Cable"

In 1856, Cyrus W. Field organized the Atlantic Telegraph Company to lay a telegraph cable across the Atlantic Ocean. The company raised $1.75 million and developed a four-inch copper cable to use in the project.

The first attempt began in August 1857, with two ships working together to lay cable as they sailed away from Ireland. Things went well for about 300 miles, but then the cable snapped.

The second attempt began in June 1858, with two ships in the mid-Atlantic. The men spliced two cables together and sailed toward opposite shores, but their cables snapped when they were only 250 miles apart.

The third attempt began in July 1858 and ended with the completion of a 1,950-mile cable across the Atlantic. But the signals were so weak that it took 67 minutes to send a 90-word message from Queen Victoria to President James Buchanan. Soon afterward, the cable was completely dead.

The fourth attempt began early in 1865, with Field aboard a large steamship called the *Great Eastern.* But after a journey of 1,186 miles, this cable also snapped.

In the spring of 1866, the *Great Eastern* finally succeeded in laying a working cable across the Atlantic. Then the men went back, retrieved the lost 1865 cable, and completed another live cable. "After nine years of setbacks and frustrations, Cyrus Field had not one but two successful telegraph cables across the Atlantic Ocean."

after 1,186 miles of cable were laid, the cable snapped. The grappling device on the ship was not able to retrieve the four-inch cable some 5,000 feet below on the ocean floor. Once more the crew returned to England.

Success at last. In the spring of 1866, Field was again on the *Great Eastern,* and this time he succeeded in laying a working cable across the Atlantic. The great steamship then traveled to the location of the lost 1865 cable. The men made some thirty attempts with an improved grappling device, and finally they retrieved the cable. They spliced another one to it and then completed the second live cable across the ocean. After nine years of setbacks and frustrations, Cyrus Field had not one but two successful telegraph cables across the Atlantic Ocean.

---

13. Improving Your Editing Skills, Part 2

The standard proofreading symbols provide a neat, efficient way to mark corrections in a manuscript. Anyone who is familiar with the marks will immediately understand what changes are intended. By contrast, look at the marks used to make changes in the following sentence.

Suddenly from the ~~S~~ky came ~~a loud~~ ⟨an⟩ earsplitting roar.

It may not be clear that *Sky* is to be changed to *sky,* for uppercase and lowercase *s* both have the same form. And scribbling out an unwanted word does not look neat at all. Can you imagine the unsightly appearance of a whole page full of such sloppy corrections? Consider too that later you may change your mind about a deleted word. How will you retain a word if it has been obliterated beyond recognition? Using the standard proofreading marks is surely much better.

The following table reviews the six proofreading marks from Lesson 7 and introduces six new marks. Below the table is a sample manuscript showing how the new marks are used. The exercises call for the proper use of all these proofreading marks.

Marks Used in Editing and Proofreading
(Introduced in first proofreading lesson)

∨ or ∧ insert (caret)	ℓ delete	.... stet (let it stand)
¶ begin new paragraph	ℓc change to lowercase (small letter)	uc change to uppercase (capital letter)

Lesson 13

Purpose: To review the previous proofreading marks, and to introduce several new marks.

Teaching Suggestions:

Review the proofreading marks studied previously, and discuss the ones introduced in this lesson. Point out that the "no ¶" symbol has the opposite effect of the "¶" symbol.

Note: There are actually several possible ways to indicate "no new paragraph." The method used by Rod and Staff copy-editors is to write "no ®" (for "no return") at the end of one paragraph and "no ¶" in the indent space of the next paragraph. Another method is to write "no ¶" in both of those places. Yet another method is to draw a line from the end of one paragraph to the beginning of the next. The method taught in this course is used to give practice with using the arrow and to avoid having to introduce the "®" symbol.

(Introduced in this lesson)

no ¶ no new paragraph	← move (arrow)	� transpose
# insert space	⌣ delete space	——— use italics

Explanations

To move a word from one line to another, it may be simplest to circle the word and use an arrow.

Words *I* and *my* are to be italicized.

Transpose symbol is used with words, letters, or punctuation.

"Delete space" symbol means the two words or word parts should be joined.

"No paragraph" symbol means the two paragraphs are to be joined.

Arrow indicates moving indented text left to the vertical line.

Extended line of the symbol # shows exactly where the space is to be inserted.

Sample Manuscript

Nebuchadnezzar did not give God His rightful place. certainly He filled his speech with I's and my's as he declared, "Is not great this Babylon, that I have built? For this reason, God caused the boast ful king to go through a very humiliating experience. no¶ |←Afterward, Nebuchadnezzar said meekly, "Those that walk in pride he [God] is able to abase" (Daniel 4:37).

There are other proofreading marks besides the ones shown in this lesson. But these twelve are the most basic symbols, and they are the ones that best apply to your work. Learn to use them accurately.

Editing Practice

A. Use the proper proofreading marks to correct two spacing errors in each sentence.

1. The Sermon on the Mount is meant for to day, not just for somefuture age.

2. If every one followed Jesus' teachings, noone would knowingly mistreat others.

3. True Christians would rather suffer wrong thanuse physical force against an other person.

4. Using physical force in cludes taking some one to court.

5. Paul rebuked the Corinthians because of their law suits against eachother.

Lesson 13 Answers

Editing Practice

(Answers are on pages 462–463.)

B. Use the proper proofreading marks to indicate one use of italics and to correct one
error of transposition in each sentence.

1. John Bunyan wrote The Pilgrim's Progress while was he in
    prison.

2. You haven't removed all the unnecessary and's from these
    paragarphs.

3. To spell accommodate, you write must two sets of double
    letters.

4. The book War-torn Valley tells a challenging story abuot
    nonresistance during the Civil War.

5. In 1927, Charles Lindbergh used the Spirit of St. Louis
    to the make first solo nonstop flight across the Atlantic
    Ocean.

C. Use the proper symbols to mark the changes indicated in parentheses.

1. The children asked if they might eat their lunches under
    the shade trees outside. (Move *outside* so that it follows *lunches.*)

2. Chastening is not pleasant; if we respond properly to it,
    however, we can benefit from the experience. (Move *however*
    and the comma after it to a position after the semicolon.)

3.   Job remained faithful to God in spite of great loss
    and suffering. (Use an arrow and a vertical line to move the indented
    text to the left.)

D. Now try your editing skills on the selection below. You will need to do the following things.
    a. Make one correction in each full line. (You will use each proofreading mark
        at least once.)
    b. Show that one word already deleted should be retained.
    c. Make the third paragraph begin in line 13 rather than line 12.
    d. Show that the term *solar constant* is to be italicized.

Sixteen changes should be marked. Can you find them all?

1.   Suppose man had to pay for all the solarpower that the

2. earth receives. At eight cents per kilowatt-hour, the Energy

3. recieved every second would cost $4 billion, or about two

4. dollars for every living person. Imagine! Each man, woman

5. and child wuld have to pay $120 per minute, which comes to

6. $7,200 per hour or $172,800 per day. how long could your

7. family afford this? ~~Yet~~ God sends solar energy completely

8. free.

9.   Remember too that the earth is but one tinny sphere

10. in the vast the solar system. The sun produces 2 billion

11. times as much energy as what the earth receives.

12.   In fact, the sun produces in one second as much energy

13. as the earth receives in about sixty years. Scientists care-

14. fully measure the soler energy reaching the earth. They

15. find that the ~~approximate~~ rate is about 5 million Horse-

16. power per acre. This is called the solar constant, for it

17. has shown hardly any measur able change over the past

18. hundred years.

---

14. Outlining Written Material

Outlining is a valuable skill. It helps a speaker or writer to organize the material he is to present. It helps a listener or reader to comprehend the material he hears or reads.

The Form and Content of an Outline

An outline is an orderly summary of something spoken or written. It shows the title, the main topics, the subtopics, the points, and so forth. An outline may consist of a paragraph summary for each idea, though that is not common. Some outlines have complete sentences to express each idea. Most outlines are topical, with a word or phrase to express each point.

Study this partial topical outline, which illustrates the rules of outline form given below it.

Old Testament Building Projects
I. Noah's ark (Genesis 6)
  A. The purpose
    1. To display God's grace and power
    2. To preserve a godly line

Lesson 14

Purpose: To review the basic pattern of outlines, and to teach *outlining as an effective study aid.

Teaching Suggestions:

Students should be familiar with the basic pattern of outlines. With the exception of Rules 10 and 11, you should spend little class time on these rules. The greater challenge at this grade level is to categorize material into main topics and lesser points. In going over the sample history lesson, have the students cover the outline while you work through it as a class. Then compare the outline you have formed with the one in the lesson.

If your students are well familiar with the basic pattern of outlines, you may wish to omit Part A of Applying the Lesson.

  B. The plan
   1. Its size
      a. 300 cubits (450 feet) long
      b. 50 cubits (75 feet) wide
      c. 30 cubits (45 feet) high
   2. Other details
      a. Made with rooms
      b. Pitched within and without
      c. Made with three stories
      d. Made with one window and one door
  C. The building time—about 100 years
   1. Because apparently not much help
   2. Because took time out to witness
   3. So that men had opportunity to repent
II. The tower of Babel (Genesis 11)
  A. The purpose
   1. To reach heaven by human effort
   2. To make themselves a name
   3. To avoid being scattered
  B. The plan

The form and structure of an outline follow a definite pattern. Notice how the sample outline above illustrates these rules.

1. Center the title above the outline.
2. Begin each line with a capital letter.
3. Indent each level equally.
4. Indent each level farther right than the previous level.
5. Put a period after each numeral or letter that marks an item. After you have used periods with *1* and *a* to mark points and subpoints, use parentheses with *1* and *a* if there are further details. On the outline above, details under "Made with one window and one door" would be marked *(1)* and *(2)*. And if those items also had details, they would be marked *(a)* and *(b)*.
6. Have at least two parts when subordinate points come under an item. If there is only one subordinate point, include it with the item above it.
7. Use either all paragraphs, all sentences, or all topics.
8. Use proper end punctuation with paragraph and sentence outlines. Omit end punctuation with topical outlines.
9. Use a logical progression from the beginning to the end of the outline.
10. Use headings that do not overlap in thought.
11. On a topical outline, keep the items of each level as nearly parallel as possible.

In relation to Rule 10, consider the first outline below. Some of the main topics overlap because essay writing includes argumentative essays and expository essays.

The second and third items should be subordinate to "Essay writing," as shown on the second outline.

Poor: Headings overlap
Composition Writing
   I. Essay writing
   II. Argumentative essays
   III. Expository essays
   IV. Story writing

Better: Headings restructured
Composition Writing
   I. Essay writing
      A. Argumentative essays
      B. Expository essays
   II. Story writing

Items that are parallel (Rule 11) are items with a basic similarity. All the items should begin with the same part of speech and be generally similar in structure. Compare the following examples.

Poor: Unparallel items
Meaningful Devotions
   I. Reading the Bible
      A. Analyzing the passage
      B. Apply the principles
   II. Prayer

Better: Parallel items
Meaningful Devotions
   I. Reading the Bible
      A. Analyze the passage
      B. Apply the principles
   II. Praying

The first outline lacks parallelism because *Reading* does not match *Prayer,* and *Analyzing* does not match *Apply.* What about *Reading the Bible* and *Praying* on the second outline? These items are not perfectly parallel, but little can be done about this, since *Reading* needs the object *Bible,* but *Praying* needs no object. The outline is acceptable because these two items are as closely parallel as possible.

Outlining as a Study Aid

Outlining is an effective study aid. The very process of outlining requires you to analyze the material you are reading. You must identify the main ideas and the lesser ideas. You must consider how the various details relate to each other. Writing an accurate, thorough outline requires diligent effort and study.

An outline continues to be a valuable aid long after you have completed it. The concentration that went into making the outline impresses the details more deeply upon your mind than if you had merely read the material. The outline also provides a good source for quick review. You can usually pick out main ideas and specific details more quickly on your outline than in your book.

Below is an example of a history lesson, with pointers to direct you through the steps of outlining it.

1. *Skim the paragraphs, and try to identify the main idea.*

Swiss Mennonite Encounters With Indians

The Swiss Mennonite settlers in colonial Pennsylvania suffered very little from the Indians before the French and Indian War. One reason for this may have been that they generally did not live on the frontier lines. By contrast, the Scotch-Irish who settled the frontiers were in frequent conflict with the Indians.

However, the larger factor contributing to peaceful relationships was the nonresistant position of the Mennonites and Amish. These peace-loving settlers treated the Indians with respect and consideration. There is no evidence that they ever used force against the Indians or that they used the forts erected by other settlers for protection. The lengthy poem "The Unbarred Door" portrays the peaceful and trusting relationship between the Indians and the Swiss settlers of the early colonial era.

The Indians who had not migrated north and west of the Blue Mountains were friendly in general. One group of Delaware Indians south of Bethlehem joined the local Mennonite (or Amish) families in their Sunday meetings. In the Lancaster area, Mennonite children played with their Indian neighbors. One of the Indian boys, Cristy, was named after someone in the Mennonite settlement, and he taught the white boys to make bows and arrows. A number of the Indians in the surrounding neighborhoods became Christians. But the Scotch-Irish on the frontier resented these peaceful relationships.

The picture changed after the Walking Purchase of 1737 and the Albany Purchase of 1754, which embittered many of the Indians. They began uniting with the French in conflict against the English settlements. This led to the bloody French and Indian War (1754–63), in which the nonresistant settlers suffered right along with the rest of the people.

One of the first Indian attacks came on October 16, 1755, at Penns Creek near Selinsgrove. The Delaware and Shawnee Indians killed, scalped, or captured all twenty-five of the settlers. Two days later, twenty-five settlers were killed five miles south of Sunbury. The massacres in 1757–58 of Mennonite families in Lebanon County, in Northkill near Hamburg, and in Page County, Virginia, are well-known incidents. On September 7, 1758, the Virginia Mennonites sent a letter to Holland stating that fifty of their number had been killed and two hundred rendered homeless. The Holland brethren gave $376.40 to assist the suffering ones.

According to the record, the early Mennonite settlers were instrumental in winning a number of Indians to the Christian faith. These Mennonites consistently upheld the doctrine and practice of nonresistance under very trying circumstances. They faithfully expressed Christian attitudes toward the Indians, whether friend or foe. Let us also express a Christlike spirit and leave a positive witness in our surrounding society.

Have you identified the main idea? Basically, this lesson discusses the relationship that the Swiss Mennonite settlers experienced with the American Indians.

2. *Read the paragraphs more carefully, trying to recognize the main divisions.* Keep a broad view as you read. Remember, you are looking for main divisions.

You should have recognized two main divisions in the lesson above: (1) the peaceful relationships between the Swiss Mennonites and the Indians before the French and Indian War and (2) the sufferings they experienced during the war. The last paragraph is a conclusion and therefore will not appear on the outline.

3. *Read the lesson again, narrowing your focus this time so that you can identify significant details and see how they relate to the main divisions.* Following these three steps should produce an outline similar to the one below.

Swiss Mennonite Encounters With Indians

I. Peaceful relationships before French and Indian War
  A. Because they did not live on frontier lines
  B. Because they practiced nonresistance
    1. Treated Indians considerately and honestly
    2. Used no force against Indians
    3. Refused protection of the forts
  C. Because the Indians living in their areas were generally friendly
    1. Group of Delawares south of Bethlehem attended Sunday meetings
    2. Mennonite children played with Indians in Lancaster area
      a. Indians named a boy Cristy, after a Mennonite
      b. Cristy taught white boys to make bows and arrows
    3. Indians in surrounding neighborhoods became Christians
II. Sufferings during French and Indian War
  A. Reasons
    1. Indians embittered by Walking Purchase (1737) and Albany Purchase (1754)
    2. Indians united with French to fight English
  B. Examples
    1. October 16, 1755, at Penns Creek—all 25 settlers killed, scalped, or captured
    2. October 18, 1755, south of Sunbury—25 settlers killed
    3. 1757–58 massacres
      a. In Lebanon County
      b. In Northkill, near Hamburg
      c. In Page County, Virginia
    4. September 7, 1758
      a. Letter sent from Virginia to Holland
        (1) 50 massacred
        (2) 200 left homeless
      b. Aid of $376.40 sent from Holland to Virginia

No two people working with the same composition are likely to produce identical outlines. But the outlines should definitely be similar in the main topics and subtopics that they portray.

Applying the Lesson

A. Improve this partial outline. Each starred line has an error.

Basic Steps in Making Bread

*I. Preparing the Dough
  A. Warm a large bowl
    1. Run hot water around inside

Lesson 14 Answers

Applying the Lesson

A. (Sample corrected outline; allow reasonable variation. Corrections are underlined.)

Basic Steps in Making Bread

I. Preparing the dough
  A. Warm a large bowl
    1. Run hot water around inside

  *2. drain off water
  *B. Pour correct amount of lukewarm water into bowl
 *C. Yeast into warm water
  D. Add sugar and stir well
  E. Cover and set aside
    *1. until it foams
    *2. Wait until it doubles in volume
  *F. Remaining ingredients mixed in well
    1. Salt
    *2. Add shortening
    *3. flour as directed
 *G. Adding remaining flour
    *1. To make soft, pliable dough
  H. Place dough on lightly floured breadboard
II. Kneading the dough
 *A. Working with lightly floured hands
  B. Knead vigorously
    *1. work toward center of dough
    2. Turn dough repeatedly
      *a. Until dough becomes smooth, springy, and satiny
 *C. Shape into a large ball.
    *1. Place in warm, greased bowl to rise

B. Write an outline of this composition.

The Island That Exploded

Krakatoa is a volcanic island in the Sunda Strait of Indonesia, between Java and Sumatra. At the beginning of 1883, this island contained about 18 square miles (47 km^2) and was populated by only a few native inhabitants. But later that year, an event occurred on Krakatoa that thousands of people heard of in a very literal way, with effects that were visible around the world for the greater part of a year.

Krakatoa's only known previous eruption had been a moderate one in 1680. But in the spring of 1883, it became clear that the volcano was stirring again. Two new fissures opened, with smoke and steam pouring out. A stream of lava cut a wide swath through the nearby jungle. The Sunda Strait was gradually covered with such a thick layer of floating cinders that by mid-August, ship captains no longer dared to sail through. On the island itself, the ground became so hot that the natives had to seek refuge in their boats.

Deep inside the island, the pressure of volcanic gases was growing more and more intense. On the afternoon of August 26, the huge rock layers in the side of the volcano—beneath the water level—suddenly buckled and broke apart, allowing white-hot lava to burst forth. Ocean water poured into the new fissure, changing instantly into steam as it contacted the hot lava; and soon a tremendous explosion ripped through the rocks. Again and again

  2. Drain off water
B. Pour correct amount of luke-warm water into bowl
C. Put yeast into warm water
D. Add sugar and stir well
E. Cover and set aside
    1. Until it foams
    2. Until it doubles in volume
F. Mix in remaining ingredients well
    1. Salt
    2. Shortening
    3. Flour as directed
G. Add remaining flour to make soft, pliable dough
H. Place dough on lightly floured breadboard
II. Kneading the dough
A. Work with lightly floured hands
B. Knead vigorously
    1. Work toward center of dough
    2. Turn dough repeatedly until dough becomes smooth, springy, and satiny
C. Shape into a large ball, and place in warm, greased bowl to rise

B. (Sample outline.)

The Island That Exploded

I. The island of Krakatoa
 A. Located in Sunda Strait of Indonesia
 B. Contained about 18 square miles
 C. Populated by a few native inhabitants
II. The explosion in 1883
 A. Events before explosion
    1. Two new fissures
    2. Wide stream of lava
    3. Thick layer of cinders in Sunda Strait
    4. Hot ground on island
 B. Explosion itself
    1. Buildup of pressure deep inside island
    2. Side of volcano blew out; seawater poured in

the ocean rushed into the opening, and time after time the island was rocked by stupendous explosions as the superheated steam shattered more and more of the massive rock layers.

Finally on the morning of August 27, the seawater reached the volcanic center of Krakatoa. The resulting explosion was so powerful that the entire northern two-thirds of the island was blown away. About 5 cubic miles (21 km³) of rock were blasted as high as 30 miles (50 km) into the air. The noise of the explosion was heard as far away as Australia, 2,200 miles distant (3,500 km); and the resulting waves were observed as far away as Africa, 5,000 miles distant (8,000 km). Clouds of smoke and dust blotted out the sun, plunging parts of Indonesia into darkness for two days.

Along with the noise came great shock waves that traveled around the world in all directions. The first of these reached London, England, some 36 hours after the explosion—arriving from the west. Then a second wave struck the city from the east. Back and forth the shock waves went, convulsing the atmosphere for more than ten days before their energy was spent.

The explosion caused widespread death and destruction. Some 36,000 people drowned when the coastal towns of nearby Java and Sumatra were struck by a wall of water 120 feet high (37 m). Red-hot ashes fell on hundreds of square miles, burying whole towns, turning rice paddies into deserts, and reducing jungles to ash-choked ruins.

Dust from the volcano was carried some 50 miles (80 km) aloft, where it hung in the atmosphere for months. Winds carried the dust over land and sea, drawing a veil across the sun and causing strange sights in the heavens. People around the world saw blue and lead-colored sunsets, green stars, and a green moon.

For months after the explosion, the little that remained of Krakatoa was utterly dead. But slowly life returned, carried by currents of air and water. The wind brought seeds, insects, and birds, and the water carried insect eggs, reptiles, and logs on which were snails and other small creatures. In fact, Krakatoa became an ideal place for scientists to observe how communities of plants and animals develop in a completely dead and isolated place. The government allowed no human visitors there except scientists; and within forty years, the island that had exploded was again teeming with plants and animals of every description.

Review Exercises

A. Write whether each statement about study skills is *true* or *false*. [9–12]
1. Before you can study at your best, you must take an interest in your work.
2. After you study a lesson, the rate at which you forget the material increases as time passes.
3. You should begin your study period by doing first what is most enjoyable.
4. Surveying a lesson before reading it gives you a helpful overview of the lesson.

3. Repeated explosions caused by steam
4. Final explosion on August 27
    a. Two-thirds of island blown away
    b. Noise heard in Australia
    c. Waves observed in Africa
    d. Parts of Indonesia plunged into darkness
C. Effects of explosion
    1. Shock waves in atmosphere
    2. Deaths caused by wall of water
    3. Destruction caused by hot ashes
    4. Strange sights caused by dust in atmosphere
III. The return of life
A. Items carried by wind
B. Items carried by water
C. Value to scientists

Review Exercises
A. 1. true   3. false
   2. false   4. true

5. You should wait until you have read a lesson before asking questions about it.
6. If you cannot recite answers to your questions about a lesson, you have not mastered that lesson.
7. When skimming a book, you should be sure to look at the preface or introduction.
8. Skillful skimming of a lesson can often take the place of studying the lesson.
9. Note-taking and summarizing promote logical thinking because the person doing these activities must understand the speaker's or writer's development.
10. Good notes should have all the main points and some of the supporting details.

B. Name the five steps in the SQ3R study method. After each one, briefly explain how to apply that step in studying a lesson. [10]

———————————

15. Outlining the Life Story of a Bible Character: Finding the Main Ideas

Christians often use outlining in their Bible study. Outlining skills serve well in preparing sermons, topics, and devotional meditations; in planning articles; and in studying Bible characters for personal benefit.

An outline of a Bible character's life story highlights the significant details of the person's birth, life, and death. The Bible does not give enough information about every character to always make an extensive outline. On the other hand, the Bible gives so many details about some characters that you would need a very long outline to include them all. Of course, the life story of many Bible characters can be outlined in more than one way. A given outline is not necessarily the only one that is correct.

The Bible study needed to form this kind of outline is not something you can do in a few minutes. First, you must study all the Scriptures that refer to the character whose life story you plan to outline. Use a concordance, topical Bible, Bible dictionary, or other reference books to find and read all those Scriptures. Be alert for name variations and for verses that do not specifically name the person. As you read those passages, think: "What short title would summarize this character's life?"

Then as you read and reflect further on those Scriptures, you must decide on the major divisions you will use. Often the simplest approach is to follow a chronological order, especially if the Bible gives details about the character's birth and childhood, his life, and his death. But the outline may also follow a topical order, emphasizing such things as influences that shaped the person's life, character traits that he illustrates, and contributions that he made to God's work.

5. false   8. false
6. true   9. true
7. true   10. true

B. Survey—Look over the lesson, noticing the headings and any pictures or diagrams.
Question—Ask questions for which you expect to find answers in the lesson.
Read—Carefully read the lesson, making sure you understand what it teaches.
Recite—Answer the questions you had asked; do the written assignment.
Review—Mentally recall the main points of the lesson.

Lesson 15

Purpose: To teach how to outline *the life story of a Bible character.

Teaching Suggestions:

Be sure to examine the students' outlines for Part B. Give help as needed so that they have a good foundation for doing the next lesson.

To illustrate the kind of outlining in focus, we will use the life of Asa, the sixth king of Judah. You would begin by reading all the verses that refer to him. *Nave's Topical Bible* lists the following references: 1 Kings 15:8–24; 1 Chronicles 3:10; 2 Chronicles 14, 15, 16; and Matthew 1:7. As you read these passages, keep thinking about a good title to use.

The verses in 1 Kings 15 and in 2 Chronicles 14 and 15 will probably impress you with the wonderful way in which King Asa led his people back to the worship of the true God. But the verses in 2 Chronicles 16 present a contrast as they describe Asa's disappointing failures later in life. So we could use this title: "Asa—Revival and Failure."

After you have chosen a title, you are ready to decide whether you will follow a chronological or a topical order of development. Consider all that the Scriptures say about the character. Can you see any general categories into which the details fit? If the Bible account includes many details of the character's life, you will probably choose a chronological order that goes through his early life, his youth, his early adulthood, and so on. If the Bible gives few details of this nature, a topical arrangement will probably be better. In that case, you will need to list the details and consider the relationships among them.

First, let us form a chronological outline of Asa's life. This means looking at his life and dividing it into logical time periods. The first division is fairly easy: his birth and early life. But where do we go from there? Does his adult life show any distinct divisions or changes? Yes, it does. After living faithfully for a number of years, Asa turned away from God. This makes a logical dividing point on our outline: first his years of faithfulness and then the time of his failure.

Asa's failure came when he was near the end of life. The remaining information is mainly about his death and burial. This gives us the following chronological outline.

Asa—Revival and Failure
    I. His birth and childhood
    II. His faithfulness
    III. His failure
    IV. His death and burial

Now let us develop a topical outline of Asa's life. We must keep our view broad and general, keeping his whole life in focus. Specific details are important only in relation to more-general observations concerning his life. What general observations can we make? Doubtless, the Bible details about this character could be grouped in a number of different ways. The following topical outline is just one possibility.

Asa—Revival and Failure
    I. Influences that shaped his life
    II. Characteristics that were evident in his life
    III. Contributions that he made to God's cause
    IV. Lessons that his life holds for us

If we were forming a topical outline of Abraham's life, one of our main topics would surely refer to his faith. An outline of Moses' life would probably have a main point concerning his meekness, and an outline of Job's life would have one about his patience. Any topical outline of a Bible character's life should definitely include his most outstanding characteristics.

Outlining the life story of a Bible character is a valuable exercise that helps us to gain a clearer overall perspective of that person. It enables us to see truths that we probably would never see by simply reading about him.

Applying the Lesson

A. Prepare to outline the life story of one of the following Bible characters by reading all the verses in the Bible which refer to that character.
1. Jephthah   4. Ruth   7. Noah
2. Esau   5. Balaam   8. Esther
3. Jonah   6. Haman

B. Begin forming your outline by choosing an appropriate title and listing the major divisions of the character's life. You may use either chronological or topical order.

---

16. Outlining the Life Story of a Bible Character: Filling In the Details

The main topics of your outline give you a sense of direction as you further study the life of a Bible character. These main ideas help you to focus on specific areas of the character's life as you add smaller details to your outline.

With your main divisions written down, read again the verses that relate to the character's life; then you will be ready to fill in the details under each main topic.

Chronological Outline

On the chronological outline of Asa's life in Lesson 15, the first main topic is "His birth and childhood." The Bible gives little information about Asa's early life, but we do find the following details. (For the material about his father, we must expand our research and read about King Abijah.)

Asa—Revival and Failure
I. His birth and childhood
  A. Was the son of Abijah
    1. Abijah's early profession of loyalty to God
    2. Abijah's later failure in true worship and godly living
  B. Was great-great-grandson of King David
  C. Was an ancestor of Jesus Christ
  D. Was born in time of widespread apostasy

Lesson 16

Purpose: To give further practice in outlining the life story of a Bible character.

Teaching Suggestions:

Perhaps you will want to finish with your students one of the outlines that is illustrated in this lesson. Here are sample completions.

Chronological development:
  III. His failure
    A. In his league with Ben-hadad
      1. Baasha's hostility
        a. Lived constantly at enmity with Asa

Lesson 15 Answers
Applying the Lesson
(All answers are individual work.)

    b. Built a fort to prevent movement between Israel and Judah
  2. Asa's request
    a. Immediately took money from the temple and his own house to persuade Ben-hadad to break his league with Baasha
    b. Apparently failed to call on the Lord
  3. Ben-hadad's response
    a. Honored Asa's request
    b. Attacked Baasha's northern cities
  4. Final results
    a. Baasha ceased building the fort
    b. Asa destroyed the fort
  B. In his treatment of the prophet Hanani
    1. Hanani's message
      a. A rebuke for failure
        (1) In relying on Syria instead of God
        (2) In forgetting past victories
        (3) In forgetting God
      b. The results of failure
        (1) Would lose the opportunity of victory over Syria
        (2) Would have constant warfare
    2. Asa's reaction
      a. Angrily threw the prophet into prison
      b. Foolishly oppressed some of the people

Now you are ready to fill in the details under the second main topic, "His faithfulness." As you consider the years when Asa was faithful to God, look for general divisions. You will see three distinct periods: his years of peace, his victory over the Ethiopians, and his leading of the people in revival. We will use these three divisions as subtopics and place the smaller details where they fit under them.

II. His faithfulness
   A. Laid a good foundation in years of peace
      1. Removed idolatry
      2. Commanded the people to seek God
      3. Fortified the cities
      4. Raised an army
   B. Led his people to victory over the Ethiopians
      1. Faced a formidable army nearly twice as large as his own
      2. Cried to the Lord for help
         a. Recognized God's ability to work through many or few
         b. Pleaded for God's help
         c. Expressed complete confidence in God
      3. Experienced a miraculous victory
      4. Pursued the enemy to complete victory
      5. Gained an abundance of spoil
   C. Led his people in spiritual revival
      1. Received encouragement from the prophet Azariah's message
      2. Continued to remove idolatry and evil from Judah
      3. Renewed true worship
      4. Provided a spiritual haven for many who sought the Lord
      5. Led the people in an outstanding worship experience
         a. An offering of 700 oxen and 7,000 sheep
         b. A renewed covenant to seek the Lord
         c. A time of great rejoicing
      6. Removed his idolatrous grandmother from being queen mother
      7. Brought into the temple that which his father and he had dedicated

To complete the outline, we would follow the same procedure for the rest of the main topics. Let us look now at the development of a topical outline.

Topical Outline

The first main topic on our topical outline is "Influences that shaped his life." This thought is related to that of the first main topic of the chronological outline above, but it represents a different viewpoint. Ask yourself: What influences do we find that would have helped to shape Asa's life? One that the Scriptures mention is his parents and grandparents. They certainly were major influences on Asa, so those points belong under this main topic.

   C. In his response to a physical ailment
      1. Became diseased in his feet
      2. Sought help from physicians
      3. Refused to seek God's help
IV. His death and burial
   A. Died in the forty-first year of his reign
   B. Was buried in his own sepulcher in Jerusalem
   C. Was greatly honored in his burial
      1. Sweet odors
      2. Various kinds of spices
      3. Great burning

Topical development:
III. Contributions that he made to God's cause
   A. Led his people in spiritual revival
      1. Removed idolatry
      2. Commanded the people to seek God
      3. Renewed true worship
      4. Provided a spiritual haven for many who sought the Lord
      5. Led the people in an outstanding worship experience
         a. An offering of 700 oxen and 7,000 sheep
         b. A renewed covenant to seek the Lord
         c. A time of great rejoicing
      6. Brought into the temple that which he and his father had dedicated
   B. Led his people in victory over the Ethiopians
      1. Faced a formidable army nearly twice as large as his own
      2. Cried to the Lord for help
         a. Recognized God's ability to work through many or few
         b. Pleaded for God's help
         c. Expressed complete confidence in God
      3. Experienced a miraculous victory
      4. Gained an abundance of spoil
IV. Lessons that his life holds for us
   A. Unwholesome childhood influences do not guarantee failure
   B. God always rewards sincere spiritual interest
   C. Times of calm are good times to prepare for future battles
   D. God honors sincere trust in His ability
   E. God expects His people to cooperate with Him in winning battles
   F. True revival attracts those who are seeking God
   G. True worship brings joy
   H. We must courageously resist evil even in those who are close to us
   I. Past faithfulness does not guarantee future faithfulness

What other factors would have influenced Asa? The low spiritual condition of Judah when he was growing up, and his acquaintance with the true God. Arranging these details under our main topic gives us the following outline.

Asa—Revival and Failure

I. Influences that shaped his life
  A. The inconsistency of his father Abijah
    1. Father showed measure of faith and loyalty
    2. Father failed in true worship and godly living
  B. The idolatry of his grandmother
  C. The apostasy of his people
  D. The God of his fathers

Now we are ready to fill in the details under the second main topic, "Characteristics that were evident in his life." As we consider this point, we remember that Asa was faithful for much of his life but then turned away from God. That suggests two divisions under this point, one for his godly qualities and one for the ungodly ones. By examining the Scriptures more closely, we can fill in further details under these two subtopics. Notice these points on our outline.

II. Characteristics that were evident in his life
  A. Godly qualities during most of his reign
    1. Spiritual interest
    2. Alertness
    3. Foresight
    4. Ability to organize
    5. Trust in the Lord
    6. Prayerfulness
    7. Perseverance
      a. In defeating the enemy
      b. In continuing the revival
    8. Courage
    9. Willingness to sacrifice for God's cause
  B. Ungodly qualities in his last years
    1. In his league with Ben-hadad
      a. Failure to trust in the Lord
      b. Confidence in a heathen king
    2. In his treatment of the prophet Hanani
      a. Anger at being rebuked
      b. Rashness in throwing the prophet into prison
    3. In his oppression of the people
    4. In his response to his physical disease
      a. Failure to trust in the Lord
      b. Confidence in the physicians

Once again, we would finish the outline by following the same procedure for all the main topics that are left.

When you have a well-rounded set of details under each point of your outline, check to see that all the points are in logical order. Also make sure you have used good form on your whole outline. Check your headings especially to see that they do not overlap in thought and that the points are as nearly parallel as possible. Finally, write the entire outline neatly.

Applying the Lesson
Follow the method described in this lesson to finish the outline you began in Lesson 15.

Lesson 16 Answers
(Individual work.)

---

17. Improving Your Speaking Style, Part 1: Eye Contact

Over the past few years, you have had several assignments in which you went to the front of the classroom and addressed your classmates as an audience. In those assignments, you worked mainly to develop a speech with good content and organization. After all, the most important part of an effective speech is having something meaningful to say.

But having something meaningful to say is not enough. You must also say it in a meaningful way. Your *speaking style* contributes greatly to the effectiveness of what you say. How well do you communicate with an audience if you speak in a mumble? Can you capture the listeners' attention if your eyes are glued to your notes? Will a dead monotone stir an audience to action? Of course not. Interesting and meaningful content requires appealing presentation to make an effective speech. This is the first of three lessons that give pointers on improving your speaking style.

Eye contact with the audience is a vital part of effective public speaking. Because many people feel self-conscious before a group, they tend to look somewhere else—at their notes, the floor, or the back wall. But meeting the eyes of your audience is so important that you dare not neglect it. Eye contact establishes an unspoken link with your listeners. It arrests their attention and shows that you are talking directly to them. It helps you to know whether you are communicating clearly. The listeners' reactions and facial expressions reveal whether you are talking loudly enough, whether your points are clear to them, and whether they enjoy what you are saying. Moreover, eye contact actually helps you to emphasize important points.

This means that you must look directly at your listeners. You are speaking to *people,* not to your notes or the walls. You are speaking to *individuals,* not to an abstract mass called an audience. Merely glancing at the group or running your eyes unseeingly over the audience is not eye contact. Look directly at individual listeners. You will know which person's eyes you meet, but that person will not know whether you are looking at him or at the person beside him. If you meet the

Lesson 17

Purpose: To introduce *the speaking style lessons, and to emphasize the need for eye contact with the audience.

Teaching Suggestions:
Point out to your students the importance of eye contact in everyday conversation. How do we feel when talking with someone whose eyes will never meet ours? Of course, we do not stare in each other's eyes through the whole conversation; but making eye contact from time to time—especially when expressing an important point—is a significant part of meaningful communication. The same principle applies to communicating with an audience.

Be sure to explain exactly how you will use the evaluation chart and whether or not you will give specific grades on these lessons.

eyes of persons in every part of the audience—in the front, in the back, to the left, and to the right—it will help each listener to feel that you have spoken directly to him.

Plan to establish eye contact with your listeners from the very beginning, with your introduction. This immediately communicates that you have something you want to tell them, something you consider worthwhile. Throughout the speech, maintain regular eye contact with your audience. However, you should not act like a programmed machine, raising your head at scheduled intervals. Rather, look at your audience naturally as you look at your friends when you talk to them.

Eye contact is especially important when you want to emphasize a certain point. Suppose in a discussion of honesty, you want to warn against exaggeration. You look down at your notes and carefully read this sentence: "We always weaken what we exaggerate." But imagine how much more effective that statement will be if you look directly at an individual in the group and say, "We always weaken what we exaggerate." Eye contact is an unobtrusive but forceful way of telling your audience, "Now, listen to this."

Finally, you should look at your audience as you conclude your speech. Though it is almost finished and you may be eager to return to your seat, your work is not quite done. Give it your best to the end. Have a well-planned conclusion, give it with fervor, look directly at your listeners—and you will end your speech on a solid, positive note.

You may think, "But I'm too nervous to look up while I'm talking. I'll get all mixed up if I do that." Those feelings are normal. But take your mind off yourself and concentrate on your subject. Think about your listeners and how they will benefit from what you have to tell them. Also remember that they are kind, sympathetic friends, who understand the difficulty you face and who want you to succeed. Like most hard tasks, this one becomes easier once you begin and also as you gain experience.

Your teacher will likely use the chart below to evaluate your speaking style assignments. This lesson introduces eye contact, so this assignment will be evaluated only for that one point of emphasis. In the next speaking style lesson, you will be evaluated on eye contact and the point of emphasis in that lesson. The third lesson will introduce a final point of emphasis, thus giving three items that your teacher will evaluate in your speaking.

Evaluation of Speaking Style

Part	*Points of Emphasis*		
	Eye Contact	*Voice Control*	*Enthusiasm*
1.	———	....	....
2.	———	———	....
3.	———	———	———

G = Good   **F** = Fair   **P** = Poor

Applying the Lesson

Prepare a talk of three to six minutes on one of the following topics or on another idea approved by your teacher. Think through your topic until it is part of you, so that you can speak confidently and wholeheartedly.

1. An accident or natural disaster experienced by your family
2. Memories of a special trip or an exciting day
3. An enjoyable family or school project

Lesson 17 Answers

(Individual work.)

---

18. Chapter 2 Review

A. List from memory the five points of the SQ3R study method.

B. Write *true* or *false* for each sentence.
1. You can develop interest in a subject by studying it as if you were interested.
2. The best time to do the hardest assignments is near the end of a study period.
3. A pleasant environment can help you study more efficiently.
4. Slouching can hinder your study because it reduces the amount of oxygen your brain receives.
5. The rate at which you forget is highest right after you have studied something.
6. The first step in studying a lesson should be to read it carefully.
7. Asking questions before reading a lesson helps you to read more purposefully.
8. Even though you have studied a lesson thoroughly, using the SQ3R method, you will need to review before taking a test.
9. When you read actively, you read to find specific information.
10. Skimming can become an effective substitute for detailed study.
11. Skimming is a good way to evaluate a book without absorbing its wrong influence.
12. When skimming a book, you need not take time to read its preface or introduction.
13. Skimming can be useful when reviewing material.
14. When skimming a book, you should occasionally read a paragraph or two.
15. Taking notes and summarizing help you to listen or read with an active mind.
16. A good rule for note-taking is "The more, the better."
17. A good summary should be written primarily in your own words.
18. A good summary should be about half as long as the original material.
19. Eye contact involves meeting the eyes of individual listeners.
20. Eye contact is important at the end but not the beginning of your talk.

Lesson 18 Answers

A. Survey. Question. Read. Recite. Review.

B.
1. true
2. false
3. true
4. true
5. true
6. false
7. true
8. true
9. true
10. false
11. true
12. false
13. true
14. true
15. true
16. false
17. true
18. false
19. true
20. false

Lesson 18

Purpose: To review the concepts taught in Chapter 2.

C. Answer these questions about study skills.
1. Why is interest the most important attitude for effective studying?
2. What are three ways to develop self-discipline in your studying?
3. For what two reasons is a regular study time important?
4. What is meant by reviewing actively?
5. What are four worthwhile purposes of skimming?
6. What are some types of significant information that you should write in your notes?
7. What are the four basic steps in summarizing?

D. Answer these questions about outlining.
1. How does outlining a lesson force a student to analyze it thoroughly?
2. What long-term benefits does outlining have?
3. When outlining the life story of a Bible character, what is the first step you must take after choosing the character?
4. What are two possible orders you may follow in outlining the life story of a Bible character?

E. Copy this partial outline, correcting all the errors.

The Art of Rug Braiding
I. What are some incentives?
  A. a simple skill to learn
  B. It is a good way to recycle old material.
  C. Can be a means to earn money
    1. High demand
      a. In craft shops
      b. Farmers' markets
    2. Flexible schedule
      a. Can be done in short snatches of time
  D. a worthwhile product to use
    1. They can fit with the décor of almost any room.
    2. come in great variety
      a. Variety of colors
      b. Various materials
      c. In a variety of shapes
        (1) Circles
        (2) In semicircles
        (3) oblongs
        (4) Can be squares
    3. Serviceable
      a. Simple to clean
      b. Reversed easily
      c. Conveniently enlarged
II. Procedures

_____

    3. Are serviceable
      a. Simple to clean
      b. Easy to reverse
      c. Convenient to enlarge
II. Procedures

C. 1. Interest helps you to apply yourself to work.
2. Start working immediately. Be prepared to work hard. Stick to your work.
3. A regular study time helps to prevent forgetfulness. It helps to condition your mind for studying at the set time.
4. Reviewing actively is recalling as many main points from memory as possible, rather than merely looking at the lesson and remembering the details.
5. to gain a bird's-eye view of a book or an article; to find information; to evaluate a book or an article; to review something studied previously
6. points that the speaker emphasizes; important definitions, figures, dates, names, and so forth; information that is new
7. Skim the material; read the material carefully; write down the main points; write the summary.

D. 1. The student must identify the main ideas and judge how the details relate to each other.
2. The increased concentration causes increased learning. The outline provides a good source for quick review.
3. Read all the Scriptures which relate to that Bible character.
4. chronological order; topical order

E. (Sample outline; accept reasonable variation.)

The Art of Rug Braiding
I. Incentives
  A. A simple skill to learn
  B. A good way to recycle old material
  C. A means to earn money
    1. High demand
      a. In craft shops
      b. In farmers' markets
    2. Flexible schedule—can be done in short snatches of time
  D. A worthwhile product to use
    1. Can fit with the décor of almost any room
    2. Come in great variety
      a. Variety of colors
      b. Variety of materials
      c. Variety of shapes
        (1) Circles
        (2) Semicircles
        (3) Oblongs
        (4) Squares

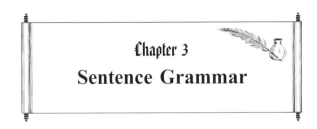

19. Complete Sentences and Sentence Skeletons

The sentence is the basic unit of language. A good grasp of sentence grammar, therefore, is essential to every kind of communication—listening, speaking, reading, and writing.

1. *A sentence is a group of words that expresses a complete thought.* It makes a statement, asks a question, gives a command, or makes an exclamation.

> Jesus Christ is Lord.
> Are we submitting to His lordship?
> Walk faithfully in His footsteps.
> If only all men would bow before Him!

2. *Every sentence can be divided into two parts: the complete subject and the complete predicate.* The complete subject tells *who* or *what* the sentence is about, and the complete predicate tells what the subject *does* or *is.*

> | complete subject | complete predicate |
> The Nelson Crider's, our neighbors for ten years, have moved to Illinois.

Sometimes the complete subject comes after the complete predicate or between parts of the complete predicate. Such a sentence is written in inverted or mixed word order, as you will see in Lesson 25. In the following sentences, the complete subject is underlined once and the complete predicate is underlined twice.

> Toward the heap of lumber streaked Brownie, our small but energetic dog.
> After a short scuffle, he came back, dragging a large woodchuck.

3. *The sentence skeleton consists of the simple subject and the simple predicate.* The simple subject is the basic part of the complete subject. It is always a substantive: a noun or pronoun, or a word, phrase, or clause used as a noun. The simple predicate is the verb or verb phrase. Either or both of these sentence parts can be compound.

4. *A fragment does not express a complete thought.* You can correct a fragment either by joining it to another sentence or by adding words to make it a complete sentence.

> **Fragments:**
> On Sunday we plan to visit Alton Mennonite Church. Where Uncle Harold's attend.
> Two pies cooling on the counter.

Lesson 19

Purpose: To review the basic structure of sentences.

Teaching Suggestions:

Sometimes students struggle to distinguish between fragments and elliptical sentences. Often the difference is in use rather than structure, for the same word group may be a fragment in one case and an elliptical sentence in another. To qualify as a proper elliptical sentence, a word group must be readily understandable by itself (as with an imperative sentence or a sentence having a clause of comparison) or in its context. In the latter case, elliptical sentences are proper only in very informal writing, such as dialogue.

In Applying the Lesson, Parts A and B are not divided in the normal odd–even manner. However, you can use the first half of the paragraphs in Part C for class practice and the second half for the written assignment.

Revisions:

> On Sunday we plan to visit Alton Mennonite Church, where Uncle Harold's attend.
> On Sunday we plan to visit Alton Mennonite Church. That is where Uncle Harold's attend.

> Two pies were cooling on the counter.
> The two pies cooling on the counter are for the Stutzman family.

5. *An elliptical sentence has one or more parts missing, but it expresses a complete thought because the missing parts are understood.* Most imperative sentences are elliptical because the subject *you* is understood. Also, many sentences with clauses of comparison are elliptical because parts of that clause are understood. Example: The Mississippi River is longer than the Susquehanna River (is long).

Other elliptical sentences are understandable because of the context. Elliptical sentences of this kind occur mainly in dialogue.

> "Are you ready to get to work?"
> "Where?"
> "In the storage room. Mother says we're cleaning it out today."

6. *A run-on error occurs when two or more sentences are joined incorrectly.* You can correct a run-on error in one of the following ways.
   a. By inserting a comma and a coordinating conjunction between the two parts. (Inserting only a comma produces a comma splice.)
   b. By inserting a semicolon between the two parts.
   c. By changing one of the clauses to a dependent clause.
   d. By dividing the incorrect sentence into two or more sentences.

   Run-on error:
   > Jesus' enemies tried to trap Him several times, He always put them to silence.

   Corrections:
   > (a) Jesus' enemies tried to trap Him several times, but He always put them to silence.
   > (b) Jesus' enemies tried to trap Him several times; He always put them to silence.
   > (c) Though Jesus' enemies tried to trap Him several times, He always put them to silence.
   > (d) Jesus' enemies tried to trap Him several times. He always put them to silence.

Applying the Lesson

A. Copy the complete subject, draw a vertical line after it, and copy the complete predicate. If the subject does not come first, rewrite the sentence in normal subject–predicate order before marking the division.
   1. God's people should be ready to sacrifice to serve others.
   2. The welfare of others holds priority over personal welfare.

Lesson 19 Answers

Applying the Lesson

A. 1. God's people | should be ready to sacrifice to serve others.
   2. The welfare of others | holds priority over personal welfare.

---

3. When God's love fills the heart, the child of God finds pleasure in helping others.
4. In the pathway of selfless service lies the way of true joy.
5. By such love for our brethren, the world can see that we love Jesus.
6. If we find selfishness crowding out kindness, we must repent.
7. Through selfishness comes much human heartache.
8. Through the power of the Gospel, every person can realize the joy of selflessness.

B. Copy the simple subject and the simple predicate of each sentence. Draw a vertical line between the two parts. (Watch for compound parts.)
1. A soft answer turns away wrath.
2. Angry words stir up bitterness.
3. A true peacemaker talks and acts in a peaceable manner.
4. By seeking peace, we can build good relationships with others.
5. Thoughtfulness and kindness are essential qualities for the peacemaker.
6. A person seeking peace not only will avoid doing unkind things but also will find ways to express good will.
7. Feelings of impatience or intolerance can quickly destroy peaceful relationships.
8. Often politeness and cheerfulness have contributed to peaceableness.
9. From Great-grandfather Gerber's excellent memory come many old-time stories.
10. Electricity and telephones came to his rural community in his childhood and dramatically changed life on his father's farm.
11. With the coming of electricity, farm jobs did often become easier.
12. With the telephone came various advantages for the farmer and his family.
13. Both the power of electricity and the convenience of telephones brought great changes and raised difficult questions for God's people.
14. The value of such new things is determined by their use.

C. These paragraphs have mistakes in joining or dividing sentences. Write the words immediately before and after each mistake, and show how to join or divide the sentences correctly. You may need to insert a conjunction.
1. The mute swan, quite common in parts of Europe and Asia, is a beautiful, graceful bird. The swan is a large bird. Attaining a length of sixty inches and a wingspan of seventy-five inches. Unlike many birds, the female generally is slightly larger than the male.
2. Mute swans are primarily herbivorous. Meaning that they feed on plant material. Since they spend most of their time on the water, their diet consists mostly of aquatic plants and roots, they also eat some small fish, frogs, and insects. An adult swan may consume as much as ten pounds of plant material in one day.
3. The swan's long, graceful neck is not merely ornamental it is essential for feeding. By stretching out its long neck, a swan is able to reach

3. The child of God | finds pleasure in helping others when God's love fills the heart.
4. The way of true joy | lies in the pathway of selfless service.
5. The world | can see that we love Jesus by such love for our brethren.
6. We | must repent if we find selfishness crowding out kindness.
7. Much human heartache | comes through selfishness.
8. Every person | can realize the joy of selflessness through the power of the Gospel.

B. 1. answer | turns
    2. words | stir
    3. peacemaker | talks, acts
    4. we | can build
    5. Thoughtfulness, kindness | are
    6. person | will avoid, will find
    7. Feelings | can destroy
    8. politeness, cheerfulness | have contributed
    9. stories | come
    10. Electricity, telephones | came, changed
    11. jobs | did become
    12. advantages | came
    13. power, convenience | brought, raised
    14. value | is determined

C. (Allow reasonable variation.)
   1. bird, attaining
   2. herbivorous, meaning
      roots. They (or roots; they)
   3. ornamental. It (or ornamental; it)
      vegetation that

far underwater to get vegetation. That other waterfowl, such as ducks and geese, cannot reach. In fact, if a swan upends itself, it can reach nearly three feet under the water.

4.　　Mute swans nest during the months of March through June. The male and the female work together at building the nest on the ground near a body of water. The male brings the sticks and reeds, the female fashions her nest from these materials. The female lays eggs every other day. Until she has from five to eight eggs. After an incubation period of thirty-six days, the cygnets hatch.

D. Show how to correct the fragments and run-on errors in this dialogue, using the same method as in Part C. Do not change elliptical sentences. If a paragraph has no mistake, write *correct*.

1. "Dorothy, will you please slice these loaves of bread? That Sister Bertha gave us?"
2. "Surely," answered Dorothy. "Everyone has been very kind to us while you've been sick, we'll need to watch for opportunities to return their kindness."
3. "Yes, indeed! It's a wonderful privilege to be part of a caring brotherhood."
4. "You're right. I remember when we first attended church here at Locust Point, we've surely learned a lot since then."
5. "Ten years," murmured Mother. "And it's been a happy ten years."
6. "Yes, it has. God has certainly blessed us. In many ways that I can hardly fathom."

Review Exercises

Write correctly each word that should be capitalized. If no capital letter is needed, write *correct*. [1]

1. magellan's ship *victoria*
2. at horst's appliance center
3. the book *in from the wasteland*
4. study bookkeeping II this winter
5. in the years before the civil war
6. see mr. horn's farm in the valley
7. in jesus' sermon on the mount
8. with my father and one of my uncles
9. some halls cough drops for sunday
10. about jeffersonian ideas in history class

4. reeds, and the (*or* reeds; the)
　　(*or* reeds. The)
　　day until

D. (Allow reasonable variation.)
1. bread that
2. sick. We'll (*or* sick; we'll)
3. correct
4. Point. We've
5. correct
6. us in

Review Exercises
1. Magellan's, <u>Victoria</u>
2. Horst's Appliance Center
3. <u>In</u>, <u>From</u>, <u>Wasteland</u>
4. Bookkeeping
5. Civil War
6. Mr. Horn's
7. Jesus', Sermon, Mount
8. correct
9. Halls, Sunday
10. Jeffersonian

20.　Sentence Complements

A *complement* is a word that *completes* the meaning of a sentence skeleton. There are three basic kinds of complements: subjective, object, and objective complements.

Subjective Complements

A *subjective complement* completes the sentence skeleton by referring to the subject. Verbs before subjective complements must be linking verbs: forms of *be* or verbs

Lesson 20

Purpose: To review subjective complements, object complements, and objective complements.

Teaching Suggestions:

Be sure to spend enough teaching time on objective complements, since the students have probably not mastered them thoroughly. Follow through the steps for the sample sentences in the lesson. Then use them together when you do some of Part C as class practice.

that can be replaced by them, such as *taste, look, grow, seem,* and *remain.*

1. A *predicate nominative* is a substantive that follows a linking verb and renames the subject.

> Our Master is the <u>Lord Jesus Christ</u>.
>> (*Lord Jesus Christ* renames *Master.*)
> Christians are <u>strangers</u> and <u>pilgrims</u> in this world.
>> (Both *strangers* and *pilgrims* rename *Christians.*)

2. A *predicate adjective* follows a linking verb and modifies the subject.

> God is altogether <u>worthy</u> of our worship.
>> (*Worthy* modifies *God.*)
> Father's voice sounded <u>calm</u> and <u>confident</u>.
>> (Both *calm* and *confident* modify *voice.*)
> Our hearts felt <u>light</u> and <u>cheerful</u>.
>> (Both *light* and *cheerful* modify *hearts.*)

Verbs like *look, turn,* and *feel* are not always linking verbs. In some sentences they are followed by adverbs, direct objects, or other sentence parts. A sentence contains a subjective complement only if the main verb expresses being rather than action, and only if the verb is followed by a substantive that renames the subject or an adjective that modifies the subject.

> The clouds turned an inky black.
>> (*Turned* expresses being; it can be replaced by *were. Black* modifies *clouds. Black* is a predicate adjective.)
> The storm has turned suddenly toward the south.
>> (*Has turned* expresses action; it cannot be replaced by *has been.* Neither *suddenly* nor *toward the south* renames or modifies *storm;* they are adverbs.)

Object Complements

An *object complement* completes the sentence skeleton by receiving the action of a transitive verb.

1. A *direct object* is a substantive that receives the action of a transitive verb directly. In a sentence with a direct object, the subject performs the action, and the direct object receives the action. To find the direct object, say the skeleton and ask *whom* or *what.*

> God created the <u>world</u> out of nothing.
>> (*World* receives the action of *created.*)
> God created the <u>heaven</u> and the <u>earth</u> in just six days.
>> (Both *heaven* and *earth* receive the action of *created.*)
> God blessed the seventh <u>day</u> and sanctified <u>it</u> as a day of rest.
>> (*Day* receives the action of *blessed,* and *it* receives the action of *sanctified.*)

2. An *indirect object* is a substantive that receives the action of a transitive verb indirectly. An indirect object comes between a verb and its direct object. To find an indirect object, say the skeleton with the direct object, and ask *to whom or what* or *for whom or what.*

> Sharon has given <u>us</u> some valuable help.
> > (Sharon has given help *to whom*? *Us* is the indirect object.)
> Leon told <u>Kevin</u> and <u>me</u> the plans.
> > (Leon told the plans *to whom*? *Kevin* and *me* are the indirect objects.)

Objective Complements

An *objective complement* is a noun or an adjective that follows and completes the direct object of a verb which expresses the idea of "making" or "considering." If the objective complement is a noun, it renames the direct object; if it is an adjective, it modifies the direct object. An objective complement is somewhat like a subjective complement. A subjective complement relates to the subject, but an objective complement relates to the direct object. Generally, you can insert the words *to be* between the direct object and the objective complement.

> The heavy rains made the creek a raging <u>river</u>.
> > (*River* is a noun that renames the direct object *creek*.)

     rains | made | creek \ river

> Meteorologists had considered a flood quite <u>likely</u>.
> > (*Likely* is an adjective that modifies the direct object *flood*.)

     Meteorologists | had considered | flood \ likely

Use the following steps to find an objective complement.
1. Identify the sentence skeleton and the direct object.
2. Determine whether the verb has the idea of "making" or "considering." If it does not, there can be no objective complement. If it does, go to Step 3.
3. Determine whether the sentence has an indirect object. If it does, there can be no objective complement. If it does not, go to Step 4.
4. Determine whether the direct object is followed by a noun that renames the direct object or by an adjective that modifies the direct object. Also determine whether you can insert the words *to be* between the direct object and the noun or adjective.

> At first we thought the idea impractical.
> > *Step 1:* Skeleton and direct object: *We thought idea.*
> > *Step 2:* The verb *thought* has the idea of "considering."
> > *Step 3:* There is no indirect object.
> > *Step 4:* The adjective *impractical* modifies *idea.* "Thought the idea to be impractical" is sensible. *Impractical* is an objective complement.

Then Father considered several other plans carefully.

Step 1: Skeleton and direct object: *Father considered plans.*

Step 2: The verb *considered* has the idea of "considering."

Step 3: There is no indirect object.

Step 4: *Plans* is not followed by a noun or an adjective that renames or modifies *plans.* There is no objective complement. (*Carefully* is an adverb.)

God has made the earth beautiful.

Step 1: Skeleton and direct object: *God has made earth.*

Step 2: The verb *has made* has the idea of "making."

Step 3: There is no indirect object.

Step 4: The adjective *beautiful* modifies *earth.* "Made the earth to be beautiful" is sensible. *Beautiful* is an objective complement.

God made Adam and Eve coats of skin.

Step 1: Skeleton and direct object: *God made coats.*

Step 2: The verb *made* has the idea of "making."

Step 3: There is an indirect object, *Adam and Eve.* There can be no objective complement.

Are you confused by the terms *subjective complement, object complement,* and *objective complement*? Remember that a subjective complement *refers* to the subject, and an objective complement *refers* to the direct object. An object complement *is* an object—either a direct object or an indirect object. But no subject *is* a complement, so there is no such thing as a subject complement.

Applying the Lesson

A. Copy each subjective complement, and label it *PN* for predicate nominative or *PA* for predicate adjective. If a sentence has no subjective complement, write *none.*

1. The Gospel message will never become outdated.
2. God's message is the answer to every man's needs.
3. Jesus' gracious words must have sounded sweet to the afflicted woman.
4. We should look often into God's Word for encouragement.
5. Two things to look for in each Bible passage are promises and commands.
6. God's Word should be growing precious and meaningful to you.
7. The warnings of the Bible should turn our minds to serious thoughts.
8. Bowser has become Richard's inseparable companion.
9. Aunt Geraldine has been a teacher or a mission worker for twenty years.
10. Judith's flower beds looked beautiful last week and have grown even more lovely since the rain.
11. The heat was high already this morning and became almost unbearable by noon.
12. Evelyn is both my cousin and my schoolmate.

B. Copy each object complement, and label it *DO* for direct object or *IO* for indirect object. If a sentence has no object complement, write *none.*

1. God's people must cultivate the Christian graces.

Lesson 20 Answers
Applying the Lesson

A. 1. outdated—PA
    2. answer—PN
    3. sweet—PA
    4. none
    5. promises—PN; commands—PN
    6. precious—PA; meaningful—PA
    7. none
    8. companion—PN
    9. teacher—PN; (mission) worker—PN
   10. beautiful—PA; lovely—PA
   11. high—PA; unbearable—PA
   12. cousin—PN; schoolmate—PN

B. 1. graces—DO

2. God faithfully describes these qualities in His Word.
3. The Lord gives His servants rich blessings of peace and joy.
4. The waffles turned a golden brown.
5. We children have been gathering walnuts and chestnuts in the pasture.
6. Grandfather Hackman made each grandchild a carved nameplate.
7. We gave Spot and Tippy baths this afternoon.
8. The boys dug potatoes and picked watermelons.
9. This morning Bonita worked on her afghan.
10. Marlene is filling the jelly dishes and the butter trays.
11. Orpha has mashed the potatoes and browned the butter.
12. Willie gave Father and the boys the message.

C. Copy the objective complements in these sentences. If a sentence has no objective complement, write *none*.
   1. God's people recognize themselves responsible to live consistently.
   2. We should be making our lives useful vessels for God's glory.
   3. The trusting soul considers God well able to meet his every need.
   4. The exercise of faith will make any trial bearable.
   5. Kelvin constructed these rabbit hutches by himself.
   6. Has Mr. Daley estimated the price of the job too high?
   7. Will Mrs. Foster make this driftwood the centerpiece of her flower arrangement?
   8. The girls worked hard all afternoon.
   9. The boys thought their work even more difficult.
   10. This dog is making himself a nuisance by his constant barking.

D. Copy each underlined complement, and label it *PN, PA, DO, IO,* or *OC.*
   1. Do you consider <u>sharks</u> dangerous <u>creatures</u>?
   2. Although tiger sharks are known <u>killers</u>, some shark experts actually consider <u>them</u> <u>gentle</u>.
   3. God gave the <u>tiger shark</u> powerful <u>jaws</u> and serrated <u>teeth</u>.
   4. Tiger sharks have keen <u>eyesight</u>, but two other senses are actually more <u>important</u> to their hunting than eyesight.
   5. With its acute sense of smell, the tiger shark is <u>able</u> to detect minute traces of blood in the water.
   6. Other creatures' nerve and muscle vibrations send the <u>shark</u> perceptible <u>messages</u> that pinpoint their location.
   7. Perhaps the strangest things found in sharks' stomachs have been license <u>plates</u> and gasoline <u>cans</u>.
   8. Tiger sharks are both <u>solitary</u> and <u>nomadic</u> in nature.

Review Exercises

For each underlined word, write *yes* or *no* to tell whether it should be followed by a comma. [2]
   1. Our God is <u>omnipotent</u> <u>omniscient</u> and omnipresent.
   2. Recognizing God's <u>greatness</u> and <u>goodness</u> we serve Him with our whole heart.

2. qualities—DO
3. servants—IO; blessings—DO
4. none
5. walnuts—DO; chestnuts—DO
6. grandchild—IO; nameplate—DO
7. Spot—IO; Tippy—IO; baths—DO
8. potatoes—DO; watermelons—DO
9. none
10. dishes—DO; trays—DO
11. potatoes—DO; butter—DO
12. Father—IO; boys—IO; message—DO

C. 1. responsible
    2. vessels
    3. able
    4. bearable
    5. none
    6. high
    7. centerpiece
    8. none
    9. difficult
    10. nuisance

D. 1. sharks—DO; creatures—OC
    2. killers—PN; them—DO; gentle—OC
    3. tiger shark—IO; jaws—DO; teeth—DO
    4. eyesight—DO; important—PA
    5. able—PA
    6. shark—IO; messages—DO
    7. plates—PN; cans—PN
    8. solitary—PA; nomadic—PA

Review Exercises
   1. yes, yes
   2. no, yes

3. Sincere <u>obedience</u> not mere lip <u>service</u> demonstrates our love for God.
4. We pray to the <u>Lord</u> with sincere <u>purpose</u> and in simple faith.
5. Lead <u>us</u> our <u>Father</u> by Thy divine grace.

3. yes, yes
4. no, no
5. yes, yes

---

21. Retained Objects and Objective Complements

You know that many verbs pass their action to another word in the sentence. If the receiver of the action is an object complement, the verb is usually in the *active voice.* But if the receiver is the subject, the verb is in the *passive voice.* (You will study voice more fully in Chapter 9.) Compare the following sentences.

Active: God <u>has given</u> bountiful <u>blessings</u>.
  (*Blessings,* the receiver, is the direct object.)
Passive: Bountiful <u>blessings</u> <u>have been given</u> by God.
  (*Blessings,* the receiver, is the subject.)

Retained Object Complements

Can a verb in the passive voice have an object complement? Yes, it can. To show how that is possible, let us first change the sentence above so that it has a direct object and an indirect object.

Active: God <u>has given</u> *mankind* bountiful <u>blessings</u>.

Now let us change this sentence to the passive voice, with the indirect object serving as the subject.

Passive: *Mankind* <u>has been given</u> bountiful <u>blessings</u> by God.

Note that *blessings* still follows the verb and receives its action, the same as in the active voice. So it is still the direct object, even though the verb is in the passive voice. Since the direct object is the same as it was in the active voice, such a sentence is said to have a *retained direct object.*

We can also rewrite the original sentence in the passive voice with the direct object serving as the subject.

Passive: Bountiful <u>blessings</u> <u>have been given</u> *mankind* by God.

Now *blessings,* the direct object, has become the subject; and *mankind,* the indirect object, has been retained in its original position. *Mankind* is now a *retained indirect object.*

As these examples show, either a direct object or an indirect object may be retained. In fact, only a sentence with both kinds of objects in the active voice can have a retained object in the passive voice. A sentence can even have an indirect object without a direct object!

Lesson 21

Purpose: To review retained direct and indirect objects, and *to introduce retained objective complements.

Teaching Suggestions:

A retained object is an object retained in the passive voice. Therefore, you should begin the class period with a thorough review of the active and passive voice of verbs. You could turn to Lesson 76 (in Chapter 9) for this review.

Unlike most lessons in this chapter, this one will likely pose a definite challenge to the students. Retained direct and indirect objects are first taught in grade 8; the students probably did not master them fully. Therefore, be prepared to give a thorough explanation of this lesson.

When you need to decide whether a sentence has a retained object, use the following steps.

1. Change the sentence so that the verb is in the active voice. (You may need to supply a subject.)
2. Identify the direct object and the indirect object. If the sentence does not have two kinds of complements, there can be no retained object.
3. See if either of these complements is an object in both active and passive voice constructions.

> **Problem:** Nehemiah was given permission to return to Jerusalem.
>   *Step 1:* The king gave Nehemiah permission to return to Jerusalem.
>   *Step 2:* Direct object: *permission;* indirect object: *Nehemiah*
>   *Step 3:* *Permission* is a direct object in both voice constructions.
> **Solution:** *Permission* is a retained direct object.

> **Problem:** Nehemiah's labors were blessed by God.
>   *Step 1:* God blessed Nehemiah's labors.
>   *Step 2:* Direct object: *labors;* no indirect object
> **Solution:** There is no retained object.

> **Problem:** Good leadership was given the people by Nehemiah.
>   *Step 1:* Nehemiah gave the people good leadership.
>   *Step 2:* Direct object: *leadership;* indirect object: *people*
>   *Step 3:* *People* is an indirect object in both voice constructions.
> **Solution:** *People* is a retained indirect object.

Retained Objective Complements

Not only object complements but also objective complements can be retained. A retained objective complement is an objective complement that is retained in a passive voice construction. Look at the following sentence. What are the direct object and the objective complement?

> God makes His will plain to the sincere seeker.
>   (*will*—direct object; *plain*—objective complement)

You could rewrite this sentence in the passive voice.

> God's will is made plain to the sincere seeker.

With the passive voice, the direct object *will* becomes the subject. What happens to the objective complement? It is retained in its original position, so now it is a *retained objective complement.*

When you need to decide whether a sentence has a retained objective complement, use the following steps.

1. Change the sentence so that the verb is in the active voice. (You may need to supply a subject.)
2. Identify the direct object and the objective complement. If the sentence does not have both a direct object and an objective complement, there can be no retained objective complement.

3. See if the same word is an objective complement in both active and passive voice constructions.

> **Problem:** Our work was made more pleasant by our singing.
> *Step 1:* Our singing made our work more pleasant.
> *Step 2:* Direct object: *work;* objective complement: *pleasant*
> *Step 3:* *Pleasant* is an objective complement in both active and passive voice constructions.
> **Solution:** *Pleasant* is a retained objective complement.

> **Problem:** The work has been done efficiently.
> *Step 1:* We have done the work efficiently.
> *Step 2:* Direct object: *work;* no objective complement
> **Solution:** There is no retained objective complement.

Applying the Lesson

A. Rewrite each sentence so that the verb is in the passive voice. Follow the directions in parentheses for retaining complements. You may omit the *by* phrase at the end of your sentence unless it is needed for clarity.
   1. Jesus gave the people many precious truths. (Retain the direct object.)
   2. Soon darkness will make the outdoor gathering impractical. (Retain the objective complement.)
   3. A young lad presented Jesus a small lunch. (Retain the indirect object.)
   4. Jesus gave each person sufficient food. (Retain the direct object.)
   5. The multitude considered Jesus a wonderful teacher. (Retain the objective complement.)
   6. The people assigned Him the position of an earthly king. (Retain the indirect object.)

B. Copy each underlined complement, and label it *DO, IO,* or *OC.* Also write *ret.* after the label if the object is retained.
   1. All creation gives <u>God</u> <u>glory</u> in one way or another.
   2. Ungodly men may think <u>themselves</u> <u>independent</u> from God.
   3. Yet even their wickedness will finally make God's <u>Name</u> <u>glorious</u>.
   4. Every man is given the <u>opportunity</u> to glorify God of his free will.
   5. God is brought acceptable <u>honor</u> only by His children.
   6. God's judgment upon the wicked brings <u>Himself</u> <u>glory</u> as right is vindicated and wrong is punished.
   7. The hot day has been made more <u>comfortable</u> by the breeze.
   8. This beautiful set of tea towels was given <u>Mother</u> for her birthday.
   9. A thorough housecleaning was given the old <u>cottage</u> by the mothers.
   10. The barn was made quite a miserable <u>ruin</u> by years of neglect.

C. Copy the retained complement in each sentence, and label it *DO ret., IO ret.,* or *OC ret.*
   1. The farmers were given an uneasy feeling by the early cold spell.
   2. Our farm is provided an adequate water supply by a large creek.

Lesson 21 Answers
Applying the Lesson

A. 1. The people were given many precious truths (by Jesus).
   2. Soon the outdoor gathering will be made impractical (by darkness).
   3. A small lunch was presented Jesus (by a young lad).
   4. Each person was given sufficient food (by Jesus).
   5. Jesus was considered a wonderful teacher (by the multitude).
   6. The position of an earthly king was assigned Him (by the people).

B. 1. God—IO; glory—DO
   2. themselves—DO; independent—OC
   3. Name—DO; glorious—OC
   4. opportunity—DO ret.
   5. honor—DO ret.
   6. Himself—IO; glory—DO
   7. comfortable—OC ret.
   8. Mother—IO ret.
   9. cottage—IO ret.
   10. ruin—OC ret.

C. 1. feeling—DO ret.
   2. supply—DO ret.

3. The whole countryside was made a winter wonderland by the freshly fallen snow.
4. A terrible scare was given Martha by a snake in the house.
5. The girls were shown several simple apron patterns by Aunt Louise.
6. We were shown the correct pronunciation of the unfamiliar word.
7. Several options were presented the congregation by the building committee.
8. The little house was made quite attractive by a new paint job.
9. The old wagon shed was made a chicken house by Uncle Laverne's brother.
10. Some good advice was offered the young man.
11. A simple but delicious meal was served the hardworking crew.
12. The report was made very interesting by the colorful details.

3. wonderland—OC ret.
4. Martha—IO ret.
5. patterns—DO ret.
6. pronunciation—DO ret.
7. congregation—IO ret.
8. attractive—OC ret.
9. (chicken) house—OC ret.
10. (young) man—IO ret.
11. crew—IO ret.
12. interesting—OC ret.

Review Exercises

A. Name the punctuation that should follow each underlined word: *colon, semicolon, ellipsis points,* or *none.* [4]
1. Father reverently read the Scripture <u>verses</u> afterward, he led us in prayer.
2. The brightest stars of the Northern Hemisphere include the <u>following</u> Arcturus, Vega, Cappella, and Procyon.
3. "Yes, Audrey, I would like to see your new place, <u>but</u>" Elaine said with a shrug.
4. When half of the corn was husked, the girls and Mother went inside to prepare it for <u>freezing</u> and we boys finished the husking, cleaned up the porch, and then helped in the kitchen.
5. Although he is only four years old, James enjoys taking care of Tabby and Mittens, our two <u>cats</u> Sport, our <u>dog</u> and Fluff, our lop-eared rabbit.

B. Write the letter of the sentence in which the boldface part is correct. [5, 6]
1. a. "Where is the verse, 'Blessed are the **peacemakers?'**" asked Father.
   b. "Where is the verse, 'Blessed are the **peacemakers'?**" asked Father.
2. a. We sang **"Loving Kindness"**; that song always inspires me.
   b. We sang **"Loving Kindness;"** that song always inspires me.
3. a. "God loveth a cheerful **giver,"** **(2 Corinthians 9:7)** and He promises to reward such.
   b. "God loveth a cheerful **giver"** **(2 Corinthians 9:7),** and He promises to reward such.
4. a. The clipper ship **"Thermopylae"** sailed from London to Melbourne, Australia, in 63 days.
   b. The clipper ship ***Thermopylae*** sailed from London to Melbourne, Australia, in 63 days.
5. a. Calvin gave a book report on ***Tips for Woodworkers.***
   b. Calvin gave a book report on **"Tips for Woodworkers."**
6. a. "Let love be without dissimulation **[pretense]**" (Romans 12:9).
   b. "Let love be without dissimulation **(pretense)**" (Romans 12:9).
7. a. "What shall we do **with—?"** Bonita dashed to the door.
   b. "What shall we do **with—"** Bonita dashed to the door.

Review Exercises

A. 1. semicolon
   2. colon
   3. ellipsis points
   4. semicolon
   5. semicolon, semicolon

B. 1. b
   2. a
   3. b
   4. b
   5. a
   6. a
   7. b

8. a. Several families will make the **three-hour** drive to the ordination.
    b. Several families will make the **three hour** drive to the ordination.
9. a. This sentence has too many **"of's"** trailing at the end.
    b. This sentence has too many *of's* trailing at the end.
10. a. We received **seventy-five-hundredths** of an inch of rain.
    b. We received **seventy-five hundredths** of an inch of rain.

8. a
9. b
10. b

---

22. Improving Your Writing Style, Part 2: Active Verbs

Originality
Active Verbs
Active Voice
Poetic Devices
Rhythm

Imagine for a moment that you are observing a large, magnificent building. You gaze in awe at the large sandstone building blocks. You examine with fascination the massive main entrance with its intricate woodwork, and then you admire the elaborate windows. You tilt your head back, your eyes moving upward.

Suddenly a small boy comes running down the sidewalk, followed closely by a barking dog and two other boys. Do you continue admiring the impressive building? Surely not. You turn your head quickly to see what is happening.

The same thing holds true in writing. Action draws attention. For this reason, we must make our writing as active as we can. We need to use plenty of specific action verbs so that the reader can see exactly what is happening.

What about the little verb *be*? It shows up time after time. Do we need this little, inactive verb? Look at these typical sentences in which this verb appears.

There <u>was</u> much sin in the city of Sodom.
All evening the children <u>were</u> outside.
Abraham <u>was</u> a man of great faith.

Used as a main verb, the forms of *be* express no action—only existence. Will this absence of action weaken our paragraphs? Should we root out *be* from all our writing? Or does this verb stand on its own merits as a verb we need, a verb with strength of its own? The following three guidelines will help you to work with this verb.

1. *Beware of using* there *followed by a form of* be. Whenever you spot a sentence beginning with *There is, There are, There was,* or *There were,* plan to revise it. Almost invariably, you can improve such sentences. Consider again the first example above.

There <u>was</u> much sin in the city of Sodom.

Remove *There was,* and the basic thought of the sentence still remains: *much sin in the city of Sodom.* Now if we add an action verb to go with it, we will have a better sentence.

Lesson 22

Purpose: To emphasize the use of lively action verbs as an element of an effective writing style.

Teaching Suggestions:

Point out that the use of lively action verbs is closely related to the use of exact verbs. What makes one verb more lively than another? The liveliness of a verb relates partly to its preciseness in saying what you want to say.

Sin <u>abounded</u> in the city of Sodom.
Much sin <u>polluted</u> the city of Sodom.
Sin <u>corrupted</u> the city of Sodom.

No longer do these sentences tell us merely that sin *was,* that it *existed* in Sodom. The verbs show what sin *did. Polluted* and *corrupted* go even further than *abounded* by showing how sin affected the city. By replacing *There was* with an active verb, we tell both what existed and what it did.

Here is another example.

During the night <u>there was</u> a heavy rain.

This time *there was* comes later in the sentence, but the problem is the same. If we remove *there was,* we have the subject of the sentence: *a heavy rain.* We must tell what the rain did, and the reader will know that the rain *was* without our saying so.

Heavy rain <u>flooded</u> our garden last night.

You will not find it easy to restructure every sentence that contains *there is* or *there was.* But if you make a special effort to weed out these phrases, you will help your sentences to "stand up and do something" rather than lying idly on the page.

2. *Examine each use of be as a main verb.* Surprisingly often, we can replace *be* with an action verb and thereby express the thought of the sentence more effectively. Look again at the second example sentence above.

All evening the children <u>were</u> outside.

So the children *were.* They existed. And they existed outside. But did they do nothing as they existed? Possibly, but not likely! They probably were *playing* or *running* or *talking* outside. Add that information to the sentence, and it takes on more life.

All evening the children <u>played</u> outside.

This does not mean that we must never use *be* as a main verb. In many cases, *be* is just the word we need. Here is the third example from the list above.

Abraham <u>was</u> a man of great faith.

Could we reword this sentence? Yes, we could write *Abraham, a man of great faith,* and add an action verb to tell what he did. We could write *Abraham obeyed God even though he did not know the outcome.* But does this revision really improve the original sentence? Not necessarily. Depending on the surrounding sentences, the revision may fit well and add vigor to the paragraph. Then again, the original sentence may fit effectively and stand in its own right.

The following paragraph concludes with a sentence using *be* as its main verb. Notice how well this sentence fills its place. (All the verbs are underlined.)

At the call of God, Abraham <u>departed</u> from Ur and <u>moved</u> away, not knowing where God <u>would lead</u> him. He <u>left</u> his father's family at Haran and <u>traveled</u> on to the land of Canaan. Even there he <u>faced</u> great tests. When God <u>commanded</u> him to sacrifice his son Isaac, he <u>obeyed</u> without hesitation. Truly, Abraham <u>was</u> a man of great faith.

3. *When* be *is a linking verb, try to replace it with a more descriptive word.* We have a number of choices in this: *sound, look, appear, taste, feel, smell, become, seem, stay, grow, turn, remain, prove,* and others. Compare the sentences in the following pairs.

Nondescriptive forms of *be:*
Father's prediction of rain <u>was</u> correct.
In days of ease, the hearts of many <u>are</u> cold toward spiritual things.
More descriptive linking verbs:
Father's prediction of rain <u>proved</u> correct.
In days of ease, the hearts of many <u>grow</u> cold toward spiritual things.

Though *proved* and *grow* are still linking verbs, they do suggest action and therefore add strength to the sentence. The small change makes a definite improvement. Now consider this example.

Although some Scripture verses *may be* difficult to comprehend, the Holy Spirit *is* our Guide into all truth.

We could say that some Scripture verses *may seem* or *may appear* difficult. But this changes the thought, suggesting that the Scriptures are not difficult to understand—they only seem that way. We probably will choose to keep the verb *may be.* And for the verb *is,* no other linking verb replaces it very well. The original sentence appears to have the best wording.

But wait. We can remove the linking verbs completely and reword the sentence with all active verbs!

Although we <u>may find</u> it difficult to comprehend some Scripture verses, the Holy Spirit <u>guides</u> us into all truth.

How do we know when to revise a sentence and when to let it stand? That is part of the art of writing. We learn by doing, by practicing, by experimenting. Examine your uses of *be,* think of other ways to express the same thought, and then use the wording you consider most effective. Sometimes it will be a new wording with an active verb, sometimes a new wording with a more descriptive linking verb, and sometimes the original sentence.

Your assignment in this lesson will be to explain or illustrate a proverb from the Bible. Below are two examples of such an explanation. Do you see how the active verbs make the second one more direct and forceful?

Paragraphs with many forms of *be:*

"A soft answer turneth away wrath: but grievous words stir up anger" (Proverbs 15:1). The story of David and Abigail <u>is</u> a clear illustration of this proverb. When David's servants asked Nabal for provisions, his answer <u>was</u> one that might have <u>been</u> a record for grievous words. "Who is David?" asked Nabal. "Shall I take the food that I have prepared for my workers, and give it to someone I do not even know?" These words <u>were</u> so insulting to David that he <u>was</u> ready to wipe Nabal and his household from the face of the earth.

As soon as Abigail <u>was</u> aware of Nabal's response, she prepared enough food to feed a small army. Soon she <u>was</u> in the presence of David with her gift, saying, "Upon me, my lord, upon me let this iniquity be"—speaking such gracious words that David immediately <u>was</u> sorry for his murderous plans. By her soft answer, Abigail <u>was</u> able to turn away David's wrath and save the lives of everyone in her household. The impression she made on David <u>was</u> so favorable that after Nabal's death, David sent a proposal to Abigail, and soon she <u>was</u> his wife.

Paragraphs with more active verbs:

"A soft answer turneth away wrath: but grievous words stir up anger" (Proverbs 15:1). The story of David and Abigail clearly <u>illustrates</u> this proverb. When David's servants asked Nabal for provisions, he <u>gave</u> an answer that might have <u>set</u> a record for grievous words. "Who is David?" asked Nabal. "Shall I take the food that I have prepared for my workers, and give it to someone I do not even know?" These words <u>stirred</u> up such anger in David that he <u>made</u> preparations to wipe Nabal and his household from the face of the earth.

As soon as Abigail <u>heard</u> of Nabal's response, she prepared enough food to feed a small army. She <u>hastened</u> with her gift to David, saying, "Upon me, my lord, upon me let this iniquity be"—speaking such gracious words that David immediately <u>repented</u> of his murderous plans. By her soft answer, Abigail <u>turned</u> away David's wrath and <u>saved</u> the lives of everyone in her household. She <u>made</u> such a favorable impression on David that after Nabal's death, David sent a proposal to Abigail, and soon she <u>became</u> his wife.

Work hard to put action into your writing style. Use descriptive, active verbs. Replace *be* if you can use something better. Remember: action draws attention.

Applying the Lesson

In 150–200 words, explain or illustrate a verse from Proverbs. You may use one of the following or choose one yourself. Put special effort into using lively action words. Also work for originality as you studied in Lesson 3.

1. "A good name is rather to be chosen than great riches, and loving favour rather than silver and gold" (22:1).

Lesson 22 Answers
(Individual work.)

2. "A word fitly spoken is like apples of gold in pictures of silver" (25:11).
3. "He that passeth by, and meddleth with strife belonging not to him, is like one that taketh a dog by the ears" (26:17).
4. "Pride goeth before destruction, and an haughty spirit before a fall" (16:18).
5. "Wealth gotten by vanity shall be diminished: but he that gathereth by labour shall increase" (13:11).

---

23. Phrases and Clauses

Some sentences consist merely of a sequence of single words, but others include phrases and clauses. Study the following examples.

> The calves bawled.
> The calves in the hutches were bawling for their breakfast before we got out of bed.

The second example has an adjective phrase (*in the hutches*), a verb phrase (*were bawling*), an adverb phrase (*for their breakfast*), and an adverb clause (*before we got out of bed*). By becoming skilled in working with phrases and clauses, you will improve your ability to communicate effectively.

Phrases

A *phrase* is a group of related words without a skeleton.

1. A *prepositional phrase* begins with a preposition (like *to, for,* or *with*), it ends with an object (usually a noun), and it includes all the modifiers of the object. A prepositional phrase is usually an adjective (modifying a substantive) or an adverb (modifying a verb or another modifier). Sometimes it is a noun because it names something.

> The tea <u>in this bed</u> came <u>from Grandmother Petre</u>.
>> (*In this bed* is an adjective phrase modifying the noun *tea. From Grandmother Petre* is an adverb phrase modifying the verb *came.*)
> <u>In the other bed</u> is the place where we planted the tea <u>from the meadow</u>.
>> (*In the other bed* is a noun phrase that names a place. It is the subject. *From the meadow* is an adjective phrase modifying *tea.*)

2. A *verbal phrase* contains a verb form used as another part of speech. The verbal phrase includes the verbal and all its modifiers and complements.
   a. A gerund phrase contains an *-ing* form used as a noun.

> <u>Standing solidly for the right</u> may not always be easy.
>> (phrase beginning with the gerund *Standing*)
> We should enjoy <u>serving the Lord</u>.
>> (phrase beginning with the gerund *serving*)

Lesson 23

Purpose: To review the definition and recognition of phrases and clauses.

Teaching Suggestions:

At first glance, this lesson may seem quite simple. However, the average student has not likely mastered noun clauses and verbal phrases. When you discuss the verbal phrases, do not stress the identification of the phrases as gerund, participial, or infinitive. The main point in this lesson is that students should recognize these word groups as phrases and identify how they function in the sentence. As you review the parts of speech in later chapters, you will emphasize the different kinds of verbals.

b.   A participial phrase contains a past form or an *-ing* form used as an adjective. It answers the question *what kind of* about a substantive.

A family <u>serving God together</u> is a great blessing.
(phrase beginning with the participle *serving*)
The family, <u>assembled for morning worship</u>, sat reverently.
(phrase beginning with the participle *assembled*)

c.   An infinitive phrase contains a basic verb form preceded by *to* and is used as a noun, an adjective, or an adverb.
(1) When used as a noun, an infinitive phrase must name an action and fill a noun function in the sentence.

Jennie has asked <u>to read this book next</u>.
(phrase beginning with the infinitive *to read* is the direct object of *has asked*)
Virgil's mistake was <u>to depend solely on Leon's story</u>.
(phrase beginning with the infinitive *to depend* is the predicate nominative renaming *mistake*)

(2) When used as an adjective, an infinitive phrase immediately follows the substantive it modifies and usually answers the question *which* or *what kind of.*

An important principle <u>to consider now</u> is that young people have a prime opportunity <u>to establish good habits</u>.
(phrase *to consider now* tells *what kind of* about *principle;* phrase *to establish good habits* tells *what kind of* about *opportunity*)

(3) When used as an adverb, an infinitive phrase may modify a verb or verbal, an adjective, or another adverb. An infinitive phrase that modifies a verb or verbal almost always tells *why.* One that modifies an adjective or adverb immediately follows the word it modifies. Usually it tells *to what degree* or *how;* sometimes it does not answer any specific question but obviously adds to the meaning of an adjective or an adverb.

Before eating, we bowed our heads <u>to pray to our heavenly Father</u>.
(tells *why* about the verb *bowed*)
Pausing <u>to recognize our heavenly Father's providence</u> is only fitting.
(tells *why* about the verbal *Pausing*)
Indeed, only God is able <u>to provide for our daily needs</u>.
(answers no specific question, but adds to the meaning of the predicate adjective *able*)
God loves us too strongly <u>to fail us in any way</u>.
(tells *to what degree* about *too strongly*)

3.   A *phrase of a single part of speech* contains several nouns or verbs working together as a unit.

<u>Grandmother Augsburger</u> now <u>is living</u> near <u>Texter Mountain</u>.

Clauses

A *clause* is a group of related words that contains a skeleton.

1. An *independent clause* expresses a complete thought and can stand alone as a sentence. Actually, every simple sentence is an independent clause, but this term is generally used only when a sentence has more than one clause.

> A wild <u>rabbit</u> <u>hopped</u> into the clearing. (simple sentence: independent clause)
> A wild <u>rabbit</u> <u>hopped</u> into the clearing, and <u>we</u> <u>watched</u> it quietly.
>   (compound sentence: two independent clauses)
> A wild <u>rabbit</u> <u>hopped</u> into the clearing while <u>we</u> <u>sat</u> quietly watching.
>   (complex sentence: first clause is independent; second is dependent)

2. A *dependent clause* does not express a complete thought but must function within an independent clause. It may function as a noun, an adjective, or an adverb.

> <u>Whoever wants God's blessing</u> must obey His Word.
>   (dependent noun clause functioning as the subject)
> God, <u>who understands humanity perfectly</u>, directs us how to live.
>   (dependent adjective clause modifying *God*)
> <u>Although the Bible reveals God's will</u>, too many people ignore its counsels.
>   (dependent adverb clause modifying *ignore*)

Applying the Lesson

A. Label each underlined phrase *prep.* (prepositional), *vb.* (verbal), or *ps.* (single part of speech). Also write the abbreviation for the part of speech that each one is.
1. The ᵃ<u>Holy Scriptures</u> ᵇ<u>will guide</u> the believer ᶜ<u>without fail</u>.
2. ᵃ<u>To benefit from that guidance</u>, we ᵇ<u>must seek</u> ᶜ<u>to understand the message of the Bible</u>.
3. ᵃ<u>Studying the Bible sincerely</u> certainly requires a willingness ᵇ<u>to do God's will</u>.
4. God's Word ᵃ<u>will endure</u> ᵇ<u>to all generations</u>.
5. Our whole family hiked ᵃ<u>up Hickory Mountain</u> and found a small clearing ᵇ<u>with a dilapidated log cabin</u>.
6. ᵃ<u>Startled by our quiet approach</u>, a doe fled ᵇ<u>with her fawns</u> to the safety ᶜ<u>of the denser woods</u>.
7. ᵃ<u>To watch the wildlife awhile</u>, we sat quietly ᵇ<u>in the brush beside the clearing</u>.
8. ᵃ<u>Within five minutes</u>, a buck ᵇ<u>with majestic antlers</u> had crossed the clearing, and a fat porcupine had waddled ᶜ<u>down the trail</u>.
9. ᵃ<u>On such occasions</u>, our goal is ᵇ<u>to increase our knowledge of nature</u>, and we also gain a renewed appreciation ᶜ<u>for God's creative power</u>.
10. ᵃ<u>Observing God's world</u> can be a definite benefit ᵇ<u>for God's people</u>.

B. Label each underlined clause *I* (independent) or *D* (dependent). If the clause is dependent, also label its part of speech.
1. "A city <u>that is set on an hill</u> cannot be hid."
2. "<u>Whosoever is angry with his brother without a cause</u> shall be in danger of the judgment."

Lesson 23 Answers

Applying the Lesson

A. 1. a. ps.—n.   c. prep.—adv.
       b. ps.—v.
    2. a. vb.—adv.   c. vb.—n.
       b. ps.—v.
    3. a. vb.—n.
       b. vb.—adj.
    4. a. ps.—v.
       b. prep.—adv.
    5. a. prep.—adv.
       b. prep.—adj.
    6. a. vb.—adj.   c. prep.—adj.
       b. prep.—adv.
    7. a. vb.—adv.
       b. prep.—adv.
    8. a. prep.—adv.   c. prep.—adv.
       b. prep.—adj.
    9. a. prep.—adv.   c. prep.—adj.
       b. vb.—n.
   10. a. vb.—n.
       b. prep.—adj.

B. 1. D—adj.
    2. D—n.

3. "If ye salute your brethren only, what do ye more than others?"
4. "Beware of false prophets, which come to you in sheep's clothing, but inwardly they are ravening wolves."
5. "A good tree cannot bring forth evil fruit, neither can a corrupt tree bring forth good fruit."
6. "If any man will come after me, let him deny himself."
7. "When ye shall see all these things, know that it is near, even at the door."
8. "All they that take the sword shall perish with the sword."

C. Label each underlined word group *phrase* or *clause.* Also label its part of speech.
1. The ªCaucasus Mountains lie ᵇbetween the Black Sea and the Caspian Sea.
2. The main range ªof the Caucasus, ᵇwhich runs roughly east and west, stretches nine hundred miles.
3. ªFor centuries, communities ᵇhave existed high in these mountains.
4. Highland glens, ªlying between steep ridges, have been populated ᵇsince very early times.
5. ªBecause these mountains rise rugged and beautiful, they have challenged mountain climbers ᵇwho have come from all parts of the world.
6. ªAlthough the Caucasus Mountains lie between two large bodies of water, only the western part of the range ᵇis blessed with abundant rainfall.
7. ªWhatever Mr. Parks sells is generally a product ᵇof high quality.
8. ªGeorge Keyes has learned ᵇthat our mud makes miserable roads.
9. ªMewing softly, Misty looked up from the corner ᵇwhere she had her nest.
10. Edward's main chore ªin the mornings is ᵇto take care of the calves.
11. ªTo ease our morning schedule, we try ᵇto have the lunches packed in the evening.
12. ªWhere Bennie cut his foot should be found ᵇso that it does not happen again.

Review Exercises
A. Copy each underlined complement, and label it *PN, PA, DO, IO,* or *OC.* [20]
1. Ceylon became the Republic of Sri Lanka in 1972.
2. From 1948 to 1972, Ceylon had been independent, but it remained a member of the British Commonwealth.
3. A population of over fourteen million gives this island a high population density.
4. The island, containing 25,332 square miles, is somewhat larger than West Virginia.
5. Sri Lanka's equatorial, oceanic location makes its climate tropical.

B. Label each underlined complement *DO ret., IO ret.,* or *OC ret.* [21]
1. By God's grace, your life can be made useful in God's service.
2. Your life can never be given true godly quality by self-help efforts.
3. We are taught the way to true greatness in God's Word.
4. God's Word must be considered authoritative so that we can trust its counsels.
5. No true help is provided man by the world's false philosophies.

3. D—adv.
4. I
5. I
6. D—adv.
7. D—n.
8. D—adj.

C. 1. a. phrase—n.   b. phrase—adv.
    2. a. phrase—adj.   b. clause—adj.
    3. a. phrase—adv.   b. phrase—v.
    4. a. phrase—adj.   b. phrase—adv.
    5. a. clause—adv.   b. clause—adj.
    6. a. clause—adv.   b. phrase—v.
    7. a. clause—n.   b. phrase—adj.
    8. a. phrase—n.   b. clause—n.
    9. a. phrase—adj.   b. clause—adj.
   10. a. phrase—adj.   b. phrase—n.
   11. a. phrase—adv.   b. phrase—n.
   12. a. clause—n.   b. clause—adv.

Review Exercises
A. 1. Republic of Sri Lanka—PN
    2. independent—PA; member—PN
    3. island—IO; density—DO
    4. larger—PA
    5. climate—DO; tropical—OC

B. 1. OC ret.
    2. DO ret.
    3. DO ret.
    4. OC ret.
    5. IO ret.

24. Appositives and Independent Elements

Appositives

An *appositive* is a substantive that identifies or explains another substantive. The appositive may be a substantive standing alone, or it may be a phrase that includes adjective modifiers. An appositive usually follows the substantive that it explains, but sometimes it precedes the other substantive.

> The apostle <u>Paul</u> carried the Gospel message on several missionary journeys. (The appositive *Paul* identifies *apostle*.)
>
> Paul, <u>the apostle to the Gentiles</u>, carried the Gospel message on several missionary journeys. (The appositive *the apostle to the Gentiles* further explains *Paul*.)
>
> <u>The apostle to the Gentiles</u>, Paul carried the Gospel message on several missionary journeys. (The appositive precedes the substantive that it explains.)

1. A *nonrestrictive appositive* merely gives additional information about a substantive, and it is set off by commas. In the example sentences above, the second and third ones contain nonrestrictive appositives.

2. A *restrictive appositive* restricts the meaning of a substantive, and it is not set off by commas. Most restrictive appositives consist of only one or two words. In the examples above, the first sentence contains a restrictive appositive.

Independent Elements

An *independent element* is a word or word group that is not grammatically related to the rest of the sentence. Usually it is set off with commas or other punctuation.

1. A *noun of direct address* names the person or thing to whom one is speaking. It may be a single noun or a noun with modifiers.

> <u>Barbara</u>, I think your bread is ready to put into the oven.
> "<u>Men of Israel</u>, and <u>ye that fear God</u>, give audience."

2. An *expletive* introduces a sentence without adding to its meaning. The two words used as expletives are *it* and *there.* You can usually reword the sentence to omit these expletives.

    a. *It* is an expletive when not used as a normal pronoun. When used as a normal pronoun, *it* has an antecedent. When used as an expletive, *it* has no antecedent.

> *It* was kind of Grandfather to give us this new sled.
>   (*It* merely introduces. The sentence can be reworded without *It:* To give us this new sled was kind of Grandfather.)
> *It* should work well with this snowfall.
>   (*It* is the subject; the antecedent is the noun *sled* in the previous example sentence. The sentence cannot be reworded without *It.*)

Lesson 24

Purpose: To give practice with appositives and independent elements, including *nominative absolutes.

Teaching Suggestions:

Most of the points in this lesson were covered in Chapter 1. There the emphasis was on punctuation; here the emphasis is on how these items relate to the structure of a sentence.

Be sure the students can tell the difference between the expletive use of *it* and *there,* and the pronoun or adverb use of these words.

Plan to spend most of your teaching time on nominative absolutes, since they were not introduced in previous years.

Note that they are called *nominative* absolutes because the main word is a substantive in the nominative case. They are called nominative *absolutes* because they stand alone, grammatically unrelated to the rest of the sentence (though the thought is related). The other independent elements are also absolute constructions.

b. *There* is an expletive when not used as an adverb telling *where.*

> *There* is a strange dog on the porch.
> > (*There* merely introduces. The sentence can be reworded without *There:*
> > A strange dog is on the porch.)
> *There* it goes across the lawn.
> > (*There* is an adverb telling *where.* The sentence cannot be reworded
> > without *There.*)

3. An *exclamation or interjection* expresses strong feeling. A few such terms are acceptable, but using them too freely can be a bad habit that mars godly speech. A mild interjection is followed by a comma; an interjection said with strong feeling is followed by an exclamation point, and the next word is capitalized.

> <u>Say!</u> Look at that red fox!   <u>Oh,</u> I didn't realize they are that small.

4. A *response* such as *yes* or *no* is sometimes used to introduce a sentence.
5. A *parenthetical expression* is a phrase such as *I believe, for example, in contrast,* or *we know.*

> Doing evil that good may come, <u>we know,</u> is never God's will.

6. A *nominative absolute* is an introductory phrase consisting of a substantive and a participle. Such a phrase is related to the thought of the sentence but is not grammatically tied to it. That is, a nominative absolute does not serve as a subject, an object, a modifier, or any other sentence part.

> <u>Heavy snow blurring his vision,</u> Father drove slowly across the mountain.
> > (substantive *snow* + participle *blurring*)
> <u>The service having already begun,</u> we took seats on the back bench.
> > (substantive *service* + participle *having begun*)
> <u>His sermon being finished,</u> Brother Lynford led the congregation in prayer.
> > (substantive *sermon* + participle *being finished*)
> <u>His sermon finished,</u> Brother Lynford led the congregation in prayer.
> > (The word *being* is often omitted from a nominative absolute.)

A nominative absolute can easily be changed to a subordinate clause, and sometimes this should be done for the clearest, most direct communication. However, the occasional use of carefully written nominative absolutes can add a special appeal to your writing. The following sentences show how the examples above can be rewritten with subordinate clauses.

> Because heavy snow blurred his vision, Father drove slowly across the mountain.
> Because the service had already begun, we took seats on the back bench.
> After his sermon was finished, Brother Lynford led the congregation in prayer.

Distinguish carefully between nominative absolutes and participial phrases. A *nominative* absolute begins with a *nominative,* but a *participial* phrase begins with a *participle.*

His <u>sermon finished</u>, Brother Lynford led the congregation in prayer.
(nominative absolute)
<u>Having finished his sermon</u>, Brother Lynford led the congregation in prayer.
(participial phrase modifying the subject)

A nominative absolute does not always come at the beginning of a sentence. It can also be a convenient way to add details at the end of a sentence.

Father drove cautiously over the mountain, <u>the snow falling thickly, the wind blowing briskly, and the temperature dropping rapidly</u>.

7. A *repeated word* may be used for emphasis or for poetic effect. This may be the repetition of the same word or of a word that names the same person or thing.

<u>Patience</u>! We surely need patience in human relationships.
(*Patience* is repeated for emphasis.)
"Thy <u>rod</u> and thy <u>staff</u> they comfort me."
(*Rod* and *staff* name the same things as *they*.)

Do not confuse this repetition with an improper expression like "Betty she drew that picture." Careless repetition of that kind merely adds clutter to a sentence. Proper repetition is deliberately planned, and it has an appealing literary effect.

Applying the Lesson

A. Copy each appositive, and label it *R* for restrictive or *N* for nonrestrictive. Commas have been omitted.
1. Respect for authority a trait sadly lacking today must characterize any young person who loves the Lord.
2. A young man of deep conviction Joseph showed great respect for Potiphar his master.
3. Daniel another youth of strong character also demonstrated respect in relating to his overseer Melzar.
4. The lad Samuel responded promptly to Eli the priest whom he served.
5. The poem "Respect in Youth" emphasizes several important principles.
6. Nevin Keeto a young man without a Christian upbringing faces many struggles that we cannot fully understand.
7. My sister Yvonne painted this picture a scene from our old place.
8. At the Spanish service we used the songbook *Himnos de la vida cristiana*.

B. Copy each independent element. Include enough words to show any needed capitalization or punctuation.
1. It is a wonderful privilege to know that God answers prayer.
2. God having commanded us to pray we can come to Him in confidence.
3. No Gary the Lord does not promise to answer the prayers of the wicked.
4. Too many people it seems expect God to answer prayer according to their own wishes.
5. Prayer how it strengthens us to face temptation!
6. Whew getting that truck out of the ditch was quite a job.

Lesson 24 Answers
Applying the Lesson
A. 1. a trait sadly lacking today—N
2. A young man of deep conviction—N; his master—N
3. another youth of strong character—N; Melzar—R
4. Samuel—R; the priest whom he served—N
5. "Respect in Youth"—R
6. a young man without a Christian upbringing—N
7. Yvonne—R; a scene from our old place—N
8. <u>Himnos de la vida cristiana</u>—R

B. 1. It
2. God having commanded us to pray,
3. No, Gary,
4. people, it seems,
5. Prayer, (*or* Prayer! How)
6. Whew! Getting

7. Mud covering us from head to foot we hurried home to clean up.
8. These roads how they try our patience!
9. The weather service I understand is predicting more rain for tomorrow.
10. Yes this is quite typical of our spring Lamar.
11. At all times to be sure we should be considerate of others.
12. Well the car started burning and headed straight toward our house.
13. What did the car actually burst into flames?
14. Father having called the fire department he and Wesley hurried outside to see what they could do the rest of us watching from a safe distance.

C. For sentences 1–6, write whether the underlined part is a *nominative absolute,* a *participial phrase,* or a *dependent clause.* Rewrite sentences 7–10, changing each underlined part to a nominative absolute.
1. The multitude seeking to make Jesus king, He departed to a mountain.
2. Evening having come, the disciples went down to the sea.
3. When they had boarded a ship, the disciples started sailing toward Capernaum.
4. Soon they ran into a storm, the wind arising and the sea becoming rough.
5. The disciples having rowed some distance, they saw Jesus walking on the water.
6. Understanding the disciples' fear, Jesus spoke comforting words to them.
7. Because Peter was imprisoned, the church prayed unceasingly for him.
8. Peter arose at the angel's command while the chains fell from his hands.
9. When the prison door opened of its own accord, the angel led Peter outside.
10. After the angel had departed, Peter went to Mary's house.

Review Exercises

A. Write *true* or *false* for each sentence. [9–12]
1. The most important attitude for good study skills is interest.
2. Removing distractions is usually better than trying to ignore them.
3. The rate at which you forget increases greatly several days after you have studied something.
4. Proper posture helps your body to be physically and mentally alert.
5. Getting a bird's-eye view of a lesson prepares you to read it more effectively.
6. If you use SQ3R faithfully, you will not need to review before taking a test.
7. By skimming, you can master your school lessons without reading them word for word.
8. When skimming, you should read beginning and ending sentences of paragraphs.
9. Taking notes can be an effective help to listening actively.
10. A summary should preserve the author's original wording as much as practical.

B. Name the five steps in the SQ3R study method. After each one, briefly explain how to apply that step in studying a lesson. [10]

---

7. Mud covering us from head to foot,
8. These roads, (*or* These roads! How)
9. service, I understand,
10. Yes,   spring, Lamar
11. times, to be sure,
12. Well,
13. What! Did
14. Father having called the fire department,

do, the rest of us watching from a safe distance

C. 1. nominative absolute
2. nominative absolute
3. dependent clause
4. nominative absolute
5. nominative absolute
6. participial phrase
7. Peter being imprisoned, the church prayed unceasingly for him.
8. Peter arose at the angel's command, the chains falling from his hands.
9. The prison door opening of its own accord, the angel led Peter outside.
10. The angel having departed, Peter went to Mary's house.

Review Exercises

A. 1. true
2. true
3. false
4. true
5. true
6. false
7. false
8. true
9. true
10. false

B. Survey—Look over the lesson, noticing the headings and any pictures or diagrams.

Question—Ask questions for which you expect to find answers in the lesson.

Read—Carefully read the lesson, making sure you understand what it teaches.

Recite—Answer the questions you had asked; do the written assignment.

Review—Mentally recall the main points of the lesson.

25. Classes of Sentences

Classes According to Use

1. *A declarative sentence makes a statement and ends with a period.*

   Jesus Christ is the Son of God.   His shed blood provides redemption.

2. *An interrogative sentence asks a question and ends with a question mark.* The subject often follows the verb or comes between two parts of the verb phrase.

   Are you laying a solid foundation for life?

3. *An imperative sentence gives a command or request and generally ends with a period.* The subject is always *you,* and it is usually understood rather than directly stated. Sentences with helping verbs like *shall, should,* or *must* may appear to be imperative; however, the verb in an imperative sentence never includes a helping verb.

   Heavenly Father, help me to grow more like Jesus. (imperative; makes a request)
   We must be growing more like Jesus. (declarative; makes a statement)

4. *An exclamatory sentence expresses strong feeling or emotion and ends with an exclamation point.* It may simply be one of the other three sentence types expressed forcefully and punctuated as an exclamation.

   Praise the Lord!   God certainly has great compassion!

Many exclamatory sentences have a special word order. The skeleton may come at the end of the sentence so that a word like *what* or *how* can come first. Or the sentence may have the form of a dependent clause that would be a fragment if it were not exclamatory.

   How wonderful is our great God!
   If only all men would submit to Him now!

Classes According to Structure

1. *A simple sentence contains one independent clause.* Although it may have compound parts, it has only one skeleton.

   The <u>mockingbird</u> <u>flew</u> to the post and <u>sang</u> a beautiful medley.

2. *A compound sentence contains two or more independent clauses.*

   The mother <u>bird</u> <u>flew</u> to the nest, and the babies' <u>mouths</u> <u>opened</u> wide.

3. *A complex sentence contains one independent clause and one or more dependent clauses.*

   While <u>we</u> <u>watched</u> the nest, the parent <u>birds</u> <u>brought</u> a total of six worms.

4. *A compound-complex sentence contains at least two independent clauses and at least one dependent clause.*

   The <u>raccoons</u> <u>have invaded</u> our sweet corn again, but before another <u>morning</u> <u>breaks</u>, <u>Father</u> <u>hopes</u> to have defeated the invaders.

Lesson 25

Purpose: To review the various classes of sentences according to their use, their structure, their word order, and their style.

Teaching Suggestions:

The average class should not need much discussion of the first two sections in this lesson. But you should give some attention to word order and even more to sentence styles. Students first learned about sentence styles in Grade 8 of this English series, so they have probably not mastered that concept.

You may want to point out that sentence style and word order are closely related. Most sentences in natural word order have a loose style; most sentences in inverted or mixed word order have a periodic style. However, word order deals primarily with the mechanical arrangement of a sentence—the placement of the subject in relation to the predicate. Style pertains to the "spirit" of a sentence—how its message is affected by different word arrangements.

Classes According to Word Order

1. *In natural word order, the complete subject precedes the complete predicate.* This is the most common word order, which we use most naturally in forming sentences.

> A large bull moose splashed across the small lake.

2. *In inverted word order, the complete predicate precedes the complete subject.* Do not separate these two sentence parts with a comma.

> Across the small lake splashed a large bull moose.

3. *In mixed word order, the complete subject comes between two parts of the complete predicate.* A comma often precedes the complete subject, especially if an adverb clause or a long adverb phrase begins the sentence. (The whole adverb clause is considered part of the predicate.)

> Across the small lake, a large bull moose splashed.
> When the moose came out the other side, he galloped away into the bush.

Classes According to Style

1. *A loose sentence gives the main idea first and the details later.* Often such a sentence could end at various points, and the thought would still be complete. The following loose sentence could end after any of the underlined words.

> We can know the truth by heeding God's Word in every detail of life, no matter how small.

Since loose sentences are the simplest kind to understand, most of your spoken sentences are naturally of this style. Most of your written sentences should also be of the loose variety.

2. *A periodic sentence gives the details first and saves the main idea until the end of the sentence.* A person must read to the *period* in order to get the main idea. Because the reader must wait, this sentence style helps to impress the main idea forcefully on his mind. Compare the following sentences with the example above. Do you see the increasing emphasis on the main idea?

> By heeding God's Word, we can know the truth.
> By heeding God's Word in every detail of life, no matter how small, we can know the truth.

An inverted sentence is often short, but you must still read to the end before you get the main idea. So the inverted sentence is also periodic.

> Beside the road sat blind Bartimaeus.

Used occasionally, periodic sentences can effectively emphasize key ideas in a paragraph. But too many periodic sentences will make a paragraph sound unnatural.

3. *A balanced sentence has two well-matched clauses.* One kind of balanced sentence has clauses beginning with words like "the more ... the more" or "the sooner ... the better." Another kind uses a slight change of wording to produce a

notable or unexpected contrast. Because of its unusual structure, a balanced sentence gives strong emphasis to the idea in focus.

> The more deeply we love God, the more deeply we will hate sin.
> Though God is blessing all our store, we must not store all our blessings.
> We are not called to see through each other; we are called to see each other through.

Note the repositioning of *through* in the last sentence. This is an example of rearranging the words to produce a striking, memorable statement. Such a sentence stands out because of its unusual structure; not many expressions can be reworded in this way. Therefore, the balanced sentence is the least common of the three sentence styles.

Changing the *style* of a sentence may have the same result as changing the *word order* of the sentence. Study the following examples.

> We must keep working until this job is finished.
>   (natural word order; loose sentence)
> Until this job is finished, we must keep working.
>   (mixed word order; periodic sentence)

Why is the change classified in two different ways? Word order deals mainly with the mechanical arrangement of words in sentences. Its primary concern is whether the subject comes at the beginning, in the middle, or at the end. Style has more to do with the "spirit" of a sentence. Its primary concern is how the message of a sentence is affected by different word arrangements.

Applying the Lesson

A. Label each sentence according to its use (*dec., int., imp., exc.*) and its structure (*S, CD, CX, CD-CX*). End punctuation has been omitted.
1. Do you carefully follow your parents' wishes, or do you do the least amount possible
2. Because respect for parents is very important, your answer to such a question tells much about your character
3. Youth who have never learned to respect their parents have difficulty learning to fear God
4. If you have godly parents, thank God for them; and if you do not, learn to fear God anyway
5. What a shame it is when one turns his back on a godly heritage
6. Did you see the beautiful display of northern lights last night
7. How delicious Mother's dinner looks and smells
8. Call Father for dinner after you have poured the water
9. Before we eat, we give thanks to our heavenly Father for His blessings
10. Do we daily praise God, who gives us our food, or do we often complain

B. Label the word order of each sentence *N* (natural), *I* (inverted), or *M* (mixed).
1. From the barn came the lowing of hungry cattle.
2. Soon we were on the way to the barn.

Lesson 25 Answers
Applying the Lesson
A. 1. int., CD
    2. dec., CX
    3. dec., CX
    4. imp., CD-CX
    5. exc., CX
    6. int., S
    7. exc., S
    8. imp., CX
    9. dec., CX
   10. int., CD-CX

B. 1. I
   2. M

3. Before we may eat our breakfast, we must take care of the animals.
4. Our morning chores usually take us about one hour.
5. We have our family worship right before breakfast.
6. To our lips spring joyful songs.
7. In confidence we pray to our Lord.
8. As we think upon God's goodness, our hearts are humbled.

C. Label the style of each sentence *L* (loose), *P* (periodic), or *B* (balanced).
   1. Before you can study to learn, you must learn to study.
   2. I can study more effectively since we have learned about study skills in Chapter 2 of this book.
   3. The more carefully I apply the principles of SQ3R, the better I remember the details of a lesson.
   4. Even though a study method like SQ3R gives much practical help for studying, effective study remains hard work.
   5. Dozens of strong thunderstorms pounded central Pennsylvania as a cold front passed through the region late yesterday afternoon.
   6. In the days of youth while you are forming habits and developing character, remember your Creator.
   7. Although evil abounds and the love of many waxes cold, sin will have its payday.
   8. We will find strength in prayer if we pray for strength.
   9. In everything we do, whether seen or unseen, we should exalt God.
   10. He who exalts himself shall be humbled, but he who humbles himself shall be exalted.

D. Rewrite sentences 1–4 in mixed order and 5–8 in inverted order.
   1. The sun triumphantly announced a new day as it burst over the eastern mountains.
   2. Its gentle rays soon warmed the chilled earth.
   3. We were ready to shed our jackets by the time we had finished the chores.
   4. The temperature had risen to eighty degrees by afternoon.
   5. A bald eagle soared high in the sky.
   6. Its shrill cry came faintly to our ears.
   7. The huge, majestic bird plummeted downward.
   8. A red-tailed hawk hung in its talons.

E. Rewrite sentences 1–4 in the periodic style. In each of sentences 5–8, copy the beginning of the second clause and add words to complete the balanced sentence.
   1. Conrad suddenly jumped and yelled during our picnic lunch by the creek in our back pasture.
   2. We understood his actions after he told us that a bee had stung him on the cheek.
   3. We welcomed a break after stacking straw in the overheated barn all afternoon.
   4. Grandfather Weinhold stayed with us during the eight weeks of recuperation from his broken leg.
   5. We must control our thoughts, or our thoughts . . .

3. M
4. N
5. N
6. I
7. M
8. M

C. 1. B
   2. L
   3. B
   4. P
   5. L
   6. P
   7. P
   8. B
   9. P
   10. B

D. 1. As it burst over the eastern mountains, the sun triumphantly announced a new day.
   2. Soon its gentle rays warmed the chilled earth.
   3. By the time we had finished the chores, we were ready to shed our jackets.
   4. By afternoon the temperature had risen to eighty degrees.
   5. High in the sky soared a bald eagle.
   6. Faintly to our ears came its shrill cry.
   7. Downward plummeted the huge, majestic bird.
   8. In its talons hung a red-tailed hawk.

E. 1. During our picnic lunch by the creek in our back pasture, Conrad suddenly jumped and yelled.
   2. After he told us that a bee had stung him on the cheek, we understood his actions.
   3. After stacking straw in the overheated barn all afternoon, we welcomed a break.
   4. During the eight weeks of recuperation from his broken leg, Grandfather Weinhold stayed with us.
   5. our thoughts will control us.

6. The Christian rejects the world and follows Christ; the carnal man...
7. The more impressed we are with God's glory, the less...
8. The more carefully we keep God's Word, the better...

Review Exercises

Label each underlined item *nominative absolute* or *participial phrase.* [24]
1. <u>The dishes washed</u>, we girls hurried to help husk the corn.
2. Kevin was quite pleased, <u>his kite having turned out nicely</u>.
3. <u>Drumming on the tin roof</u>, the rain drowned out our voices.
4. <u>The river having overflowed its banks</u>, we were forced to turn back.
5. I enjoy watching the goats <u>frisking around the pasture</u>.

6. the carnal man rejects Christ and follows the world.
7. the less impressed we are with our own (the world's) glory.
8. the better God's Word can keep us.

Review Exercises

1. nominative absolute
2. nominative absolute
3. participial phrase
4. nominative absolute
5. participial phrase

26. Improving Your Editing Skills, Part 3

With the basic proofreading symbols that you have learned, you can mark most of the corrections commonly needed in manuscripts. However, you will soon encounter some situations where you are not sure exactly how to mark the changes. Consider the following example. Which is the best way to show the inserted dash?

```
The energy from the sun but I have mentioned that before.
                        ^
The energy from the sun-but I have mentioned that before.
                        ^
The energy from the sun but I have mentioned that before.
                         ^
```

We could use any of these ways, but we will understand one another's work more easily if we all follow the same pattern. This proofreading lesson and the next one show some specific patterns for using several of the proofreading marks. These patterns are the ones you should use throughout this course.

Marks Used in Editing and Proofreading

∨ or ∧ insert (caret)	ℐ delete	. . . . stet (let it stand)	_____ use italics
¶ begin new paragraph	no ¶ no new paragraph	*lc* change to lowercase (small letter)	*uc* change to uppercase (capital letter)
# insert space	⌒ delete space	← move (arrow)	⊓⊔ transpose

Lesson 26

Purpose: To provide proofreading practice.

Explanations

Ellipsis points, like periods and commas, are inserted by writing them below the caret. All other punctuation is written above the caret.

If there is room, these other marks may be written where they would normally go. If not, they must be written in the space above the words.

Loop for delete symbol curves up if there is room in the space above, and down if there is not. Curving down also works well for deleting a word and a comma or period after it.

Inserted dash must be long enough to distinguish it from a hyphen.

Sample Manuscript

"For sin shall not have dominion over you: for ye are under grace" (Romans 6:14) What does this verse mean?

An Indian in Oklahoma traveled by train to a pastors' conference. The theme of the conference was this subject: "Living Under Grace." A number of prominent speakers were there, and as they delivered profound messages on law and grace, the Indian pastor listened carefully.

Afterward he said, "It would seem to me that those train station represents law law and this conference represents grace. At the train station, men are spitting on the floor even though a sign said, 'Do not spit.' Here we have no sign, yet no one spits."

This simplehearted Indian pastor illustrated the truth well perhaps more clearly than any of the honored speakers.

Editing Practice

A. Use proofreading marks to add the missing punctuation. In each sentence, one mark will go above the caret and one below.

1. "Boys have you finished digging the red beets" asked Mother.

2. John (the only cousin my age will be visiting our farm this coming Saturday

3. "Then Jonah prayed unto the Lord out of the fish's belly" (Jonah 21).

4. You are welcome to eat lunch with us however we have only sandwiches and apples.

5. The fire chief had one main goal to determine, if possible the cause of the fire.

Lesson 26 Answers

Editing Practice

(Answers are on pages 464–465.)

B. Use proofreading marks to insert one hyphen or dash and to make one deletion in each sentence. Make the loop curve down for at least two of your deletions.

1. I'll show you you, how to prune this young peach tree it's
   a fairly simple procedure.

2. Be sure to use well sharpened shears, for clean cuts heal
   more readdily than jagged ones.

3. A broken branches will be a long term liability; remove it.

4. If branches are tangled together this does happen often—
   leave only the branch
   that is growing most
   directly from the trunk
   off the tree.

5. Now trimm, off those high
   reaching shoots.

6. Just a few more cuts, and
   we will but I see that
   it's time time to quit.

C. Use proofreading marks to correct the fourteen errors in these paragraphs. No line contains more than one error.

1.   The universe is so large that our mind's falter when

2. we consider its vast extent. To begin, consider the

3. number of of individual stars. We can see about 3,000

4. stars with the unaided eye; and by using a telescope,

5. we can see many, many more. But our galaxie (the Milky

6. Way) contains an estimated 200 billion stars—a number

7. that defies are comprehension. And scientists calculate

8. that there are than more 10 billion galaxies in the

9. observ able part of the universe!

10.   When we consider the distances involved in the universe,

11. our minds again stagger. Consider this. Even at the grate

12. speeds attained by space craft, it takes three days to reach

13.   the moon. Traveling to Jupiter would take 2 years, and
14.   going to Pluto would require 15 years. But these figures
15.   pail when we compare the distance to the stars. Reaching
16.   Alpha Centauri, the nearest star, would mean a trip almost
17.   100,000 years—and the spacecraft would still be deep
18.   inside the Milky way!
19.   No Design is greater than its designer. As we consider
20.   the mind boggling size of the universe, we begin to grasp
21.   the greatness and power of the God who created it.

---

27. Chapter 3 Review

A. Write the words immediately before and after each mistake in this dialogue, and show how to join or divide the sentences correctly. Add words only where necessary; do not change elliptical sentences.
  1. "Father, who was the stranger that came to the barn? And talked with you for a while?" asked Laban.
  2. "Right after lunch? That was Mr. Jack, he's a salesman for Hamilton Supply," replied Father.
  3. "A new salesman? Is he replacing Mr. Keedy? When he retires in a few weeks?"
  4. "Yes, that's what Mr. Jack said. He started to work for Hamilton Supply two months ago. And seems to know his products well."
  5. "Good. It's nice to have good salesmen, they've often given us sound advice."

B. Copy the simple subject and the simple predicate of each sentence. Draw a vertical line between the two parts.
  1. The Lord is gracious to His children.
  2. He is daily pouring out His blessings upon us.
  3. From our Father comes every good gift of life.
  4. The ungrateful receive good things from God but fail to return thanks to Him.
  5. You and I should be filled with thanksgiving to our great God.

C. Copy each complement, and label it *PN, PA, DO, IO,* or *OC.*
  1. The sunset is becoming gorgeous; the whole western sky is a display of rich colors.
  2. The squirrels are making their nests secure for the coming winter.
  3. Brother Yoder found some interesting information and gave us a summary of it.

Lesson 27 Answers

A. (Allow reasonable variation.)
  1. barn and
  2. Jack. He's
  3. Keedy when
  4. ago and
  5. salesmen; they've

B. 1. Lord | is
   2. He | is pouring
   3. gift | comes
   4. ungrateful | receive, fail
   5. You, I | should be filled

C. 1. gorgeous—PA; display—PN
   2. nests—DO; secure—OC
   3. information—DO; us—IO; summary—DO

Lesson 27

Purpose: To review the concepts taught in Chapter 3.

4. That bird must consider us a threat to her nest.
5. Father gave Leland and me clear instructions.

D. Copy each retained object, and label it *DO ret., IO ret.,* or *OC ret.*
   1. A warm welcome was given the visitors from Belgium.
   2. These chickens are fed laying mash every day.
   3. The children were told a story by Uncle Myron.
   4. The story was made especially interesting by his lively style.

E. Copy the appositives, and label them *R* (restrictive) or *N* (nonrestrictive). Commas have been omitted.
   1. Joshua Strite a former member of our church gave a report of the mission work in India a land of many contrasts.
   2. My brother Lamar plans to accompany Brother Aaron Yoder our bishop on a visit there next month.
   3. The story "Where Is Linda?" was captivating.

F. Copy each independent element, and add any punctuation that is needed after it. Also write correctly any other word with which there is an error in capitalization or punctuation.
   1. Great this snow I believe will be perfect for sledding!
   2. Do you remember Doris what Grandmother used to say in times like these?
   3. It is certainly an answer to prayer to hear that Donna is getting better.
   4. The electricity having gone off an hour ago Mother could prepare only a cold lunch.
   5. These modern conveniences how much we have come to depend on them!

G. Label each underlined word group *prep.* (prepositional phrase), *vb.* (verbal phrase), *ps.* (phrase of a single part of speech), *D* (dependent clause), or *I* (independent clause). Also label the part of speech that each phrase or dependent clause is.
   1. The safety bicycle, ^ahaving equal-sized wheels and pneumatic tires, was developed ^bin the late 1800s.
   2. Because such bicycles ^acould be ridden easily by anyone, ^bthey quickly became popular.
   3. The ^aUnited States Census Bureau stated ^bthat "few articles ever used by man have ever created so great a revolution in social conditions."
   4. ^aTo supply the demand, over three hundred companies were manufacturing bicycles by 1895; indeed, the largest manufacturer, ^bwhich operated five factories, produced about one bicycle every minute.
   5. The bicycle gave many the freedom ^ato travel greater distances, for ^bone could travel much faster on a bicycle than on foot.
   6. ^aTraveling on horseback could also be speedy, but a horseman always needed ^bto feed and water his horse.
   7. ^aWhat helped most for nighttime biking was the 1895 invention ^bof the carbide lamp, which allowed the cyclist to see the ruts and holes ^cin the road.
   8. ^aBy the turn of the century, the bicycle's popularity waned ^bas electric trains provided efficient transportation between towns and cities.

4. us—DO; threat—OC
5. Leland—IO; me—IO; instructions—DO

D. 1. visitors—IO ret.
   2. mash—DO ret.
   3. story—DO ret.
   4. interesting—OC ret.

E. 1. a former member of our church—N; a land of many contrasts—N
   2. Lamar—R; our bishop—N
   3. "Where Is Linda?"—R

F. 1. Great! This   snow, I believe,
   2. remember, Doris,
   3. It
   4. The electricity having gone off an hour ago,
   5. These modern conveniences,

G. 1. a. vb.—adj.   b. prep.—adv.
   2. a. ps.—v.   b. I
   3. a. ps.—n.   b. D—n.
   4. a. vb.—adv.   b. D—adj.
   5. a. vb.—adj.   b. I
   6. a. vb.—n.   b. vb.—n.
   7. a. D—n.
      b. prep.—adj.
      c. prep.—adj.
   8. a. prep.—adv.   b. D—adv.

H. Label each sentence according to its use (*dec., int., imp., exc.*) and its structure (*S, CD, CX, CD-CX*). End punctuation has been omitted.
1. What a privilege we have to carry our burdens to the Lord in prayer
2. When we pray in simple faith, God promises to hear and answer us
3. Cast your burdens on the One who is omnipotent, and trust His gracious care
4. Did you seek God's blessing today, or did you foolishly step forth in your own strength
5. If we expect to handle life by ourselves, we are bound to be bitterly disappointed

H. 1. exc., S
   2. dec., CX
   3. imp., CD-CX
   4. int., CD
   5. dec., CX

I. Label the word order of each sentence *N* (natural), *I* (inverted), or *M* (mixed).
1. Joseph was a truly remarkable young man.
2. In his life are found many types of Christ.
3. Because he feared God, he resisted temptation.
4. Through strange circumstances, God directed Joseph's life.
5. From his lips came words of good advice for Pharaoh.

I. 1. N
  2. I
  3. M
  4. M
  5. I

J. Label the style of each sentence *L* (loose), *P* (periodic), or *B* (balanced).
1. It is good to focus on a noble aim; it is better to keep aiming for that focus.
2. By persevering diligently to the end of life, we can reach our final goal.
3. Life holds rich meaning to those who follow God in commitment to His will.
4. The more sincerely we purpose to follow the Lord, the more easily we can follow His purposes.
5. Although many declare that man is becoming more intelligent, that the world is getting better, and that a utopia lies just around the corner, the human race is actually degenerating.

J. 1. B
  2. P
  3. L
  4. B
  5. P

K. Rewrite these sentences according to the directions in parentheses.
1. We can see Mount Parnell when the sky is clear. (Change to mixed word order.)
2. A diamond dewdrop sparkled on every blade of grass. (Change to inverted word order.)
3. A cat sprang from the bushes just as the little rabbit disappeared into its hole. (Change to periodic style.)
4. You must cut the glass carefully, or… (Finish as a balanced sentence.)
5. As we kneel more humbly before God, we can stand more courageously before men. (Change to a balanced sentence beginning with "The more humbly we kneel…")

K. (Allow reasonable variation.)
1. When the sky is clear, we can see Mount Parnell.
2. On every blade of grass sparkled a diamond dewdrop.
3. Just as the little rabbit disappeared into its hole, a cat sprang from the bushes.
4. the glass will cut you.
5. The more humbly we kneel before God, the more courageously we can stand before men.

L. Rewrite each sentence, using a more active verb.
1. There were a few deer in our bean patch yesterday.
2. Sometimes Fido is loud at night.
3. This pie is delicious.

L. (Sample sentences.)
1. A few deer devoured some of our beans yesterday.
2. Sometimes Fido barks loudly at night.
3. This pie tastes delicious.

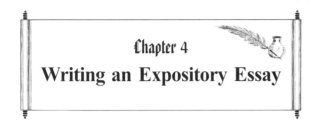

28. Understanding an Expository Essay

An expository essay is an essay that explains. We have all explained—or tried to explain—many things to others. Whether we told our grandparents how we learned to ride a bicycle or informed a friend why an accident occurred or showed a younger brother how to tie his shoe, we were explaining. Actually, giving and receiving explanations has occupied a large part of our lives.

This means writing an expository essay should come naturally, doesn't it? In some ways it probably will. But in other ways, you will benefit greatly from having some specific directions to guide you.

The Nature of an Exposition

The noun *exposition* comes from the verb *expose.* Thus, an exposition is writing that *exposes.* It takes something not seen or understood by others and holds it up to clear view. This immediately suggests a limitation in the topics that are suitable for expository writing. Why explain something that everyone already understands? You are in a position to explain a subject only when you understand things about it that your readers do not. Some of this understanding you gain through personal experience. Some of it you gain through reading and research.

In writing exposition, you must present your topic with complete clarity and precise order. You may report new information (as in your sixth grade report on alligators); you may explain how something works; you may show how to do something; or you may describe the steps in a process. Whatever the topic, you must present everything as clearly as possible. Anything unfamiliar to the reader must be laid out before him in plain language. The goal of all expository writing is to lead the reader to say, "I understand."

Much of your writing in previous grades was exposition. In grade 6, as already mentioned, you wrote a report about alligators. You have also written many single paragraphs of explanation. You will now use your background knowledge and experience to produce a final expository essay.

Below is a sample exposition. As you read it, can you sense that the writer knows what he is talking about? Does the essay present the explanation in a clear and precise manner?

The Beautiful Nuisance

1   The water hyacinth is a tropical water plant with large, elegant lavender flowers. It floats on air-filled sacs, and it reaches a height of about 2 feet (61 cm) above the surface of the water. When thousands of water

Lesson 28

Purpose: To teach the nature and general structure of an expository essay, and to teach the *purpose of footnotes and bibliographies.

Teaching Suggestions:

In this lesson, the students are introduced to footnotes. Technically, a footnote is placed at the bottom of the page containing the text to which it refers. It is called an endnote if it is placed at the end of the entire essay. For simplicity, this chapter uses *footnote* in referring to all notes of this kind.

hyacinths grow together, they form a mat so thick that it can support a man's weight.

2   But for all its striking beauty, the water hyacinth has some very ugly behavior. The plants multiply with amazing speed, sometimes doubling in number every ten days. Just 10 plants can increase to a mat of more than 600,000 in one growing season,[1] and the mat continues to spread until it completely covers the surface of the water. In this way, the plant makes itself such a nuisance that it has been called the purple curse.

3   The water hyacinth does its mischief in a multitude of forms. It decreases the oxygen content of water so much that fish suffocate. When canals are choked with hyacinths, boats cannot get through and irrigation water cannot flow freely. The mats make ideal homes for mosquitoes that carry malaria. And high winds will sometimes roll mats of hyacinths into great dams, backing up waterways and flooding the surrounding countryside.

4   Man himself is actually to blame for the purple curse. Water hyacinths grow naturally in South America, where various diseases and insects keep the plant in check. But in 1884 the plant was displayed at the New Orleans Exposition, where gardeners were delighted by its beauty. Some of them took seedlings home for their garden pools, and eventually the plant invaded streams and creeks. By 1900, the water hyacinth had spread all the way from Florida to Texas and as far west as California. Even the Panama Canal has been invaded; it must be cleared regularly to keep the plants from choking off canal traffic.[2]

5   Nor has the water hyacinth limited its domain to the Americas. It reached Australia in 1895 and India around 1900—probably transported by people fascinated with its beauty. A missionary is said to have carried it to Africa around 1950, where it infested the Congo River and then spread rapidly to many other African waterways.[3]

6   People soon discovered that the water hyacinth is no easy enemy to defeat. They fought it first with pitchforks and then with dynamite. They used arsenic, but it killed crops and cattle as readily as hyacinths. Government engineers devised a seagoing "lawn mower" that cut a swath 40 feet wide (12 m), but cutoff pieces floated away and spread the hyacinth to new locations. One scientist even experimented with a flamethrower. The next year, however, the burned plants sprouted first and grew taller than before!

7   Finally in the late 1940s, scientists found that 2,4-D[4] is an effective weapon against water hyacinths. This chemical made it possible to clear thousands of acres of hyacinth-infested water in Florida and Louisiana, and it soon became an important tool for keeping waterways passable in the South. But no one is comfortable with such widespread use of 2,4 D year after year.

8   Because of the chemical danger, scientists are investigating natural methods of control. They have learned that the manatee, or sea cow, is able to eat enough of the plants to keep river mouths clear. Other possibilities include beetles that eat hyacinth leaves, moths that cause rot by boring into the roots, and certain grasshoppers and caterpillars that eat hyacinths.

9   To be sure, the water hyacinth has a few good points. Because the plants are excellent absorbers of chemicals, some scientists think that polluted water might be purified by passing it through tanks full of water hyacinths.[5] Also, a way might be found to make cattle feed from dried hyacinths. But until a safe and effective method is found to control this weed, it will continue to plague tropical waters around the world.

Notes

[1] James Poling, "The World's Most Exotic Nuisance," in *Our Wonderful World of Nature* (Pleasantville, N.Y.: Reader's Digest Association, 1969), p. 109.

[2] *Compton's Encyclopedia*, 1992, article "Panama Canal."

[3] Poling, "Exotic Nuisance," p. 110.

[4] This herbicide has natural hormones that kill broadleaf plants but not grasses.

[5] *World Book Encyclopedia*, 1983, article "Water Hyacinth."

Bibliography

Compton's Encyclopedia. "Panama Canal." 1992.

Poling, James. *Our Wonderful World of Nature*. Pleasantville, N.Y.: Reader's Digest Association, 1969.

World Book Encyclopedia. "Water Hyacinth." 1983.

This essay includes footnotes and a bibliography. The main purpose of footnotes is to show the sources of information in case the reader wants to verify a particular statement. Sometimes a footnote simply gives an added explanation, as illustrated by footnote 4 above. The purpose of a bibliography is to list all the sources from which the writer obtained information for the essay. You will learn more about footnotes and bibliographies in later lessons.

The Structure of an Exposition

1. *The introduction.* Like most compositions, an expository essay consists of three parts: introduction, body, and conclusion. The introduction of a shorter composition may be only a sentence or two. In an exposition of 500–600 words, it will be a complete paragraph. The introduction has several purposes. First, it must appeal to the reader's interest. If it fails to do this, no one will read the essay and it will not explain anything to anyone! Second, it must tell what object or concept will be explained and must introduce it in a general way.

Examine the introductory paragraph in the exposition above. Notice first that it begins with a general statement: *The water hyacinth is a tropical water plant with large, elegant lavender flowers.* This is followed by several other descriptive details about the water hyacinth. These opening sentences do not directly introduce the theme of the essay—that the beautiful water hyacinth has become a serious nuisance. But they give basic information that is needed to understand the essay, and this information is presented in a way that should appeal to the reader's interest.

The sample exposition does not introduce the theme until the beginning of the second paragraph. Other patterns are also possible. You may find the theme at the end of the first paragraph, with the second paragraph going into the first of the main supporting points. Especially in a longer essay, the topic may be such that two paragraphs are required for the basic information. Then the theme may appear at the end of the second paragraph or the beginning of the third.

The introduction of an exposition is like a funnel. It is wide at the beginning—with a general statement—and then it narrows down to the theme of the essay.

2. *The body.* With the main idea introduced, the body of an exposition goes on to develop the explanation. In the body, the writer lays out exact details that will help the reader to understand. Here it is that his exposition succeeds or fails. Therefore, he must be sure to use precise, accurate information and to follow a clear, logical order.

The writer must use specific facts that he finds by careful research. It is not enough to guess and reason; he must provide concrete information so that the reader gains a clear picture of what he is explaining. Each paragraph must develop one aspect of the theme, one step in the process, or some other block of supporting information.

Notice the many specific details in the sample essay. Paragraph 2 does not say merely that a few plants can multiply into thousands in a short time. It says that *10 plants* can increase to *more than 600,000* in *one growing season.* Paragraph 3 says the water hyacinth *decreases the oxygen content of water so much that fish suffocate,* and it gives four other specific forms of mischief. Paragraph 4 states the exact year when the plant was brought to the United States, and paragraph 5 gives the years when it was carried to other continents. Note also the many specific details about the methods used to combat the water hyacinth.

The details in the essay are presented in a clear, logical order. To achieve this, of course, a writer must develop and follow a good outline. You will study this further in later lessons.

3. *The conclusion.* Having stated his theme and explained it as clearly as possible, the writer is ready to close his exposition. How can he bring the essay to a smooth and satisfying conclusion? In the sample essay, this is done by using a contrast. The closing paragraph shows that the water hyacinth is not all bad—again by giving specific details—but then it returns to the idea that the plant is, after all, a serious nuisance. The last sentence is a general statement about the future outlook in relation to water hyacinths.

Other patterns are also possible. A good conclusion might summarize the main points and give a final observation. It might contain a quotation that is especially fitting. Or it might call the reader to some kind of response in relation to the information presented.

Remember that the introduction is like a funnel that narrows down to the theme of the essay. The conclusion is like an inverted funnel, narrow at the beginning and broadening to general ideas. Below is an illustration showing this pattern in the form of a diagram.

Introduction
    General ideas narrowing to statement of theme

Body
    Supporting details presented and clarified

Conclusion
    Theme summarized or otherwise reinforced, followed by general ideas

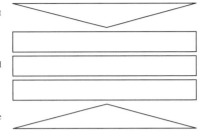

A good exposition is carefully planned and well organized. It clearly exposes a theme by presenting specific facts in an orderly way. Fix these principles firmly in your mind, and let them guide you in planning and writing your expository essay.

Applying the Lesson

A. Answer these questions about expositions.
  1. What is the goal of all expository writing?
  2. One specific purpose of an exposition is to report new information. What are three other specific purposes for which expositions may be written?
  3. What kind of topic is *not* suitable for an expository essay?
  4. Instead of directly stating the theme, what do the opening sentences often provide?
  5. Where is a common place to find the statement of the theme?
  6. In the body, why must the writer present specific facts rather than guessing and reasoning?
  7. How can the writer make sure that he presents his facts in a clear, logical order?
  8. How is the introduction like a funnel? How is the conclusion like an inverted funnel?

B. Below are three introductions for expository essays. Tell which one is *good,* which one *has no general opening ideas,* and which one *does not lead to the theme.*

  1.   **How Airplanes Fly**
       One of the four forces affecting an airplane is thrust, which is usually provided by propellers or jet engines. Propellers drive a plane by cutting into air as a screw cuts into wood. Jet engines drive a plane with a powerful exhaust of burning gases. The plane is driven forward with a force equal to that of the gases shooting out the back.

  2.   **Animals That Hibernate**
       Wild animals have various ways of surviving cold winters. Many birds leave their summer homes and fly to warmer regions. Some animals store away food, and a few simply expand their feeding grounds. Wild animals also grow heavier coats to keep warm in winter.

Lesson 28 Answers
Applying the Lesson
A. 1. to explain something (*or* to lead the reader to say, "I understand")
  2. to explain how something works, to show how to do something, to describe the steps in a process
  3. a topic that everyone already understands
  4. basic information that is needed to understand the essay
  5. at the end of the first paragraph or the beginning of the second
  6. so that the reader gains a clear picture of what the writer is explaining
  7. by developing and following a good outline
  8. The introduction begins with general ideas and then narrows down to the theme of the essay.
     The conclusion summarizes the theme and then broadens to general statements.

B. 1. has no general opening ideas
  2. does not lead to the theme

3.
Changing a Flat Tire

     If you are ever a driver, and if your driving experience is normal, you will someday have a flat tire. This event announces itself in various ways. Sometimes you will simply notice a strange vibration or find that steering is difficult. Less frequently—and less fortunately if it occurs at high speed—the tire will go flat with a loud bang. Whatever the circumstances, you will have a great advantage if you know how to change a flat tire.

3. good

C. The conclusions below are for the essays introduced in Part B. Note how the conclusions progress from narrow to general ideas. Then write whether a *summary*, a *contrast*, or a *quotation* precedes the general ideas.

1.   Not all vehicles affected by thrust and lift will rise from the ground and fly. But when men learned how to use these forces to overcome drag and gravity, they were able to build airplanes of many different types and sizes.
2.   In Psalm 36:6, David wrote, "O Lord, thou preservest man and beast." This verse reminds us that God cares for the animals as well as the people in His creation. Hibernation is just one of the many ways that God has designed to preserve wild animals.
3.   Though a flat tire is an inconvenience, it is no reason for panic. Just remember to drive well off the road; then jack up the car and replace the flat tire with the spare. You will probably be back on the road in less than thirty minutes.

C. 1. contrast
   2. quotation
   3. summary

---

29. Choosing a Limited Topic

    Remember that an *exposition* has that name because it *exposes* facts or information to others. It is not a narrative that teaches a lesson by telling a story. Rather, an exposition defines, clarifies, or explains something to help readers understand it more fully.

Choosing a General Field of Information

    In many cases, the writer of an exposition does not need to choose his subject. Instead, the subject presents itself through his work or through an incident in his life. He may be asked to write a report to explain a situation or happening to others. A minister may feel the need to write an article explaining a Bible doctrine or clarifying the position of the church on a particular issue. This suggests that church periodicals contain much expository writing.

    In this chapter, however, you will need to decide on your own subject. Choose a general field of information that interests you. This matter of interest is important; for without it you will have little motivation, and your work will be dull and tedious.

    The range of possible fields of information is as wide as the scope of human knowledge. Are you interested in your father's vocation: farming, carpentry, or mechanics?

Lesson 29

Purpose: To teach the method of choosing a topic for an expository essay.

Teaching Suggestions:

    Be sure to check students' choices of topics for Part B. Evaluate each topic to see that it is limited sufficiently, but not too much, for the essay that will be assigned. Also consider whether your school library has enough reference material for the students to write meaningfully about their topics. If not, find out where they expect to find the needed information. Careful planning at this stage will help to prevent frustration and wasted time later.

Do you have a personal hobby such as crocheting, woodworking, or stamp collecting? Did you especially enjoy a visit to a museum, a cave, or some other point of interest? Has your curiosity been stirred by some detail in a history or science lesson? by some natural phenomenon that you have witnessed? by some invention or discovery? These questions suggest a few of the general fields that you could choose to explore.

A list of all the available fields would be almost endless. However, there are some subjects that may be best not to choose. First, you should avoid a topic that involves only your personal knowledge and experience. You need to be somewhat familiar with the topic, of course, but you should be able to do research and learn something new about it. Second, avoid topics that you can hardly research because they are too uncommon or because you do not have access to sufficient material. Third, avoid topics that are controversial. This essay is to be an exposition, not an argument.

Limiting the Scope of Your Topic

After you have decided on a general field of information, you must limit the topic to an idea that you can cover in an essay of 500–600 words. The topic must be limited enough so that you must do more than state generalities. Your essay must give specific details that will truly inform. On the other hand, you do not want a topic so narrow that you can hardly find enough information.

To limit the topic, think of the more general field of information as the title of a book. But you do not intend to write a book! So you must think of a subtopic that might make a chapter title in that book. Even this may be too broad for your purpose here. You may need to further limit the subtopic to something that could be part of a chapter. Sometimes a topic almost automatically narrows down as you begin reading and researching for your essay. For instance, you may find sufficient information about only one aspect of the topic. Or you may become inspired by a topic that is a little to the side of your original topic.

Note the narrowing process in the following examples. The italicized topics would make suitable titles for an essay such as you will be expected to write.

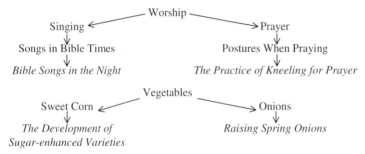

The wording of the limited topic you choose will serve as your working title during the research and early writing stages. Later you might adjust that title or replace it entirely. But you should not spend much time on the title now. Indeed, your research may lead to a slight shift in emphasis that calls for a new title anyway.

Stating the Purpose of the Essay

After you have chosen a limited topic, you should state the purpose of your essay. Even a limited topic could likely be developed in various ways. Your statement of purpose will indicate exactly how you plan to develop your essay. This statement will then help you stay on track as you select information in your research. Study the following examples.

> **Limited Topic:** The Practice of Kneeling for Prayer
> **Statement of Purpose:**
>   To explain why it is a good practice to kneel for prayer.

> **Limited Topic:** Raising Spring Onions
> **Statement of Purpose:**
>   To show the steps to be followed in raising spring onions.

The lessons throughout this chapter will develop the following topic and statement of purpose.

> **Limited Topic:** The Pharisees of Jesus' Day
> **Statement of Purpose:**
>   To explain the significant place of the Pharisees in Jewish life during the time when Jesus was on earth.

Deciding on Main Topics

Often you can determine what main topics your essay will develop even before you begin gathering information. In fact, deciding on those main topics first will be a definite help in guiding your research. For example, in preparing for the topic "The Pharisees of Jesus' Day," you might anticipate finding information that will come under the following main topics.

> I. Their origin
> II. Their beliefs
> III. Their relationship to Jesus

All the steps in this lesson are preliminary. They will not show directly in your final essay. But they will show! The first steps in any process are of major importance, and writing a well-developed expository essay is no exception.

Applying the Lesson

A. For any five of the following topics, write one specific, limited topic that would be suitable for an expository essay of 500–600 words.

1. The Age of Exploration
2. The Inca Indians
3. Weather
4. Small Engines
5. Wildlife in Africa
6. Making Paper
7. History of Virginia (Missouri, etc.)
8. Angels
9. Nonresistance
10. The Bible

B. As you work through this chapter, you will produce an expository essay. Begin now to consider possible topics on which you might write an essay of 500–600

Lesson 29 Answers
Applying the Lesson

A. (Sample limited topics.)
1. a. The Purposes of the Explorations
   b. Effects of the Age of Exploration
   c. The First (or Second, etc.) Voyage of Christopher Columbus
   d. The Voyage of Vasco da Gama (or Ferdinand Magellan, etc.)
2. a. Inca Settlements in Peru (or Ecuador, etc.)
   b. The Government of the Inca Empire
   c. The Religion of the Inca Indians
   d. The Fall of the Inca Empire
3. a. Cold Fronts (or Warm Fronts)
   b. Weather Systems in the Eastern United States (or the Midwest, etc.)
   c. How Hurricanes Form
   d. How Jet Streams Influence Weather
4. a. Troubleshooting for Small Four-cycle (or Two-cycle) Engines
   b. How a Small Four-cycle (or Two-cycle) Engine Works
   c. The Development of the Two-cycle Engine
   d. Unique Uses of Two-cycle Engines
5. a. Wildlife in the Sahara (or Along the Nile, etc.)
   b. The African Elephant (or Leopard, etc.)
   c. Preservation of Endangered Species in Africa
6. a. Early Egyptian Papermaking
   b. The Development of Modern Papermaking
   c. Inside a Paper Mill
7. a. Early Settlements in ———— County, Virginia (or another county and state)
   b. History of [local area]
   c. Mennonite Settlements in ————
8. a. The Nature of Angels
   b. The Ministry of Angels
   c. Various Orders of Angels
9. a. Nonresistance in the Revolutionary War (or World War I, etc.)
   b. Peacetime Nonresistance
   c. Old Testament Types of Nonresistance
10. a. A Survey of the Book of Esther (or Job, 1 Timothy, etc.)
    b. Contrasts Between the Old and the New Testament
    c. Bible Poetry
    d. Why We Use the King James Version

B. (Individual work.)

words. Write two limited topics that you would consider using, along with a statement of purpose for each. Then for each topic, make an outline with three to five main topics that would be suitable for your essay.

The score on the essay you write will make up a considerable part of your Chapter 4 test score.

Review Exercises

A. Name the five steps in the SQ3R study method. After each one, briefly explain how to apply that step in studying a lesson. [10]

B. Write whether each of these sentences about studying is *true* or *false*. [9–12]
  1. An uncomfortable environment promotes efficient study.
  2. Good posture is helpful because it allows an adequate supply of oxygen to reach the brain.
  3. Asking questions before reading a lesson helps you to read with purpose.
  4. If you use the SQ3R method, you will not need to review before taking a test.
  5. When you read actively, you read to find specific information.
  6. Skimming can be an effective substitute for detailed study.
  7. Skimming can be useful when reviewing material.
  8. When skimming a book, you should avoid actually reading any whole paragraphs.
  9. Taking notes helps you to listen or read with an active mind.
  10. When taking notes, you should be sure to write something from every paragraph in a lesson.

Review Exercises

A. Survey—Look over the lesson, noticing the headings and any pictures or diagrams.
  Question—Ask questions for which you expect to find answers in the lesson.
  Read—Carefully read the lesson, making sure you understand what it teaches.
  Recite—Answer the questions you had asked; do the written assignment.
  Review—Mentally recall the main points of the lesson.

B. 1. false   6. false
   2. true   7. true
   3. true   8. false
   4. false   9. true
   5. true   10. false

---

30. Taking Notes for an Expository Essay

After you have limited the topic for an expository essay, you must do research. You will need to dig for facts and bring them together. This information is the raw material for your finished product. The quality of that final product depends heavily on the quality of your research and notes.

Reference Sources

You need to find information in a variety of reference sources. The most important source of information is the Bible, for it contains both specific information about many subjects and important principles relating to every subject. Other reference sources include Bible dictionaries, Bible handbooks, encyclopedias, and so forth. Books on your particular topic usually have more details than you will find in general reference sources such as encyclopedias. When looking for information in a book, put to practice the skimming skills that you learned in Chapter 2.

You should plan to use at least two or three different sources of information. Drawing from several sources helps to balance your essay because it gives you a wider scope of details. In addition, blending the details from several sources helps you to express your ideas in your own words. Using several sources of information also helps

Lesson 30

Purpose: To review the steps involved in gathering information for an expository essay.

Teaching Suggestions:

As stated in the Purpose, this material is review. A writer's ability to take good notes will directly affect the success of his final essay. So do not shortchange your class by failing to cover the lesson thoroughly.

The lesson indicates that using ideas from other people is not considered plagiarism as long as the writer expresses those ideas in his own words. You may want to point out that this refers to the field of common knowledge, in which

no individual can claim title to a certain idea. However, if a person devises a new theory or interpretation that is not established as common knowledge, other writers are guilty of plagiarism if they use that idea without giving proper credit to the source. One saying (perhaps oversimplified) puts it this way: "If you get it from just one source, it's plagiarism. If you get it from two sources, it's research." A writer also commits plagiarism if he merely paraphrases someone else's writing. He should rather be working on his own, putting ideas together according to a plan that he himself has developed.

Although the written assignment may appear quite simple, writing a good set of notes for a 500-word essay is a you to verify the information that you find. If more than one source gives a particular detail, you can be fairly sure that it is accurate. Finally, drawing from several sources helps you to avoid misinterpreting facts. The particular wording in one source may give you a wrong impression that another source may correct.

Guidelines for Taking Notes

1. *Take careful notes.* Include only information that relates directly to your topic, and indicate exactly where you found each item. You will need this later if you write a footnote for that item, or if you want to check the accuracy of your notes. Include the title and page number if the information is from a book, the title of the article if it is from an encyclopedia, and the date of issue if it is from a periodical.

2. *Avoid plagiarism.* It is plagiarism to copy another person's writing and pass it off as your own. Using *ideas* from other people is all right, as long as you express those ideas in your own words. Therefore, your notes should consist primarily of short phrases rather than whole sentences or paragraphs. Of course, you may copy a short quotation from a reference source and use it in your essay if you give proper credit within the text of the essay or in a footnote. Be sure to place exact quotations in quotation marks.

3. *Write sufficient notes.* You need a broad understanding of your subject to write an effective essay. Therefore, you should expect to write more notes than you will actually use, rather than writing barely enough. It is always easier to discard some notes than to go back through your reference sources looking for more information.

Of course, you should also avoid the other extreme. Do not get yourself bogged down by taking far more notes than you can use. With experience, you will develop a sense of when you have enough notes for the purpose at hand.

Below are notes for the topic "The Pharisees of Jesus' Day." These notes are simply shown as a list; you will probably write your notes on note cards as you did in Grade 8.

— began in third century B.C. in resistance to Hellenization (Halley's Bible Handbook, p. 411; Henry H. Halley; Zondervan Publishing House, Grand Rapids, Mich., 1965)
— wanted to keep their national identity intact and to keep alive the strict adherence to Mosaic Law (HBH, p. 411)
— included more adherents and had greater influence than any other Jewish sect (HBH, p. 445)
— mostly "known for their covetousness, self-righteousness, and hypocrisy" (HBH, p. 445)
— arose in time of Maccabeans, chiefly from the scribes, whereas the Sadducees came primarily from the priests (The New Unger's Bible Dictionary, p. 997; Merrill F. Unger; Moody Press, Chicago, Ill., 1976)
— surfaced in Jewish life when Maccabeans no longer stood for loyalty to the Law (NUBD, p. 997)

major task. You should allow several days for the students to complete this assignment.

Note: Tell students that along with their notes, they must be sure to write the necessary information about the sources. When they write the footnotes and the bibliography, they will need the following information: the author's name, the title of the book or article, and the publication facts. For a detailed list, see Lesson 35.

— some beliefs of the Pharisees: acknowledged judgment upon sinners; resurrection to life for saints (Josephus, <u>Ant.</u> 18.1.3; cited in <u>NUBD</u>, p. 998)

— recognized cooperation of divine will and human will in human affairs (Schürer, <u>History of the Jewish People in the Time of Christ</u>, div. 2, 2:15; cited in <u>NUBD</u>, p. 998)

— were primarily a spiritual party, not a political party; involved in politics only when their freedom to obey Law was threatened (<u>NUBD</u>, p. 998)

— numbered about 6,000 (<u>NUBD</u>, p. 999)

— name first appears in time of John Hyrcanus (Mattathias Maccabeus's grandson) (<u>Explore the Book</u>, p. 50; J. Sidlow Baxter; Zondervan Publishing House, Grand Rapids, Mich., 1966)

— were spiritual successors of the Chasidim ("Pious Ones") who had resisted Antiochus Epiphanes's efforts to destroy Judaism 30 to 40 years before (<u>EB</u>, p. 50)

— name, which means "Separatists," likely was given by those who despised "their pious but proud and often petty exclusiveness" (<u>EB</u>, p. 51)

— admired by common people, who considered them very righteous (<u>EB</u>, p. 51)

— most influential in keeping alive the Messianic hope in years before Christ's coming (<u>EB</u>, p. 52)

— had influence far greater than numbers would warrant because of popularity with common people (<u>EB</u>, p. 52)

— believed in resurrection, angels, and spirits (Acts 23:8)

— practiced frequent fasting (Matt. 9:14; Luke 18:12)

— believed washing of hands and eating utensils to be important (Matt. 15:1–3; Mark 7:1–5)

— basically right in beliefs, but inconsistent in doing right (Matt. 23:3)

— hypocrisy denounced by John the Baptist (Matt. 3:7–10) and by Jesus (Matt. 23)

— made desperate efforts to trap Jesus with questions (Matt. 19:3; 22:15–21; Mark 8:11; Luke 11:54; 20:20; John 8:3–11)

— some followed Jesus (John 3:1; Acts 15:5; Phil. 3:5)

Remember that these notes are the raw material for an essay. In the next lesson, you will study the process of converting this raw material into a meaningful form.

Applying the Lesson

In Lesson 29, Part B, you wrote two limited topics that you would consider using for an expository essay. Decide exactly what topic you will write about, and take notes from at least two sources on that topic. Save your notes for use in the next several lessons.

Lesson 30 Answers
(Individual work.)

31. Organizing Your Material

Organization is one key to success in writing an expository essay. If an essay is to define, clarify, or explain in a meaningful way, it must follow a logical order. Otherwise, it will be a rambling hodgepodge of ideas that hardly communicates anything worthwhile.

Use the following three steps to organize your material for an expository essay.

1. *Finalize the main topics for your outline.* The main topics that you chose earlier may need adjustment to make them suitable for your essay. Change them in any way necessary so that your notes fit logically under them. The notes in Lesson 30 can be grouped into four main ideas: the Pharisees' origin, their relationship to the Jews in general, their beliefs, and their relationship to Jesus.

2. *Arrange the main topics in a logical order.* Sometimes this is totally arbitrary; you have no specific reason for the order you choose. But often the topic has a natural order of chronology, space, or importance. In what order would you place the four main ideas in the example above? The following order is not the only logical one, but it does make a good arrangement.

     I. Their origin
     II. Their beliefs
     III. Their relationship to Jews in general
     IV. Their relationship to Jesus

3. *Fill in the outline with details from your notes.* Again, several different arrangements may be acceptable; but you do need to give careful thought to the order of the details. Try to have a logical reason for the order you choose. Study the following partial outline.

The Pharisees of Jesus' Day

Purpose:
To explain the significant place of the Pharisees in Jewish life during the time when Jesus was on earth.
I. Their origin
  A. The conflict of the Maccabean era
    1. Were spiritual successors of the Chasidim ("Pious Ones") who had resisted Antiochus Epiphanes's efforts to destroy Judaism 30 to 40 years before
    2. Came chiefly from the scribes, whereas the Sadducees came primarily from the priests
    3. Surfaced when Maccabeans no longer stood for loyalty to the Law
    4. Opposed Hellenization
  B. The significance of their name
    1. Appeared first in time of John Hyrcanus (Mattathias Maccabeus's grandson)
    2. Means "Separatists"
    3. Was likely first given by those despising "their pious but proud and often petty exclusiveness"

Lesson 31

Purpose: To review the steps of organizing notes into an outline.

Teaching Suggestions:

If you feel that your students need additional practice with outlining, you could have them finish the outline for "The Pharisees of Jesus' Day." A sample outline appears below.

This assignment is again a major task. Allow at least two days for the students to complete their outlines.

Sample Completed Outline:
III. Their relationship to Jews in general
  A. Were primarily a spiritual party, not a political party; involved in politics only when their freedom to obey Law was threatened
  B. Included more adherents and had greater influence than any other Jewish sect
  C. Numbered about 6,000
  D. Were admired by common people, who considered them very righteous
  E. Had influence far greater than numbers would warrant because of popularity with common people
  F. Were most influential in keeping alive the Messianic hope in years before Christ's coming
IV. Their relationship to Jesus
  A. Were denounced by Jesus for their hypocrisy
  B. Made desperate efforts to trap Jesus with questions
  C. Had some who followed Jesus

C. Their twofold goal
  1. To keep their national identity intact
  2. To keep alive the strict adherence to Mosaic Law
II. Their beliefs
  A. Believed washing of hands and eating utensils to be important
  B. Believed frequent fasting to have definite merit
  C. Acknowledged judgment upon sinners and resurrection to life for saints
  D. Acknowledged the existence of angels and spirits
  E. Recognized the cooperation of divine will and human will in human affairs
  F. Were basically right in beliefs, but were inconsistent in doing right

When such an outline is completed, it provides the framework needed to write a well-organized expository essay.

Applying the Lesson

A. Using the information you gathered in Lesson 30, write a basic outline of three or four main points. Show this outline to your teacher before you do Part B.

B. Use additional information from your notes to make a more detailed outline.

Lesson 31 Answers

Applying the Lesson
(All answers are individual work.)

32. Writing an Expository Essay

Now that you have gathered your raw material and organized it into an outline, you are ready to start shaping the finished product. As with other compositions you have written, an expository essay consists of three main parts: an introduction, a body, and a conclusion. In an essay of the length in focus here, both the introduction and the conclusion should be short paragraphs. These two parts are not apparent on the outline. Rather, the outline serves as the skeleton for the body—the main part of the essay.

Follow the steps below to write the first draft of your expository essay.

1. *Write an introduction that leads naturally to the theme of your essay.* Remember that the introduction should resemble a funnel, opening with a broad, general statement and then narrowing to the theme of the essay. The first several sentences must catch the reader's attention and lead him to the idea you plan to develop. The last sentence should directly state the theme of the essay. Usually that can be done by weaving in the statement of purpose that you wrote when you chose the topic.

Where can you find ideas for those first sentences? Sometimes they come easily. Other times you must work much harder to develop an opening that you like. You can begin your search for a meaningful opening by looking at the main words in your statement of purpose. What general comment can you make that relates to those key words, that appeals to your readers, and that leads naturally toward your theme?

Below is the statement of purpose for the sample topic being developed in these lessons. The key words are in italics.

Lesson 32

Purpose: To present guidelines for writing the first draft of an expository essay from an outline.

Teaching Suggestions:

This lesson teaches how to write footnotes, something your students have not done before in this English series. Be sure to explain carefully why and how footnotes are used. They are most common in scholarly writing of a technical nature, rather than in articles like those in the *Christian Contender.* Show the class several articles or other manuscripts that include footnotes. One example is the series "Introductory Study of the *Martyrs' Mirror*," by James W. Lowry, in the 1994–95 *Christian School Builder.*

> To explain the significant place of the *Pharisees* in *Jewish life* during the *time when Jesus was on earth.*

Any of the following sentences could serve as the springboard of the introductory paragraph.

> By the time of Jesus' earthly life, the Pharisees had degenerated greatly from their original position.
>
> The religious life of the Jews demonstrated many contrasts in the time of Jesus.
>
> Jesus lived in a time of great religious zeal.

Once you have a broad idea for your opening, you must find a way to move logically from that idea to your specific theme. You may need to try several times before you develop a satisfactory introduction. Do not be surprised at that; rather, approach it as a puzzle to be solved. Enjoy the challenge of making unruly words fall into line. Try and try again until you succeed.

Developing a general statement from key words in the purpose is only one way to begin an introductory paragraph. You can use any opening statement that allows you to move logically toward the theme of your exposition. The limit is your imagination.

Think of it this way. Your introduction is like bait. You are trying to attract your reader so that he will read your exposition. If he does not take the bait, he fails to read your exposition and it will mean nothing to him. So you must make your introduction as appealing as possible!

2. *Write the body of the essay, based on your outline.* For this first draft, write only on every other line so that you can proofread more easily in Lesson 34. Express each important point of the outline in a clear topic sentence. As you develop each paragraph, you may discover that one main idea needs to be developed in several paragraphs. Perhaps each of the subpoints deserves a full paragraph of development.

If your essay is to succeed as an exposition, you must develop your paragraphs with plenty of concrete details. Use specific facts that tell *what,* sound reasons that tell *why,* and clear illustrations that show *how.* Keep inspecting your work for generality and vagueness, the two enemies of good expository writing. Both enemies can be overcome by the use of clear, specific details.

When developing these paragraphs, remember the important qualities of good paragraphs. Keep the paragraphs unified with every sentence clearly developing the topic sentence. Keep the paragraphs coherent with logical order of development, with good use of transitional words, with effective repetition of key words, and with clear pronoun reference. Finally, provide smooth transitions between the paragraphs.

Write brief notations for all direct quotations and for all important statements that you have summarized from your reference sources. Put these notations in parentheses right within the paragraphs, writing just enough for you to recognize the sources. (See the notations in the first draft of "Who Were the Pharisees?" at the end of the lesson text.) When you write the final draft, you will transform these notations into footnotes that come at the end of your essay.

As you write, you may wonder how you can decide when a footnote is needed, since almost every sentence may draw directly from your notes. But you hardly expect to have a footnote for every sentence! The following list will help you to determine when to make a notation for a footnote.

    a. *For direct quotations.* Of course, if you credit the source right within the text, no footnote is needed.

    b. *For details that the reader might question.* The footnote helps to validate a detail by showing that it is not just your opinion; the idea comes from an established source.

    c. *For technical information, such as definitions and statistics.* The footnote will enable the reader to do further research if he so desires.

3. *Write a smooth, satisfying conclusion.* In your introduction, you tried to catch the reader's attention. In the body, you tried to present a clear, logical discussion of your theme. Now in your conclusion, you must wrap up your exposition in a way that impresses the theme upon the reader's mind. Below are some ideas for doing this, illustrated mostly with examples from elsewhere in the chapter.

    a. *Summarize the steps, and describe the outcome or finished product.* This is a good way to conclude an exposition when the main points can be condensed into one or two statements. If this cannot be done, a summary can easily become repetitious.

> Though a flat tire is an inconvenience, it is no reason for panic. Just remember to drive well off the road; then jack up the car and replace the flat tire with the spare. You will probably be back on the road in less than thirty minutes.

    b. *Emphasize the importance or usefulness of what has been explained.* For example, if you have presented the steps in a process, you could mention a few instances when the process is useful in everyday life. The sample conclusion above points out that a knowledge of the steps described should keep a driver from being seriously delayed by a flat tire.

    c. *Use a contrast.* Such a conclusion might describe how things would be in the absence of the thing explained, or it might give a few points that contrast the main emphasis of the essay. Note that using a contrast is one way to conclude an essay by broadening to general ideas.

> To be sure, the water hyacinth has a few good points. Because the plants are excellent absorbers of chemicals, some scientists think that polluted water might be purified by passing it through tanks full of water hyacinths. Also, a way might be found to make cattle feed from dried hyacinths. But until a safe and effective method is found to control this weed, it will continue to plague tropical waters around the world.

    d. *Use a quotation.* A fitting Bible verse can be especially effective in the conclusion. An impressive statement from another source may also be suitable if it matches the theme well. For best results, a quotation should be woven smoothly into the closing paragraph.

In Psalm 36:6, David wrote, "O LORD, thou preservest man and beast." This verse reminds us that God cares for the animals as well as the people in His creation. Hibernation is just one of the many ways that God has designed to preserve wild animals.

e. *Call for some kind of response.* The conclusion may call the reader to a specific action in relation to what has been explained. It may simply call him to appreciate the thing explained, or it may urge him not to forget the facts presented.

The next time you start a fire with a simple flick of the wrist, think about our ancestors of a few centuries ago. Remember how hard they worked to light and maintain the fires that gave them light, kept them warm, and cooked their food.

Several of these methods may be combined in the conclusion of an essay. For example, you might combine a summary with a statement of how useful the process can be, as is done in the first sample conclusion above. Or you might combine a quotation with a call for a certain response. Your main goal is to write a smooth, satisfying conclusion that clinches the theme of your essay.

4. *Write an appealing title.* The title of your essay should be short—not more than five words if possible. It should relate directly to the theme of your exposition, and it should catch the reader's interest. Writing a good title is often a challenge all its own. What is the secret of making it fresh and catchy? A good title often has rhyming words, alliteration, or an interesting word combination. Sometimes it is a question. If the title is appealing enough that it causes a person to read the essay, it will have accomplished its purpose.

Look at the following titles. Can you tell why the second one in each pair is better than the first?

(1) a. **Fair:**   How to Make an Attractive Birdhouse
   b. **Better:** Building Beautiful Birdhouses
(2) a. **Fair:**   Bible Happenings in the Jordan Valley
   b. **Better:** Bible Highlights of the Jordan Valley
(3) a. **Fair:**   Hardships of Early Voyages to America
   b. **Better:** Braving the Waves to Reach America

Title (1)b holds definite appeal because of the strong alliteration. But some of its appeal is also in its directness. With a little effort, you can usually improve a title that begins with *How to.* Title (2)b contains an interesting play on words. The essay describes *highlights* about a *low* place. Title (3)b has the appeal of assonance as well as originality. To speak of braving the waves carries an air of freshness and vitality in contrast to the commonplace wording of the first title.

The following paragraphs show the beginning of the first draft of an expository essay based on the outline in Lesson 31. The final draft of the entire essay appears in Lesson 35. Notice that the working title has been changed to a question.

Who Were the Pharisees?

The religious life of the Jews demonstrated many contrasts in Jesus' day. No doubt Simeon and Anna represented a large group of righteous Jews. But we also meet in the Scriptures the worldly-minded Sadducees, promoting their policy of assimilation into the surrounding Greek culture. On the other hand, we read much more about the narrow-minded Pharisees, who clung to a corrupted form of conservatism. Let us take a closer look at these Pharisees. Who were they, and what was their significance in Jewish life at the time of Christ?

To understand that significance, we should first consider the origin of the Pharisees. This group emerged as a distinct sect during the conflict of the Maccabean era. The Pharisees were spiritual successors of the Chasidim, or "Pious Ones," who had resisted Antiochus Epiphanes's efforts to destroy Judaism at least thirty years before. (EB, p. 50) The Pharisees drew primarily from the ranks of the scribes, in contrast to the Sadducees, who came primarily from the priests. Specifically, they surfaced when the Maccabeans no longer stood for loyalty to the Law. They opposed the Hellenizers' goal of adopting Greek culture. (HBH, p. 411)

The very name Pharisee reveals something significant about their origin. The term (which first appears in the time of John Hyrcanus, the grandson of Mattathias Maccabeus) means "separatist." Likely, this name was given by those who despised the "pious but proud and often petty exclusiveness" (EB, p. 51) of the group. These early Pharisees, however, espoused a noble twofold goal. Against the threat of Hellenization, they determined to keep Jewish national identity intact. Closely related, they committed themselves to keeping alive a strict adherence to the Mosaic Law. These two goals, of course, represented every faithful Jew's faith in God and hope for the Messiah.

An expository essay exposes a block of information little by little. You need to work step by step so that your readers will gain a clear and complete view of that information.

Applying the Lesson

Write an expository essay based on the outline you made in Lesson 31.

Lesson 32 Answers
(Individual work.)

33. Improving Your Editing Skills, Part 4

For people to communicate successfully, they must use symbols that they understand in the same way. Misunderstandings result when a symbol means different things to different people. Some misunderstandings are humorous. Others are quite serious. For example, suppose you found a box lying along the road, and it was marked with the symbol shown at the right. Would you open the box to see what was inside? You had better not, for this symbol indicates a dangerous radioactive substance!

Failure to understand proofreading symbols could result in serious communication errors. In this lesson you will again see some specific patterns to follow in the use of these symbols.

Marks Used in Editing and Proofreading

˅or˄ insert (caret)	ℒ delete	.... stet (let it stand)	—— use italics
¶ begin new paragraph	no ¶ no new paragraph	ℓc change to lowercase (small letter)	uc change to uppercase (capital letter)
# insert space	⌒ delete space	← move (arrow)	⌐⌐ transpose

Sample Manuscript

Explanations

Symbol for "transpose" may involve items in two different lines.

It may be better to delete and insert than to use the transpose or move symbol.

When a letter is deleted within a word, the symbol for "delete space" may be used to show that no space is to remain—although this is optional.

Transpose symbol may be used with more than two words or letters.

The story is told of a Bible scholar named Bengel, who was lying on his death-bed. One day a friend quoted a Bible familiar verse to him. Actually, He misquoted the verse actually by adding an extra word. "I know in whom I have believed," said the friend.

"No, no," responded the dying man.

"Do not allow a preposition even to come between my Savour and me. 'I know whom I have believed!'"

Editing Practice

A. Correct the two errors of transposition in each sentence. Notes in parentheses give specific instructions for correcting some errors.

Lesson 33

Purpose: To provide proofreading practice.

Teaching Suggestions:

The first correction in the sample manuscript is the insertion of a hyphen in *deathbed,* a closed compound divided at the end of a line. In such a case, it is actually better to use the "delete space" symbol, for *deathbed* may not come at the end of a line when the manuscript is rewritten. The "delete space" symbol clarifies that this is a closed compound, not a hyphenated compound.

If a hyphenated compound like *self-taught* occurs at the end of a line, the standard method is to underline the

Lesson 33 Answers

Editing Practice

(Answers are on pages 466–467.)

hyphen (‐). This symbol means "retain hyphen." For simplicity, however, this course teaches only the normal insertion of omitted hyphens. The standard methods are shown below for your information.

1. For a division between syllables, such as *stability:* **stabil‐ ity**

2. For a closed compound, such as *blackboard:* **black board**

3. For a hyphenated compound, such as *clear-cut:* **clear‐ cut**

1. On our trip to the Midwest, we visited Colby, Wisconsin, place the where Colby cheees was first made.

2. Mr. Zeiger, who has just moved to a nursing home, an old friend, requested that our family him visit often. (Use delete and insert symbols to make *an old friend* come immediately after *Mr. Zeiger.* Omit the comma after *friend.*)

3. The above two sentences are both decarlative, not imperative. (Use the transpose symbol to make *above* follow *sentences.*)

4. The rich man was albe to buy a new, large, expensive car every year. (Use the transpose symbol to make *new* come immediately before *car.* Delete the comma after *new.*)

5. "The secret of faithfulness under test really not is hard to understand", said Brother Arnold. (Use the transpose symbol to make *is* come before *really.*)

6. The three couragoues Hebrews simply determined that they would do what was right regradless of the consequences.

B. Use the "delete space" symbol twice in each sentence. Some uses will be in connection with a letter that you should delete.

1. When Father returned from South America, he arrived at the air port late on Friday evenning.

2. Christians should be grateful for the priviledge to spread the Gospel with out government interference.

3. Every one was impressed by the extra ordinary abilities revealed by Pedro's work.

4. Our prayers should include petition, praise, confesssion, thanks giving, and intercession.

C. Use proofreading marks to correct the thirteen errors in the following paragraphs. No line has more than one error.

1. If our galaxy (the Milky Way) so large that spacecraft

2. would require almost 100,000 years to reach the nearest

3. star, how large is the whole universe. Suppose we could

4. reduce the known universe one trilion times. This would

5. make the sun the size of a pinhead, and the entire solar

6. system would fit in side your classroom. How close would

7. the nearest star be now? It would be 26 miles (42 km)

8. away. And the Milky Way still be would about 600,000 miles

9. (970,000 km) in diameter!

10.   Let us reduce everything again, this time untill the

11. Milky Way is the size of large pie pan. How big would that

12. make the known universe? The greatest dinstace that man

13. has peered into outerspace would be 30 miles (48 km) away.

14.   What a grate and mighty God we serve! "Thou art worthy,

15. O Lord, to recieve glory and honour and power: for thou

16. hast created allthings, and for thy pleasure they are

17. and were created" (Revelation 4:11.)

---

34. Proofreading an Expository Essay

Almost without exception, producing a good finished essay requires proofreading and rewriting. Check the essay you wrote in Lesson 32, using the following questions to direct you.

Content and Organization

1. Does your essay include the three distinct parts: introduction, body, and conclusion?
2. Does the introduction lead naturally to the theme? Is the theme woven effectively into the introduction?
3. Are the main points in logical sequence?
4. Do the paragraphs of the body develop the main points carefully and completely?
5. Does every paragraph have unity and coherence?
6. Does the thought flow smoothly from one paragraph to the next?
7. Have you made the necessary notations from your reference sources for footnotes?
8. Does the conclusion bring the essay to a positive, satisfying end?
9. Does your essay have an appealing title?

Lesson 34

Purpose: To review guidelines for proofreading the first draft of an essay.

Teaching Suggestions:

Be careful not to neglect this lesson. Students are familiar with the concept of proofreading, but they need frequent reminders to proofread their own work with diligence and purpose. Challenge them to correct and improve their work until it is positively the best that they can do.

Style

1. Do you see any sentences that you should write with more freshness and originality?
2. Do you see any vague, general terms that you could replace with exact, descriptive words?
3. Do you see any weak or passive verbs that you could make more active?

Mechanics

1. Have you used any unnecessary or repetitious words?
2. Have you omitted any words or phrases that are needed to make the meaning clear?
3. Have you transposed or misplaced any words, phrases, or clauses?
4. Have you misspelled any words? Especially check spellings like *ei* and *ie, ai* and *ia, ent* and *ant,* and so forth. Double-check your use of homonyms like *your—you're* and *their—there—they're.* Make sure that you have spelled technical terms and proper nouns correctly. Pay close attention to words that you have difficulty spelling correctly.
5. Have you used proper capitalization and punctuation?
6. Have you followed the rules of correct grammar and word usage?

Do not imagine that you can evaluate all these points at one time. Since the points under "Content and Organization" form a sequence, you should consider them in the order they occur. For "Style," you will probably need to evaluate your essay on each point separately. For the points under "Mechanics," it will take several readings to do a thorough job. Concentrate first on points 1–3, next on point 4, then on point 5, and finally on point 6.

Applying the Lesson
Proofread the essay that you wrote in Lesson 32.

Lesson 34 Answers
(Individual work.)

---

35. Writing the Final Draft

After you have proofread your essay and marked the changes on your first draft, you must rewrite the essay. This essay is to be set up in a formal manner, with footnotes and a bibliography. Follow these guidelines for writing the final draft of your expository essay.

The Standard Layout
Type or recopy the essay according to the following standards.
1. Use 8½-by-11-inch typing paper or standard, lined composition paper.
2. Type on only one side of a sheet. If writing by hand, follow your teacher's direction about using one or both sides of the paper.
3. If typing, double-space. (Spacing of 1½ lines may be used if the typewriter has that capability.) If writing by hand, use blue or black ink and write on every line.
4. Leave a margin of about one inch along all four edges of each page.

Lesson 35

Purpose: To present guidelines for writing the final draft of an essay.

Teaching Suggestions:
This is your students' final opportunity to make this essay their best possible work. Help them to understand that much of their former work is wasted if they slack off now.

5. Center the title. Allow some extra space between the title and the first line of the essay.
6. Indent paragraphs five spaces for typed copy or one inch for handwritten copy.
7. Beginning with page 2, number each page in the upper-right corner.

The Footnotes

As you write the final draft, change the notations from your reference sources into footnotes. Number the footnote locations throughout the entire essay. The number referring to a footnote should appear immediately after the text to which the footnote applies. Elevate the number slightly from the main text.

The footnotes themselves are commonly listed at the end of the essay. It is also correct to write each one at the bottom of the page to which it applies, but you will probably find it more convenient to list all the footnotes together at the end. If you place them at the bottom of the page, you will need to plan ahead to see how much space your footnotes will require. Begin each footnote with the appropriate number, again elevated slightly. Indent the first line in the normal manner for a paragraph. Each footnote should end with a period, whether or not it is a complete sentence.

The following guidelines give further help for writing footnotes. Pay careful attention to the punctuation of these samples.

1. a. For information from a book or pamphlet, the first reference to a particular source should give the author's name, the title, the place of publication, the publisher, the copyright date, and the page number(s) referred to. (The state is included with a less familiar city such as Grand Rapids, but not with a well-known city such as Chicago.)

    [1]J. Sidlow Baxter, <u>Explore the Book</u> (Grand Rapids, Mich.: Zondervan Publishing House, 1966), p. 50.

   b. Later references to the same source should include just enough information for simple identification. In these later references, write only the author's last name, one or two key words from the title, and the page number(s).

    [2]Baxter, <u>Explore</u>, p. 52.

   c. If the book has been compiled by an editor, use the editor's name instead of the author's name, and write *ed.* after it.
   d. If the author's name is not given, the footnote simply begins with the title.

2. a. For information from an article in a magazine or some other periodical, the first reference to a particular source should list the author's name, the title of the article, the name and date of the publication, and the page number(s) referred to.

    [3]David K. Siegrist, "Basic Map Skills," <u>The Christian School Builder</u>, March 1990, pp. 178, 179.

   b. Later references to the same source should include just the author's last name, one or two key words from the publication name, and the page number(s).

    [4]Siegrist, <u>Builder</u>, p. 183.

3. For information from encyclopedia articles, write the name of the encyclopedia, the edition number or copyright date, and the title of the article.

> [5]<u>Compton's Encyclopedia</u>, 1995, article "Inquisition."

4. For information from the Bible, write the reference in its usual form.

> [6]Matthew 23:3.

5. If part of a reference is included in the text, you do not need to repeat it in the footnote. For example, if the author's name is mentioned in the text, the footnote may begin with the second part of the entry.

6. If a footnote refers to the same source as the preceding footnote, write *ibid.* and the page number(s). This abbreviation stands for the Latin word *ibidem* (ib'·i·dem'), which means "in the same place."

> [7]Henry H. Halley, <u>Halley's Bible Handbook</u> (Grand Rapids, Mich.: Zondervan Publishing House, 1965), p. 411.

> [8]Ibid., p. 445.

7. If a footnote refers to information from some other source within the source you consulted, give the original source first and then the source in which you found it.

> [9]Josephus, <u>Ant</u>. 18.1.3, cited in Merrill F. Unger, <u>The New Unger's Bible Dictionary</u> (Chicago: Moody Press, 1988), p. 998.

8. If a footnote is simply a comment by the author, write it in normal paragraph form.

> [10]The English word <u>martyr</u> comes from a form of the Greek <u>martus</u>, which means "witness."

The Bibliography

Your finished expository essay should include a *bibliography,* a complete listing of all the sources (except the Bible) that you consulted in writing your essay. The bibliography shows all the works from which you obtained information, whether or not you actually quoted from all of them. The following guidelines will help you to write the bibliography correctly.

1. The sources should be listed in alphabetical order according to the last names of the authors. If you used more than one reference source from the same author, group those sources alphabetically by title. If no author's name is given, list the source alphabetically according to the title.
2. Each entry for a book should have the following information in the order given. Place a period after the information for each lettered item below.
   a. The author(s), editor(s), or organization that did the writing. The author's last name should be first.
   b. The title of the book.
   c. The volume number of a book in a series. For an encyclopedia, the title of the article is sufficient.

d. The place of publication, the publisher, and the copyright date. Place a colon between the name of the city and the publisher, and a comma between the other two items. For an encyclopedia, only the copyright date is needed.

3. Each entry for a periodical should have the following information in the order given. Place a period after the information for each lettered item below.

a. The author(s), editor(s), or organization that did the writing. The author's last name should be first.

b. The title of the article.

c. The name of the periodical and the date of issue. Place a comma between these two items.

4. Entries of more than one line are arranged with hanging indents. In a hanging indent, the first line extends to the left and the remaining lines are indented. (This is the opposite of a normal paragraph indent. All the rules in this list are arranged with hanging indents.)

Below is the final draft of the expository essay illustrated throughout this chapter, with the footnotes and bibliography.

Who Were the Pharisees?

The religious life of the Jews demonstrated many contrasts in Jesus' day. No doubt Simeon and Anna represented a large group of righteous Jews. But the Scriptures also tell of the worldly-minded Sadducees, who favored assimilation into the surrounding Greek culture. On the other hand, we read much more about the narrow-minded Pharisees, with their hypocrisy and corrupted form of conservatism. Take a closer look at these Pharisees. Who were they, and what was their significance in Jewish life at the time of Christ?

The Pharisees first emerged as a distinct sect during the conflict of the Maccabean era. They were the spiritual successors of the Chasidim, or "Pious Ones," who had resisted Antiochus Epiphanes's efforts to destroy Judaism at least thirty years before.[1] The Pharisees drew primarily from the ranks of the scribes, whereas the Sadducees came primarily from the priests. Specifically, the Pharisees surfaced when the Maccabeans no longer stood for loyalty to the Law. They opposed the Hellenizers' goal of adopting Greek culture.[2]

The very name _Pharisee_ reveals something significant about their origin. The term (which first appeared in the time of John Hyrcanus, the grandson of Mattathias Maccabeus) means "separatist." Quite likely, this name was given by those who despised the "pious but proud and often petty exclusiveness"[3] of the group. These early Pharisees, however, espoused a noble twofold goal. Against the threat of Hellenization, they determined to keep Jewish national identity intact. Closely related, they committed themselves to keeping alive a strict adherence to the Mosaic Law. These two goals, of course, represented every faithful Jew's belief in God and hope for the Messiah.

From the New Testament Scriptures and from other sources, we can discover the basic beliefs of these Pharisees. We learn, for example, that they placed a strong emphasis on the ceremonial washing of hands and of eating utensils. It also appears that they considered frequent fasting to have definite merit. Furthermore, they acknowledged the reality of judgment upon sinners and of the resurrection to life for the saints. We know that they believed in the existence of angels and of spirits. And they recognized the cooperation of the divine will and the human will in human affairs.[4] Jesus indicated that their beliefs were basically right but that they were inconsistent in doing right.[5]

What was the relationship of the Pharisees to the Jews in general at the time of Christ? First, they were primarily a spiritual party, not a political party. They became involved in politics only when their freedom to obey the Law was threatened.[6] Although they numbered only about 6,000,[7] they apparently included more adherents and held greater influence than any other Jewish sect.[8] They were greatly admired by the common people, who considered them very righteous; therefore, they had an influence far greater than their actual numbers would warrant. Above all, the Pharisees held the strongest influence in keeping alive the Messianic hope in the years before Christ's coming.[9]

More important than the Pharisees' relationship to the Jews in general was their relationship to Jesus. From early in Jesus' ministry until His crucifixion, the Pharisees appear numerous times in the Gospel accounts. On the one hand, Jesus scathingly denounced their hypocrisy. In fact, Matthew 23 records some of the sternest denunciations in the Gospels, leveled against Pharisaic hypocrisy. On the other hand, the Pharisees made desperate efforts to trap Jesus by using trick questions. Yet a few of the Pharisees did follow Jesus. Nicodemus secretly believed in Him before

His crucifixion. The most influential Pharisee to become a follower of Jesus, no doubt, was the apostle Paul. And Acts 15:5 indicates that a sizable number of Pharisees joined the early church.

In summary, the Pharisees constituted a force that figured largely in Jewish life. From their noble origin as defenders of Judaism against Hellenization, they clung to a core of beliefs that were basically right. But their response to Jesus varied from outright rejection to loyal commitment. The Pharisees stand as a reminder that a noble beginning never guarantees that a group will continue on a right course.

Notes

[1] J. Sidlow Baxter, Explore the Book (Grand Rapids, Mich.: Zondervan Publishing House, 1966), p. 50.

[2] Henry H. Halley, Halley's Bible Handbook (Grand Rapids, Mich.: Zondervan Publishing House, 1965), p. 411.

[3] Baxter, Explore, p. 51.

[4] Schürer, History of the Jewish People in the Time of Christ, div. 2, 2:15, cited in Merrill F. Unger, The New Unger's Bible Dictionary (Chicago: Moody Press, 1988), p. 998.

[5] Matthew 23:3.

[6] Merrill F. Unger, The New Unger's Bible Dictionary (Chicago: Moody Press, 1988), p. 998.

[7] Unger, Dictionary, p. 999.

[8] Halley, Handbook, p. 445.

[9] Baxter, Explore, p. 52.

Bibliography

Baxter, J. Sidlow. Explore the Book. Grand Rapids, Mich.: Zondervan Publishing House, 1966.

Halley, Henry H. Halley's Bible Handbook. Grand Rapids, Mich.: Zondervan Publishing House, 1965.

Unger, Merrill F. The New Unger's Bible Dictionary. Chicago: Moody Press, 1988.

Applying the Lesson

A. Write the following footnotes correctly. Use the exercise numbers as footnote numbers.

   1. Christian Literature Crusade, Fort Washington, Pa., Made According to the Pattern, page 90, Charles W. Slemming, 1974.

Lesson 35 Answers
Applying the Lesson

A.   [1] Charles W. Slemming, Made According to the Pattern (Fort Washington, Pa.: Christian Literature Crusade, 1974), p. 90.

2. Glenn M. Jones, <u>Big Ten Tabernacle Topics</u>, pp. 18–20, Moody Press, Chicago, Ill. 1977
3. Charles W. Slemming, <u>Pattern</u>, p. 93.
4. <u>Moses and the Gods of Egypt</u>, John J. Davis, Grand Rapids, Mich., Baker Book House, 1986, pages 275, 276.

B. Compile a bibliography for the footnotes above.

C. Write the final draft of your expository essay. Include your footnotes neatly and correctly.

D. Compile the bibliography for your essay.

Your teacher may use the following evaluation chart to grade your expository essay. Remember, your score on this essay will make up a considerable part of your Chapter 4 test score.

Evaluation of an Expository Essay

Points possible Points earned

Title
  _3_ ____ Short and appealing
  _3_ ____ Directly related to theme

Introduction
  _3_ ____ Interesting; catches attention
  _3_ ____ Leads naturally to statement of theme

Body
  _3_ ____ All points of exposition are clear
  _3_ ____ Consists of well-developed paragraphs
  _3_ ____ Gives points in logical order

Conclusion
  _3_ ____ Brings theme into clear focus
  _3_ ____ Summarizes or otherwise reinforces main points
  _3_ ____ Ends with effective concluding sentence

Style
  _3_ ____ Freshness and originality
  _3_ ____ Active verbs and other exact, descriptive words

Mechanics
  _3_ ____ Correct spelling
  _3_ ____ Correct capitalization and punctuation
  _3_ ____ Correct grammar
  _3_ ____ Avoids careless repetition, omitted words, transpositions
  _48_ ____ **Total points**

[2]Glenn M. Jones, <u>Big Ten Tabernacle Topics</u> (Chicago: Moody Press, 1977), pp. 18–20.
[3]Slemming, <u>Pattern</u>, p. 93.
[4]John J. Davis, <u>Moses and the Gods of Egypt</u> (Grand Rapids, Mich.: Baker Book House, 1986), pp. 275, 276.

B.   Davis, John J. <u>Moses and the Gods of Egypt</u>. Grand Rapids, Mich.: Baker Book House, 1986.
  Jones, Glenn M. <u>Big Ten Tabernacle Topics</u>. Chicago: Moody Press, 1977.
  Slemming, Charles W. <u>Made According to the Pattern</u>. Fort Washington, Pa.: Christian Literature Crusade, 1974.

C. (Individual work.)

D. (Individual work.)

Lesson 36 Answers (Continued)

C.   [1]John C. Wenger, <u>The Mennonite Church in America</u> (Scottdale, Pa.: Herald Press, 1966), p. 358.
  [2]Harry A. Brunk, <u>History of Mennonites in Virginia: 1900–1960</u>, vol. 2 (Verona, Va.: McClure Printing Co., Inc., 1972), pp. 25–28.
  [3]Ibid., pp. 505–507.
  Jesse Neuenschwander, "Perpetuating Biblical Nonconformity," <u>The Eastern Mennonite Testimony</u>, December 1990, p. 6.
  [5]Wenger, <u>Mennonite Church</u>, p. 360.

D. Brunk, Harry A. <u>History of Mennonites in Virginia: 1900–1960</u>. Vol. 2. Verona, Va.: McClure Printing Co., Inc., 1972.
  Neuenschwander, Jesse. "Perpetuating Biblical Nonconformity." <u>The Eastern Mennonite Testimony</u>, December 1990.
  Wenger, John C. <u>The Mennonite Church in America</u>. Scottdale, Pa.: Herald Press, 1966.

36. Chapter 4 Review

A. Write the correct word or phrase for each blank.
1. An expository essay has that name because it ——— facts or information in order to define, clarify, or explain something.
2. Before you begin doing research, it will help you to select the right information if you write down the ——— of your essay.
3. Three types of information for which you should write footnotes are ———, ———, and ———.
4. For the final draft of your essay, leave a margin of about ——— along all four edges of the pages.
5. In a footnote for a quotation, the first item of information is usually the name of the ———.
6. The abbreviation *ibid.* means ———.
7. A list of the sources of information for an essay is called a ———.

B. Answer these questions.
1. What are three kinds of subjects that you should avoid when choosing a topic for an expository essay?
2. What are three things you can do to make sure you are not guilty of plagiarism?
3. How should the introductory paragraph begin, and how should it end?
4. One good way to develop paragraphs is by using specific facts that tell *what.* What are two other good ways?
5. What are two good ways to conclude an expository essay?
6. In what two places may footnotes appear?
7. When do you *not* need to write a footnote for a direct quotation?
8. What are three general characteristics of an appropriate title?
9. What are three specific ways to make a title appealing?
10. What three guidelines determine the order of the reference sources in a bibliography?

C. Write the following set of footnotes correctly, using the proper form and avoiding unnecessary repetition.
1. The Mennonite Church in America, p. 358, John C. Wenger, Herald Press, Scottdale, Pa., 1966
2. Harry A. Brunk, History of Mennonites in Virginia: 1900–1960, Vol. 2, McClure Printing Co., Inc., Verona, Va., 1972. pages 25–28
3. Harry A. Brunk, History of Mennonites in Virginia: 1900–1960, Vol. 2, McClure Printing Co., Inc., Verona, Va., 1972. pages 505–507
4. Jesse Neuenschwander, The Eastern Mennonite Testimony, "Perpetuating Biblical Nonconformity," December, 1990, p. 6
5. John C. Wenger, The Mennonite Church in America, p. 360

D. Compile a bibliography for the footnotes above.

Lesson 36

Purpose: To review the concepts taught in Chapter 4.

Lesson 36 Answers
Applying the Lesson

A. 1. exposes
2. purpose
3. direct quotations, details that the reader might question, technical information
4. one inch
5. author
6. "in the same place"
7. bibliography

B. 1. subjects involving only your personal knowledge and experience; subjects that you can hardly research; subjects that are controversial
2. Use others' ideas, not their exact words. Take notes in short phrases rather than whole sentences or paragraphs. Place direct quotations in quotation marks and credit them properly.
3. It should begin with a broad, general opening sentence. It should end with a sentence that directly states the theme of the essay.
4. Give sound reasons that tell *why.* Give clear illustrations that show *how.*
5. (Any two.) by summarizing the steps or main points; by emphasizing the importance or usefulness of what has been explained; by using a contrast; by using a quotation; by calling for a response from the reader
6. at the end of the essay; at the bottom of the page with which each one belongs
7. when you credit the source within the essay itself
8. is short; relates directly to the theme; catches the reader's interest
9. (Any three.) Use rhyming words. Use alliteration. Use an interesting word combination. Use a question.
10. List the sources in alphabetical order according to the last names of the authors. If more than one reference source from an author is used, list them alphabetically by title. If no author's name is given, list the source alphabetically according to the title.

(Parts C–D are on page 140.)

Chapter 5
Glossary of Usage

Book 1 Word List

Part 1

ability, capacity
accompanied by, with
adverse, averse
affect, effect
agree to, with
all the farther, faster
allusion, illusion
already, all ready
altogether, all together
among, between

Part 2

and etc.
anyways, nowheres,
    somewheres
as
at, to (*with* where)
awful, awfully
bad, badly
being as, that
beside, besides
better
but that, what

Part 3

cannot help but
complement, compliment
contend against, for, with
correspond to, with
credible, credulous
different(ly) from, than
discover, invent
disregardless, irregardless
emigrate, immigrate
envelop, envelope

Part 4

exalt, exult
farther, further
fewer, less
figure (out)
formally, formerly
get
had (hadn't) ought
hardly, scarcely
have got to
healthful, healthy

Part 5

hear to
in, into
incredible, incredulous
interior, superior
kind, kinds
later, latter
learn, teach
literally
lot, lots
mad

Part 6

mighty
muchly
nohow
nowhere near
of
part from, with
piece
plus
pretend like
principal, principle

Part 7

real, really
reckon
right
said, same
sight
so, such
sometime, some time
statue, stature, statute
suppose
suspect, suspicion

Part 8

taunt, taut
their, there, they're
to, too, two
type
valuable, invaluable
wait for, on
want that
where
who's, whose
you all, you'ns, you's

Book 2 Word List

Part 1 (Lesson 37)

above
accept, except
adapt, adopt
advice, advise
ain't
all
all right
allude, elude, refer
almost, most
altar, alter

Part 2 (Lesson 38)

always, all ways
amount, number
angry about, at, with
anymore, any more
as (if), like
awhile, a while
believe, feel
be sure and
burst, bursted, busted
can, may

Part 3 (Lesson 40)

censor, censure
compare to, with
comprehensible, comprehensive
contemptible, contemptuous
continual, continuous
could (should, would) of
council, counsel
differ from, with
dilemma
disinterested, uninterested

Part 4 (Lesson 41)

eminent, imminent, immanent
enormity
enthuse, enthused
everyday, every day
fabulous
flaunt, flout
good, well
haven't but, only
heap, heaps
hopefully

Part 5 (Lesson 42)

how come
impact
imply, infer
in back of
ingenious, ingenuous
its, it's
kind (sort) of
lay, lie
let, leave
loose, lose

Part 6 (Lesson 43)

maybe, may be
momentarily
nice
notable, noted, noteworthy, notorious
OK, okay
over with
persecute, prosecute
perspective, prospective
poorly
precede, proceed

Part 7 (Lesson 45)

propose, purpose
quote
raise, rise
receipt, recipe
respectable, respectful, respective
right along
set, sit
some, somewhat
stationary, stationery
straight, strait

Part 8 (Lesson 46)

than, then
them
this (these) here, that (those) there
transpire
try and
want in, off, out, through
way, ways
what for
worst kind, sort, way
your, you're

37. Correct Word Usage, Part 1

This chapter contains a listing of commonly misused or confused words. Book 1 of this set contains a companion listing of other words. Each lesson includes ten items with brief explanations and illustrations to show how the words should be used.

Some example sentences are marked with labels that indicate levels of usage. *Standard* usage refers to what is proper for all speech and writing. Words and meanings in this category are shown in the dictionary without any special label. *Informal* usage is acceptable for everyday speech and for personal writing (such as friendly letters), but it is not recommended for public speaking or for compositions such as reports and explanations. Compare the following sentences.

> **Informal:** Carl acted <u>like</u> he was <u>enthused</u> about the suggestion.
> **Standard:** Carl acted <u>as if</u> he was <u>enthusiastic</u> about the suggestion.

Many example sentences in this chapter are simply labeled *correct* if they represent standard usage, and *incorrect* if they do not. Study the illustrations below.

> **Incorrect:**
> Everyone <u>accept</u> Norman thought the idea would work <u>alright</u>.
> **Correct:**
> Everyone <u>except</u> Norman thought the idea would work <u>all right</u>.

Above

Most people have no difficulty with *above* when it is a preposition (*above* the clouds). When used as an adjective, it should follow the noun it modifies (the clouds *above,* the paragraph *above*). Using *above* before the modified noun is proper in legal or business writing, but it should be avoided otherwise. Also avoid using *the above* to mean "something already referred to."

> All <u>the statistics above</u> have been verified. (not *the above statistics*)
> Read <u>the agreement above</u> before signing your name. (not *the above*)

Accept, Except

Accept is a verb meaning "to receive" or "to agree with." This word has the prefix *ac-,* which is a form of *ad-.* When you *accept* something, you *add* it to what you already have.

Except is usually a preposition meaning "not including." It is sometimes a verb meaning "to leave out; exclude." Note that *except* has the prefix *ex-,* which means "out of."

> We must <u>accept</u> responsibility for our actions.
> No man <u>except</u> Jesus has ever lived a sinless life.
> God does not <u>except</u> anyone from His requirements for salvation.

Adapt, Adopt

Adapt means "to adjust" or "to make suitable." (The root *apt* means "fitting.")
Adopt means "to accept" or "to make one's own." (The root *opt* means "to choose.")

Lesson 37

Purpose: To reinforce correct usage in a variety of applications.

Teaching Suggestions:

The rules for English usage are constantly changing because languages change. Godly people do well to be slow in accepting these changes; however, they also need to remember that language change is not a moral issue and therefore is not wrong in itself. (The moral issue is in the careless attitudes that result in many language changes.) Because of these changes, some items in this glossary may be outdated in a few years—especially the distinctions between standard and informal usage. Generally, these distinctions are maintained in writing and public speaking but not in everyday settings.

In this chapter, the exercises are not divided in the normal odd–even manner. But each usage lesson has Parts A, B, and C; so if you do not assign all the exercises as written work, you can use Part A for class practice and the other parts for the written assignment.

Because some exercises require answers of the students' own choosing, a number of their answers may differ from those in the answer key. In such cases, the answer key generally gives two answers joined by *or.*

We <u>adapted</u> the words of the poem for this occasion.
The Swiss Anabaptist immigrants did not readily <u>adopt</u> the English language.
Misty <u>adopted</u> the orphaned kittens and cared well for them.

Advice, Advise

Advice is a noun meaning "counsel." The last three letters spell *ice,* which is also a noun in most cases.

Advise is a verb meaning "to give counsel." It has the same ending as verbs like *revise* and *surmise.* This word may mean "inform" in legal or business writing, but that use is generally not appropriate.

Young people should listen to the <u>advice</u> of those more experienced.
Godly parents <u>advise</u> their children to guard their friendships carefully.
Mother <u>informed</u> us that dinner was ready. (not *advised*)

Ain't

The contraction *ain't* is not standard English. Use *am not, are not (aren't),* or *is not (isn't).*

Incorrect:
I <u>ain't</u> ready yet, and Harvey <u>ain't</u> either.
Correct:
I <u>am not</u> ready yet, and Harvey <u>isn't</u> either.

All

The word *all* should not be used to mean things like "all gone," "all consumed," or "all done."

Incorrect: The sugar in the canister is <u>all</u>.
When the work was <u>all</u>, we went home.
Correct: The sugar in the canister is <u>all gone</u>.
The sugar in the canister is <u>all used up</u>.
When the work was <u>all done</u>, we went home.

All right

The correct spelling is *all right,* not *alright.* (*All right* is the antonym of *all wrong.*)

Incorrect: I feel <u>alright</u> now that I have rested.
Correct: I feel <u>all right</u> now that I have rested.
These answers are <u>all right</u>.

Allude, Elude, Refer

Allude means "to refer to indirectly" or "to hint." When a person alludes to something, he does not identify it specifically because he assumes that the listener or reader is familiar with it.

Elude means "to escape from by evading or avoiding." (The prefix *e-* is a form of *ex-*.)

Refer means "to mention specifically." This word (rather than *allude*) should be used for speaking directly about a person or thing.

> By describing his escape as a "Red Sea experience," Mr. Golitsyn <u>alluded</u> to Israel's deliverance from the Egyptians.
> Several times he <u>eluded</u> the secret police who were pursuing him.
> He often <u>refers</u> to his grandmother, who was a true believer.

Almost, Most

Almost is an adverb meaning "nearly." Avoid using *most* for this definition.

> **Incorrect:** <u>Most</u> everyone has heard of the patience of Job.
> **Correct:**   <u>Almost</u> everyone has heard of the patience of Job.

Altar, Alter

Altar is a noun meaning "an elevated structure on which offerings are made."
Alter is a verb meaning "to change." To al<u>ter</u> something is to conv<u>ert</u> it.

> Abraham built an <u>altar</u> almost everywhere he went.
> God's Word will never <u>alter</u> to suit man's changing ways.

Applying the Lesson

A. Choose the standard expressions in these sentences.

1. When Brother Edward told us not to hide under a juniper tree, he was (alluding, eluding, referring) to the experience of Elijah.
2. We must always be ready to (altar, alter) our ways to follow the Bible way.
3. Although he tried hard, Darius could not (accept, except) Daniel from the penalty that his law decreed.
4. (Almost, Most) every book of the Bible refers to the Messiah.
5. This morning Brother Alvin (advised, informed) us that our memory work is due on Thursday.
6. My assigned work was (all, all finished) before Father returned.
7. Everything seemed (all right, alright) again after Father came home.
8. A careful reading of the (above paragraph, paragraph above) should answer your questions.
9. We (ain't, aren't) getting more cereal until this cereal is (all, all gone).
10. Mr. White (advised, informed) us that the fox which had (alluded, eluded) our traps was now hanging in his shed.
11. The board members discussed the (above, paragraph above) and agreed to (adapt, adopt) it as a statement of their position.
12. Mr. Chadwick (ain't, isn't) here now, but he will probably (accept, except) your offer.
13. It is not enough to have (almost, most) everything on the (altar, alter) of sacrifice.
14. This tropical weather may suit you (all right, alright), but I can hardly (adapt, adopt) to it.

Lesson 37 Answers
Applying the Lesson

A. 1. alluding
2. alter
3. except
4. Almost
5. informed
6. all finished
7. all right
8. paragraph above
9. aren't, all gone
10. informed, eluded
11. paragraph above, adopt
12. isn't, accept
13. almost, altar
14. all right, adapt

B. Write the standard word or words for the underlined part of each sentence. If it needs no improvement, write *correct*.

1. The worldly wiseman does not <u>except</u> the Bible as God's authoritative Word.
2. We must be cautious lest we <u>adopt</u> the world's values and standards.
3. We know that things will come out <u>all right</u> in the end, for God is on the throne.
4. We can never <u>altar</u> an unpleasant truth by ignoring it or misrepresenting it.
5. No man can <u>allude</u> Satan's snares without godly faith and commitment.
6. The Bible teaches that ignorance does not <u>except</u> a person from accountability.
7. If the cookies are <u>all</u>, please serve the cupcakes.
8. Jerry fell off the wagon, but he thinks he will be <u>alright</u>.
9. Brother Wesley <u>adopted</u> this mobile home to serve as an office.
10. These chickens <u>ain't</u> laying very well anymore.
11. I did not write the <u>above</u>, but I know who did.
12. Brother Philip often <u>eludes</u> to his experiences on the mission field in Guatemala.
13. People who refuse to listen to good <u>advice</u> usually meet disaster.
14. We had <u>almost</u> all the work finished before noon.
15. I <u>ain't</u> sure what Father's surprise is, but he acts as if we will enjoy it.
16. Tell Father that the heifer feed is almost <u>all</u>.
17. <u>Most</u> every calf hutch needs fresh bedding tonight.
18. Father <u>advised</u> us that he has special plans for tomorrow.
19. The apostle Paul mentioned the Athenians' <u>altar</u> "TO THE UNKNOWN GOD."
20. Did you read the <u>above</u> carefully before you tried to answer the questions?

B.
1. accept
2. correct
3. correct
4. alter
5. elude
6. correct
7. all gone
8. all right
9. adapted
10. aren't
11. paragraph(s) above (*or* material above)
12. alludes *or* refers
13. correct
14. correct
15. am not
16. all gone
17. Almost
18. informed
19. correct
20. paragraph(s) above (*or* material above)

C. Write enough words to show how each sentence should be improved according to the rules you have studied. If a sentence needs no improvement, write *correct*.

1. Oliver Evans, born in 1755, invented several machines that worked alright; but his greatest invention was the high-pressure steam engine.
2. When he was seventeen years old, one of his brothers advised him about something that the blacksmith's son had done.
3. The boy had blocked the touchhole of a gun barrel, put water into it, and plugged the muzzle with wadding—which usually ain't wise at all!
4. Having altared the barrel in this way, the lad put it into the smith's fire; and soon the steam pressure shot out the wadding with great force.
5. Oliver immediately recognized that this idea could be adapted to make a useful steam engine.
6. However, it was most thirty-three years later before his dream materialized, and he completed the first steam-powered vehicle to run on American roads.
7. He named his weird-looking contraption *Orukter Amphibolos,* eluding to its ability to travel both on land and in water.

C.
1. all right
2. informed
3. isn't
4. altered
5. correct
6. almost
7. alluding

8. Evans built his machine after excepting a contract to dredge out the Philadelphia harbor.
9. He appealed to President Jefferson for relief when his money was nearly all.
10. We learn from the above that useful ideas sometimes come from unexpected sources.

8. accepting
9. all gone
10. story above (*or* account above)

Review Exercises

Write whether the underlined sentence part is a nominative absolute (*NA*) or a participial phrase (*PP*). [24]

1. <u>The storm having passed</u>, we went outside to see what damage it had done.
2. <u>Looking around</u>, we saw many leaves and twigs on the ground.
3. One tree, <u>having withstood many previous storms</u>, now lay prostrate on the ground.
4. The bark of another tree was split open, <u>the tree having been struck by lightning</u>.
5. <u>God alone having power to control the weather</u>, man must simply accept what comes.

Review Exercises

1. NA
2. PP
3. PP
4. NA
5. NA

---

38.   Correct Word Usage, Part 2

Always, All ways

Always is an adverb meaning "every time," "all the time," "forever," or "at any time."

The expression *all ways* means "every way." It often follows a preposition.

> Myron is <u>always</u> ready to help others.
> God will <u>always</u> be sovereign over His creation.
> The book was attractively designed in <u>all ways</u>.

Amount, Number

Use *amount* with a noun that refers to a single mass—something that cannot be counted. *Amount* goes with the same nouns that *much* (rather than *many*) goes with.

Use *number* with nouns that refer to individual items—things that can be counted. *Number* goes with the same nouns that *many* (rather than *much*) goes with.

> We covered a large <u>amount</u> of material in our history classes this week.
>   (Compare: *much material,* not *many material*)
> We covered a large <u>number</u> (not *amount*) of pages in our history classes this week. (Compare: *many pages,* not *much pages*)

Angry about, at, with

A person may be *angry with* another person, *angry about* a situation or an event, and *angry at* an animal or an inanimate object.

Lesson 38

Purpose: To reinforce correct usage in a variety of applications.

God is <u>angry with</u> the wicked every day.
Jonah was <u>angry about</u> the destruction of the gourd.
Balaam became <u>angry at</u> his donkey.

Anymore, Any more

In standard usage, *anymore* is an adverb meaning "any longer" or "at the present," and it occurs mainly in negative constructions and questions. It is used informally to mean "nowadays."

Informal: <u>Anymore</u>, Grandmother Bricker hears very poorly.
Standard: Grandmother Bricker cannot hear well <u>anymore</u>.
    (negative statement)
    Do Eskimos build igloos <u>anymore</u>? (question)

The phrase *any more* should be used only in the sense of "some additional." It should not be used as an adverb.

Incorrect: We do not live in Virginia <u>any more</u>.
Correct: We do not live in Virginia <u>anymore</u>.
    We do not have <u>any more</u> maple syrup.

As (if), Like

In standard English, *as* and *as if* are conjunctions and *like* is a preposition. *Like* has become accepted as a conjunction in informal usage.

Informal: God does not treat us <u>like</u> we sometimes treat our fellow men.
    Too often we treat others <u>like</u> they have no feelings.
Standard: God does not treat us <u>as</u> we sometimes treat our fellow men.
    Too often we treat others <u>as if</u> they have no feelings.
    We should conduct ourselves <u>like</u> humble servants of Jesus Christ.

Awhile, A while

Awhile is an adverb meaning "for a short time."
The expression *a while* often follows a preposition. Avoid using the adverb *awhile* as the object of a preposition.

This evening we plan to visit Grandfather <u>awhile</u>.
This evening we plan to visit Grandfather for <u>a while</u>. (not *for awhile*)

Believe, Feel

Believe means "to think" or "to be convinced of." A valid belief is based on fact.
Feel indicates a perception based on emotion or opinion and not necessarily on fact.

Poor: We <u>feel</u> that Sunday is the proper day of worship.
Better: We <u>believe</u> that Sunday is the proper day of worship.
    Because of our great privileges, we should <u>feel</u> that we are richly blessed. (Note the emotional aspect.)

Be sure and

The expression *be sure and* should be replaced with *be sure to.*

> **Incorrect:** We must <u>be sure and</u> fix that broken window.
> **Correct:**   We must <u>be sure to</u> fix that broken window.

Burst, Bursted, Busted

The three principal parts of the verb *burst* are *burst, burst, burst.* The forms *bursted, bust,* and *busted* are not standard English verbs.

> **Incorrect:** The dam <u>bursted</u> and flooded the valley below.
>   The water pipes <u>busted</u> during the cold snap.
> **Correct:**   The dam <u>burst</u> and flooded the valley below.
>   The water pipes <u>burst</u> during the cold snap.

Can, May

Can means "to be able to." It refers to ability.

May means "to be permitted to." The distinction between *can* and *may* is illustrated in this sentence: You *may* get a drink if you *can.*

> **Incorrect:** <u>Can</u> I use your pen?
> **Correct:**   <u>May</u> I use your pen?

Sometimes *may* indicates possibility. For example, "They may go" could mean "They are permitted to go" or "It is possible that they will go." If the meaning of *may* is uncertain, replace it with *might* or *must* or some other verb.

> **Unclear:**
> We <u>may</u> hike in the woods this afternoon.
> We <u>may</u> not allow the fear of man to control our actions.
> **Clear:**
> We <u>are allowed to</u> hike in the woods this afternoon. (permission)
> We <u>might</u> hike in the woods this afternoon. (possibility)
> We <u>must</u> not (or *dare not*) allow the fear of man to control our actions.

Applying the Lesson

A. Choose the standard expressions in these sentences.
1. Youth who do (as, like) their godly parents request are (always, all ways) happier than those who insist on their own way.
2. If you feel like becoming angry (about, at, with) someone who has wronged you, be (sure and, sure to) crucify those feelings.
3. God is (always, all ways) able to (burst, bust) our balloon of pride if we exalt ourselves.
4. We (believe, feel) that God hears the prayers of saints, but sometimes His answer does not come for (awhile, a while).
5. Although many do not uphold Bible principles (anymore, any more), we must be (sure and, sure to) keep on obeying God.

Lesson 38 Answers
Applying the Lesson
A. 1. as, always
   2. with, sure to
   3. always, burst
   4. believe, a while
   5. anymore, sure to

6. A large (amount, number) of Bible verses warn us not to live (as, like) the world does.
7. (Can, May) we walk to the back pasture this afternoon?
8. We do not have (anymore, any more) snow on the ground.
9. Grandmother Bicher will live with us (awhile, a while) this winter.
10. Due to an acute ear infection, Melanie's eardrum (burst, bursted, busted).
11. Even though the heifers are contrary, you must not become angry (about, at, with) them.
12. Mother said that we (can, may) make blueberry cobbler for dessert.
13. With only a small (amount, number) of visitors, our little church building is soon full.
14. Job must have (believed, felt) that God had forsaken him; for he said, "Oh that I knew where I might find him!"

6. number, as
7. May
8. any more
9. awhile
10. burst
11. at
12. may
13. number
14. felt

B. Write the standard word or words for the underlined part of each sentence. If it needs no improvement, write *correct.*
1. If we desire God's blessing, we must be sure and follow His will.
2. Our heavenly Father is always watching over us lovingly.
3. We may face trials for awhile in life, but heaven will be worth it all.
4. A large amount of songs in the German *Ausbund* deal with the theme of persecution.
5. We should live each day like it might be our last.
6. Do you have anymore prayer requests?
7. The water line burst because the pressure regulator had stuck.
8. Did Brother Alan say that we can eat outside today?
9. Do you feel that kindness is an essential quality for God's people?
10. If you trust in the Lord, you cannot be angry about a change in your plans.
11. Self-pity will cause you to feel that nobody cares about you.
12. I wonder if Aunt Charlotte has any more of those crocheted afghans ready.
13. Suddenly the tire bursted with a tremendous bang.
14. Leslie managed to work in the shop awhile this morning.
15. Viola can go along to the store if she wants to.
16. That strange man seems quite angry at Father.
17. We almost all ways see several deer in this pasture in the evening.
18. Mother wants to be sure and send a get-well card to Sister Annette.
19. We had a record amount of thunderstorms this summer.
20. It seems like many thunderstorms follow the mountain ridge behind our farm.

B. 1. be sure to   11. correct
2. correct   12. correct
3. a while   13. burst
4. number   14. correct
5. as if   15. may
6. any more   16. angry with
7. correct   17. always
8. may   18. be sure to
9. believe   19. number
10. correct   20. as if

C. Write enough words to show how each sentence should be improved according to the rules you have studied. If a sentence needs no improvement, write *correct.*
1. During the American Revolution, many items were all ways in short supply.
2. In 1779, at the age of fourteen, Eli Whitney felt that he could supply some of the demand for nails.
3. "Can I make a forge in our workshop?" Eli asked his father.
4. Eli's father let him make a forge like he requested.

C. 1. always
2. correct *or* believed
3. May
4. as

5. Soon young Eli could not meet the demand any more.
6. He hired a helper to increase the number of nails he could produce.
7. The war ended in 1783, bringing cheaper nails from England and busting the bubble of his success.
8. Instead of becoming angry with the circumstances, Eli started making hat-pins and walking canes.
9. He continued this business only for a while; then at eighteen years of age he began teaching school.
10. Be sure and read more about Eli Whitney's inventive career.

5. anymore
6. correct
7. bursting
8. about
9. correct
10. sure to

Review Exercises

Write enough words to show how each sentence should be improved according to the rules you have studied. If a sentence needs no improvement, write *correct*. [37, 38]

1. In 1527, George Wagner was arrested at Munich because he refused to adapt the position of the state church on four articles of faith.
2. George was held in prison for awhile as the authorities urged him to recant.
3. An astounding amount of people tried to make George change his mind.
4. Even George's wife and child were brought to the prison to see if they could persuade him to alter his beliefs.
5. However, George felt that he must remain loyal to God if he was to be saved in the end.
6. When the prince finally decided that George would not except deliverance, he condemned him to death.
7. George wanted to be sure and testify about the truth before everyone present at his execution.
8. With a smile, George went bravely to his death; he was not angry with his persecutors.
9. The sheriff, however, did not consider his work to be all; he determined to arrest more of the brethren.
10. But the sheriff could not allude God's judgment, and that night he died in bed.

Review Exercises
1. adopt
2. a while
3. number
4. correct
5. believed
6. accept
7. be sure to
8. correct
9. all done (*or* finished)
10. elude

---

39. Improving Your Writing Style, Part 3: Active Voice

In the previous two writing style lessons, you learned that originality and the use of active verbs characterize good writing style. That is, an effective writer looks for fresh, colorful ways of expressing himself, and he strives to use verbs that put life and action into his writing.

Another element of good writing style is the deliberate use of verbs in the active voice. You should remember that transitive verbs can be active or passive. In the active

Lesson 39

Purpose: To emphasize that use of the active voice is an element of an effective writing style.

Teaching Suggestions:

This writing style lesson may require a bit more class time than some of the others. Although previous books in this series have taught students to avoid the passive voice as much as possible, do not pass over this material too quickly. Most people do not shake off the passive voice habit very easily.

voice, the subject *performs* the action of the verb. But in the passive voice, the subject merely *receives* the action.

Active voice: The presidents and princes <u>hated</u> Daniel.
    They <u>persuaded</u> the king to make a foolish law.
Passive voice: Daniel <u>was hated</u> by the presidents and princes.
    The king <u>was persuaded</u> to make a foolish law.

The active voice puts energy into writing because it makes the subject do something. The presidents and princes *hated* Daniel; they *persuaded* the king. In contrast, the passive voice introduces a passive subject that never gets into the action! Daniel did nothing; he simply *was hated.* The king did nothing; he merely *was persuaded.*

This difference between active voice and passive voice makes a great contrast in writing. While the passive voice is dull and sluggish, the active voice is lively and energetic. We can understand this; but unless we think carefully as we write, the passive voice will slip into our sentences and snuff out the action. See how that happens in the following example.

After feeding the five thousand, Jesus sent His disciples across the Sea of Galilee. Before they reached the other side, however, a mighty tempest arose. The ship and every person in it were being threatened. But Jesus was not neglecting His loved ones! Above the roar of the storm, the Master's voice was heard: "Be of good cheer."
Peter responded, "Lord, if it is You, bid me come to You on the water."

Did you catch it? *The Master's voice was heard.* Why should we record this action with a passive verb? Jesus Himself spoke words of comfort to His distressed disciples. We want to capture that action: Above the roar of the storm, *the Master called,* "Be of good cheer." Or we could say that *the disciples heard a voice.* Either way, we are using the active voice, and the action puts life into the writing style.

You see this, but did you see the other use of the passive voice in the example? *The ship and every person in it were being threatened.* Again we have a subject with no action; the ship and those in it are merely being acted upon. How can we write this in the active voice? To answer that question, consider *what action* was taking place and *who* or *what* was doing it. *The stormy waves were threatening the ship and every person in it.* Now we have action; now we have life.

Of course, the passive voice does exist for a good reason. Sometimes there is no clear doer of the action, and sometimes we deliberately avoid naming the doer. Also, the passive voice may fit well in a sentence that pictures someone as the victim of a tragedy or disaster: *Samson was blinded and imprisoned.* But the passive voice nearly always weakens writing style because it allows a person to write in vague generalities without saying exactly *who* does the things he describes.

For this reason, you need to make a special effort to detect passive verbs in your writing and replace them with active verbs. This point is so important that you will try to avoid the passive voice completely in your written work for this lesson.

Applying the Lesson

A. Read the story below, and do the following exercises in class.

1. Find the one passive verb in each paragraph, and notice how it spoils the action. Suggest how to improve that sentence or clause with a verb in the active voice.

2. Tell whether each underlined expression has a *good* or *poor* effect on the story. If it is good, tell whether it illustrates *originality* or an *active verb*. If it is poor, suggest how to improve it.

How Nevin Helped

(1)   Mother sighed as she glanced out the window at the ᵃhaze-blanketed August sky. "What a day!" she thought as beads of sweat were wiped from her forehead. Father had left early that morning to attend the ministers' meeting. He would not return before evening, so Mother had some of his work to do in addition to her own regular duties.

(2)   Mother's shoulders sagged as tomatoes were cut to make tomato juice. She must hurry. ᵇThere were many jobs pressing upon her. She thought over the many interruptions of the morning. Several times the doorbell had rung. Mother needed to stop her work to see who had come. How ᶜmany precious minutes fled with each person at the door! How small the heap of cut tomatoes looked beside the big pile awaiting the ᵈwork of her deft hands!

(3)   "Oh!" exclaimed Mother. "That washer has stopped already. How time flies! I guess the wash must be hung up by Nevin."

(4)   Mother turned to call her fourteen-year-old son. But then she turned back to the sink. "I promised Nevin that he could work at his pine hutch this afternoon. And this will surely be called a girl's job. ᵉI feel just too tired to deal with complaints now. Maybe I can hang up the wash later."

(5)   Another juicy red tomato was cut by Mother. Then she shook her head. "No," she decided. "I have a son ᶠwho can be a helper. And he must learn to help cheerfully."

(6)   The button of the intercom was pressed. Hearing no ᵍnoise, Mother called, "Nevin, would you please come to the house?"

(7)   "Sure, Mother," Nevin returned. "Be there shortly. Some clamps on the side panels that I've just glued are being set by me."

(8)   "What do you want, Mother?" Nevin asked as the kitchen was entered a few minutes later.

(9)   "I'm sorry, Nevin, but your help is needed," Mother told him, ʰa little sunlight coming from her knife. "Please hang up that load of towels for me."

(10)   "Sure," Nevin answered. He ⁱwhistled like a bird as the clean, wet towels were pulled from the washer.

(11)   ʲMother smiled as Nevin's cheerful whistle was heard from the clothesline. "Thank You, Lord, for his cheerful attitude right now when

Lesson 39 Answers

Applying the Lesson

A. 1. (Answers are numbered according to paragraphs.)

(1) were wiped; as she wiped beads of sweat

(2) were cut; as she cut tomatoes

(3) must be hung; Nevin must hang up the wash

(4) will be called; he will surely call this

(5) was cut; Mother cut another

(6) was pressed; Mother pressed the button

(7) are being set; I am setting some clamps

(8) was entered; as he entered the kitchen

(9) is needed; I need your help

(10) were pulled; as he pulled

(11) was heard; as she heard Nevin's cheerful whistle (*or* as Nevin's cheerful whistle came)

2. a. good; originality

b. poor; Many jobs were pressing

c. good; originality

d. good; originality

e. good; active verb

f. poor; who can help

g. poor; saw whining (*or* sander humming)

h. poor; a glint of sunlight sparkling from her knife

i. poor; whistled like a merry teakettle

j. poor; A smile played on Mother's lips

k. good; originality

I'm feeling so pressured," Mother whispered. ^k<u>Some of her tension melted away, and the mountain of tomatoes steadily melted too.</u>

B. Write a story of 200–300 words about a time when you or someone else helped another person, perhaps in a small or hidden way. *Use no passive voice* in your writing. Also put special effort into applying the other elements of writing style that you have studied: originality and active verbs.

B. (Individual work.)

-----

40. Correct Word Usage, Part 3

Censor, Censure

Censor (sen′·sər) means "to examine (speech or writing) and remove objectionable content."

Censure (sen′·shər) means "to express strong disapproval of" or "to condemn harshly."

> Father <u>censored</u> some slang words from the book before he gave it to me.
> The angry woman <u>censured</u> the boy for ruining her flowers.

Compare to, with

Use *compare with* to speak of comparing things in order to observe literal similarities or differences.

Use *compare to* for making figurative comparisons.

> How does your weather in northern Ontario <u>compare with</u> ours here in Alberta?
> The New Testament <u>compares</u> the Christian life <u>to</u> a warfare.

Comprehensible, Comprehensive

Comprehensible means "intelligible; understandable."
Comprehensive means "of a large scope" or "inclusive."

> After I learned the meanings of a few key words, the directions became <u>comprehensible</u>.
> This book gives a <u>comprehensive</u> survey of beekeeping.

Contemptible, Contemptuous

Contemptible means "deserving contempt; despicable." It should generally be used to describe actions rather than people.

Contemptuous means "expressing contempt; scornful." It may describe words, actions, or people.

> Judas committed the <u>contemptible</u> deed of betraying Jesus for money.
> Sanballat spoke <u>contemptuous</u> words when the Jews began rebuilding the wall.

Lesson 40

Purpose: To reinforce correct usage in a variety of applications.

Continual(ly), Continuous(ly)

Continual means "occurring repeatedly at frequent intervals."
Continuous means "occurring constantly without interruption."

> God has blessed us with <u>continual</u> showers this spring.
> It has rained <u>continuously</u> for the past twelve hours.

Could (Should, Would) of

In informal speech, contracted forms like *could've, should've,* and *would've* sound like *could of, should of,* and *would of.* Inexperienced writers sometimes write these verbs with *of* rather than *have.*

> **Incorrect:** We <u>should of</u> started sooner; then we <u>would of</u> been here earlier.
> **Correct:**　We <u>should have</u> started sooner; then we <u>would have</u> been here earlier.

Council, Counsel

A *council* is a group of people who serve in some official position, as in a state church or in civil government.

As a noun, *counsel* means "advice" or "an exchanging of ideas." As a verb, *counsel* means "to give advice" or "to exchange ideas."

> The Jewish <u>council</u> sought false witnesses to testify against Jesus.
> Mother <u>counseled</u> me to discuss the question with Father.
> A preparatory service before Communion is often called a <u>counsel meeting</u>.
> 　　(not *council meeting*)

Differ from, with

Differ from means "to be unlike," usually with no indication of conflict.
Differ with means "to disagree with." It usually refers to people with conflicting ideas.

> The Spanish alphabet <u>differs from</u> the English alphabet in several ways.
> Mr. Hilbert <u>differed with</u> us when we discussed nonresistance.

Dilemma

The primary meaning of *dilemma* is "a circumstance requiring one to choose between two equally undesirable options." (The prefix *di-* means "two.") In standard writing, avoid using *dilemma* to mean simply "problem" or "difficulty."

> Pilate faced a <u>dilemma</u>. Should he crucify an innocent man or risk a riot by the Jews?
> The pioneers met one <u>difficulty</u> after another as they traveled through the mountains. (not *dilemma*)

Disinterested, Uninterested

The primary meaning of *disinterested* is "impartial; having no special preference concerning the outcome of an issue." For example, a good judge is disinterested in the outcome of a trial. His main interest is to have a fair and just trial.

Uninterested means "having no interest in," "not paying attention," or "indifferent."

The neighbors asked a <u>disinterested</u> person to help settle their disagreement.
Mr. Scott appears quite <u>uninterested</u> in the Gospel.

Applying the Lesson

A. Choose the standard expressions in these sentences.
   1. Because of the (dilemma, problem) that Moses faced, Jethro suggested that he appoint (disinterested, uninterested) judges to help settle disputes among the Israelites.
   2. The Pharisees differed (from, with) the Sadducees because their doctrines differed (from, with) the Sadducees' doctrines.
   3. The faithful priests (censored, censured) Uzziah when he offered incense.
   4. Ever since his fall, Satan has maintained a (continual, continuous) warfare against God.
   5. Ephesians 6 presents a (comprehensible, comprehensive) list of the armor that a Christian should wear.
   6. Compared (to, with) the Old Testament, the New Testament upholds the same faith in God but a new way of approaching God.
   7. David's (contemptible, contemptuous) sin gave the enemies of the Lord an occasion to blaspheme.
   8. Haman built a gallows at his wife's (council, counsel), and Mordecai might (have, of) been hanged on it if Haman's scheme had worked.
   9. Paul differed (from, with) Barnabas over the wisdom of taking John Mark on another missionary journey.
   10. The (contemptible, contemptuous) children who mocked Elisha were punished severely.
   11. Jesus spoke of a rich man who was (disinterested, uninterested) in the welfare of his soul.
   12. The school board will (censor, censure) these books before putting them into the library.
   13. We have been praying (continually, continuously) for rain.
   14. The note was barely (comprehensible, comprehensive), but we understood its main idea.
   15. My brother compared the writing (to, with) chicken scratches.
   16. We should (have, of) been more careful when we planted these rows of peas.

B. Write the standard word or words for the underlined part of each sentence. If it needs no improvement, write *correct.*
   1. Though many people consider the Bible a mysterious book, it is easily <u>comprehensive</u> to those who sincerely want to know God.
   2. The prophets <u>censored</u> God's people for their unfaithfulness.
   3. Animal sacrifices, <u>continuously</u> offered during the Old Testament years, could not provide full salvation for man.

Lesson 40 Answers
Applying the Lesson
A. 1. problem, disinterested
   2. with, from
   3. censured
   4. continuous
   5. comprehensive
   6. with
   7. contemptible
   8. counsel, have
   9. with
   10. contemptuous
   11. uninterested
   12. censor
   13. continually
   14. comprehensible
   15. to
   16. have

B. 1. comprehensible
   2. censured
   3. continually

4. The attitudes of the world <u>differ from</u> those of God's people.
5. Father gave careful, <u>uninterested</u> consideration to both sides of the story.
6. We <u>should of</u> listened more carefully to what Mother said.
7. Anabaptists were often brought before a church <u>council</u> and questioned about their beliefs.
8. The people laughed <u>contemptibly</u> when Jesus said that Jairus's daughter was sleeping.
9. <u>Compared with</u> our farm in Virginia, this farm has much better soil.
10. The fireman faced the <u>dilemma</u> of letting the child perish and saving his own life, or trying to rescue the child and risking two lives.
11. After Brother Wilmer had <u>censured</u> the newspaper clipping, he posted it on the bulletin board.
12. With a casual, <u>disinterested</u> shrug of his shoulders, the man walked away.
13. Even though Mr. Clark was so <u>contemptuous</u>, we need to forgive him.
14. In building our new shop, we faced a number of <u>dilemmas</u> that had no simple solutions.
15. Father often sought <u>counsel</u> from Brother Wayne, an experienced builder.
16. Your recipe <u>differs with</u> mine in only a few details.
17. In Walter's poem, the flowers are <u>compared with</u> smiling faces.
18. I need a more <u>comprehensible</u> concordance than the small one in the back of my Bible.
19. We <u>could of</u> worked a little longer, but we had come to a good place to stop.
20. The fans do not run <u>continually</u>; they are thermostatically controlled.

C. Write enough words to show how each sentence should be improved according to the rules you have studied. If a sentence needs no improvement, write *correct*.
1. In 1792, Eli Whitney arrived in Georgia, where he would of tutored Major Dupont's children.
2. Compared to the salary he had been promised, however, he found that he might receive only half as much money.
3. Whitney moved to a different plantation, where he heard about the dilemma that faced cotton growers in the South.
4. As he listened to the plantation owners' discussions, he gained a comprehensible view of the strong market for cotton and the great need for a speedier process of cleaning cotton.
5. A lady gave this council: "Mr. Whitney can build a machine to clean cotton"; and within two weeks, he had built a cotton gin.
6. Whitney's gin differed with others in several important ways, and it was able to clean the green seed cotton that other gins could not clean.
7. Moving teeth on a roller continuously pulled the cotton through narrow slits that prevented the seeds from coming through.
8. A number of dishonest men, seemingly contemptible of patent laws, made cotton gins modeled after Whitney's without paying for the right to do so.
9. In a letter to a fellow inventor, Whitney bitterly censured those who profited at his expense.

4. correct
5. disinterested
6. should have
7. correct
8. contemptuously
9. correct
10. correct
11. censored
12. uninterested
13. correct
14. problems *or* difficulties
15. correct
16. differs from
17. compared to
18. comprehensive
19. could have
20. continuously

C. 1. would have
2. Compared with
3. problem *or* difficulty
4. comprehensive
5. counsel
6. differed from
7. correct
8. contemptuous
9. correct

10. Although many southern states did authorize payments to Whitney, an uninterested observer will soon recognize that he did not earn what he deserved from this invention.

Review Exercises

Write enough words to show how each sentence should be improved according to the rules you have studied. If a sentence needs no improvement, write *correct*. [37–40]

1. Leonhard Keyser, a Roman Catholic priest, could not be satisfied any more with the corruption in the church.
2. He made quite a comprehensive study of Lutheran, Zwinglian, and Anabaptist doctrines.
3. In 1525, Leonhard joined the Anabaptist movement like many others were doing.
4. He served zealously as a minister among the Anabaptists, all ways undaunted by the severe persecution.
5. After he was arrested, the authorities advised him that he would be burned on the Friday before Saint Lawrence Day.
6. On the way to the execution, the priests spoke to Leonhard in Latin because otherwise the common people would of understood them.
7. Leonhard plucked a flower and told the judge that if they could burn the flower and his body, their way was all right and his was wrong.
8. Twice the executioners built an enormous fire; yet when the wood was all, Leonhard's body and the flower remained unharmed.
9. The executioners then did a contemptible deed: they cut Leonhard's body into pieces and tried to burn them.
10. When the pieces of his body would not burn, the terrified judge resigned his office and moved away; but the judge's servant adapted the Anabaptist faith and lived in godliness until death.

10. a disinterested

Review Exercises

1. anymore
2. correct
3. as many others
4. always
5. informed (*or* correct, if viewed as having a legal connotation)
6. would have
7. correct
8. all gone (*or* consumed)
9. correct
10. adopted

---

41. Correct Word Usage, Part 4

Eminent, Imminent, Immanent

Eminent (em′·ə·nənt) means "high-ranking," "conspicuous," or "prominent."

Imminent (im′·ə·nənt) means "likely to occur at any moment."

Immanent (im′·ə·nənt) means "indwelling" and refers mainly to a person. It has the same root (*man*) as the word *remain.* Note that *imminent* and *immanent* are pronounced alike; they are homonyms.

Menno Simons was respected as an <u>eminent</u> church leader.
We must not lose sight of Jesus' <u>imminent</u> return for the saints.
The <u>immanent</u> Holy Spirit directs the life of a Christian.

Lesson 41

Purpose: To reinforce correct usage in a variety of applications.

Enormity

Enormity means "extremely great wickedness" or "outrageousness." To refer to greatness of size, scope, or influence, use *enormousness* or *immensity.*

> Overwhelmed by the <u>enormity</u> of his sin, David pleaded for God's forgiveness.
> The <u>immensity</u> of outer space boggles our finite minds. (not *enormity*)

Enthused

The word *enthused* is derived by folk etymology from *enthusiasm. Enthused* is informal but undignified because it suggests an outward emotional display. In standard English, it should be replaced by a word such as *excited* or *enthusiastic.*

> **Informal:** The children were <u>enthused</u> about visiting Grandmother.
> **Standard:** The children were <u>enthusiastic</u> (or *excited*) about visiting Grandmother.

Everyday, Every day

The word *everyday* means "daily," "relating to ordinary days," or "commonplace." It is an adjective.

The expression *every day* means "each day." It functions as an adverb.

> My <u>everyday</u> chores include feeding the chickens.
> Pack two sets of <u>everyday</u> clothes for the trip.
> We have family worship <u>every day</u> before breakfast. (not *everyday*)

Fabulous

Fabulous, derived from *fable,* means "incredible," "imaginary," or "known only through fables." It is informal for "outstanding" or "marvelous."

> **Informal:** Myra did a <u>fabulous</u> job on these posters.
> **Standard:** Myra did an <u>outstanding</u> job on these posters.
> The neighbor boy told a <u>fabulous</u> story about killing a wolf barehanded.

Flaunt, Flout

Flaunt means "to make a bold, showy, or defiant display of."
Flout means "to show bold disregard for (a rule or standard)."

> The Pharisees often <u>flaunted</u> their piety before others.
> Many of their practices <u>flouted</u> the clear commandments of God.

Good, Well

Good is an adjective with many meanings, such as "right," "proper," and "satisfactory."

Well usually modifies an action verb by indicating "in a good manner." It is sometimes an adjective meaning "healthy," "proper," or "prudent."

> The children's <u>good</u> behavior made the baby-sitting job a pleasure.
> Listen <u>well</u> so that you will know exactly what to do.

If Aunt Mae feels <u>well</u> enough, she will help us make applesauce.

It is <u>good</u> (or *well*) that you asked for advice.

Haven't but, only

Haven't but is a double negative because *but* has a negative meaning in this construction.

The phrase *haven't only* sometimes occurs in expressions like "we haven't only." This indicates either that we have more than the amount specified or that we have none at all. The correct expression is "we have only."

> **Incorrect:** We <u>haven't but</u> two bushels of apples left, and we <u>haven't only</u> one bushel of pears.
>
> **Correct:**   We <u>have but</u> two bushels of apples left, and we <u>have only</u> one bushel of pears.

Heap, Heaps

A *heap* is a pile. The word is used informally to mean "many," "large amount," or "multitude."

> **Informal:** We had a <u>heap</u> of trouble pushing the van out of the mud.
> This area must have had <u>heaps</u> of rain.
>
> **Standard:** We had <u>great</u> difficulty pushing the van out of the mud.
> This area must have had a <u>large amount</u> of rain.
> The farmer repaired his lane with stones from the <u>heap</u> of gravel.

Hopefully

Hopefully means "in a hopeful manner." Avoid using *hopefully* as a sentence modifier meaning "it is hoped" or "if all goes well."

> **Poor:**
> <u>Hopefully</u>, we will finish harvesting the wheat tomorrow.
> **Better:**
> <u>If all goes well</u>, we will finish harvesting the wheat tomorrow.
> We looked <u>hopefully</u> at the approaching clouds, but they brought no rain.

Applying the Lesson

A. Choose the standard expressions in these sentences.
1. Because of the (enormity, enormousness) of Israel's sin, God brought severe judgment upon the nation.
2. Although the people of Judah knew about this, they brazenly continued to (flaunt, flout) their own wickedness.
3. The prophets did their work (good, well), but most of the Jews paid little heed to their warnings.
4. Finally the (eminent, imminent, immanent) presence of the Lord departed from the temple.
5. When one is (enthused, enthusiastic) about his assignment, he can work efficiently.

Lesson 41 Answers
Applying the Lesson
A. 1. enormity
   2. flaunt
   3. well
   4. immanent
   5. enthusiastic

6. We (haven't only, have only) one life to live, so we must live it in godly fear.
7. We have had rain (everyday, every day) so far this week.
8. I think Susan did a (fabulous, remarkable) job on her embroidery patch.
9. If you (flaunt, flout) good advice today, you will regret it tomorrow.
10. The (enormity, immensity) of the ocean amazes me every time I see it.
11. By steady perseverance, the (fabulous, remarkable) tortoise won the race with the hare.
12. Since Mother is not feeling (good, well), she is resting this afternoon.
13. The Alabama coast was in (eminent, imminent, immanent) danger from a violent hurricane.
14. Chasing heifers should not be an (everyday, every day) occurrence, but every dairy farmer will need to chase heifers.
15. The Christian (hasn't but, has but) one overall goal: to please the Lord.
16. Are you as (enthused, enthusiastic) about gaining approval from the Lord as from your friends?

B. Write the standard word or words for the underlined part of each sentence. If it needs no improvement, write *correct.*
1. A Christian has the <u>imminent</u> presence of the Holy Spirit.
2. The Book of Jude describes false teachers who <u>flout</u> Gospel principles and follow their own self-centered ways.
3. God lavishes rich blessings upon us <u>everyday</u>.
4. <u>Hopefully</u>, we remember to praise His Name frequently.
5. The <u>enormity</u> of the dense forest frightened the little children.
6. The destitute refugees <u>hadn't only</u> enough food for one scant meal.
7. Over lunch hour, Market Square is crowded with a <u>heap</u> of office workers.
8. The idea of selling cantaloupes <u>enthused</u> Steven immensely.
9. Those who <u>flaunt</u> their knowledge have a poor concept of true wisdom.
10. Benjamin Franklin, an <u>eminent</u> statesman of his day, published hundreds of wise sayings.
11. According to Miss Orndorf's <u>fabulous</u> account, her parents grew tons of produce every year in their small backyard garden.
12. Do your work <u>good</u> the first time, and you will not need to go back and redo it.
13. Tractor breakdowns have been almost <u>every day</u> occurrences lately.
14. The <u>enormity</u> of the crime shocked the community.
15. We <u>haven't but</u> one load of straw to stack now.
16. Nobody seemed very <u>enthused</u> about dinner because of the high heat and humidity.
17. <u>Hopefully</u>, the temperature will cool down a bit before tomorrow.
18. Mr. Eisenberger owns <u>a heap of</u> real estate in this area.
19. Because he has strep throat, Wesley is not <u>good</u> enough to go along tonight.
20. With all the rain this summer, we have a <u>fabulous</u> stand of field corn.

6. have only
7. every day
8. remarkable
9. flout
10. immensity
11. fabulous
12. well
13. imminent
14. everyday
15. has but
16. enthusiastic

B. 1. immanent
2. correct
3. every day
4. It is hoped that
5. enormousness *or* immensity
6. had only
7. multitude
8. excited
9. correct
10. correct
11. correct
12. well
13. everyday
14. correct
15. have but
16. enthusiastic
17. It is hoped that
18. much (*or* a large amount of)
19. well
20. remarkable *or* exceptional

C. Write enough words to show how each sentence should be improved according to the rules you have studied. If a sentence needs no improvement, write *correct*.

1. Cyrus McCormick's father Robert was an immanent man at Walnut Grove, Virginia; he owned over one thousand acres, two gristmills, two sawmills, a limekiln, a distillery, and a blacksmith shop.
2. Robert McCormick had tried for many years to devise a mechanical harvester, but there were heaps of problems to overcome.
3. Although his father gave up, Cyrus remained enthused about the idea.
4. By the age of twenty-two, Cyrus had developed a machine that worked well enough to harvest as much grain in a few hours as three men could cut by hand in a day.
5. Although others had tried to build mechanical reapers before McCormick, none of the other machines worked as fabulously as the McCormick reaper did.
6. At this time the McCormicks invested most of their capital in an iron-smelting venture, which hadn't only begun production when the Panic of 1837 hit.
7. The enormity of their losses plunged them into debt, so Cyrus began building and selling reapers again.
8. So great was his success that within a few years he paid his family's debt and made the reaper an every day piece of machinery on American farms.
9. However, McCormick seemed to enjoy flouting his patent rights in court as he engaged in suing and countersuing his rivals.
10. Hopefully, we can learn from his perseverance without following his ungodly ways.

Review Exercises

Write enough words to show how each sentence should be improved according to the rules you have studied. If a sentence needs no improvement, write *correct*. [37–41]

1. At Kitzbuehl in the province of Tyrol, the authorities arrested a fairly large amount of believers in 1527.
2. The tyranny of the persecutors succeeded so good that a number of the believers recanted.
3. These authorities publicly censured the Anabaptists by saying, "How finely your teachers and pastors now give their lives for you!"
4. Then Thomas Hermann, apparently one of the leaders, bursted from the crowd.
5. He advised the authorities that he had taught the people the truth and that he was ready to testify to the truth with his blood.
6. Thomas excepted his coming death so calmly that on the way to his martyrdom, he composed and sang a hymn.
7. This execution differed with many others, for Thomas's heart would not burn; so his enemies threw it into a nearby lake.

C.
1. eminent
2. many problems
3. enthusiastic
4. correct
5. well *or* excellently
6. had only
7. enormousness *or* immensity
8. everyday
9. flaunting
10. It is hoped that

Review Exercises
1. number
2. well
3. correct
4. burst
5. informed
6. accepted
7. differed from

8. The town clerk declared that he would not lay down his head in peace until he had helped exterminate these people; and his vow was fulfilled, but not like he had expected.
9. He was not able to elude God's judgment; for in making a turn with his sleigh, the town clerk was thrown out, and his brains were dashed out against a wall and an oak tree.
10. This account reminds us that God all ways has the last word when men blaspheme Him or persecute His people.

8. as
9. correct
10. always

---

42. Correct Word Usage, Part 5

How come

How come is an informal expression for "how is it that?" or "why?"

Informal: How come we never have liver or spinach anymore?
Standard: Why do we never have liver or spinach anymore?

Impact

Impact is often a noun that refers to the force of a collision or an influence. As a verb it means "to strike forcefully" or "to pack in." Avoid using *impact* as a verb with the meaning "to affect or influence."

Poor:
The rising corn prices strongly impacted the farmers in our area.
Correct:
The rising corn prices strongly affected the farmers in our area.
The rising corn prices had a strong impact on the farmers in our area.
I cleaned the impacted mud from the grooves in my shoe soles.

Imply, Infer

Imply means "to express indirectly." Implying is done by a person who is writing, speaking, or acting.

Infer means "to reach a conclusion by reasoning." Inferring is done by a person who is reading, listening, or observing.

Mr. Peterson implied that he appreciated our Gospel signs.
Father inferred from his words that several other neighbors were displeased with them.

In back of

Do not use *in back of* for *behind.* However, it is correct to use *in the back of* when referring to the back part of a place.

Incorrect: We looked in back of the shed for Lela's doll.
Correct: We looked behind the shed for Lela's doll.
In the back of the room is Warren's stamp collection.

Lesson 42

Purpose: To reinforce correct usage in a variety of applications.

Ingenious, Ingenuous

Ingenious (in·jēn′·yəs) means "skillful," "clever," or "resourceful."
Ingenuous (in·jen′·yü·əs) means "simple and trustful; not cunning or suspicious."

An <u>ingenious</u> mechanic is a valuable asset on the mission field.
The <u>ingenuous</u> youth was easily persuaded by the smooth-tongued salesman.

Its, It's

Its is a possessive case pronoun that means "belonging to it."
It's is a contraction for "it is" or "it has."

The angry bull shook <u>its</u> massive head and pawed the ground.
<u>It's</u> high time to get out of here!

Kind (Sort) of

Kind of and *sort of* should not be used to mean "rather" or "somewhat." Also, the article *a* or *an* should not follow *kind of, sort of,* or *type of* when referring to a class of items.

Incorrect: I was <u>sort of</u> surprised that Bennie would say such a thing.
What <u>kind of a</u> goat is this?
Correct: I was <u>rather</u> surprised that Bennie would say such a thing.
What <u>kind of</u> goat is this?

Lay, Lie

Lay is a transitive verb meaning "to put or place (something)." Its principal parts are *lay, laid, (have) laid.*

Lie is an intransitive verb meaning "to rest, recline, or remain in a flat position." Its principal parts are *lie, lay, (have) lain.* One reason for confusing these words is that the form *lay* is the first principal part of *lay* and also the second principal part of *lie.*

If plans carry, we shall <u>lay</u> the linoleum this afternoon.
Apparently this book <u>lay</u> out in the rain all morning.

Let, Leave

Let means "to allow or permit." Its principal parts are *let, let, (have) let.* This verb is always followed by an infinitive without *to,* which tells what is being permitted. Sometimes the infinitive is understood from the context.

Leave means "to depart, go away from, or allow to remain." Its principal parts are *leave, left, (have) left.* Unlike *let,* the verb *leave* is not followed by an infinitive.

Sometimes Father <u>lets</u> me drive the car out the lane to get the mail.
(*Let* is followed by the infinitive *to drive* with *to* omitted.)
I wanted to drive the car into the garage, but Father would not <u>let</u> me.
(The infinitive *to drive* is understood.)
Do not <u>leave</u> the car windows open.

Loose, Lose

   Loose is an adjective that means "not tight; not fastened or restrained." As a verb it means "to release" or "to set free." This word has the same ending as the rhyming words *goose, moose,* and *noose.* You might also remember that in the phrase "loose tooth," both words have double *o*'s.

   Lose is a verb that means "to be deprived of; to have (something) taken away." Its past form is *lost;* note that the present and past forms both have just one *o.*

   If you carry <u>loose</u> change in your pocket, you are likely to <u>lose</u> some of it.

Applying the Lesson

A. Choose the standard expressions in these sentences.
   1. We (imply, infer) that a spirit of self-sufficiency was (behind, in back of) Nebuchadnezzar's boastful words.
   2. To humble Nebuchadnezzar, God (let, left) him become insane and (loose, lose) his kingdom for a time.
   3. Jesus was not so (ingenious, ingenuous) that the scribes and Pharisees could trap Him.
   4. The disciples were (kind of, rather) weak in faith at times.
   5. The labors of the apostle Paul strongly (impacted, influenced) the early church.
   6. (Its, It's) hard to imagine what would have happened to the church without his efforts.
   7. I wondered (how come, why) Luann was not helping, but then I saw the cast on her leg.
   8. She told me that she had experienced a bad fall on (loose, lose) gravel.
   9. During the sultry afternoon, the cattle (laid, lay) under the shade trees or stood in the creek.
   10. The brief shower hardly (impacted, affected) the temperature at all.
   11. Father said that you should (let, leave) the disabled wagon in the field.
   12. (Behind, In back of) Mr. Jenkin's rough manners, you will find a friendly man.
   13. What (kind of, kind of a) turtle is this?
   14. Mrs. Stacy (implied, inferred) in various ways that she wished she still lived on a farm.
   15. (How come, Why) are we starting the chores early this evening?
   16. Using an (ingenious, ingenuous) whistle code, the villagers kept their only Bible hidden from the authorities.
   17. (Behind, In back of) even the stormiest clouds shines the sun.
   18. When people strive for earthly riches, they often (loose, lose) sight of the riches in heaven.
   19. Covetousness, with (its, it's) related sinful attitudes, robs man of true happiness.
   20. The choice to be content or to be covetous (lays, lies) with each person.

Lesson 42 Answers
Applying the Lesson
A. 1. infer, behind
    2. let, lose
    3. ingenuous
    4. rather
    5. influenced
    6. It's
    7. why
    8. loose
    9. lay
    10. affected
    11. leave
    12. Behind
    13. kind of
    14. implied
    15. Why
    16. ingenious
    17. Behind
    18. lose
    19. its
    20. lies

B. Write the standard word or words for the underlined part of each sentence. If it needs no improvement, write *correct.*
1. The conduct of older children strongly <u>impacts</u> their younger brothers and sisters.
2. You should not be too <u>ingenious</u>, but neither should you be unduly suspicious.
3. There is no greater loss than to <u>lose</u> one's soul.
4. Be careful not to <u>imply</u> an idea that the speaker did not actually intend.
5. If we have failed, we know the problem <u>lays</u> with us rather than God.
6. Since our family is <u>kind of</u> outdoors-oriented, we enjoy hiking in the woods.
7. Our woods is not large, but <u>its</u> beautiful in all seasons.
8. If warm air rises, <u>how come</u> are mountain peaks cooler than lowlands?
9. The answer <u>lays</u> in the fact that air cools as its pressure decreases.
10. The low pressure of air at the top of a mountain has a direct <u>impact</u> on its temperature.
11. Father did not see the post <u>in back of</u> the truck, so he backed right into it.
12. Marvin <u>let</u> some bags of feed on the truck to unload at the other shed.
13. Wilmer wonders <u>how come</u> this heifer feed is different from that heifer feed.
14. Did you know that the billy goat has gotten out of <u>it's</u> pen again?
15. You should <u>leave</u> the wooden chairs in the house.
16. The man standing <u>in back of</u> Uncle Howard is Brother Silas Wenger.
17. Please <u>lose</u> the horse so that he can go to the watering trough.
18. This article wrongly <u>implies</u> that the United States is a Christian nation.
19. What <u>kind of a</u> government would a Christian nation have?
20. No matter how <u>ingenuous</u> the leaders may be, they cannot set up a truly Christian nation.

C. Write enough words to show how each sentence should be improved according to the rules you have studied. If a sentence needs no improvement, write *correct.*
1. Although rubber fascinated Charles Goodyear when he was yet a schoolboy, he little imagined then how he would impact the development of useful rubber.
2. The practical uses of uncured rubber are sort of limited.
3. Even though its waterproof, uncured rubber is brittle in cold weather and tacky in warm weather.
4. For over six years, the problem of making a useful, all-weather rubber lay heavy on Goodyear's mind.
5. The conviction that the Creator wanted him to devote his life to this pursuit stood in back of his perseverance.
6. In January 1839, Goodyear was heating a compound of rubber and sulfur when he accidentally left some drop onto the hot stovetop.

B. 1. affects *or* influences
2. ingenuous
3. correct
4. infer
5. lies
6. somewhat *or* rather
7. it's
8. why
9. lies
10. correct
11. behind
12. left
13. why
14. its
15. correct
16. behind
17. loose
18. correct
19. kind of
20. ingenious

C. 1. influence *or* affect
2. rather *or* somewhat
3. it's
4. correct
5. behind
6. let

7. From what he saw, he immediately implied that he had discovered the long-sought key for curing rubber into a consistently useful material.
8. Chemists still cannot explain how come heat and sulfur produce a chemical reaction in rubber that makes it strong and flexible in both heat and cold.
9. After perfecting this process, known as vulcanization, Goodyear did not loose much time in finding ways to use his new rubber.
10. This ingenuous man might have become wealthy if he had received all the royalties that he deserved, but he actually lived and died in poverty.

7. inferred
8. why
9. lose
10. ingenious

Review Exercises

Write enough words to show how each sentence should be improved according to the rules you have studied. If a sentence needs no improvement, write *correct*. [37–42]

1. In 1529, seven brethren in southwestern Germany were arrested because their beliefs differed with the doctrines of the state church.
2. Among them was a fourteen-year-old lad who had a fabulous faith.
3. He was kept in prison for most a whole year.
4. During this time the authorities continually tried to persuade him to recant.
5. However, the young man did not leave any of their appeals move him.
6. While he was awaiting execution by the sword, an imminent person rode up to him.
7. This man offered the lad a regular payment of money if he would adapt the teachings of the state church.
8. The youth steadfastly refused to altar his convictions.
9. He would rather have suffered on earth than loose his inheritance in heaven.
10. Like him, we should be more enthused about our heavenly home than about earthly riches.

Review Exercises

1. differed from
2. remarkable
3. almost
4. correct
5. let
6. eminent
7. adopt
8. alter
9. lose
10. enthusiastic

---

43. Correct Word Usage, Part 6

Maybe, May be

Maybe is an adverb meaning "perhaps" or "possibly."
May be is a verb phrase that expresses possibility.

> <u>Maybe</u> Aunt Lela will come tomorrow.
> Grandmother <u>may be</u> able to come along.

Momentarily

The primary meaning of *momentarily* is "for a moment; briefly." This word is sometimes used to mean "in a moment" or "soon," but that usage should be avoided because it may be unclear.

Lesson 43

Purpose: To reinforce correct usage in a variety of applications.

Unclear: The clerk promised to wait on us <u>momentarily</u>.
                        (Would the clerk wait on us for only a moment?)
Clear: The clerk promised to wait on us <u>in a moment</u>. (or *soon*)
                        I was <u>momentarily</u> blinded by the bright lights.

Nice

Nice is an overworked, vague adjective. Choose more specific and colorful words
such as *pleasant, thoughtful, kind, desirable,* and *delightful.*

Poor: The Wallaces have been <u>nice</u> neighbors.
               This is a <u>nice</u> day for a hike to the falls.
Better: The Wallaces have been <u>friendly</u> neighbors.
               This is a <u>pleasant</u> day for a hike to the falls.

Notable, Noted, Noteworthy, Notorious

Notable, noted, and *noteworthy* mean "famous," "well-known," or "remarkable."
Notorious means "well-known for an unfavorable reason; infamous."

Gideon won a <u>notable</u> victory over the Midianites.
Boaz was <u>noted</u> for his kindness and benevolence.
David made a <u>noteworthy</u> contribution to Israel's spiritual life.
Abigail admitted that Nabal was <u>notorious</u> for his churlishness.

OK, Okay

OK and *okay* are informal for "all right" or "in good condition."

Informal: After a brief rest, I felt <u>OK</u> (or *okay*) again.
Standard: After a brief rest, I felt <u>all right</u> again.

Over with

Do not use *over with* to mean "over," "finished," or "past."

Incorrect: We were glad when that hard task was <u>over with</u>.
Correct: We were glad when that hard task was <u>over</u>. (or *finished*)

Persecute, Prosecute

Persecute means "to harass or oppress, usually for one's beliefs."
Prosecute means "to take legal action against."

The Jews <u>persecuted</u> the early church.
The attorney general <u>prosecuted</u> the leader of the crime network.

Perspective, Prospective

Perspective means "a visible scene" or "a mental view; an outlook."
Prospective means "of or in the future" or "potential."

The whole valley lay in <u>perspective</u> before us.
From our <u>perspective,</u> the Anabaptists faced very trying circumstances.
Some of you are <u>prospective</u> teachers, writers, and editors.

Poorly

Poorly is an adverb meaning "in a poor manner." It is used informally as an adjective meaning "in poor health."

Informal:
> Great-aunt Lucinda has been <u>poorly</u> in recent weeks.

Standard:
> Great-aunt Lucinda has been <u>in poor health</u> in recent weeks.
> Even with medication, her heart has been functioning <u>poorly</u>.

Precede, Proceed

The basic meaning of *precede* is "to go before" (*pre-*, before, + *cede*, to go). This word uses the most common spelling of the *cede* root, which also occurs in words like *concede, recede, secede, antecedent,* and *intercede.*

The basic meaning of *proceed* is "to go forth or forward" (*pro-*, forth or forward, + *ceed*, an alternate spelling of *cede*, to go). *Proceed, exceed,* and *succeed* are the only English words with the *cede* root spelled *ceed;* in all other words it is spelled *ced* or *cede.*

> In the New Testament, the Gospels <u>precede</u> the Epistles.
> You may <u>proceed</u> with the special project if all your assignments are completed.

Applying the Lesson

A. Choose the standard expressions in these sentences.

1. Before David came into the camp, Saul's army was too fearful to (precede, proceed) in the battle against the Philistines.
2. David's (notable, notorious) victory, however, produced a marked change.
3. David's (perspective, prospective) was quite different from that of the others because he trusted in the Lord.
4. The giants that we face (maybe, may be) less recognizable than Goliath, but they are no less formidable.
5. The disgruntled man (persecuted, prosecuted) his Christian neighbors in various small ways.
6. Since he did not believe in God, he thought everything would be (okay, all right) in the end.
7. We must remember that no matter how hardened a person may seem, he is still a (perspective, prospective) believer in Jesus.
8. Even a persecutor as (noteworthy, notorious) as Saul became a devoted follower of Christ.
9. The gray skies and the northeast wind suggest that (maybe, may be) a blizzard is coming.
10. The police could not find enough evidence to (persecute, prosecute) their suspect.
11. Prisoner's base is (okay, all right), but I would rather play freeze tag.
12. Sufficient planning must (precede, proceed) the writing of a worthwhile story.

Lesson 43 Answers

Applying the Lesson

A. 1. proceed
2. notable
3. perspective
4. may be
5. persecuted
6. all right
7. prospective
8. notorious
9. maybe
10. prosecute
11. all right
12. precede

B. Write the standard word or words for the underlined part of each sentence. If it needs no improvement, write *correct.*

1. We must keep a heavenly <u>prospective</u> if we expect to win the race of life.
2. The righteous are often <u>persecuted</u> by wicked people who hate the truth.
3. Many saints have found that glory in heaven is <u>proceeded</u> by suffering on earth.
4. The righteous may not have everything <u>nice</u>, but they do enjoy God's rich blessing.
5. One of the most <u>notorious</u> blessings is a free conscience.
6. It is also a great blessing to know that someday all temptations will be <u>over with</u>.
7. <u>Maybe</u> we recognize that too often we take these blessings for granted.
8. The Cretians were <u>notable</u> for their deceit and slothfulness.
9. The next wagonload of hay should be coming <u>momentarily</u>.
10. Grandmother Boll has been <u>poorly</u> ever since she had a stroke last winter.
11. These pancakes taste <u>okay</u>, but I like whole-wheat pancakes better.
12. There still <u>maybe</u> time to make a batch of cookies this morning.
13. We will miss Uncle Joel's family when their visit is <u>over with</u>.
14. Although the bolt of lightning lasted only <u>momentarily</u>, it started a forest fire that raged for several days.
15. Our congregation made a sunshine box for Caroline Wenger, who has been <u>poorly</u> for several weeks.
16. Except for a few minor difficulties, the work has <u>preceded</u> well.
17. The setting sun spread its <u>nice</u> colors across the western sky.
18. Father is interviewing a <u>perspective</u> hired man today.
19. Although Mr. Harrison has not paid his bill, we will not <u>persecute</u> him.
20. My head was hurting this morning, but I feel <u>okay</u> now.

B.
1. perspective
2. correct
3. preceded
4. pleasant *or* easy
5. noteworthy *or* notable
6. over *or* past
7. correct
8. notorious
9. soon (*or* in a moment)
10. in poor health
11. all right
12. may be
13. over
14. correct
15. in poor health
16. proceeded
17. lovely *or* beautiful
18. prospective
19. prosecute
20. all right

C. Write enough words to show how each sentence should be improved according to the rules you have studied. If a sentence needs no improvement, write *correct.*

1. In the early life of Samuel F. B. Morse, there maybe little to suggest that he would become an important inventor.
2. Even at the age of thirty-four, when his wife was poorly and then died, he had made no significant mark as an inventor.
3. Both of his parents died within the next three years, and in 1829 he sailed for Europe to renew his courage and precede with his halting career as an artist.
4. On his return trip in 1832, a discussion about electricity provided the inspiration for his most notorious invention: the electric telegraph.
5. When he learned that electricity can travel over long wires, he concluded that messages could be transmitted momentarily over great distances.
6. Immediately after dinner, he started sketching the design of a perspective telegraph system.
7. But it was not until 1836 that he completed a crude device that worked okay.
8. In later years, Morse was not very nice to Professor Joseph Henry, from whom he had often received scientific advice and public support.

C.
1. may be
2. in poor health
3. proceed
4. notable *or* noteworthy
5. in a moment
6. prospective
7. all right
8. kind *or* thoughtful

9. In fact, Morse and Henry prosecuted each other over patent rights.

10. When the legal battles were over with, Samuel F. B. Morse emerged as the owner of the patent for the telegraph.

9. correct
10. over

Review Exercises

Write enough words to show how each sentence should be improved according to the rules you have studied. If a sentence needs no improvement, write *correct*. [37–43]

1. About 1538, two cousins from Flanders were persecuted for their faith.

2. These youths became enthused about studying the Bible, and soon they were convinced that the Scriptures teach believer's baptism.

3. They went to Germany to seek fellow believers, but they stayed there only for awhile because they could find nobody who shared their convictions.

4. Back home with their parents, these young men sought to live the kind of a life that would please the Lord.

5. However, the authorities suspected that they were heretics, and they imprisoned the young men under conditions most beyond description.

6. When a sister brought them some new shirts, they told her that they could not keep the worms from eating their clothes any more.

7. John Styaerts, one of the youths, was released for a time because he was poorly.

8. He probably could of escaped during that time, but he willingly returned to prison to die with his brother in Christ.

9. When no amount of suffering could change their minds, the young men were put to death by the sword.

10. Hopefully, we shall be able to stand faithfully for the Lord no matter what circumstances we face.

Review Exercises

1. correct
2. enthusiastic
3. a while
4. kind of life
5. almost
6. anymore
7. in poor health
8. could have
9. correct
10. It is hoped that

---

44. Improving Your Editing Skills, Part 5

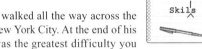

The story is told of a man who walked all the way across the United States, from California to New York City. At the end of his journey, someone asked, "What was the greatest difficulty you encountered on your way? Was it the steep mountains you had to climb?"

"No, it was not that," the traveler assured him.

"Perhaps the swollen rivers that crossed your trail were the greatest hazard," the inquirer suggested.

"It was not that either," replied the traveler. Then after a pause, he said, "What almost defeated me on my journey across the continent was the sand in my shoes."

Lesson 44

Purpose: To provide proofreading practice.

Many things in real life are just like that. Often we are defeated not by great problems but by little nagging difficulties that we face day after day.

In writing, it is seldom whole sentences and paragraphs that hinder communication. It is usually the little things instead—details like spelling, punctuation, and word usage. Errors in these details are the "sand" that will hinder the message of your writing. That is why you are making a special study of word usage in this chapter.

In this lesson you will again practice the use of proofreading marks. See if you can find *every* mistake in the exercises.

Marks Used in Editing and Proofreading

$\lor$ or $\land$ insert (caret)	delete	.... stet (let it stand)	use italics
¶ begin new paragraph	no ¶ no new paragraph	*lc* change to lowercase (small letter)	*uc* change to uppercase (capital letter)
# insert space	⌒ delete space	← move (arrow)	transpose

Editing Practice

A. Use proofreading marks to correct the two capitalization or punctuation errors in each sentence.

1. In Math we learned that one acre contains 43560 square feet.

2. When an inch of rain falls 3,630 cubic feet of water is dumped on one Acre.

3. "I have read that the weight of water varies slightly, said conrad.

4. One cubic foot of water weighs an average of 62.4 pounds, thus, one inch of rain on one acre weighs about: 113 tons.

5. "Can you convert that figure to gallons," asked brother Henry.

6. The Total comes to more than 27000 gallons of water.

7. "What a tremendous amount of water falls in just a small Spring shower," exclaimed Carol.

Lesson 44 Answers

Editing Practice

(Answers are on pages 468–469.)

8. Water is precious to people of desert region's like the
   sahara.

9. One Missionary in africa wrote that even the children
   knelt in gratitude when he gave them a drink of water.

10. "As cold waters to a thirsty soul, so is good news from
    a far country (Proverbs 25 25).

B. Use proofreading marks to correct the two usage errors in each sentence.

 1. Whitcomb L. Judson was enthused about most any kind of new gadget.

 2. He invented a considerable amount of useful every day items.

 3. One of his friends had a dilemma that would of been a trial for anyone.

 4. Because of his stiff back, this friend all ways had a heap of trouble putting on his shoes.

 5. The ingenuous inventor devised a slide fastener that differed with any fastener ever made before.

 6. This invention left a person fasten or lose his shoes by using just one hand.

 7. Judson's fastener alluded popular notice until an imminent manufacturer used it in a line of boots called Zippers.

 8. Be sure and notice that its the slide fasteners rather than the boots that are called zippers today.

C. Use proofreading marks to correct the sixteen errors in the following paragraphs. No line has more than one error.

1. Early astronomers believed that the earth was at the
2. center of the universe. This fit good with their view of man
3. and his importance. About A.D. 150, a Greek astronomer name
4. Ptolemy produced a work of thirteen volumes on based on
5. this theory. He described a stationary earth with the sun,
6. the moon and the stars all revolving around it. For nearly
7. 1,500 years, people considered Ptolemys theory to be fact.
8. In 1543, Nicolaus Copernicus propposed that the sun
9. rather than the earth was the center of the universe,

10. and that the the earth and other planets revolve around

11. the sun. His ideas still were not alright, but they

12. were closer to the truth than Ptolemy's were. This

13. new theory stirred up a storm of opposition. Men who

14. excepted it were charged with heresy, and at least one

15. was burned the at stake. Galileo with his telescope

16.   observed four moons of Jupiter revolving around that

17. Planet, which provided further support for the Copernican

18. theory. But in 1633, Roman catholic officials forced

19. Galileo to confess that he was in error!

20.   Astronomers continued to study the haevens until they

21. proved beyond doubt that the planets in deed revolve

22. around the sun. Instead of being at the center, man and

23. his World are a mere speck in the grand universe that

24. God created.

---

45. Correct Word Usage, Part 7

Propose, Purpose

Propose is a verb meaning "to suggest." If an action is proposed, it is generally stated in a *that* clause which follows *propose*.

Purpose is a verb meaning "to determine" or a noun meaning "aim or goal." Either an infinitive or a *that* clause may follow *purpose*.

> I <u>propose</u> that we make a scrapbook for Sister Melody.
> Our <u>purpose</u> would be to cheer her lonely days.
> Like Daniel, we must <u>purpose</u> that we will not defile ourselves.

Quote

Quote is usually a verb. It is used informally as a noun meaning "quotation."

> **Informal:** This <u>quote</u> from Proverbs is especially fitting now.
> **Standard:** This <u>quotation</u> from Proverbs is especially fitting now.

Raise, Rise

Raise is a transitive verb meaning "to cause (something) to go up or grow up." Its principal parts are *raise, raised, (have) raised*.

Lesson 45

Purpose: To reinforce correct usage in a variety of applications.

Rise is an intransitive verb meaning "to get up or go up." Its principal parts are *rise, rose, (have) risen.*

> We shall <u>raise</u> our voices to the Lord in joyful song.
>
> As our praises have <u>risen</u> to the Lord, we have received rich blessing.

Receipt, Recipe

Receipt (ri·sēt′) is the noun form of *receive.* It means "the act of receiving," "a quantity received," or "a written acknowledgment that something has been received."

Recipe (res′·ə·pē) means "formula" or "method."

> I found the <u>receipt</u> at the bottom of the bag.
>
> This <u>recipe</u> calls for too much sugar.

Respectable, Respectful, Respective

Respectable means "worthy of respect."

Respectful means "showing respect or esteem."

Respective means "individual; particular."

> Evan has developed a <u>respectable</u> character in spite of his background.
>
> Darlene gave consistently <u>respectful</u> answers to Mrs. Hawsley's sharp accusations.
>
> Put these peaches, pears, and plums into their <u>respective</u> compartments in the cooler.

Right along

The expression *right along* is used informally to mean "steadily" or "with little hindrance."

> **Informal:**
>
> The work on the new shed has been progressing <u>right along</u>.
>
> **Standard:**
>
> The work on the new shed has been progressing <u>steadily</u>.

Set, Sit

Set is usually a transitive verb meaning "to put or place (something)." It also has the following intransitive meanings: "to move below the horizon," "to keep eggs warm for hatching," and "to become firm." Its principal parts are *set, set, (have) set.*

Sit is an intransitive verb meaning "to rest or be seated." Its principal parts are *sit, sat, (have) sat.*

> Please <u>set</u> the bags of groceries on the table.
>
> The moon has just <u>set</u> beyond the western mountains.
>
> Biddy has been <u>setting</u> for a week.
>
> Has the glue <u>set</u> well yet?
>
> We <u>sat</u> breathlessly watching the deer eat.

Some, Somewhat

The adverb *some* is informal when it has the meaning "somewhat."

Informal:

This tree has grown <u>some</u> taller since we moved here.

Standard:

This tree has grown <u>somewhat</u> taller since we moved here.

Stationary, Stationery

Stationary means "fixed; unmoving." Think of something station<u>a</u>ry as st<u>a</u>nding in a fixed position.

Stationery means "writing materials." Think of station<u>e</u>ry as including pap<u>e</u>r.

We tied the wagon to a <u>stationary</u> post.
Grandmother gave Elaine a box of <u>stationery</u>.

Straight, Strait

Straight is a modifier that means "not curved," "level," "direct," or "directly."

The noun *strait* refers to a narrow stretch of water. *Strait* is also an archaic modifier that means "narrow" or "strict."

We should not expect to travel <u>straight</u> to heaven without facing obstacles.
The <u>Strait</u> of Magellan lies at the southern tip of South America.
"Enter ye in at the <u>strait</u> gate" (Matthew 7:13).

Applying the Lesson

A. Choose the standard expressions in these sentences.

1. We (set, sat) in (respectable, respectful, respective) silence as Father read the Scripture passage.
2. The Bible informs us that nobody can (raise, rise) himself to a (respectable, respectful, respective) standing with God by his own strength.
3. "Did not we (straightly, straitly) command you that ye should not teach in this name?" (Acts 5:28).
4. When the (stationary, stationery) front finally moved out, the weather became (some, somewhat) cooler.
5. I have (proposed, purposed) to acknowledge the (receipt, recipe) of every get-well card that arrives.
6. Louella (proposed, purposed) an interesting plan for helping the Leids.
7. Lolita's new (stationary, stationery) has a beautiful rose design.
8. The prices have (raised, risen) to record highs because of the drought.
9. Caleb finished his chores (some, somewhat) earlier than he had expected.
10. Hold your drill (straight, strait) to drill these dowel holes.
11. The "Never-Fail Cake" was a total failure even though Gloria followed the (receipt, recipe) exactly.
12. For a long time the owl (set, sat) on a branch of the old oak tree.

Lesson 45 Answers

Applying the Lesson

A. 1. sat, respectful
   2. raise, respectable
   3. straitly
   4. stationary, somewhat
   5. purposed, receipt
   6. proposed
   7. stationery
   8. risen
   9. somewhat
   10. straight
   11. recipe
   12. sat

B. Write the standard word or words for the underlined part of each sentence. If it needs no improvement, write *correct.*
1. Do you know where to find the <u>quote</u>, "Be subject unto the higher powers"?
2. Christians must maintain <u>respective</u> attitudes even toward oppressive civil authorities.
3. Jesus broke the power of sin when He <u>raised</u> from the dead.
4. Jesus Christ is <u>sitting</u> at the Father's right hand to intercede for us.
5. Father <u>proposed</u> that we visit Brother Henry this evening.
6. Although he is feeling <u>some</u> better, Brother Henry still cannot go to church.
7. Our peach harvest is almost finished, and the apple harvest is increasing <u>right along</u>.
8. The speeding truck collided with a <u>stationary</u> car.
9. Neighbors said that the car had been <u>setting</u> there for two days.
10. Mother often bakes cookies without looking at a <u>receipt</u>.
11. In the open Midwest, many roads run <u>strait</u> for miles on end.
12. Cutting off the corn and packing it into freezer boxes is progressing <u>right along</u>.
13. We are <u>some</u> closer to Mother's goal for frozen corn than we had been earlier.
14. "And he <u>straitly</u> charged them that they should not make him known" (Mark 3:12).
15. Airmail <u>stationary</u> is lightweight to keep down the postage price.
16. Donald <u>proposed</u> to improve his penmanship.
17. Mother checked the <u>receipt</u> to make sure it contained no errors in calculation.
18. The smoke from the burning barn <u>raised</u> in a huge cloud, visible for many miles.
19. You should verify this <u>quote</u> from Isaiah 53.
20. God sets the members of the church in their <u>respective</u> places.

C. Write enough words to show how each sentence should be improved according to the rules you have studied. If a sentence needs no improvement, write *correct.*
1. In the early 1800s, even respectful adults often rode hobbyhorses for recreation.
2. These wheeled horses were not stationery as many children's horses are today.
3. A person would set on the horse and push himself along with his feet.
4. A Scottish blacksmith named Kirkpatrick Macmillan decided that the hobbyhorse could be used for a more worthwhile purpose.
5. The receipt, he thought, was to devise a way to turn the wheels with pedals.
6. Macmillan's work progressed right along, and soon he completed a two-wheeled machine that he called a bicycle.
7. This machine had pedals that drove a strait rod connected to the back wheel.
8. In 1840, Macmillan pedaled his bicycle seventy miles in ten hours—an "astounding achievement" according to one quote.

B.
1. quotation
2. respectful
3. rose
4. correct
5. correct
6. somewhat
7. steadily *or* continuously
8. correct
9. sitting
10. recipe
11. straight
12. steadily
13. somewhat
14. correct
15. stationery
16. purposed
17. correct
18. rose
19. quotation
20. correct

C.
1. respectable
2. stationary
3. sit
4. correct
5. recipe
6. steadily
7. straight
8. quotation

9. But his success was marred some, for he accidentally knocked down a young lady and was jailed for reckless driving!
10. Macmillan's invention raised to such popularity that within his lifetime, thousands of people in different countries were riding bicycles.

9. somewhat
10. rose

Review Exercises

Write enough words to show how each sentence should be improved according to the rules you have studied. If a sentence needs no improvement, write *correct*. [37–45]

1. Two men named George Vaser and Leonhard Sailer, whose lives differed with those of people around them, were passing through Neudorf, Austria.
2. They were arrested and taken to the nearby town of Metling, where they were held in prison continuously for almost a year.
3. Although it seems hardly comprehensive, these brethren had testified boldly on the way to Metling, and the authorities had been too amazed to stop them.
4. Cast into the common prison, these godly men faced the dilemma of enduring the gross wickedness of their fellow prisoners.
5. In fact, they would rather have been forced to set in an offensive dungeon than in that prison with such company.
6. They still were able to impact the lives of the others, for they answered many questions about their faith.
7. These Anabaptists boldly declared that those who flout the teachings of the Bible will face God's wrath.
8. Their fabulous faith gave them a sincere desire to depart, and they manfully and boldly expected death at any hour.
9. Having maintained their faith very good, the two men were marvelously delivered after nearly a year in prison.
10. These notorious brethren came to the church at Trasenhofen, where they were received joyfully.

Review Exercises

1. differed from
2. correct
3. comprehensible
4. problem *or* difficulty
5. sit
6. influence *or* affect
7. correct
8. remarkable *or* amazing
9. well
10. notable *or* noteworthy

---

46. Correct Word Usage, Part 8

Than, Then

Than is a conjunction used to introduce the second part of a comparison.

Then is an adverb with meanings that include "at that time," "in that case," "therefore," and "next in time, space, or order."

> Our history test proved easier <u>than</u> I had expected.
> <u>Then</u> why did you not make a better score on your test?

Lesson 46

Purpose: To reinforce correct usage in a variety of applications.

Them

Them should never be used as a demonstrative to replace *those.*

> **Incorrect:** <u>Them</u> apples are deliciously sweet.
> **Correct:**   <u>Those</u> apples are deliciously sweet.

This (These) here, That (Those) there

The demonstratives *this, that, these,* and *those* must not be followed by *here* or *there.*

> **Incorrect:** <u>This here</u> rosebush is lovely.
> **Correct:**   <u>This</u> rosebush is lovely.

Transpire

Transpire means "to leak out" or "to become known to many people." It has a pretentious tone when used for the meaning "to happen; occur."

> **Poor:**
> Walton's accident <u>transpired</u> last evening.
> **Correct:**
> Walton's accident <u>occurred</u> last evening.
>
> Water vapor <u>transpires</u> through the leaves of plants.
> The news of Aunt Lena's plans to teach school has <u>transpired</u> already.

Try and

The expression *try and* should be replaced with *try to.*

> **Incorrect:**
> We should <u>try and</u> finish splitting this wood before dark.
> **Correct:**
> We should <u>try to</u> finish splitting this wood before dark.

Want in, off, out, through

An expression like "want in" should be revised so that an infinitive such as *to come* or *to get* comes after *want.*

> **Incorrect:** That cat always <u>wants in</u> at mealtime.
>   The man on that tractor <u>wants through</u> this gate.
> **Correct:**   That cat always <u>wants to come in</u> at mealtime.
>   The man on that tractor <u>wants to get through</u> this gate.

Way, Ways

Ways is an informal word for "distance." Use *way* or *distance* in standard writing.

> **Informal:**
> We have quite a long <u>ways</u> to the mountain from our place.
> **Standard:**
> We have quite a long <u>way</u> to the mountain from our place.

What for

The expression *what for* should not be used to mean "what kind of." *What for* can also mean "for what reason," but that meaning is not always clear. It is generally better to use *why*.

Poor:
> What for book are you reading?
> What are you going outside for?
> > (Could mean "For what item are you going outside?" or "For what reason are you going outside?"

Better:
> What kind of book are you reading?
> Why are you going outside?

Worst kind, sort, way

Expressions with *worst* should not be used to mean "very much" or "in the highest degree."

Incorrect:
> Linda wants in the worst way to finish sewing her dress before the weekend.

Correct:
> Linda wants very much to finish sewing her dress before the weekend.

Your, You're

Your is a possessive pronoun that means "belonging to you."
You're is a contraction for *you are*.

> Is this your sweater?
> You're supposed to put it away.

Applying the Lesson

A. Choose the standard expressions in these sentences.
1. God has blessed us far more (than, then) what we deserve.
2. If we would (try and, try to) count those blessings, time would fail us.
3. (What for, What kind of) attitudes do you express toward your parents?
4. If (your, you're) insubmissive at home, you cannot be truly happy.
5. Every sincere Christian recognizes that he is a long (way, ways) from reaching perfection.
6. (Them, Those) people who consider themselves superior fail to realize how foolish they are.
7. Do you know when the next solar eclipse is supposed to (transpire, occur)?
8. With godly grandparents living near (your, you're) home, you have a definite privilege.
9. Both sets of my grandparents live a long (way, ways) from my home.
10. Your little brother is crying, but I don't know (what for, why).
11. We shall (try and, try to) start cleaning the school early this evening.

Lesson 46 Answers
Applying the Lesson
A. 1. than
2. try to
3. What kind of
4. you're
5. way
6. Those
7. occur
8. your
9. way
10. why
11. try to

12. If we start early, (than, then) we should be able to finish early.
13. Do you know where (them, those) runaway steers belong?
14. What a strange event (transpired, occurred) last night!

12. then
13. those
14. occurred

B. Write the standard word or words for the underlined part of each sentence. If it needs no improvement, write *correct*.
1. Our congregation often conducts services at <u>this here</u> rest home.
2. This one has more guests <u>then</u> any other rest home in our area.
3. Nelson and I will <u>try and</u> pick all our tomatoes before the end of the week.
4. Since we had only two days to finish the job, we needed to make <u>them</u> days count.
5. You can drive this car a long <u>ways</u> after the fuel gauge shows empty.
6. Justin wanted <u>in the worst way</u> to run the baler.
7. <u>What for</u> experience has he had with baling hay?
8. Man and animals use the oxygen that <u>transpires</u> from green plants.
9. If <u>you're</u> chores are finished early, we shall leave early.
10. <u>That there</u> new barn is the one Uncle Melvin is building.
11. We all hurried <u>in the worst way</u> so that we would finish in time.
12. Some groundhogs were trying to get through this fence, and it's easy to guess <u>what for</u>.
13. They <u>wanted through</u> so that they could eat our vegetables.
14. When <u>your</u> driving in the West and first see a town ahead, it is still many miles away.
15. <u>Then</u> after a long time, you finally arrive at the town.
16. Even though we had entered Missouri, we were still a long <u>ways</u> from Uncle Walter's house.
17. You will need hot, soapy water to wash <u>them</u> greasy dishes clean.
18. I will <u>try and</u> memorize these verses perfectly.
19. We told the bus driver that we <u>wanted off</u> at the King Street Market.
20. Things <u>transpired</u> so rapidly that we wondered what would happen next.

B. 1. this
2. than
3. try to
4. those
5. way *or* distance
6. very much (*or* intensely)
7. What kind of
8. correct
9. your
10. That
11. very much
12. why
13. wanted to get through
14. you're
15. correct
16. way *or* distance
17. those
18. try to
19. wanted to get off
20. happened *or* occurred

C. Write enough words to show how each sentence should be improved according to the rules you have studied. If a sentence needs no improvement, write *correct*.
1. In the 1850s, a man named Linus Yale wanted in the worst way to make a good lock.
2. Most locks in them days were crude and fairly easy to open.
3. If a burglar wanted into a house, there was hardly any way to keep him out.
4. What for lock could one make that would be more secure?
5. Yale devised a lock that was much better then all others of his time.
6. That there lock had a cylinder with a number of pins which were all of different lengths.
7. To try and open such a lock, one must use a key with a pattern of notches cut into it.
8. Each notch lifts one pin just a small ways; but if it is too little or too much, the lock will not open.

C. 1. very much
2. those days
3. wanted to get into
4. What kind of lock
5. than
6. That lock
7. try to open
8. way *or* distance

9. Eventually it transpired that Yale had gotten the idea for his lock from the ancient Egyptians, who had also used locks with pins of varying lengths.

10. Quite likely, many of you're family's possessions are secured by locks based on the principle of the Yale lock.

Review Exercises

Write enough words to show how each sentence should be improved according to the rules you have studied. If a sentence needs no improvement, write *correct.* [37–46]

1. In 1544, an Anabaptist maiden named Maria van Beckum was driven out of her home because her mother would not leave her stay there anymore.

2. She fled to the house of her brother John, whose wife Ursula shared her prospective of faith.

3. When a large group of men came to arrest Maria, she was compelled to raise from bed and face them.

4. Seeing the large amount of people, Maria asked Ursula if she would go along with her.

5. Ursula answered, "I am willing to go if John says that I can."

6. John gave his consent, and them two sisters in the Lord went with the persecutors to face the afflictions that awaited.

7. After enduring many trials and sufferings, Maria and Ursula were sentenced to death by the council in Delden.

8. As the time of their execution drew near, these notorious sisters prayed that God would forgive the judges who would be guilty of their blood.

9. When Ursula stepped up to the stake, the wood was not very stationery, and she almost slipped off.

10. The priest thought that may be she wanted to recant, but Ursula assured him that she would "constantly adhere to Christ"; and thus both sisters remained steadfast until death.

---

47. Chapter 5 Review

A. Choose the standard expressions in these sentences.

1. We must (always, all ways) be ready to (altar, alter) our ways to please the Lord.

2. Others can (imply, infer) much about your character from your (everyday, every day) speech habits.

3. Using a great (amount, number) of interjections and casual expressions shows the lack of a godly (perspective, prospective).

4. (Its, It's) never (all right, alright) to (flaunt, flout) the instruction of godly parents.

5. If you are (disinterested, uninterested) in wise (council, counsel), you will suffer for it.

Lesson 47

Purpose: To review the concepts taught in Chapter 5.

9. correct
10. your

Review Exercises

1. let
2. perspective
3. rise
4. number
5. may
6. those
7. correct
8. notable *or* noteworthy
9. stationary
10. maybe

Lesson 47 Answers

A. 1. always, alter
2. infer, everyday
3. number, perspective
4. It's, all right, flout
5. uninterested, counsel

6. Even though another person may be angry (about, at, with) us, we must (raise, rise) above our natural feelings and treat him (good, well).

7. We (believe, feel) that God will (let, leave) no insurmountable test come our way, so we willingly (accept, except) the most trying circumstances.

8. When we (propose, purpose) to (adapt, adopt) ourselves to God's will (as, like) we should, we have found the (receipt, recipe) for true joy.

9. Many people who do not esteem the Bible (anymore, any more) do (allude, elude) to it in more ways (than, then) they may realize.

10. Mr. Barnes seems to have a (comprehensible, comprehensive) knowledge of (almost, most) every subject, yet he is not (contemptible, contemptuous) toward us common folks.

11. Although Father feels (some, somewhat) better now, he still does not (set, sit) up (continually, continuously) for more than twenty minutes.

12. When we compare our lives (to, with) the lives of many others, we conclude that we are a long (way, ways) from poverty.

13. When we differ (from, with) others in our opinions, we should not (censor, censure) them (as if, like) we are much wiser than they.

14. Even if God does not answer our prayers for (awhile, a while), we must not (loose, lose) faith in Him.

15. It looks as though (maybe, may be) a deer has (laid, lain) here recently.

16. Father said that we (can, may) go to the neighbors for milk if we come (straight, strait) home again.

17. The township supervisors intend to (persecute, prosecute) the persons responsible for the (burst, bursted, busted) water line.

18. When Curvin came home, we (advised, informed) him about the letter that had arrived on the (preceding, proceeding) day.

19. Is the equipment in (your, you're) workshop all run by this (stationary, stationery) engine?

20. The students took their (respectable, respectful, respective) places with (noteworthy, notorious) quietness.

B. Write enough words to show how each sentence should be improved according to the rules you have studied. Every sentence needs two improvements.

1. If you try and do your best, you may impact others for good.

2. We faced a dilemma that was intensified because there were heaps of possible solutions.

3. Grandfather Fox has been sort of poorly for several weeks.

4. Aunt Mary is recuperating right along since she had that operation and began taking them heart pills.

5. If you have read the above, you know that Mr. Brian's special offer will soon be over with.

6. Hopefully Alvin has not become too enthused about buying those rabbits.

7. He wanted in the worst way to buy them regardless of his older brother's council.

8. Does anyone know how come the wheelbarrow is in back of the garage?

6. with, rise, well
7. believe, let, accept
8. purpose, adapt, as, recipe
9. anymore, allude, than
10. comprehensive, almost, contemptuous
11. somewhat, sit, continuously
12. with, way
13. with, censure, as if
14. a while, lose
15. maybe, lain
16. may, straight
17. prosecute, burst
18. informed, preceding
19. your, stationary
20. respective, noteworthy

B. 1. try to do, influence
2. problem, many
3. rather (or somewhat) in poor health (or in rather poor health)
4. steadily, those heart pills
5. the material (or paragraph[s]) above, over
6. It is to be hoped that, enthusiastic
7. very much, counsel
8. why, behind

9. You should be sure and check the accuracy of that quote.
10. We will be there momentarily to see your fabulous stamp collection.
11. The feed is all, and the cattle want out into the pasture.
12. This corn ain't as nice as some that we have sold.
13. I haven't only one picture that shows the enormity of the rock we saw.
14. In spite of the way things transpired, everything turned out okay.

C. Write the correct words for these sentences.
    1. The ——— voice puts more energy into writing than the ——— voice does.
    2. In the ——— voice, the subject is acted upon.
    3. In the ——— voice, the subject does something.
    4. The passive voice may be useful when there is no clear ——— of the action, when we want to avoid naming the ———, or when the subject is the victim of a ———.
    5. Choose the more lively verb in each sentence.
        a. The sun (disappeared, was hidden) behind thick clouds.
        b. Even strong trees (bowed, were bowed) in the fierce wind.

9. sure to check, quotation
10. in a moment (*or* soon), remarkable *or* wonderful
11. all gone, want to go out
12. isn't, desirable
13. have only, immensity *or* enormousness
14. occurred *or* happened, all right

C. 1. active, passive
    2. passive
    3. active
    4. doer, doer, tragedy *or* disaster
    5. a. disappeared
        b. bowed

Whatsoever thy hand findeth to do,

do it with thy might.

Ecclesiastes 9:10

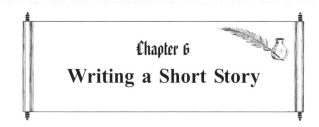

Chapter 6
Writing a Short Story

48. The Writer of a Story

No doubt you have read dozens of stories; and some of them, consciously or sub-consciously, you labeled good. You have also read stories that you labeled boring or stiff or unrealistic. What makes the difference? What are the keys to writing a good story? This chapter should help to answer these questions. First, however, we shall take a look at the person who writes the story.

What kind of individual is a storywriter? He is not one with unique experiences that nobody else has, neither does he have a special pen from which fascinating stories flow effortlessly. Instead, he is generally a common person just like you. If a story is especially interesting, it is because the writer has used the time and effort needed to make the story interesting.

The Contribution of a Storywriter

A writer of short stories should understand the important role that stories fill. God chose to reveal much truth through stories in the Bible, and this illustrates the high value that He places on stories. Most of the Old Testament books contain stories. The Gospels and Acts—over half the New Testament—tell story after story about Jesus and His disciples. Even the New Testament Epistles relate a few stories.

A good short story fills an important place because it teaches a worthwhile lesson. The writer who loves God and His kingdom has a higher purpose than merely to entertain. Yes, he seeks to capture the reader's attention, but his most important goal is to communicate a Bible principle or to persuade the reader to pursue a noble course of action.

Furthermore, a story has certain advantages over an essay in presenting truth. Because a reader identifies with the story characters, he may accept truth in story form more readily than if it were expressed in a sermon or an essay. And because the reader's emotions become involved in the story, the truth tends to penetrate deeper and stick longer than if it had been expressed in another way. For instead of presenting an abstract theory, a story shows how truth works in real life. You can probably think of at least one time in your own experience when a story helped you to deal properly with a difficult or perplexing situation.

The Resources of a Storywriter

A short-story writer should cultivate an alertness for story material. Beware of thinking that good stories must be about extraordinary happenings. The fact is that worthwhile stories portray either true or true-to-life experiences. They are easy to

Lesson 48

Purpose: To describe the characteristics and resources of a short-story writer.

Teaching Suggestions:

In a typical set of six ninth and tenth grade students, at least one student enjoys writing stories and at least one student considers himself incapable of writing stories. Most students fall somewhere between those extremes. Your challenge is to inspire and motivate those students who think they cannot write stories.

One way to do that is to discuss how stories capture people's attention. Have the students ever found their minds wandering from a sermon until an illustration brought them back? Did they ever find it hard to study when the teacher was telling a story to a different class?

Another way to motivate students to write stories is to discuss the ever-pressing need for good stories in church periodicals. Let the students name some familiar story periodicals, estimate the number of stories in one issue, and then estimate the number of stories needed in a year's time. Your students may be writing some of those stories in a few years.

identify with. And it is the common, everyday happenings that meet this requirement most naturally.

Where will you find your prospective story material? Remember first of all that every story deals with a problem to be solved. Then watch the actions and reactions of people around you—acquaintances as well as strangers—as they face various problems. Every problem-solving situation has some degree of potential for a story.

The problems and conflicts in your own life are one major resource. Here are some things you may have experienced and forgotten: eating a certain food for the first time, getting calves (or pigs) back into their pen, facing a strong temptation, learning to ride a bicycle, making ice cream, playing with the neighbor children, baking a cake (as a boy), or driving a tractor (as a girl). You can write best about familiar happenings because you know them best.

Of course, you may want to write about other people's experiences. Grandpa may have told you many interesting stories such as the time the horses ran away with three children alone in the wagon, or the time an aunt who was not a Christian wanted to adopt his little sister.

You can also get story ideas from books. They describe things like fighting forest fires in Oregon, farming by the square mile in Australia, nursing in African mission hospitals, and suffering persecution in Anabaptist days. They tell of many people outside your own little circle of friends. Books stir your writing imagination.

But remember, the people and happenings you know best will be the easiest for you to write about. The following story beginning comes from a shopping trip on an ordinary day.

"Do you see what I see?" Mother pointed to the ignition switch inside the locked car. There hung the car keys. "I guess we can't go home yet, after all. Well, I'll just take this ironing board back to the store and ask them to keep it for us. Then we'll need to find someone to open the door."

An hour later, after a mechanic had used a wire to unlock the car, Mother and Beth were finally on their way home. The town lay three miles behind them when Beth was struck by a sudden thought. "Mother, where is our ironing board?"

"Just where we left it," Mother replied calmly as she stepped on the brake. "In Hodges' Department Store."

So they returned to the store and picked up the ironing board. But just as Mother and Beth settled themselves in the car again, they heard a tapping on the window. Quickly Mother rolled down the window to see what the woman standing there wanted.

"I'd like to know what that white cap is that you're wearing on your head," the woman said.

The writer may base his story directly on a real-life experience. He may use an actual happening as the foundation but then add or adjust details to make the story interesting and instructive. Or he may write a story based entirely on his imagination. However it originates, the story will be most effective if it deals with a practical, true-to-life experience.

The Qualities of a Storywriter

A storywriter needs a large measure of humility. If he is proud, he will find it hard to accept corrections and suggestions for changes from his teacher and later from an editor. Few indeed are the writers whose work is so nearly perfect that an editor accepts it without making changes. Also remember that only what is done in humility can truly bring glory to God. A writer motivated by selfish ambition may write a story that is interesting and even worthwhile, but he will miss the blessing of serving the Lord.

A storywriter also must be willing to work hard at improving his skills. Do you think that you have little or no story-writing ability? Do your best to improve the ability you do have. Do you enjoy writing stories? Do you think that you have already written some good stories? Determine to learn techniques that will make your stories even better. The lessons in this chapter will give specific helps on writing worthwhile, appealing short stories.

Applying the Lesson

A. Do these exercises.
1. How does the Bible show the valuable place of stories?
2. What important goal should a person have in writing a short story?
3. Why can stories often communicate truth more effectively than essays?
4. What are the three sources of story material mentioned in this lesson?
5. This lesson emphasizes that you would probably find it easiest to write about what type of subject: grand, familiar, or mysterious?
6. About which two of the following subjects could an upper grade student probably write the best stories?
   a. kings and castles
   b. family life and daily chores
   c. pioneers and covered wagons
   d. doctors and famous medical discoveries
   e. classrooms and playgrounds
7. For what two reasons is humility essential for writing effective short stories?

B. Write the numbers of the following items that should make good, profitable stories.
1. Ruth overhears one classmate softly telling another that some incorrect answers on a history test were not marked wrong. Should she ignore the incident or talk to the person?
2. Aunt Ellen spends an enjoyable day working in her garden.
3. Three evenings in a row, Nathan's baseball glove is hidden when he is ready to go home. "I know who did it," he thinks, "and I'll think of some way to get even."
4. Seventeen-year-old Oscar hears Linda urgently calling him. Running to the house, he finds little Anthony lying unconscious where he has fallen on the concrete porch. He keenly remembers Father's words as he and Mother left: "Well, Oscar, take care of everything."

Lesson 48 Answers
Applying the Lesson

A. 1. The Bible contains many stories that convey truth.
   2. to communicate a Bible principle or to persuade readers to pursue a noble course of action
   3. Readers identify with the story characters (and their emotions become involved). A story shows how truth works in real life.
   4. the writer's own experiences, other people's experiences, books
   5. familiar
   6. b, e
   7. A writer must be humble to accept his teacher's or editor's corrections. Only what is done in humility can truly serve to God's glory.

B. 1, 3, 4, 6

5. Katrina enjoys knitting on a grassy place beside the creek. The sound of the flowing water is relaxing, and numerous birds and other wild creatures feed, drink, and play within sight.
6. Arlin is anticipating a trip to the zoo with his family and Uncle Myron's family. But on the evening before the trip, his younger brother makes a careless mistake and breaks his leg.

C. Write three examples of your own for good story possibilities, following the pattern of the good examples in Part B. Save this work for use in later lessons.

C. (Individual work.)

Review Exercises

A. Label each sentence according to its use (*dec., int., imp., exc.*) and its structure (*S, CD, CX, CD-CX*). End punctuation has been omitted. [25]
1. Do you know what dry ice is, and can you explain its formation
2. Read this simple description of transforming carbon dioxide into dry ice
3. Gaseous carbon dioxide is cooled at high pressure; this causes the gas to liquefy
4. After the carbon dioxide is cooled and compressed through several stages, it is allowed to expand quickly, which causes rapid evaporation
5. What drastic cooling this evaporation causes
6. The sudden cooling changes about one-third of the liquid carbon dioxide into carbon dioxide "snow," which is pressed into blocks of dry ice; and the remaining two-thirds is returned to the cooling and compressing process

B. Label the word order of each sentence *N* (natural), *I* (inverted), or *M* (mixed). [25]
1. If our affection is set on heavenly things, we will not pursue the pleasures of this world.
2. Throughout the fabric of our lives must run the fear of God.
3. Simple trust in the Lord produces rest and calmness.
4. By the fruits of our lives, others can discern something about our hearts.

C. Label the style of each sentence *L* (loose), *P* (periodic), or *B* (balanced). [25]
1. The optimist sees something good in the darkest circumstances; the pessimist sees something bad in the brightest circumstances.
2. A man of faith believes that God's hand is at work throughout the varied experiences of life.
3. Even when the sun of God's love seems hidden by gloomy clouds, God cares.
4. We must overcome evil, or evil will overcome us.

Review Exercises
A. 1. int., CD-CX
   2. imp., S
   3. dec., CD
   4. dec., CX
   5. exc., S
   6. dec., CD-CX

B. 1. M
   2. I
   3. N
   4. M

C. 1. B
   2. L
   3. P
   4. B

---

49. The Message of a Story

Foundational to every worthwhile story is a worthwhile message. A story without a message would be like an expository essay without a theme. The message is the thread that holds a story together from beginning to end.

Read the two sample stories below. You will refer to them several times in this lesson and in later lessons.

Lesson 49

Purpose: To describe the purposes and themes of good stories, and to describe the difference between stories of fact and stories of fiction.

Sample Story 1

Terry's Temper

"Three months to enjoy the farm!" Terry voiced his thoughts to twelve-year-old Walter. The previous day had marked the last day of his ninth year in school. A pleasant mid-May sun smiled on the lush growth of grass. Terry took deep breaths of the fresh, exhilarating air. Brushing his hand across his well-combed hair, he glanced at Walter's unkempt hair.

"This grass sure needs a good haircut. Looks almost as bad as your hair," Terry said. "Wonder if that old mower will last all summer. Father said maybe we'll get a riding mower, and I hope we do soon."

Some time later, Terry was resolutely pushing the old mower back and forth across the Gehmans' spacious yard. The front lawn was nearly finished when the sputtering engine coughed and died.

Terry's temper flared. "You old mower! You belong on the junk heap," he snarled. "Wish Father would buy a decent mower right now."

The gas and oil checked, Terry gave the starter cord several vigorous pulls. Nothing. He checked the spark plug. It looked fine. He looked at the air cleaner. It was clean. Red-faced and grim, he grabbed the starter cord and yanked it again. *Clunk!* Throwing the torn starter cord against the mower, Terry spun around, his face a thundercloud.

"Father's probably in the shop," he muttered to himself as he stalked across the lawn.

"Better calm down a bit," Terry thought uncomfortably as he neared the shop. He took several deep breaths. Stopping at the outside faucet, he splashed cold water over his face.

Forty-five minutes later, Terry was mowing grass again.

One morning several days later, Father said, "Terry, I want you to fill the feed bin for the calves. Walter scraped out the last feed this morning."

This job Terry enjoyed. He thrived on the challenge of mixing the feed precisely, and he enjoyed running any farm machinery. Before long, the auger was carrying the feed from the mixer to the bin with a rhythmical *clankety-clank.*

"Stop! Stop!" Walter's urgent shouts jolted Terry like an electric shock. "The feed is pouring out on the barn floor," Walter gasped. "I forgot to shut the door."

Quickly Terry pulled the lever, stopping the auger. "Walter Jay Gehman! Of all things! You're always forgetting to close the door!"

Sure enough, a mountain of feed covered the floor below the feed bin chute. "Well, you may as well get the feed bags and a shovel," Terry said grimly as he struggled to slide the door shut. "Get to work while I finish emptying the mixer." He threw the words over his shoulder as he stalked away.

Terry was back in a few minutes. "Come on, shovel faster!" he snapped at his brother. "I ought to make you clean it up alone."

"I'm sorry, Terry," Walter said. "The breakfast bell rang just as I finished emptying the bin. Then I forgot all about it," he finished lamely.

"Obviously," stormed Terry.

"Terry." Father's stern voice broke in upon the scene. "You must not talk and act like this."

Turning to Walter, he said, "You are excused for a while."

"Now, son," Father said, and his penetrating gaze searched Terry's face. "Sit down here on this feed bag. Perhaps you can explain what's going on."

Unable to meet Father's gaze, Terry dropped his eyes. "I guess Walter forgot to close the door," he faltered, "and the feed spilled out on the floor, and . . ."

"And what?" Father prompted.

"And—well—I—I guess I got upset at him." Terry's troubled eyes met Father's kind ones.

"Yes. I've noticed recently that you get quite impatient when something doesn't suit you. Have you thought about the selfishness of your impatience? You think everything must suit *you.* And you're not being considerate of other people's feelings. I want you to think about this. And you *must* learn to control your temper.

"Now, you clean up this mess by yourself. And I expect you to apologize to Walter for your unkindness."

The following day, the heifers found a weak spot in the fence and were soon romping in the alfalfa. "Oh, the heifers are out!" Mother dropped her basket of laundry.

"Terry! Walter! The heifers are out!" Mother cupped her hands and called toward the barn.

"Oh, no!" groaned Terry as he and Walter stepped outside the milk house. "Why did those miserable animals—" Terry's voice dripped with annoyance.

"Looks like they're having fun," commented Walter.

"I guess they are having fun!" Terry retorted. "It sure won't be fun for us!"

For a few moments, Terry stood beside the barn, his hands clenched, his jaw set, and his anger rising. Suddenly in his mind's eye, he saw Father's serious but kind face. And he heard Father's words, "You *must* learn to control your temper."

Slowly Terry's anger melted, and he glanced sheepishly at Walter. "Well, I guess there's nothing to do but bring them in.

"Mother, open the gate. You and the girls guard the lane. Come, Walter. Let's circle around and chase the heifers through the back yard and in the gate." Terry's quick mind laid out a plan as the boys dashed across the lane.

But the heifers had other plans. Up went their heads and tails, and away they raced across the field toward the woods.

"Look at those heifers run!" Terry sighed. "We might as well use the tractor. How about it, Walter? Want to drive?"

"Sure," answered Walter, surprised at Terry's offer.

Forty minutes later, two exhausted boys chased the last heifer through the gate just as Father drove in the lane.

The boys rehearsed the story while they helped Father fix the fence. "Well, boys, it sounds as if you had quite a chase. I'm glad you got them all back in," said Father. "But that isn't the best part of the story," he added, looking at Terry. "The best thing I've heard is that you didn't lose your temper."

Sample Story 2
"He Rides Upon the Storm"

My hands were mechanically cutting apples into neat halves when Mother's words burst into my thoughts. "Grandmother Fry called this morning. She asked if it would suit for you to spend the weekend with her. She said you help her to feel secure because she knows you are dependable. There'll be no school Friday, so you could go on Thursday evening. We'd pick you up again on Sunday afternoon."

My mind whirled into high gear. "Of course, I dearly love Grandmother," I thought. "But would she want me to come if she knew how insecure I feel sometimes? What if I can't fit into her schedule? What if . . ."

"Oh, Mother, I don't know what to say," I finally answered.

"Why not? What's wrong, Wanda?" Mother's steady voice calmed my tumultuous thoughts somewhat.

"Well," I began slowly, "well, I suppose it would be all right. But, Mother, didn't she say just the other week that she gets up at four o'clock? Will she expect me to get up that early too?"

"Oh, I doubt it," answered Mother. "She spends some of that time in Bible reading and prayer. In fact," Mother continued, "I remember her saying recently that she eats breakfast at seven o'clock."

"What about her special diet? Will I have to eat without sugar and salt?"

"Would that be so bad?" Mother's voice held a tone of humor. "But, seriously, no. She has sugar and salt that you can add to your food. Just trust in the Lord, and He will be with you."

"I suppose I can try it if you're sure everything will be all right," I finally answered hesitantly.

Friday and Saturday were busy days at Grandmother's house. We made tomato juice, ketchup, and applesauce. But we had time for a leisurely walk over to Uncle Jacob's farm for milk on Saturday afternoon.

After a simple Sunday lunch of potato soup, Grandmother said, "I've surely enjoyed your help and your company these days, Wanda."

"Not more than I've enjoyed being here," I returned. As I looked at Grandmother's neatly veiled, silvery hair shining in the sunlight, love filled my heart. Even her wrinkled face looked more beautiful than ever. "To think I was uneasy about coming," I thought. "But I trusted God, and He blessed me with peace and a pleasant time."

The following Saturday, I hurried from the flower bed I was weeding and burst into the kitchen. "Alta," I gasped, "there's a man coming in the lane. A bushy-haired, scary-looking man! Whatever will we do?" I wailed.

Father's parting words flashed across my mind: "Well, Alta, you'll be in charge for a few hours. Wanda, you pitch in and help take care of the little ones. In case of an emergency, call Uncle Ralph's. Above all, trust in the Lord." Then he and Mother had left to visit Aunt Mattie in the hospital.

Alta glanced out the window. "We'll trust the Lord," she said. The man had nearly reached the house.

"Shall I call Uncle Ralph's?" I asked desperately. But a firm knock sounded just then, sending a shiver down my spine.

"Good morning," said Alta politely. "Can I help you with something?"

"I'm sorry to bother you, ma'am." The soft, polite voice contrasted sharply with the man's appearance. "My car choked off just past your lane, and I can't get it started again. Do you have a phone I could use?"

"Yes," Alta replied. "In fact, my uncle Ralph owns Witmer's Garage just one mile up the road. Should I call him?"

"Sounds great! I'll just walk back to my car then," the man replied. With a bow, he was gone.

"Whew!" I breathed. "I didn't know what to expect. My heart's still racing!"

"But God is with us," answered Alta. "He's well able to care for us, isn't He?"

"Yes, but . . ." I hesitated. "I—I guess I should learn to trust Him more."

That very night I suddenly sat bolt upright in bed, my heart pounding wildly. "What was that?" I wondered bewilderedly. In answer, there came a brilliant flash of lightning, followed closely by a sharp crash of thunder. All sleepiness chased away, I lay down, closed my eyes, and shivered.

Soon one flash after another kept the sky lit almost continuously. Tremendous crashes of thunder rattled the windows and shook my bed. The howling wind whipped the trees outside my window. The rain and the hail combined into one mighty, oceanlike roar.

And there stood Alta at the window, as calm as if she were watching a summer sunset! "Are you awake, Wanda?" she asked, beckoning me to stand beside her.

Hesitantly I climbed out of bed and crossed the room. "Aren't you afraid?" I asked as another streak momentarily blinded our eyes.

"Not really," she answered with her usual calmness. "But I find it awesome to see this display of God's power. Just think! Some people can watch a storm like this and still declare that there is no God!" Alta shook her head.

"I guess I never thought of it that way," I admitted. The storm raged for a while longer. Then as suddenly as it had come, it moved on.

"'What a mighty God we serve!'" I breathed as I climbed back into bed. Then I prayed, "Help me, heavenly Father, to trust Thee more completely."

A Worthwhile Purpose

A story with a worthwhile message must be written for a worthwhile purpose. People write stories for all kinds of purposes, including many that are not profitable. The following paragraphs describe three noble purposes.

1. *To help readers acknowledge their own weaknesses and shortcomings.* A reader may see the fault of a story character and condemn him for it—only to realize that he himself has the same fault. With such an indirect approach, the reader is often able to acknowledge his fault when he might have rebelled at a more direct approach.

In 2 Samuel 12, the prophet Nathan needed to help David acknowledge the great sin he had committed against Uriah and Bathsheba. Rather than confronting the king with a direct rebuke, Nathan began by telling a story from everyday life. David strongly condemned the rich man in the story for his great injustice—only to realize that he himself had done something much worse. The story fulfilled its purpose as David responded by repenting and confessing his sin.

Jesus also told stories to show people their shortcomings. His story of the Good Samaritan made it clear that the Samaritan obeyed God's command to "love thy neighbour as thyself," while the priest and the Levite did *not* obey that command.

2. *To inspire noble ideals and godly living.* Just as an experience in our own lives can inspire and encourage us, so an experience we encounter in a story can serve the same purpose. Through stories we can benefit from the experiences of other people. The following story should inspire greater love for God in all who read it.

Once there was a Christian man who became seriously ill. As he lay in bed, he grew troubled because he felt so little love for God in his heart. He expressed his concern to a Christian brother one day.

"My friend," replied the other, "when I leave here, I expect to go home to my family. We have a baby whom I love more than words can tell. But she loves me little. If my heart were breaking with sorrow, it would not disturb her sleep. If my body were racked with pain, it would not interrupt her play. In fact, if I died, she would forget me in a very short time.

"Even so, there is not enough money in the whole world for someone to buy my baby. Do I say that because she loves me or because I love her? Do I withhold my love until I know she loves me? Do I wait for her to do something worthy of my love before I extend it to her? Of course not! And God loves us in the same way except that His love is infinitely greater."

This illustration so affected the sick man that tears began rolling down his face. "Oh, now I see!" he exclaimed. "It is not my love for God but His love for me that I should be thinking of. And I do love Him now as I have never loved Him before."

3. *To show God at work.* As we go through the daily routines of life, what God does for us may become commonplace. We tend to forget or overlook God's workings in our lives and surroundings. A story can bring the overruling hand of God into sharp focus and clearly remind us of what God does. Consider the following example.

A good many years ago, I was sailing in the desolate seas off Cape Horn, hunting whales. One day we were beating directly south in the face of a hard wind. We had been tacking this way and that all the morning and were making very little headway.

About eleven o'clock, as I stood at the wheel, the idea suddenly came into my mind, "Why batter the ship against these waves? There are probably as many whales to the north as to the south. Suppose we run with the wind instead of against it?"

In response to that sudden idea, I changed the course of the ship and began to sail north instead of south. One hour later, at noon, the lookout at the masthead shouted, "Boats ahead!"

Presently, we overtook four lifeboats in which were fourteen sailors, the only survivors of the crew of a ship that had burned to the water's edge ten days before. Those men had been adrift in their boats ever since, frantically praying to God for rescue; and we arrived just in time to save them. They could not have survived another day.

Consider the two sample stories in this lesson. Which of the three purposes above do those stories fulfill? "Terry's Temper" helps to show readers their own shortcomings as it portrays them in Terry. "'He Rides Upon the Storm'" should inspire trust in God in facing the circumstances of life.

One Central Theme

Another basic part of the story message is a theme—a lesson that the story teaches. A worthwhile theme communicates a specific Bible principle applied to life. Your goal is to convince the reader of the importance of that principle.

A good short story develops only one central theme. After you have decided what it will be, seek to have every detail of your story point to that theme. Every character trait, every description of the setting, and every point in the conflict should contribute to the lesson you want to teach. Although the story may naturally hint at other themes, avoid the temptation to weave them deliberately into the story. A short story is too limited to develop more than one theme effectively. Trying to do so will spoil the unity of the story.

Is your theme thoughtfulness to parents? Then refrain from sticking in little lessons about diligence in school or friendliness to neighbors. These other ideas will detract from the main theme.

Consider again the sample stories in this lesson. Can you identify the theme in each one? They may be stated as follows:

> Learning to control one's temper is an important part of maturing emotionally and spiritually.
> Simple trust in the Lord brings peace even in uncertain and frightening circumstances.

Although the theme should run through the entire story, it should not be directly stated in the story. A story is neither a sermon nor an essay; rather, it works in a more subtle way. As the reader follows the main character through the story, he should subconsciously absorb the theme that you have woven in.

Fact and Fiction

A good short story may be either fact or fiction. A factual story develops a specific, actual happening. Very few stories, however, are totally factual. A writer may change the names of characters and places, as well as other details, to avoid embarrassing the people involved. Also, a writer must often use his imagination to supply details of action, dialogue, and thoughts that will carry the story along.

If a story is fiction, it often contains a combination of fact and imagination. A writer may combine details from various events and conversations into one story. Even though every detail may have occurred at one time or another, the story is fiction because those details do not represent one actual event.

An author may also build a story from a snatch of conversation that he hears or a snapshot of action that he observes. In this case again, the story is fiction because it does not describe an actual happening. Of course, a writer may develop a story completely from his imagination. He chooses a story theme that he wants to convey and then creates the characters, events, and dialogue to portray that theme.

The writer of worthwhile fiction must take great care to write realistically. Even though the story is not true, it must be true to life. A reader should not have reason to conclude that the story could not have happened to real people.

Applying the Lesson

A. Do these exercises.
1. List three noble purposes for worthwhile stories.
2. What is a story theme?
3. Why should a short story develop only one central theme?
4. The theme of a good story is not stated directly. Then how does the theme become clear to the reader?
5. What is the difference between a story of fact and a story of fiction?
6. In what ways might a factual story be changed?
7. List several things that may serve as the seed for a story of fiction.
8. What must the writer of fiction be especially careful to do?

Lesson 49 Answers
Applying the Lesson
A. 1. to help readers acknowledge their own weaknesses and shortcomings;
   to inspire noble ideals and godly living;
   to show God at work
2. the lesson that a story teaches
3. A short story is too limited to develop more than one theme effectively.
4. The theme runs through the entire story in such a way that the reader absorbs it subconsciously.
5. A story of fact is based on an actual happening.
   A story of fiction may be a combination of events and imagination.
6. by changing the names of characters and places to avoid embarrassment;
   by using imaginary actions, dialogue, and thoughts to carry the story along
7. actual events and conversations from the experiences of various people;
   a snatch of conversation;
   a snapshot of action;
   imagination
8. He must be especially careful to make his story realistic.

B. Write a possible theme for each of the following story openings.
1. Flying snow filled the air as two snow shovels moved steadily. The snowbanks on either side of the drifted lane rose higher.

    "Really deep," grunted Mark, tossing another shovelful of snow.

    "Uh-huh," Jesse agreed. "Packed too. I hope we'll be able to get the lane open before the milk truck comes."

    "I hope so too," said Mark. "I prayed about it."
2. Recess was nearly over. Joyce backed up far beyond second base, prepared to catch a fly ball, for Alvin was coming up to bat. He selected his favorite bat and swung it experimentally. "Think I can hit a home run before the bell rings?"
3. "I wish I could do as I please for once," commented Doris.

    "Oh, I don't think that would make you happy," replied Mother.

    "Well, I think it would. Couldn't we try it, just once?" coaxed Doris.
4. Jonathan whistled a merry tune as he hurried to the barn through the rain. "It surely has rained often this summer," he thought. He glanced at the cornfield, which was already starting to turn yellow. Then his eyes swept across the field of hay that they had planned to bale today. Jonathan was glad when he could step into the warm, dry barn.

    "Good morning," his father greeted him. "Looks like a rainy day today, so the hay will have to wait a little longer."
5. "Oh, David, what could have happened?" I asked with concern. "Edward still isn't home."

    "I can't understand it." David frowned and scratched his head. "Edward said they'd come back early today."
6. "Ernest Swalm?" asked the major as Ernest entered the room.

    "Yes, sir."

    "You refuse to put on your uniform?"

    "Yes, sir. I am a Christian. I cannot kill my enemies, for the Scriptures say, 'Love your enemies.' Nor can I wear the uniform of an organization whose business it is to kill."

C. Choose one of the possibilities you wrote in Lesson 48 as the basis of a story that you will write in this chapter, or another idea approved by your teacher. Write the theme that you will develop in your story. (Save this work for use in later lessons.)

Review Exercises
A. Write whether the underlined sentence part is a nominative absolute (*NA*) or a participial phrase (*PP*). [24]
1. The dishes finally finished, we walked out to the orchard.
2. Walking among the apple trees, we breathed in the sweet smell of ripening apples.
3. Several apples having fallen to the ground, each of us enjoyed a snack.

B. (Sample answers.)
1. God answers prayer.
    Faith includes hard work.
2. Do not be too sure of yourself.
    Playing fairly is more important than winning.
3. Contentment is found in filling the place God has for us.
    Submission to parents brings true contentment.
4. We must learn to trust God's all-wise control of the weather.
5. God cares for His own.
    Faith in God removes fear and anxiety.
6. God's grace is sufficient even in severe testing.
    Christian love is stronger than carnal force.

C. (Individual work.)

Review Exercises
A. 1. NA
   2. PP
   3. NA

4. Later we headed back to the house, <u>the air having grown chilly</u>.

5. The mothers visited together for a time, <u>sharing their girlhood memories</u>.

B. Rewrite each sentence, changing the underlined subordinate clause to a nominative absolute. [24]

1. <u>Because the grass has grown tall</u>, Delmar plans to mow the lawn this afternoon.

2. <u>After her first batch of cookies burned</u>, Katrina paid closer attention to the clock.

3. <u>Because Mollie's milk is rich in cream</u>, we make plenty of butter.

4. NA

5. PP

B. 1. The grass having grown tall, Delmar plans to mow the lawn this afternoon.

2. Her first batch of cookies having burned, Katrina paid closer attention to the clock.

3. Mollie's milk being rich in cream, we make plenty of butter.

---

50. Improving Your Editing Skills, Part 6

When you proofread a composition, you must give full attention to the work at hand. You will not detect errors very well if you have a preoccupied mind or you try to proofread in a distracting environment. This may be the reason that even professional proofreaders occasionally let errors get into print.

Overlooked errors can sometimes be humorous. Someone surely was not concentrating on his work when he allowed the following mistakes to slip through.

In an advertisement for a lawn mower:
"Riding mower, 42' cut."

In a recipe printed with a magazine article:
"Spoon topping over cake until all is absorbed. Leave cake in pain."

Just one mark or one letter is incorrect in each case. But what a difference those errors make!

In this lesson you will again proofread a number of sentences and paragraphs. Give full attention to your work so that you can find *every* mistake in these exercises.

Marks Used in Editing and Proofreading

∨ or ∧ insert (caret)	ℒ delete	. . . . stet (let it stand)	—— use italics
¶ begin new paragraph	no ¶ no new paragraph	*lc* change to lowercase (small letter)	*uc* change to uppercase (capital letter)
# insert space	⌒ delete space	← move (arrow)	⌐⌐ transpose

Lesson 50

Purpose: To provide proofreading practice.

Teaching Suggestions:

For extra interest and variety, you may wish to let students work in pairs for some of these proofreading lessons. (Professional proofreaders usually work in teams.) Paired students should be of equal competence so that less able students do not gain an unfair advantage.

Editing Practice

A. Use proofreading marks to correct the two errors of spelling or spacing in each sentence.

1. God has given sevral kinds of fish strange waysof caring for their young.

2. Sum African fish carry their eggs around in their mouths be fore they hatch.

3. In some speceis the male caries the eggs, and in others the female does.

4. The eggs hach in afew days, and the young continue to live in the adult's mouth.

5. Ocassionally the parent fish spits out the young, and they swim near by.

6. When any danger thretens, the young dart back into the adult's protectin mouth.

7. In a few weeks, howver, the little fish grow to large for the parent to carry.

8. The young are than left to care for them selves.

9. During those weaks of caring for their young, the adult fish eats no thing.

10. By the time the young are one their own, the pour adult is quite thin and weak.

B. Use proofreading marks to correct the errors in word order in these sentences.

1. Monsoons are great convectional currents that between winter and summer reverse their direction.

2. During the winter cool months, the oceans remain warmer than the continents.

3. So the winds blow out to the ocean and keep the land dry mostly.

4. When the continent becomes warmer during the summer than the ocean, the winds blow inland from the ocean.

Lesson 50 Answers

Editing Practice

(Answers are on pages 470–471.)

5. These winds bring heavy rain to the land, being laden
   with moisture.

6. The best-known monsoons occur in India probably.

7. From December through March, a typical dry winter monsoon
   only brings about five inches of rain to a given region.

8. In April, the winds change and five inches of rain
   approximately may fall in that month.

9. When the moist summer monsoon blows from May through
   October, the rainfall may exceed one hundred inches
   actually.

10. Then as the monsoon changes during November again, another
    five inches may fall.

C. Use proofreading marks to correct all the errors in this essay. Your corrections
   should include one use of the stet symbol and one joining of two paragraphs. No
   line has more than one error.

1.   God created the earth "to be inhabited (Isaiah 45:18).

2. This required that the earth have an atmosphere.

3.   The atmosphere provides oxygen for breatheing. But

4. that is only a small part of the picture. The atmosphere

5. serves to to regulate the surface temperature of the

6. earth. Like a huge blanket, it surrounds us, allowing

7. sunlight to pass ~~through~~ but preventing heat from escaping

8. freely into Space.

9.   By contrast, the atmosphere of Venus traps so much solar

10. heat that the surface tempature of that planet is scorching

11. hot. And the moon, which has no atmosphere, endures blister

12. ing noontime temperatures and freezing nights

13.   But there is more. meteors burn up and disintegrate in

14. the atmosphere. If this did not ~~really~~ happen, even a small

15. meteoric particel no larger than a dust speck would strike

16. the earth with the force of a shot from a revolver.

17.   Since billions of such particles strike the atmosphere

18.   everyday, we surely need its protection!

19.   In addition to these all services, the atmosphere is a

20.   shield against deadly radiation from space. Truely, our

21.   atmosphere is the handiwork of an all knowing Creator.

---

51. The Structure and Elements of a Story

"Oh, girls." Doris glanced around the warm auditorium and instinctively lowered her voice. *"Did you hear the latest news?"*

Betty fidgeted self-consciously while several other girls leaned forward eagerly. *"What should I do?"* Betty wondered.

A short story must get right down to business. This sample beginning does. It hints at the theme of the story, which you studied in Lesson 49. It also pictures the setting briefly, it introduces the main characters, and it suggests the conflict. These are the three main elements of every good story.

The Setting

A short story should include just enough details about the setting to make the story clear. The first few paragraphs should make some reference to the setting. As the story moves along, you may add more details to help explain the story. Often the setting helps a reader to understand why the characters act as they do.

One main part of the setting is *where* the story occurs. You can usually indicate this with incidental details (like "the barn door" or "the kitchen sink") that show whether the story happens at home or elsewhere. Or you can make a brief reference to the geographical location (such as "the Kansas prairie"). Detailed information is necessary only if the reader is probably unfamiliar with the setting and if those details are important to the story. You must be well familiar with the location of the story so that all the details will be consistent.

Another part of the setting is *when* the story occurs. Brief descriptions, such as "a spring morning" or "the setting sun," are usually enough to indicate the time. Specific dates may be important for historical interest or value.

The setting also includes the emotional or spiritual atmosphere in the story. If the moods of significant characters are important to the development of the story, the opening paragraphs should give that information. Often it takes just a few words ("whistled merrily" or "fumed to herself") to indicate whether the atmosphere is pleasant or unpleasant.

The details of the setting often reflect the attitudes or actions of the main character. Is your story about an inner turmoil of conscience? The setting may include turbulent clouds overhead. A setting of morning countryside beauty may reflect

Lesson 51

Purpose: To review the basic elements that make up a short story.

Teaching Suggestions:

Be sure the students understand the sequence of Lessons 49 and 51. Deciding on a general purpose and a specific theme provide a writer with the foundation of a story. Developing details of the setting, the characters, and the conflict provide the framework for the story.

Note that Lesson 52 gives more thorough treatment on the portraying of the story characters.

the peace of a soul yielded to God. Sometimes, however, the details of the setting differ sharply from the attitudes or actions of the main character. A peaceful setting, by its very contrast, may emphasize the irritability or perplexity of the main character.

Look again at the story opening at the beginning of this lesson. What hints do you find about the place, time, and atmosphere of the story? In the second sentence, the mention of a *warm auditorium* reveals that the story takes place at church, probably in summer. The opening further suggests that the atmosphere is less than ideal, with the two characters displaying opposite moods.

The Characters

Characters are central to the action and conflict of a story. Although you might produce a story with no allusion to a physical setting, you certainly cannot produce a story without characters. In fact, they are so important that the entire next lesson deals with the portraying of story characters.

Story characters must be realistic. If you present the main character as a noble example, he must uphold high ideals. However, he must not be so idealistic that your reader can hardly identify with him. What real-life teenager (or any other person) is so good that he never does anything wrong, never considers a wrong response, and never even faces a strong temptation to do wrong? If you portray such characters in a story, you will destroy its realism and the reader will probably discredit the whole story.

If your story is about people you actually know, you must be especially careful to portray their characteristics fully and clearly. You will tend to interpret details of your story by your background knowledge of the characters, but your reader knows only what you reveal to him in the story. As a result, what seems perfectly clear to you may be confusing or baffling to your reader when he first meets a character. Read the following example.

Carla had just finished her drawing when Ivan walked into the room. "I'd be ashamed of a picture like that," he declared.
Carla smiled happily and sat up a little straighter.

Are you surprised at Carla's reaction? Surely she heard what her brother said. Is she such a cheerful person that criticism does not bother her? No, Carla is a normal girl; but Ivan has a habit of speaking in irony, and he was actually praising his sister's work. If you had known that, you would have understood Carla's reaction immediately. In the same way, your reader must have all the necessary details about your characters in order to understand why they act as they do.

Story characters must not only be realistic but also remain consistent throughout the story. If conflict in the story changes the main character, the change should generally be in a gradual way and in the same direction. Any sudden or unexpected change should be the result of a crisis in the story, or the character will not seem realistic.

Story characters should also generate an emotional response from the reader. If your main character is a good example, his reactions throughout the conflict should cause your reader to respond with definite approval. If he is a poor example, he should provide reasons for definite disapproval of his reactions. Be sure to portray the characters in a manner that directs the reader's sympathy in the right way. A poor example may actually draw the reader's sympathy to himself if he is constantly ridiculed and mistreated by the other story characters.

The Conflict

A conflict involving the main character must be the framework of your story. This struggle or problem that the main character faces is what holds the reader's interest and makes the story theme live.

This does not mean that you must write about robberies or sinking ships or burning hospitals. Many less dramatic experiences build up interest quite well. The important thing is to tell the story in the right order, making the conflict grow stronger as you go along. For example, Jane looks up from her test and sees Miriam looking in her direction. She knows Miriam would not be trying to copy from her test, so she thinks nothing of it. Later she looks up again, and Miriam is still looking in her direction. After several more glances, she hardly knows what to think because Miriam is still looking. Do you see the buildup?

1. *Types of conflict.* The conflict in a story is one or more of three different types. One common type is conflict between the main character and another character. The story of Isaac and his wells is a familiar Bible story with this kind of conflict. Isaac, the *protagonist* (main character), must relate to the unfair demands of the Philistines, who are the *antagonists* (persons opposing the main character). Other examples of this type of conflict might include a main character who struggles to appreciate a classmate; one who rejects the advice of an authority figure; or one who resists the wrong influence of another person.

A second type of conflict is that between the main character and his circumstances. For instance, Paul and the other passengers faced this type of conflict when a tempest battered their ship for days and finally destroyed it. Other examples include a main character who must accept a change of plans, who must cope with a handicap or hardship, or who must accomplish some task against contrary circumstances. Although other characters may play a part in the story, this type of conflict is brought on by a circumstance rather than by a person.

A third type is conflict between the main character and himself. This type is illustrated by the story of Moses' hesitation when God called him to lead Israel out of Egypt. Other examples would include a main character's struggles in overcoming a temptation or a bad habit; in clearing his conscience by confessing a wrong or making restitution; or in facing a difficult decision. Sometimes in this type of conflict, you may almost conclude that God is the antagonist opposing the main character. But this is not true; God is rather prompting the main character to respond rightly. The conflict rages between the main character's proper desire to do right and his carnal desire to take the easiest way.

2. *Development of conflict.* The conflict should be introduced as early as possible in the story. Avoid a long introduction that merely gives background or setting

information but involves no action or conflict. Suppose your story is about strange guests who appeared at bedtime asking for a place to sleep. You do not need to tell what you had for supper that evening or what your family discussed at the table. Start the story with the timid knock on the front door.

"But," you say, "I have to start back in the afternoon so that the setting is clear. Father was not at home, because he was away at a meeting. He said that he wouldn't be back until late, and he told us not to disturb Mother unless it was positively necessary. She was in bed with a bad sore throat."

What you can do is begin with the action of the story and slip those facts in later as a flashback. There may be several flashbacks, each one introducing background information as it is needed. The flashbacks in the following example are underlined.

> There we were, with strangers on the front porch asking for lodging. Wilbur, Helen, and I looked at each other questioningly.
>
> "Oh, I wish Mother could be up," I sighed. "But she just told me that her sore throat isn't much better than it was this morning."
>
> "We can make out this time without her help, can't we?" Wilbur replied. "Father did say we shouldn't disturb Mother unless it's really necessary. Remember?"
>
> "Sure we can manage," Helen said cheerfully. Wilbur returned to the door to invite the guests inside.

Once you have started with a good conflict, keep the story moving. Increase the intensity of the conflict throughout the main part of the story. Unless the story is very short, the main character should face his conflict at least two times before it is resolved. Each incident of the conflict should involve stronger emotion than the preceding incident. This, along with the recurrence of the conflict, increases the reader's suspense as the story progresses. The most intense incident of the conflict is the climax, at which point the main character's response brings either victory or defeat.

After the conflict is resolved, a short conclusion should round out the story and clinch the theme. The reader is satisfied. He knows how the problem was solved and is ready for the story to end. And the theme of the story should be clear to him. If it is not, a direct statement will only dull the point and spoil his interest. So if the lesson is vague, revise your story until you do not need to explain the theme at the end. Your closing should contain just enough to tie the story together, like this:

> The rain had slowed to a fine drizzle when Mr. Smith dumped the last bucket of water down the drain. "People say I procrastinate," he muttered, "but I know one job I'm not going to put off again. I'm going to be up on the roof patching those leaks bright and early tomorrow morning."
>
> He looked at the clock.
>
> "Not tomorrow," he said. "Today."

Applying the Lesson

A. Do these exercises.

1. Where should the setting of a story be portrayed?
2. What three things make up the setting of a story?
3. Why is it important to make story characters realistic?
4. In a story about actual people, why might a writer neglect to portray the characters clearly enough for his reader?
5. If a main character changes in a sudden, drastic way, how can you make the change seem realistic?
6. What is the story conflict?
7. What are the three common types of story conflict?
8. Where should the conflict begin?
9. What is the purpose of a flashback?
10. What should happen to the conflict as the story unfolds?
11. What two things cause a buildup of intensity in the conflict?
12. What two things should the conclusion do for the story?

B. Answer these questions about the sample story "Terry's Temper" in Lesson 49.

1. What information about the place and time do the first two paragraphs provide?
2. Is the setting a reflection of or a contrast to the conflict?
3. The main character changes in this story. How is that change kept realistic?
4. What is the conflict in the story?
5. Which of the three types of conflict does the story portray?
6. How many incidents of conflict occur in the story?
7. What are some things that make the climax (final incident) the most intense?
8. How does the conclusion clinch the story theme?

C. Answer these questions about the sample story "'He Rides Upon the Storm'" in Lesson 49.

1. What information about the place, time, and atmosphere is given in the first three paragraphs?
2. What is the conflict in the story?
3. Which of the three types of conflict does this story portray?
4. How many incidents of conflict occur in the story?
5. How does the conclusion clinch the story theme?

Review Exercises

Do these exercises on expository essays. [28–32]

1. What is the general purpose of an expository essay?
2. Write the letters of the two topics that are limited enough for an expository essay.
   a. Weather Systems
   b. The Formation of Hurricanes
   c. Effects of Weather on Agriculture
   d. Weather Patterns in Canada
   e. Typical Blizzards of the Great Plains

3. conflict between the main character and herself (*or* between the main character and circumstances)
4. three
5. Wanda's thoughts and especially her prayer show a definite determination to trust the Lord rather than to fear.

Review Exercises

1. to define, clarify, or explain something
2. b, e

Lesson 51 Answers
Applying the Lesson

A. 1. in the first several paragraphs
   2. place, time, and emotional or spiritual atmosphere
   3. If the story characters are not realistic, the reader will probably discredit the whole story.
   4. Because of his familiarity with the people, a writer may overlook important details that must be specifically mentioned before readers will understand the characters' actions.
   5. by portraying the change as the result of a crisis
   6. the struggle or problem that the main character faces
   7. conflict between the main character and another person, between the main character and his circumstances, and between the main character and himself
   8. as near to the beginning as possible
   9. to provide background information needed to understand the story
   10. The conflict should become more intense.
   11. the recurrence of the conflict and the increased emotion in the incidents
   12. The conclusion should round out the story and clinch the story theme.

B. 1. *Place:* A farm; an area in which grass is growing well in mid-May.
      Time: Middle of May; the first day of summer vacation.
   2. a contrast
   3. The change is gradual, and it is in the same direction.
   4. Terry struggles to control his temper when things go wrong.
   5. conflict between the main character and himself
   6. three
   7. Father is not at home to help. The heifers run away when the boys try to chase them in. It takes forty minutes to get all the heifers in.
   8. Father commends Terry for the progress in controlling his temper.

C. 1. *Place:* In the kitchen; in a locality where apples grow.
      Time: Late summer or early fall (school in session; during apple harvest).
      Atmosphere: A busy, loving home atmosphere.
   2. Wanda struggles to overcome her tendency to be anxious and fearful.

3. Write whether each statement about expository essays is true (*T*) or false (*F*).
   a. A good set of notes draws from at least two sources.
   b. A good set of notes contains no direct quotations from reference sources.
   c. Good notes include many sentences and paragraphs.
   d. The introductory paragraph should begin with a statement of the theme.
   e. Credits for direct quotations are noted in the bibliography.
   f. The conclusion should summarize or otherwise reinforce the main points of the essay.

3. a.	T	d.	F
b.	F	e.	F
c.	F	f.	T

---

52. Characterization in a Story

A story lives if its characters live. Therefore, a writer must pay close attention to his characters and portray them in a way that shows their traits as clearly as possible. The process of portraying story characters is *characterization.*

Three Classes of Characters

Every story character fits into one of three classes: major, minor, and background. The *major characters* carry the development of the story conflict. They are the ones that the reader should come to know by reading the story. Every story has at least one major character—whom you have known before as the main character. Another name for this main character is *protagonist.* The entire story generally comes to the reader through the protagonist's eyes. Many stories also include a second major character, the *antagonist.* The antagonist is the protagonist's opponent. (Note the prefix *ant-,* meaning "against.")

The number of major characters in a short story must be strictly limited. Since each one deserves to be characterized clearly, the story simply does not have room for more than three major characters. For example, the story of David killing the giant has two major characters: David and Goliath.

The *minor characters* contribute to the development of the conflict without carrying it directly. These are generally named, and they should be characterized only as much as necessary. Normally, this means the portraying of only one character trait.

The *background characters* are simply a part of the setting; they do not contribute to the actual story conflict. So they should not be characterized, and usually they should not even be named. Background characters often occur in groups. For example, siblings referred to in a family setting or students in a school setting are background characters. Even in writing a factual story, you are not required to mention every character in order to be honest. You are writing a *story,* not giving a *report.*

The story of David and Goliath illustrates these three classes of characters. David and Goliath, of course, are the major characters—the protagonist and the

Lesson 52

Purpose: To teach principles of effective characterization.

Teaching Suggestions:

This lesson builds strongly upon the lesson on characterization in the Grade 8 book. The idea of background characters, however, is new for this series. Also new is the point that showing a character's reputation is a method of characterization.

Emphasize the important place of characters in a story. If students fail to grasp the impact of this lesson, their stories will likely fall flat.

antagonist. Saul, Jesse, and Eliab are the minor characters. The background characters include David's unnamed brothers, the Israelite soldiers, and the Philistine soldiers.

Direct and Indirect Characterization

Direct characterization generally uses adjectives to tell what story characters are like. Here are two examples of direct characterization.

> Mary Jane was very active.
> Susan was quiet and gentle.

In a good story, however, things need to keep moving. The characters must engage in specific actions and say specific words. They will seem lifeless if you paint portraits of them! Direct characterization slows the forward movement of a story. Any sentence that merely *tells* what a character is like will hinder the action of the story.

Furthermore, direct characterization tends to be dull. Why say that Mary Jane *is* active or that Susan *is* quiet and gentle? The reader wants to know what is *happening.* So the value of direct characterization in stories is very limited. It is usually effective only for minor characters, and only if it is a brief description important to the story.

Much more effective is indirect characterization, which *shows* what story characters are like. This is accomplished by including the characterizing right with the flow of the story action. As a further advantage, indirect characterization gives the reader the satisfaction of drawing his own conclusions by reading between the lines.

> Mary Jane came skipping down the steps, humming to herself.
> I looked up to see Susan rearranging the flowers on the table. "Why, I didn't even hear you come downstairs," I said.

Methods of Characterization

You can use five basic methods to accomplish your goal of indirect characterization. Not every story will include all five; but as you write, you should look for ways to include as many of them as possible.

1. *Show the character's actions.* Jesus said, "By their fruits ye shall know them." A character's actions are a significant part of that fruit. Carefully chosen words that show how a character walks, works, plays, or drives can paint vivid pictures of your character's traits. A proud person would strut down the sidewalk, while a rebellious person might swagger and a determined person might stride. A careful driver will accelerate smoothly and use his turn signals, but a hostile one might go roaring down the road with his tires squealing.

2. *Show the character's speech.* Again Jesus said, "Out of the abundance of the heart the mouth speaketh." In similar circumstances, one character might complain while another gives thanks, thus displaying contrasting character traits. A character who uses polite, respectful, or gracious words reveals much about his true self.

In addition to *what* a character says, the explanatory words that tell *how* he spoke are also revealing. Compare the following examples. What does each one reveal about the speaker?

> "I'll show him what happens to people who cross my path," growled the man.
>
> "We must forgive as Christ did," the man said gently. "We must always forgive."

3. *Show the character's thoughts.* This method is used far less than the previous two. In fact, many stories do not show the characters' thoughts at all. But thoughts are one of the best indicators of what a character is really like. "As [a man] thinketh in his heart, so is he."

In the following paragraph from the second sample story, the main character's thoughts reveal her tendency to be anxious and fearful.

> My mind whirled into high gear. "Of course, I dearly love Grandmother," I thought. "But would she want me to come if she knew how insecure I feel sometimes? What if I can't fit into her schedule? What if . . ."

4. *Show the character's appearance.* Again, this method is used only occasionally. But a passing comment about a character's tousled or neatly combed hair, about his dirty or clean clothes, or about his stern or friendly face can certainly add to the total picture of a character's inner traits.

5. *Show the character's reputation.* This method is used the most infrequently of all. However, the words and actions of others in relation to a certain character can help the reader to understand that character and see why other characters respond to him as they do. Consider the following example from the Book of Acts.

> And there was a certain disciple at Damascus, named Ananias; and to him said the Lord in a vision, Ananias. And he said, Behold, I am here, Lord.
>
> And the Lord said unto him, Arise, and go into the street which is called Straight, and enquire in the house of Judas for one called Saul, of Tarsus: for, behold, he prayeth. . . .
>
> Then Ananias answered, Lord, I have heard by many of this man, how much evil he hath done to thy saints at Jerusalem: and here he hath authority from the chief priests to bind all that call on thy name.
>
> But the Lord said unto him, Go thy way: for he is a chosen vessel unto me, to bear my name before the Gentiles, and kings, and the children of Israel.

We know that a person's reputation is not a foolproof indicator of his character. A reputation may match a person's true character, or it may not (as in the example above). And a skillful writer can make good use of this very fact. The contrast between a character's reputation and his true self can make a strong impression about that character.

Know Your Characters Well

Obviously, if you are to portray your story characters effectively, you must know them well before you write the first sentence of the story. If the story is about real people whom you know, choose one or two specific traits that best match your story theme. Then stick to them, and emphasize only those traits. If your story is fiction, you must gain a clear mental image of the characters that will make up the story. Visualize the kinds of persons who will develop your theme effectively. Then list details about each major and minor character's appearance and inner traits to make them true to life.

Be sure to keep these details consistent. Some of the details in your list will never be mentioned in the story. But you still need to write them down so that you yourself will have a well-rounded picture of the characters. Unless you have such a picture, you may write something inconsistent about a character without even realizing it.

Applying the Lesson

A. Do these exercises.
1. What is characterization?
2. Explain the terms *protagonist* and *antagonist.*
3. Write *major, minor,* or *background* to tell which class of characters fits each description.
    a. Should be named but not characterized very much.
    b. Should be no more than three in number.
    c. Should be characterized fully.
    d. Are often grouped together.
    e. Have an effect on the conflict, but do not carry it.
    f. Are part of the setting rather than the conflict.
    g. Carry the development of the conflict.
4. What is the difference between direct and indirect characterization?
5. Which two methods of characterization should you use in every story?
6. Name three other methods that you might use occasionally.

B. Do these exercises on the sample story "Terry's Temper" in Lesson 49.
1. List all the story characters, grouped in the three classes.
2. Give specific example details that characterize Terry, as indicated below.
    a. Two examples of action. (Identify each one, and describe the trait revealed.)
    b. Three examples of speech. (Identify each one, and describe the trait revealed.)
    c. One example of thoughts. (Identify it, and describe the trait revealed.)
    d. Two examples of appearance. (Identify each one, and describe the trait revealed.)
3. Give specific examples that characterize the following characters, as indicated below. Your answers should follow the same pattern as in exercise 2.
    a. Walter: one example each of action and appearance.
    b. Father: one example each of speech and appearance.

    d. (Any two. Traits revealed will vary.)
    His hair was well combed—carefulness.
    His face was red and grim—frustration.
    His face looked like a thundercloud—anger.
    He looked sheepishly at Walter—shame.
3. a. (Sample answers. Traits revealed will vary.)
    Action: He forgot to shut the feed bin door—thoughtlessness.
    Action: He worked rather slowly—sluggishness.
    Appearance: His hair was unkempt—thoughtlessness.
    b. (Sample answers. Traits revealed will vary.)
    Speech: He spoke sternly—sternness.
    Speech: He explained Terry's problem to him—concern.
    Speech: He commended Terry for his victory—goodwill.
    Appearance: His eyes looked kind—kindheartedness.

Lesson 52 Answers
Applying the Lesson
A. 1. the process of portraying a story character
2. The protagonist is the main character, and the antagonist is the character that opposes him.
3. a. minor   e. minor
   b. major   f. background
   c. major   g. major
   d. background
4. In direct characterization, the writer uses adjectives to describe a character directly.
   In indirect characterization, he uses the character's words and actions to show what he is like.
5. actions and speech
6. thoughts, appearance, and reputation

B. 1. *Major:* Terry
   Minor: Walter, Father
   Background: the girls
   (Mother may be listed as a minor or background character.)
2. a. (Any two. Traits revealed will vary.)
   He pushed the mower resolutely—displeasure.
   He yanked the starter cord so hard that it tore—impatience.
   He stalked across the lawn—disgust.
   He stalked away from Walter—anger.
   His hands were clenched and his jaw set—anger.
   b. (Any three. Traits revealed will vary.)
   He said the mower belonged on the junk heap—disgust.
   He muttered to himself as he walked away—disgust.
   He scolded Walter—impatience.
   He said that Walter was always forgetting to close the door—unkindness.
   He threw his words over his shoulder—anger.
   He said he should make Walter clean up the mess by himself—anger.
   He gave a sharp retort when Walter said the heifers were having fun—impatience.
   c. (Any one. Other traits may be correct.)
   He thought uncomfortably that he should calm down—guilt.
   In his mind he saw Father's serious but kind face and heard Father's words—shame.

C. Do these exercises on the story "'He Rides Upon the Storm'" in Lesson 49.
  1. List all the story characters, grouped in the three classes.
  2. Give specific examples that characterize Wanda, as indicated below.
    a. Two examples of action.
    b. Three examples of speech.
    c. Three examples of thoughts.
    d. One example of reputation.
  3. Give specific examples that characterize the following persons, as indicated.
    a. Mother: two examples of speech.
    b. Alta: one example of action and two examples of speech.

---

53. The Point of View and Plot of a Story

Two different artists painting the same farm could produce pictures that look quite different. How is that? Suppose one painter stood to the northwest on a small hill, and the other stood to the southeast at a place level with the farm. Their pictures might look so different that you could hardly recognize them as portraying the same place.

Likewise, two people could tell entirely different stories about the same event. The story told by a ten-year-old child would be so different from that of a forty-year-old father, that it might be hard to imagine how they could represent the same incident. In both illustrations, the contrast results from a difference in the painters' or storytellers' point of view.

Point of View

Every story is written from a certain perspective, or *point of view.* The three most common points of view are first person, third person, and omniscient.

1. *First person point of view.* With this viewpoint, the main character is the author himself. He uses first person pronouns like *I, me, us,* and *our* in referring to himself; and the reader may not find out what his name is in the story until another character speaks to him. Of course, other characters may also use *I* and *me* in direct quotations, but then the pronouns do not refer to the storyteller.

The main advantage of the first person point of view is its strong impression of reality. The writer has firsthand information. He was really there. On the other hand, this point of view also has several disadvantages because the writer must limit himself to the view of the character-narrator. First, he can include only what this character (the *I* in the story) can realistically see, hear, or know. Second, since the main character is the narrator, he has the difficulty of portraying his good qualities without appearing to be proud.

The story "'He Rides Upon the Storm'" (Lesson 49) is written from the first person point of view. The narrator is the main character, Wanda. The story reveals Wanda's thoughts several times, but it does not reveal any other character's

C. 1. *Major:* Wanda
    Minor: Mother, Grandmother, Alta, strange man
    Background: Uncle Ralph, Father, Aunt Mattie
  2. a. (Any two.)
      She cut the apples into neat halves.
      She burst into the kitchen.
      She closed her eyes and shivered during the storm.
      She climbed out of bed hesitantly.
    b. (Any three.)
      Her words showed anxiety and hesitation.
      She wailed, "Whatever will we do?"
      She admitted her need to trust the Lord more.
      She wondered if Alta was not afraid of the storm.
    c. (Any three.)
      Her mind whirled into high gear, full of anxious questions.
      She recognized that God had blessed her trust.
      She prayed for the ability to trust the Lord more.
    d. Grandmother considered her dependable.
  3. a. She spoke steadily.
      Her voice held a tone of humor.
    b. *Action:* She watched the thunderstorm with calm interest.
      Speech: (Any two.)
        She told Wanda that they would trust the Lord.
        She spoke politely to the strange man.
        She reminded Wanda that God was caring for them.
        She spoke of the thunderstorm as a display of God's power.

Lesson 53

Purpose: To introduce *three common points of view used in short stories, and to describe the *two kinds of plots in short stories.

thoughts. What you know of the other characters is only what Wanda herself can observe. So the author can write the first of the example sentences below; for as Wanda saw it, Alta did seem to be enjoying the scene. In contrast, the author would not have been consistent if he had presented any detail from Alta's viewpoint, as in the second example below.

Consistent with first person point of view:
There stood Alta at the window, apparently enjoying the scene.
Not consistent with first person point of view:
There stood Alta at the window, pondering the greatness of God.

2. *Third person point of view.* This is like the first person point of view in that the author must limit himself to the viewpoint of the main character in the story. He must always stay at that character's side, as it were, portraying the things he observes but omitting anything he cannot observe. Because the author is not writing about himself, he can more easily reveal the good qualities of the main character.

The story "Terry's Temper" (Lesson 49) is written from the third person point of view. This story is portrayed through Terry's eyes. What you know of the other characters is totally from Terry's viewpoint. So the author can write the first example sentence below, but not the second.

Consistent with third person (Terry's) point of view:
"Better calm down a bit," Terry thought uncomfortably as he neared the shop.
Not consistent with third person (Terry's) point of view:
"I forgot to shut the door," thought Walter.

3. *Omniscient point of view.* With this viewpoint, the author writes as an outside observer, seeing everything as God does in the real world. Since the happenings are not presented as seen through any one character's eyes, the author has the advantage of being able to describe events at various places. For example, he may describe what is happening at home while Mother is in the hospital. Then he might change the scene to the hospital and show what is happening there. However, this viewpoint tends to be impersonal because it does not bring the reader to identify with any character in the story.

The following examples illustrate how the same incident can be presented with these three different viewpoints.

First person:
I picked up the telephone and dialed Mrs. Perry's number. "Hello," came our neighbor's voice across the line. She sounded more cheerful than when I had called the day before.

Third person:
Cheryl picked up the telephone and dialed Mrs. Perry's number. "Hello," came the neighbor's voice across the line. She sounded more cheerful than when Cheryl had called the day before.

Omniscient:

Cheryl picked up the telephone and dialed Mrs. Perry's number. "Hello," the neighbor lady answered brightly. She had just come inside from a walk in the bright spring sunshine, and she was feeling more cheerful than usual.

4. *Subjective and objective viewpoints.* The third person and the omniscient viewpoints can be either subjective or objective. With the third person subjective point of view, the author sees into the mind of the one character through whose eyes the story unfolds. He reveals the thoughts of that character but not of any other character in the story.

With the third person objective point of view, the author does not see into the mind of any character. He goes with the main character through the story, portraying his words and actions but not his thoughts. Since it is difficult to write in this way, very few stories represent the third person objective point of view.

With the omniscient subjective point of view, the author writes about the thoughts of any character. If he uses the objective approach, he does not write about any character's thoughts.

The sample story "Terry's Temper" is written in the third person subjective point of view. The following examples show a portion of that story written in two other viewpoints. Compare the underlined words with the sample story.

Omniscient subjective:

"Stop! Stop!" Walter's urgent shouts jolted Terry like an electric shock. "The feed is pouring out on the barn floor," Walter gasped. "Because I forgot to shut the door," he thought. "Wonder what Terry will say now?"

Quickly Terry pulled the lever, stopping the auger. "Walter Jay Gehman! Of all things! You're always forgetting to close the door!". . .

Terry was back in a few minutes. "Come on, shovel faster!" he snapped at his brother. To himself he fumed, "I ought to make him clean it up alone."

Omniscient objective:

"Stop! Stop!" Walter's urgent shouts made Terry jump. "The feed is pouring out on the barn floor," Walter gasped. "I forgot to shut the door."

Quickly Terry pulled the lever, stopping the auger. "Walter Jay Gehman! Of all things! You're always forgetting to close the door!". . .

Terry was back in a few minutes. "Come on, shovel faster!" he snapped at his brother. "I ought to make you clean it up alone."

The following chart summarizes the points of view that stories can have.

First Person	Limited to the viewpoint of the author, who is the main character. Uses the pronouns *I* and *me*. Gives a strong impression of reality.
Third Person	Limited to the viewpoint of the main character. Can reveal the main character's good qualities. *Subjective:* Reveals the thoughts of the main character only. *Objective:* Does not reveal the thoughts of any character.
Omniscient	Views happenings as an outside observer. Tends to be impersonal. *Subjective:* Reveals the thoughts of any character. *Objective:* Does not reveal the thoughts of any character.

Plot

A short story should develop a plot. The plot is the overall development of the story conflict. Most short stories have either a complication plot or a loose plot.

With a ***complication plot,*** the conflict builds up to a definite climax. This is the type of conflict that you worked with in the previous books of this series. The story "Terry's Temper" illustrates the complication plot. Below is a brief outline of a complication plot.

1. A brief beginning introduces the main character, establishes the setting, and presents an opening problem that hints at the theme.
2. The middle includes the main part of the story. The main character faces his conflict in a series of episodes, each increasing the suspense. The suspense builds to the climax, in which the main character either prevails or fails.
3. A brief conclusion shows the outcome of the conflict and leaves the main character with the results of his climaxing decision.

With a ***loose plot,*** the conflict moves through several incidents relating to the problem in the story, without building to a definite climax. The story "'He Rides Upon the Storm'" illustrates the loose plot.

A story with either kind of plot has a beginning, a middle, and a conclusion. With the loose plot, however, there is only a loose connection between the incidents in the middle of the story. Each incident also resembles a miniature story in itself, with the conflict basically resolved before the story moves on. The loose plot tends to represent real life more accurately than the complication plot, for most everyday problems do not involve a buildup that parallels a complication plot in a short story.

Applying the Lesson

A. Do these exercises.

1. What is meant by the point of view of a story?
2. Write *first, third,* or *omniscient* to identify the point of view described by each statement. For some, you will need to write two answers.
   a. The author writes as if he is constantly with a certain character in the story.
   b. The main character is the author himself.
   c. The author writes as if he can see all aspects of the story at once.
   d. The story seems especially realistic because it shows what the author actually observed.
   e. The author can write either subjectively or objectively.
   f. The author may find it awkward to portray the main character's good qualities.
   g. The main character's actual name may be hard to find.
   h. The author is limited to one character's perspective.
3. What is the difference between a subjective and an objective point of view?
4. What is the plot of a short story?
5. Write *complication, loose,* or *both* to tell which kind of plot is described in each statement.
   a. The story has a beginning, middle, and conclusion.
   b. The story is particularly true to life.
   c. Each incident increases the buildup of suspense.
   d. Each incident resembles a miniature story.

B. Name the point of view used in each of these excerpts. Include *objective* or *subjective* if it applies.

1.   "You could never guess who I saw in town last week." My sister Millie dropped this challenge into the middle of our chicken-dressing project. Her eyes were sober when she raised them to mine.

   I paused for a moment with my knife in midair. "No, I probably couldn't. How about a hint?"

   "I saw an old friend of yours; one you haven't seen for years. And it wouldn't make you happy to see her now."

2.   "So it's true!" Alvin mused as he lay across his bed, his thoughts going back to the close of the prayer service held that evening. He thought again of Brother Mark's announcement that the Martin Weaver family would soon move to the new area into which their congregation was expanding.

   "That means Titus and I won't be together as much," he realized. "Forty miles really isn't very close—" He stopped as a new thought dawned upon him. "Brother Mark mentioned that an ordained brother would be asked to move there also! What if that is Uncle Wilbur's? If they move, no other boy my age will live here anymore!"

Lesson 53 Answers

Applying the Lesson

A. 1. the perspective from which the story is written
   2. a. third   e. third, omniscient
      b. first   f. first
      c. omniscient   g. first
      d. first   h. first, third
   3. Story characters' thoughts are revealed in a subjective point of view but not in an objective point of view.
   4. the overall development of the story conflict
   5. a. both   c. complication
      b. loose   d. loose

   Teacher: You may wish to identify different kinds of story plots in Rod and Staff's Eighth Reader. Stories with complication plots include Lesson 1 ("The Dime Store Cotton") and Lesson 46 ("We'll Let Them Borrow"). Stories with loose plots include Lesson 12 ("Micha's Thanks") and Lesson 32 ("The Boy and Hushwing").

B. 1. first
   2. third person, subjective

3.   "Will you come out to church some Sunday?" Faith invited. "We would be happy to have you." For a moment Joyce again stared dumbfounded and then replied, "I have a church to attend." . . .

After walking up and down the hospital hallway a few minutes to relieve tired, aching muscles, Faith returned to her room and spent the day with her mother, and in prayer for Joyce. "Help her find the way. Give me more opportunities and the right words to speak," she prayed. Joyce's troubled face had impressed her with the deep need in her life, the unsatisfied longings, and the lack of peace with God. . . .

At home that evening, Joyce felt restless and discontented. A new longing possessed her to find the way to God. An entirely new concept of God had been awakened in her heart. . . .

Joyce's thoughts were in a turmoil. "She's just trying to convert me to her religion," she decided.

4.   An hour later Calvin was again on the steps at the side porch. "We're finished now," he announced when Dorie came to the door. "And here's the bill."

"What!" exclaimed Dorie. "It's higher than last time."

"That's because we trimmed the hedge this time," reminded Calvin gently.

"Well, okay then; just wait a minute till I get the money." When she returned, she handed the money to Calvin and then closed the door without a word.

The boys loaded their equipment and soon left. But Lloyd, the boys' employer, received a call from Dorie Baner just a few hours later.

"Those boys of yours!" she said angrily. "They can do all right sometimes, but this time they didn't. I just knew there couldn't be any boys around that are always good as gold!"

C. Read this story, and do the exercises after it.

Twenty Pounds

"Grandmother is very sick, and I must go over to stay with her," Mother told the children.

"Please take us all along. We can sleep on the kitchen floor," twelve-year-old Timothy pleaded.

"No, son, not this time," Mother said firmly. "You must be brave. You are the oldest. Little Joseph is too sick to be taken out on a cold night like this, and the girls are scarcely over the whooping cough. You must stay at home and help Donna take care of the little ones."

The two oldest children listened attentively to the directions and sadly nodded their heads.

"Remember, God is with you," Mother whispered as she went to the door after the four youngest had fallen asleep. "Now you two go to bed and try to sleep. I will be only a few hundred yards away. If anything

3. omniscient, subjective

4. omniscient, objective

happens so that I need to come home, just turn the porch light on, and I should soon see it. I am sure I won't sleep much, the way Grandmother is."

"If only their father were with us, how different it would be," Mother thought wistfully as she went on her way. Her faithful Christian husband had died two years earlier.

The night hours dragged, and the sick woman did not sleep much. Toward morning she became more rational but also weaker. Her voice was scarcely more than a whisper.

"Marla," the sick woman called tremulously, "I will not be here much longer. God has been good to me. Trust Him. He has been my faithful companion, and He will be yours." Her eyes rested lovingly on her only daughter. "I know you have seen hard times and will likely see more. I have nothing to leave you but this small house with the half acre of land. Maybe you will be able to sell or rent it to someone."

Marla knew it was doubtful that anyone would buy or even rent the small rundown, two-room house so near their own.

"Marla," her mother continued when she had rallied enough strength to talk more, "over there on the table is a coffee can; in it you will find a twenty-pound note. It has been dedicated to the Lord. Take it to the bank, cash it, and send the money to that faithful little mission in Scotland. God laid it on my heart to send it to them. I know you could use it, but it is the Lord's money. Send it as I have requested, and the Lord will return it to you a hundredfold."

"Twenty pounds!" thought Marla. "My mother does not know that her own dear grandchildren have not had sufficient food these past months, that there is no food in the house for breakfast and no flour to bake bread, and that they haven't had milk or eggs for weeks. If only I could ask her to lend it to me to feed my family, just until I could earn enough to pay it back."

Marla waited quietly for her mother to finish her instructions, but that was all. She lay perfectly motionless. Marla bent forward. Her mother was not breathing; she had quietly slipped away to her reward.

The first streaks of red were glowing in the eastern sky as Marla softly pulled the covers up over the dear form on the bed, so lifeless and still. She tiptoed out of the room and closed the door. Tears streamed down her cheeks as she hurried home.

The children were all sleeping quietly when she arrived. As Marla gazed upon their peaceful faces, the note came again to her mind. "Twenty pounds! Would it be wrong to keep it? Could the mission in Scotland possibly need it as badly as my own family does? Couldn't they wait? Surely sometime I could pay it back."

Softly Mother called, "Timothy, Timothy."

The lad stirred on his cot beside Joseph's crib.

"Come out in the hall so we don't wake the baby," Mother said as the boy sat up and rubbed his eyes.

Donna awoke too and joined them in the hall, stretching and yawning sleepily. "Is it morning?" she asked.

"Yes," replied Mother. "Grandmother suffered a lot and was very weak. Early this morning God took her home to her eternal reward.

"Timothy," Mother added, "I want you to harness Old Steady and ride over to the Millers. They are our nearest neighbors who have a telephone. I'll write them a note, telling them whom I want them to call about Grandmother. Donna, when the children awake, dress them and tell them that Mother will soon be home with some breakfast for them," Mother instructed as she prepared to return to Grandmother's little cottage.

At Grandmother's house, Mother looked around and sized up the situation. She and Timothy could carry Grandmother's cot over for Donna to sleep on so that all four girls would not have to sleep in one bed. Then there was Grandmother's old rocker and the table. Oh, yes, there was the coffee can. She must take care of the twenty-pound note.

"Twenty pounds!" Mother sighed wistfully. Her mind pictured the milk and eggs and flour and many other things her family desperately needed. "Oh, what shall I do?" her troubled thoughts raced. "Is it right to neglect my dear children? Couldn't I use the money for now and give it to the mission later?"

"No, this will never do." Quickly Mother stuffed the twenty-pound note into her apron pocket. Of course, she would obey her mother's parting instructions.

"The Lord will return it to you a hundredfold," Grandmother had said. That was hard to understand.

Immediately after breakfast, Mother saddled Old Steady and hurried into town. In obedience to her mother's directions, she obtained a money order for the twenty pounds and sent it to the mission in Scotland. She never told the children about that money or the gift to Scotland.

Work was not easy to find, and the family's condition grew worse. The children tried to help all they could. Mother often thought of her own mother's last words: "I know you could use it, but it is the Lord's money. Send it as I have requested, and the Lord will return it to you a hundredfold."

Mother's heart was broken when Timothy rejected her faith, took his own way, and joined the army. "I can't find any way to help you support the family here. At least this way you will have one less mouth to feed," he justified himself.

The sad and weary mother grieved and wept and slaved for the sake of her children. She prayed constantly for Timothy, as her wayward son was traveling somewhere far away. She had not heard from him for many months.

She often envisioned that little piece of paper, a money order dated 1935, sent to the mission in Scotland. Oh, how she needed that money! As time went on and things grew worse, doubts stormed her mind. "Did I do the right thing? If only I had that twenty pounds now!" Often she did not know which way to turn, but God always supplied their need in some way.

One day a letter came, postmarked in Scotland. Mother's mind turned immediately to the faithful mission in Scotland and, along with it, to the twenty-pound note. The handwriting looked familiar.

Inside was a single sheet. Her eyes ran quickly to the signature at the bottom. *Timothy* stood out in bold letters, along with *Mother, I love you.*

Her heart leaped for joy as her oldest son explained how he had come under conviction after he had wandered into a little mission in Scotland. There the truth of God's Word was taught exactly as his own dear mother had taught him at home, and there he had received salvation. Timothy would soon be returning home.

The last paragraph especially gripped her attention. "Mother, this little mission has been here for fifty years," wrote Timothy. "They told me it nearly closed down nine years ago. The country was in such desperate straits, and there was no money to pay the rent to keep the mission open. The pastor wept and prayed all night, pleading with God for funds to keep it open. Many souls had been saved there. He asked God for the twenty pounds they needed, and God sent it from some foreign country—he couldn't remember where—but he knew it was sent from God to keep the mission open. He said, 'Had that twenty-pound money order not arrived in the winter of 1935, there would be no mission here today.' Suppose it had been closed," he added. "I wouldn't be writing this letter today."

The letter ended with these words: "I thank God for that faithful giver who lives somewhere, though I will probably never know who it was."

Mother felt that she could stand no more. Her joy overflowed in tears of humility and gratitude. A twenty-pound money order in the winter of 1935, sent to the mission in Scotland! A son saved, for whom she had labored in tears and prayers! And her mother's words!—"Send it as I have requested, and the Lord will return it to you a hundredfold."

"Ah, my dear mother could have said a millionfold, and that would not have been enough," said Mother. "For this one soul is worth more than the whole world."

1. Identify the point of view from which the story is written. Include *subjective* or *objective* if it applies.
2. Choose the letters of the three main incidents of conflict in the story. Also write the letter of the climax, and circle it.
   a. Mother thinks of her faithful husband and wishes he were still with her.
   b. Mother is tempted to keep the twenty pounds immediately after Grandmother's death.
   c. Mother needs to tell the children about Grandmother's death.
   d. Mother is tempted to keep the twenty pounds when she gathers some of Grandmother's things for her family.

C. 1. third person, subjective
   2. b, d, g; (h)

e. Mother sends the twenty pounds to the mission in Scotland.

f. Mother is heartbroken when Timothy rejects her faith and joins the army.

g. Mother struggles for years with doubts about the twenty pounds sent to the mission.

h. Mother's doubts melt away when she learns of how the twenty pounds contributed to her son's salvation.

i. Mother acknowledges that one soul is worth more than the whole world.

---

54. Developing a General Plan for a Story

Now that you have studied the different aspects of a short story, it is time to put your understanding into practice. Before you begin writing, however, you must make a plan. This lesson will guide you in writing a general plan for your story. In the next lesson, you will fill in the details.

Follow these steps in developing a general plan for a short story. Refer to the first sample story in Lesson 49, "Terry's Temper," as you study these steps.

1. *Write a theme for your story.* If you are writing a factually based story, you must determine what particular theme (perhaps out of several possibilities) you want to emphasize. If your story is fiction, choosing a theme is a good place to begin. In either case, you must have a definite goal for the story if you expect to write something worthwhile.

This statement of your theme will never actually appear in the finished product, but it is essential to the unity of the story. Then as you plan and write, you should review your theme several times. Otherwise, your story is likely to wander from that theme.

The theme of "Terry's Temper" may be stated like this:

Theme:
   Learning to control one's temper is an important part of maturing emotionally and spiritually.

2. *Determine the age level of your reading audience.* You need to do this because the main character should usually be about the same age as the readers for whom you write the story. In your school assignments, you will write to your own age level unless otherwise directed. You are naturally most familiar with the interests and characteristics of your own age group.

Writing for children of a younger age level is a special challenge. You need to thoroughly familiarize yourself with their mannerisms and vocabulary. Give your descriptions of the appearance and behavior of children on their own level, not as it appears to you. For example, be careful about calling them *little, cute, silly,* and so forth. Children like to think of themselves as big, and they do *not* consider themselves silly.

Lesson 54

Purpose: To teach a simple, practical way to plan the basic framework of a story.

Teaching Suggestions:

Be sure to look over the next lesson before teaching this lesson. You should have a good understanding of both the general plan and the detailed plan in order to present this lesson most effectively.

Whether you write to your own age level or to a different age level, you must plan and write consistently. Ask yourself frequently, "Will my readers be able to involve themselves in this story?" The age level for the first sample story may be written like this:

Age level:
early and mid teens

3. *Determine the basic identity of the major characters.* With rare exceptions, you should put the main character on the age level of your intended audience. This is an important part of aiming your story at your audience. Do not attempt to describe these characters at this point. In fact, you need not even name them now.

The basic identity of the major characters in the first sample story may be written as follows:

Major characters:
a fifteen-year-old boy, his twelve-year-old brother, and his father

4. *Decide from what point of view you will write the story.* Consider the advantages and disadvantages of each point of view that you studied in Lesson 53; they are summarized below. Also decide whether you want your story to be subjective or objective.

First person:
Gives strong impression of reality; limits writer to one character's viewpoint; makes it difficult to portray the main character's good qualities.
Third person:
Limits writer to one character's viewpoint; makes it easier to portray the main character's good qualities.
Omniscient:
Allows writer to report on different characters at various places; does not bring the reader to identify with any character in the story.

5. *Write a sentence summarizing the conflict.* This sentence should not describe the individual incidents in the conflict; it should merely give a general view of the conflict. A suitable conflict must be typical of the age level you are writing to. It should also appear difficult for the main character to handle. Remember that a suitable conflict does not need to be something unusual or dramatic. Here is a statement of conflict for the first sample story.

Conflict:
Terry struggles to overcome his tendency to become angry when things do not go as he wishes.

Developing a general plan like this will force you to take an overall view of your story. This overall view, in turn, will help you to produce a unified, smooth-flowing story. The following example brings together all the points in the general plan for the first sample story.

Theme:
>   Learning to control one's temper is an important part of maturing emotionally and spiritually.

Age level:
>   early and mid teens

Main character:
>   a fifteen-year-old boy

Other major characters:
>   boy's twelve-year-old brother and boy's father

Point of view:
>   third person, subjective

Conflict:
>   Terry struggles to overcome his tendency to become angry when things do not go as he wishes.

Applying the Lesson

Write a general plan for the story possibility you chose in Lesson 49, which will be the basis of a story that you will write in this chapter.

Lesson 54 Answers
(Individual work.)

---

55. Planning the Details of a Story

The general plan you developed in Lesson 54 represents an important beginning to your story writing. But you still are not ready to write the actual story. You need to do the more detailed planning that this lesson describes.

Use the following steps to plan the details of your short story.

1. *Write descriptions of all the major characters.* For each character, you will make two lists. In the first one, list some details about the character's appearance. Look each character over carefully in your mind's eye, and then describe him in detail. Is he tall or short? muscular or slight? What color is his hair? Is it neatly combed? Not all of these details will receive even a passing comment in the story, but you should list them to give yourself a well-rounded view of your character, especially if the story is fictitious.

In your second list, write some traits of inner character. Is the person shy? impulsive? greedy? diligent? honest? The more familiar you are with the characters of your story, the more realistically you will be able to have them act in the story. Be careful, though. The traits you list must give a consistent picture of a real-life or true-to-life individual.

If your characters are real people whom you know, this step may be quite easy. However, you could consider changing some details about a character's appearance or even his inner traits if you wish to conceal the true identity of the characters. If they are fictitious, you will need to spend extra time learning to know them in your mind.

Lesson 55

Purpose: To teach how to write a detailed plan of a story.

Here is this part of the detailed plan for the first sample story, "Terry's Temper."

Appearance:	Inner traits:
Light brown hair	Diligent
Blue eyes	Tends toward being perfectionistic
Strong, muscular build	Not very talkative
Medium height	Sensitive

2. *Plan the opening.* Write a short description of the setting. Include the time, place, and atmosphere. Briefly describe the opening scene. Begin as near to the first scene of conflict as possible. Remember, you can often include important background information in a flashback more effectively than in the opening. And do not forget to hint at the theme and the conflict of the story.

Here is a plan for the opening of the first sample story.

Setting:
> A south-central Pennsylvania farm, on a pleasant day in mid-May. A fine Christian family atmosphere.

Opening scene:
> Terry and Walter are outside on the first day of summer vacation. Terry comments that the lawn needs to be mowed and then that their worn-out mower might not last the whole season.

3. *Plan each scene in the conflict.* In a brief paragraph, describe the basic events of each scene and the outcome of that scene. Be sure these incidents grow directly out of the conflict, that they develop the theme, and that they reveal the characters' traits. If you are using a complication plot, arrange the scenes in order of increasing importance to the final outcome and of increasing difficulty for the main character to solve.

Give special attention to the climaxing scene, for this is the most critical point in the story. At this point, the main character makes his final decision for or against the right course. Here is a plan for the scenes of conflict in the first sample story.

Incident 1:
> The mower quits working before Terry finishes mowing. He becomes angry and jerks the starter cord so hard that it tears.

Incident 2:
> Walter forgets to close the door to the feed bin chute after emptying the bin. When Terry tries to fill the bin, a huge pile of feed spills out on the barn floor. Terry scolds his brother harshly, but Father hears him and rebukes him.

Incident 3:
> The heifers get out and give Terry and Walter quite a chase. Terry is strongly tempted to become angry, but he overcomes the temptation and responds properly.

4. *Plan the ending.* Briefly describe the main character's actions in carrying out the climaxing decision. Then in closing, describe the final outcome. Show and impress upon the reader the story theme through the main character's responses. If any important questions about the major characters have not been answered, briefly dispose of them. Do not include distracting remarks about minor characters or about later events involving the main character.

Here is a plan for the ending of the first sample story.

Ending:
> Father comes home just as the boys are getting the last heifer back in. He commends Terry for keeping his temper under control.

Below is the complete plan for the details in the sample story "Terry's Temper."

Appearance:	**Inner traits:**
Light brown hair	Diligent
Blue eyes	Tends toward being perfectionistic
Strong, muscular build	Not very talkative
Medium height	Sensitive

Setting:
> A south-central Pennsylvania farm, on a pleasant day in mid-May. A fine Christian family atmosphere.

Opening scene:
> Terry and Walter are outside on the first day of summer vacation. Terry comments that the lawn needs to be mowed and then that their worn-out mower might not last the whole season.

Incident 1:
> The mower quits working before Terry finishes mowing. He becomes angry and jerks the starter cord so hard that it tears.

Incident 2:
> Walter forgets to close the door to the feed bin chute after emptying the bin. When Terry tries to fill the bin, a huge pile of feed spills out on the barn floor. Terry scolds his brother harshly, but Father hears him and rebukes him.

Incident 3:
> The heifers get out and give Terry and Walter quite a chase. Terry is strongly tempted to become angry, but he overcomes the temptation and responds properly.

Ending:
> Father comes home just as the boys are getting the last heifer back in. He commends Terry for keeping his temper under control.

Applying the Lesson
Write a detailed plan for your story, following the steps in this lesson.

Lesson 55 Answers
(Individual work.)

56. Writing a Story

Now that you have planned your story in detail, you are ready to write. But remember that your plan is a guide, not a set of ironclad rules. You may well discover in the actual writing process that you need to add or delete ideas in some parts of the story. You may find that the incidents are not in the best order and should be rearranged. You may even decide that a certain incident in the story needs to be completely reworked. Make whatever changes are needed, shaping and reshaping the story as you work.

Use the following steps in writing your story.

1. *Write your opening scene.* If the first paragraph is dull, a reader may lay your story aside without even reading it. So begin with action, dialogue, or an unusual statement. Read again the opening paragraphs from the two sample stories in Lesson 49. Notice how each one begins.

Begins with dialogue:

"Three months to enjoy the farm!" Terry voiced his thoughts to twelve-year-old Walter. The previous day had marked the last day of his ninth year in school. A pleasant mid-May sun smiled on the lush growth of grass. Terry took deep breaths of the fresh, exhilarating air. Brushing his hand across his well-combed hair, he glanced at Walter's unkempt hair.

Begins with an unusual statement:

My hands were mechanically cutting apples into neat halves when Mother's words burst into my thoughts. "Grandmother Fry called this morning. She asked if it would suit for you to spend the weekend with her. She said you help her to feel secure because she knows you are dependable. There'll be no school Friday, so you could go on Thursday evening. We'd pick you up again on Sunday afternoon."

Besides attracting attention and interest, the opening paragraphs should also introduce the main character. In fact, the first character to speak, to do something, or to be introduced should usually be the main character. Look again at the opening paragraphs in the examples above. The main character is speaking in the first example and acting in the second.

Sometimes the opening paragraphs weave in a few details of the setting. In the first example, you learn that the story occurs on a farm in mid-May. In the second example, you can deduct that the story occurs in a kitchen (that is the most likely place to be cutting apples into halves) in the fall (apples are a fall crop and school has begun). The second example also hints at the emotional mood by using the words *mechanically* and *burst.*

2. *Write the scenes in the conflict.* Be careful to characterize the story characters consistently. Refer to your detailed descriptions of the major characters before writing each incident in the conflict. Keep asking yourself, "Are these characters' words, actions, and appearances consistent with the way I have described them?"

Provide smooth transitions from one incident to the next. For example, in the story "Terry's Temper," the second incident begins with the words "One morning several

Lesson 56

Purpose: To review how to write the first draft of a story.

Teaching Suggestions:

Give any pointers needed as your students work on their stories. Note that they will be writing only the first draft in this chapter. The second draft will not be assigned until the end of Chapter 8, which teaches various methods for improving stories. You may wish to collect the first drafts and file them for use in Chapter 8.

Note: Chapter 7 is intended to provide a break in the work on stories. If you prefer not to have a break, you may go directly from Chapter 6 to Chapter 8, and study Chapter 7 later.

days later." This shows the relationship between the two incidents. The third incident begins with the words "The following day." In the story "'He Rides Upon the Storm,'" the second incident begins with the words "The following Saturday." And the third incident begins with the words "That very night." Each of these transitions helps the reader to move from one incident to the next without confusion.

Use occasional flashbacks to provide important background information. "'He Rides Upon the Storm'" has a flashback at the beginning of the second incident. It is underlined in the following excerpt.

> The following Saturday, I hurried from the flower bed I was weeding and burst into the kitchen. "Alta," I gasped, "there's a man coming in the lane. A bushy-haired, scary-looking man! Whatever will we do?" I wailed.
>
> Father's parting words flashed across my mind: <u>"Well, Alta, you'll be in charge for a few hours. Wanda, you pitch in and help take care of the little ones. In case of an emergency, call Uncle Ralph's. Above all, trust in the Lord." Then he and Mother had left to visit Aunt Mattie in the hospital.</u>
>
> Alta glanced out the window. "We'll trust the Lord," she said. The man had nearly reached the house.

3. *Write the ending.* After the climax, the reader should be satisfied. Bring your story to a prompt close. Make the ending *show* the theme of the story; do not directly state it. If the reader has not caught the theme throughout the story, he will not be impressed by a direct statement at the end. The following sentence would *not* be a good one to include in the last paragraph of the second sample story: "These experiences helped to teach me that simple trust in the Lord brings peace even in uncertain and frightening circumstances."

4. *Write an interesting title.* The title should hint at the story theme without giving away the outcome. It should be short, generally not more than five words, and it should be fresh and original. Alliteration, rhyming words, and unusual word combinations can increase the appeal of titles. Compare the following titles for the stories in this chapter.

Good titles:

Terry's Temper
  (is short; uses alliteration)

"He Rides Upon the Storm"
  (uses an interesting quotation)
Worrying Wanda
  (is short; uses alliteration)

Twenty Pounds
  (is short; is appealing because *pounds* can mean different things)

Poor titles:

Terry Learns to Control His Anger
  (is long; gives away outcome)
Terry's Misplaced Energy
  (misses story theme)

"Above All, Trust in the Lord"
  (is long; states theme too directly)
Wanda Learns to Trust
  (gives away outcome)

Mother's Faith Is Rewarded
  (gives away outcome)
How Twenty Pounds Became Worth a Million (is long; gives away outcome)

Applying the Lesson

Write the first draft of your story, following the steps in this lesson. Write on every other line to allow room for revising. Your story should have 700–1,000 words.

Be sure to save this first draft. You will do further work with it in Chapter 8.

Lesson 56 Answers
(Individual work.)

---

57. Improving Your Speaking Style, Part 2: Voice Control

In Lesson 17 you learned that eye contact is one important element of an effective speaking style. Look directly at individuals in your audience. Establish eye contact early in your speech, use eye contact to emphasize major points throughout the speech, and close the speech on a solid note with eye contact.

Your *voice control* also affects your speaking style. Actually, your voice reveals many things about you. It shows whether you are careless or careful, tense or relaxed, timid or confident. This becomes especially important when you speak to a group. The listeners should sense that you are eager to communicate something worthwhile to them. If your voice suggests that you are bored with your subject, the listeners will be bored too!

The following paragraphs discuss four important elements of proper voice control.

1. *Articulation.* You need to open your mouth well and pronounce each word distinctly, for your talk will lose its effect if the listeners cannot understand you. They may be able to miss a considerable number of sounds and still understand what you mean; but the greater the number of sounds missed, the greater the chance of misunderstanding.

Of course, you must also avoid the extreme of exaggerated articulation. Your voice sounds best when it is clear, natural, and relaxed.

2. *Volume.* This is probably the first thing you think of when you consider voice control. Be sure to speak loudly enough so that your listeners need not strain to hear you. No matter how many other good qualities your voice may have, your talk will not be effective if the audience cannot hear what you say.

On the other hand, speaking too loudly is just as ineffective as speaking too softly. Your voice must not be so loud that your listeners feel uncomfortable. Rather, you should have a pleasant variety, using the greatest volume for your most important points. This variety will help you to avoid a boring manner of speech.

Look at the following sentences. What pattern of volume would be appropriate for each one?

Does this mean that we should compromise principle for peace? God forbid!
God forbid that we ever compromise principle for peace.

Lesson 57

Purpose: To give students practice in speaking before a group, and *to teach voice control as an element of effective speaking style.

Teaching Suggestions:

Ask the students to think about a person whom they consider an effective speaker. Have them list details about the way he uses his voice, which help to make his talk effective.

Another way to emphasize the points of this lesson would be to illustrate them negatively. Speak several sentences with careless articulation, with too much or too little volume, in a boring monotone, and too rapidly. Then illustrate the points positively.

Sometimes we may feel like compromising. But true peace is never gained that way.

The first example should begin with moderate volume and build up to strong volume for the words *God forbid.* The reverse pattern should be used in the second example—beginning loud and gradually becoming softer. In the third example, the volume should increase through the word *compromising* and then decrease. These differences in volume help to put proper emphasis where it belongs.

3. *Pitch.* This aspect of the voice is directly affected by emotions. When you are calm and confident, your voice pitch is generally lower than when you are excited or anxious. Therefore, make a deliberate effort to relax and use the lower tones in your voice range.

You must modulate your pitch according to what you are saying. In everyday speech, do you state a fact, ask a question, and make an exclamation with every word at the same pitch? Of course not—and neither should you do that in speaking to a group. Raise and lower the pitch of your voice to communicate as you would in a normal conversation. Few things deaden a talk more than a voice droning on and on in a monotone.

Pitch and volume generally go together, with high pitch accompanying strong volume and lower pitch accompanying lower volume. Notice how this is true as you again read the sample sentences above. When you do use falling pitch and volume (especially at the end of a sentence), be careful not to reduce them too much. Otherwise, your listeners will fail to catch the last words.

4. *Speed.* Regulating your flow of speech is another aspect of voice control. Try to speak at the same comfortable speed that you use in conversation. You should not have long, awkward pauses, but neither should you try to fill in pauses by using *uh*'s and *ah*'s. Try to use a natural variety, speaking faster to express excitement or enthusiasm and slowing down to emphasize major points.

Which of the following sentences should be spoken slowly? Which should be spoken more rapidly? The answers should be obvious.

> To understand that significance, we should first consider the origin of the Pharisees. (major point)
> The Pharisees drew primarily from the ranks of the scribes, in contrast to the Sadducees, who came primarily from the priests. (supporting detail)

Some voices just naturally sound more pleasant than others; there is little we can do about that. But regardless of the natural sound of your voice, you will communicate at your best if you speak clearly and use a variety of volume, pitch, and speed. A well-modulated voice is constantly changing to express the meanings known and *felt* by the speaker. If you follow these guidelines and put your heart into your message, you will communicate well with your audience.

Applying the Lesson

A. Two sample stories appear in Lesson 49: "Terry's Temper" and "'He Rides Upon the Storm.'" Practice reading paragraphs from these stories in class, with good voice control as taught in the lesson.

Lesson 57 Answers
(All answers are individual work.)

B. Choose a story that you know well and that you can tell in three to five minutes. It may be from your own experience, or it may be an incident you have heard or read. After your teacher approves your story, prepare to tell it to your class. Concentrate on effective voice control, and remember also to maintain eye contact with your listeners.

---

58. Chapter 6 Review

A. Write the correct words to complete these statements.
1. The most important goal for writing any short story should be to ———.
2. You will find it easiest to write about ——— subjects.
3. A short story does not need to be about some ——— subject; it can deal with common, everyday happenings.
4. The lesson a story teaches is the ——— of the story.
5. A short story should develop ——— theme rather than several themes.
6. The setting should be introduced in the ———.
7. The setting includes the ———, the ———, and the ———.
8. The struggle or problem that the main character faces is the story ———.
9. If the main character struggles to overcome the habit of gossip, the story conflict is between the main character and ———.
10. If the main character struggles to accept the handicap of a crippling disease, the story conflict is between the main character and ———.
11. If the main character must resist the wrong influence of some worldly cousins, the story conflict is between the main character and ———.
12. The overall development of a story conflict is the ———.
13. With a complication plot, the conflict should ——— as the story progresses.
14. The process of portraying story characters is called ———.
15. The main character of a story is sometimes called the ———.
16. A person opposing the main character is called the ———.
17. Characters that should be named but not characterized very much are ——— characters.
18. Characters that should be clearly characterized are ——— characters.
19. Characters that are often not even named are ——— characters.
20. Every story portrays the characters by their ——— and ———.
21. In addition to the methods above, characters may be portrayed by their ———, ———, or ———.
22. The perspective from which an author writes a story is the ——— of that story.
23. When the author writes as if he is able to see every character equally well, he is writing from the ——— point of view.
24. When the author uses *I* and portrays himself as the main character, he is writing from the ——— point of view.

Lesson 58 Answers
A. 1. teach a lesson
    2. familiar
    3. dramatic *or* unusual
    4. theme
    5. one
    6. opening paragraphs (*or* beginning)
    7. place, time, atmosphere
    8. conflict
    9. himself
   10. his circumstances
   11. another person
   12. plot
   13. intensify *or* increase
   14. characterization
   15. protagonist
   16. antagonist
   17. minor
   18. major
   19. background
   20. actions, speech
   21. thoughts, appearance, reputation
   22. point of view
   23. omniscient
   24. first person

Lesson 58

Purpose: To review the concepts taught in Chapter 6.

25. When the author follows one particular character through the story, he is writing from the ———— point of view.
26. The ———— point of view carries a strong impression of reality.
27. If a story reveals any character's thoughts, its viewpoint is ————.
28. If a story does not reveal any character's thoughts, its viewpoint is ————.
29. The four elements of voice control are ————, ————, ————, and ————.
30. You should have variety in all the elements of voice control except ————.

25. third person
26. first person
27. subjective
28. objective
29. articulation, volume, pitch, speed
30. articulation

B. For each of these samples, write a suitable theme that it would be likely to develop.
   1.   A few minutes' work by the experienced woodsmen brought the giant maple crashing down, shaking the earth beneath their feet. Then suddenly John and his crew found themselves listening to the greatest torrent of profanity that they had ever heard from Graham McIntosh. The huge tree was hollow; and Graham was expressing his displeasure.

   Brother John slowly moved over to stand beside Graham. When the volley of vulgar words finally ended, John turned to face him. "Graham, why do you swear?" he asked simply.

   "Why, I—I—I—" Graham's face flushed, and his hands went in and out of his pockets. "I—I—I don't swear near as much as some men do. And, anyhow—well—what does it matter how I talk, anyway?"

   "Did you know," John asked softly, "the Bible says that 'every idle word that men shall speak, they shall give account thereof in the day of judgment'?"

   Graham had nothing further to say, and after a few moments of silence, John returned to his chain saw. Graham watched the men for a few minutes more; and then, with his usual call of "Don't work too hard," he left.

   A week later, John and his wife were driving through a neighboring town when they saw Graham on the sidewalk. He raised his hand in friendly greeting as they passed.

   "You know," John mused, "Graham has really seemed different the last while. Especially since he's so careful about his language when we're working for him."

   2.   Thomas walked briskly as he headed toward the barn. It seemed that extra jobs always awaited him on the family dairy farm. So this Saturday he planned a head start for next week. And a prompt start would mean more time this evening for the Sunday school lesson.

   "Father and Mother have an errand to run today. He suggested that I use the day at my discretion. That points to the calf pens. Their cleaning is overdue. I can hustle through the Saturday chores by nine o'clock and finish the pens by midafternoon. Then if I finish writing that story before milking time, I won't have to take the time from next week," Thomas thought as he mentally planned his day.

B. (Sample answers.)
   1. God can use a simple testimony to touch another person's life.

   2. We should always be willing to sacrifice to help others.

Whistling cheerfully, Thomas finished washing the milkers. He trotted through the barn, grabbed a straw bale with each hand, and began bedding the heifers. The rumble of a car motor alerted his thoughts. "Likely a neighbor passing; no reason to stop and look." But the sound did not move on. "Well, I'll have to check," he decided, reluctantly dropping his bale.

Yes, it was Mrs. Berry, their widowed neighbor.

"Good morning," he greeted.

"My goat is out again." Her aging voice trembled. "I was wondering if you had time to help me catch her."

"Certainly," agreed Thomas. "I'll be right over."

3. Breathing a prayer for wisdom and patience, I went to the door. "Good afternoon, Mr. Daley," I said pleasantly as a cool fall breeze blew in.

"Good afternoon, nuthin'!" Mr. Daley thundered. His six-foot, three-hundred-pound frame towered above me on the porch. Disheveled hair, tobacco-stained beard, and grimy clothes accentuated the harsh voice. "Think you gonna put your fence three feet on my side of the line, eh? Well, you just take those posts off my property 'fore mornin', or else!"

"I'm sorry, Mr. Daley," I answered, trying hard to keep my voice calm. "I'm putting the fence exactly where it was before."

"Yep, I know. That fence's always been on my side of the line, and I'm tired of it. I won't have a new fence put there. Leastways not by a Bible-quoting sissy of a Mennonite!"

"Well, Mr. Daley, if you have a few minutes, let's just go right down there now and mark where that line should be," I suggested.

4. Debra blinked, but the tears multiplied faster than she could blink them away. "If only I could hike along with the other girls tomorrow up to Vista Peak. Wish Father would be more reasonable."

But then her conscience smote her. "That's not fair to your father. You know quite well that with Mother ill, you're needed at home. What about that verse you read this morning about honoring your parents?"

"Oh, I know." At Debra's voice, Princess perked up her ears and wagged her tail. "Lord, help me to be respectful," Debra prayed as she looked up to the beautiful mountains that rose abruptly behind the family farm.

"Well, Princess, I'd better get back in the house and finish the dishes." Debra gave her pet a final caress and resolutely strode for the kitchen. Soon her voice swelled with the words "Count your many blessings."

Through Mother's bedroom door came the sound of Debra's melodious voice. "Praise the Lord!" Mother said to herself. "That sounds like Debra's usual, cheerful self again." The lines on her face relaxed, and soon she was sleeping peacefully.

3. "Blessed are the peacemakers."

4. Submission is the way to true joy.

C. Answer these questions about the setting of the samples in Part B.
   1. a. What is the day of the week in sample 2?
      b. In what season of the year does sample 3 occur?
      c. Does sample 4 occur during warm weather or cold weather?
   2. What do you learn about the place of sample 4?
   3. How would you describe the atmosphere of sample 4?

D. For each sample in Part B, write whether the main character's conflict is with *another person, circumstances,* or *himself.*

E. Do these exercises about the characters of the samples in Part B.
   1. In sample 1, who is the main character? Who is another major character? Who are the background characters?
   2. In sample 2, who is the main character? Who is the minor character? Who are the background characters?
   3. Give two specific examples of characterization by actions. (Give the characters, the actions, and the traits revealed.)
   4. Give three specific examples of characterization by speech. (Give the characters, the speech, and the traits revealed.)
   5. Give two specific examples of characterization by thoughts. (Give the characters, the thoughts, and the traits revealed.)
   6. Give one specific example of characterization by appearance. (Give the character, the appearance, and the trait revealed.)
   7. Give two specific examples of characterization by reputation. (Give the characters, the reputation, and the traits revealed.)

F. For each sample in Part B, write which point of view is used. Include *subjective* or *objective* where applicable.

They . . . expounded unto

him the way of God more perfectly.

Acts 18:26

C. 1. a. Saturday
      b. in fall
      c. during warm weather (warm enough for hiking up a mountain)
   2. The story occurs on a farm in a mountainous area.
   3. The atmosphere seems to be a loving Christian home.

D. *Sample 1:* another person
   Sample 2: circumstances
   Sample 3: another person
   Sample 4: himself

E. (Sample answers given for numbers 3–7.)
   1. *Main character:* John
      Another major character: Graham McIntosh
      Background characters: John's crew, John's wife
   2. *Main character:* Thomas
      Minor character: Mrs. Berry
      Background characters: Father and Mother
   3. *John:* waited until Graham stopped talking—patience.
      Thomas: walked briskly—diligence; whistled cheerfully—cheerfulness.
      "I" of sample 3: breathed a prayer—prayerfulness.
      Debra: blinked back tears—sensitivity.
   4. *Graham:* used profanity—anger, ungodliness.
      John: "Graham, why do you swear?"—concern for souls.
      Thomas: "Good morning"—friendliness.
      "I" of sample 3: "Good afternoon, Mr. Daley"—pleasantness.
      Debra: "Lord, help me to be respectful"—prayerfulness, conscientiousness.
   5. *Thomas:* "I can hustle through the Saturday chores by nine o'clock and finish the pens by midafternoon"—diligence, helpfulness.
      Debra: "You know quite well that with Mother ill, you're needed at home"—sense of duty.
   6. *Mr. Daley:* disheveled hair, grimy clothes—untidiness, carelessness.
   7. *"I" of sample 3:* was called a Bible-quoting sissy—love for the Bible, nonresistance.
      Debra: was called her usual cheerful self—cheerfulness.

F. *Sample 1:* third person, objective
   Sample 2: third person, subjective
   Sample 3: first person
   Sample 4: omniscient, subjective

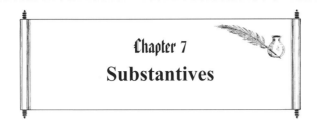

59. Identifying Nouns

As you have known for years, a noun is the name of a person, place, thing, or idea. Nouns constitute the backbone of language. To a large extent, we use nouns to express the main ideas in our communication.

Concrete and Abstract Nouns

A noun names a person, place, thing, or idea. Nouns are either concrete or abstract. A concrete noun names a person, place, or thing, usually with physical substance that we can perceive through the senses. An abstract noun names an idea that does not have physical substance and that we cannot perceive through the senses.

Concrete:

carpenter	church	grass
Edward	Potter County	automobile

Abstract:

job	mercy	courage
parable	humility	righteousness
idea		

Names referring to God, spiritual beings (like *cherubim*), and spiritual places (like *paradise*) are also concrete nouns. Although they do not have physical substance that we can perceive through our senses, they are real persons, places, and things.

Common and Proper Nouns

Nouns are either common or proper. A common noun is the general name of a person, place, or thing. It is the name *common* to a group of items, and it is not capitalized. A proper noun is the particular name of a person, place, or thing. It is the name *proper* for one specific item, and it is capitalized. In Lesson 1 you studied ten groupings of proper nouns.

Gender of Nouns

All nouns have gender. Masculine gender refers to persons or animals that are male (*boy, father, buck*). Feminine gender refers to persons or animals that are female (*girl, mother, doe*). Common gender refers to persons or animals that are either male or female, or to a group that may include any combination of genders (*child, parent, deer*). Neuter gender refers to nonliving objects or to abstract nouns, which can be neither male nor female (*door, river, cheerfulness*).

Lesson 59

Purpose: To review the basic facts about nouns.

Noun-forming Suffixes

Many nouns, especially abstract nouns, end with noun-forming suffixes. The following are common noun-forming suffixes: *-ment, -ity, -ness, -ion, -ation, -dom, -ance, -ence, -ude, -al, -ship, -hood, -er, -or,* and *-ar.* The pairs of words below illustrate how these suffixes are used to form nouns from other parts of speech or from other nouns.

appoint—appointment   solitary—solitude
free—freedom   deprive—deprival, deprivation
continue—continuation, continuance   child—childhood

Other Words Used as Nouns

A word is classified as a certain part of speech not only because of its basic meaning but also because of how it is used in a sentence. When used with their normal meanings, some words are always nouns, some are never nouns, and some may be either nouns or other parts of speech. Can you place each of the following words into one of those three categories?

right   apple   near   calmness
sweetly   reliance   look   retain

Calmness and *reliance* are always nouns. *Sweetly, near,* and *retain* are never nouns. *Right, apple,* and *look* are sometimes nouns and sometimes other parts of speech.

Perhaps you notice that *apple* can actually serve as an adjective sometimes, as in *apple tree.* But dictionaries generally do not label *apple* as an adjective. This is an example of an attributive noun—a noun that precedes another noun and functions as an adjective. In its basic essence, however, such a word is a noun.

Applying the Lesson

A. Copy each noun, and label it *C* (concrete) or *A* (abstract).
1. Sincere worship and praise ascend to God like the sweet incense that Aaron offered.
2. The true believer feels his unworthiness and insufficiency.
3. A careful study of the Scriptures increases our spiritual understanding.
4. Faithful characters of the Old Testament are an inspiration to us today.
5. While the dough was slowly rising, Mother heated the oven.
6. After dinner the boys will cut the thistles in the pasture.
7. As we entered the damp cave, an uneasy feeling caused our hearts to beat more rapidly.
8. The confidence of our guide soon dispelled our fears.

B. Copy each noun, and write *M* (masculine), *F* (feminine), *N* (neuter), or *C* (common) to label its gender.
1. In humble devotion, Mary approached her beloved Master.
2. Breaking her alabaster box, she poured precious ointment on His feet.

Lesson 59 Answers
Applying the Lesson
A. 1. worship—A; praise—A; God—C; incense—C; Aaron—C
2. believer—C; unworthiness—A; insufficiency—A
3. study—A; Scriptures—C; understanding—A
4. characters—C; Old Testament—C; inspiration—A
5. dough—C; Mother—C; oven—C
6. dinner—C; boys—C; thistles—C; pasture—C
7. cave—C; feeling—A; hearts—C
8. confidence—A; guide—C; fears—A

B. 1. devotion—N; Mary—F; Master—M
2. box—N; ointment—N; feet—N

3. The disciples thought that the act of this worshiper was a great waste.
4. She could have sold her gift and used the money to help the poor.
5. Jesus praised the woman for her noble sacrifice of such a great gift.
6. At the request of Balaam, King Balak offered seven bullocks and seven rams on seven altars.
7. The aged bishop addressed the members of the church with tender affection.
8. The matron at Grand View Children's Home supervises the activities of the children.

C. Add a noun-forming suffix to each word in parentheses so that it fits in the sentence.
1. Thomas Edison, a famous (invent), possessed great (determine) and (persevere).
2. His (develop) of the light bulb came only after thousands of (fail) and (disappoint).
3. Scientists had made the (declare) that the (construct) of Edison's light was an (impossible).
4. Edison's (hard) were repaid when he and his assistants watched in (elate) the gentle (radiate) of the first successful bulb.
5. In the (Create), God produced (illuminate) by His simple (command) that there be light.
6. God did not need to exercise (persevere), for through His infinite (able) He could make light immediately without a single (err).
7. Edison's first (achieve) of success produced a light that burned about forty-five hours; but God's light (produce), the sun, has been in (exist) for nearly six thousand years.
8. In (compare) to the work of God, Edison's light fades into (pale) and (insignificant).

D. Write whether each word is *always, never,* or *sometimes* a noun.
1. idea
2. contrast
3. swallow
4. contain
5. salvation
6. jump
7. solidify
8. preacher
9. spoken
10. generally
11. cook
12. childhood

Review Exercises

A. Identify the structure of each sentence as simple (*S*), compound (*CD*), complex (*CX*), or compound-complex (*CD-CX*). [25]
1. Beware of a person who says he hates gossip.
2. By perseverance the snail reached the ark.
3. A lie travels around the world while truth is putting on her boots.
4. Confess that you were wrong yesterday; it will show that you are wiser today.
5. Carry an appetite to God's house, and you will be fed.

3. disciples—M *or* C; act—N; worshiper—F *or* C; waste—N
4. gift—N; money—N; poor—C
5. Jesus—M; woman—F; sacrifice—N; gift—N
6. request—N; Balaam—M; King Balak—M; bullocks—M; rams—M; altars—N
7. bishop—M; members—C; church—C; affection—N
8. matron—F; Grand View Children's Home—N; activities—N; children—C

C. 1. inventor, determination, perseverance
2. development, failures, disappointments
3. declaration, construction, impossibility
4. hardships, elation, radiation *or* radiance
5. Creation, illumination, commandment
6. perseverance, ability, error
7. achievement, producer, existence
8. comparison, paleness *or* pallor, insignificance

D. 1. always   7. never
2. sometimes   8. always
3. sometimes   9. never
4. never   10. never
5. always   11. sometimes
6. sometimes 12. always

Review Exercises

A. 1. CX
2. S
3. CX
4. CD-CX
5. CD

B. Identify the word order of each sentence as natural (*N*), inverted (*I*), or mixed (*M*). [25]
  1. Christ's soldiers fight best on their knees.
  2. When everybody talks, nobody hears.
  3. After the cup of affliction comes the cup of consolation.
  4. Guilt on the conscience puts grief on the countenance.
  5. On a long journey, even a straw is heavy.

C. Identify the style of each sentence as loose (*L*), periodic (*P*), or balanced (*B*). [25]
  1. Children may make a rich man poor, but they make a poor man rich.
  2. If you want a boy to move fast, say, "Now, my man!"
  3. Do not leave your heart at home when you go to worship.
  4. Holiness is not the way to Christ, but Christ is the way to holiness.
  5. The best book about Christ is His living biography, written out in the words and actions of His people.

B. 1. N
  2. M
  3. I
  4. N
  5. M

C. 1. B
  2. P
  3. L
  4. B
  5. L

---

60. Verbals and Clauses as Nouns

Most nouns are single words or compound words whose normal, basic meanings make them nouns. Sometimes, however, other words and word groups serve to name persons, places, things, or ideas. The most common of these are verbals, verbal phrases, and clauses. Study the following sentences. In each one, the subject is underlined.

<u>Faith</u> is essential to a life that pleases God. (simple single word)
<u>To believe</u> is not enough in itself. (infinitive)
<u>Obeying the Bible</u> must complement a profession of faith. (gerund phrase)
<u>How a person lives</u> determines the truth of his profession. (noun clause)

Verbals as Nouns

Verbals hold two jobs. On the one hand, they are verb forms that have many characteristics of verbs. On the other hand, they function in a sentence as some other part of speech. Two kinds of verbals can function as nouns: the gerund and the infinitive. When the gerund or the infinitive has adverb modifiers or complements, the word group is a verbal phrase. The entire verbal phrase then functions as a noun.

1. *Gerunds and gerund phrases.* A gerund is the present participle (the *-ing* form) of a verb used as a noun. It functions as the subject of a sentence, as a verb complement, or as the object of a preposition. Rather than expressing action, as a verb does, the gerund *names* an action.

<u>Studying</u> requires a great deal of concentration.
    (The subject *Studying* names an action; it is a gerund.)

Lesson 60

Purpose: To review the basic facts about verbals and clauses used as nouns.

Teaching Suggestions:

Review what the students know about verbals and dependent clauses. (See Lesson 23.) Students may also remember things that they learned in previous years.

Aunt Thelma enjoys <u>painting these colorful scenes</u>.

    (The direct object *painting these colorful scenes* names an action; it is a gerund phrase.)

Grandfather Weaver's hobby is <u>carving</u>.

    (The predicate nominative *carving* names an action; it is a gerund.)

Brother Elmer added a room to his shop for <u>storing lumber</u>.

    (The object of the preposition, *storing lumber,* names an action; it is a gerund phrase.)

Sentence diagrams can help you to evaluate the place that a verbal or verbal phrase fills in a sentence. Remember that a verbal used as a noun is diagramed on a pedestal. Observe specifically the noun position filled by each gerund.

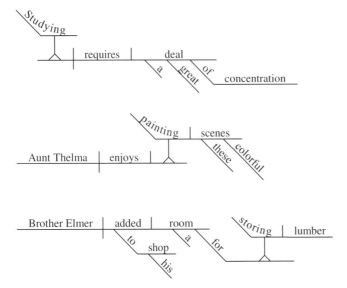

Be especially careful that you do not confuse a gerund functioning as a predicate nominative with the present participle form of a true verb. In both cases the *-ing* form may follow a form of *be.* If the word is a gerund, however, it must name an action and rename the subject. If the word is part of the verb phrase, it will express the action that the subject is performing. Examining the meaning of the sentence and reading the skeleton should help you decide which it is.

    Sister Ruth's main responsibility at the rest home is <u>keeping the residents' rooms clean</u>. (*Keeping the residents' rooms clean* renames the subject *responsibility;* it is a gerund phrase.)

Her job certainly is <u>keeping</u> her busy.

    (*Keeping* does not rename the subject *job;* it expresses the action that the subject is performing; it is part of the verb phrase.)

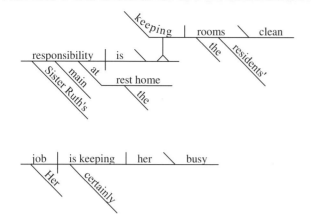

2. *Infinitives and infinitive phrases.* An infinitive is the basic form of a verb preceded by *to*. An infinitive is a noun when it names an action and fills a noun function in the sentence.

> <u>To persevere</u> requires determination and endurance.
>> (The subject *To persevere* names an action; it is an infinitive.)
>
> God promises <u>to bless His faithful servants</u>.
>> (The direct object *to bless His faithful servants* names an action; it is an infinitive phrase.)
>
> God's desire has always been <u>to preserve a people for Himself</u>.
>> (The predicate nominative *to preserve a people for Himself* names an action; it is an infinitive phrase.)

Notice on each diagram how the infinitive fills the place of a regular noun in each sentence.

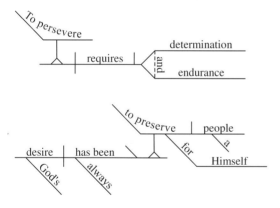

Do not confuse infinitives with prepositional phrases that begin with *to. To* plus the basic form of a verb makes an infinitive. *To* plus a noun or pronoun makes a prepositional phrase.

Nancy plans to bake bread, and she will take some to Grandmother Smith.
(*To bake bread* is *to* plus a basic verb form; it is an infinitive phrase. *To Grandmother Smith* is *to* plus a noun; it is a prepositional phrase.)

Noun Clauses

A noun clause is a dependent clause with a noun function in a complex sentence. Unlike an adjective or an adverb clause, a noun clause is a basic part of the independent clause except when it serves as the object of a preposition. In a complex sentence containing a noun clause, therefore, the two clauses are sometimes hard to identify.

When a sentence contains a noun clause used as a verb complement, the two clauses are usually quite easy to identify. Especially obvious are the clauses that function as direct and indirect quotations. Almost always they are noun clauses used as direct objects. In the following sentences, the noun clauses are in brackets and the skeletons of both clauses are underlined.

Grandfather said [that his arthritis was bothering him].
(The clause in brackets is the direct object of *said.*)

Mrs. Kendig offered [whoever was thirsty] a drink of cold tea.
(The clause in brackets is the indirect object of *offered.*)

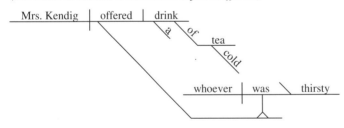

This rain is [what the crops desperately needed].
    (The clause in brackets is a predicate nominative renaming *rain*.)

When a sentence contains a noun clause used as a subject, the two clauses may be difficult to identify. The entire noun clause serves as the subject of the independent clause; therefore, the skeleton of that independent clause may be difficult to detect. In the following sentences, the noun clauses are again in brackets. The skeletons of the noun clauses are underlined, and the verbs of the independent clauses are underlined.

[Whoever wants salvation] must believe the Gospel.
    (The clause in brackets is the subject of the independent clause.)

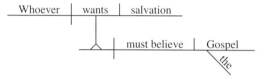

[Whose sweater this is] remains a mystery to us.
    (The clause in brackets is the subject of the independent clause.)

A noun clause functioning as the object of a preposition is not a basic part of the independent clause. Therefore, the two clauses should be easy to identify. The following sentences show the noun clauses in brackets, with the skeletons of both clauses underlined.

Louis Pasteur took a great interest in [what causes diseases].

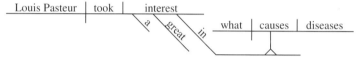

Today we benefit greatly from [what he discovered].

Applying the Lesson

A. If the underlined item is a noun phrase, identify its function by writing *subject, direct object, predicate nominative,* or *object of a preposition.* If it is not a noun phrase, write *none.*
1. The ultimate purpose for every created being is to glorify the Creator.
2. Peace with one's own self and with others requires living in peace with the Lord.
3. Overcoming temptation in our own strength is a foolish endeavor.
4. The only way to victory over sin is through the power of the Lord.
5. A godly man wants to receive the wisdom of God.
6. To view life from God's point of view means that we must take our eyes off self.
7. However, too many people are thinking too much of themselves.

Lesson 60 Answers
Applying the Lesson
A. 1. predicate nominative
   2. direct object
   3. subject
   4. none
   5. direct object
   6. subject
   7. none

8. True fullness of life comes by <u>emptying ourselves of all that is selfish</u>.
9. We can find true happiness in <u>seeking the happiness of others</u>.
10. The Christian's greatest joy will be <u>seeing his Saviour face to face</u>.

B. Copy each verbal or verbal phrase, and write whether it is a gerund (*G*), a gerund phrase (*GP*), an infinitive (*I*), or an infinitive phrase (*IP*).
1. Stacking those boxes that high is not wise.
2. The lame horse has finally managed to stand.
3. This evening Maryann's job will be to wash the dishes.
4. Helping in Grandfather's small-engine shop is Nevin's chief delight.
5. We can often learn many things by listening.
6. To sleep is to refresh the body's energy and alertness.
7. Working can often relax a body that is tired from study or nervous strain.
8. By thinking ahead, we can often spare ourselves the pain and shame of foolish mistakes.
9. To procrastinate is rarely a reasonable option for facing difficult circumstances.
10. Sledding is practically unknown in this flat country.

C. If the underlined word group is a noun clause, identify its function by writing *subject*, *direct object*, *indirect object*, *predicate nominative*, or *object of a preposition*. If it is not a noun clause, write *none*.
1. Mortal man will never fully understand <u>how the physical world works</u>.
2. <u>Whoever considers himself wise</u> knows nothing yet as he ought to know.
3. Your character is <u>what your choices have made it to be</u>.
4. By now you should recognize <u>why even life's little choices are important</u>.
5. We should seek to glorify God by <u>whatever we do, say, or think</u>.
6. <u>Whenever a person goes against better knowledge,</u> he damages his conscience.
7. We give <u>whoever sent this gift of food</u> our sincere thanks.
8. This truck is <u>what we call a rattletrap</u>.
9. <u>How long it will keep working</u> remains to be seen.
10. Give this message to <u>whomever you can find in the shop</u>.
11. We shall leave <u>when everyone is ready</u>.
12. Our loud noises must have given <u>whatever was disturbing the chickens</u> a good scare.

D. Copy each noun clause.
1. How Cousin Alvin can paint with his arthritic hands is truly amazing.
2. He will put into rich color and exquisite detail a scene of what you describe to him.
3. Have you discovered whose dog was chasing your sheep?
4. The outside dimensions of the bookcase must be whatever fits well in that corner.
5. Michael gave whichever calf was coughing a shot.
6. Whose idea this was is not hard to guess.
7. I could not read the chalkboard from where I was sitting.

B.
1. Stacking those boxes that high—GP
2. to stand—I
3. to wash the dishes—IP
4. Helping in Grandfather's small-engine shop—GP
5. listening—G
6. To sleep—I;
   to refresh the body's energy and alertness—IP
7. Working—G
8. thinking ahead—GP
9. To procrastinate—I;
   facing difficult circumstances—GP
10. Sledding—G

C.
1. direct object
2. subject
3. predicate nominative
4. direct object
5. object of a preposition
6. none
7. indirect object
8. predicate nominative
9. subject
10. object of a preposition
11. none
12. indirect object

D.
1. How Cousin Alvin can paint with his arthritic hands
2. what you describe to him
3. whose dog was chasing your sheep
4. whatever fits well in that corner
5. whichever calf was coughing
6. Whose idea this was
7. where I was sitting

8. Although confined to a wheelchair, Grandfather Horning gives whoever visits him more inspiration than they give to him.
9. A good time to visit him can be when you are feeling discouraged.
10. The visitor could not remember if he had met any of us before.

Review Exercises

For each underlined word, write *yes* or *no* to tell whether it should be followed by a comma. [2]

1. <u>Gertie</u> our pet <u>goat</u> is a most frolicsome creature.
2. Grazing out in the <u>meadow</u> she looks as <u>placid</u> as a sheep.
3. Let the boys play out in the <u>meadow</u> <u>however</u> and you will see what a tease she can be!
4. If they play <u>tag</u> you can be sure that <u>Gertie</u> enjoying herself <u>immensely</u> will run and jump with them.
5. The <u>game</u> that she enjoys <u>most</u> is hide-and-seek.

8. whoever visits him
9. when you are feeling discouraged
10. if he had met any of us before

Review Exercises

1. yes, yes
2. yes, no
3. yes, yes
4. yes, yes, yes
5. no, no

---

61. Plural and Possessive Nouns

Plural Forms

Most one-word nouns show number; that is, their form shows whether they are singular or plural. The following rules will help you to write the plural forms of nouns correctly.

1. *General rules.*
   a. To form the plurals of most nouns, add *-s.*

      paper—papers
      stream—streams
      state—states
      explanation—explanations

   b. To form the plural of a noun ending with *s, sh, ch, x,* or *z,* add *-es.* You may need to double a final *s* or *z.*

      gas—gases *or* gasses
      church—churches
      tax—taxes
      quiz—quizzes

2. *Nouns ending with* y.
   a. To form the plural of a noun ending with *y* after a vowel, add *-s.*

      bay—bays
      chimney—chimneys
      envoy—envoys

Lesson 61

Purpose: To review the rules for making plural and possessive forms of nouns.

Teaching Suggestions:

Students at this level should be quite familiar with the plural and the possessive forms of nouns. They should need little more than a brief review of the rules, along with some practice in applying them. However, the use of possessive nouns before gerunds is a new concept.

Note: Words such as *fish, trout,* and *elk* may have plurals ending with *-s* or *-es* (*fishes, trouts, elks*). In modern usage, these forms usually indicate a diversity of species, such as "the food fishes."

b. To form the plural of a noun ending with *y* after a consonant, change the *y* to *i* and add *-es.*

> cherry—cherries
> enemy—enemies

3. *Nouns ending with* f *or* fe.
a. For many nouns, change the *f* to *v* and add *-s* or *-es.*

> wolf—wolves
> sheaf—sheaves

b. For other nouns, simply add *-s.*

> strife—strifes
> gulf—gulfs
> chief—chiefs

c. For most nouns ending with *ff,* simply add *-s.*

> bluff—bluffs
> plaintiff—plaintiffs

d. Sometimes either ending is correct for a word.

> hoof—hoofs *or* hooves
> handkerchief—handkerchiefs *or* handkerchieves

4. *Nouns ending with* o.
a. To form the plural of a noun ending with *o* after a vowel, add *-s.*

> patio—patios
> portfolio—portfolios
> zoo—zoos

b. To form the plural of a noun ending with *o* after a consonant, add *-s* or *-es.* Sometimes either ending is correct.

> tomato—tomatoes
> silo—silos
> zero—zeros *or* zeroes

c. For most musical terms ending with *o,* simply add *-s.*

> soprano—sopranos
> trio—trios

5. *Compound nouns.*
a. In general, change the most important word to the plural form.

> daughter-in-law—daughters-in-law
> inspector general—inspectors general
> bondwoman—bondwomen

   b. Simply add -s to nouns ending with -*ful*.

       mouthful—mouthfuls   bucketful—bucketfuls

   c. For a few nouns, each part of the compound word is made plural.

       manservant—menservants
       womanservant—womenservants

6. *Nouns with irregular plural forms.*

   a. In only seven nouns, the internal vowels are changed for the plural forms. Of course, if a compound word contains one of these roots, the plural is formed in the same way.

       foot—feet; tooth—teeth; goose—geese
          (forefoot—forefeet *but* mongoose—mongooses)
       louse—lice; mouse—mice (dormouse—dormice)
       man—men; woman—women (fireman—firemen)

   b. Four plural nouns have an archaic -*en* ending.

       child—children; ox—oxen (still used today)
       brother—brethren (used within the church, but archaic otherwise)
       hose—hosen (archaic; found once in the King James Bible)

   c. Some nouns have the same form whether singular or plural.

       trout—trout   sheep—sheep
       deer—deer   series—series

7. *Nouns with foreign plural forms.*

     A number of nouns borrowed from foreign languages have retained their foreign plural forms. In addition, the regular English pattern is often acceptable.

Singular Ending	Plural Ending	Example
-is	-es	oasis—oases
-ex *or* -ix	-ices	apex—apices *or* apexes
-a	-ae	vertebra—vertebrae *or* vertebras
-us	-i	narcissus—narcissi *or* narcissuses
-um *or* -on	-a	paramecium—paramecia

Possessive Forms

    Possessive nouns show possession or ownership. The following rules will help you to write possessive forms correctly.

1. *Singular nouns.*

   a. Make the possessive form of most singular nouns by adding 's. This includes nouns that end with a single *s* sound.

       the visitor's question   James's reputation

b. If a singular noun contains two *s* or *z* sounds in the last syllable, add only an apostrophe. Adding a third *s* or *z* sound makes the word awkward to pronounce.

   Jesus' disciples   Xerxes' rule

2. *Plural nouns.*
   a. If a plural noun does not end with -*s,* add *'s.*

   the women's waterpots   the deer's tails

   b. If a plural noun ends with -*s,* add only an apostrophe.

   the girls' purses   the monkeys' antics

3. *Compound nouns and noun phrases.*
   Make the last word in the compound possessive.

   his mother-in-law's kindness   the passerby's wave

Usage of Possessive Nouns

1. Normally, only nouns naming persons or animals are written in possessive forms. For inanimate objects, you should generally use a prepositional phrase. Exceptions include poetic or figurative language and various common expressions, such as those used for measures of time or money.

   a spider's web
   the hands of the clock (*not* the clock's hands)
   a day's wages; a moment's delay; five dollars' worth

2. Show joint ownership of several nouns by making only the last noun possessive. Show separate ownership by making each noun possessive.

   Joint ownership:
      Have you ridden Samuel and Aaron's bicycle?
         (one bicycle owned by two boys together)
   Separate ownership:
      Have you ridden Samuel's and Aaron's bicycles?
         (two bicycles owned by two boys separately)

3. A noun coming before a gerund should usually be possessive. To see why, replace the gerund with a regular noun form. It is clear that the preceding noun should be possessive.

   Moses' interceding turned away God's fierce wrath.
      (*Interceding* was what turned away God's wrath. *Moses'* modifies *interceding* by telling whose. Compare: Moses' intercession, *not* Moses intercession.)
   John's studying for the test enabled him to make a perfect score.
      (*Studying* was what enabled him. *John's* modifies *studying* by telling whose. Compare: John's preparation, *not* John preparation.)

Do not confuse this with a noun followed by a participle.

> We all saw <u>John</u> studying for the test.
>> (The sentence does not mean that we saw *John's studying*, but that we saw *John* in the action of *studying*. The participle *studying* modifies the direct object *John*.)

Applying the Lesson

A. For each noun, write the singular possessive, the plural, and the plural possessive forms. Use the foreign plural spellings for numbers 31–40. If possessive forms should generally not be used, write *none*.

1. sheriff	15. alto	28. valley
2. company	16. kinsman	29. louse
3. post office	17. roof	30. ox
4. calf	18. Angeleno	31. emphasis
5. child	19. sheep	32. appendix
6. embargo	20. mongoose	33. nebula
7. brother (church)	21. bondservant	34. cactus
8. lioness	22. titmouse	35. bacterium
9. family	23. son-in-law	36. basis
10. manservant	24. inspector general	37. vertex
11. placebo	25. goose	38. formula
12. trout	26. clef	39. octopus
13. alloy	27. bush	40. criterion
14. spoonful		

B. Write correctly each phrase that has an error. If it is correct, write *correct*.

1. Judas' desire for money
2. Matthew's and Mark's Gospels
3. strife between Abram and Lot's herdsmen
4. the corn's ears
5. the blind mans plea
6. her mother's-in-law's direction
7. disobeyed Samuel's orders
8. for a day's wages
9. the two prophet's miracles
10. sprinkled handfuls of ashes
11. James's, Joses', Judas's, and Simon's brother
12. foretold Peter denying his Lord
13. went to Zacchaeus's house
14. the tabernacle's coverings
15. found Jesus talking with the Jewish teachers
16. married seven hundred wifes
17. six potsful of water
18. grieved by the children's mocking
19. at the years end
20. three mens' visit to Abraham

11. James, Joses, Judas, and Simon's brother
12. foretold Peter's denying his Lord
13. correct
14. the coverings of the tabernacle
15. correct
16. married seven hundred wives
17. six potfuls of water
18. correct
19. at the year's end
20. three men's visit to Abraham

Lesson 61 Answers
Applying the Lesson

A.
1. sheriff's, sheriffs, sheriffs'
2. company's, companies, companies'
3. none, post offices, none
4. calf's, calves, calves'
5. child's, children, children's
6. none, embargoes, none
7. brother's, brethren, brethren's
8. lioness's, lionesses, lionesses'
9. family's, families, families'
10. manservant's, menservants, menservants'
11. none, placebos *or* placeboes, none
12. trout's, trout, trout's
13. none, alloys, none
14. none, spoonfuls, none
15. alto's, altos, altos'
   (*or* none, altos, none)
16. kinsman's, kinsmen, kinsmen's
17. none, roofs, none
18. Angeleno's, Angelenos, Angelenos'
19. sheep's, sheep, sheep's
20. mongoose's, mongooses, mongooses'
21. bondservant's, bondservants, bondservants'
22. titmouse's, titmice, titmice's
23. son-in-law's, sons-in-law, sons-in-law's
24. inspector general's, inspectors general, inspectors general's
25. goose's, geese, geese's
26. none, clefs, none
27. none, bushes, none
28. none, valleys, none
29. louse's, lice, lice's
30. ox's, oxen, oxen's
31. none, emphases, none
32. none, appendices, none
33. none, nebulae, none
34. none, cacti, none
35. none, bacteria, none
36. none, bases, none
37. none, vertices, none
38. none, formulae, none
39. octopus's, octopi, octopi's
40. none, criteria, none

B.
1. Judas's desire for money
2. correct
3. strife between Abram's and Lot's herdsmen
4. the ears of the corn
5. the blind man's plea
6. her mother-in-law's direction
7. correct
8. correct
9. the two prophets' miracles
10. correct

Review Exercises

A. Identify each underlined word as a direct object (*DO*), an indirect object (*IO*), a predicate nominative (*PN*), a predicate adjective (*PA*), or an objective complement (*OC*). [20, 21]
   1. No one considered my plan <u>workable</u>.
   2. Brother Mark always gave us sufficient <u>time</u> to do our lessons.
   3. A good beginning is an important first <u>step</u> in any project.
   4. The children showed <u>Sister Mary</u> a spider in the garden.
   5. John, your shoes are <u>muddy</u>.
   6. The Bible calls hatred a terrible <u>sin</u>.

B. Identify each underlined word as a retained direct object (*DO ret.*), a retained indirect object (*IO ret.*), or a retained objective complement (*OC ret.*). [21]
   1. After the fire, Brother Albert was given much <u>assistance</u> by the church.
   2. Outside work was made <u>difficult</u> by the bitter wind.
   3. The answer to the riddle was told <u>us</u> by little Jacob.
   4. The harmless water snake was declared a dreadful <u>creature</u> by our visitors.
   5. Christian women are asked numerous <u>questions</u> about their veilings.
   6. Bread and meat were provided <u>Elijah</u> by the ravens.

Review Exercises

A. 1. OC   4. IO
   2. DO   5. PA
   3. PN   6. OC

B. 1. DO ret.   4. OC ret.
   2. OC ret.   5. DO ret.
   3. IO ret.   6. IO ret.

---

62. Personal and Compound Personal Pronouns

A *pronoun* is a word that takes the place of a noun. The noun to which a pronoun refers is its *antecedent.* This lesson reviews two of the six classes of pronouns, and the next lesson deals with the other four classes.

Personal Pronouns

Personal pronouns are words like *he, you,* and *them,* which often refer to persons. The pronouns in this class are probably the first ones that come to your mind when you think of pronouns. Personal pronouns have different forms to show person, number, case, and gender.

1. *Person.* The person of a pronoun shows the relationship between the pronoun and the speaker. First person pronouns (*I, me, my, mine, we, us, our, ours*) refer to the speaker himself. Second person pronouns (*you, your, yours*) refer to the person that the speaker is talking to. Third person pronouns (*he, him, his, she, her, hers, it, its, they, them, their, theirs*) refer to the person or thing that the speaker is talking about.

2. *Number.* The number of a pronoun shows whether it is singular or plural. First and third person pronouns have different forms according to number, but second person pronouns do not.

3. *Case.* The case of a pronoun relates to its use in the sentence. The three cases in the English language are nominative, objective, and possessive.

Lesson 62

Purpose: To review the characteristics and usage of personal and compound personal pronouns, and to introduce *subjects of infinitives.

Teaching Suggestions:

Students should be familiar with most of the material in the lesson. Your main emphasis should be on the importance of using the correct case forms of pronouns.

Be sure to give sufficient explanation of an infinitive with a subject (a new concept) and to clarify that such a subject must be in the objective case. To help students understand this grammatical construction, you might point out that an infinitive

with a subject can sometimes be reworded as a noun clause, which also has a subject.

Father asked <u>me to paint the woodshed</u>.
Father asked <u>that I paint the woodshed</u>.

Note: Although the lesson indicates that *ourself* is an incorrect form, that word does have an accepted use in referring to the "editorial *we*"—that is, a writer's use of *we* to avoid using *I.* Example: "We [the writer] have often had such an experience ourself." But since *ourself* is incorrect in most everyday uses, students are told to avoid it.

The *nominative case* pronouns are as follows: *I, you, he, she, it, we, they.* These pronouns function as subjects, predicate nominatives, or appositives to one of these. Be especially careful to use the nominative case in compound structures of these sentence parts.

> Titus and <u>I</u> raked the leaves in the front yard. (subject)
> The visitors, Audrey and <u>she</u>, are signing the guest book.
>   (appositive to subject)
> <u>We</u> girls will help Aunt Mary clean her house.
>   (subject followed by appositive)
> The men to serve on the building committee would be <u>they</u>.
>   (predicate nominative)

The King James Bible uses the archaic forms *thou* (singular) and *ye* (plural) as second person pronouns in the nominative case.

> "When <u>thou</u> hast brought forth the people out of Egypt, <u>ye</u> shall serve God upon this mountain."

The *objective case* pronouns are as follows: *me, you, him, her, it, us, them.* They function as object complements, objects of prepositions, or appositives to any of these. Be careful to use the objective case in compound structures of these sentence parts and with appositives.

> The teacher commended Laura and <u>her</u> for their interesting essays.
>   (direct object)
> Brother Robert has given <u>you</u> and <u>me</u> an interesting assignment.
>   (indirect objects)
> The request came from <u>us</u> boys.
>   (object of preposition followed by an appositive)

The objective case is also used as the *subject of an infinitive.* This is a new grammatical construction for you, but since you are familiar with infinitives, you should find it easy to understand. Begin by considering this sentence with a simple infinitive phrase.

> Father wants <u>to paint the woodshed</u>.

Father wants what? *To paint the woodshed.* The infinitive phrase is the direct object in the sentence. Look at the diagram of this sentence.

To this same sentence we will add one more word.

> Father wants *me* to paint the woodshed.

Now find the direct object. Father wants what? *To paint the woodshed?* No, he wants *me* to paint it! *Me to paint the woodshed* is clearly the thing that Father wants—the direct object. *Me* is the subject that will perform the action of the infinitive. A diagram may help to show this more clearly.

The direct object in each of the following sentences is an infinitive phrase with a subject. Notice that each of these subjects is in the objective case, not nominative.

> Brother Myron told <u>him to open the windows</u>.
> Aunt Matilda is teaching <u>us to knit slippers</u>.
> Mother let <u>me try another recipe</u>.

In the last sentence above, the main verb is *let* and the word *to* is understood: *let me (to) try another recipe.* (Compare "allowed me to try another recipe.") In former years you learned that *let* is always used with another verb form that tells what action is permitted. This verb form is always an infinitive with a subject and with *to* understood.

The King James Bible uses the archaic forms *thee* (singular) and *you* (plural) as the second person pronouns in the objective case.

> "And the eye cannot say unto the hand, I have no need of <u>thee</u>: nor again the head to the feet, I have no need of <u>you</u>."

The *possessive case* pronouns are as follows: *my, mine, your, yours, his, her, hers, its, our, ours, their, theirs.* These pronouns show ownership. Most possessive case pronouns function as adjectives, modifying the nouns they precede. Absolute possessive pronouns function as substantives, representing both the possessor (the antecedent) and the thing possessed (the understood noun that could be stated).

> <u>Their</u> farm is more productive than <u>ours</u>.
> > (*Their* functions as an adjective modifying *farm. Ours* is an absolute possessive pronoun that stands for *our farm,* thus representing both the speaker and the speaker's farm.)

The King James Bible uses the archaic forms *thy* and *thine* as second person singular pronouns in the possessive case. *Thy* precedes consonant sounds, and *thine* precedes vowel sounds. In archaic usage, *my* also precedes consonant sounds, and *mine* precedes vowel sounds.

"<u>Thy</u> prayers and <u>thine</u> alms are come up for a memorial before God."
"Thou knowest <u>my</u> downsitting and <u>mine</u> uprising."

4. *Gender.* The gender of a pronoun is *masculine, feminine, neuter,* or *common.* This is the same as for nouns, as you studied in Lesson 59. Only third person singular pronouns have specific forms for gender. They are as follows: *he, him, his* (masculine); *she, her, hers* (feminine); *it, its* (neuter). All other personal pronouns are of common gender.

5. *Agreement of pronouns and antecedents.* A pronoun must agree with its antecedent in person, number, and gender. In the following sentence, the pronouns are underlined and the antecedents are italicized.

Felix Manz lost <u>his</u> life because he opposed the *Zwinglians* and <u>their</u> teachings.
(*His* is third person singular, masculine gender, to agree with *Felix Manz.*
Their is third person plural, common gender, to agree with *Zwinglians.*)

Compound Personal Pronouns

The compound personal pronouns end with *-self* or *-selves.* Below is a table showing the nine compound personal pronouns (including one archaic form).

	Singular	**Plural**
First person:	myself	ourselves
Second person:	yourself (thyself)	yourselves
Third person:	himself, herself, itself	themselves

Be sure to use the correct forms of compound personal pronouns. The following forms should be avoided: *ourself, themself, hisself, theirselves.*

A compound personal pronoun can serve in two ways. If it is *intensive,* it serves to add intensity or emphasis to another noun or pronoun. Such a pronoun serves as an appositive, emphasizing a person or thing by referring to it a second time.

If a compound personal pronoun is *reflexive,* it shows an action done by the subject to itself. In this use, the pronoun functions as the direct object, the indirect object, or the object of a preposition and shows an action *reflected* back to the subject.

Intensive: We *ourselves* are responsible for this predicament.
　　　　　　The girls *themselves* put up the new curtains.
　　　　　　The girls put up the new curtains *themselves.*
Reflexive: Roger gave *himself* a severe scolding. (indirect object)
　　　　　　You boys may take a short hike by *yourselves.*
　　　　　　　(object of preposition)

Usage of Personal and Compound Personal Pronouns

1. *Use the proper case when a pronoun follows* than *or* as. Such a pronoun is either a subject or an object in an elliptical clause. Therefore, you must consider what the completed construction of the clause would be, and choose the correct pronoun case to fit that construction. Sometimes either case is correct, depending on the meaning.

> Sandra is more artistic than I.
> > (Completed construction: than *I am artistic. Me* does not fit.)
> We meet the Millers more often than them.
> > (Completed construction: more often than *we meet them.*)
> We meet the Millers more often than they.
> > (Completed construction: more often than *they meet the Millers.*)

2. *Never use apostrophes with personal pronouns in the possessive case.* The possessive forms of some other classes of pronouns require apostrophes. With personal pronouns, however, use apostrophes only to form contractions.

> He's doing his assignments, but yours and hers are completed already.

3. *When you speak about another person and yourself, refer to the other person first and yourself last.* This not only represents correct grammar but also complements the Bible principle, "In honour preferring one another."

> Mr. Totter, our neighbor, wants Brian and me to shovel his snow this winter.

4. *Do not use compound personal pronouns to replace personal pronouns.* Use them only as intensive or reflexive pronouns, as illustrated above.

> **Incorrect:** Harry and myself turned out a baseball bat on the old lathe.
> > Cleon's family and ourselves traveled together to Niagara Falls.
> **Correct:** Harry and I turned out a baseball bat on the old lathe.
> > Cleon's family and we traveled together to Niagara Falls.

Applying the Lesson

A. Copy each personal pronoun, including any possessive form used as an adjective. Label its person (*1, 2, 3*), number (*S, P*), case (*N, O, P*), and gender (*M, F, N, C*).
1. When Samuel heard God's voice, he thought Eli was calling him.
2. At the people's request, Aaron made them a golden calf, and they worshiped it.
3. Jesus said, "I am the way, the truth, and the life: no man cometh unto the Father, but by me."
4. The man who displays his giving receives from the world its applause and praise.
5. Our good deeds can never gain for us a position in heaven.
6. We know that the woman who touched Jesus' garment was healed because of her faith in Jesus.
7. If you sow wild oats, my friend, they will grow to produce a bitter harvest.
8. Children, treat your parents with utmost respect, for they deserve it.

Lesson 62 Answers
Applying the Lesson
A. 1. he—3, S, N, M; him—3, S, O, M
2. them—3, P, O, C; they—3, P, N, C; it—3, S, O, N
3. I—1, S, N, C; me—1, S, O, C
4. his—3, S, P, M; its—3, S, P, N
5. Our—1, P, P, C; us—1, P, O, C
6. We—1, P, N, C; her—3, S, P, F
7. you—2, S, N, C; my—1, S, P, C; they—3, P, N, N
8. your—2, P, P, C; they—3, P, N, C; it—3, S, O, N

B. Write a personal pronoun to fit each description.
1. first person, plural, objective case
2. third person, plural, nominative case
3. second person, possessive case (2 forms)
4. first person, singular, possessive case (2 forms)
5. third person, singular, objective case, feminine gender
6. third person, singular, possessive case, neuter gender

C. Copy each compound personal pronoun, and write whether it is intensive (*I*) or reflexive (*R*).
1. We continually reminded ourselves of the warm house we would find at the end of the hike.
2. Mother said herself that she planned to invite company on Sunday.
3. Jacob hurt himself when he slipped on the wet floor.
4. The girls prepared the entire meal by themselves.
5. We owe everything we have to God Himself.
6. The Nile River itself was turned to blood.
7. If you find yourself groping for answers, ask for advice.
8. We must forbear with others, for we have some shortcomings ourselves.

D. Diagram these sentences, which contain infinitives with subjects.
1. Father asked Henry to hold the wrench.
2. The children watched him tighten the bolts.
3. He let them start the motor.
4. Then they helped him to mow the lawn.

E. Find the errors in pronoun usage, and write the correct words or phrases. If a sentence has no error, write *correct*.
1. Brother Melvin prepared for the demonstration by hisself.
2. The students gathered theirselves around his desk.
3. He told ourselves that the bowl contained water.
4. He then asked I to connect the wires to a battery.
5. We saw for ourself that the test tubes were filling with gas.
6. As different students asked questions, Brother Melvin answered them himself.
7. Me and Jeffrey noticed that one tube had collected twice as much gas as the other one.
8. Brent declared that the tube with more gas contained oxygen; Stephen was not as sure as him about that.
9. The teacher asked Brent and he to tell us the formula for water.
10. They did not have their books, so Miriam loaned them her's.
11. When us students heard the formula H_2O, we began to understand.
12. Brother Melvin hisself explained, "Every decomposed water molecule produces twice as much hydrogen as oxygen."
13. Was there any way for him to prove which gas was which?
14. Us girls were extremely curious as he collected the gases in two new test tubes.

B. 1. us
2. they
3. your, yours
4. my, mine
5. her
6. its

C. 1. ourselves—R
2. herself—I
3. himself—R
4. themselves—R
5. Himself—I
6. itself—I
7. yourself—R
8. ourselves—I

D. 1.

2.

3.

4.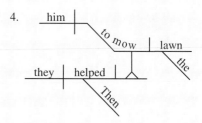

E. 1. himself
2. themselves
3. us
4. me
5. ourselves
6. correct
7. Jeffrey and I
8. he
9. him
10. hers
11. we
12. himself
13. correct
14. We

15. The ones who held the tubes were Paul and him.
16. The boys themself helped to get a wood splint burning.
17. Brother Melvin blew out the splint and said, "Paul, I'm ready for your's."
18. When he inserted the glowing splint into the tube, everyone except me and Elizabeth heard a distinct bark.
19. "Hydrogen is known as the barking gas," he said; so we were all as sure as him that this tube had contained hydrogen.
20. The ones who tested the other tube were George and him; this time the glowing splint burst into flame.

15. he
16. themselves
17. yours
18. Elizabeth and me
19. he
20. he

Review Exercises

A. Write the letters of the correct plural forms in each sentence. [61]
1. From the (ᵃchimneys, ᵇchimnies) poured huge (ᵃpuffs, ᵇpuffes) of smoke.
2. The (ᵃeditors in chief, ᵇeditor in chiefs) carefully examined the (ᵃleafs, ᵇleaves) of the books.
3. Many huge (ᵃbison, ᵇbisons) thundered across the prairie with pounding (ᵃhoof, ᵇhooves).
4. Before (ᵃworkmans, ᵇworkmen) could complete the Panama Canal, they had to reduce the great numbers of (ᵃmosquitoes, ᵇmosquito).
5. Please put out two (ᵃcupsful, ᵇcupfuls) of seed for those (ᵃtitmouses, ᵇtitmice).
6. For one measure in the song, the (ᵃsopranos, ᵇsopranoes) rested while the (ᵃaltos, ᵇaltoes) carried the melody.
7. Our (ᵃfamilys, ᵇfamilies) attend Bible-believing and Bible-obeying (ᵃchurchs, ᵇchurches).
8. The (ᵃneighbors, ᵇneighbores) spend many hours relaxing on their (ᵃpatioes, ᵇpatios).

B. Write the letter for the correct foreign plural form of each singular noun. [61]
1. nova   a. novae   b. novum
2. vortex   a. vorta   b. vortices
3. thesis   a. thesae   b. theses
4. hippopotamus   a. hippopotami   b. hippopotama
5. podium   a. podia   b. podii
6. appendix   a. appendi   b. appendices

Review Exercises

A. 1. a, a
2. a, b
3. a, b
4. b, a
5. b, b
6. a, a
7. b, b
8. a, b

B. 1. a
2. b
3. b
4. a
5. a
6. b

---

63. Other Pronoun Classes

Demonstrative Pronouns

The four demonstrative pronouns (*this, that, these, those*) point out specific persons or things. A demonstrative pronoun is a pronoun only when it functions as a substantive. If it precedes and modifies a noun, it is an adjective telling *which* rather than a pronoun.

Lesson 63

Purpose: To review the characteristics and usage of demonstrative, relative, interrogative, and indefinite pronouns.

Teaching Suggestions:

Only two details in this lesson are new to this English series: relative pronouns introducing noun clauses and compound relative pronouns. Neither of these details represents a major or difficult concept.

The community in which you teach will influence which usage points of the lesson you must especially emphasize. Consider what errors you hear frequently; or better yet, ask your students to tell which ones they tend to make.

God has always rewarded faith in Him, and *that* will never change.
  (subject of clause: pronoun)
This truth gives us hope for the future.
  (precedes and modifies a noun: adjective)

Two rules for correct usage of demonstrative pronouns deserve special mention.
1. Never use *them* as a demonstrative pronoun.
2. Do not say *this (these) here* or *that (those) there.*

Incorrect: <u>Them</u> are outstanding heroes of faith.
    We must be like <u>those there</u> men.
Correct: <u>Those</u> are outstanding heroes of faith.
    We must be like <u>those</u> men.

Relative Pronouns

There are six relative pronouns: *who, whom, whose, which, what, that.* You learned in previous years that a relative pronoun introduces an adjective clause which modifies the antecedent of the relative pronoun.

Noah, <u>*who feared God,*</u> built an ark on dry ground.
  (The relative pronoun *who* introduces an adjective clause that modifies
    Noah, the antecedent of *who.*)

You have learned that the same pronouns may introduce noun clauses. They are also classed as relative pronouns when they function in that way. A relative pronoun has no antecedent when it introduces a noun clause.

Do you know <u>*what motivated him in that hard task*</u>?
  (The relative pronoun *what* introduces a noun clause that is the direct object
    of *you Do know.* There is no antecedent for *what.*)

That is a relative pronoun only when it has a substantive function. If it simply introduces a clause, it is a conjunction.

The apples <u>that</u> we bought are Golden Delicious.
  (direct object in adjective clause: relative pronoun)
I think <u>that</u> they were picked too green.
  (no substantive function; simply introduces noun clause: conjunction)
I think <u>that</u> spoils their taste. (subject in noun clause: relative pronoun)

Correct usage of the relative pronouns requires that *who* and *whom* refer only to people, *which* refer only to things, and *that, what,* and *whose* refer to either people or things. In the King James Bible, however, *which* often refers to people.

Youth <u>who</u> can resist temptation have learned a valuable lesson.
  (not *youth which*)
Those two kittens, <u>which</u> we found on our front porch, have entertained the
    children for hours. (not *kittens who*)
The man <u>that</u> was blind possessed an understanding <u>that</u> the Pharisees lacked.
"Come, see a man, <u>which</u> told me all things that ever I did" (John 4:29).

Three of the relative pronouns actually are different forms of the same word, used to show different cases. *Who* is nominative, *whom* is objective, and *whose* is possessive.

> Andrew Smith, <u>who</u> painted our house, has thirty years of experience.
>> (nominative *who* for subject of clause)
> Mrs. Graham, from <u>whom</u> we buy our eggs, keeps a small flock of chickens.
>> (objective *whom* for object of preposition)
> I do not know <u>whose</u> shoes are making these black marks.
>> (possessive *whose* for adjective)

Compound relative pronouns are formed by adding *-ever* or *-soever* to simple relative pronouns. They introduce only noun clauses.

> <u>Whoever</u> drinks of the water of life has inner peace in <u>whatever</u> circumstances he faces.

Interrogative Pronouns

The interrogative pronouns (*who, whom, whose, which, what*) introduce questions. Each of these pronouns also serves a specific function in the sentence, such as a subject or a direct object. When *who, whom, whose,* and *which* are interrogative pronouns, the same usage rules apply as when they are relative pronouns. The only exception is that the interrogative pronoun *which* can refer to persons as well as things.

> <u>Who</u> is coming down the stairs?
>> (*Who* acts as a subject and refers to a person.)
> <u>Whom</u> shall we invite for dinner?
>> (*Whom* acts as a direct object and refers to a person.)
> <u>Whose</u> can we borrow? (*Whose* acts as a direct object and refers to a person.)
> <u>Which</u> is your brother? (*Which* acts as a subject and refers to a person.)
> <u>What</u> is she asking for?
>> (*What* acts as the object of a preposition and refers to a thing.)

Indefinite Pronouns

The indefinite pronouns, as their name suggests, do not refer to definite persons, places, or things. Unlike most other pronouns, they often have no specific antecedents. Many indefinite pronouns are always singular: *each, either, neither, one, another, anybody, anyone, anything, everybody, everyone, everything, somebody, someone, something, nobody, no one, nothing.* Most of the pronouns in this group contain the singular word element *other, one, thing,* or *body.*

When one of these singular pronouns functions as a subject, a prepositional phrase with a plural object often comes between the subject and the verb. Be careful to make the verb agree with the subject, not with the object of the preposition. If any other pronoun refers to the singular subject, it must also be singular.

> <u>Each</u> of the articles <u>presents</u> *its* message clearly and effectively.
> <u>Everyone</u> in our churches <u>has</u> *his* personal responsibilities to fulfill.

A few indefinite pronouns are always plural: *both, few, many, others, several.* Use plural verbs with these pronouns, and use plural pronouns in referring to them.

<u>Several</u> of the farmers <u>were selling</u> *their* produce at local markets.

A few indefinite pronouns may be either singular or plural: *some, any, none, all, most.* The number of the pronoun depends on the number of its antecedent. When one of these pronouns is used as a subject, that antecedent often occurs in a prepositional phrase between the subject and the verb. If the antecedent is singular, the indefinite pronoun is singular because it refers to a certain portion of that one thing. If the antecedent is plural, the indefinite pronoun is plural because it refers to certain individual items in that set of things.

<u>Some</u> of this *market* <u>is</u> in the open air.
    (A portion of this one thing is in the open air.)
<u>Some</u> of these *markets* <u>are</u> in the open air.
    (Some items in this set of things are in the open air.)

<u>None</u> of this *fruit* <u>comes</u> from another state.
    (No portion of this one thing comes from another state.)
<u>None</u> of these *fruits* <u>come</u> from another state.
    (No items in this set of things come from another state.)

Make the possessive forms of indefinite pronouns by adding *'s.* This is different from the possessive forms of personal pronouns, which do not have apostrophes.

<u>Everyone's</u> composition is lying on <u>his</u> desk.

The words listed as indefinite pronouns are pronouns only if they have a substantive function in a sentence. Many of these words also function as modifiers, and then they are adjectives.

I ate <u>both</u> of the buns for breakfast. (pronoun used as direct object)
I ate <u>both</u> buns for breakfast. (adjective modifying direct object)

Applying the Lesson
A. Copy each pronoun, and write whether it is personal (*P*), compound personal (*CP*), demonstrative (*D*), indefinite (*ID*), interrogative (*IR*), or relative (*R*). Include the possessive pronouns used as adjectives.
1. We show ourselves to be good or poor sports by many of our actions on the playground.
2. One must play graciously, without scolding his teammates for the errors that they make.
3. Who enjoys playing with someone who has not learned this?
4. Let others play their parts by themselves; that allows everyone to enjoy the game.
5. Even when you are winning, control yourself and guard against comments which could make someone on the other team feel bad.

Lesson 63 Answers
Applying the Lesson
A. 1. We—P; ourselves—CP; many—ID; our—P
   2. One—ID; his—P; that—R; they—P
   3. Who—IR; someone—ID; who—R; this—D
   4. others—ID; their—P; themselves—CP; that—D; everyone—ID
   5. you—P; yourself—CP; which—R; someone—ID

6. Which is more important to me, winning the game or helping all to enjoy themselves?

B. Choose the correct words in parentheses.
1. Both of my parents (was, were) advising me to try.
2. Each of the ministers (take, takes) part in the morning service.
3. One of the brethren (lead, leads) the singing.
4. Most of us (have, has) a priceless Christian heritage.
5. Everyone (enjoy, enjoys) the fellowship during and after the service.
6. Have you ever met anybody who considers (himself, themselves) indispen-
sable?
7. Some of my friends (think, thinks) the work is too difficult.
8. Several of these cauliflower heads (is, are) beginning to turn brown.
9. (Is, Are) any of the cake left for me?
10. (Have, Has) all of those cakes been eaten already?
11. Either of your suggestions (offer, offers) a reasonable solution.
12. Another of the trees (have, has) been blown over.

C. Write one or two words to show how to correct each error. If the sentence is correct, write *correct.*
1. Brother Mahlon is the man who you should ask about the oil leak.
2. You will ruin that there engine if you run it without oil.
3. The mechanic which serviced your car did not tighten the drain plug.
4. We can avoid most mistakes if everyone does his work carefully.
5. This composition is full of life, but them use the passive voice too much.
6. I have a very good idea whom the writers were.
7. All of my aunts and uncles are planning to be at the reunion.
8. Should a nonresistant Christian have a dog who would viciously attack an
intruder?
9. We should bear one anothers burdens.
10. Them are my books, but you are welcome to borrow a few.
11. I have no idea whom the author is.
12. Mr. Morgan is a salesman who you can trust.

Review Exercises

Write the letters of the correct forms in each sentence. [61]
1. When Brother ([a]Amos', [b]Amos's) neighbor visited our church, he especially
enjoyed the ([a]congregation, [b]congregation's) singing.
2. After ([a]a moment's hesitation, [b]the hesitation of a moment), Ellen lifted ([a]the
trap's arm, [b]the arm of the trap) and removed the dead mouse.
3. The ([a]boy, [b]boy's) talking to your brother is as tall as ([a]Wanda's, [b]Wandas')
father.
4. ([a]Womens', [b]Women's) purses and ([a]girls', [b]girls's) shoes are on sale this
week.
5. ([a]Brother Edgar, [b]Brother Edgar's) and Sister Marie's family will be helping
to clean ([a]Aunt Alice, [b]Aunt Alice's) and Sister Carol's houses this fall.

6. Which—IR; me—P; all—ID;
themselves—CP

B. 1. were
2. takes
3. leads
4. have
5. enjoys
6. himself
7. think
8. are
9. Is
10. Have
11. offers
12. has

C. 1. whom
2. that engine
3. who
4. correct
5. those
6. who
7. correct
8. that *or* which
9. another's
10. Those *or* They
11. who
12. whom *or* that

Review Exercises
1. b, b
2. a, b
3. a, a
4. b, a
5. a, b

6. (ᵃRuth's, ᵇRuths') faithfulness was ample reward for all her (ᵃmother's-in-law, ᵇmother-in-law's) sacrifices.
7. Brother Levi asked his (ᵃministers's, ᵇministers') advice before he agreed to his (ᵃson, ᵇson's) serving in Guatemala.
8. It is ironic that the Jews cried for (ᵃJesus', ᵇJesus's) crucifixion and accepted (ᵃBarabbas', ᵇBarabbas's) release.

6. a, b
7. b, b
8. a, b

64. Improving Your Writing Style, Part 4: Using Poetic Devices

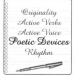

To develop an effective writing style, you must put much time and effort into your work. You need to look for ways to weave original, creative expressions into your sentences. And you must take special care to put energy into your verbs—by choosing lively action verbs instead of linking verbs, and by using the active voice rather than the passive voice.

Yet another way to add appeal to your writing is by the use of poetic devices. The words of poetry have a distinct musical quality. By borrowing a few devices from poetry, we can put some of that music into our prose writing. Three of these devices are described below.

1. *Alliteration.* This is the repetition of beginning consonant sounds. Poems often use this repetition to produce a musical effect. Feel the music in the example below.

Day is dying in the west,
Heaven is touching earth with rest;
Wait and worship while the night
Sets her evening lamps alight
Through all the sky.

Just as alliteration adds appeal to poetry, it can add appeal to prose. For the most striking effects, weave alliteration into the more significant words of your sentences. Also consider that different sounds add different musical tones. The repetition of sharp, cutting sounds like /b/, /d/, or /k/ can add a tone of harshness and increase the tempo of a sentence. On the other hand, the repetition of slow, soft sounds like /f/, /m/, or /s/ can add a note of mildness and slow the speed of a sentence.

Read the following sentences. Each pair says basically the same thing, but note the music in the second set of sentences because of their alliteration.

Without alliteration:
Bitterness damages the hearts of those it controls.
Grandmother's pleasant face gives cheer wherever she goes.

Lesson 64

Purpose: To teach the use of *poetic devices as an element of an effective writing style.

Teaching Suggestions:

You could begin class by asking the students to name some elements of poetry, and discussing how these elements make poems musical. The students should be familiar with the poetic devices reviewed in this lesson.

With alliteration:

Bitterness becomes a blight on the inner being of those it controls.
(The repetition of the hard /b/ matches the idea of bitterness.)
Grandmother's smiling face spreads sunshine wherever she goes.
(The repetition of soft /s/ sounds matches the idea of cheer.)

2. *Rhyming words.* We can also borrow from poetry the music of rhyme. We will not do this often; but in the few places where it is suitable, rhyme will add a few notes of melody to our writing. The rhyming words should come fairly close together for the best effect. As with alliteration, we need to choose significant words for the rhymes.

Read the following pairs of sentences. Observe how rhyme adds to their appeal.

Without rhyming words:

Christians commit themselves to obey truth and to share it with others.
Godly fear and worldly mirth never abide in the same heart.

With rhyming words:

Christians commit themselves to live and to give the message of truth.
Godly fear and worldly cheer never abide in the same heart.

3. *Onomatopoeia* (on′·ə·mat′·ə·pē′·ə). This is the use of a word having an imitative sound. Onomatopoeia appeals especially to children, but a limited use of it can contribute to an effective style in any type of writing.

Can you hear the music added to each of these sentences by their onomatopoeia? (The last example uses both rhyme and onomatopoeia.)

Without onomatopoeia:

The boasting of pride and the complaining of self-pity war against the soul.
Let nothing turn you aside, whether it be the world's approval or disapproval.

With onomatopoeia:

The blustering of pride and the murmuring of self-pity war against the soul.
Let nothing turn you aside, whether it be the world's hooting and jeering or its clapping and cheering.

Your assignment in this lesson will be to write a paragraph of description. In such a paragraph, the topic sentence should give a brief, basic sketch of what is being described. The rest of the paragraph should expand the topic sentence by giving details that clarify or illustrate it.

Read the following paragraph. Can you see how the poetic devices add musical appeal to the description?

The children huddled around the fireplace, trying to keep warm as the blizzard raged. It howled and growled, rattling the windows, rumbling in the chimney, and rocking the small cabin. Snow swished against the walls and sifted through cracks around the door. Mother had set one kerosene lamp on a windowsill, but it was only a feeble light in the dark night. Before going to bed, the family knelt and prayed that Father would find his way home safely.

Applying the Lesson

A. Improve the style of the following sentences by using alliteration, rhyming words, and onomatopoeia. Be ready to compare your work with that of your classmates, to see the various things that can be done.
1. The market resounded with the sounds of dogs, sheep, and cattle.
2. In order to live as you should, you must forsake wrong.
3. Amid the noisy activities of daily life, do not forget to enjoy the sounds of the wind and the brook.
4. Faith perceives the unseen, accepts the unbelievable, and obtains the impossible. (The second and third verbs should rhyme with *perceives,* and all the direct objects should begin with *i.*)
5. To do things "decently and in order," do them readily, correctly, and patiently. (Use three adverbs beginning with *p.*)

B. Write a paragraph of description on one of the following topics. Put special effort into using poetic devices and applying the other elements of effective writing style that you have studied.
1. the family car
2. the kitchen (or another room) in your home
3. the woods (or another outdoor place) where you live

Review Exercises

Write the letters of the sentences with the better writing style. [3, 22, 39]
1. a. The gentle rain made the flowers look brighter again.
   b. The gentle rain washed the dainty face of each flower.
2. a. I wish I had given my tongue a vacation.
   b. I wish I had not talked so much.
3. a. The plumber thanked me profusely for helping him carry his tools to his truck.
   b. The plumber heaped upon me a truckload of unmerited thanks for helping him convey his occupational equipment to his work vehicle.
4. a. The setting sun was making the waves sparkle like diamonds.
   b. The setting sun was skipping stars across the waves.
5. a. Soon the evening sky was a shining pink and gold.
   b. Soon the evening sky glowed with pink and gold.
6. a. The visiting speaker gave numerous illustrations from nature.
   b. Numerous illustrations from nature were given by the visiting speaker.

Lesson 64 Answers
Applying the Lesson

A. (Sample answers. Give students the opportunity to read their sentences in class, so that everyone can evaluate and enjoy the poetic devices that are used.)
1. The market resounded with <u>barking</u> dogs, <u>bleating</u> sheep, and <u>bellowing</u> cattle.
2. In order to <u>live right</u>, you must <u>leave wrong</u>.
3. Amid the <u>clatter</u> and <u>clangor</u> of daily life, do not forget to enjoy the <u>whisper</u> of the wind and the <u>gurgling</u> of the brook.
4. Faith <u>perceives</u> the <u>invisible</u>, <u>believes</u> the <u>incredible</u>, and <u>receives</u> the <u>impossible</u>.
5. To do things "decently and in order," do them <u>promptly</u>, <u>properly</u>, and <u>patiently</u>.

B. (Individual work.)

Review Exercises
1. b
2. a
3. a
4. b
5. b
6. a

65. Identifying Substantives

Nouns and pronouns have specific functions in sentences: subjects, direct and indirect objects, predicate nominatives, and so forth. Words, phrases, or clauses that you would not necessarily identify as nouns or pronouns can also function in these ways. The term *substantive* is used for any word or word group that names something and serves as a noun or pronoun.

1. *Single-word nouns and compound nouns are substantives.* This includes all the words that obviously name persons, places, or things. You would recognize them as nouns without knowing how they were used in a sentence.

> Jesus Christ gave His life for the sins of mankind.

2. *Pronouns are substantives.* This includes the words in all six classes of pronouns that you reviewed in Lessons 62 and 63. However, a possessive pronoun that modifies a noun is not considered a substantive, for it functions as an adjective.

> We serve a God who reveals His power in everything He created.
> > (*His* is an adjective, not a substantive.)

3. *Infinitives and infinitive phrases may be substantives.* An infinitive is the basic form of a verb preceded by *to.* When an infinitive has a subject, the subject is part of the substantive. Infinitives and infinitive phrases used as adjectives or adverbs are not substantives.

> To listen is a good way to learn many things.
> > (*To listen* is an infinitive used as a subject. *To learn many things* is an infinitive phrase used as an adjective.)
> The doctor told Mother to rest for several days.
> > (*Mother to rest for several days* is an infinitive phrase with a subject; it is used as a direct object.)

4. *Gerunds and gerund phrases are substantives.* A gerund is the present participle of a verb (the *-ing* form) used as a noun. But remember that the present participle can also be used as a main verb or as an adjective.

> Our family enjoys singing when we are traveling.
> > (*Singing* is a gerund used as a direct object. *Traveling* is a main verb.)
> Lester's favorite pastime, reading history books, gives him a growing understanding of the present. (*Reading history books* is a gerund phrase used as an appositive to the subject. *Growing* is an adjective.)
> The giggling girls failed to realize the seriousness of being too lighthearted.
> > (*Being too lighthearted* is a gerund phrase used as the object of a preposition. *Giggling* is an adjective.)

5. *Prepositional phrases may be substantives.* Such a phrase names a place or a thing and usually functions as the subject of a sentence with a linking verb.

> In the furnace room is a good place to dry your gloves.
> > (prepositional phrase used as a subject)

Lesson 65

Purpose: To review the concept of substantives, and to review the various items that can be substantives.

Teaching Suggestions:

The term *substantive* can be somewhat abstract. Be sure to emphasize that this is not a separate part of speech.

6. *Noun clauses are substantives.* A noun clause is a dependent clause that functions as a substantive in a complex sentence.

> Whatever we do should be done as unto the Lord. (clause used as a subject)
> Even a child is known by what he does.
>   (clause used as the object of a preposition)
> The slothful man wishes that he would not need to work.
>   (clause used as a direct object)

7. *Any item used as a subject of discussion is a substantive.* Such an item is not being used in its normal sense; it is referred to as a symbol, a letter, a word, or a word group. Remember that a word or a letter used as a subject of discussion should be italicized (underlined).

> Three *e's* are buried in the word *cemetery*.
>   (The first underlined item is the subject, and the second is an appositive.)
> Should I pronounce *vehement* with a silent *h*?
>   (The first underlined item is the direct object, and the second is the object of a preposition.)

8. *Any title is a substantive.* Such a substantive may also be called a noun phrase.

> "My Old Bible" is my favorite poem about the Bible. (title used as a subject)
> The book *When Father Was a Boy* describes the growing-up years of Edward Sanger. (title used as an appositive to the subject)

The term *substantive* is a convenient label that includes nouns, pronouns, and any other expressions that serve as nouns. When you look for substantives in a sentence, first find the largest elements (the clauses) and then look for verbals and other kinds of noun phrases. Last of all, find the nouns, pronouns, and other small elements that serve as substantives.

Applying the Lesson

A. Copy all the words (including noun phrases) that function as substantives in these sentences.
1. All who view Niagara Falls are confronted with clear evidence of a mighty Creator.
2. Christians share God's love and mercy with those in need.
3. *Mississippi* has four *i*'s, yet it can see nothing.
4. We found some of this information in *Nature Friend,* a magazine for children.
5. What were the causes of the accident on Ridge Avenue?
6. Which is the most strongly accented syllable in the word *ambiguity*?

B. Copy the phrases and verbals that function as substantives in these sentences.
1. By imitating those around him, a small child quickly learns to do many things.
2. To read the preface of a book is a good way to evaluate its contents.
3. In the incinerator is the best place for sweepstakes offers.

Lesson 65 Answers
Applying the Lesson

A. 1. All, who, Niagara Falls, evidence, Creator
   2. Christians, love, mercy, those, need
   3. Mississippi, i's, it, nothing
   4. We, some, information, Nature Friend, magazine, children
   5. What, causes, accident, Ridge Avenue
   6. Which, syllable, word, ambiguity

B. 1. imitating those around him, to do many things
   2. To read the preface of a book
   3. In the incinerator

4. To have students who enjoy learning makes teaching a highly rewarding occupation.
5. Most people like to read, but they need more time to do it.
6. Before 6:00 is the best time to call Brother Harlan.

C. Copy the clauses and titles that function as substantives in these sentences.
1. The book *Our Solar System* tells how the gravity of the moon affects the earth.
2. According to what I have read, its pull causes the earth to flex.
3. What really surprises me is that the earth keeps its shape more rigidly than steel.
4. "The Planet Earth" is a good article for whoever wants to find more interesting facts.

D. Copy all the substantives in these sentences. Do not list separately a substantive within another substantive phrase or clause.
1. During the presidency of Richard M. Nixon, American astronauts amazed the world by landing on the moon.
2. Who would have thought that men could do such a thing?
3. They had left the earth itself and gone out into the heavens.
4. The president of the United States declared that it was the greatest event in history.
5. Neil Armstrong called the first small step which he took on the moon a giant leap for mankind.
6. Does anyone know the message on the plaque that the astronauts placed on the moon?
7. "We came in peace for all mankind."
8. Reading that message may remind us of something that happened long ago.
9. Jesus Himself left the heavens to come down to the earth.
10. The purpose of His coming was to bring peace and goodwill to men.
11. We know how the world rejected Jesus, and His mission seemed like a failure.
12. On the cross was a shameful place for Him to die.
13. Now I want you to answer a question.
14. Which of these two events was greater?

Review Exercises

A. Choose the correct words in these sentences. [62]
1. Brother Mark appointed Harvey and (he, him) as editors for our school newspaper.
2. He also wants Martha and (she, her) to help proofread the articles.
3. The artists for this project will be (me and Sidney, Sidney and I, Sidney and me).
4. Brother Mark said that the principal and (he, himself) will need to approve all the articles.
5. (We, Us) students will surely be busy now.
6. Since the students at Maple Hill School began their paper two weeks sooner than (we, us), their paper will be finished before (ours, our's).

C. 1. Our Solar System,
how the gravity of the moon affects the earth
2. what I have read
3. What really surprises me,
that the earth keeps its shape more rigidly than steel
4. "The Planet Earth,"
whoever wants to find more interesting facts

D. 1. presidency, Richard M. Nixon, astronauts, world, landing on the moon
2. Who, that men could do such a thing
3. They, earth, itself, heavens
4. president, United States, that it was the greatest event in history
5. Neil Armstrong, step, which, he, moon, leap, mankind
6. anyone, message, plaque, that, astronauts, moon
7. We, peace, mankind
8. Reading that message, us, something, that
9. Jesus, Himself, heavens, earth
10. purpose, coming, to bring peace and goodwill to men
11. We, how the world rejected Jesus, mission, failure
12. On the cross, place, Him to die
13. I, you to answer a question
14. Which, events

Review Exercises
A. 1. him
2. her
3. Sidney and I
4. he
5. We
6. we, ours

B. Choose the correct words in these sentences. [63]
   1. We meet many people (who, which) have poor listening habits.
   2. Too many are like sponges, (who, which) soak up everything they meet.
   3. The problem is that (these, these here) people absorb the bad as well as the good.
   4. On the other hand are those people (who, whom) we might call funnel-listeners.
   5. (They, Them) are at fault because they do not catch anything—it all goes right through!
   6. And surely none of us (want, wants) to be sieve-listeners, catching the bad while all the good passes through.
   7. If each of these (is, are) so bad, how then shall we listen?
   8. Make your mind like a colander in which all of the good things (remain, remains) while the unprofitable things drain away.

B. 1. who
    2. which
    3. these
    4. whom
    5. They
    6. want
    7. is
    8. remain

Discretion shall preserve thee, understanding shall keep thee.

Proverbs 2:11

66. Chapter 7 Review

A. Copy each noun, and write whether it is concrete (*C*) or abstract (*A*). Also label its gender (*M, F, N, C*).
1. Margaret was writing a story about the childhood of her grandmother.
2. Through the years, my teachers have demanded the best of all their students.
3. If a person will not do a humble task, he is not worthy of greater responsibilities.
4. Adam's sin in the Garden of Eden brought eternal consequences.
5. The widow of Nain received her son raised to life again.
6. In Galatians, Paul referred to Hagar and Sarah in his discussion of spiritual freedom.

B. Write the plural form of each noun. Use the foreign plural spellings for numbers 15–24.

1. grief	9. turkey	17. diagnosis
2. species	10. brother (two forms)	18. thesaurus
3. attorney at law	11. solo	19. index
4. tornado	12. pocketknife	20. crisis
5. eyetooth	13. trout	21. curriculum
6. footman	14. panoply	22. vertex
7. child	15. phenomenon	23. fungus
8. mother-in-law	16. antenna	24. memorandum

C. Write the possessive form of each noun.

1. Ulysses	5. hostess	8. Josephus
2. geese	6. daughter-in-law	9. patrolman
3. giraffes	7. visitors	10. king
4. chief of staff		

D. Copy each pronoun, and write whether it is personal (*P*), compound personal (*CP*), demonstrative (*D*), indefinite (*ID*), interrogative (*IR*), or relative (*R*). Include the possessive pronouns used as adjectives.
1. One never raises himself by pushing others down.
2. What can be done to help those who will not admit their mistakes?
3. You had better keep your eye on the man whom dogs distrust.
4. Few of our inconveniences are as serious as we often think.
5. That is not what I was expecting.
6. This must be done by some of the girls themselves.

E. Copy each substantive in these sentences, and label it *N* (one-word or compound noun), *Pron.* (pronoun), *G* (gerund or gerund phrase), *I* (infinitive or infinitive phrase), *Prep.* (prepositional phrase), *C* (clause), *T* (title), or *S* (subject of discussion). If a substantive is within a substantive phrase or clause or within a title, do not list it separately.
1. The moderator said that Brother Jason would conduct our devotions.
2. He sought to inspire us with the greatness of God.
3. *Uncle Ben's Quote Book* contains many short, forceful quotations.
4. By displaying Gospel tracts, we offer help to whoever may be seeking.

Lesson 66

Purpose: To review the concepts taught in Chapter 7.

Lesson 66 Answers

A. 1. Margaret—C, F; story—C, N; childhood—A, N; grandmother—C, F
2. years—A, N; teachers—C, C; best—A, N; students—C, C
3. person—C, C; task—A, N; responsibilities—A, N
4. sin—A, N; Garden of Eden—C, N; consequences—A, N
5. widow—C, F; Nain—C, N; son—C, M; life—A, N
6. Galatians—C, N; Paul—C, M; Hagar—C, F; Sarah—C, F; discussion—A, N; freedom—A, N

B.
1. griefs	13. trout
2. species	14. panoplies
3. attorneys at law	15. phenomena
4. tornadoes	16. antennae
5. eyeteeth	17. diagnoses
6. footmen	18. thesauri
7. children	19. indices
8. mothers-in-law	20. crises
9. turkeys	21. curricula
10. brothers, brethren	22. vertices
11. solos	23. fungi
12. pocketknives	24. memoranda

C.
1. Ulysses'	6. daughter-in-law's
2. geese's	7. visitors'
3. giraffes'	8. Josephus's
4. chief of staff's	9. patrolman's
5. hostess's	10. king's

D. 1. One—ID; himself—CP; others—ID
2. What—IR; those—D; who—R; their—P
3. You—P; your—P; whom—R
4. Few—ID; our—P; we—P
5. That—D; what—R; I—P
6. This—D; some—ID; themselves—CP

E. 1. moderator—N;
that Brother Jason would conduct our devotions—C
2. He—Pron.;
to inspire us with the greatness of God—I
3. Uncle Ben's Quote Book—T;
quotations—N
4. displaying Gospel tracts—G; we—Pron.; help—N; whoever may be seeking—C

5. The word *bullheaded* suggests refusing stubbornly to change one's mind.
6. "Loving Kindness" is the song which Uncle Jerry selected, and we plan to sing it now.
7. In the attic is our starting place; Mother wants us to find her old diary.
8. Before your test is the time to learn the spelling of the word *ambidextrous*.

F. Write the underlined items correctly. If an item has no error, write *correct*.
1. The Americans fighting a Civil War was a great calamity, and each of the battles were a tragedy.
2. Angela and me learned that this country of our's experienced much anguish and suffering.
3. There were over 600,000 men which died in the war, and most of the Southern families were bereft of a father, son, or brother.
4. The Northerners theirselves had offered a position of leadership to Robert E. Lee, who the South chose as their commander.
5. Me and Herman discovered that this was the first time photographers followed a war's progress.
6. This here opened the eyes of the nation to the horrors of war, even though none of the photographs was of actual battle scenes.
7. Since a subject had to hold hisself motionless for several minutes, Matthew Brady's and others' photographs were of soldiers posing between battles.
8. At a battle's end, they took pictures of the dead, often after some of the bodies were rearranged to make the pictures more striking.
9. Even though these here pictures shocked men and women, selfish and sinful men continue to fight those who they cannot get along with.
10. When Gerald's and Jolene's teacher goes to Bible school, we do not know whom the substitute will be.
11. Everyone except Sharon and herself was working faster than me.
12. Me and Julia made these cookies, but them were made by someone else.
13. Father bought these brown coats for Samuel and me, and that blue one is your's.
14. Even though the old tree's nectarines were knotty and bitter, the hogs who ate them were soon looking for more.
15. I don't know who raised these cantaloupes, but them on the truck came from New Jersey.
16. Sheila and myself have never done as well in algebra as him.

G. Write the correct words for these sentences about writing style.
1. Poetic devices have a ———— quality that adds appeal to writing.
2. The repetition of beginning consonant sounds is ————.
3. Repetition of sharp sounds like /b/ and /k/ will (increase, decrease) the tempo of a sentence, while repetition of soft sounds like /m/ and /s/ will (increase, decrease) the tempo.
4. A phrase like "believing and receiving" uses ———— to add appeal to writing.
5. The use of words having an imitative sound is ————.

5. word—N; bullheaded—S; refusing stubbornly to change one's mind—G
6. "Loving Kindness"—T; song—N; which—Pron.; Uncle Jerry—N; we—Pron.; to sing it now—I
7. In the attic—Prep.; place—N; Mother—N; us to find her old diary—I
8. Before your test—Prep.; time—N; spelling—G; word—N; ambidextrous—S

F. 1. Americans' fighting, was
2. Angela and I, ours
3. who, correct
4. themselves, whom
5. Herman and I, the progress of a war
6. This, were
7. himself, correct
8. the end of a battle, correct
9. these, whom
10. Gerald and Jolene's teacher, who
11. her, I
12. Julia and I, those
13. correct, yours
14. the nectarines from the old tree, that
15. correct, those
16. Sheila and I, he

G. 1. musical
2. alliteration
3. increase, decrease
4. rhyme
5. onomatopoeia

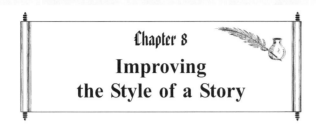

Chapter 8
Improving
the Style of a Story

67. Make a Story Live

To be interesting, a story must contain an appealing plot and conflict. Even if these things are present, however, a story may fail to appeal to readers if its style is poor. This chapter will teach you a number of methods for improving the style of stories you write. At the end of the chapter, you will apply those methods to the first draft of the story you wrote in Chapter 6.

A writer's style can make his story live or die. If his story lives, readers will reach out to receive its message. If his story dies, they will lay it aside and its message will have no effect on them. This lesson will help you to add vigor and energy to your story.

Use Natural Dialogue

Dialogue is an important element of effective stories. Without dialogue, a story becomes a mere account—much like a report or description. But just having the story characters communicating with each other is not enough. Their dialogue must sound natural—the way real people talk. Below are three points that will help you to write natural-sounding dialogue.

1. *Keep the tone informal.* Few people speak in the formal tone that marks an essay. Can you imagine visiting with your friends after school and talking like this?

"That was a very difficult history test, was it not?" asked Marlene.

"It certainly was a very difficult test!" declared Susan. "I am almost sure that I will have some wrong on those matching sets. Those essay questions were hard too! I could not remember even one thing for that last question!"

"Oh, I know those essay questions were hard." Marlene sighed. "I will be afraid even to look at my test when Brother Marcus returns it."

No, that is hardly the way you talk to your friends. Rather than using carefully structured, complete sentences, everyday speech contains contractions, interruptions, and elliptical sentences. The conversation above would be much more likely to sound like this:

"Quite a history test, wasn't it?" asked Marlene.

"Certainly was!" declared Susan. "I'm almost sure I'll have some wrong

Lesson 67

Purpose: To describe ways to make a story fresh and lively.

Teaching Suggestions:

If you filed the students' stories from Chapter 6, you might use them to emphasize the points of this lesson. You could read excerpts from the stories to illustrate strengths or weaknesses in relation to the lesson concepts.

None of the points of this lesson are new. All but the first, however, are new in the sense of applying these principles specifically to story writing.

on those matching sets. And those essay questions! I couldn't remember a thing for that—"

"Oh, I know." Marlene sighed. "I'll be afraid to even look at my test when Brother Marcus hands it back."

Establishing an informal tone, however, does not mean that you must use poor grammar, sloppy language, and slang. You might use poor grammar or sloppy language sparingly to characterize a specific person as being careless and unconcerned. But otherwise, such language is beneath the dignity of Christian writing.

2. *Change speakers frequently.* When people speak together, one person usually does not talk on and on. Instead, one person says a few things; then another asks a question or makes a comment, and so forth. Especially in a story, keep the quotations short. Long quotations stall the forward movement of a story.

3. *Use descriptive explanatory words.* Although *said* and *asked* are good words to use sometimes, a great variety of other terms can express *how* the characters said or asked their words. For example, words like *shout, call, demand, whisper, murmur, mutter, mumble, comment, prompt, agree, continue, answer, inquire,* and *question* can make an otherwise mediocre dialogue come alive.

Explanatory words must refer to things that can actually be done with words. People can *invite* with words, and they can *beg, call, shout, argue,* and so on. But no one can *hum, whistle, pause, point, smile,* or *frown* with words.

> **Incorrect:**
> "Come right on in," smiled Father.
> "Well, I just came to ask if I may borrow your tractor," paused Mr. Nelson.
> **Correct:**
> "Come right on in," Father invited with a smile.
> "Well, I just came to ask if I may borrow your tractor." Mr. Nelson paused.
> > (In the last sentence, *paused* is correct because it tells what Mr. Nelson did, not how he spoke. Note that it is in a separate sentence.)

Although explanatory words often contribute to the descriptiveness and smoothness of a story, they are not necessary in every paragraph of an extended dialogue. If the identity of the speakers is clear without stating who is speaking and you do not need to describe how they spoke, you may well omit the explanatory words altogether. The following example illustrates this point.

> Late that night Mervin heard a loud knock at the door. He jumped out of bed and ran to his parents' bedroom. "Father!" he gasped. "There's someone at the door!"
> Quickly Father got up, dressed, and hurried downstairs. Turning on the porch light, he saw a policeman standing outside!
> Father opened the door. "Good evening; what can I do for you?" he asked.

"Who's shooting around here?" demanded the policeman.

"I don't know," replied Father calmly.

"Do you have any boys?"

"Yes, six."

"Are they home?"

"Yes, they are all in bed. But Mervin heard the shooting. If you want to talk with him, I can call him."

Use Straightforward Language

Clear, straightforward language also adds life to the writing style. But if your story contains many uncertain expressions, it will appear weak to your readers. Notice the underlined words in the following excerpt.

"Melvin, you must take care of that boy of yours." Mr. Winters, the neighbor man, spoke in a loud, harsh-sounding voice. "Last evening he was down here throwing stones at my horses."

"Well," replied Melvin rather uneasily, "I know he does things like that sometimes. I guess I'll have to talk with him." He shuffled around a bit as if somewhat unsure of what to do next.

It is easy to see that Melvin is a weak and indecisive father. You may use indefinite expressions in the speech of a character like that, but be careful not to let them creep into the narrative itself. Compare the following version of the excerpt above.

"Melvin, you must take care of that boy of yours." Mr. Winters, the neighbor man, spoke in a loud, harsh voice. "Last evening he was down here throwing stones at my horses."

"Well," replied Melvin uneasily, "I know he does things like that sometimes. I guess I'll have to talk with him." He shuffled around as if unsure of what to do next.

Here is a list of uncertain expressions and endings that you should treat with suspicion.

a little (a bit)	fairly	probably	-ish
about	maybe	rather	-looking
almost	perhaps	seemed	-seeming
around	possibly	somewhat	

These expressions do have a proper use, of course, but you must exercise good judgment. For example, suppose you are writing about Nelson, whose height is 5 feet 11 inches. You may well describe him as being "almost six feet tall," since *six feet* is an exact measure. But if you describe him less precisely, say that he is "tall," not "somewhat tall." The word *tall* is already inexact, and *somewhat* only makes it more so. A story with numerous expressions like these cannot convey a clear, forceful theme.

Use Fresh, Original Language

You need to avoid clichés in the narrative parts of a story—the parts that describe what is happening. As you saw in Lesson 3, a cliché is an expression which has been repeated so often that it no longer has its original force. Though the expression had once been vivid and sparkling, it is now weak and dull.

Many clichés are worn-out figures of speech. If you find such an expression in your writing, replace it with an original figurative comparison. Otherwise, use clear, direct language to express your idea.

Poor: Uses clichés
> Though his face was <u>as white as a sheet</u>, George tried to make his voice to sound <u>as bold as a lion</u>.

Better: Uses an original comparison and direct language
> Though his face was <u>as pale as a wax figure</u>, George tried to make his voice to sound <u>strong and bold</u>.

Remember, though, that people often use clichés in everyday speech. So it is proper to include a limited number of clichés in dialogue. In fact, a cliché is sometimes the best choice because an original expression may sound unnatural. Consider the following examples.

> "That screw had been right here on the bench, <u>as plain as day</u>," Arnold declared. "Trying to find it now will be <u>like looking for a needle in a haystack</u>." (Clichés sound natural in dialogue.)

> "That screw had been right here on the bench, <u>as plain as a clock on the wall</u>," Arnold declared. "Trying to find it now will be <u>like looking for one grain of oats in a wheat bin</u>." (Original expressions often sound unnatural in dialogue.)

This does not mean that you should purposely use clichés to make your story dialogue sound natural. It simply means that you may have a story character use a cliché if that is the most natural expression for a given situation.

Appeal to the Five Senses

Close your eyes and plug your ears. Now try to enjoy a conversation with your friends. Try to enjoy the outside scenery. Try to enjoy *anything* happening around you. Your chances of succeeding are quite low, for we learn about the world around us through our senses. Without them, we would lose touch with our surroundings.

Remember this when you are writing a story, and strive to stimulate the senses of your reader. Appeal to his sense of sight by giving clear and vivid descriptions. Appeal to his sense of hearing by portraying the sighs and screeches and other sounds of your story. Show the smells and describe the tastes that go along with the action. Make the reader feel the heat or shiver with cold.

When the reader lives with your story characters—seeing, feeling, smelling, hearing, and tasting along with them—your story comes to life. Notice how this is accomplished in the following paragraphs. The parts that especially appeal to the senses are underlined.

> These descriptions show graphically the warmth and the cold. The reader can hardly help feeling with Fred as he faces the bitter elements outside.
>
> Not only does the writer mention the smells, but he goes on to describe them so temptingly that we feel as if we are stepping into the warm kitchen with Fred.

With a glance toward the barn two hundred feet away, Fred resolutely stepped out of the <u>cozy comfort</u> of the house. Immediately the <u>cold north wind bit</u> into the exposed flesh of his face. It <u>knifed through</u> his heavy coat. It stung his nose and burned his lungs.

Two hours later, <u>delicious breakfast smells</u> welcomed Fred back into the snug house. He could almost taste the <u>bacon sizzling</u> in the cast-iron frying pan as it filled the atmosphere with its aroma. More faintly, the <u>fragrance of freshly baked cornmeal muffins</u> floated across the room.

Here is another paragraph, this one appealing to the reader's sense of hearing.

> *Crash* and *tinkling* help the reader to hear the same sounds that poor Edna heard.

Suddenly Grandma Kramer's prized platter slipped from Edna's hands. It landed with a <u>crash</u>, followed by the <u>tinkling</u> of myriad pieces of china. Edna blinked back tears as she stared in horror at the ruins.

Remember: Have your characters speak with true-to-life expressions. Use straightforward language without *maybe*'s and *somewhat*'s. Think for yourself and avoid clichés. And aim for the five senses of your reader. The added life in your stories is well worth your extra efforts.

Applying the Lesson

A. Rewrite this story excerpt, following as many points of the lesson as possible to make the dialogue more natural. For one change, have Mother interrupt the speaker's detailed explanation in the third paragraph.

"What is wrong?" I asked as Mother replaced the telephone receiver.

In a tremulous voice, she said, "Keith has had an accident. Where is Father?"

"He is seeding alfalfa," I said. "That is what he said yesterday that his plans are. He would like to finish today because tomorrow it is supposed to rain."

"Take the pickup, and tell Father that Keith is in the hospital," Mother said.

"Thank You, Lord," I said in a whisper as I saw Father coming toward the near side of the alfalfa field.

Leaping from the truck, I sprinted across the field. "Father!" I said. "Keith is in the hospital. They have just transferred him to Springfield Medical Center."

Lesson 67 Answers
Applying the Lesson

A. (Improvements are underlined.)

"<u>What's</u> wrong?" I asked as Mother replaced the telephone receiver.

In a tremulous voice, she <u>responded</u>, "<u>Keith's</u> had an accident. <u>Where's</u> Father?"

"<u>Seeding</u> alfalfa," I replied. "<u>That's</u> what he said yesterday—"

"Take the pickup, and tell Father that <u>Keith's</u> in the hospital," Mother <u>directed</u>.

"Thank You, Lord," I <u>whispered</u> as I saw Father coming toward the near side of the alfalfa field.

Leaping from the truck, I sprinted across the field. "Father!" I <u>shouted</u>. "<u>Keith's</u> in the hospital. <u>They've</u> just transferred him to Springfield Medical Center."

B. Rewrite the underlined parts of these paragraphs, removing or replacing the clichés and indefinite expressions. If an underlined item needs no improvement, write *correct*.

"Young man." The gentleman addressed Ralph [1]in a fatherly-sounding voice. "Young man, the world has a place for talented, decent people like you. Have you ever considered going to college?" He surveyed Ralph [2]with kind-looking eyes.

"Well—ah—sir . . ." Ralph [3]hesitated a little and then [4]spoke somewhat more firmly. "Well, sir, I'm a Christian. I—"

"Of course," the man [5]answered as quick as a flash. "That's exactly why you could serve the world. You haven't ruined your life [6]in sowing wild oats as so many young people are doing today."

"It's only by the grace of God," replied Ralph, thinking of [7]his fairly sheltered life in a godly home. "But, sir, as for having a place in this world, I am not looking for that. I simply want to do God's will as faithfully as I can." Ralph had no desire to [8]blow his own horn; he would let the Lord choose the place where he should serve.

C. Follow the instructions to improve these story excerpts.
1. Rewrite to add appeal to the sense of hearing. (Add several words to indicate sounds.)

Darla stirred in her sleep. Then she sat bolt upright. "Is someone knocking at the door?" she wondered. Sure enough, the knocking sounded again.

Darla quickly crossed the hall and stood at her parents' bedroom door. "Father, Mother," she called, "someone's knocking at the front door."

2. Rewrite to add appeal to the sense of sight. (Add sentences describing what Father saw.)

Father looked anxiously at the clouds gathering in the west. Glancing back over the pepper patch, he urged, "Boys, we'd better hurry. Looks like a thunderstorm brewing."

3. Finish the second paragraph to describe Wendell's lunch in a way that appeals to the sense of taste. (Add sentences giving details of what Wendell enjoyed as he ate the lunch.)

When the sun stood high overhead, Grandpa said, "Time to eat, Wendell." Leaning their axes against the pile of split wood, the two made their way to the sugaring shack to eat lunch.

After a prayer of thanks to the Provider of life, health, and daily food, Wendell opened his lunch bag.

D. You wrote the first draft of an original story in Chapter 6. In Chapter 8, you will either write the second draft or write a new story. As you learn in this chapter how to improve stories, think of specific ways to apply those methods to your own story. (You may want to write down some ideas.) Your score on the second draft of the story will make up a considerable part of your Chapter 8 test score.

B. (Some answers may vary.)
1. in a fatherly voice
2. with kind eyes
3. hesitated
4. spoke more firmly
5. answered without hesitation
6. correct
7. his sheltered life
8. make a name for himself

C. (Sample answers.)
1. *Knock! Knock!* Darla stirred in her sleep. Then she sat bolt upright. "Is someone knocking at the door?" she wondered. *Knock! Knock!* Sure enough, the knocking sounded again.

   Darla quickly crossed the hall and stood at her parents' bedroom door. "Father, Mother," she called, "someone's knocking at the front door."

2. Father looked anxiously toward the west. A billowing mass of clouds was rapidly pushing its way in. Cirrus anvils loomed above the higher towers, and streaks of lightning danced among the darker folds. Glancing back over the pepper patch, Father urged, "Boys, we'd better hurry. Looks like a thunderstorm brewing."

3. After a prayer of thanks to the Provider of life, health, and daily food, Wendell opened his lunch bag. With a sigh of pleasure, he bit into the thick sandwich Mother had made. The hearty flavor of fried liver blended perfectly with the wholesome taste of Mother's homemade bread. A crisp dill pickle added its tangy savor to the delicious sandwich. Soon Grandma's buttermilk cookies were melting in his mouth, and the steaming cocoa from his thermos filled him with its soothing warmth. The sweet-tart of a Grimes Golden apple added the finishing touch to his meal.

D. (Individual work.)

Review Exercises

A. Write the correct term to match each description. [28–30]
1. Copying another's writing and passing it off as your own.
2. The main point of an essay.
3. A list of the sources used in preparing an essay.
4. A comment about a detail in the essay.

bibliography
exposition
footnote
plagiarism
theme

B. Write *true* if the statement is true, or *false* if it is false. [28–35]
1. The purpose of an exposition is to convince the reader of your idea or viewpoint.
2. The introductory paragraph of an exposition should resemble a funnel, with general ideas narrowing to a statement of the theme.
3. If a topic is too general, an essay is likely to be too detailed.
4. The abbreviation *ibid.* means "in the same place."
5. The entries in a bibliography should be numbered.
6. You should write a footnote for every detail that you draw directly from your notes.

Review Exercises

A. 1. plagiarism
2. theme
3. bibliography
4. footnote

B. 1. false
2. true
3. false
4. true
5. false
6. false

---

68. Keep the Action Flowing

A well-written story picks up the reader right at the beginning, carries him at a comfortable speed through the entire story, and sets him down with a satisfied feeling at the conclusion. Therefore, an important element of an effective story is a smooth flow of action. This lesson describes four ways to keep the action flowing.

Use Lively Action Verbs

Verbs are the engines of sentences. If you use sluggish engines, your story will move sluggishly. But powerful engines will make your story move briskly and energetically. In previous books of this series, you learned that verbs in the active voice give much more life and vigor to sentences than do linking verbs and passive verbs.

Linking verbs convey no movement. They suggest stationary characters and events. Passive verbs do express action, but they weaken its force because things happen automatically—the story characters do little or nothing. Read the following paragraphs, noticing how the underlined linking and passive verbs deaden the action.

> The sky <u>was</u> perfectly cloudless. Since there <u>was</u> not even the slightest breeze, the atmosphere <u>was heated</u> to an almost unbearable temperature by the blazing sunshine. The bean rows <u>appeared</u> almost endless.
> "I <u>am</u> dreadfully thirsty," sighed Dennis.

Lesson 68

Purpose: To describe ways to keep the story action moving forward.

Teaching Suggestions:

The first two parts of the lesson should be familiar to the students. They have worked with lively action verbs before (though not specifically in relation to story writing); and they were told in Chapter 6 to avoid painting portraits in a story. The other two parts of the lesson are new material.

"Yes," agreed Father, "the work certainly <u>is made</u> harder in this heat." Their progress <u>was surveyed</u> briefly, and then a welcome announcement <u>was made</u>. "Time for a break, boys."

Verbs in the active voice, as well as many intransitive complete verbs, do much better at keeping things brisk and interesting. Furthermore, using these strong verbs tends to draw out picturesque details in a way that linking verbs do not. As you read the following paragraphs, you should feel the stronger sense of movement produced by the active verbs.

Not a single cloud <u>graced</u> the sky. Not the slightest breeze <u>moderated</u> the blazing sunshine, which <u>heated</u> the atmosphere to an almost unbearable temperature. The bean rows <u>stretched</u> endlessly across the produce patch.
"I am dreadfully thirsty," sighed Dennis.
"Yes," agreed Father, "this heat certainly <u>makes</u> the work harder." He surveyed their progress briefly and then announced, "Time for a break, boys."

Notice that the improved version retains one linking verb: "I *am* dreadfully thirsty." Linking verbs portray a state of being, which is certainly true here. To rewrite this sentence with an active verb would produce a strained effect ("I have dreadful thirst").

Active voice and intransitive complete verbs generally make stronger engines than other verbs, but not all such verbs have equal "horsepower." So choose the most dynamic and descriptive verbs that fit the context. Compare the following examples.

Poor: Weak Verbs

"Wherever can that water be coming from?" asked Dawn.

"The bathroom!" Lois Ann <u>called</u> over her shoulder as she <u>went</u> up the steps two at a time. She <u>pushed</u> open the bathroom door with a *whoosh*.

A stream of warm water from the base of the faucet <u>was running</u> over the floor. Lois Ann <u>waited</u> but a moment; then she <u>put</u> her hand under the sink and <u>turned</u> the hot water shutoff valve.

Better: Strong Verbs

"Wherever can that water be coming from?" asked Dawn.

"The bathroom!" Lois Ann <u>flung</u> the words over her shoulder as she <u>raced</u> up the steps two at a time. She <u>threw</u> open the bathroom door with a *whoosh*.

A stream of warm water from the base of the faucet <u>was spraying</u> over the floor. Lois Ann <u>hesitated</u> but a moment; then she <u>reached</u> under the sink and <u>twisted</u> the hot water shutoff valve.

Limit Static Description

Every story includes a certain amount of static description. This is description that does not move the story forward, such as details about the setting or characters. A good story has as few such details as necessary. When static description is needed, try to slip it into a phrase or clause within a sentence that does carry the story action. Compare the following examples.

Poor: Too much static description

Terry stood outside the barn on the <u>dairy farm</u> where he lived, and <u>twelve-year-old Walter</u> stood nearby. The previous day had marked the last day of Terry's ninth year in school. Today was a <u>pleasant day in mid-May.</u> The <u>air was fresh and exhilarating</u>, and the sun shone brightly on the lush growth of grass. <u>Terry's hair was neatly combed</u>, but Walter had <u>unkempt hair.</u>

Better: Description woven into action

"Three months to enjoy the <u>farm!</u>" Terry voiced his thoughts to <u>twelve-year-old Walter</u>. The previous day had marked the last day of his ninth year in school. A <u>pleasant mid-May sun</u> smiled on the lush growth of grass. Terry took deep breaths of the <u>fresh, exhilarating air</u>. Brushing his hand across his <u>well-combed hair</u>, he glanced at Walter's <u>unkempt hair.</u>

Both paragraphs contain the same details (underlined), but note the contrast in how they are presented. In the better description, Terry *voiced his thoughts* rather than merely standing outside the barn. A pleasant mid-May sun *smiled* on the grass, and Terry *took deep breaths* of the fresh air. Terry was *brushing his hand* across his well-combed hair, and he *glanced* at Walter's unkempt hair. This is much more appealing than merely saying that it *was* a pleasant day, the air *was* fresh and exhilarating, Terry's hair *was* neatly combed, and so on. As much as possible, include such details in the action rather than presenting them as static description.

Avoid Arrested Action

A subtle snare that stalls story action is to have characters *begin* or *start* to do things rather than actually doing them. If Mother washed the dishes, do not write that she merely *began washing* them. If Susan swept the floor, avoid saying that she *started to sweep.* True, doing something always includes a beginning; but if you say that a story character merely *began* to do something, you arrest the action. Consider the following example.

Nolan whistled cheerily as he climbed the ladder to the haymow. At the top, he swung his leg over the beam and pulled himself onto the hay. Then he walked across the mow, grabbed a bale in each hand, and came back toward the edge of the mow.

"I'd better be careful," he said to himself. "Don't want to knock these end bales loose."

But even as he spoke, Nolan felt the bales shift beneath his feet. He threw himself backward and grabbed desperately for a handhold, but the entire edge of the mow had given way. With a sickening lurch, he plunged over the edge and landed with the hay bales on the floor below.

Father was just outside the milk house when he <u>began to hear</u> Nolan calling for help. He <u>started running</u> toward the barn as fast as he could.

Did Father actually hear Nolan, or did he only *begin* to hear him? Did he run to the barn or merely *start* running? Poor Nolan needed help, and we surely hope that Father indeed ran all the way to the barn. The following sentences keep the story moving without arresting the action.

> Father was just outside the milk house when he <u>heard</u> Nolan calling for help. He <u>ran</u> toward the barn as fast as he could.

Of course, *begin* and *start* do have valid uses. Sometimes an action is truly interrupted. And sometimes you may want to emphasize the time when an action began.

> Father <u>began to plow</u> the back field, but a hydraulic hose burst.
> Since Father <u>began plowing</u> the back field soon after lunch, he should be almost finished.

Match the Pace to the Action

On some occasions, things happen rapidly and time flies. On others, the activity around us almost stops and time seems to crawl. This difference shows up in stories too. Things happen at different speeds. As we write about these circumstances, we must match our story style to the speed of the action.

For example, suppose we are writing about a busy Saturday morning scene. A telephone call has just announced unexpected visitors for lunch. Suddenly much work must be done in a very short time. How can we write in a way that creates the feeling of hustle-and-bustle that would be present on such an occasion? As you read the following paragraphs, try to identify what it is that makes the action move rapidly.

> "All right, then. We'll be glad to see you folks again." As Father hung up the telephone receiver, all eyes focused on him.
> "Well, this is going to change our morning plans drastically," announced Father. "Brother Abner Krahn's are on their way to Lancaster County. Their trip went better than they had expected, and they want to visit with us for a few hours. They'll be here for lunch."
> "Oh, dear," wailed Melanie. "How will we ever get ready for company that fast?"
> "And whatever will we do with all those apples?" asked Ferne.
> "Some of them may just wait until Monday," Mother replied calmly to Ferne. "And," turning to Melanie, "we can easily prepare for company in four hours!"
> "Yes," agreed Father. "Everyone finished with breakfast? You're all excused. Clarence, finish feeding the stock. Nevin, mow the grass. James and Dallas, clean up around the house and barn. Then check with Mother."
> Suddenly the kitchen became a beehive of activity. The boys dashed outside. Father followed at a brisk walk. Melanie whisked the plates and cups off the table. Ferne plopped the dishpans and the draining rack into place. And Mother snatched the cookbook off the shelf.

Notice how short most of the sentences are. In the entire selection, the average is about eight words per sentence. But in the last two paragraphs, the sentences average only six words each. These short sentences give a distinct feeling of bustling activity.

In addition to the shortness of the sentences, the author's choice of words in the last paragraph pictures speed, energy, and excitement. Note the words *beehive, dashed, whisked, plopped,* and *snatched.*

Now suppose we are writing about a very different Saturday morning scene. Father and Mother had left for the hospital before breakfast because Grandfather was sick. The rest of the family is at home, waiting for news about Grandfather. How can we write in a way that emphasizes the slower action and dragging time on such a morning? Read the following paragraphs, noting how they differ from the example above.

> "Well, that's the latest breakfast I ever remember eating." Clarence sighed as he glanced around the table.
>
> "That's for sure," agreed Nevin. "Guess I didn't realize how much work Father does." He smiled sheepishly as he pushed his chair back from the table.
>
> Melanie nodded understandingly. "Same thing here in the kitchen, wasn't it, Ferne?"
>
> "Yes," answered Ferne. "I'm glad Mother isn't gone every morning." She paused and cleared her throat; then she added, "I sure wonder how Grandpa is doing."
>
> "So do I," stated Clarence. "But Father will call as soon as he has anything to report, so we may as well get started with the morning work. We have too many things to do to just sit here and talk."
>
> He rose from his chair and scratched his head thoughtfully. "Nevin, if you help me feed the livestock, you can start mowing while I do the other chores at the barn. James and Dallas should clean up around the house and barn. Do you girls have any work for them after that?"
>
> "Yes, they'll be a big help to us," replied Ferne.
>
> Listlessly the boys got up from the table and headed for their various chores. With a long sigh, Melanie picked up her cup and stacked it with the others. Ferne pulled the dishpans out from under the sink. Gazing out the window, she idly sloshed her hands in the water that slowly filled the dishpan.

Notice how much longer these sentences are than in the previous sample. In the entire selection, the sentences average about eleven words each. In the last three paragraphs, the average is thirteen words per sentence.

Again, the author's choice of words contributes to the pace of the story. Note the words *paused, listlessly, long sigh, idly,* and *slowly.*

As you can see, short sentences and lively words speed up the action of a story; but long sentences and sluggish words slow down the action. By using these devices, we can create a mood and pace that matches the action in a story.

Applying the Lesson

A. Rewrite this story excerpt, removing as many linking verbs and passive voice verbs as practical.

"Sure, Mrs. Nelson," Father responded. "Splitting and stacking your wood was enjoyed by the boys."

"Well, their work was greatly appreciated again. You folks are helpful to me in so many ways. Yet you're never fully repaid for your kindness." These words were spoken with deep emotion.

"Oh, but you're mistaken, Mrs. Nelson," Father said softly. "We are well rewarded by the Lord. Your praise should be given to Him."

On the way home, Father's statement was pondered by two tired boys. Finally the thoughts on their minds were expressed by Raymond. "Father, I wish Mrs. Nelson's offer to pay us for our work would be accepted. That would be better than the reward you talked about."

"Why, Raymond!" Father exclaimed. "That was surely said without thinking. How can anything be more valuable than the blessing of the Lord?"

B. Find each sentence with an example of arrested action, and write enough words to show how it can be improved.

1.   a"Well, girls," Mother declared after breakfast, "we must start cleaning the house and preparing dinner. bUncle Lamar's will be here before we're ready."

c"Yes," agreed Father as he began to push his chair back from the table. d"You boys have plenty to do too in the furniture shop. eFred, you start working at cleaning up the finishing room. fMervin, I want you to start turning that stock for McKee's order. gIt must be finished by tomorrow."

2.   a"Mother, this iron is starting to give me trouble again," Melinda called. b"It isn't staying hot like it should."

cMother began to sigh. d"Oh, no," she said. e"If the iron quits working too, what will we do?" fBut she had barely spoken when she began to think of some Bible promises assuring the saints of God's care.

3.   aI was at the far end of my trapline when I started to notice that the previously bright sunshine was dimming fast. bI glanced at the sky and checked the wind. cA cold deeper than the rising wind at the sub-zero temperature began to grip my heart. dA blizzard was brewing, and I had been too absorbed in my work to notice!

e"Dear Lord," I prayed as I began to hurry homeward, "protect me if it be Thy will."

C. Rewrite these story excerpts, following the directions for each.

1. This scene contains a number of static descriptions (underlined). Rewrite the scene to include those details within sentences that carry the story action. Begin your paragraph with the starred sentence.

It was a pleasant day in June. The uncles and aunts and cousins were sitting around the picnic tables at Uncle Raymond's farm.

Lesson 68 Answers
Applying the Lesson

A. (Sample answer. Improved verbs and their subjects are underlined.)

"Sure, Mrs. Nelson," Father responded. "The boys enjoyed splitting and stacking your wood."

"Well, I greatly appreciated their work again. You folks help me in so many ways. Yet I can never fully repay you for your kindness." Mrs. Nelson spoke these words with deep emotion.

"Oh, but you're mistaken, Mrs. Nelson," Father said softly. "The Lord rewards us well. You should give your praise to Him."

On the way home, two tired boys pondered Father's statement. Finally Raymond expressed the thoughts on their minds. "Father, I wish you'd accept Mrs. Nelson's offer to pay us for our work. That would be better than the reward you talked about."

"Why, Raymond!" Father exclaimed. "You surely said that without thinking. How can anything have more value than the blessing of the Lord?"

B. 1. a. we must clean the house and prepare dinner (May be considered acceptable.)
      c. he pushed his chair
      e. you work at cleaning up
      f. I want you to turn that stock
   2. a. is giving me trouble
      c. Mother sighed.
      f. she thought of some Bible promises
   3. a. I noticed
      c. gripped my heart
      e. I hurried homeward

C. (Sample answers.)
   1.   A solemn hush fell over the group as Grandfather Bender stood and lifted a shaky hand for silence. He

*A solemn hush fell over the group as Grandfather Bender stood and lifted his hand for silence. <u>His hair was snow-white,</u> and <u>his hands were shaky.</u> "It is a pleasure to come together like this again," he said. <u>His voice was tender,</u> and it trembled a bit more than usual. "The Lord has richly blessed us. We have a godly heritage. And we have plenty of food and clothing. Let us bow our heads and give thanks to our heavenly Father."

2. For this scene, suppose that Grandmother had just called and asked for Nancy's help in the afternoon. Rewrite the scene to change the slow-moving action to the more rapid action that would result. Change and add details to make things consistent.

"Now what shall I do next?" Nancy murmured to herself. Staring at the clock, she stifled a sigh. "Only ten o'clock!" Her words echoed in the kitchen that usually bustled with family activity.

"I never imagined that I would become so lonely this soon!" she declared to herself. Her mind went back to the morning two days before when Father and Mother and all the children except Abigail and her had left for New York. "Well, this is Saturday." Nancy sighed. "So it's just today and Monday to spend alone here, doing all the work. I guess I'd better get started with making the butter."

Review Exercises

A. Write the correct term to match each description. [49–53]
1. The lesson that a story teaches.
2. The process of portraying story characters.
3. The perspective from which an author writes a story.
4. The main character of a story.
5. The struggle or problem that the main character faces.
6. The time, place, and atmosphere of a story.

antagonist
characterization
conflict
point of view
protagonist
setting
theme

B. Write *true* if the statement is true, or *false* if it is false. [48–53]
1. Many effective stories are written about common, everyday happenings.
2. The first person point of view carries the strongest impression of reality.
3. The two most common methods of portraying characters are showing their actions and their appearance.
4. In the third person point of view, the author writes as if he were able to see every character equally well.
5. In a subjective point of view, the author reveals the thoughts of characters.
6. Background characters may be named, but they should not be characterized.

looked over the uncles and aunts and cousins sitting around the picnic tables at Uncle Raymond's farm. "It is a pleasure to come together like this again," said Grandfather in a tender voice. The pleasant June sun gleamed on his snow-white hair, and his voice trembled a bit more than usual. "The Lord has richly blessed us. We have a godly heritage. And we have plenty of food and clothing. Let us bow our heads and give thanks to our heavenly Father."

2. "What shall I do next?" Nancy wondered as she glanced at the clock. "Ten o'clock already!" she gasped. Her words echoed in the kitchen that usually bustled with family activity.

"I didn't imagine time would fly so fast!" she declared to herself. Her mind went back to the morning two days before. Father and Mother and all the children except Abigail and her had left for New York. "Since it's Saturday," Nancy declared, "I have only this forenoon and Monday to get the work done. Guess I'd better get started with the butter."

Review Exercises

A. 1. theme
2. characterization
3. point of view
4. protagonist
5. conflict
6. setting

B. 1. true
2. true
3. false
4. false
5. true
6. true

69. Paint Descriptive Details

A good story holds the reader's interest. While this is often due to the nature of the story and the development of its plot, the writer's choice of words also plays a major part. For just as a painter needs brilliant, sharp colors to make an attractive painting, so an author needs descriptive words to write an effective story.

Exact, Descriptive Words

Vagueness clouds writing and obscures its message. The only way to avoid such haziness is to use exact, descriptive words. Pay special attention to nouns and verbs, the two most important parts of speech. Whenever possible, use a precise noun or verb rather than a general word with modifiers. Your dictionary or thesaurus will help you to find the best possible word choices.

Compare the following sentences. Notice the precise nouns and verb forms that are underlined in the second example.

> **Vague:** The men forcefully threw the burning things from the building.
> **Clear:** Father and Uncle Charles flung the flaming rags from the shop.

Although modifiers are not as basic to our communication as nouns and verbs, they are also important. You need to choose colorful adjectives and adverbs to make the picture as clear as possible. Notice in the sample above that *burning* is changed to *flaming* because that paints a sharper picture. We could also add adjectives to describe *shop.*

> Father and Uncle Charles flung the flaming rags from the crowded furniture shop.

Remove every weak modifier. If a sentence would benefit from additional details, change the weak modifier to an appropriate adjective or adverb, or choose a more precise noun or verb. Be especially suspicious of the following weak modifiers.

anyway	exactly	really	some
certainly	just	right	such
definitely	maybe	so	very
even	quite		

Now compare the following sentences. Notice the improvement made by deleting or replacing the weak modifiers.

> **Weak modifiers:**
> Because the boys were very much involved in their game, they definitely failed to notice the really black clouds gathering in the west.
> **Exact modifiers:**
> Because the boys were deeply involved in their game, they failed to notice the inky clouds gathering in the west.

Simple, Familiar Words

Occasionally, a writer falls into the trap of thinking that many large and unusual words add to effective description. That is not necessarily true. In fact, simple,

Lesson 69

Purpose: To describe ways to enhance the descriptiveness of a story.

familiar words are generally the best. These words the reader will readily understand. If you do use an occasional larger or less familiar word, be sure the context makes the word easy to understand.

Here are two versions of a paragraph from the story "'He Rides Upon the Storm'" in Chapter 6. Observe the difference in the underlined words.

Poor: Uses uncommon words and expressions

> That very night I suddenly sat bolt upright in bed, my heart <u>beating apace</u>. "What was that?" I wondered bewilderedly. In <u>rejoinder</u>, there came a <u>resplendent</u> flash of lightning, followed <u>instantaneously</u> by a sharp crash of thunder. All <u>slumber having departed</u>, I <u>reclined</u>, closed my eyes, and shivered.

Good: Uses simple, familiar words

> That very night I suddenly sat bolt upright in bed, my heart <u>pounding wildly</u>. "What was that?" I wondered bewilderedly. In <u>answer</u>, there came a <u>brilliant</u> flash of lightning, followed <u>closely</u> by a sharp crash of thunder. All <u>sleepiness chased away</u>, I <u>lay down</u>, closed my eyes, and shivered.

Imagery

Imagery includes similes, metaphors, personification, and hyperboles. By making apt, striking comparisons, these figures of speech paint vivid word pictures. They are high-powered tools of descriptive writing. In the discussion below, the examples are from stories in Chapter 6.

A simile makes a figurative comparison by using *like* or *as.*

> Walter's urgent shouts jolted Terry <u>like an electric shock</u>.
> The rain and the hail combined into one <u>mighty, oceanlike roar</u>.

A metaphor makes a figurative comparison without using *like* or *as.* Some metaphors contain a form of *be* and say that one thing is another thing when that is not literally true. Other metaphors use literal terms to describe something that happens only in a figurative sense.

> "This grass sure needs a good <u>haircut</u>."
> Throwing the torn starter cord against the mower, Terry spun around, his face a <u>thundercloud</u>.
> He <u>threw the words</u> over his shoulder as he stalked away.
> Terry's voice <u>dripped</u> with annoyance.
> My mind <u>whirled into high gear</u>.

In personification, a thing or quality is pictured as if it had the characteristics of a living creature.

> The front lawn was nearly finished when the sputtering engine <u>coughed and died</u>.

A hyperbole is what might be called an artistic exaggeration. It gives an overstated description—not to deceive someone, but to create a vivid picture in the mind.

Sure enough, a <u>mountain</u> of feed covered the floor below the feed bin chute.

Challenge yourself to make your story so clear and colorful that readers feel as if they are personally involved in the action.

Applying the Lesson

A. Write words that are more exact and descriptive, which could replace the underlined words in this story excerpt. If an underlined item should be deleted, show that by writing the words immediately before and after it.

Grandmother always seemed happy, using her [1]<u>equipment</u> to [2]<u>work on</u> clothes for others. She was sitting there when I stepped into the [3]<u>room</u>.

With a [4]<u>tired sound</u>, I [5]<u>sat down</u> on a nearby chair. "What do you do, Grandmother, when someone [6]<u>just</u> deliberately tries to [7]<u>make you feel bad</u>?"

Calmly Grandmother finished the [8]<u>line of stitches</u>. Then she turned to look at me. "Is Trudy Walters [9]<u>getting after</u> you again?"

"Yes. I [10]<u>really</u> don't understand why she should [11]<u>be against</u> me. I'm [12]<u>just</u> sure I've never done anything to [13]<u>cause her resentful feelings</u>."

"From what you've said before, Arlene, I wonder if [14]<u>maybe</u> Trudy's problem is that your [15]<u>good</u> testimony is [16]<u>making her feel guilty</u>."

B. Write simple, familiar words that could replace the underlined words in this story excerpt.

"Does your head still feel [1]<u>congested</u>?" Mother asked [2]<u>solicitously</u> as she turned to face her oldest daughter. "If it does, I can [3]<u>transport</u> you to the doctor and go shopping while I wait."

"That would be [4]<u>charitable</u>," Rhoda answered. "I surely would [5]<u>take no pleasure in</u> driving today."

The waiting room was [6]<u>overpopulated</u>. Rhoda [7]<u>anticipated</u> a long wait as she [8]<u>traversed</u> the room to find an [9]<u>unoccupied</u> chair. About an hour passed before a nurse [10]<u>summoned</u> her to see the doctor.

C. Write suitable figures of speech that could replace four of the underlined expressions in this story excerpt.

Carla stood on the porch a few minutes, gazing about [1]<u>with an expression of awe</u>. "How I enjoy this secluded valley with the mountains [2]<u>all around us</u>," she whispered. "And the beautiful blue sky with the [3]<u>fluffy white</u> clouds." As she stood there [4]<u>gazing at</u> the beauty, a Carolina wren [5]<u>expressed itself</u> in a sweet song. "Thank You, Lord, for the beautiful world You have made," Carla whispered again.

"Carla, hang up that wash!" Mother's harsh voice shattered Carla's reverie. "You have too much work to do to stand there gawking!"

"Yes, Mother," responded Carla quietly. "This beauty impressed me so greatly that I had to praise the Creator."

[6]<u>Her heart felt heavy</u> as she hurried out to the clothesline. "If only Mother were a Christian," Carla said with a sigh.

Lesson 69 Answers
Applying the Lesson
A. (Sample answers.)
1. sewing machine
2. make
3. living room
4. sigh
5. slumped
6. someone deliberately
7. irritate you
8. seam
9. bothering
10. I don't
11. dislike
12. I'm sure
13. offend her
14. if Trudy's
15. Christian
16. convicting her

B. (Sample answers.)
1. stuffy
2. sympathetically
3. take
4. nice, considerate
5. not enjoy
6. crowded
7. expected
8. crossed
9. empty
10. called

C. (Sample answers.)
1. with awe written on her face
2. holding us in their arms
3. cotton
4. drinking in
5. poured out its heart
6. The burden on her heart outweighed the laundry basket

70. Improving Your Editing Skills, Part 7

As the title of this lesson indicates, editing involves a number of skills—things that you must practice in order to do them well. One important skill is to see what is actually written on the page, rather than what you expect to see. Consider the following example.

```
Two scientists in Europe, working separately, discovered

    oxgyen in the 1770s.
```

Is everything in order? The proper noun is capitalized, *separately* is spelled properly, and the independent element and *1770s* are punctuated correctly. But there is one mistake! If you did not catch it, you saw the misspelled word *oxgyen* as *oxygen.* It is because proofreaders see what they expect to see that they sometimes overlook mistakes—even if they think they are fully concentrating on their work.

When you proofread, you need to inspect each word and punctuation mark separately. Put special effort into seeing what is actually written so that you can correct *every* mistake.

Marks Used in Editing and Proofreading

⌄ or ⌃ insert (caret)	⎯ℐ delete	.... stet (let it stand)	⎯⎯⎯ use italics
¶ begin new paragraph	no ¶ no new paragraph	*lc* change to lowercase (small letter)	*uc* change to uppercase (capital letter)
# insert space	⌒ delete space	← move (arrow)	⊓⊔ transpose

Editing Practice

A. Use proofreading marks to correct the two capitalization or punctuation errors in each sentence.

```
1. A new commission for patents was established shortly before

   the thirteenth State signed the constitution.

2. The first commission consisted of: Thomas Jefferson, Henry

   Knox and Edmund Randolph.

3. Opening for business on april 10, 1790 this commission

   required a working model with each application for a patent.
```

Lesson 70 Answers

Editing Practice
   (Answers are on pages 472–473.)

Lesson 70

Purpose: To provide proofreading practice.

4. An unmanageable number of models had accumulated by 1807, therefore, a new Law specified that the commissioner would determine whether a model was needed.

5. It appears, however that the commissioner felt inadequate to decide, for the accumulation of models didnt decline.

6. Because of the large number of models the patent office had been moved to Blodgett's hotel in 1810.

7. When the British burned the capital city during the war of 1812 this was the only government building spared.

8. Dr William Thornton headed the patent office at that time and he deserves the credit for saving its treasures.

9. News of the danger to the office raised Thorntons ire so much that he ignored self interest and raced to the city.

10. He dissuaded the British from burning the building—what a waste that would have been! by comparing such an action to the Turks destruction of the Alexandrian Library.

B. Use proofreading marks to correct the one or two usage errors in each sentence.

1. If we maintain a heavenly prospective, we will continue to feel that the Bible always applies to present-day living.

2. Read often in the Book of Proverbs, and leave those practical precepts influence your life.

3. If your not enthused about a job, do the best you can anyway.

4. For three days a stationery front set over the region, producing heavy rains.

5. Loretta's answer implied that she is progressing right along with her work.

6. Father is doing some better, but the doctor said that he will be in bed for awhile yet.

7. I wonder how come Duchess wants out of her pen so much.

8. Our neighbor's dog is notable for continually disturbing the neighborhood chickens, lambs, and other animals.

9. Milford's idea surely differed with mine, but I know he is more familiar with those there tools than I am.

10. There is nothing in back of you, so you should back strait to the loading dock.

C. Use proofreading marks to correct all the errors in this essay. Your corrections should include one use of the stet symbol and one joining of two paragraphs. No line has more than one error.

1.   Our sun is an average-sized star. That is, in comparing

2. it to most other stars in the universe, we find that it

3. is similar in size. But lets consider a star that is not

4. average—one that is much more larger than the sun.

5.   Scientists classify Betelgeuse (bēt′·əl·jüz′), a bight

6. star in the constellation Orion, as a red supergiant. The

7. star is red (rather than yellow like the sun because its

8. surface temperature is half only as hot. This star goes

9. through cycles of expanding and shrinking. With an average

10. diameter 460 times that of the sun, it has an enormity

11. that we can hardly fathom.

12.   If this star could be placed in the center of our solar

13. system, it would ~~completely~~ engulf the orbits of Mercury,

14. Venus, earth, and Mars!

15.   The diameter of Betelgeuse, varies by about 100 million

16. miles, which is more than the distance from the earth to

17. the sun. If our sun were a variablestar like that, life

18. as we know it wouldn't hardly be possible. Truly we can

19. be glad for the Sun as God made it—a steady star that

20. provides a constant, depend able supply of heat and light.

71. Proofreading and Rewriting the Story

You probably put much time and effort into the first draft of the story you wrote in Chapter 6. In the present chapter, you have studied various methods by which a story can be improved. Now you will put those methods to practice in proofreading and rewriting your story.

Proofreading

In proofreading the first draft of your story, use proofreading marks to show your corrections. The following checklist can help in this process.

1. Does the story have a worthwhile theme?
2. Does the story open effectively with action, dialogue, or an unusual statement?
3. Does the opening promptly introduce the main character, establish the setting, and hint at the theme and conflict? Does the story open as near to the first scene of conflict as possible?
4. Does it portray the characters effectively and consistently?
5. Is the conflict clear and forceful? Does it build up to a climax that occurs near the end of the story?
6. Is the conclusion brief and satisfying?
7. Does the story have a fresh, original title that does not give away the outcome?
8. Have you consistently adhered to the point of view that you have chosen?
9. Does the story have smooth transitions between scenes?
10. Does it have natural dialogue, straightforward expressions, and fresh, original language? Does it appeal to the five senses?
11. Have you kept the action moving by using lively action verbs, by limiting static description, and by avoiding arrested action?
12. Have you used exact, descriptive words while avoiding large unfamiliar words?
13. Have you used apt figures of speech?
14. Are there any awkward sentences that you should reword?
15. Have you used correct spelling, punctuation, and grammar?

Rewriting

The final step, of course, is to rewrite the story, incorporating the corrections and changes you have made in your proofreading. For the final draft, you should write on every line. Strive for a neat paper: use your best penmanship, keep the left margin straight, and keep the right margin as straight as practical.

Applying the Lesson

A. Do one of the following things.
1. Proofread the first draft of the story that you wrote in Lesson 56. Use the questions listed in this lesson, and mark changes by using the proofreading symbols you have learned.

Lesson 71 Answers
Applying the Lesson
(All answers are individual work.)

Lesson 71

Purpose: To review methods of evaluating and improving stories.

Teaching Suggestions:

Give the students several days to do a thorough job of proofreading. Insist that they go over their stories several times.

2. Start over by writing a new story, following the pattern taught in Chapter 6. Lay your story aside for a day or so, and then proofread it as described in number 1 above.

B. Write the second draft of your story, making the improvements that you marked. Use every line, write as neatly as you can, and keep neat margins. Your teacher may use the evaluation chart below to grade your story. Remember, your score on this story will make up a considerable part of your Chapter 8 test score.

Evaluation of a Story

Points possible   Points earned

Title
- 2 ____ Short and appealing
- 2 ____ Relates to theme without revealing the outcome

Theme
- 3 ____ Introduces theme in an interesting way
- 3 ____ Worthwhile; evident without being directly stated
- 3 ____ Consistent throughout story

Structure
- 3 ____ Opens effectively with action, dialogue, or unusual statement
- 3 ____ Has at least three incidents of conflict
- 3 ____ Conflict intensifies or consists of satisfactory individual incidents
- 3 ____ Has consistent point of view throughout story
- 3 ____ Ends with a satisfying conclusion

Characterization
- 3 ____ Major characters portrayed consistently throughout story
- 3 ____ Uses several methods of characterization
- 3 ____ Minor and background characters presented appropriately

Style
- 3 ____ Natural dialogue, straightforward language, appeals to five senses
- 3 ____ Active verbs; other exact, descriptive words; avoidance of unfamiliar words
- 3 ____ Apt figures of speech

Mechanics
- 3 ____ Correct spelling
- 3 ____ Correct capitalization and punctuation
- 3 ____ Correct grammar
- 3 ____ Avoidance of careless repetition, omitted words, transpositions

- **58** ____ **Total points**

72. Chapter 8 Review

A. Write the correct words for these descriptions.
   1. Words like *said, asked,* and *exclaimed.*
   2. The voice of verbs that adds life and vigor to a story.
   3. A figurative comparison that uses *like* or *as.*
   4. A figurative, artistic exaggeration.
   5. Imagery that uses literal terms to describe something that happens only in a figurative sense.
   6. Imagery that pictures a thing or quality as having the characteristics of a living creature. ·
   7. A once-vivid expression that has become stale through overuse.
   8. The error of having story characters merely *begin* or *start* to do things.

B. Rewrite this story excerpt, making the dialogue more natural as you studied in Lesson 67.
   "Oh, Tina," said Lillie, "you ought to read *Caught in the Web.* It is quite interesting."
   "Should I really read it?" said Tina. "Is it your book?"
   "No, it is not mine," said Lillie. "It belongs to my cousin Suzanne. Do you remember her? She is from Pennsylvania. She was at church last summer when her family visited us."
   "Yes, I remember her." Tina said thoughtfully. "She was rather worldly, was she not?"
   "Well, yes, she was a bit worldly," Lillie said. "But this book is a good, Christian story."
   "What is the story about?" said Tina.
   "It is about a Christian girl who grew cold spiritually, ran away from home, and got tangled up in some wrong things," Lillie said. "Toward the end of the book, she repented and got things straightened out again."
   "It does sound interesting," Tina said. "Of course, I would want my parents to review it first."

C. Rewrite the numbered phrases, replacing the clichés, removing the indefinite expressions, and making a stronger appeal to the five senses. Several notes in brackets give specific directions.
   "This spot is beautiful," declared Fred ¹in rather awed tones. "That waterfall sounds ²really loud." [Use a simile.]
   "I'd like to go down closer," suggested Melvin.
   "We can't climb down here," returned Fred. He pointed toward ³the steep-looking bank.
   "I know a path we can take," offered Albert. "It's almost as steep as a ladder. But if you watch your step, it's not too bad."
   ⁴As quick as a wink, the boys were clambering down the trail. ⁵They made a beeline for the waterfall ⁶almost as soon as they reached the bottom.

Lesson 72

Purpose: To review the concepts taught in Chapter 8.

Lesson 72 Answers
Applying the Lesson

A. 1. explanatory words   5. metaphor
   2. active voice   6. personification
   3. simile   7. cliché
   4. hyperbole   8. arrested action

(Answers for Parts B–H may vary somewhat.)

B. (Improvements are underlined.)
   "Oh, Tina," declared Lillie, "you ought to read *Caught in the Web.* It's quite interesting."
   "Really?" asked Tina. "Is it your book?"
   "No," replied Lillie. "It belongs to my cousin Suzanne. Remember her? She's from Pennsylvania. She was at church last summer when her family visited us."
   "Yes," Tina said thoughtfully. "She was rather worldly, wasn't she?"
   "Well, yes," Lillie admitted. "But this book is a good, Christian story."
   "What's the story about?" asked Tina.
   "A Christian girl who grew cold spiritually, ran away from home, and got tangled up in some wrong things," Lillie explained. "Toward the end of the book, she repented and got things straightened out again."
   "Does sound interesting," Tina commented. "Of course, I'd want my parents to review it first."

C. 1. in awed tones
   2. like thunder
   3. the steep bank
   4. Immediately
   5. They headed straight toward
   6. as soon

"Look at this pool!" exclaimed Melvin. "The water [7]is really clear." [Use a simile.]

[8]"I can feel the spray from the waterfall way out here," Fred commented. [Have Fred tell how the spray feels.]

D. The following excerpt contains several linking verbs and passive verbs. For each numbered sentence, write enough words to show how to improve those sentences with lively action verbs.

[1]"Yes, Allen is a hard worker," stated Sister Arlene. "I'm not sure how I would get along without his strong arms. Since Paul passed away . . ."

[2]"His dedication is deeply appreciated by all of us," she was assured by Sister Brenda.

[3]"Nearly all the farm work is managed by him now," Sister Arlene commented further. [4]"Uncle Dale is here occasionally to check on things. [5]He is called by Allen whenever there is a problem."

[6]The conversation was ended by Allen's sudden appearance. [7]"Good afternoon, Sister Brenda," the visitor was addressed politely. "This is surely a warm day, isn't it?"

E. Rewrite this story excerpt, removing all examples of arrested action. Also remove the static descriptions, or include them within sentences that carry the story action.

Mildred Lefever was sixteen years old. She had blue eyes and blond hair. She had been crippled in a car accident and was now confined to a wheelchair. On this warm June day, she was soaking in the warmth of the sunshine as she sat on the spacious front porch.

"Oh, how nice!" Mildred's face began to light up with joy as Uncle William's car drove up the lane. "An afternoon with Louise and Alma will be wonderful!"

Before long, the two cousins had started setting up a small folding table for a game of Scrabble.

F. Write more exact and descriptive words that could replace the underlined words.

Paul [1]took the [2]tool and [3]moved it swiftly through the air. *Crack!* The sharp blade [4]divided the wood neatly. Quickly he [5]put another [6]piece in place. *Crack!* That one too was soon split.

"At this rate," he said to himself as he wiped the [7]moisture from his [8]face, "I'll finish [9]this job by noon. Then I can work on my [10]project for a while."

G. Write simple, familiar words that could replace the underlined expressions.

"This large [1]institution of learning is quite different from the small one we were [2]accustomed to [3]heretofore," Priscilla commented as she and Edward [4]ambulated homeward.

"I [5]concur with that," Edward replied. [6]"Gaining acquaintance with all these students is [7]intimidating, but I will enjoy the recesses."

7. is as clear as crystal
8. The spray from the waterfall feels cool and refreshing

D. 1. Allen works hard
2. We all deeply appreciate his dedication;
Sister Brenda assured her
3. He manages nearly all the farm work
4. Uncle Dale comes occasionally
5. Allen calls him
6. Allen's sudden appearance ended the conversation.
7. he addressed the visitor

E. Sixteen-year-old Mildred Lefever sat in her wheelchair on the spacious front porch, soaking in the warmth of the June sunshine. "Oh, how nice!" she exclaimed, her blue eyes lighting up with joy as Uncle William's car drove up the lane. "An afternoon with Louise and Alma will be wonderful!"

Before long, the two cousins had set up a small folding table for a game of Scrabble.

F. 1. gripped   6. chunk
2. ax   7. sweat
3. swung   8. forehead
4. split   9. splitting this wood
5. stood   10. rabbit hutch

G. 1. school   5. agree
2. used   6. Learning to know
3. before   7. scary
4. walked

"Yes, and the class [8]dialogues will be [9]far superior too. Back at Walnut Valley, it was quite [10]infrequent to have more than four students in one class."

As the two reached the top of the last [11]prominence in the road, they broke into a run for their [12]residence.

H. Write suitable figures of speech that could replace the underlined expressions.

Vernon glanced up from his book as the wind [1]blew vigorously outside. It [2]made wild noises around the corners of the house, and it [3]blew the deep snow into intricate shapes.

In the center of the room stood the cast-iron stove, [4]warming the house. Through its glass doors, Vernon watched the flames [5]moving upward around the oak logs. As his gaze [6]passed over his surroundings, Vernon's heart filled with thanksgiving.

"Thank You, Lord," he breathed, "for a cozy house. Thank You even more for a fine Christian family."

Then his thoughts turned to the Swartz family down the road. He remembered Sylvan's longing words, "You fellows have it so nice. Every time I'm with you, why, it seems so very peaceful. The atmosphere in my home is [7]tense."

8. discussions
9. much better
10. rare
11. hill
12. home

H. 1. raged
    2. howled and shrieked
    3. carved
    4. cheering the house with its warmth
    5. licking
    6. swept
    7. a balloon ready to pop

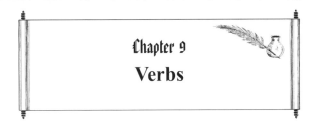

73. Verbs and the Principal Parts of Verbs

Nouns and verbs make up the core of language. Nouns give substance to language by naming persons, places, things, and ideas. Verbs are the engines of language, making the nouns act or exist in specific ways.

Basic Facts About Verbs

1. *A verb expresses action or being to tell what the subject does or is.* The verb joins with the subject to make the basic framework, or skeleton, of a sentence.

> <u>Isaac</u> willingly <u>gave</u> up his wells.
> <u>Isaac</u> <u>is</u> an example for us.

2. *Every clause has a verb, which is the simple predicate of the clause.*

> The Philistines <u>had mistreated</u> Isaac.

In an elliptical clause, the verb may be understood. Elliptical sentences are found mainly in dialogue.

> Which two Bible characters never <u>died</u>?
> Enoch and Elijah. (Enoch and Elijah never <u>died</u>.)

3. *Many simple predicates are verb phrases, consisting of the main verb and one or more helping verbs.* The main verb always comes last in a verb phrase.

Other words often interrupt a verb phrase. Many of these are adverbs like *not, never, hardly, always, ever,* and *surely.* In a contraction like *don't,* the *n't* is also an adverb. In a question, the subject often comes between the helping verb and the main verb.

> Elaine <u>has</u> surely <u>increased</u> her typing speed this year.
> She <u>hasn't</u> <u>managed</u> to type without numerous errors.
> <u>Does</u> she really <u>deserve</u> a good score on this paper?

4. *Sometimes the simple predicate is a compound verb, in which two or more verbs are joined by a conjunction.* The parts of a compound verb share the same subject. They may also share the same helping verb, which may appear only before the first main verb.

> The students <u>sat</u> tensely and <u>waited</u> for the starting signal.
> Soon they <u>were typing</u> rapidly, <u>trying</u> to avoid errors, and <u>listening</u> for the signal to stop.

Lesson 73

Purpose: To review the basic facts about verbs and their principal parts.

Teaching Suggestions:

Understanding the facts about principal parts is not difficult, but ingrained habits can be hard to change. Therefore, you should plan to spend sufficient time on the second part of the lesson, in order to touch the common errors of the community in which you are teaching. For a more complete list of the principal parts of verbs, use an English handbook or look at the list in Grade 8 of this English series.

One way to make this lesson practical is to start a classroom list of errors in the use of principal parts. Add to the list as either you or the students call attention to an error.

Principal Parts of Verbs

5. *Verbs have three principal parts, which are used to form the different tenses:* the first principal part (present form), the second principal part (past form), and the third principal part (past participle).

Present	Past	Past Participle
walk	walked	(have) walked
ring	rang	(have) rung

6. *The first principal part is the basic form of a verb—the form you would use* with *to*.

walk	see	ring	build	run

7. *The second and third principal parts of most verbs are formed by adding* -ed *to the first principal part.* Other spelling changes may also be necessary. If the verb ends with *e*, drop the *e* before adding -ed. If the verb ends with *y* after a consonant, change the *y* to *i*. If a one-syllable verb ends with a single consonant after a short vowel, double the final consonant.

Present	Past	Past Participle
comb	combed	(have) combed
bake	baked	(have) baked
carry	carried	(have) carried
chop	chopped	(have) chopped

8. *The second and third principal parts of some verbs have irregular forms.* The correct forms of a few of the commonly misused ones follow. Use an English handbook or a dictionary to find the correct forms whenever you are in doubt.

First (Present)	Second (Past)	Third (Past Participle)	First (Present)	Second (Past)	Third (Past Participle)
awake	awoke	(have) awoke	know	knew	(have) known
	or awaked	(have) awaked	lay	laid	(have) laid
bid	bade	(have) bidden	leave	left	(have) left
	or bid	(have) bid	let	let	(have) let
blow	blew	(have) blown	lie	lay	(have) lain
bring	brought	(have) brought	raise	raised	(have) raised
burst	burst	(have) burst	rise	rose	(have) risen
come	came	(have) come	see	saw	(have) seen
creep	crept	(have) crept	set	set	(have) set
dig	dug	(have) dug	shrink	shrank	(have) shrunk
do	did	(have) done		*or* shrunk	(have) shrunken
drag	dragged	(have) dragged	sit	sat	(have) sat
drink	drank	(have) drunk	swim	swam	(have) swum
drown	drowned	(have) drowned	swing	swung	(have) swung
forbid	forbade	(have) forbidden	tag	tagged	(have) tagged
	or forbad	(have) forbid	take	took	(have) taken
go	went	(have) gone			

9. *In addition to the three principal parts, most verbs have two other forms—the present participle and the -s form. The present participle, which ends with -ing, is used in progressive verb forms. The -s form is used with third person singular subjects in the present tense.*

Mother <u>is baking</u> bread today. She <u>bakes</u> ten loaves every week.

Applying the Lesson

A. List all the verbs and verb phrases. Underline the main verb in each verb phrase.
1. "The words of a talebearer are as wounds, and they go down into the innermost parts of the belly."
2. "A good man obtaineth favour of the LORD: but a man of wicked devices will he condemn."
3. "Trust in the LORD with all thine heart; and lean not unto thine own understanding."
4. "Counsel in the heart of man is like deep water; but a man of understanding will draw it out."
5. A Christian driver will be obeying the traffic laws and showing courtesy to other motorists.
6. He dims his lights for oncoming traffic, follows other cars at a proper distance, and keeps his vehicle in a safe condition.
7. Did you stop completely at that intersection?
8. Has Harold been studying for his driver's test?

B. Write the correct form of each underlined verb; do not change the tense. If it is correct, write *correct.*
1. After the water pipes had <u>froze</u>, we needed to carry water in buckets.
2. The students <u>raised</u> their hands to volunteer for the job.
3. When the dog <u>seen</u> me coming, he started to bark fiercely.
4. These stockings have <u>shrank</u> so much that I can no longer wear them.
5. I was sure that I had <u>laid</u> the knife beside my plate.
6. Howard <u>tug</u> three of the prisoners and set them free.
7. The wind is so strong that it has <u>blew</u> down several of our pine trees.
8. It looks as if Mrs. Walters has <u>came</u> for some more eggs.
9. The allurements of evil have <u>drawn</u> many away from the Lord.
10. By this time most of the robins have <u>flew</u> north for the summer.
11. Our neighbor lady planned to visit our church, but her husband <u>forbad</u> it.
12. After you have <u>hanged</u> the wash on the line, sweep off the porch.

C. Write the correct past form of each verb in parentheses. Use the past participle only if there is a helping verb in the sentence.
1. You have again (forget) to close the door.
2. We (throw) the empty box into the incinerator.
3. After everyone had (shake) hands, we sat down to visit.
4. The congregation has (kneel) for prayer.
5. David (slay) Goliath with the giant's own sword.
6. The boy who has (steal) a penny will likely steal much larger things.

Lesson 73 Answers

Applying the Lesson

A. 1. are, go
2. obtaineth, will <u>condemn</u>
3. Trust, lean
4. is, will <u>draw</u>
5. will be <u>obeying</u>, <u>showing</u>
6. dims, follows, keeps
7. Did <u>stop</u>
8. Has been <u>studying</u>

B. 1. frozen
2. correct
3. saw
4. shrunk *or* shrunken
5. correct
6. tagged
7. blown
8. come
9. correct
10. flown
11. correct
12. hung

C. 1. forgotten
2. threw
3. shaken
4. knelt *or* kneeled
5. slew
6. stolen

7. Slowly and quietly, we (creep) toward the large bullfrog.
8. Never before had we (ride) in a jet.
9. The borrower is servant to the man who has (lend) him money.
10. Mary polished the apple until it (shine).

Review Exercises

Write the letters of the correct forms in each sentence. [61]

1. When Jesus fed the five thousand, twelve (ᵃbasketsful, ᵇbasketfuls) of food were left after the (ᵃpeople's, ᵇpeoples') hunger was satisfied.
2. The three (ᵃbailiff's, ᵇbailiffs') terms lasted until (ᵃthe decade's end, ᵇthe end of the decade).
3. We put (ᵃten dollars' worth, ᵇthe worth of ten dollars) of gasoline into (ᵃthe car's tank, ᵇthe tank of the car).
4. Both of my (ᵃbrother-in-laws, ᵇbrothers-in-law) know what a (ᵃday's laborer, ᵇday laborer's) life is like.
5. An (ᵃindividual's, ᵇindividuals') looks and intelligence are not reliable (ᵃindicae, ᵇindices) of his character.
6. The (ᵃdormice, ᵇdormouses) disappeared into the (ᵃbushes' leaves, ᵇleaves of the bushes).
7. Some brook (ᵃtrout's, ᵇtrouts') bodies are as much as eighteen (ᵃinches, ᵇinches') long.
8. Ancient (ᵃRoman's, ᵇRomans) served the tongues of (ᵃflamingo's, ᵇflamingos) as a delicacy.
9. In both (ᵃgentlemen's, ᵇgentlemens') opinions, these (ᵃanalysa, ᵇanalyses) are fair and accurate.
10. The (ᵃnuclea, ᵇnuclei) of all the (ᵃamoebae, ᵇamoebi) were clearly visible in the photograph.

7. crept
8. ridden
9. lent
10. shone

Review Exercises

1. b, a
2. b, b
3. a, b
4. b, b
5. a, b
6. a, b
7. a, a
8. b, b
9. a, b
10. b, a

74. Simple and Perfect Tenses

Verbs have different forms to indicate action or existence in the past, present, or future. English verbs have three simple tenses and three perfect tenses.

Simple Tenses

1. *The present tense shows action or existence in the present.* It also records a statement of general truth, even if the context of the sentence is past. Present tense uses the first principal part (present form). The third person singular form ends with -s.

Jonathan Burkholder, who <u>lives</u> next door, <u>is</u> a minister at our church.
Jesus testified that He <u>is</u> the Son of God.

2. *The past tense shows action or existence in the past.* It uses the second principal part (past form).

Daniel Kauffman <u>edited</u> the book *Doctrines of the Bible.*

Lesson 74

Purpose: To review the formation and uses of the six tenses of verbs.

Teaching Suggestions:

Be prepared to call special attention to the following points in the lesson.

Point 3: The formal use of *shall* and *will,* and especially the reversed pattern of these helping verbs to show determination, strong desire, or promise.
Point 4: The difference between simple past and present perfect.
Points 5 and 6: The uses of the past perfect and future perfect tenses.

Note: The conjugation of *help* does not include all the possible forms of this verb. It does not show the progressive, emphatic, or passive forms, which are taught in Lesson 77. Neither does it show verb phrases with *may, might, must, can, could, should,* and *would.* These helping verbs (and some others) appear to be remnants of main verbs that formerly were used with infinitives. For example, "He will help" most likely comes from "He wills to help." "He should help" probably comes from a construction that meant "He is indebted to help" (compare the German *Schuld,* debt). Today these verbs serve as helping verbs to express ideas like the ones shown below. Verbs in other languages have special moods to express such ideas.

3. *The future tense shows action or existence in the future.* The future tense uses the first principal part (present form) with the helping verb *shall* or *will*. In formal writing, use *shall* for first person subjects and *will* for second and third person subjects. In general usage, *will* is acceptable for all three persons.

I shall call you tomorrow if you will be home then.

To show determination, strong desire, or promise, reverse the normal pattern of *shall* and *will* in formal English.

I shall go now, and you will come later. (simple future tense statement)
I will go now, and you shall come later. (statement of determination)

The King James Bible uses formal English. Understanding the distinctions between *shall* and *will* contributes to a clear understanding of many Bible verses. Study the following examples.

"Moses said unto the people, Ye have sinned a great sin: and now I will [strong desire] go up unto the LORD; peradventure I shall [simple future] make an atonement for your sin" (Exodus 32:30).
"Now I will [determination] come unto you, when I shall [simple future] pass through Macedonia: for I do pass through Macedonia" (1 Corinthians 16:5).

Perfect Tenses

4. *The present perfect tense shows an action or a condition that began in the past and is completed as of the present or continues into the present.* This tense uses the third principal part (past participle) with the helping verb *have* or *has*.

Both the simple past and the present perfect tenses refer to things that happened before the present. The simple past, however, merely indicates that an action or existence occurred at some past time. The present perfect indicates that what began in the past is now completed or is still continuing.

Simple past: The boys split the firewood yesterday.
Present perfect: The boys have split all the firewood.

Simple past: Brother Heisey answered many questions.
Present perfect: In his years of teaching, Brother Heisey has answered many
                     questions.

5. *The past perfect tense shows an action or a condition that was completed by a certain time in the past.* This tense uses the third principal part (past participle) with the helping verb *had*.

The past perfect tense requires that two past actions or conditions be expressed or implied. That which was completed first must be expressed in the past perfect tense.

Incomplete: Only one past action
It had snowed for several hours.

Other verb forms:

Permission:	You may go.
Possibility:	You might go.
Obligation:	You must go.
Actual ability:	You can go.
Conditional ability:	You could go.
Duty:	You should go.
Potential:	You would go.

Complete: Two past actions stated
   It <u>had snowed</u> for several hours before darkness <u>fell</u>.
Complete: One past action stated and one implied
   It <u>had snowed</u> for several hours before dark.

Use the past perfect tense either to clarify which of two past actions or conditions occurred first or to emphasize that one action or condition was completed at the time of the other. Compare the differences in meaning and emphasis in the following sentences.

Unclear: Sounds as if the two actions occurred at the same time
   We <u>opened</u> our Bibles to the passage that Brother Harold <u>announced</u>.
Clear: Clarifies that the announcing came first
   We <u>opened</u> our Bibles to the passage that Brother Harold <u>had announced</u>.

Completed action not emphasized: Both verbs in simple past tense
   Brother Harold <u>read</u> all the verses before he <u>explained</u> them.
Completed action emphasized: First action in past perfect tense
   Brother Harold <u>had read</u> all the verses before he <u>explained</u> them.

6. *The future perfect tense shows an action or a condition that will be completed by a certain time in the future.* This tense uses the third principal part (past participle) with either *shall have* or *will have* as helping verbs.

The future perfect tense requires that two future actions or conditions be expressed or implied. That which will occur first or whose completion is to be emphasized must be expressed in the future perfect tense; the other may be expressed in the simple future or simple present tense.

Incomplete: Only one future action
   Our school <u>will have operated</u> for twenty-six years.
Complete: One future condition implied and one future action stated
   By the end of this school term, our school <u>will have operated</u> for twenty-
      six years.

The future perfect tense serves a function similar to that of the past perfect tense. Use it either to clarify which of two future actions or conditions will occur first, or to emphasize that one action or condition will be completed at the time of the other. Compare the differences in meaning and emphasis in the following sentences.

Unclear: Sounds as if we shall travel *after* the stated time
   At the end of our trip, we <u>shall travel</u> two thousand miles.
Clear: Clarifies that our traveling will be completed at the stated time
   At the end of our trip, we <u>shall have traveled</u> two thousand miles.

Completion of action not emphasized: Both verbs in simple tenses
   Before this week <u>ends</u>, we <u>shall sing</u> at the rest home.
Completion of action emphasized: Completed action in future perfect tense
   Before this week <u>ends</u>, we <u>shall have sung</u> at the rest home.

A *conjugation* is a listing of certain forms of a verb. Here is a conjugation of *help* in the simple and perfect tenses.

Help

Person	Singular	Plural
Present Tense		
First:	I help.	We help.
Second:	You help.	You help.
Third:	He helps.	They help.
Past Tense		
First:	I helped.	We helped.
Second:	You helped.	You helped.
Third:	He helped.	They helped.
Future Tense		
First:	I shall help.	We shall help.
Second:	You will help.	You will help.
Third:	He will help.	They will help.
Present Perfect Tense		
First:	I have helped.	We have helped.
Second:	You have helped.	You have helped.
Third:	He has helped.	They have helped.
Past Perfect Tense		
First:	I had helped.	We had helped.
Second:	You had helped.	You had helped.
Third:	He had helped.	They had helped.
Future Perfect Tense		
First:	I shall have helped.	We shall have helped.
Second:	You will have helped.	You will have helped.
Third:	He will have helped.	They will have helped.

Applying the Lesson

A. Copy each verb or verb phrase, and write which tense it is.
1. Father has sharpened the chain saw, and soon he will fill the fuel tank.
2. That old locust tree is not dead, but it leans over the driveway.
3. After Father had examined the tree, he noticed some nearby wires.
4. The wires run along the driveway, but they seem a safe distance away.
5. Before Father cuts down the tree, he will have checked more carefully.
6. The tree easily cleared the wires just as Father had expected.
7. Locust wood burns well, but we have no need for firewood.
8. The neighbor will bring his truck this evening; by then we shall have sawed the wood into two-foot pieces.

B. Write the correct verb form for the tense shown in italics.
1. If you memorize one Bible verse each day, you (memorize) over three hundred verses by the end of the year. *future perfect*

Lesson 74 Answers
Applying the Lesson
A. 1. has sharpened—present perfect; will fill—future
2. is—present; leans—present
3. had examined—past perfect; noticed—past
4. run—present; seem—present
5. cuts—present; will have checked—future perfect
6. cleared—past; had expected—past perfect
7. burns—present; have—present
8. will bring—future; shall have sawed—future perfect

B. 1. will have memorized

2. Remembering Scripture passages (require) frequent review. *present perfect*
3. By the time I was in ninth grade, I (gain) a great store of Bible verses. *past perfect*
4. By the middle of January, the students (finish) chapter 15. *future perfect*
5. Most of our visitors this month (comment) on the attractive bulletin board. *present perfect*
6. I was encouraged by the comment that the teacher (write) on my paper. *past perfect*

C. In each sentence, changing one verb to a perfect tense would make the meaning clearer or would put more emphasis on the completion of one action. Write that verb in the correct perfect tense.
1. The wise men followed the star for many miles before they came to Jerusalem.
2. King Herod learned from them that an infant king came into his domain.
3. We shall read about the conflict between these two kings before our devotional period ends.
4. When the wise men arrive at Bethlehem, they will follow the star to the end of their search.
5. The diligent seekers worshiped the King that they found.
6. Joseph took Jesus and His mother to Egypt before Herod killed the children in Bethlehem.
7. I shall read the rest of the account when I reach the end of Matthew 2.
8. When we learn to submit cheerfully, we shall gain a valuable character trait.

D. Write short sentences for these descriptions, using pronouns and the correct verb forms.
1. First person singular, present tense of *think.*
2. Second person, present perfect tense of *ride.*
3. Second person, future tense of *go.*
4. Third person plural, past tense of *wring.*
5. Third person singular, feminine, past perfect tense of *forget.*
6. First person plural, present tense of *keep.*
7. First person plural, future perfect tense of *seek.*
8. First person singular, past perfect tense of *shut.*
9. Third person plural, past tense of *eat.*
10. Third person singular, masculine, future perfect tense of *cut.*

Review Exercises

Write the letter of the correct form in each sentence. [61]
1. (^{a}James and John's, ^{b}James's and John's) mother came to Jesus with a special request.
2. She asked Jesus for the favor of her (^{a}sons, ^{b}sons') sitting at His right hand and left hand in His kingdom.
3. Jesus first asked about the (^{a}brothers, ^{b}brothers') being able to drink of the cup that He would drink.

2. has required
3. had gained
4. will have finished
5. have commented
6. had written

C. 1. had followed
2. had come
3. shall have read
4. will have followed
5. had found
6. had taken
7. shall have read
8. shall have gained

D. 1. I think.
2. You have ridden.
3. You will go.
4. They wrung.
5. She had forgotten.
6. We keep.
7. We shall have sought.
8. I had shut.
9. They ate.
10. He will have cut.

Review Exercises
1. a
2. b
3. b

4. Then He said that His Father, not Jesus Himself, would be the ([a]one, [b]one's) granting that position.
5. At the Last Supper, Peter objected strongly to ([a]Jesus, [b]Jesus') washing his feet.
6. ([a]Peter and John's, [b]Peter's and John's) ideas about the heavenly kingdom were much clearer after Pentecost than before.
7. The apostles continued boldly preaching the Gospel even after the Jewish council prohibited ([a]their, [b]them) speaking in the Name of Jesus.
8. We stayed at my ([a]aunt's and uncle's, [b]aunt and uncle's) home while Mother was sick.
9. While she recuperated, Mother liked to listen to the ([a]birds, [b]birds') singing cheerily outside.
10. She especially enjoyed the ([a]bluebird and robin's, [b]bluebirds' and robins') songs.

4. a
5. b
6. b
7. a
8. b
9. a
10. b

---

75. Moods of Verbs

A *mode* is a manner of doing something. When people want to go somewhere, they can choose among several different modes of travel. They can walk, ride a bicycle, drive a car, or travel by plane—to name a few possibilities. They choose the mode that best fits their purpose.

Just as there are different modes of travel, there are different modes of verbs. However, we generally use the term **mood** instead of *mode* when referring to verbs. The mood of a verb is its manner of communicating, as determined by the intention of the speaker or writer. For example, a preacher during his sermon communicates in several different ways. The following sentences are some of the things he might say; each underlined verb is in a different mood.

> Abraham <u>showed</u> remarkable faith in offering his son Isaac.
> <u>Open</u> your Bibles to Genesis 22.
> If I <u>were</u> Abraham, could I pass such a test?

In the first sentence, the speaker intends simply to state a fact. So he uses a declarative sentence, which declares that something is true. The mood of this verb is indicative (in·dik′·ə·tiv) because it indicates a fact about Abraham.

In the second sentence, the speaker intends that his listeners do something. He expresses his intention by using an imperative sentence. Since the sentence is imperative, the verb is in the imperative mood.

What is the speaker's intention in the third sentence? He is making no request, neither is he indicating that something is true. In fact, he is expressing an idea that could *not* be true: "If I were Abraham" (when obviously he is not Abraham). The verb in this clause is in the subjunctive mood.

These examples illustrate the three moods of English verbs: indicative, imperative, and subjunctive.

Lesson 75

Purpose: To teach that the three *moods of verbs are indicative, imperative, and subjunctive.

Teaching Suggestions:

Emphasize that the indicative mood is by far the most common in speech and writing, and that the subjunctive mood is by far the least common. Since the subjunctive mood is so uncommon, however, it poses the greatest problem both because of its unusual forms and because it has largely been replaced by the indicative mood (with the use of helping verbs like *should* and *would*).

To show the importance of the subjunctive mood, make some comparisons between verbs in that mood and in the indicative mood. Point out that the clause "if I *was* you" implies that I could be you, which is not even logical. Likewise, "if Satan *rises* up against himself" suggests that he might do such a thing, which again is illogical. These examples show that the subjunctive mood is not just extra baggage, but that it is sometimes needed to express the meaning accurately.

Observe that not every verb in an *if* clause is subjunctive. If a student asks about this, explain that the subjunctive mood is used in an *if* clause mainly when it expresses a condition contrary to a known fact. When an *if* clause simply expresses a condition on which something else depends, the indicative mood is used. Compare the following sentences.

The Indicative Mood

The **indicative mood** states a fact or asks a question. Since we generally use language to *indicate* real actions or conditions, we use the indicative mood far more often than any other mood. The verbs in most declarative and interrogative sentences are indicative.

> Great Britain <u>became</u> the northernmost province of the Roman Empire.
> What peoples <u>invaded</u> Great Britain after the Romans <u>left</u>?

The Imperative Mood

The **imperative mood** gives a command or makes a request. The verbs in all imperative sentences are imperative.

> <u>Find</u> more information about this invasion.
> Please <u>tell</u> us what you have discovered.

A verb in the imperative mood may appear to ask a question even though it actually makes a request. A sentence with such a verb ends with a period rather than a question mark because the verb is imperative.

> <u>Will</u> the owner of this pickup please <u>move</u> his truck away from the doors.
> <u>Shall</u> we <u>kneel</u> for prayer.

The Subjunctive Mood

You have probably used the **subjunctive mood** even if you have never heard of it before. Have you ever made a statement like this one?

> If I were you, I would try to finish by noon.

Why do you say "I were"? Have you not learned that the correct expression is "I was"? Yet here it is—"if I were you"—and it sounds quite natural. You use the form *were* because this verb is in the subjunctive mood.

The subjunctive mood does not tell or ask about something that actually happens. Rather, it often expresses a condition contrary to fact, as in the example above. I am not you, and I can never be you. I will always be me! The subjunctive mood may also express a doubt, a wish, or a recommendation.

The subjunctive mood is much less common today than it was long ago. It is still required in a few expressions like "if I were you," and it may be used in certain other phrases. But today we often use helping verbs like *would* and *should* for ideas that formerly were expressed with the subjunctive mood.

You have studied verbs in the indicative and imperative moods ever since you studied declarative and imperative sentences. So these moods generally pose no problem for you. But the subjunctive mood requires more careful attention because a few of its forms are less familiar to you.

Subjunctive Verb Forms

Actually, almost all the subjunctive verb forms are identical to those of the indicative mood. There are only three places where they differ. Learning the correct subjunctive verb forms for these three exceptions will help you to use the subjunctive mood properly. The following paragraphs describe these three situations.

> If it <u>were</u> raining, we would need to stay inside. (We know it is not raining; *if* clause expresses condition contrary to known fact; subjunctive mood is used.)
> If it <u>is</u> raining, we will need to stay inside. (It may or may not be raining; *if* clause simply expresses a condition on which something else depends; indicative mood is used.)

Note: Many verb forms in the subjunctive mood are the same as in the indicative mood. What makes them subjunctive is that a verb used in a *present* setting may actually be a *past* form, and a verb used in a *past* setting may actually be a *past perfect* form. Consider the following examples.

> I <u>do</u> not <u>know</u> the answer right now, but I wish I <u>knew</u> it.
> (*Do know* is present; *knew* is a past form used in the same present setting.)
> I <u>did</u> not <u>know</u> the answer yesterday, but I wish I <u>had known</u> it.
> (*Did know* is past; *had known* is a past perfect form used in the same past setting.)

This is the reason for the verb form in a clause like "if you had gotten up sooner." The fact is that "you *did* not *get* up sooner" (past indicative); but "if you *had gotten* up sooner" (past perfect subjunctive used in a past setting), "you would not need to hurry so much."

1. *The verb* be *in the present tense.* In the indicative mood, we must use three different forms for the verb *be* in the present tense. In the subjunctive mood, however, we use only the form *be.* Notice this difference on the chart below. (The conjunction *if* is included with the subjunctive forms because subjunctive verbs are common in *if* clauses.)

Present Tense		**Present Tense**	
(Indicative Mood)		*(Subjunctive Mood)*	
I am	we are	(if) I <u>be</u>	(if) we <u>be</u>
you are	you are	(if) you <u>be</u>	(if) you <u>be</u>
he is	they are	(if) he <u>be</u>	(if) they <u>be</u>

Again, note that the subjunctive mood uses the word *be* no matter what the subject. Here are some examples of this usage.

> "And I, if I <u>be</u> lifted up from the earth, will draw all men unto me."
> (subjunctive *I be* rather than indicative *I am*)
> "Will ye plead for Baal?... If he <u>be</u> a god, let him plead for himself."
> (subjunctive *he be* rather than indicative *he is*)

2. *The verb* be *in the past tense.* Here the indicative mood uses *was* and *were.* As with the present tense, the subjunctive mood again uses a single form, this time *were.* Study the difference between the two forms in the chart below.

Past Tense		**Past Tense**	
(Indicative Mood)		*(Subjunctive Mood)*	
I was	we were	(if) I <u>were</u>	(if) we were
you were	you were	(if) you were	(if) you were
he was	they were	(if) he <u>were</u>	(if) they were

Here the subjunctive mood is the same as the indicative mood except for two places: *I were* and *he were.* These may sound strange; but in examples such as the following, you will probably recognize that you have heard and even used them yourself.

> If I <u>were</u> at home right now, I would be doing my chores.
> (subjunctive *I were* rather than indicative *I was*)
> "If this man <u>were</u> not of God, he could do nothing."
> (subjunctive *man were* rather than indicative *man was*)

3. *Third person singular verbs in the present tense.* In the present tense, indicative mood, verbs always add -*s* for the third person singular. He *eats.* He *sees.* He *thinks.* The subjunctive mood, however, does not add this -*s.* The following chart shows the forms for the verb *go.*

Present Tense		**Present Tense**	
(Indicative Mood)		*(Subjunctive Mood)*	
I go	we go	(if) I go	(if) we go
you go	you go	(if) you go	(if) you go
he goes	they go	(if) he <u>go</u>	(if) they go

Concerning the imperative mood, you may notice that a sentence like "Shall we stand to our feet" has a verb phrase. How can this be, since imperative sentences never include helping verbs? Observe two things about this sentence: it has the helping verb *Shall,* and the subject is not *you.* So we must conclude that an imperative *verb* does not necessarily make an imperative *sentence.* (This sentence is declarative.) But the concept of mood is so unfamiliar that you should probably not try to explain this to the students unless someone asks about it.

Note: This lesson is not as important as some others. It could be omitted, but it does provide an interesting challenge. A study of moods will also give valuable insight that students may be glad for later, especially if they ever study a foreign language.

He go is the only place the subjunctive mood is different. Following this pattern with other verbs, we would have *he eat, he see, he think,* and so forth. Such usage is not as common as the subjunctive uses of *be,* yet these examples should have a familiar ring to them.

> "If thy presence go not with me, carry us not up hence."
>> (subjunctive *presence go* rather than indicative *presence goes*)
> If Mother go away for a month, how would we manage?
>> (subjunctive *Mother go* rather than indicative *Mother goes*)

For the second example, we may be more likely to say, "If Mother were to go away for a month." Even then we would be using the subjunctive mood, *Mother were,* rather than the indicative mood, *Mother was.*

The English of the King James Bible follows the rules of formal usage. Also, the subjunctive mood was used much more in the 1600s than it is today. For these reasons, the King James Bible contains many examples of subjunctive verbs. Understanding the subjunctive verb forms described above will help you to understand some of the "unusual" verb forms in the King James Version, and thus it will make the Bible clearer to you.

Using the Subjunctive Mood

1. *Use the subjunctive mood in the following situations.* The subjunctive mood occurs most often in a clause introduced by *if, whether, as if, as though,* or *that.* In the example sentences below, the underlined verbs are in the subjunctive mood.

   a. Expressing doubt or uncertainty.

   > "All men mused in their hearts of John, whether he were the Christ, or not."
   > "Now therefore, if it displease thee, I will get me back again."

   b. Expressing a wish or desire.

   > "Peace be with thee."   I wish he were more careful.

   c. Expressing a supposition, a condition contrary to fact, or something unlikely.

   > I would be cautious too if I were in his shoes.
   > "If Satan rise up against himself, and be divided, he cannot stand."

   d. Expressing recommendation, request, command, or necessity in a *that* clause.

   > I move that the trustees be authorized to repair the roof.
   > The doctor recommended that Grandfather have a checkup.

2. *In a* that *clause expressing recommendation, request, command, or necessity, use the present subjunctive form even if other verbs in the sentence are in a different tense.*

> Father will request that he be exempted from jury duty.
>> (*Be exempted* is present tense even though *will request* is future tense.)

God has directed that the Christian <u>live</u> in holiness.
>   (*Live* is present tense even though *has directed* is present perfect tense.)
The Lord commanded that Abram <u>move</u> out of Ur.
>   (*Move* is present tense even though *commanded* is past tense.)

3.   *Use the subjunctive mood to avoid unnecessary* would *phrases.* When a sentence has a dependent *if* or *that* clause, the main clause often uses *would* as a helping verb. *Would* may seem to fit in the dependent clause too, but that is not a standard usage. You will avoid repeating *would,* and you will express your idea more concisely, if you use the subjunctive mood in the *if* or *that* clause. Study these examples and explanations.

Two *would* phrases:
>   If I <u>would be</u> you, I *would* set my alarm a bit earlier.
Improved with subjunctive:
>   If I <u>were</u> you, I *would* set my alarm a bit earlier.
>>   (Subjunctive form *I were* fits in a statement that is contrary to fact.)

Two *would* phrases:
>   I *would* like to suggest that Brother James <u>would be appointed</u> as the leader.
Improved with subjunctive:
>   I *would* like to suggest that Brother James <u>be appointed</u> as the leader.
>>   (Subjunctive form *be appointed* is used in a recommendation. Also note that the recommendation is given in the present tense.)

Two *would* phrases:
>   If you <u>would have gotten</u> up sooner, you *would* not need to hurry so much.
Improved with subjunctive:
>   If you <u>had gotten</u> up sooner, you *would* not need to hurry so much.
>>   (*If you had gotten up sooner* is a statement contrary to fact. This requires using the subjunctive mood. Is *had gotten* a subjunctive form? Yes, because the subjunctive and the indicative forms are exactly the same. Remember, subjunctive mood differs from indicative mood only in the three situations listed earlier in this lesson.)

The verbs in most sentences are in the indicative mood—the mood that tells or asks about things as they really are. But a verb in the imperative mood is necessary for telling someone to do something, and a verb in the subjunctive mood is useful for speaking of something that is doubted, wished, or supposed.

Applying the Lesson

A. Copy each underlined verb, and write whether its mood is indicative (*ind.*), imperative (*imp.*), or subjunctive (*sub.*).

1. God <u>commands</u> that everyone <u>obey</u> His Word.
2. If I <u>were</u> not <u>trusting</u> in the Lord, these temptations would overwhelm me.

Lesson 75 Answers
Applying the Lesson
A. 1. commands—ind.; obey—sub.
    2. were trusting—sub.

3. <u>Raise</u> your hand if you have a question or comment.
4. "If God <u>be</u> for us, who <u>can be</u> against us?"
5. A proud person often <u>acts</u> as if he <u>were entitled</u> to the last word.
6. Never <u>act</u> as if God <u>were</u> on vacation.
7. The Lord <u>preserve</u> you from all evil.
8. <u>Will</u> you please <u>clean</u> up this clutter.
9. If I <u>be</u> at fault, I <u>want</u> to know.
10. I <u>move</u> that the chairman <u>appoint</u> a committee to study the problem.
11. That bull <u>sounds</u> as if he <u>were</u> ready to charge.
12. The government inspectors <u>recommend</u> that major repairs <u>be made</u> to the bridge.
13. <u>Suppose</u> your little brother <u>were</u> to find this knife on the floor.
14. If indeed the work <u>be finished</u>, I <u>shall go</u> home.

B. Choose the words that are correct for the subjunctive mood.
1. Suppose this (was, were) your last opportunity to visit Grandfather Stauffer.
2. Our neighbor worked as if he (was, were) afraid of having a heart attack.
3. The company recommends that the equipment (be, is) serviced annually.
4. God's grace (be, is) with you until we meet again.
5. If any man (hear, hears) God's voice, let him pay close heed.
6. I wonder if indeed this (be, is) the best explanation.
7. If he (do, does) his best, I will be satisfied.
8. Lazarus would not have died if Jesus (was, had been) present, but He received more glory by raising Lazarus from the dead.
9. That rooster acts as if he (was, were) the king of the barnyard.
10. If Sheila (was, were) to help us, we could finish in a few minutes.
11. The teacher required that everyone (be, was) prepared.
12. If this work (prove, proves) successful, I shall be surprised.
13. The building inspector requested that the electrician (make, made) a small change.
14. I wish that Duke (was, were) more friendly to the children.
15. Even if David (would have made, had made) an unreasonable request, Nabal should have responded more courteously.
16. If Abigail (would not have taken, had not taken) prompt action, Nabal's whole household would have been destroyed.

C. Write a subjunctive verb or verb phrase to replace each underlined *would* phrase.
1. We would leave at three o'clock in the morning if that <u>would be</u> practical.
2. I would appreciate if these directions <u>would be</u> a little clearer.
3. I move that the secretary <u>would mail</u> out copies of the minutes.
4. Brother Alvin asked that the noise level <u>would be lowered</u>.
5. If we <u>would have made</u> better plans, things would not have turned out this way.
6. If Grandfather <u>would have been</u> able, he would surely have come to the services.

Answers:

3. Raise—imp.
4. be—sub.; can be—ind.
5. acts—ind.; were entitled—sub.
6. act—imp.; were—sub.
7. preserve—sub.
8. Will clean—imp.
9. be—sub.; want—ind.
10. move—ind.; appoint—sub.
11. sounds—ind.; were—sub.
12. recommend—ind.; be made—sub.
13. Suppose—imp.; were—sub.
14. be finished—sub.; shall go—ind.

B. 1. were
2. were
3. be
4. be
5. hear
6. be
7. do
8. had been
9. were
10. were
11. be
12. prove
13. make
14. were
15. had made
16. had not taken

C. 1. were
2. were
3. mail
4. be lowered
5. had made
6. had been

Review Exercises

A. Choose the correct words in these sentences. [62, 63]
1. I am older than my brother Carl, but he is a little taller than (I, me).
2. One day Father told (we, us) boys to burn some trash.
3. He had often warned Carl and (I, me) to be careful with fire.
4. I started the fire by lighting some gasoline-soaked rags from (someones, someone's) cleanup project.
5. The flames roared up very suddenly, almost burning (me, myself) in the face.
6. It was a good lesson for (me and Carl, Carl and I, Carl and me).

B. Choose the correct words in these sentences. [62, 63]
1. Elijah was a man (who, which) had feelings and desires just like ours.
2. (This, This here) was the prophet who prayed that rainfall would cease in Israel.
3. All of us generally (prefer, prefers) prosperous times.
4. But (them, those) were days when the people had become extremely wicked.
5. Elijah so greatly desired that (they, them) return to the true God, that he was willing to endure a great drought along with the sinful people.
6. Each of us (need, needs) to care about other people as Elijah did.

Review Exercises

A. 1. I
2. us
3. me
4. someone's
5. me
6. Carl and me

B. 1. who
2. This
3. prefer
4. those
5. they
6. needs

76. Transitive and Intransitive Verbs

Verbs are classified according to their tense, their form, and their mood. They are also classified as either transitive or intransitive.

Transitive Verbs

The word *transitive* comes from a Latin word that means "passing over." A transitive verb passes its action to a substantive in the sentence. Transitive verbs are in the *active voice* or the *passive voice*, depending on the receiver of their action.

1. *A transitive verb in the active voice passes its action to the direct object.* The subject performs the action, and the direct object receives the action. A verb with a direct object may also have an indirect object or an objective complement.

God answered Solomon's prayer for wisdom.
    (*Prayer* is the direct object of *answered.*)
God gave Solomon wisdom to rule his kingdom.
    (*Wisdom* is the direct object of *gave,* and *Solomon* is the indirect object.)
God made Solomon wise above all other men.
    (*Solomon* is the direct object of *made,* and *wise* is the objective complement.)

The direct object may be a verbal, a verbal phrase, or a noun clause.

Every Christian needs to pray. (verbal)
Every Christian needs to pray without ceasing. (verbal phrase)
Every Christian realizes that he needs to pray without ceasing. (noun clause)

Lesson 76

Purpose: To review transitive, intransitive linking, and intransitive complete verbs.

Teaching Suggestions:

One way to help your students remember the different kinds of verbs is to provide them with a simple outline.

Kinds of Verbs

I. Transitive verbs pass action
   A. Active voice passes action to direct object
   B. Passive voice passes action to subject
II. Intransitive verbs pass no action
   A. Intransitive complete expresses action without passing it to a receiver
   B. Intransitive linking expresses condition or state of being

2. *A transitive verb in the passive voice passes its action to the subject.* In the passive voice, the subject receives the action rather than performing it. Often the doer of the action is named later in the sentence, by a substantive in a phrase beginning with *by.* A verb in the passive voice consists of the past participle with a form of *be* as a helping verb.

> Solomon's prayer for wisdom was answered by God.
> > (*Prayer* receives the action of *was answered.*)
> Wisdom to rule his kingdom was given to Solomon by God.
> > (*Wisdom* receives the action of *was given.*)

Intransitive Verbs

Just as *transitive* means "passing over," so *intransitive* means "not passing over." An intransitive verb does not pass its action to a substantive in the sentence. Intransitive verbs divide into two groups: intransitive complete and intransitive linking.

1. *An intransitive complete verb expresses action but does not pass the action to a receiver.* The meaning of the skeleton is complete without a complement.

> During the night, two inches of snow <u>fell</u>.
> In silence we <u>waited</u> for his answer.

Some intransitive complete verbs may seem to pass their action to the subject. However, both the meaning of the sentence and the form of the verb show that the subject actually is performing the action.

> Slowly the ice cube in my cup <u>melted</u>.
> > (intransitive complete; *melted* means the ice cube turned to liquid; subject performs this action; verb is simple past form)
> The ice cube <u>was melted</u> by the warm water.
> > (transitive verb in the passive voice; subject receives the action performed by the *warm water;* verb consists of a past participle with a form of *be* as a helping verb)

Some verbs may be either transitive or intransitive complete, depending on their use in a sentence. Most dictionaries give specific definitions for both transitive and intransitive uses of such verbs.

> We <u>learned</u> three new songs in music class.
> > (transitive; *songs* receives the action)
> The students <u>learned</u> very rapidly.
> > (intransitive complete; no receiver of the action)

2. *An intransitive linking verb expresses a condition or a state of being.* Such a verb often has little meaning of its own; it serves mainly to link the subject to the subjective complement. The subjective complement may be either a predicate nominative, which renames the subject, or a predicate adjective, which modifies the subject.

Teacher: Intransitive complete verbs usually express action. But they may also express existence (with forms of *be*) and be complete in themselves.

> God <u>is</u>.
> The children <u>were</u> in school.

The most common linking verbs are the forms of *be: am, is, are, was, were, be, been, being.* Linking verbs also include verbs of sense (*taste, feel, smell, sound, look, appear*) and some other verbs (*grow, seem, stay, become, remain, turn, prove*).

> Joseph Funk <u>was</u> an early Mennonite music teacher.
> (*Teacher* is a predicate nominative renaming *Joseph Funk.*)
> His introduction of shaped notes <u>proved</u> very beneficial.
> (*Beneficial* is a predicate adjective modifying *introduction.*)

Do not confuse a linking verb followed by an adjective with an intransitive complete verb followed by an adverb or with a transitive verb in the active or passive voice. Except for the forms of *be,* most of the linking verbs can also function as transitive verbs or as intransitive complete verbs. A verb is intransitive linking only when it expresses a condition or a state of being rather than an action.

> Students sometimes <u>grow</u> restless in the springtime. (*Grow* expresses a condition; it links *Students* and *restless. Grow* is intransitive linking.)
> Many students <u>grow</u> rapidly during the year. (*Grow* expresses action; there is no receiver of the action. *Grow* is intransitive complete.)
> My brothers <u>grow</u> watermelons to sell at the market. (*Grow* expresses action; *watermelons* receives the action. *Grow* is transitive active.)
> These watermelons were <u>grown</u> on our own farm. (*Grown* expresses action; *watermelons* receives the action. *Grown* is transitive passive.)

A sentence diagram can help you to quickly tell whether a verb is transitive or intransitive. If a direct object follows the verb, it is a transitive verb in the active voice. If the verb is a past participle with a form of *be* as a helping verb, it is a transitive verb in the passive voice. If the verb is not passive and it has no complement, it is an intransitive complete verb. And if a predicate nominative or predicate adjective follows the verb, it is an intransitive linking verb.

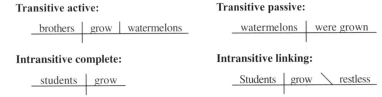

Transitive active:

brothers | grow | watermelons

Transitive passive:

watermelons | were grown

Intransitive complete:

students | grow

Intransitive linking:

Students | grow \ restless

Applying the Lesson

A. Copy each verb and the substantive that receives its action. Label the verb *active* or *passive.*

1. Early in his ministry, Daniel Kauffman visited the Sugar Creek congregation in Wayland, Ohio.
2. His supper was eaten at the home of the bishop, Sebastian Gerig.
3. During the meal, very little was said by Kauffman.
4. Because of this, Bishop Gerig's hired man did not expect a very forceful sermon that evening.

Lesson 76 Answers
Applying the Lesson
A. 1. visited, congregation—active
   2. was eaten, supper—passive
   3. was said, little—passive
   4. did expect, sermon—active

5. On the way to church, young Kauffman expressed indecision about what to use for his subject.
6. Several simple texts were suggested by the somewhat uneasy bishop.
7. To Brother Gerig's surprise, the subject of the resurrection was used for that night's message.
8. Kauffman's powerful sermon made a vivid impression on the congregation.

B. Write whether each underlined verb is transitive (*T*) or intransitive complete (*IC*).
   1. Our visitor <u>had</u> very poor hearing.
   2. In each ear he <u>wore</u> a hearing aid.
   3. As he explained how they work, we <u>listened</u> with interest.
   4. When only one hearing aid <u>was operating</u>, he could not identify the direction from which a sound came.
   5. Why <u>do</u> we <u>need</u> two ears?
   6. A sound <u>rings</u> more loudly in the ear closer to the source.
   7. The sound also <u>arrives</u> a little sooner in that ear than in the other ear.
   8. Our brain <u>uses</u> the difference in volume and time to discern the direction of the sound.

C. Copy each linking verb and the words that it links.
   1. The Book of Psalms has always been a source of great inspiration.
   2. This book was the hymnal of the Jewish people.
   3. To the New Testament saint, it remains fresh and meaningful.
   4. The parallelism of Hebrew poetry is truly beautiful.
   5. Some of the psalms are acrostics.
   6. The psalms have grown sweet to many Bible readers.

D. Copy each verb, and label it *TA* (transitive, active voice), *TP* (transitive, passive voice), *IC* (intransitive complete), or *IL* (intransitive linking).
   1. The Hans Herr House is the oldest building in Lancaster County, Pennsylvania.
   2. Hans Herr, a Mennonite minister, came to Pennsylvania from the German Palatinate.
   3. The Mennonites first settled in Lancaster County in 1710.
   4. Actually, this house was built by Hans Herr's son Christian.
   5. The stone above the door bears the date 1719.
   6. This house served as a residence and as a Mennonite meetinghouse.
   7. Its construction follows the style of Swiss–German architecture.
   8. The roof of this stone house is very steep.
   9. A long fireplace and large chimney are located in the center of the house.
   10. The raised floor of the fireplace kept children out of the fire.
   11. For about one hundred years, the house was a neglected structure.
   12. It was restored during the years 1970–1972.

Review Exercises

Name the tense of the underlined verb in each sentence. [74]
   1. By the early 1700s, Isaac Newton <u>had</u> already <u>demonstrated</u> that sunlight contains the seven colors of the rainbow.

---

5. expressed, indecision—active
6. were suggested, texts—passive
7. was used, subject—passive
8. made, impression—active

B. 1. T
   2. T
   3. IC
   4. IC
   5. T
   6. IC
   7. IC
   8. T

C. 1. has been—Book (of Psalms), source
   2. was—book, hymnal
   3. remains—it, fresh (and) meaningful
   4. is—parallelism, beautiful
   5. are—Some, acrostics
   6. have grown—Psalms, sweet

D. 1. is—IL
   2. came—IC
   3. settled—IC
   4. was built—TP
   5. bears—TA
   6. served—IC
   7. follows—TA
   8. is—IL
   9. are located—TP
   10. kept—TA
   11. was—IL
   12. was restored—TP

Review Exercises

1. past perfect

2. To this day, however, scientists <u>have</u> not <u>been</u> able to explain light fully.
3. Light is a form of energy that <u>travels</u> even through a vacuum.
4. Light leaving the sun <u>will have passed</u> through millions of miles of vacuum by the time it reaches the earth.
5. Since vibrating molecules <u>carry</u> sound, it cannot pass through a vacuum.
6. Sound passing through air <u>will travel</u> about 1,100 feet every second.
7. An echo is the reflection of a sound that <u>occurred</u> just a moment earlier.
8. When lightning <u>has struck</u>, its one brief discharge sets off a series of echoes that we call thunder.

2. present perfect
3. present
4. future perfect
5. present
6. future
7. past
8. present perfect

---

77. Forms of Verbs

All verbs have six tenses—three simple and three perfect. Within these tenses, verbs also have three different forms that give them slightly different shades of meaning. The three forms are *simple, progressive,* and *emphatic.* We use these different verb forms to give precise expression to the ideas we want to convey.

Verb Forms in the Active Voice

1. *The simple form of a verb expresses an action or a condition as simply as possible.* The only helping verbs used with the simple form are *shall* and *will* (for the simple future tense) and forms of *have* (for the perfect tenses). The simple form is the one you immediately think of when you are asked to give a particular verb in any tense. In all the previous lessons of this chapter, the focus has been on the simple form of verbs.

Simple form:
 Present: I <u>help</u> my father.
 Past: I <u>helped</u> my father.
 Future: I <u>shall help</u> my father.
 Present perfect: I <u>have helped</u> my father.
 Past perfect: I <u>had helped</u> my father.
 Future perfect: I <u>shall have helped</u> my father.

2. *The progressive form uses the present participle with a form of* be *as a helping verb.* In contrast to the simple form, the progressive form emphasizes that an action or a condition is in progress. Each of the six tenses has a progressive form.

Progressive form:
 Present: I <u>am helping</u> my father.
 Past: I <u>was helping</u> my father.
 Future: I <u>shall be helping</u> my father.
 Present perfect: I <u>have been helping</u> my father.
 Past perfect: I <u>had been helping</u> my father.
 Future perfect: I <u>shall have been helping</u> my father.

Lesson 77

Purpose: To review the simple, progressive, and emphatic forms of verbs.

Teaching Suggestions:

For Part D of the exercises, the students may fill in the charts on pages 27 and 28 of *Tests and Editing Sheets.* If you do not have the booklet, you may wish to photocopy the chart on page 482.

3. *The emphatic form uses the first principal part with a form of* do *as a helping verb.* As its name suggests, this form gives added emphasis, perhaps in response to a question or a doubt. Only the present and past tenses have emphatic forms, because sentences like "I do will help" and "I did had helped" would be extremely awkward.

Emphatic form:
> **Present:** I <u>do help</u> my father.
> **Past:**   I <u>did help</u> my father.

The helping verbs *do* and *did* are also used in questions and negative statements. The verb form in such a sentence is simple rather than emphatic.

> <u>Do</u> you <u>help</u> your father? (present tense, simple form)
> I <u>did</u> not <u>help</u> my father. (past tense, simple form)

Verb Forms in the Passive Voice

4. *The simple form of a verb in the passive voice is the past participle with a form of* be *as a helping verb.* This is the simplest verb form that will pass an action to the subject of a sentence.

Simple form:
> **Present:** I <u>am helped</u> by my brother.
> **Past:**   I <u>was helped</u> by my brother.
> **Future:** I <u>shall be helped</u> by my brother.
> **Present perfect:** I <u>have been helped</u> by my brother.
> **Past perfect:**   I <u>had been helped</u> by my brother.
> **Future perfect:** I <u>shall have been helped</u> by my brother.

5. *The progressive form of a verb in the passive voice is made with the addition of* being *as a helping verb.* As in the active voice, the verb phrase contains a present participle—but the *-ing* is added to *be* rather than the main verb. Such a verb phrase contains two forms of *be:* a form like *am, is,* or *was* for the passive voice, and *being* for the progressive form. In the passive voice, the progressive form commonly occurs only in the present and past tenses. The other forms are too awkward because of the many helping verbs required.

Progressive form:
> **Present:** I <u>am being helped</u> by my brother.
> **Past:**   I <u>was being helped</u> by my brother.

> (Forms seldom used because of their awkwardness)
> **Future:** I <u>shall be being helped</u> by my brother.
> **Present perfect:** I <u>have been being helped</u> by my brother.
> **Past perfect:**   I <u>had been being helped</u> by my brother.
> **Future perfect:** I <u>shall have been being helped</u> by my brother.

6. *The emphatic form never occurs in the passive voice, because it is too awkward and illogical.* The emphatic form would require constructions like *I do am helped* and *I did was helped.*

Study the following chart, which compares the three forms of verbs in both the active voice and the passive voice.

Comparison of Verb Forms
Active Voice

	Simple Form	Progressive Form Made with a form of *be* and *-ing*	Emphatic Form Made with a form of *do*
Present:	I help.	I <u>am</u> help<u>ing</u>.	I <u>do</u> help.
Past:	I helped.	I <u>was</u> help<u>ing</u>.	I <u>did</u> help.
Future:	I shall help.	I shall <u>be</u> help<u>ing</u>.	(too awkward)
Pr. perf.:	I have helped.	I have <u>been</u> help<u>ing</u>.	
Past perf.:	I had helped.	I had <u>been</u> help<u>ing</u>.	
Fut. perf.:	I shall have helped.	I shall have <u>been</u> help<u>ing</u>.	

Passive Voice

	Simple Form Made with a form of *be* and a past participle	Progressive Form Made with two forms of *be* and a past participle	Emphatic Form (not used at all)
Present:	I <u>am</u> <u>helped</u>.	I <u>am</u> <u>being</u> <u>helped</u>.	
Past:	I <u>was</u> <u>helped</u>.	I <u>was</u> <u>being</u> <u>helped</u>.	
Future:	I shall <u>be</u> <u>helped</u>.	(too awkward; seldom used)	
Pr. perf.:	I have <u>been</u> <u>helped</u>.		
Past perf.:	I had <u>been</u> <u>helped</u>.		
Fut. perf.:	I shall have <u>been</u> <u>helped</u>.		

Applying the Lesson

A. Identify the form of each underlined verb as *simple, progressive,* or *emphatic.*
  1. I do belie<u>ve</u> that a storm <u>is coming</u> soon.
  2. The birds that <u>come</u> to the feeder <u>have been fighting</u> more than usual.
  3. That blue jay <u>has chased</u> all the other birds away and <u>does</u> not <u>let</u> them come back.
  4. We <u>invited</u> Mr. Smith to our services, and he <u>will be coming</u> next Sunday.
  5. The boys <u>did lock</u> the gate, but somehow the heifers <u>pushed</u> it open.
  6. <u>Have</u> you <u>heard</u> that Sister Dorcas <u>broke</u> her arm?

B. Write the progressive form and the emphatic form of each underlined verb. If such a form is awkward or nonexistent, write *none.* Do not change the tense of the verb.
  1. Amos <u>hopes</u> to finish the job by noon.
  2. Our neighbors <u>plan</u> to move to Indiana in the spring.
  3. Henry <u>was questioned</u> by the officer about his accident.
  4. Tomorrow the students <u>will take</u> their science test.
  5. No one <u>has tried</u> successfully to solve this equation.
  6. Before the window <u>had been washed</u>, we could hardly see through it.

C. Identify the tense, voice, and form of each underlined verb.
  1. "In the beginning God <u>created</u> the heaven and the earth."
  2. We <u>have been receiving</u> heavy rains for several days.

Lesson 77 Answers
Applying the Lesson
A. 1. emphatic, progressive
   2. simple, progressive
   3. simple, simple
   4. simple, progressive
   5. emphatic, simple
   6. simple, simple

B. 1. is hoping, does hope
   2. are planning, do plan
   3. was being questioned, none
   4. will be taking, none
   5. has been trying, none
   6. none, none

C. 1. past, active, simple
   2. present perfect, active, progressive

3. I <u>do believe</u> that your brother is learning to be patient.
4. While the book <u>was being written</u>, the author did more research.

D. Copy the chart below, and fill in the blanks with all the forms for the following two skeletons.
   1. He finds.
   2. You hear.

Verb Forms
Active Voice

Simple Form	Progressive Form	Emphatic Form
Present: _____	_____	_____
Past: _____	_____	_____
Future: _____	_____	
Pr. perf.: _____	_____	
Past perf.: _____	_____	
Fut. perf.: _____	_____	

Passive Voice

Simple Form	Progressive Form	Emphatic Form
Present: _____	_____	
Past: _____	_____	
Future: _____		
Pr. perf.: _____		
Past perf.: _____		
Fut. perf.: _____		

Review Exercises

A. Write whether the underlined sentence part is a nominative absolute (*NA*) or a participial phrase (*PP*). [24]
   1. <u>Mild weather having come</u>, we heard geese honking already in January.
   2. <u>Flying in great V formations</u>, the geese were heading northward.
   3. <u>Surprised to see geese so early</u>, we wondered how they would fare if frigid weather came.
   4. <u>God having promised His care</u>, we should not worry as much as we sometimes do.

B. Rewrite each sentence, changing the underlined subordinate clause to a nominative absolute. [24]
   1. <u>Because the creek had flooded</u>, we had to find a different way home.
   2. Soon we had to change our course again <u>because a tree had fallen across the road</u>.

3. present, active, emphatic
4. past, passive, progressive

D. 1.
Verb Forms
Active Voice

Simple Form	Progressive Form	Emphatic Form
Present:		
He finds.	He is finding.	He does find.
Past:		
He found.	He was finding.	He did find.
Future:		
He will find.	He will be finding.	xxx
Pr. perf.:		
He has found.	He has been finding.	xxx
Past perf.:		
He had found.	He had been finding.	xxx
Fut. perf.:		
He will have found.	He will have been finding.	xxx

Passive Voice

Simple Form	Progressive Form	Emphatic Form
Present:		
He is found.	He is being found.	xxx
Past:		
He was found.	He was being found.	xxx
Future:		
He will be found.	xxx	xxx
Pr. perf.:		
He has been found.	xxx	xxx
Past perf.:		
He had been found.	xxx	xxx
Fut. perf.:		
He will have been found.	xxx	xxx

2.
Verb Forms
Active Voice

Simple Form	Progressive Form	Emphatic Form
Present:		
You hear.	You are hearing.	You do hear.
Past:		
You heard.	You were hearing.	You did hear.
Future:		
You will hear.	You will be hearing.	xxx
Pr. perf.:		
You have heard.	You have been hearing.	xxx
Past perf.:		
You had heard.	You had been hearing.	xxx
Fut. perf.:		
You will have heard.	You will have been hearing.	xxx

Passive Voice

Simple Form	Progressive Form	Emphatic Form
Present:		
You are heard.	You are being heard.	xxx
Past:		
You were heard.	You were being heard.	xxx
Future:		
You will be heard.	xxx	xxx
Pr. perf.:		
You have been heard.	xxx	xxx
Past perf.:		
You had been heard.	xxx	xxx
Fut. perf.:		
You will have been heard.	xxx	xxx

Review Exercises

A. 1. NA
   2. PP
   3. PP
   4. NA

B. 1. The creek having flooded, we had to find a different way home.
   2. Soon we had to change our course again, a tree having fallen across the road.

3. <u>Since our route extended over twice the normal distance</u>, the trip took much longer than usual.
4. <u>After my homework was finished</u>, I played with my little brother for a while.

3. Our route extending over twice the normal distance, the trip took much longer than usual.
4. My homework (being) finished, I played with my little brother for a while.

---

78. Subject–Verb Agreement

For the vast majority of sentences, you have very little problem with subject–verb agreement. Some situations, however, do deserve special attention. The following rules give you specific direction in these problem areas.

1. *When the verb precedes the subject, think ahead to the subject and make the verb agree with it.* In many questions and in most sentences beginning with *there* or *here,* the verb or a part of the verb phrase precedes the subject.

> <u>Are</u> the <u>women</u> <u>washing</u> all the windows?
> There <u>was</u> a steady <u>rain</u> <u>falling</u> throughout the day.

2. *Make the verb agree with the subject, not with some other substantive in the sentence.* Be especially careful when a prepositional phrase comes between the subject and the verb, and when a subject and its predicate nominative differ in number.

> A huge <u>flock</u> of blackbirds <u>has landed</u> in the wheat field.
> The <u>emu</u>, along with the ostrich and the penguin, <u>is</u> a bird that cannot fly.
> One <u>attraction</u> at the Baltimore zoo <u>is</u> the monkeys.
> The <u>monkeys</u> <u>are</u> an irresistible attraction to the children.

3. *Use a contraction as you would use the words it represents.* Be especially alert to the contractions *here's, there's, how's, what's,* and *don't.*

> **Incorrect:** <u>Here's</u> (Here is) the answers to our questions.
>   This cow <u>don't</u> (do not) give much milk.
> **Correct:**   <u>Here are</u> the answers to our questions.
>   This cow <u>doesn't</u> give much milk.

4. *Use a plural verb with a compound subject joined by* and. The conjunction *and* means that the verb expresses action or condition for all parts of the subject.

> <u>Sodium</u> and <u>chlorine</u> <u>combine</u> to form salt. (Two <u>elements</u> <u>combine</u>.)
> A <u>stone</u> and a <u>sling</u> <u>were</u> the only weapons David needed.
>   (<u>Both</u> <u>were</u> weapons.)

Sometimes a compound subject names only one person or thing, as when one person holds two positions or one dish is composed of two foods. In this case, the verb is singular and an article or a possessive pronoun is used only before the first noun. In contrast, if the compound subject names two different persons

Lesson 78

Purpose: To review rules for subject–verb agreement.

Teaching Suggestions:

Rules 1–11 have been introduced through Grade 8 of this English series. In general, the students know the rules fairly well but may fail to apply them in their everyday speaking and writing. Be prepared to review and explain subject–verb agreement in relation to collective nouns (rule 10). Rules 12–14 are new for Books 1 and 2.

or objects, the verb is plural and an article or a possessive pronoun is used before each of the nouns.

The <u>farmer</u> and <u>minister</u> <u>was</u> humbly <u>serving</u> the Lord.
  (One <u>man</u> <u>was serving</u> the Lord.)
The <u>farmer</u> and the <u>minister</u> <u>were discussing</u> Sunday's sermon.
  (Two <u>men</u> <u>were discussing</u> the sermon.)
<u>Macaroni</u> and <u>cheese</u> <u>is</u> a favorite at our house. (One <u>dish</u> <u>is</u> a favorite.)

5. *Follow these rules for compound subjects joined by* or *or* nor.
   a. If both subjects are singular, use a singular verb.

   Neither <u>fire</u> nor <u>sword</u> <u>is</u> able to stop the Gospel message.

   b. If both subjects are plural, use a plural verb.

   Cruel <u>trials</u> or angry <u>mockings</u> <u>do</u> not deter Christians from their purpose.

   c. If one subject is singular and one is plural, make the verb agree with the subject that is nearer to the verb.

   Neither <u>Joseph</u> nor his <u>brothers</u> <u>were</u> aware of God's purposes.
   Neither his <u>brothers</u> nor <u>Joseph</u> <u>was</u> aware of God's purposes.

6. *Use a singular verb with a singular indefinite pronoun.* These pronouns are as follows: *each, either, neither, one, another, anybody, anyone, anything, everybody, everyone, everthing, somebody, someone, something, nobody, no one, nothing.*

   <u>Neither</u> of the prisoners <u>was</u> able to interpret his dream.
   <u>Nothing</u> <u>is</u> impossible when we trust in God.

7. *Use the correct verb with indefinite pronouns that may be either singular or plural.* These include *some, any, none, all,* and *most.* Such a pronoun is singular if its antecedent is singular. (The antecedent is usually stated in a prepositional phrase after the pronoun.) The indefinite pronoun then means a certain portion of that one thing and takes a singular verb. But the pronoun is plural if the antecedent is plural. Then the indefinite pronoun means certain individual items in that set of things, and it takes a plural verb.

   <u>Most</u> of the lawn <u>has</u> been mowed.
   <u>Most</u> of the lawns <u>have</u> been mowed.

8. *Use a singular verb with a noun that is plural in form but singular in meaning.* This includes nouns like *news* and *gallows,* names of diseases like *measles* and *mumps,* and words ending with *-ics* like *civics* and *ethics.*

   For many years <u>checkers</u> <u>has been</u> a favorite game.
   <u>Mathematics</u> <u>is</u> one of our most important school studies.

9. *Usually a plural verb is used with a noun that names an item made of paired parts.* This includes words like *shears, trousers, pliers, glasses, tweezers,* and *tongs.*

If the subject is *pair* followed by one of these nouns in a prepositional phrase, the verb must agree with the singular *pair.*

> Mary's new glasses <u>have helped</u> to relieve her headaches.
> Mary's new pair of glasses <u>has helped</u> to relieve her headaches.

10. *If a collective noun refers to a group acting as a unit, use a singular verb. If a collective noun refers to individual members of the group acting separately, use a plural verb.* A collective noun names a collection of individuals. Some common collective nouns are *group, family, congregation, herd, flock,* and *swarm.* In many sentences, a word like *its* or *our* helps to show whether the group is acting unitedly or separately.

> The <u>class</u> <u>is studying</u> about the early Indians of Central America.
>> (Class acting as a unit, doing the same thing.)
> The <u>class</u> <u>are preparing</u> their reports about the early Indians of Central America.
>> (Class members acting individually, doing different things; note the plural *their.*)

11. *Use a singular verb with a title or a word that is a subject of discussion.*

> <u>Fire Among the Zurich Hills</u> <u>tells</u> of early Swiss Anabaptists.
> <u>Emphases</u> <u>is</u> the plural of *emphasis.*

12. *Use a singular verb with a subject that is plural in form but which indicates a quantity or is regarded as a unit.*

> <u>Five dollars</u> <u>was</u> missing from her purse.
>> (This <u>amount</u> <u>was</u> missing from her purse.)
> <u>Eight miles</u> <u>is</u> too far to walk tonight. (This <u>distance</u> <u>is</u> too far to walk tonight.)

13. *Make the verb after a relative pronoun agree with the antecedent of the relative pronoun.*

> Our farm has a small spring <u>which</u> <u>gives</u> clear, pure water.
> Our farm has several springs <u>which</u> <u>give</u> clear, pure water.

Sometimes a relative pronoun follows a phrase like *the only one.* Then the antecedent is singular, and the verb in the relative clause should be singular.

> Judas was the *only one* of the disciples <u>who</u> <u>was</u> a traitor.
>> (*Who was a traitor* modifies *one;* the antecedent of *who* is the singular *one.* The sentence indicates that only one <u>disciple</u> <u>was</u> a traitor.)
> Peter was *one* of the disciples <u>who</u> <u>were</u> with Jesus in the garden.
>> (*Who were with Jesus in the garden* modifies *disciples;* the antecedent of *who* is the plural *disciples.* The sentence indicates that several <u>disciples</u> <u>were</u> with Jesus in the garden.)

14. *For words like* plenty, abundance, *and* rest *and for fractions followed by a phrase beginning with* of, *the object of the preposition following the subject determines the number of the subject.*

The <u>rest</u> of the day <u>was spent</u> cultivating the corn.
The <u>rest</u> of the days <u>were spent</u> cultivating the corn.

Three-fourths of the work <u>is</u> done.
Three-fourths of the jobs <u>are</u> done.

Applying the Lesson
A. Choose the correct word or phrase.
1. (There's, There are) many truths we can learn from the tabernacle of Moses.
2. One of the things that (impress, impresses) us is the single opening in the outer court.
3. Neither man nor woman (come, comes) to God through any way other than the one He has designed.
4. Many of the sacrifices (was, were) brought to the brazen altar.
5. A clear type of Christ (is, are) the many blood sacrifices that were offered here.
6. Our class (is, are) studying some Bible lessons about the tabernacle.
7. The cleansing of believers (is, are) portrayed by the priests' washing at the laver.
8. Some of the tabernacle types (relate, relates) to the different kinds of metals.
9. *Big Ten Tabernacle Topics* (indicate, indicates) that the gold was typical of Christ's deity.
10. An abundance of types (shine, shines) forth from the furniture of the holy place.
11. There (have been, has been) a few differences of opinion on some of these things.
12. Neither Herod nor his soldiers (was, were) able to destroy the Christ child.
13. Some of Jesus' worshipers (was, were) wise men from the East.
14. Simeon and Anna (stand, stands) as godly saints who rejoiced to see their Saviour.
15. A host of enemies (have, has) tried numerous ways to get around their accountability to a holy God.
16. Many teachings of the Bible (come, comes) to us from simple things.
17. The ant or the coney (teach, teaches) us to prepare ahead of time.
18. The spider (don't, doesn't) give up even after its web is destroyed by enemies.
19. The locusts, which (have, has) no king, challenge us to work together in humility and unity.
20. One of the differences between the twins (is, are) their personalities.
21. Our neighbor and accountant (fill, fills) out our tax returns each year.
22. The chickadees or titmice (visit, visits) our feeder each morning.
23. Eleanor's glasses (have, has) so many scratches that she needs new ones.
24. My trousers (seem, seems) too short since Mother washed them the last time.

Lesson 78 Answers
Applying the Lesson
A. 1. There are
2. impress
3. comes
4. were
5. is
6. is
7. is
8. relate
9. indicates
10. shine
11. have been
12. were
13. were
14. stand
15. have
16. come
17. teaches
18. doesn't
19. have
20. is
21. fills
22. visit
23. have
24. seem

25. You are the only one of my cousins who (was, were) not told about the accident.
26. Five days (pass, passes) very slowly when you are sick in bed.
27. Neither sickness nor other hardships (mean, means) that God has forsaken us.
28. Civics (was, were) very important to Mr. Johnson.
29. In my opinion, fifty dollars (is, are) an exorbitant price to pay for that purse.
30. *Arthropods* (was, were) the answer the teacher expected.
31. Each of my brothers (work, works) at home on our farm.
32. Stella is the only one of the students who (type, types) more than fifty words per minute.
33. Song leaders and moderators (fill, fills) an important place in our services.
34. A visit or a letter often (mean, means) very much to shut-ins.

B. Rewrite each sentence, following the directions in parentheses and changing the verb as needed to agree with the subject. Do not change the tense of the verb.
1. The heavy spring showers were flooding our garden. (Begin the sentence with *Each of.*)
2. Mr. Springfield is one of our neighbors who work on Sunday. (Insert *the only* before *one.*)
3. Neither my brothers nor my sister remembers Grandfather Martin. (Reverse the order of the subjects.)
4. There's a swarm of bees in the cherry tree. (Change *a swarm* to *thousands.*)
5. Most of these years have been unusually wet. (Change *these years* to *this year.*)
6. The family was eating a quiet dinner together. (Change the ending to *telling about their various experiences of the day.*)
7. This pair of trousers has a torn pocket. (Change *This pair of trousers* to *These trousers.*)
8. These stories haven't been revised yet. (Insert *One of* before *These.*)
9. The car and the truck use too much oil. (Change *and* to *or.*)
10. I have read all of the book that tells about Fanny Crosby's life. (Change *book* to *library books.*)
11. Two-thirds of the work is completed. (Change *work* to *chores.*)
12. This pair of pliers is broken. (Change *This pair of pliers* to *These pliers.*)
13. Susan is one of those girls who make friends easily. (Insert *the only* before *one.*)
14. Most of these boys know how to change a flat tire. (Change *these boys* to *this group.*)
15. The visitors that were present paid close attention. (Change *visitors* to *visitor.*)
16. Henry and Emma gather the eggs. (Change *and* to *or.*)
17. There's excellent cooperation among the students. (Change *cooperation* to *relationships.*)
18. Either the driver or the passengers were watching for the hidden lane. (Reverse the order of the subjects.)

25. was
26. passes
27. mean
28. was
29. is
30. was
31. works
32. types
33. fill
34. means

B. (Verbs with changes are underlined.)
1. Each of the heavy spring showers <u>was</u> flooding our garden.
2. Mr. Springfield is the only one of our neighbors who <u>works</u> on Sunday.
3. Neither my sister nor my brothers <u>remember</u> Grandfather Martin.
4. There <u>are</u> thousands of bees in the cherry tree.
5. Most of this year <u>has</u> been unusually wet.
6. The family <u>were</u> telling about their various experiences of the day.
7. These trousers <u>have</u> a torn pocket.
8. One of these stories <u>hasn't</u> been revised yet.
9. The car or the truck <u>uses</u> too much oil.
10. I have read all of the library books that <u>tell</u> about Fanny Crosby's life.
11. Two-thirds of the chores <u>are</u> completed.
12. These pliers <u>are</u> broken.
13. Susan is the only one of those girls who <u>makes</u> friends easily.
14. Most of this group <u>knows</u> how to change a flat tire.
15. The visitor that <u>was</u> present paid close attention.
16. Henry or Emma <u>gathers</u> the eggs.
17. There <u>are</u> excellent relationships among the students.
18. Either the passengers or the driver <u>was</u> watching for the hidden lane.

19. These vehicles don't use much fuel. (Insert *One of* before *These.*)
20. The rest of my friends were just around the corner. (Change *friends* to *luggage.*)
21. The softball team were taking their places on the field. (Change the ending to *winning the game by four runs.*)
22. These alarm clocks wake a sound sleeper. (Insert *Neither of* before *These.*)

Review Exercises

Choose the words that are correct for the subjunctive mood. [75]

1. It would be a great blessing if every person (was, were) a student of the Bible.
2. If a man (know, knows) not where to find truth, he is indeed in great darkness.
3. We could have attended every service if the meetings (would not have been, had not been) so far away.
4. Some people were acting as if it (was, were) cold in the auditorium.
5. Brother David requested that someone (turn, turns, turned) up the heat.
6. The chairman recommended that the decision (be, is, was) postponed until the next meeting.
7. He considered it important that each board member carefully (think, thinks, thought) through the proposal.
8. If the captain (would have known, had known) about the danger, he would have tried to prevent the accident.
9. An accused man should be set free if he (be, is) found innocent.
10. If every person (was, were) completely honest, court trials would be unnecessary.

19. One of these vehicles <u>doesn't</u> use much fuel.
20. The rest of my luggage <u>was</u> just around the corner.
21. The softball team <u>was</u> winning the game by four runs.
22. Neither of these alarm clocks <u>wakes</u> a sound sleeper.

Review Exercises

1. were
2. know
3. had not been
4. were
5. turn
6. be
7. think
8. had known
9. be
10. were

79. Improving Your Editing Skills, Part 8

We use alarm clocks to waken us in the morning. As long as we get up when the alarm rings, the system works well. But we all know what happens to a person who ignores his alarm clock. The more often he turns the alarm off and goes back to sleep, the less sensitive he becomes to its warning. Finally, the time will come when he continues to sleep while the alarm continues to ring!

Your editing skill works in an amazingly similar way. The more careful you are to use correct English in everyday speech and writing, the sharper you become in detecting errors. But if you excuse your errors and say or write things you know are incorrect, you will grow less sensitive. Do you allow yourself to use expressions like "Him and I plan to go" or "That don't matter" or "I seen him yesterday"? If so, you will find it hard to catch all the mistakes when you are editing—especially those that involve a fine detail of English grammar.

Lesson 79

Purpose: To provide proofreading practice.

Whenever you become aware of an error in your use of English, you need to consciously raise yourself to a proper use of the language. This is the only way to develop a high degree of skill in editing.

Marks Used in Editing and Proofreading

$\lor$ or $\land$ insert (caret)	⟋ delete	. . . . stet (let it stand)	————— use italics
¶ begin new paragraph	no ¶ no new paragraph	*lc* change to lowercase (small letter)	*uc* change to uppercase (capital letter)
# insert space	⌒ delete space	← move (arrow)	⌐⌐⌐ transpose

Editing Practice

A. Use proofreading marks to correct the ten spelling or spacing errors in this selection.

1.   George R. Brunk was an influental Mennonite bishop in
2. Virginia. He served the church faith fully until his death
3. in 1938. In one of his sermons, he denouced the infidel
4. ity of men like Robert G. Ingersoll, a promanent agnostic.
5. After the service, one of the brethern from the audience
6. came to Brother Brunk with an intresting question. He
7.   asked if it was allright to buy an Ingersoll watch.
8. The quick-thinking bishop smiled and replied, "Certianly;
9. Ingersoll will do for time, but not for eternity."

B. Use proofreading marks to make these corrections in the paragraph below.
   a. Divide the selection into two paragraphs.
   b. Correct two errors in sentence division.
   c. Improve the word order in two places.

1.   George Brunk was visiting one day a brother who was
2. lying in the hospital, after speaking to him words of
3. comfort, the minister turned to a man in a bed nearby
4. and asked him about the state of his soul. The man
5. replied gruffly, "If God wants me, let Him come and

Lesson 79 Answers

Editing Practice
   (Answers are on pages 474–475.)

6. get me!" "Listen," said Brother Brunk. "If you don't

7. concern yourself about your soul's salvation and do

8. something about it. Somebody will come and get you—

9. and it won't be God either."

C. Use proofreading marks to correct all the errors in these paragraphs. No line has more than one error.

1.   Whereas some stars are much larger then the sun, others

2. are much more smaller. One of these is Sirius B, which is a

3. companion of the bright star called Sirius (the Dog Star).

4. Scientists classsify Sirius B as a white dwarf. Because

5. of its white color, they think its surface temperature is

6. hoter than that of the sun.

7.   Though the diameter of Sirius B appears to be about

8. equal to that of the earth. Scientists believe its total

9. mass is equal to that of the sun. Compressing so much

10. mass into such a small sphere produces a extremely great

11. density. According to one estimate, a brick made of

12. substance from Sirius B weigh would thirty tons. That

13. is the weight of six full grown elephants!

14.   According to scientists, the reason for differences in

15. stars is that they are in different stages of developement.

16. White dwarfs, they say, are millions of years older than

17. "young stars" like the gaint Betelgeuse. The Bible teaches

18. that God made all the stars on the forth day of Creation.

19. It also says, "One star differeth from another star in

20. glory (1 Corinthians 15:41). The stars are different, not

21. because they are in variuos stages of evolution, but

22. because God made them that way.

80.   Chapter 9 Review

A. Copy each verb or verb phrase, and write which tense it is. Also write whether it is *simple, progressive,* or *emphatic* in form.
1. Over the years men have used water for many different things.
2. We do drink water, of course, and we are continually washing ourselves and our clothes.
3. We shall always need water for our plants.
4. Have you been thinking about its use for transportation?
5. Oh, yes, I had forgotten about its use in baptism.

B. Most of these sentences have mistakes in the use of verb principal parts. Write the correct verb, or write *correct.*
1. The dam at Johnstown had bursted after days of heavy rainfall.
2. I seen the mistake as soon as he handed me his paper.
3. Nobody else had did as much of the work as little Samuel.
4. I do believe that this shirt has shrunken with every washing.
5. As soon as you have tug someone else, he will be it.

C. Rewrite each sentence, changing one verb to a perfect tense so that the meaning is clearer or a completed action is emphasized.
1. Before we saw the other car, it crashed into our back fender.
2. By the time you finish your homework, the rest of the family will go to bed.
3. When I ate my lunch, I went outside to play.

D. Copy each underlined verb, and write whether its mood is indicative (*ind.*), imperative (*imp.*), or subjunctive (*sub.*).
1. Ahab <u>coveted</u> the vineyard of his neighbor Naboth.
2. How he wished that he <u>were</u> the owner of the land.
3. Always <u>guard</u> against an envious spirit.
4. <u>Do</u> you <u>think</u> that Ahab really needed the vineyard to be happy?
5. Jezebel ordered that Naboth <u>die</u> so that the king could have what he wanted.

E. Choose the words that are correct for the subjunctive mood.
1. "If God (is, be) for us, who can be against us?"
2. The doctor recommended that Grandfather (take, takes) a stress test.
3. Brother Sanford moved that the trustees (fix, fixed) the roof.
4. If we (were, would be) earlier, we would stop and visit Sister Emma.
5. Suppose this car (was, were) to run out of fuel.

F. Copy each verb, and label it *TA* (transitive, active voice), *TP* (transitive, passive voice), *IC* (intransitive complete), or *IL* (intransitive linking).
1. Three different arks are mentioned in the Scriptures.
2. The first one is Noah's large boat.
3. Next Moses' mother built a very small ark.
4. The ark of the covenant comes third.
5. The materials used for each ark were different.
6. Different items were placed into each of the arks.

Lesson 80 Answers

A. 1. have used—present perfect, simple
   2. do drink—present, emphatic; are washing—present, progressive
   3. shall need—future, simple
   4. Have been thinking—present perfect, progressive
   5. had forgotten—past perfect, simple

B. 1. had burst
   2. saw
   3. had done
   4. correct
   5. have tagged

C. 1. Before we saw the other car, it had crashed into our back fender.
   2. By the time you finish your homework, the rest of the family will have gone to bed.
   3. When I had eaten my lunch, I went outside to play.

D. 1. coveted—ind.   4. Do think—ind.
   2. were—sub.   5. die—sub.
   3. guard—imp.

E. 1. be
   2. take
   3. fix
   4. were
   5. were

F. 1. are mentioned—TP
   2. is—IL
   3. built—TA
   4. comes—IC *or* IL
   5. were—IL
   6. were placed—TP

Lesson 80

Purpose: To review the concepts taught in Chapter 9.

7. Each ark served as an instrument of preservation.
8. Like an ark today, the Christian home protects its inhabitants from many surrounding dangers.

7. served—IC
8. protects—TA

G. If the underlined verb or contraction does not agree with the subject, write the correct form. If it does agree, write *correct.*

1. Brother Brendon or Brother Wesley <u>are scheduled</u> to conduct the Wednesday devotional period.
2. The apple tree and the pear tree <u>needs</u> pruning this spring.
3. This pair of shears <u>are</u> too dull to do the job well.
4. Fifty pounds <u>is</u> the average weight of a fertilizer bag.
5. Approximately one-third of our watermelon plants <u>wilts</u> if we fail to spray them.
6. Nothing about his comments <u>suggest</u> that he felt mistreated.
7. *Thrilling Escapes by Night* <u>recounts</u> the experiences of William Tyndale.
8. <u>Does</u> your mother's parents still live near Mount Aetna?
9. English is the only one of my subjects that <u>seem</u> fairly easy.
10. My favorite breakfast <u>is</u> pancakes and syrup.
11. The family <u>was</u> working at their hobbies last evening.
12. He declares that it <u>don't</u> make any difference whether he comes or not.
13. Most of the building <u>has</u> been destroyed by the fire.
14. Neither the lettuce nor the onions <u>appeals</u> to my sense of taste.
15. All of the wall that <u>was</u> painted should have a second coat.
16. My friend and helper <u>are</u> holding the board in place.
17. The nail clippers <u>were</u> lost somewhere in the drawer.
18. Baby sheep or goats <u>adds</u> a great deal of interest around a place.
19. Our class <u>has</u> just finished a study of the Great Pyramid of Egypt.
20. <u>There's</u> no dull moments when Uncle Henry is present.

G. 1. is scheduled
2. need
3. is
4. correct
5. wilt
6. suggests
7. correct
8. Do
9. seems
10. correct
11. were
12. doesn't
13. correct
14. appeal
15. correct
16. is
17. correct
18. add
19. correct
20. There are

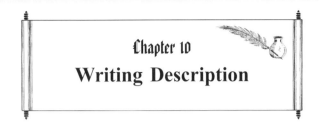

Chapter 10
Writing Description

81. Employing Descriptive Language

A writer of description uses words to sketch the details of a scene or an event. In describing a scene, he depicts the details of a particular place. In describing an event, he portrays the points of a particular happening. The more skillfully he draws his word pictures, the more appealing and fascinating they will be to the reader.

Almost invariably, writers weave descriptive writing into their stories, expositions, and arguments. Without it, the paragraphs would be flat, dull, and lifeless. Occasionally, however, a writer may produce an entire essay of description. Such an essay has as its purpose to paint a distinct picture in the reader's mind. You will produce such an essay in this chapter. But first, in this lesson, you will review the qualities that make writing truly descriptive.

Rich Detail

Effective description consists of rich detail. A paragraph of fuzzy generalities is about as satisfactory as a photograph that is out of focus. Clear details produce a sharp, meaningful picture.

What can you do to ensure that your writing contains that richness of detail? Above all, you must develop an eye for detail in the things around you. Look at things as if you had never seen them before. Analyze them carefully and thoroughly. Instead of taking a sweeping view, stop and consider exactly what you are seeing. Notice the people, their faces, their clothes, their postures. Notice specific objects and their variations of color, shape, and size. Pay attention to the things that are happening around you. You cannot hope to add rich detail to your writing unless you first exercise keen observation.

Consider this example, apparently written by a traveler in a Central American country.

> Looking at each other dubiously, we boarded the old, rickety bus. Soon we were jolting down the rough road.

The writer has described his experience simply, clearly, and honestly. But before he lays his pencil down, he should answer a few questions. How could he tell that the bus was old? By recognizing it as a 1945 model? By its faded paint? What was rickety about the bus? Was it missing a hood? Were the windows cracked and rattly? Did the floor have holes? And can he show us that the road really was rough?

Lesson 81

Purpose: To review pointers for writing description.

Teaching Suggestions:

The first section of this lesson is foundational. The very essence of description is detail that creates a mental image of a person, a place, or an object. The other sections review elements of description that the students have studied previously in this English series, including some in Chapter 8 of this book (in relation to story writing).

While students generally need urging to use vivid, descriptive language, there is also room for a caution against overdoing it—especially in describing negative aspects of a person or thing. We need to remember the Golden Rule and to describe other people and their things just as charitably as we want others to describe us and our things.

If he fills in these answers, he will produce a description with rich details that stimulate our imagination and help us enjoy what he has observed. Read the description below, with these details added.

Looking at each other dubiously, we boarded the dented, rust-eaten bus. The door sagged on its hinges, and we soon noticed that it refused to close completely. What padding the seats may have contained in some ancient past had disappeared or compacted so tightly that the seats felt more like knotty boards than bus seats worthy of the name. The engine coughed and almost died as the driver coaxed the bus to drag itself forward. Each bump and pothole (of which there were many!) made its whole rheumatic body twist and groan with pain.

Vivid, Concrete Words

Effective description uses vivid, concrete words. Exact nouns paint a sharper picture than general nouns modified by adjectives. Why write *huge rock* when *boulder* makes the picture clear? Or why write about a *sudden, heavy downpour* when *cloudburst* paints a sharp image? Look at the exact nouns in the paragraph above. The writer chose the word *padding* rather than *soft material*. He wrote *driver,* not *the man who was driving.* These exact nouns contribute to the descriptiveness of the paragraph.

Expressive verbs also add to the sparkle of the word picture. As much as practical, use strong, vivid action verbs. Linking verbs, passive verbs, and weak action verbs tend to tarnish a description. Compare the underlined verbs in the following sentences with the ones used in the paragraph above.

We got onto the dented, rust-eaten bus.
The door was crooked and was impossible to close completely.
What padding there may have been in the seats in some ancient past was gone.
The bus was coaxed to drag itself forward.
Its whole rheumatic body was caused to twist and groan with pain.

Truly picturesque modifiers can add further color and sharpness to exact nouns and expressive verbs. The paragraph about the old bus contains a number of such picturesque words. Notice the italicized modifiers in the following expressions from that paragraph: Looking at each other *dubiously,* refused to close *completely,* in some *ancient* past, like *knotty* boards, its whole *rheumatic* body.

Imagery

Similes, metaphors, hyperboles, personification, and onomatopoeia help to make a description especially appealing. A skillful sprinkling of these figures throughout your composition adds spice and freshness that tickle the taste buds of a reader's mind. How many of these kinds of imagery caught your attention in the sample paragraph?

Simile:
the seats felt more like knotty boards than bus seats worthy of the name

Hyperbole:

What padding the seats may have contained <u>in some ancient past</u>...

Personification:

The door... <u>refused to close completely</u>.

The engine <u>coughed and almost died</u> as the driver <u>coaxed the bus to drag itself forward</u>.

Each bump... <u>made its whole rheumatic body twist and groan with pain</u>.

Onomatopoeia: twist and <u>groan</u> with pain

Used with discretion, onomatopoeia adds a special appeal to descriptive writing. Unless the writing is geared to young children, you should use very few onomatopoeic exclamations like *Crash!* and *Moo!* or expressions like "the box rolled *bumpity-bump* down the steps." Rather, use more subtle forms of onomatopoeia like *groan* in the sample paragraph.

Appeal to the Five Senses

What is true for story writing (Chapter 8) is just as true for description: sensory details help the reader to live what the author is describing. Most descriptive writing appeals primarily to the sense of sight. But put forth special effort to include details that appeal to the other senses. In the description of the bus, the writer deliberately included details that appeal to three of our senses.

Sight: It was a dented, rust-eaten bus.

The door sagged on its hinges and did not close tight.

The padding of the seats was worn thin.

Sound: The engine ran rough and almost choked off.

The bus made groaning sounds as it bounced over the rough road.

Feeling: The seats were hard and lumpy.

Applying the Lesson

A. From these paragraphs, write examples that illustrate the indicated elements of description.

Suddenly the Sunday afternoon peace was shattered by screams of pain and fright. Father and I dashed outside to see three-year-old Bennie racing for the house with all the speed he could muster. Like a windmill gone berserk, his arms were flailing at his face, his stomach, and his legs. Around him swarmed an army of yellow jackets, furiously injecting their red-hot, poisoned needles into his flesh.

Grabbing a nearby water hose, Father dispersed most of the army. Quickly he and I removed Bennie's shirt, killing several more of the zealous warriors. Then Father picked up the little boy, who was swelling rapidly, and raced for the house. "Brian," he shouted, "get the van out of the garage. We must go to the hospital!"

1. An exact noun for loud noises.
2. An exact noun for clothing.
3. A verb that describes vigorous whirling motions.

Lesson 81 Answers

Applying the Lesson

A. 1. screams
   2. shirt
   3. flailing

4. Five other clear, vigorous verbs or verbals.
5. Two picturesque adjectives.
6. Two picturesque adverbs.
7. One simile.
8. Three metaphors.
9. Two details that appeal to the sense of sight.
10. Two details that appeal to the sense of hearing.

B. Write a more descriptive word for each underlined expression in this paragraph. Use personification in two of your answers, as noted in brackets.

The mountain road went on and on, sometimes ¹going around hairpin curves and sometimes ²going swiftly downward [personification] into narrow ravines. Then a ³very lovely view presented itself. Almost directly below us, a huge lake ⁴showed an image of the bright blue heavens. A few small fishing boats ⁵moved lazily on its ⁶undisturbed surface. Several small farms ⁷were in the verdant valley beyond the lake. In the distance, ⁸nice hayfields ⁹went up [personification] the slope for only a short distance before another mountain range abruptly cut them off.

C. Write a descriptive paragraph about two of these scenes or events. Include as many of the elements of description as practical.
1. Your younger siblings playing school.
2. The view from your house.
3. A place of interest that you have visited.
4. Your classroom at lunchtime.
5. Several puppies (kittens, lambs) playing together.
6. The aftermath of a flood (hurricane, tornado).

82. Selecting and Arranging the Details

Imagine that you are drawing a picture of your schoolroom. To make the picture accurate, will you draw everything that you can see? Indeed not! You will not draw all the cracks between the boards in the floor. Neither will you include all the lines of the wood grain in the teacher's desk, nor every speck and irregularity on the chalkboard. If you try to draw everything you can observe, you will succeed only in producing a grand and ungracious clutter.

Now imagine that you are writing a description of your schoolroom. Will you include everything that you can see, hear, smell, and feel? The lines in the floor? The rustling of papers? The squeaking of shoes? The smoothness of your desk top? No, of course not. Such a description would become a meaningless assortment of trivial details.

Whether drawing a picture with lines or with words, we must limit the details that we include.

Lesson 82

Purpose: To teach the importance of selecting details carefully.

Teaching Suggestions:

You should plan to spend most of your teaching time on the first part of the lesson. The matter of spatial and chronological order has been covered several times before.

One effective way to teach the lesson would be to work together at writing a descriptive paragraph. You might describe the scene from your classroom window or some other scene or event with which all your students are familiar. Decide on a theme, list your details, and write at least a few sentences together.

4. (Any five.) shattered, dashed, racing, swarmed, injecting, Grabbing, dispersed, swelling, raced, shouted
5. (Any two.) red-hot, poisoned, zealous
6. (Any two.) furiously, Quickly, rapidly (*Berserk* may also be accepted, even though it is a predicate adjective. Students may not recognize *gone* as a linking verb.)
7. Like a windmill gone berserk
8. (Any three.)
   peace was shattered;
   an army of yellow jackets;
   injecting their red-hot, poisoned needles;
   several more of the zealous warriors
9. (Any two.)
   Bennie racing for the house;
   his flailing arms;
   yellow jackets swarming around him
10. Bennie's screams of pain and fright; Father's shouted instructions

B. (Allow reasonable variation.)
1. leading
2. diving
3. magnificent, gorgeous
4. mirrored, reflected
5. floated, drifted
6. still
7. dotted
8. luxuriant, green
9. climbed

C. (Individual work.)

Selecting the Details

To write effective description, you must select details carefully. First you must learn to recognize the important details. Which items in the scene catch your attention? Which other items fit with them to create the scene? Or which movements in an event stand out most? Which other movements blend with them as the significant happenings? Since you cannot use every detail, you must choose those that are central to your description.

In essence, every detail in a description should contribute to one specific impression. This is the theme of the description. In Lesson 81, for example, the paragraph about the rickety bus focuses only on the rundown condition of the bus. The author did not include details about how crowded it was or about the dust blowing in the open windows. He did not describe the driver, the cattle on the road, or anything else outside. The paragraph is intended to impress the reader with the condition of the bus itself; therefore, any other details would detract from that theme.

Two descriptions may give two different impressions about the same scene or event. For example, compare the following paragraphs, which describe the same kitchen scene.

As usual, the kitchen extends a cozy welcome to each family member on this blustery winter evening. From its place in the corner, the large wood stove cheers the whole room with its friendly warmth. A large kettle on its surface diffuses the spicy aroma of hot apple cider. Eli and Conrad sit on the floor, playing contentedly with their tractors and farm animals. The three older girls enjoy the comfort of the sofa. Dorcas is engrossed in the experiences of *War-torn Valley.* A steady stream of words issues from Esther's pen as she writes to one of her friends. And the skein of yarn at Sarah's feet gradually takes shape as a sweater for baby Miriam, who coos and giggles from her walker. I turn back to the English lesson waiting patiently on the kitchen table. A warmth more precious than that of the cozy kitchen fills my heart as I thank God for my Christian home.

As usual, the kitchen presents a busy but orderly appearance on this blustery winter evening. Mother has banished any dirt that was bold enough to gather on the floor. Her zeal is also evident in the sparkle of the wood stove standing in the corner. Now Mother's industrious needle is steadily changing a basketful of torn items into neat stacks of mended clothing. All the children are busily occupied too—the younger ones with their toys, and the older ones with reading, writing, and knitting. The books on the library shelves stand stiff and straight in orderly array. The sink and countertops smile at me with the joy of cleanliness. Once more the scene thrills me as I return to work on my English lesson.

Do you see the difference? In the first paragraph, the focus is on the warm pleasantness of the kitchen. So this paragraph presents details to match that theme, such as the friendly warmth of the wood stove, the spicy aroma of hot apple cider, and the amusement of two small boys. The second paragraph deals with the "busy but orderly" aspects of the kitchen. It develops that theme by mentioning things like Mother's banishing of dirt, her polishing of the wood stove, and the busyness of the children. Thus the paragraphs convey two different impressions even though they describe the same scene.

Arranging the Details

Once you have selected the details, you must consider how you will arrange them. For most descriptive paragraphs, you will choose either spatial or chronological order. Use spatial order to describe a scene. You may move from left to right, from near to distant, from a central figure to the less important details, or in any other logical progression. The sample paragraphs above follow spatial order.

Be sure to maintain a consistent point of view in your description. For example, if you are viewing a barn from the front, you must describe everything as seen from there. You could not tell about the back of the building. If you were to describe the barn as you walk around it, however, it would be appropriate to describe the back of the barn as your circuit takes you there.

Use chronological order to describe an event. In Lesson 81, the description about Bennie and the yellow jackets is in chronological order.

Applying the Lesson

A. Read this descriptive paragraph, and do the exercises that follow.

Aunt Viola's garden stands as a monument to her industry. In the left half is her bed of strawberries, forming a plush carpet that covers about a fourth of the garden. They are bearing exceptionally well this year, and a multitude of berries smile out from their leafy homes. Beyond the strawberries, a number of tomato plants gaze in wonder at the huge cages surrounding them. In the right half, a number of rows run the full length of the garden, as straight as latitude lines. They include a luscious stand of peas supported by four-foot-high poultry wire, as well as lettuce, carrots, beets, onions, radishes, green beans, and lima beans. Throughout the entire garden, not a single weed is bold enough to thrust its head into view.

1. Summarize the main impression about Aunt Viola's garden that this paragraph conveys.
2. Copy the first three words of the sentence that should be deleted because it does not contribute to that impression.
3. Name the order of development that is used in this paragraph.

B. Write two paragraphs describing the same scene or event, creating two different impressions. The following suggestions may help you.
1. An old barn: its neat simplicity, its sturdiness, its great size.
2. Sawing firewood: its noisiness, its bustling activity, its danger.
3. A cleaning day at church: its efficiency, its improvements, its large amount of work.
4. Moving day: its disorder, its excitement, its uncertainties.
5. A deep snow: its beauty, its hindrances to work, its chill.

Lesson 82 Answers
Applying the Lesson
A. 1. Aunt Viola's garden is neat and well cared for
   2. They are bearing
   3. spatial

B. (Individual work.)

83. Writing Description Within Other Compositions

When we find out that someone we know has just purchased a farm or a car, or has simply gotten another dog, we immediately want more information. Where is the farm? How big is it? Or, what kind of car did he buy? What year? And the dog—is it full-grown, or is it only a puppy?

Just as descriptive information adds meaning to real life, so it adds to writing. Description fills an important place in narrative essays (stories), expository essays, and argumentative essays. However, descriptive writing does not often stand alone as separate paragraphs in these other kinds of writing. It is usually woven right into the compositions.

Description Within Narratives

Description fills a vital role in narratives. The story setting represents descriptive information about the time, place, and mood of the story. The story incidents themselves should involve ample use of the elements of description. And the process of characterization relies heavily on the elements of descriptive writing.

Indeed, description is so important to narratives that in Chapter 8 you had several lessons devoted specifically to various elements of description in improving the style of a story. Notice the many descriptive details in the following excerpt.

> Being new in the area, Alfred was apprehensive about his first venture to the village. He stepped quietly under the awning of the blacksmith shop, and through the open door he surveyed its smoky interior. Scraps of iron and various crude works of art cluttered the corners. A great forge stood to one side. It crackled and belched smoke as the smith's assistant piled on fresh coal. Scattered here and there were various implements awaiting repair. Mr. Davis himself was hammering out a piece of steel destined to be part of a plow.
>
> Remembering his errand, Alfred stepped timidly into the shop and approached the men. The assistant jerked his thumb toward the smith. "He'll see to you shortly. Just sit and watch a spell." With that, he continued pumping the old leather bellows vigorously. Alfred watched as sparks leaped upward in the furious heat of the forge.

Description Within Exposition

Exposition often employs description. In writing exposition, you explain how something works or what something consists of. To do that effectively, you must include illustrations, examples, and other details. And that means you must write descriptively. Furthermore, to write your exposition interestingly, you should employ the various elements of description.

You will remember the following paragraphs from the exposition in Lesson 28. Notice now how much description the writer used in explaining what the water hyacinth is like.

Lesson 83

Purpose: To teach how descriptive writing enhances stories, expositions, and arguments.

Teaching Suggestions:

Using descriptive writing in stories received specific emphasis in Chapter 8, so it is merely mentioned here. Including descriptive language often proves more challenging in expositions and arguments than in stories because stories are naturally more suitable for descriptive development than are the other two kinds of writing.

If you have saved the students' expository essays from Chapter 4, you might be able to use both positive and negative examples to illustrate the lesson teaching. And if any argumentative essays from Book 1 are available, you might use them in the same way.

The water hyacinth is a tropical water plant with large, elegant lavender flowers. It floats on air-filled sacs, and it reaches a height of about 2 feet
(61 cm) above the surface of the water. When thousands of water hyacinths
grow together, they form a mat so thick that it can support a man's weight.

But for all its striking beauty, the water hyacinth has some very ugly behavior. The plants multiply with amazing speed, sometimes doubling in number
every ten days. Just 10 plants can increase to a mat of more than 600,000
in one growing season, and the mat continues to spread until it completely
covers the surface of the water. In this way, the plant makes itself such a nuisance that it has been called the purple curse.

In Lesson 81 you studied four elements of description. See how the writer incor-
porated them in the paragraphs above.

1. *Rich detail.* Notice some of the specific details. Water hyacinths float on air-
filled sacs and reach a height of about two feet. Water hyacinths sometimes double
every ten days, and a mere ten plants can increase to 600,000 plants in one growing
season. These details add to the quality of the exposition, for they help you to see
exactly what the author is writing about.

2. *Vivid, concrete words.* The paragraphs use exact nouns: *mat, beauty, nuisance.* Notice the expressive verbs: *grow, form, support, multiply, increase.* They
add more strength than would verbs of being or passive voice verbs. And several
colorful modifiers make their contribution as well: *elegant, lavender, striking,
amazing.*

3. *Imagery.* The second paragraph begins by attributing some *very ugly behavior* to this beautiful plant. Plants do not behave, of course, but we enjoy this imaginative description of what the plant does. The concluding sentence also suggests that
the plant *makes itself a nuisance.* Again, the suggestive implication adds interest and
appeal.

4. *Appeal to the five senses.* These paragraphs include language that appeals to
your sight. In fact, those visual details constitute the very essence of the exposition.
As you see those details, you understand the exposition. Since none of the other senses
are involved in observing the hyacinth, the essay includes no details that appeal to
them.

Clearly, the inclusion of descriptive writing has helped to make the exposition
about the water hyacinth clear, effective, and interesting.

Description Within Argument

Arguments may also include description. True, the strength of an argument lies
in its sound reasoning and its supporting facts. But the supporting evidence includes
illustrations, examples, and other details that involve description. As with exposition, that description again contributes greatly to the overall effectiveness of the
essay.

Notice the descriptive details in the following paragraphs from an argumentative essay.

> Owning a small flock of laying hens assures your family a steady supply of eggs. For their room and board, twenty good layers pay between fifteen and eighteen eggs a day for two to four months. During those peak months, that accumulates to nine or ten dozen cartons of economical nutrition every week. This should provide breakfast several times a week for a family with six to eight children, in addition to supplying plenty of eggs for cooking and baking. Even when production declines to only ten eggs a day, you should still be gathering about six dozen eggs per week. Your family will seldom suffer an egg shortage if you have a small flock of layers.
>
> A small flock of laying hens will also give your family the assurance of knowing that you are eating fresh eggs. Unfortunately, eggs from the store can hardly make any reasonable claim to freshness. Indeed, most of those eggs have probably spent several weeks in storage before they get their first glimpse of a store shelf. By the time they are sizzling in your frying pan, they are definitely suffering from old age. But you can trust your own eggs. You know when you gathered them. So a family flock of layers makes sense for people who prefer eating fresh eggs.

All four elements of descriptive language shine in these paragraphs. They are categorized below, along with examples from the essay.

Specific details: twenty good layers, between fifteen and eighteen eggs a day, two to four months, nine or ten dozen cartons, six to eight children, several weeks in storage

Vivid, concrete words: small flock, peak months, breakfast, cooking and baking, egg shortage, fresh eggs, frying pan, old age

Imagery: their room and board, nine or ten dozen cartons of economical nutrition, their first glimpse of a store shelf, suffering from old age

Appeal to the five senses: sizzling in your frying pan

Some description is written purely to give the reader a mental picture of what the writer has observed. Within other kinds of composition, descriptive writing adds color and interest to the narrative, exposition, or argument.

Applying the Lesson

Read the following essay, and show how to make it more descriptive by following the directions below. (Exercise letters correspond to the letters of sentences in the essay.) You need to write only enough of the appropriate sentences to show your improvements.

1. Include the following specific details in the sentences indicated.
    f. The pool of Siloam has an oblong shape.
    h. The water in the pool has a somewhat brackish taste.
    n. The underground conduit is 1,750 feet long.

Lesson 83 Answers
(Allow reasonable variation.)
1. f. This oblong pool
   h. The water in the pool of Siloam, which has a somewhat brackish taste, comes
   n. through solid rock for 1,750 feet

2. Replace each of the following expressions with a specific noun.
   i. steep face of rock
   l. effort to capture the city by surrounding and blockading it
   o. words inscribed
3. In sentences *c, d, i,* and *k,* replace the passive verbs and linking verbs with more expressive verbs in the active voice.
4. Replace the following expressions with imagery.
   i. rises above (personification)
   n. travels a twisted course (personification)

The Pool of Siloam

[a]In a notable display of His power, Jesus healed a man who had been born blind. [b]But He did not merely speak the word of healing as He usually did. [c]Rather, clay was made and was spread on the man's eyes. [d]Then the blind man was commanded, "Go, wash in the pool of Siloam" (John 9:1–7).

[e]Archaeologists and Bible scholars generally identify the pool of Siloam with the modern Birket Silwan, southeast of Mount Zion. [f]This pool is in a basin about fifty-three feet long, eighteen feet wide, and nineteen feet deep. [g]It lies partly in hewn rock and partly in masonry construction. [h]The water in the pool of Siloam comes from the Gihon Spring. [i]Flowing from the steep face of rock that rises above the Kidron Valley, this spring was the only unfailing source of fresh water for ancient Jerusalem. [j]The spring flows intermittently, however, sending its tribute to the pool from three to five times daily in winter, about twice a day in summer, and about once a day in autumn.

[k]Because of the strategic importance of this spring, an extraordinary feat of excavation was performed by men of ancient times. [l]Apparently in preparation for the Assyrian effort to capture the city by surrounding and blockading it, Hezekiah "stopped the upper watercourse of Gihon, and brought it straight down to the west side of the city of David" (2 Chronicles 32:30). [m]In the words of 2 Kings 20:20, "he made a pool, and a conduit, and brought water into the city." [n]This underground conduit travels a twisted course through solid rock. [o]According to the words inscribed on the channel wall near the pool of Siloam, workmen using picks dug from both ends and met in the middle.

2. i. cliff
   l. siege
   o. inscription
3. c. Jesus made clay and spread it
   d. He commanded the blind man
   i. this spring provided
   k. men of ancient times performed an extraordinary feat of excavation
4. i. looks down on
   n. snakes

---

84. Planning a Descriptive Essay

You saw in the previous lesson that descriptive writing adds color and interest to narratives, expositions, and arguments. But sometimes a whole essay consists of description. Such an essay has the general purpose of giving the reader a mental picture of what the writer has observed, and the specific purpose of giving a certain impression about the scene or event described.

Lesson 84

Purpose: To review the steps in planning a description.

Teaching Suggestions:

Stress to your students that they must be thoroughly familiar with the scene or event that they plan to describe. Unless they can first see, hear, feel, smell, and taste the details, they will not be able to paint word pictures that lead a reader to identify with the scene or event. Emphasize also the importance of having a theme—a focus on one specific impression.

You should plan to review the students' choices for Part A before they begin working on Part B. You may have some helpful criticism or changes to suggest before they have expended much energy in listing details.

As with other kinds of writing, a descriptive essay calls for careful planning. The following five steps will help you to plan a descriptive essay.

1. *Choose a scene or an event to describe.* This should be something familiar that interests you. You cannot write a good descriptive essay about something you have never observed unless you write about an imaginary scene or event. A description is not an exposition that presents facts about a subject. It is rather a word picture, giving specific details that will paint in the mind of the reader the picture that the writer sees.

The subject of a good description need not be something extraordinarily beautiful or exciting. With a little imagination and writing skill, you can make interesting descriptions even of everyday scenes and events. For example, you could probably give quite an interesting description of your family at the dinner table.

2. *Decide on the theme of your description.* Remember that the theme is the main impression you want to convey. With many scenes, you can write a description focusing on one of several different impressions. For example, the essay in Lesson 85 emphasizes the great size of Grandfather Hoover's farmhouse. The author could have included details about the neatness of the house or the simplicity of its structure and furnishings. But an essay is better if it focuses on only one theme.

3. *List details about the scene or the event.* Look for details that will paint concrete word pictures. List details that appeal to as many of the five senses as practical. Generally, details that appeal to the sight come quite naturally. But you should also put special effort into capturing details that appeal to the other senses.

If you have already decided on the theme of your description, you will limit the details to those that convey the impression you want. If you have not yet decided, list all the details that are outstanding to you. Your list should be helpful in deciding on a suitable theme.

4. *Examine your list of details, and delete any that do not contribute to the theme.* Even if you have been selective in making your list, you will probably find some details that are insignificant or that are not as well related as you had thought earlier. The following list shows some details that could be written for an essay about a large farmhouse. Notice how the deleted details do not fit. Although they are interesting, they do not develop the impression of the great size of the house.

> Massive front door—7½ feet by 4 feet
> Five-foot-wide hallway through length of house
> Wide spiral stairway in center of hallway
> ~~Paintings of old farm machinery on two parlor walls~~
> Kitchen wood stove ~~with well-padded rocking chair beside it~~
> Half-bathroom in corner of kitchen

5. *Organize your details into an outline.* A description of a scene should follow spatial order, and you must be consistent with your point of view. A description of an event should follow chronological order.

Study the following outline for a descriptive essay about a large farmhouse.

Room for Sixteen Children

I. Entrance
   A. Massive front door—7½ feet by 4 feet
   B. Stone walls nearly two feet thick
   C. Five-foot-wide hallway running length of house
   D. Wide, spiraling stairway in center of hall

II. Parlor
   A. Stale odor from little use
   B. Ten-foot ceiling
   C. Echoing sound from paneling and hardwood floor

III. Master bedroom
   A. Large bed in center of far wall
   B. Wide dresser with large round mirror along right wall
   C. Cedar chest in near right corner

IV. Kitchen
   A. Countertop with double sink and spacious cabinets along left wall
   B. Half-bathroom in far left corner
   C. Countertop along a third of right wall
   D. Wood stove in far right corner
   E. Door to living room centered in right wall
   F. Extension table in center

V. Living room
   A. Study in near right corner
      1. Desk at far wall
      2. Bookshelves along both walls to left
   B. L-shaped living room itself
      1. Plants along wall to left
      2. Recliner in far left corner
      3. Walnut hutch along wall beyond
      4. Toy box and table along opposite wall

VI. Second story and attic
   A. Five rooms on second floor—three on left, two on right
   B. Center room on left—bathroom and storeroom
   C. Attic over entire floor space of lower two stories
   D. Attic ceiling—six feet high at peak, four feet at eaves

Applying the Lesson

A. In the next lesson, you will be asked to write a descriptive essay. Choose a scene or an event to describe, and decide what impression you want to convey about it.

B. List a number of details about the scene or event you have chosen to describe, and organize the details into an outline. The score on your finished essay will make up a considerable part of your Chapter 10 test score.

———————————————

Lesson 84 Answers
Applying the Lesson
(All answers are individual work.)

85. Writing a Descriptive Essay

Writing a descriptive essay is much like writing any other essay. You gather and organize information, and then you write the first draft. Later you proofread and revise your essay, and finally you write the second draft.

A descriptive essay contains the same three parts found in other essays: an introduction, a body, and a conclusion. However, the introduction and the conclusion may consist of only a single sentence each—one to introduce the theme (general impression) and one to clinch the theme.

In writing a descriptive essay, follow your outline. The outline should keep you on track in the proper spatial or chronological order. It will also help you to include all the important details that you have observed. Your outline, of course, is your guide for writing the essay.

In each paragraph, describe one general section of a scene or one connected movement in an event. Generally, each main topic on your outline (I, II, III, . . .) should constitute one paragraph in your essay. If a main topic includes many details, each subtopic (A, B, C, . . .) might constitute a separate paragraph. But if a main point has only a few supporting details, all the subtopics may be covered in a single paragraph. You can see actual examples of this by comparing the essay below with the outline in Lesson 84.

Your essay will also need a title. The title should be short (five words or less), and it should relate to the theme in an appealing way.

Read the following essay. The first sentence is the introduction, the last is the conclusion, and all the material in between is the body. Then compare the essay with the outline in Lesson 84. Notice how it describes the entrance to the house in the first paragraph, the parlor in the second, the master bedroom in the third, and so forth. The last paragraph describes both the second story and the attic because so little detail is given about those parts of the house.

Room for Sixteen Children

Grandfather Hoover's live in an old farmhouse that dwarfs any other house I have ever entered. To begin our tour, we shall enter the front door—a massive oak slab measuring seven and one-half feet by four feet. As we move through the doorway, we notice that the stone walls are almost two feet thick! We have stepped into a great hallway five feet wide, running the whole length of the house. Every footstep echoes in the vast, almost empty space. Our eyes immediately focus on a wide stairway in the exact center of the hallway. It spirals from the ground floor all the way to the attic.

To the left of the hallway are two large rooms: the parlor and the master bedroom. A slightly stale odor greets us as we enter the parlor, for it is used only when a large number of visitors come. As in all the rooms of the first and second stories, the ceiling of the parlor soars above us at an altitude of ten feet. So in spite of the padded parlor furniture, the wood paneling and the hardwood floor make this room an effective resonator, echoing every sound.

Lesson 85

Purpose: To review how to write the first draft of a descriptive essay.

Now we step into the master bedroom. A large bed is centered on the far wall, but the room is so spacious that the bed almost looks small. Along the wall on our right, a wide dresser with a large round mirror surveys the scene. Squatting beside it in the near corner is a small cedar chest—or does it only look small? A full bathroom completely fills the near corner to our left.

Across the hall from the master bedroom, we come to the kitchen—which I usually consider the most important room of the house. Along the wall to our left is a long countertop with a large double sink in the center and with spacious cabinets above and below. A half-bathroom occupies the far left corner. Another large countertop embraces a third of the wall to our right, and the old wood stove beams a warm welcome from its place in the far right corner. Centered along the wall to our right is the door to the living room. Today the shrunken table huddles forlornly in the space directly before us. But when the table spreads its broad back to bear the food at our family gatherings, it fills the center of the kitchen quite comfortably.

We pass through the door from the kitchen to the living room. Shortly after he was ordained forty years ago, Grandfather walled off the entire corner to our right for his study. As we step through its doorway, which stands immediately to our right, we see his large desk sitting solemnly along the far wall. Grandfather's extensive library fills both walls to our left.

Now we step back into the L-shaped living room. Even with one corner walled off, this room still makes us feel small. The broad wall to our left is loaded with Grandmother's plants—cherry tomatoes, small strawberries, and a great variety of flowers—enough to start a fair-sized garden. In the corner beyond the plants, a recliner bids a pleasant welcome to anyone who yearns to sit back and relax. Centered between this chair and the hallway door, a wide walnut hutch stands almost like a throne, with a pair of heavy wooden chairs guarding its two sides. Along the opposite wall sits a large toy box and a long table, where we grandchildren often play games.

We go through the hall door and climb the steps to the second story. Here we find five large rooms, three on the left of the hallway and two on the right. Years ago, Grandfather divided the center room on the left into a spacious bathroom and storeroom. The mammoth attic sprawls over the entire floor space of the lower two stories, but its ceiling is only six feet high at the peak and four feet at the eaves. As we descend the long stairway, we are again impressed with the immensity of this house in which Grandfather Hoover's raised their sixteen children.

As you write, strive to employ the four qualities of descriptive writing that you studied in Lesson 81: rich detail; vivid, concrete words; imagery; and appeal to the five senses. Use descriptive language throughout your essay to clearly show the details you are portraying.

Applying the Lesson

Write the first draft of your descriptive essay, following the steps in this lesson. Write on every other line to allow room for revising. Your essay should have 500–700 words.

Lesson 85 Answers

(Individual work.)

---

86. Improving Your Editing Skills, Part 9

Many English words have a variety of meanings and uses. In most cases, we can combine words in more than one way to communicate our thoughts. But occasionally a certain word combination can produce an *ambiguous* sentence. Such a sentence may be seriously misleading—or embarrassingly humorous.

The following item once appeared as a headline in a newspaper.

TWO CARS COLLIDE, ONE SENT TO HOSPITAL

The ambiguity, of course, results from the different ways in which *one* can be used. We often use this pronoun to mean "one person." But in the headline, *one* appears to mean "one of the cars." Are we expected to think that a car was actually sent to the hospital? We know better.

This time we can smile and pass on. But some ambiguous statements are confusing or misleading, so you need to make it your responsibility to detect and change such statements. A person should not need to be a detective to understand what he is reading.

In this lesson and in all your proofreading, make sure every sentence is clear and easily understandable.

Marks Used in Editing and Proofreading

˅or˄ insert (caret)	ℒ delete	. . . . stet (let it stand)	———— use italics
¶ begin new paragraph	no ¶ no new paragraph	*lc* change to lowercase (small letter)	*uc* change to uppercase (capital letter)
# insert space	⌒ delete space	← move (arrow)	⌐⌐ transpose

Editing Practice

A. Use proofreading marks to correct the two errors of capitalization or punctuation in each sentence.

Lesson 86 Answers

Editing Practice

(Answers are on pages 476–477.)

Lesson 86

Purpose: To provide proofreading practice.

1.   Leopards are large members, of the Cat family. They
2. live throughout most of Africa, the middle East, southern
3. Asia and eastern Asia. When a leopard is born it weighs
4. only about one pound, and is quite helpless. A young
5. leopard generally stays with its Mother until it is two
6. years old; then it becomes self supporting.

7.   did you know that people are a greater danger to leop-
8. ards than leopards are to people. Actually these animals
9. seldom attack human-beings. But after they discover that
10. people are easy victims: they may become a serious threat
11. to Man. Poachers, herdsmen and shepherds have ruthlessly
12. hunted leopards, however, the species is protected today.

B. Use proofreading marks to correct the fifteen usage errors in these paragraphs,
according to the rules you studied in Chapter 5.

1.   Have you ever considered the enormity of the assign-
2. ment that Noah excepted from God? Because the Flood was
3. immanent, he needed to build an ark of fabulous size. Also,
4. he and his family had to stand all alone in a society that
5. flaunted the principles of godliness. A quote from 2 Peter
6. infers that Noah warned his fellow men while he worked,
7. but they were disinterested in his message. Apparently
8. none of them wanted into the ark.

9.   What are some notorious lessons that we can learn
10. from this here account? First, Noah felt that God's words
11. would surely come to pass. He did not loose his faith
12. even though many years passed before the Flood came.
13. Second, Noah committed himself to obeying God regardless
14. of what transpired. It is all ways best to believe and
15. obey God, no matter what other people may do.

C. Use proofreading marks to correct all the errors in these paragraphs, including the ones that are specifically mentioned below. No line has more than one error.

    a. In the first sentence of paragraph 1, "more and more elaborate telescopes" could mean "a greater and greater number of elaborate telescopes." Make it clear that the telescopes are becoming more and more elaborate.

    b. In line 12, change the position of *only* so that its meaning is clear.

    c. In the first sentence of paragraph 3, it sounds as if the mirror was *hauled* at an altitude of 7,200 feet. Make it clear that *Cerro Tololo* is at that altitude.

1.   In their effort to learn more about the heavens, men
2. have built more and more elaborate telescopes. The great
3. telescope at the Cerro Tololo Inter-American Observatory
4. in chile is one outstanding example. This huge instrument
5. has a mirror with a diameter of 4 meters (158 inches)—more
6. then 13 feet!
7.   When the molten glass was poured for this mirror; its
8. total wait was 25 tons. The huge mass first had to be
9. cooled for many months—very gradually, to keep it from
10. cracking. Then work men began to grind the glass into a
11. concave shape. They labored for 2½ years, and they remove
12. so much material that the finished mirror only weighed
13. 17 tons. In the perfecting process, technicians used a
14. laser so accurate that it detect ed irregularities as
15. slight as 5 millionths of an inch.
16.   The finished mirror was hauled to Cerro Tololo, at an
17. altitude of 7,200 feet (2,200 m). Scientists chose this
18. place because of its clear stable air and because of its
19. location South of the equator. The site is ideal for
20. studying the centeral portions of the Milky Way galaxy,
201. which are best observed from the Southern Hemisphere.

87. Proofreading and Rewriting
a Descriptive Essay

As with other types of writing, you need to give the first draft of your descriptive essay a thorough evaluation. Check the essay that you wrote in Lesson 85, using the following questions to help you find ways to improve it.

Content and Organization

1. Does the description give a clear mental picture of the scene or event? (If possible, have someone else read your first draft and give his comments.)
2. Does the description give details in a logical order?
3. Is the description full of rich detail and vivid, concrete words? Does it use effective imagery? Does it appeal to the five senses?
4. Is the point of view consistent?
5. Are the paragraphs unified and coherent? Is there smooth transition between paragraphs?
6. Does the essay have an introduction, a body, and a conclusion?

Style

1. Do you see any sentences that you should write with more freshness and originality?
2. Do you see any vague, general terms that you could replace with exact, descriptive words?
3. Do you see any passive verbs that you could change to the active voice?

Mechanics

1. Have you used any unnecessary or repetitious words?
2. Have you omitted any words or phrases that are needed to make the meaning clear?
3. Have you transposed or misplaced any words, phrases, or clauses?
4. Have you misspelled any words? Especially check spellings like *ei* and *ie, ai* and *ia, ent* and *ant,* and so forth. Double-check your use of homonyms like *your—you're* and *their—there—they're.* Make sure that you have spelled technical terms and proper nouns correctly. Pay close attention to words that you have difficulty spelling correctly.
5. Have you used proper capitalization and punctuation?
6. Have you followed the rules of correct grammar and word usage?

Do not imagine that you can evaluate all these points at one time. You could begin by checking your essay with the points under "Content and Organization," in the order they appear. Next, you could review your essay for improvements by using the points under "Style." For the points under "Mechanics," you might concentrate first on points 1–3 and then on points 4–6.

Applying the Lesson
A. Proofread the descriptive essay that you wrote in Lesson 85.

Lesson 87 Answers
Applying the Lesson
(All answers are individual work.)

Lesson 87

Purpose: To review guidelines for proofreading and rewriting a descriptive essay.

Teaching Suggestions:
Give the students several days to do a thorough job of proofreading. Insist that they go over their essays several times.

B. Recopy your essay in your best handwriting. Your teacher may use the following evaluation chart to grade your essay. Your score on this essay will make up a considerable part of your Chapter 10 test score.

Evaluation of a Descriptive Essay

Points possible   Points earned

Title

_3_ ____ Short and appealing

_3_ ____ Directly related to theme

Introduction

_3_ ____ Introduces theme in an interesting way

Body

_3_ ____ Clear mental pictures

_3_ ____ Consistent point of view

_3_ ____ Well-developed paragraphs

_3_ ____ Logical order (spatial or chronological)

Conclusion

_3_ ____ Clinches theme effectively

Elements of description

_3_ ____ Single theme

_3_ ____ Effective imagery

_3_ ____ Rich details that appeal to the five senses

Style

_3_ ____ Freshness and originality

_3_ ____ Active verbs and other exact, descriptive words

Mechanics

_3_ ____ Correct spelling

_3_ ____ Correct capitalization and punctuation

_3_ ____ Correct grammar

_3_ ____ Absence of careless repetition, omitted words, transpositions

_51_ ____ **Total points**

---

88. Chapter 10 Review

A. Write the correct word or phrase for each blank.

1. The author of description paints ———.
2. Effective description employs the vivid language of ——— nouns, ——— verbs, and ——— modifiers.
3. The careful use of ——— makes meaningful comparisons and adds color to a description.

Lesson 88 Answers

A. 1. word pictures
   2. exact, expressive, picturesque
   3. imagery

Lesson 88

Purpose: To review the concepts taught in Chapter 10.

4. By appealing to the ———, a writer can help the reader to live what he has described.

5. A description of a scene usually follows ——— order; a description of a happening usually follows ——— order.

6. The ——— of a description is the one main impression that it emphasizes.

B. Answer these questions.

1. What two important considerations must you remember as you select the details for a descriptive essay?

2. Why must you choose a familiar subject when you plan a descriptive essay?

3. What three parts should a descriptive essay have?

4. If a whole essay consists of description, what is its general purpose? What is its specific purpose?

C. Read this description, and do the exercises that follow.

Kate did not run across that railroad bridge. She did not even walk. She crawled! On hands and knees, she fought physical and mental terrors as she pushed ahead for about five hundred feet to the far side of the bridge, groping through darkness, her lips trembling in prayer. From time to time, her skirt became entangled in spikes, nearly toppling her off balance. Other spikes and splinters cut and bruised her hands and knees. Every moment she was fearful of seeing the headlight of the eastbound train shine full in her face.

Panic gripped Kate when, about halfway across, she saw a huge tree, its roots thickly matted with earth clods, bearing down upon her like a giant battering ram. The tree was so big that she felt sure it would engulf and drag her down to a watery grave when it smashed the bridge. But somehow it passed harmlessly between the piers, spraying her with leaves and spume; and she continued to creep toward the end of the bridge, which appeared so very far away.

1. Write exact nouns that are used instead of the following general words or phrases.

   a. great fears   d. chunks of material sticking together

   b. large nails   e. supporting posts

   c. sudden overwhelming fear   f. watery foam

2. Write expressive verbs or verbals that are used for the following actions.

   a. Kate was feeling her way.   d. Fear came forcefully upon her.

   b. Her skirt got caught.   e. The tree would have struck the bridge

   c. She almost fell over.   with crushing force.

3. Copy the phrase that more expressively communicates this idea: enclose her and pull her down and drown her.

4. Copy the picturesque modifiers that describe these words.

   a. lips   c. roots

   b. tree   d. passed

5. Copy the simile that is used.

---

4. senses

5. spatial, chronological

6. theme

B. 1. Recognize important details.
Choose details that match your theme (the specific impression you want to give).

2. because a descriptive essay gives personal impressions about a scene or an event

3. introduction, body, conclusion

4. *General Purpose:* to give the reader a mental picture of what the writer has observed

Specific Purpose: to give a certain impression about the scene or event described

C. 1. a. terrors   d. clods

    b. spikes   e. piers

    c. Panic   f. spume

2. a. groping   d. gripped

    b. entangled   e. smashed

    c. toppling

3. engulf and drag her down to a watery grave

4. a. trembling   c. matted

    b. huge   d. harmlessly

5. like a giant battering ram

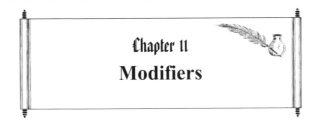

Chapter 11
Modifiers

89. Recognizing Adjectives

To modify something is to change it. Teachers modify their lesson plans to fit the needs of different classes. Weather forecasters modify their reports as weather patterns change. Hog farmers modify their feeding program in an effort to make their hogs grow faster. Students modify their reports to make them clearer and more interesting.

In grammar, too, we are familiar with modifiers. Adjectives and adverbs modify the meanings of other words to make them more descriptive and more precise. Adjectives modify substantives by telling *which, whose, how many,* or *what kind of.* These modifiers include two main classes: limiting and descriptive.

Limiting Adjectives

A *limiting adjective* limits a substantive by telling *which, whose,* or *how many.* The following six groups of words may function as limiting adjectives.

1. *The articles are always limiting adjectives.* *A* and *an* are indefinite articles because they indicate no specific nouns. *The* is a definite article because it indicates a specific noun.

> <u>a</u> minister of the Gospel (any minister)
> <u>the</u> minister of the Gospel (a certain one)

2. *Number words are often used as limiting adjectives.*
   a. Cardinal numbers (*one, two, three,* and so forth) tell *how many.*

   > <u>one</u> Lord   <u>three</u> psalms

   b. Ordinal numbers (*first, second, third,* and so forth) tell *which.*

   > <u>first</u> day   <u>fourth</u> king of Israel

3. *Indefinite pronouns are sometimes used as limiting adjectives.* These words are adjectives only when they precede substantives to tell *which* or *how many.* When they stand alone and function as substantives, they are pronouns.

   > <u>every</u> promise   <u>several</u> questions

4. *Demonstrative pronouns are sometimes used as limiting adjectives that tell which.*

   > <u>that</u> mistake   <u>these</u> mountains

Lesson 89

Purpose: To review basic facts about adjectives.

Teaching Suggestions:

Students should be familiar with all the points in this lesson. However, they may not have thoroughly mastered the use of verbals. The term *attributive noun* may also be unfamiliar to them. You may wish to point out that some dictionaries label nouns that are often used attributively.

5. *The interrogative pronouns* whose, which, *and* what *are sometimes used as limiting adjectives.*

<u>which</u> rivers   <u>what</u> lakes

6. *Possessive nouns and pronouns are often used as limiting adjectives that tell* whose. Remember to use apostrophes with nouns and indefinite pronouns, but not with personal pronouns.

<u>Herbert's</u> essay   <u>somebody's</u> heifers
the <u>families'</u> contributions   books that are <u>ours</u>

Descriptive Adjectives

Descriptive adjectives describe substantives by telling *what kind of.* These are the words that shade and shape our language. Descriptive adjectives can be classified according to their structure.

1. *Some words in their simplest form are descriptive adjectives.*

<u>brilliant</u> sunsets
<u>simple</u> truths

2. *Some descriptive adjectives can be identified by adjective-forming suffixes.* The following list includes some of the most common of these suffixes.

-ish:	foolish, greenish	**-less:**	toothless, tasteless
-al:	parental, tidal	**-like:**	Christlike, summerlike
-ic:	basic, academic	**-ous:**	momentous, bulbous
-ive:	elusive, subjective	**-some:**	winsome, troublesome
-y:	steamy, marshy	**-ant, -ent:**	tolerant, absorbent
-ful:	bountiful, masterful	**-able, -ible:**	replaceable, accessible
-ary:	primary, customary	**-an, -en:**	European, earthen

3. *Some descriptive adjectives are formed by changing the spellings of nouns.* In general, adjectives of this kind are proper nouns.

Switzerland—Swiss
Wales—Welsh

4. *Nouns are often used as descriptive adjectives without any spelling change.* These are known as attributive nouns.

<u>country</u> store   <u>window</u> frame
<u>tin</u> roof   <u>Gothic</u> letters

5. *Present and past participles may be used as descriptive adjectives.*

<u>running</u> water   <u>written</u> message

6. *Infinitives may be used as descriptive adjectives.* Such an infinitive immediately follows the substantive it modifies.

a promise <u>to keep</u>   a story <u>to write</u>

Remember to separate with commas two or more descriptive adjectives used in a series and having equal rank. If necessary, review the specific details of this rule in Lesson 2.

Several <u>warm</u>, <u>sunny</u> days melted the late snow quickly.

Positions of Adjectives

An adjective may occur in three positions relative to the substantive it modifies. An *attributive adjective* precedes the substantive it modifies. The adjective *attributes* (assigns) a quality to the substantive that follows. Most adjectives appear in this position.

A <u>small</u>, <u>neat</u> school squatted under a <u>mighty</u> oak.

An *appositive adjective* follows the substantive it modifies. This places special emphasis on the adjectives. Appositive adjectives often come in pairs, in which case they are set off by commas.

Each classroom, <u>simple</u> yet <u>attractive</u>, breathes an atmosphere of dignity.

A single adjective may also follow the substantive, especially when it refers to position or when it is modified by an adverb phrase.

An open playroom <u>downstairs</u> is used on rainy days.

The playground, <u>small</u> by some standards, serves the school well.

In the first example above, *downstairs* is an adjective because it tells which playroom. (Compare "the downstairs playroom.") Since *downstairs* tells which, it is a limiting adjective.

A *predicate adjective* follows a linking verb and modifies the subject. You can usually tell that it is a predicate adjective because the word would also fit in the attributive position, before the subject.

The new furnace is <u>quiet</u> and <u>efficient</u>.
(Compare: quiet and efficient furnace)

Applying the Lesson

A. Copy each underlined adjective. First label it *L* (limiting) or *D* (descriptive); then label it *AT* (attributive), *AP* (appositive), or *PR* (predicate).
1. <u>Your</u> character, <u>invisible</u> to <u>man's</u> view, displays itself in <u>the</u> <u>little</u>, <u>everyday</u> actions of life.
2. <u>Noble</u> conduct, <u>displaying</u> <u>wholesome</u> character, earns <u>the</u> respect of others.
3. <u>Acceptable</u> words will be <u>truthful</u> and <u>gracious</u>.
4. <u>Many</u> <u>Bible</u> characters, <u>facing</u> <u>severe</u> temptations <u>to compromise</u>, endured in <u>godly</u> fear.
5. <u>Three</u> boxes <u>to fill</u> are standing beside <u>that</u> pile of <u>wood</u> scraps <u>outside</u>.
6. <u>Which</u> picture <u>above</u> shows <u>the</u> <u>first</u> tractor that Grandfather bought for <u>this</u> <u>thriving</u> farm?

Lesson 89 Answers
Applying the Lesson
A. 1. Your—L, AT; invisible—D, AP; man's—L, AT; the—L, AT; little—D, AT; everyday—D, AT
2. Noble—D, AT; displaying—D, AP; wholesome—D, AT; the—L, AT
3. Acceptable—D, AT; truthful—D, PR; gracious—D, PR
4. Many—L, AT; Bible—D, AT; facing—D, AP; severe—D, AT; to compromise—D, AP; godly—D, AT
5. Three—L, AT; to fill—D, AP; that—L, AT; wood—D, AT; outside—L, AP
6. Which—L, AT; above—L, AP; the—L, AT; first—L, AT; this—L, AT; thriving—D, AT

B. Copy each adjective and the word that it modifies.
1. Our Father above continually showers us with numerous gifts.
2. Some gifts, common and often overlooked, still are great blessings.
3. We should be thankful for abundant food to eat and for work to do.
4. The daily ration of many people is several ounces of rice.
5. Multitudes do not have any regular income because they are sick or have no jobs.
6. Simply having fresh air to breathe is a notable blessing.

C. Copy these sentences, replacing each *L* or *D* with a limiting or descriptive adjective other than an article. Add commas as needed.
1. *L* cookies *D* and *D* make a *D* treat.
2. *L* lambs, *D* in the *D* meadow, seem quite *D*.
3. William is making *D D* mottoes in the *D* woodshop *L*.
4. The *D D* water flows from the spring *L* to this *D* pond.
5. The *D* snowdrifts, *D* into *D* shapes, look *D*.
6. Although *L D* mountain looks *D*, it is actually quite *D*.

D. For each word in parentheses, write an adjective form that fits in the sentence.
1. The (office) name of the southernmost (Scandinavia) country is the Kingdom of Denmark, which correctly indicates its (presence) form of government.
2. The Danes have a (constitution) monarchy, with a (parliament) system actually (response) for the (base) governing.
3. The land of Denmark includes a (prominence) peninsula, (know) as Jutland, as well as hundreds of islands of (vary) sizes.
4. The (prevalence) features on Jutland are the long, (roll) hills that are often quite (knob).
5. Many (finger) fiords, (break) up the coastline, give Denmark several (size) seaports that contribute to the country's (prosper) fishing industry.
6. Most regions of Denmark contain (product) grainfields, (fruit) produce farms, or (luxuriate) pastures.

Review Exercises
Write the correct word in each set of parentheses. [62, 63]
1. We know that God is much wiser than (we, us).
2. Anyone who thinks (he, they) can direct (his, their) life without God's wisdom is deceived.
3. Only the person (who, which) trusts the Lord can walk safely the highway of life.
4. God's power is infinite, but (ours, our's) is limited.
5. (Who, Whom) but God can we trust for power to overcome our enemy?
6. God and (I, myself) can be victorious, but I alone cannot be.
7. God's Word contains many promises and warnings, and (them, these) are powerful helps for us.
8. (Everyones, Everyone's) faith would be strengthened if he were to rely wholly on the Lord.

B. 1. Our—Father; above—Father; numerous—gifts
2. Some—gifts; common—gifts; overlooked—gifts; great—blessings
3. thankful—We; abundant—food; to eat—food; to do—work
4. The—ration; daily—ration; many—people; several—ounces
5. any—income; regular—income; sick—they; no—jobs
6. fresh—air; to breathe—air; a—blessing; notable—blessing

C. (Sample adjectives are underlined, along with commas that are to be added.)
1. These cookies, sweet and spicy, make a delicious treat.
2. Those lambs, frisking in the verdant meadow, seem quite healthy.
3. William is making colorful, attractive mottoes in the small woodshop downstairs.
4. The clear, sparkling water flows from the spring above to this quiet pond.
5. The deep snowdrifts, carved into strange shapes, look beautiful.
6. Although that high mountain looks smooth, it is actually quite rugged.

D. (Answers may vary somewhat.)
1. official, Scandinavian, present
2. constitutional, parliamentary, responsible, basic
3. prominent, known, various (*or* varying)
4. prevalent, rolling, knobby
5. fingerlike, breaking, sizable, prosperous
6. productive, fruitful, luxuriant

Review Exercises
1. we
2. he, his
3. who
4. ours
5. Whom
6. I
7. these
8. Everyone's

9. If (these, these here) small trials shake our faith, what shall we do when we face severe tests?
10. We live daily with things of this world, but we must love heaven more than (they, them).

9. these
10. them

---

90. Adjective Phrases and Clauses

Not only single words but also phrases and clauses can function as adjectives in a sentence. Adjective phrases come in a variety of forms: prepositional, participial, and infinitive.

Prepositional Phrases

A prepositional phrase consists of a preposition and its object, along with any modifiers of the object. When a prepositional phrase serves as an adjective, it usually comes right after the substantive it modifies.

> Men of faith consider the order within the universe a testimony to God's creative skill.

Participial Phrases

The present and past participles of most verbs end with *-ing* or *-ed.* (A few past participles end with *-t* or *-en,* such as *lost* and *hidden.*) These verb forms are called participles when they serve as adjectives. If a participle has modifiers or complements, it is a participial phrase. A participial phrase may come before or after the word it modifies.

> Even unbelievers, observing that order, have come to humble submission before God.
>
> Convinced of God's existence, a man may come to trust in Jesus as his Saviour.

Participles can show three different tenses. Use the present participle to express action or being that occurs at the same time as that of the main verb in the sentence.

> The rain, pouring down in torrents, flooded the low-lying areas.
> (The rain flooded the areas at the same time it poured down.)

The past participle can also express an action that occurs at the same time as that of the main verb. In addition, it may express a completed action.

> The streams, affected immediately by the downpour, rose rapidly.
> (The streams were affected at the same time they rose rapidly.)
> The river, swollen by heavy rains earlier in the week, soon overflowed its banks. (The river was swollen before and during the time it overflowed.)

Lesson 90

Purpose: To review prepositional phrases, participial phrases, infinitive phrases, and dependent clauses used as adjectives.

Teaching Suggestions:

Nothing in this lesson is new for this English series. Plan to spend most of your teaching time on the two types of verbals. You may also need to spend time reviewing the difference between restrictive and nonrestrictive phrases and clauses. Be sure to clarify that some phrases and clauses that may look like adjectives are nouns or adverbs.

In doing Part A, your students may find it helpful to first look for participial and infinitive phrases. Then check for prepositional phrases, including those that may lurk within the verbal phrases. Remind them also to check each prepositional phrase to determine if it is part of a longer phrase or if it contains a shorter phrase.

The present perfect form indicates that the action or being occurs before that of the main verb in the sentence. The present perfect form consists of the past participle preceded by *having*.

> <u>Having risen rapidly</u>, the flooded streams caught many travelers by surprise. (Indicates that the streams had risen before they caught travelers by surprise.)
> <u>Having been warned not to drive through high water</u>, the driver went a different way. (Indicates that the driver was warned before he went a different way.)

Infinitive Phrases

An infinitive phrase, consisting of an infinitive and its modifiers and complements, can be used as an adjective. (Infinitives can also be used as substantives or adverbs.) An infinitive used as an adjective immediately follows the substantive it modifies, and it usually tells *which* or *what kind of*.

> The Bible passage <u>to memorize this week</u> is Romans 12:1–5. (The infinitive phrase tells *which* passage.)
> The best way <u>to remember Bible verses</u> is to review them often and put them to practice. (The infinitive phrase tells *what kind of* way.)

Adjective Clauses

An adjective clause is a dependent clause that modifies a substantive. Either a relative pronoun or a relative adverb introduces an adjective clause. The relative pronouns are *who, whom, whose, which,* and *that;* the relative adverbs are *when, where,* and *why.* These words are called relative pronouns and relative adverbs because they *relate* the adjective clause to the substantive that the clause modifies. Therefore, adjective clauses are sometimes called relative clauses.

> Those people <u>whom Father helped</u> had never heard of people <u>who practiced nonresistance</u>.
> The town <u>where they live</u> has several churches but apparently few consistent Christians.

Sometimes the relative pronoun or the relative adverb is omitted, making the clause harder to identify.

> The story <u>Great-grandfather told</u> was about a time <u>he went to town on horseback</u>. (Compare: story <u>that Great-grandfather told</u>; time <u>when he went to town on horseback</u>)

The words listed as relative pronouns and relative adverbs do not always introduce adjective clauses. Relative pronouns may also introduce noun clauses, and *when* and *where* may introduce noun or adverb clauses.

> <u>When I walked past the old shed</u>, I saw <u>that wild morning glories are taking over</u>. (*When I walked past the old shed* is an adverb clause telling *when* about *saw. That wild morning glories are taking over* is a noun clause serving as the direct object of *saw.*)

Restrictive and Nonrestrictive Modifiers

Participial phrases and adjective clauses may be restrictive or nonrestrictive. If the phrase or clause restricts the meaning of a substantive by identifying *which one,* it is restrictive. A restrictive phrase or clause is essential to the meaning of the sentence and is not set off with commas.

> That big dog <u>running around our yard</u> belongs to the family <u>who lives across the road</u>.

In the example above, the participial phrase restricts the meaning of *dog* by telling *which one.* Not all the dogs belong to that family—only the one running around our yard. The adjective clause restricts the meaning of *family* by telling *which one.* The sentence is not referring to all the families—only the one across the road. The underlined modifiers are not set off with commas, for they are necessary to the meaning of the sentence.

If the modifying phrase or clause simply gives additional information about the substantive, it is nonrestrictive. A nonrestrictive phrase or clause does not identify a substantive by telling *which one.* Since it is not essential to the meaning of the sentence, it is set off with commas.

> <u>Rising to his feet</u>, Eugene offered his chair to Grandfather, <u>who had just entered the room</u>.

In this example, the participial phrase does not identify *Eugene* by saying "the Eugene rising to his feet." It simply gives additional information about *Eugene.* The adjective clause does not identify *Grandfather* by saying "the Grandfather who had just entered the room." It simply gives additional information about *Grandfather.* The underlined modifiers are set off with commas, for they are not necessary to the meaning of the sentence.

Modifiers Within Other Modifiers

One adjective phrase or clause may contain other adjective phrases or clauses. The object of a preposition, the complement of a participle or an infinitive, and any substantive in an adjective clause may have a phrase or clause modifier. Study the following sentences, in which arrows point from the underlined modifiers to the words modified.

> The owl <u>that is hooting from yonder tree</u> wants a meal <u>for the young ones in its nest</u>.
>
> <u>Filled with many examples of noble character</u>, this book is a treasured gift <u>from my grandfather who recently passed away</u>.

The ability to understand adjective phrases and clauses will help you to construct sentences that express your thoughts clearly and precisely. Learn to recognize and use them well.

Applying the Lesson

A. Copy each adjective phrase. If a phrase is part of a longer phrase, include it with the longer phrase and also copy it separately. Label each phrase *prep.* (prepositional), *part.* (participial), or *inf.* (infinitive).

1. Recognizing God's sovereignty, we do not fear those things disturbing the natural man's tranquillity.
2. Self-worship, also labeled as pride, never fulfills man's need to worship God.
3. True worship, centered on God alone, gives man the motivation to become more godly.
4. The commitment required for steadfastness through trial can be a reality known to all.
5. Our plans to visit our neighbors down the road might provide an occasion to learn some new things about Switzerland.
6. The family's move to a new country has brought many changes, but their desire to find a Bible-believing church may bring the greatest changes.
7. Their faith, having grown over the past several years, is finding a new opportunity to flourish freely.
8. Having found this home in our community, the Muellers have recognized their need to obey the entire Bible and are taking steps to adopt a Biblical lifestyle.

B. Copy the correct participles in parentheses.

1. The bread (rising, having risen) sufficiently, Mother slid it carefully into the oven.
2. The King James Bible, (proving, having proved) itself over several centuries, holds for us a place of high appreciation.
3. (Roasting, Roasted) to juicy tenderness, the chicken made a delicious meal for us.
4. The pork chops, slowly (barbecuing, barbecued) over the charcoal, will soon be finished.
5. (Being, Having been) fed, the puppies lay down to sleep.
6. (Sliding, Having slid) into the ditch, Mother climbed out of the car and went for help.

C. Copy each adjective clause.

1. Anyone who loves the Lord must renounce certain things that this world highly esteems.
2. The Holy Bible, which is God's message to mankind, sanctifies all whose hearts are open to its message.
3. In homes where God's Word holds its rightful place, you will discover that peace reigns.
4. The letter Mother just read stated that Uncle Myron's had two feet of snow last week.

Lesson 90 Answers
Applying the Lesson

A. 1. Recognizing God's sovereignty—part.; disturbing the natural man's tranquillity—part.
2. also labeled as pride—part.; to worship God—inf.
3. centered on God alone—part.; to become more godly—inf.
4. required for steadfastness through trial—part.; through trial—prep.; known to all—part.
5. to visit our neighbors down the road—inf.; down the road—prep.; to learn some new things about Switzerland—inf.; about Switzerland—prep.
6. to a new country—prep.; to find a Bible-believing church—inf.
7. having grown over the past several years—part.; to flourish freely—inf.
8. Having found this home in our community—part.; in our community—prep.; to obey the entire Bible—inf.; to adopt a Biblical lifestyle—inf.

B. 1. having risen   4. barbecuing
2. having proved   5. Having been
3. Roasted   6. Having slid

C. 1. who loves the Lord; that this world highly esteems
2. which is God's message to mankind; whose hearts are open to its message
3. where God's Word holds its rightful place
4. Mother just read

5. The visiting preacher, whom I remember hearing before, was Sue Troyer's grandfather.
6. In the days when Grandfather was young, many modern conveniences were unknown.

5. whom I remember hearing before
6. when Grandfather was young

D. Write whether each underlined phrase or clause is restrictive (*R*) or nonrestrictive (*N*). Also copy each word that should be followed by a comma, and add the comma.
 1. The spotted hyena <u>which lives in the region south of the Sahara</u> is a badly misunderstood animal.
 2. Its howl <u>which sounds like eerie laughter</u> helps to make it one of Africa's most-hated creatures.
 3. The notion <u>that hyenas follow lions to eat their leftovers</u> is also quite common.
 4. The Dutch scientist Hans Kruuk <u>studying hyenas in the wild</u> learned much about these mysterious nocturnal animals.
 5. Soon the determined scientist <u>whose equipment included binoculars, cameras, and a sturdy station wagon</u> observed a group of hyenas as they killed a zebra.
 6. Several lions, however, seized the kill <u>that these hyenas had made</u>.
 7. Kruuk also played into the night air recordings <u>made of hyenas at a kill</u> as well as some of lions at a kill.
 8. His lion recording <u>played near a group of hyenas</u> created not the least stir of interest.
 9. But lions <u>hearing the recorded sound of hyenas at a kill</u> came on the run.
10. So the animal <u>widely viewed as a thief</u> is actually the victim.

D. 1. N; hyena, Sahara,
    2. N; howl, laughter,
    3. R
    4. N; Kruuk, wild,
    5. N; scientist, wagon,
    6. R
    7. R
    8. N; recording, hyenas,
    9. R
   10. R

Review Exercises

A. Identify each underlined complement by writing *PN, PA, DO, IO,* or *OC*. [20]
 1. This rain will give our <u>gardens</u> and <u>fields</u> a much-needed <u>boost</u>.
 2. I consider the <u>miracle</u> of growing things a <u>testimony</u> of the Creator's skill.
 3. The rooster's crowing sounded <u>haughty</u> and <u>challenging</u>.
 4. Brilliant sunshine warmed the <u>earth</u> and cheered our <u>spirits</u>.
 5. The busy schedule challenged <u>us</u> at first but soon became a familiar <u>routine</u>.

B. The underlined words are retained complements. Identify each one by writing *DO ret., IO ret.,* or *OC ret.* [21]
 1. A kind helping hand has been given <u>us</u> through this time of trial.
 2. Our burdens have been made <u>lighter</u> by the help of so many friends.
 3. Their help has been considered a <u>blessing</u> from the Lord.
 4. We have been given many <u>encouragements</u> by the Lord.

Review Exercises

A. 1. IO, IO, DO
    2. DO, OC
    3. PA, PA
    4. DO, DO
    5. DO, PN

B. 1. IO ret.
    2. OC ret.
    3. OC ret.
    4. DO ret.

91. Recognizing Adverbs

Though adjectives modify the substantives in sentences, adverbs modify—or change the meanings of—other words to make them more descriptive and more precise. The points in this lesson and the next will help you to recognize adverbs.

1. *Adverbs modify verbs.* Most adverbs modify verbs by telling *how, when,* or *where* something happened or existed.

> We can <u>continually</u> serve the Lord <u>faithfully</u>, for Jesus <u>ever</u> lives to intercede for us.

The words *not, never, ever, almost, always, hardly, scarcely,* and *seldom* are always adverbs. Often they qualify verbs by limiting or altering their meanings. Even if the word *not* is compounded with *can* in *cannot* or joined with a verb in a contraction ending with *n't,* it is an adverb.

> Man can<u>not</u> resist the devil in his own strength; moreover, he is<u>n't</u> able to subdue his own carnal nature.

2. *Adverbs modify adjectives and other adverbs.* Adverbs of this kind are often called adverbs of degree because they tell *to what degree.* Almost without exception, they come immediately before the words they modify. The following words are commonly used as adverbs of degree.

almost	especially	quite	thoroughly
completely	extraordinarily	rather	too
dangerously	extremely	so	unusually
definitely	greatly	somewhat	very
entirely	partly	surprisingly	

Study the following sentences. Note especially how the underlined words are diagramed.

> We should be <u>deeply</u> grateful to the Lord, for He has blessed us <u>very</u> richly.

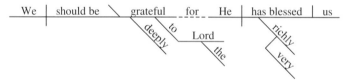

> The <u>formerly</u> eminent man is <u>almost</u> completely unknown now.

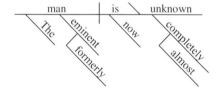

Lesson 91

Purpose: To review basic facts about adverbs.

Teaching Suggestions:

When discussing the adverbs of degree, be sure to point out that they sometimes modify predicate adjectives (as in "We should be *deeply* grateful"). Adverbs in that position may be more easily overlooked than some others.

In relation to adverbs modifying verbals, point out that verbals, although they function as nouns or adjectives or adverbs, retain certain characteristics of verbs. One such characteristic is that they can be modified by adverbs.

Also be ready to spend ample time with infinitives used as adverbs.

3. *Adverbs modify verbals.* These adverbs tell *how, when, where,* or *to what degree* about the action or existence indicated by the verbal. Remember that verbals include gerunds, infinitives, and participles. In the following examples, the verbals are italicized and the adverbs modifying the verbals are underlined.

Flying <u>gracefully</u> <u>overhead</u>, the swans soon disappeared.
    (*Gracefully* tells *how* and *overhead* tells *where* about the participle *Flying.*)

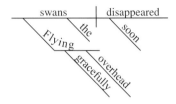

Carving the picture frame <u>well</u> was not a job *to do* <u>hurriedly</u>.
                  (*Well* tells *how* about the gerund *Carving.*
                   Hurriedly tells *how* about the infinitive *to do.*)

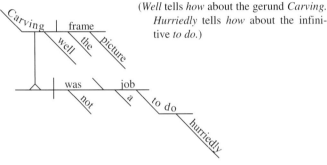

Forms of Adverbs

Many adverbs are adjectives to which the suffix *-ly* has been added. However, an *-ly* ending is not a sure indicator of an adverb, because some words ending with *-ly* are other parts of speech. And some words *not* ending with *-ly* are adverbs—especially those that tell *when* or *where.* You must observe how a word is used in a sentence before you can decide what part of speech it is.

Those who <u>zealously</u> stand for truth will <u>surely</u> face temptations to compromise.
If we <u>always</u> trust in the Lord, we shall move <u>forward</u> in His will.
    (In both examples above, all the underlined words are adverbs.)
A <u>lowly</u> attitude toward self gives one a <u>friendly</u> outlook toward others.
    (The underlined words are adjectives.)

Many adverbs can also function as adjectives or prepositions, without any change in form.

Last night was quite cold, but tonight the temperature might drop even <u>lower</u>.
    (*Lower* is an adverb modifying *might drop.*)

These <u>lower</u> temperatures may be common <u>up</u> north, but they are unusual
here. (*Lower* is an adjective modifying *temperatures; up* is a preposition.)
The weathermen expect the temperature to move <u>up</u> again tomorrow.
(*Up* is an adverb modifying *to move.*)

When there are two adverb forms like *quick* and *quickly,* the *-ly* form is usually
better in standard English.

Informal: "Come <u>quick</u>," Laura shouted.
Standard: Blizzards can descend very <u>quickly</u> on a prairie region.

Infinitives can be used as adverbs. An infinitive that modifies a verb almost always
tells *why.*

The family gathered reverently <u>to worship</u>.
(*To worship* tells *why* about *gathered.*)
<u>To pray</u>, they always knelt at their places.
(*To pray* tells *why* about *knelt.*)

An infinitive that modifies an adjective usually follows the adjective and tells *to
what degree* or *how* (that is, *in what way*). Sometimes it may not answer any specific
question, but it definitely modifies the adjective by telling *to do what* about it.

Anyone who is determined <u>to endure</u> must put on the whole armor of God.
(*To endure* modifies the predicate adjective *determined* by telling *in what
way.*)
The Bible contains many warnings important <u>to consider</u>.
(*To consider* modifies the adjective *important* by telling *to do what* about it.)
Too numerous <u>to count</u>, God's blessings should inspire us to faithfulness.
(*To count* tells *to what degree* about the adjective unit *Too numerous.*)

In the last example, note that the infinitive modifies the unit *Too numerous.* These
words are considered a unit because it is not logical to say that the infinitive modifies either word separately ("Too *to count*" or "numerous *to count*"). Below is the diagram of this sentence.

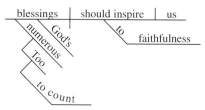

An infinitive that modifies an adverb usually follows the adverb and tells *to what
degree* or *how.* Again, the infinitive may merely qualify the adverb by telling *to do*

what about it. And the infinitive almost always modifies an adverb unit similar to that in the last example above.

> You have spoken too softly <u>to understand</u>.
>> (*To understand* tells *to what degree* about the adverb unit *too softly*. *Too* is also an adverb modifying *softly*.)
> Perhaps you did not stand close enough <u>to hear</u>.
>> (*To hear* qualifies the adverb unit *close enough*. *Enough* is also an adverb modifying *close*.)

Applying the Lesson

A. Copy each underlined adverb, and write whether it modifies a verb (*v.*), an adjective (*adj.*), an adverb (*adv.*), or a verbal (*vbl.*).

1. God promises His <u>abundantly</u> sufficient grace to all who <u>sincerely</u> seek His face.
2. Man <u>naturally</u> thinks that he is <u>well</u> able to handle the circumstances of life <u>effectively</u>.
3. Man <u>certainly</u> can<u>not</u> live without God's help, yet he <u>too</u> <u>often</u> resents God's will.
4. The Christian who <u>very</u> <u>humbly</u> looks to God <u>continually</u> receives divine grace.
5. Standing <u>motionlessly</u> in the water, a great blue heron peered <u>downward</u>, waiting <u>patiently</u> for a fish to swim <u>near</u>.
6. Scattered <u>profusely</u> over the hillside, the <u>beautifully</u> blooming wildflowers made a <u>most</u> lovely sight.
7. To raise produce <u>profitably</u> requires a <u>significantly</u> large investment in hard work, coupled with God's blessing.
8. The girls are working <u>unusually</u> <u>fast</u> <u>today</u>, and by noon should be done sufficiently well <u>to be excused</u>.
9. Did those wild animals know in some way impossible <u>to explain</u> that the storm would strike <u>so</u> <u>severely</u>?
10. God has <u>marvelously</u> provided them with the ability to sense <u>keenly</u> some things that man can<u>not</u> perceive.

B. Copy each adverb, and write the word or words that it modifies.

1. Unexpectedly seeing a wild turkey in a forest glade is a highly interesting experience.
2. A tom turkey often struts stiffly and gobbles noisily as if boldly declaring that he owns the forest.
3. Wild turkeys frequently gather to feed contentedly under the relatively peaceful shade of the trees.
4. The swan's gracefully curved neck contributes quite definitely to its overall beauty.
5. God obviously designed the swan to swim, and it swims almost constantly.
6. The swan's relatively short legs make it a very awkward bird on land.
7. The boys are still looking for Daniel's truck that disappeared overnight.

8. Snow fell thickly today, yet the roads stayed mostly clear and safe to travel.
9. As dusk settled in, the temperature dropped slightly; but the wind later shifted suddenly to the northwest, causing the temperature to drop sharply.
10. Can we accurately measure this wildly drifted snow that unexpectedly blanketed the earth?

Review Exercises

A. Identify the form of each underlined verb as simple (*S*), progressive (*P*), or emphatic (*E*). [77]
 1. The Lord <u>does remember</u> those who put their trust in Him.
 2. I <u>believe</u> the promises of God.
 3. We <u>should be seeking</u> to grow in the qualities of righteousness.
 4. <u>Do</u> you <u>consider</u> yourself perfect?
 5. I <u>do know</u> that I have much room for improvement.

B. Change each underlined verb to the form shown in italics. Do not change the tense. [77]
 1. The day swiftly <u>comes</u> to a close. *progressive*
 2. We <u>recognize</u> that the time to labor for the Lord is now. *emphatic*
 3. Jesus <u>promised</u> His continual presence with the faithful. *emphatic*
 4. We <u>look</u> for the eternal morning to dawn. *progressive*
 5. Jesus <u>has prepared</u> a place for us. *progressive*

---

8. thickly—fell; today—fell; mostly—clear; to travel—safe
9. in—settled; slightly—dropped; later—shifted; suddenly—shifted; sharply—to drop
10. accurately—Can measure; wildly—drifted; unexpectedly—blanketed

Review Exercises

A. 1. E
  2. S
  3. P
  4. S
  5. E

B. 1. is coming
  2. do recognize
  3. did promise
  4. are looking
  5. has been preparing

---

92. Recognizing Other Adverbs

In Lesson 91 you saw that adverbs modify verbs, adjectives, adverbs, and verbals. These are the most common functions of adverbs. This lesson covers less common functions of adverbs. In fact, the last two points of the lesson introduce functions of adverbs that you likely have never considered before.

1. *Adverbs introduce questions.* Such adverbs also modify the verb in the question.

> <u>Where</u> are Uncle Sherman's moving?
> <u>When</u> can we visit them?

2. *Adverbs join independent clauses.* When adverbs function in this way, they are called conjunctive adverbs and always modify the verb of the second clause. You will study conjunctive adverbs further in Chapter 13.

> The sunflower seeds and suet are attracting many birds; <u>indeed</u>, we have already counted over twenty different kinds at the feeding station.
> (*Indeed* connects two clauses and modifies *have counted,* the verb of the second one.)

Lesson 92

Purpose: To review that adverbs may introduce questions, and to teach that *adverbs may modify prepositions, conjunctions, and whole sentences.

Teaching Suggestions:

This lesson contains two concepts that are new for this English series: that adverbs can modify prepositions and conjunctions, and that they can modify entire sentences. In relation to the second point, be sure to discuss how such adverbs modify the thought of the entire word group instead of modifying any specific word. This is illustrated by changing the word group to a *that* clause in a sentence beginning with "It is ——— that…"

3. *Adverbs modify prepositions and conjunctions.* Both prepositions and conjunctions show relationships between words. But sometimes a connecting word alone does not express the relationship accurately enough; a modifier is needed to show it more precisely. Then an adverb may be used to modify the conjunction or preposition. Observe how this is done in the following examples.

Henry's ball landed in the water <u>almost</u> beyond Father's reach.
 (The preposition *beyond* is not precise enough because the ball did not actually land beyond Father's reach. *Almost* modifies *beyond* and helps to show the exact relationship between the landing of the ball and Father's reach.)

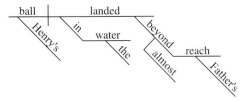

The salesman came <u>right</u> after Father left.
 (The conjunction *after* is not precise enough to indicate that Father had barely left when the salesman came. *Right* modifies *after* and helps to show the exact relationship between Father's leaving and the salesman's coming.)

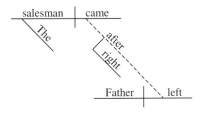

4. *Adverbs modify whole sentences.* An adverb does not always modify a specific word. Sometimes it modifies an entire sentence. Study the following example.

<u>Clearly</u>, the stranger misinterpreted our words.
 (*Clearly* modifies the entire sentence, *the stranger misinterpreted our words,* by indicating that its idea is clear. To say that it modifies *misinterpreted*—"misinterpreted clearly"—would not be sensible.)

Here are some adverbs that can modify whole sentences.

certainly	providentially	surprisingly
clearly	regrettably	tragically
interestingly	sadly	understandably
obviously	strangely	

Note that when an adverb modifies a whole sentence, it is usually the first word. But an introductory adverb can also modify just the verb. How can you tell the difference? Here is a method that you should find helpful.

Change the introductory adverb to its adjective form, and use that form in the following expression: "It is ——— that..." Continue with the rest of the original sentence. If the resulting sentence means the same as the original, the introductory adverb modifies the entire sentence. If the meaning is different, the introductory adverb modifies only the verb.

    Problem: Strangely, many can behold the wonders of creation and still deny God.
      Think: It is strange that many can behold the wonders of creation and still deny God. (This sentence has the same meaning.)
    Solution: *Strangely* modifies the entire sentence.

    Problem: Sadly the old man told his story of woe.
      Think: It is sad that the old man told his story of woe.
        (This sentence has a different meaning.)
    Solution: *Sadly* modifies the verb *told.* (The old man told his story sadly.)

    Problem: Sadly, the whole store burned to the ground.
      Think: It is sad that the whole store burned to the ground.
        (This sentence has the same meaning.)
    Solution: *Sadly* modifies the entire sentence.

Applying the Lesson

A. Copy each underlined adverb, and write whether it modifies a verb (*v.*), a preposition (*p.*), or a conjunction (*c.*).
1. <u>When</u> will the first strawberries ripen if we had snow and cold <u>almost</u> into May?
2. <u>Just</u> as the capering calf was heading for its hutch, little Jason shouted; <u>consequently</u>, we had another ten-minute chase.
3. The forecasters did not know <u>exactly</u> where the hurricane would strike, but it seemed <u>nearly</u> beyond a doubt that it would hit the East Coast sometime on Wednesday.
4. <u>Why</u> does Shep bark and growl <u>far</u> into the night so often?
5. <u>Soon</u> after Grandmother arrived to spend a few weeks with us, she became quite sick; <u>however</u>, in a few days she was feeling much better again.
6. The deer bounded <u>high</u> over the fence and <u>straight</u> into the forest.

B. Each sentence has two adverbs that modify prepositions or conjunctions. Copy those adverbs, and write *p.* or *c.* after each to tell what part of speech it modifies.
1. Immediately after Jesus was born, angels brought a heavenly message directly to the shepherds.
2. Almost before they realized it, these lowly men were heading straight toward Bethlehem.

Lesson 92 Answers
Applying the Lesson
A. 1. When—v.; almost—p.
  2. Just—c.; consequently—v.
  3. exactly—c.; nearly—p.
  4. Why—v.; far—p.
  5. Soon—c.; however—v.
  6. high—p.; straight—p.

B. 1. Immediately—c.; directly—p.
  2. Almost—c.; straight—p.

3. God's wisdom is not slightly above man's comprehension; it extends far beyond the highest of man's wisdom.
4. Man tries to delve deep into the mysteries of life, but he shall stop exactly where God decrees.
5. Lee is speaking exactly as I believe, but Lamar thinks his ideas are somewhat beside the point.
6. We had battled the fire nearly to the point of exhaustion, but a fresh breeze fanned the flames just as we thought we were winning.
7. The car was heading straight for the ditch, but the driver regained control just before it was too late.
8. Uncle Lester's came soon after ten o'clock, but they had to leave long before nightfall.

C. Write whether each underlined adverb modifies a *verb* or an entire *sentence.*
   1. Obviously, man's natural inclinations stand opposed to God's holy purposes.
   2. Sadly Father described the end of those who reject God's way.
   3. Gladly the Lord will pardon every sinner who turns to Him in true penitence.
   4. Regrettably, few backsliders return to the Lord and seek His forgiveness.
   5. Strangely, no one saw the fire until most of the building was aflame.
   6. Providentially, the fire did not spread to the paint store.
   7. Tragically the waifs told their story.
   8. Understandably, our hearts were deeply touched by their pathetic story.

Review Exercises

A. Name the punctuation that should follow each underlined word: *colon, semicolon, ellipsis points, dash,* or *none.* [4, 6]
   1. At the root of most sin lies one evil pride.
   2. "Man really has no basis for being proud," Father mused, "but still"
   3. Pride began with Lucifer's attempt to dethrone God it will cease when Satan and all his followers are cast into the lake of fire.
   4. We receive much encouragement to humility through the teaching of the Bible, the counsel of our parents, and the example of the godly.
   5. "Everyone should strive to be more humble than well, no, that doesn't make sense," said Elmer.
   6. We do not strive to be more humble than others however, we do seek to become more humble than we have been.

B. Write the letter of the sentence in which the boldface part is correct. [5, 6]
   1. a. "Were you living up to the Bible standard to be subject 'for conscience **sake'?"** asked Father.
      b. "Were you living up to the Bible standard to be subject 'for conscience **sake?'"** asked Father.
   2. a. "The powers that be are ordained of **God (Romans 13:1),"** and we should not speak evil of them.
      b. "The powers that be are ordained of **God" (Romans 13:1),** and we should not speak evil of them.

---

3. slightly—p.; far—p.
4. deep—p.; exactly—c.
5. exactly—c.; somewhat—p.
6. nearly—p.; just—c.
7. straight—p.; just—c.
8. soon—p.; long—p.

C. 1. sentence
   2. verb
   3. verb
   4. sentence
   5. sentence
   6. sentence
   7. verb
   8. sentence

Review Exercises

A. 1. colon
   2. ellipsis points
   3. semicolon
   4. none
   5. dash
   6. semicolon

B. 1. a
   2. b

3. a. The chapter **"Nonconformity to the World"** gives much practical help on the subject.
   b. The chapter *Nonconformity to the World* gives much practical help on the subject.
4. a. This **all purpose** glue works remarkably well.
   b. This **all-purpose** glue works remarkably well.
5. a. Thomas Jefferson said, "The hole and the patch should be commensurate **[of corresponding size].**"
   b. Thomas Jefferson said, "The hole and the patch should be commensurate **(of corresponding size).**"
6. a. Because of the flu epidemic, nearly **one-third** of the students are absent.
   b. Because of the flu epidemic, nearly **one third** of the students are absent.
7. a. "Did Father ask, 'Is everyone ready for family **worship'?**"
   b. "Did Father ask, 'Is everyone ready for family **worship?'**"
8. a. The *Titanic,* at first a symbol of man's ability, has become a symbol of man's foolish pride.
   b. The **"Titanic,"** at first a symbol of man's ability, has become a symbol of man's foolish pride.
9. a. As soon as we saw the **mud-covered** truck, we knew why Father was late.
   b. As soon as we saw the **mudcovered** truck, we knew why Father was late.
10. a. You had too many **"ah's"** in your speech.
    b. You had too many *ah's* in your speech.

3. a
4. b
5. a
6. a
7. b
8. a
9. a
10. b

---

93. Adverb Phrases and Clauses

Like adjectives, adverbs come not only as single words but also as phrases and clauses. Adverb phrases may be either prepositional or infinitive.

Prepositional Phrases

A prepositional phrase may be an adverb. When such a phrase modifies a verb or a verbal, it answers questions like *how, when, where,* and *why.*

> God has revealed Himself <u>through His Word</u> <u>for man's eternal well-being</u>.
> (*Through His Word* tells *how* about the verb *has revealed; for man's eternal well-being* tells *why* about the verb *has revealed.*)
> God's Word, forever settled <u>in heaven</u>, shall continue to guide God's people <u>until the eternal age</u>. (*In heaven* tells *where* about the participle *settled; until the eternal age* tells *when* about the infinitive *to guide.*)

A prepositional phrase that modifies an adjective or an adverb tells *to what degree, how,* or *how much.* It usually comes immediately after the word it modifies.

Lesson 93

Purpose: To review prepositional phrases, infinitive phrases, and clauses used as adverbs.

Teaching Suggestions:

Nothing in this lesson is new for this English series. However, you should probably give special attention to the following two points: distinguishing several adverb phrases occurring in succession, from one adverb phrase that includes adjective phrases; and understanding elliptical adverb clauses.

Sometimes an adverb prepositional phrase modifies an adjective or an adverb unit like *too friendly* or *too quickly.*

Saul, jealous <u>in the extreme</u>, pursued David even though he was innocent <u>of any wrong</u>. (*In the extreme* tells *to what degree* about the adjective *jealous. Of any wrong* tells *how* about the adjective *innocent.*)

Saul served the Lord too halfheartedly <u>for any lasting usefulness</u>.
　　(*For any lasting usefulness* tells *to what degree* about the adverb unit *too halfheartedly.*)

Some sentences have several prepositional phrases in succession. Sometimes these phrases are a series of adverb phrases, each modifying the same word independently of the others. Study the following sentence, in which arrows point from the underlined modifiers to the word modified.

Great-grandfather Weber often traveled <u>across the mountain</u> <u>on foot</u> <u>in favorable or unfavorable weather</u>.

At other times, the first preposition introduces the whole string of prepositional phrases, which work together as one adverb. Each of the other prepositional phrases is an adjective modifying the object in the previous phrase. When prepositional phrases occur in succession, you must think carefully about each one to decide whether it is an adjective or an adverb phrase.

Great-grandfather Weber served <u>as the bishop</u> <u>over three congregations</u> <u>in this valley</u>.

Infinitive Phrases

An infinitive phrase, consisting of an infinitive and its modifiers and complements, can be used as an adverb. (Infinitives can also function as substantives and as adjectives.) An infinitive that modifies a verb almost always tells *why.*

We should rise in the presence of the elderly <u>to give them due respect</u>.
　　(*To give them due respect* tells *why* about *should rise.*)

<u>To give due honor to the Lord</u>, we must give due honor to our fellow men.
　　(*To give due honor to the Lord* tells *why* about *must give.*)

An infinitive that modifies an adjective or an adverb tells *to what degree* or *how.* Usually, it immediately follows the word it modifies. Again, these infinitives sometimes modify a unit like *too loud.*

Grandmother Wenger is always glad <u>to help us with our work</u>.
　　(*To help us with our work* tells *how* about the predicate adjective *glad.*)

This bread dough is rather stiff <u>to handle nicely</u>.
　　(*To handle nicely* tells *how* about the adjective unit *rather stiff.*)

Finally the wind is blowing hard enough <u>to spin the windmill</u>.
　　(*To spin the windmill* tells *to what degree* about the adverb unit *hard enough.*)

Adverb Clauses

An adverb clause is a dependent clause that modifies a verb, an adjective, or another adverb. An adverb clause begins with a subordinating conjunction. The following list contains some of the most common subordinating conjunctions.

after	even if	than	when
although	even though	that	whenever
as	how	though	where
as if	if	till	wherever
because	since	unless	whether
before	so that	until	while

Just like single-word adverbs and adverb phrases, adverb clauses can modify verbs, verbals, adjectives, or adverbs. Many adverb clauses answer the basic adverb questions *how, when,* and *where.* In addition, they can answer the questions *why, how long, how much, to what degree, in spite of what,* and *under what condition.* Adverb clauses can also modify adjective or adverb units like *as soon* or *so long.*

You should form noble habits <u>while you are still young</u>.
> (*While you are still young* tells *when* about the verb *should form.*)

Youth must develop conviction to do right <u>even though others are doing wrong</u>.
> (*Even though others are doing wrong* tells *under what condition* about the verbal *to do.*)

A Christian, joyous <u>although hardships beset him</u>, is the truly happy person.
> (*Although hardships beset him* tells *in spite of what* about the adjective *joyous.*)

We should strive to live so faithfully <u>that others can find no fault with us</u>.
> (*That others can find no fault with us* tells *to what degree* about the adverb unit *so faithfully.*)

When *as* or *than* introduces an adverb clause of comparison, the clause is often elliptical.

Norma does not write poems as often <u>as stories</u>.
> (as often *as she writes stories*)

Glenford can run a little faster <u>than Lowell</u>.
> (a little faster *than Lowell can run*)

Punctuation With Adverb Phrases and Clauses

Use a comma after an introductory adverb phrase or clause (unless it is a short prepositional phrase). An adverb clause at the end of a sentence needs no comma. If an adverb clause comes in the middle of a sentence, use a comma before and after it. Only a short clause should occur in the middle; a long clause usually mars sentence coherence.

With several feeders on the trees behind our house, we feed many wild birds.
To bring in a large number of birds, hang out several feeders.

If you put different types of seed in the feeders, you should attract a wide variety of birds.

These many birds, when snowy weather comes, flock to the feeders.

We enjoy feeding the birds while their natural food supply is limited.
(no comma)

Applying the Lesson

A. Copy each prepositional phrase used as an adverb, including any adjective phrase that may be in it. Write the word or word group that the phrase modifies.
   1. In six days of creative work, God made the world, complex beyond man's understanding.
   2. After centuries of investigation, many facts continue to baffle man by their complexity in spite of man's scientific advances.
   3. Accepting the Bible account by simple faith provides the only foundation solid enough for true scientific understanding.
   4. Evolutionary theories are detrimental to man's learning process; indeed they are responsible for many foolish conclusions among the worldly-wise.
   5. Many additional responsibilities fell on Charlotte's shoulders during Mother's illness, but she handled them quite well for a sixteen-year-old girl.
   6. Warm weather had stayed in our region for a long time, but yesterday the temperature dropped too low for comfort.

B. Copy each infinitive phrase used as an adverb, and write the word or word group that the phrase modifies.
   1. We must develop God's point of view to understand anything properly.
   2. To develop God's point of view, we must become well acquainted with His Word.
   3. Creation speaks of God's glory clearly enough to convince any honest person of His existence.
   4. However, many are too proud to accept their accountability before God.
   5. A wise person is slow to accept new ideas.
   6. Sometimes new ideas are too impractical to prove themselves valuable.
   7. Sound wisdom includes the discretion necessary to test new ideas.
   8. The Bible warns us against deception often enough to spur us to great carefulness.

C. Copy each adverb clause, and write the word or word group that the clause modifies.
   1. If you look at a physical map of South America, the Andes Mountains stand out more sharply than any other feature does.
   2. This mountain range, greatly varying as it extends along the west coast, passes through many degrees of latitude.
   3. The Andes range, much wider than it appears on a map, is so rugged that it makes an effective barrier.
   4. The southern Andes lie where the west winds carry much moisture from the Pacific, but the moisture condenses thoroughly enough that little remains for the lands beyond.

Lesson 93 Answers
Applying the Lesson

(Allow reasonable variation in deciding whether a phrase or clause modifies a single word or a unit such as too fast.)

A. 1. In six days of creative work—made; beyond man's understanding—complex
   2. After centuries of investigation—continue; by their complexity—to baffle; in spite of man's scientific advances—to baffle;
   3. by simple faith—Accepting; for true scientific understanding—solid enough
   4. to man's learning process—detrimental; for many foolish conclusions among the worldly-wise—responsible
   5. on Charlotte's shoulders—fell; during Mother's illness—fell; for a sixteen-year-old girl—quite well
   6. in our region—had stayed; for a long time—had stayed; for comfort—too low

B. 1. to understand anything properly—must develop
   2. To develop God's point of view—must become
   3. to convince any honest person of His existence—clearly enough
   4. to accept their accountability before God—too proud
   5. to accept new ideas—slow
   6. to prove themselves valuable—too impractical
   7. to test new ideas—necessary
   8. to spur us to great carefulness—often enough

C. 1. If you look at a physical map of South America—stand; than any other feature does—more sharply
   2. as it extends along the west coast—varying
   3. than it appears on a map—much wider; that it makes an effective barrier—so rugged
   4. where the west winds carry much moisture from the Pacific—lie; that little remains for the lands beyond—thoroughly enough

5. Early explorers faced the laborious task of traversing the Andes when the only roads across were steep, narrow paths.
6. Although highways and railroads cross the Andes today, they follow paths so tortuous that they require much patience.

D. Copy each word that should be followed by a comma, and add the missing comma. If no comma is needed, write *correct.*
1. To be a noble example to others we must follow our perfect example—Jesus Christ.
2. Youth because they are inexperienced should especially look for noble examples to follow.
3. We can never truly love the Lord if we love the things of this world.
4. Within the boundaries of God's will for our lives we find true satisfaction.
5. Whenever a person chafes at God's purposes he becomes vulnerable to evil suggestions.
6. We must daily die to self so that we might live unto God.
7. Brother Alvin though he is eighty years old is still quite active and healthy.
8. As spring slowly chases away the winter cold we anticipate the first fresh strawberries.
9. On the far edge of this stand of trees we often pick raspberries and blackberries.
10. To be ready in time for church we shall start chores early.

Review Exercises
A. Write whether the mood of each underlined verb is indicative (*ind.*), imperative (*imp.*), or subjunctive (*sub.*). [75]
1. If it be too late, we shall wait until tomorrow.
2. Brother Gerald requested that each person walk more quietly in the hall.
3. If Spot were more aggressive, imagine how many groundhogs he could have caught.
4. Barbara has been acting as if she were too busy to help Margaret with the cleaning.
5. Suppose everyone were as careless as you.
6. Shall we rise for the benediction.

B. Write the words that are correct for the subjunctive mood. [75]
1. If the stranger (be, is) a Mexican, your Spanish will be useful.
2. That raccoon acts as if it (was, were) rabid.
3. The police officers demanded that everyone (stand, stood) back.
4. If the dictionary (approves, approve) your pronunciation, I shall be surprised.
5. I wish the neighbor man (was, were) more respectful toward God.
6. If he (had been, would have been) more alert, this accident would likely not have happened.

---

5. when the only roads across were steep, narrow paths—traversing
6. Although highways and railroads cross the Andes today—follow;
that they require much patience—so tortuous

D. 1. others,
2. Youth, inexperienced,
3. correct
4. lives,
5. purposes,
6. correct
7. Alvin, old,
8. cold,
9. trees,
10. church,

Review Exercises
A. 1. sub., ind.
2. ind., sub.
3. sub., imp.
4. ind., sub.
5. imp., sub.
6. imp.

B. 1. be
2. were
3. stand
4. approve
5. were
6. had been

94. Improving Your Writing Style, Part 5: Sentence Rhythm

Originality
Active Verbs
Active Voice
Poetic Devices
Rhythm

You have studied several different ways to make your writing style more effective. First you considered the importance of putting a touch of originality into your writing. You learned next to harness the energy of lively action verbs and of verbs in the active voice. Then you studied several poetic devices like alliteration, rhyme, and onomatopoeia, which add a musical touch to writing.

A fifth element of effective writing style is sentence rhythm. Now you may immediately think, "Rhythm belongs to poetry, not prose." And poetry does use strong, regular rhythm. Good prose, however, also has a certain rhythm. Though it is not the regular meter found in poetry, it is nevertheless a pleasing flow of sounds and syllables.

Ordinarily, most people speak and write smooth-flowing, rhythmic sentences. We have a natural feel for what sounds right and what sounds awkward. Most of the time, therefore, sentence rhythm poses no problem. But just as we make mistakes in other areas of life, we sometimes construct sentences that have a disturbing lack of rhythm. One of the best ways to identify such problems in our writing is to read it aloud. What looks fine on paper may sound jarring to the ear.

Consider two points that affect sentence rhythm.

1. *Beware of unintentional repetition of similar or identical syllables or words.* The previous writing style lesson directed you to use repetition by means of poetic devices like alliteration and rhyme. These add appeal to writing. But sometimes we repeat words or sounds without realizing it, and then it can be a problem. Such repetition of sounds is often more awkward than appealing.

If you did not purposely use repetition, then you will not even realize it is there. How can you recognize it? Here is where it becomes especially helpful to read aloud what you have written. As you study the following examples, read them aloud for the best understanding.

> **Poor:**   Sometimes the repetition of a <u>sound</u> <u>sounds</u> awkward.
> **Better:** Sometimes the repetition of a sound becomes awkward.

Here two forms of *sound* occur in immediate succession. This repetition does not please the ear. Further disrupting the sentence is the fact that the first form of *sound* is a noun and the second is a verb, requiring the reader to switch definitions in mid-sentence.

> **Poor:**   Jesus taught <u>beside</u> the <u>seaside</u> <u>outside</u> the city.
> **Better:** Jesus taught along the seaside near the city.

By the time a reader gets past these three *sides*—be*side,* sea*side,* out*side*—he may be *side*tracked from the meaning of the sentence. This repetition would be fine if the identical syllables occurred in some kind of parallel relationship, as in the series "the left side, the right side, and the upper side." But since the repetition is obviously unplanned, it is clumsy and distracting.

Lesson 94

Purpose: To teach *sentence rhythm as an element of an effective writing style.

Teaching Suggestions:

The effect of rhythm in a sentence is a bit more abstract than that of the other elements in this series of writing style lessons. It often depends on a subtle sense of what sounds pleasant; and not even skilled writers will always agree whether a particular sentence has good rhythm. However, the points in this lesson should at least open the door for the students to consider this element of effective style in their writing.

To stimulate interest, have your students say *unique New York* three times in succession: "unique New York, unique New York, unique New York." Few sentences will twist a reader's tongue this much, but a writer should aim to produce sentences and word combinations that read smoothly, and to avoid any word arrangements that are awkward or distracting for readers.

Poor: The accident happened <u>probably</u> <u>only</u> an hour ago.
Better: Probably the accident happened only an hour ago.
         The accident happened probably no more than an hour ago.

This example illustrates the common problem of two *-ly* words occurring next to each other. While the resulting rhythm is not intolerable, it does lack strength. A similar problem is the occurrence of two *-ing* words together, as in "*practicing spelling words.*"

In the examples above, the first rewording separates the *-ly* words so that the repeated syllable is no longer noticeable. The second simply replaces one of the *-ly* words.

2. *For words or phrases in a compound construction, you can often improve the rhythm by having the longer item come second.* A different arrangement is not necessarily awkward, but the rearrangement often stands as an improvement.

Fair: The Israelites could trust in God, or they could rely on their own <u>warriors</u> and <u>wits</u>.
Better: The Israelites could trust in God, or they could rely on their own <u>wits</u> and <u>warriors</u>.

Warriors and wits does not actually sound bad, but *wits and warriors* has an increased smoothness that sharpens the sentence. This along with alliteration produces a very pleasing rhythm.

Fair: James 5 gives encouragement to <u>fervent prayer</u> and <u>patience</u>.
Better: James 5 gives encouragement to <u>patience</u> and <u>fervent prayer</u>.

Here again, the rearrangement improves the rhythm because the longer item comes second. This arrangement also makes it clear that *fervent* modifies only *prayer;* the phrase does not mean "fervent prayer and fervent patience."

In some ways, sentence rhythm is like the arrangement of furniture in a room. Not everyone will agree on what is most appealing, and some people will like what others consider poor. Yet there are certain combinations that everyone will agree should not be used. So read your sentences aloud, evaluate them to the best of your ability, and change the wording when you spot a construction that sounds rough or distracting.

Applying the Lesson

A. Improve the style of the following sentences according to the guidelines in this lesson. Be ready to compare your work with that of your classmates, to see the various possibilities for improvement.
1. Brother Milford's charitable, wise words have often proved full of insight and fitting.
2. Nothing on earth can equal the glories of heaven, but many will miss this bliss because of sin.
3. Usually the scene of a gold find finds many undesirable prospectors present.
4. The two friends met with a hearty and hale handshake.
5. What we laugh about says much about what our character is all about.

Lesson 94 Answers
Applying the Lesson
A. (Sample answers. Improvements are underlined.)
1. Brother Milford's <u>wise, charitable</u> words have often proved <u>fitting and full of insight</u>.
2. Nothing on earth can equal the glories of heaven, but many will <u>fail to attain its bliss</u> because of sin.
3. Usually the scene of a gold <u>find attracts many undesirable prospectors</u>.
4. The two friends met with a <u>hale and hearty</u> handshake.
5. What we laugh <u>at reveals much about our character</u>.

6. This picture shows a boat afloat in the moat surrounding a city.
7. With temperatures so low, no snow will melt very fast.
8. By the edge of the hedge sat a discouraged, poor orphan.

B. The following paragraphs have poor sentence rhythm in a number of places. Find at least five of those places, and write enough words to show how to improve the rhythm.

   ¹On a windy, cold day you may need to take deliberate steps to prevent frostbite. ²Understanding frostbite right might be the best way to avoid it. ³This condition most often occurs in the nose, ears, cheeks, fingers, and toes. ⁴Therefore, usually simply covering the body well will prevent frostbite.

   ⁵Preventing frostbite also means avoiding hindering the proper circulation of blood. ⁶Ill-fitting and tight clothes sometimes cut off circulation to the extremities. ⁷Keeping moving is important if you must go outside in extremely cold weather. ⁸This will help to fight frostbite by increasing the flow of blood to the muscles.

C. Write a brief narrative on one of the following topics or a different subject that your teacher approves. Underline at least four phrases that you consider to have good rhythm. Remember also to apply the other elements of effective writing style that you have studied.
   1. Elijah praying for rain on Mount Carmel
   2. Jesus stilling the storm on the Sea of Galilee
   3. Your first hour (or day) in a new school
   4. Enjoying the task of chopping wood (or some other job)
   5. Your activities on a snow day (or another vacation day)

Review Exercises

Write *originality, active verbs, active voice,* or *poetic devices* to tell why the second sentence in each pair has a better style than the first. [3, 22, 39, 64]

   1. a. There are many promises in the Bible that are inspirational.
      b. The Bible contains many promises to inspire us onward.
   2. a. The Bible should remove our fears and cause us to have an unwavering trust in God.
      b. The Bible should dispel our fears and impel us to an unwavering trust in God.
   3. a. A jet made a line as straight as an arrow across the sky.
      b. A jet was writing across the sky in disappearing ink.
   4. a. The noise of chain saws and axes indicated that the brethren were transforming Sister Ada's pile of logs into a neat stack of firewood.
      b. The buzzing of chain saws and the ringing of axes proclaimed that the brethren were transforming Sister Ada's pile of logs into a neat stack of firewood.
   5. a. With so many willing hands, the job was finished in two hours.
      b. The many willing hands finished the job in two hours.

---

6. <u>The boat in this picture is in the moat</u> surrounding a city.
7. With <u>such low</u> temperatures, <u>none of the snow</u> will melt very fast.
8. By the <u>side of the hedge</u> sat a <u>poor, discouraged</u> orphan.

B. (Sample answers. Improvements are underlined.)

   ¹On a <u>cold, windy</u> day you may need to take deliberate steps to prevent frostbite. ²<u>Properly understanding frostbite is probably</u> the best way to avoid it. ³This condition most often occurs in the nose, ears, cheeks, fingers, and toes. ⁴Therefore, <u>simply covering the body properly will usually</u> prevent frostbite.

   ⁵Preventing frostbite also means <u>being careful not to hinder</u> the proper circulation of blood. ⁶<u>Tight and ill-fitting</u> clothes sometimes cut off circulation to the extremities. ⁷<u>It is important to keep moving</u> if you must go outside in extremely cold weather. ⁸This will help to <u>prevent frostbite</u> by increasing the flow of blood to the muscles.

C. (Individual work. You may find it profitable to have students examine each other's work and look for sentences with poor rhythm. Class discussion of ways to improve specific sentences could be valuable in emphasizing this matter to students.)

Review Exercises
   1. active verbs
   2. poetic devices
   3. originality
   4. poetic devices
   5. active voice

95. Forms of Comparison for Modifiers

Basic Definitions and Forms

Many adjectives and adverbs have three degrees of comparison: positive, comparative, and superlative. The following chart illustrates these three degrees.

Positive	Comparative	Superlative
near	nearer	nearest
dim	dimmer	dimmest
friendly	friendlier	friendliest
precious	more precious	most precious
bountifully	more bountifully	most bountifully

The positive degree describes without comparing. This is the simplest form of a modifier.

Alan's dart struck <u>close</u> to the bull's-eye.
Sheba is a <u>friendly</u> dog.
Our gardens yielded <u>bountifully</u> this year.

The comparative degree compares two items. For regular modifiers, it ends with -er or includes the word *more*. Use -er with most one-syllable and some two-syllable words. If necessary, double the final consonant or change a final *y* to *i* before adding -er. For most two-syllable words and for all longer words, use *more*. Use the word *less* for negative comparisons of all words.

Mervin's dart struck <u>closer</u> to the bull's-eye than Alan's did.
Princess is even <u>friendlier</u> than Sheba.
Our gardens yielded <u>more bountifully</u> this year than they did last year.

The superlative degree compares more than two items. For regular modifiers, it ends with -est or includes the word *most*. Follow the same rules for using -est and *most* (or *least*) as those for the comparative degree.

Of all the darts, Wilmer's struck <u>closest</u> to the bull's-eye.
Tippy is the <u>friendliest</u> dog I know.
Our gardens yielded the <u>most bountifully</u> this year of all the past five years.

Some common modifiers have irregular forms of comparison.

Positive	Comparative	Superlative
good, well	better	best
bad, badly, ill	worse	worst
far	farther	farthest
much, many	more	most
little (amount)	less	least
little (size)	littler	littlest

Grandfather felt <u>ill</u> this morning, but he feels even <u>worse</u> this evening.
We had <u>little</u> rainfall this summer, Oakdale had even <u>less</u> rainfall, and Mapleton
    had the <u>least</u> rainfall in our county.

Lesson 95

Purpose: To review the three degrees of comparison for adjectives and adverbs.

Teaching Suggestions:

Most likely, your students will have little difficulty in understanding the points of this lesson or in applying those points to the exercises. Just as likely, however, they make numerous mistakes with regard to these points in their normal conversations and even in their writing. Your work will include challenging your students to use these modifiers correctly.

Usage Guidelines

As you work with forms of comparison, observe the following guidelines.

1. *Avoid the common mistake of using the superlative form to compare only two items.*

> **Incorrect:** I can hardly decide whether Linda's or Wanda's cookies are the <u>most delicious</u>.
>
> Both Frank and Henry worked hard at shoveling, but Henry shoveled the <u>most</u>.
>
> **Correct:** I can hardly decide whether Linda's or Wanda's cookies are <u>more delicious</u>.
>
> Both Frank and Henry worked hard at shoveling, but Henry shoveled <u>more</u>.

2. *Do not make a double comparison.*

> **Incorrect:** Jezebel was <u>much more bolder</u> in doing evil than Ahab was.
>
> **Correct:**   Jezebel was <u>much bolder</u> in doing evil than Ahab was.

3. *A modifier that expresses an absolute quality cannot logically have degrees of comparison.* The following adjectives (and their adverb forms) are some examples of modifiers that may express absolute qualities: *square, straight, round, fatal, dead, perfect, true, unanimous, unique.*

> **Incorrect:**
>
> The moon is <u>rounder</u> tonight than it was last night.
>
> This is the most <u>unique</u> book that I have ever read about the Flood.
>
> (If something is truly unique, it is the only one of its kind.)
>
> **Correct:**
>
> The moon is <u>more nearly round</u> tonight than it was last night.
>
> This is the most <u>remarkable</u> book that I have ever read about the Flood.

Some of the words listed above may express qualities that are not absolute, and then they may logically have degrees of comparison. For example, the phrase *more perfectly* is correct when it means "more fully" or "in greater detail." This is its meaning in the following verse.

> "And he said, The Jews have agreed to desire thee that thou wouldest bring down Paul to morrow into the council, as though they would enquire somewhat of him <u>more perfectly</u>" (Acts 23:20).

4. *When comparing one thing with a group of which it is part, do not omit the word other or else.* If you omit these words, you will say that something is bigger or better than itself.

> **Illogical:** I enjoy geometry better than any branch of mathematics.
>
> To love God and our neighbor is more important than anything.
>
> **Logical:** I enjoy geometry better than any <u>other</u> branch of mathematics.
>
> To love God and our neighbor is more important than anything <u>else</u>.

5. *Do not change an adverb to an adjective when using a comparative or superlative form.* This is something rather common that people do with *-ly* adverbs. Some tend to drop the *-ly* and add *-er* or *-est* to the *adjective* form of the word.

> **Incorrect:** You must play quieter while Brenda is napping.
> **Correct:** You must play more quietly while Brenda is napping.

Applying the Lesson

A. Write the comparative and superlative degrees of these adjectives and adverbs.

1. little (size)
2. far
3. badly
4. little (amount)
5. carefully
6. lowly
7. slim
8. masterful
9. happy
10. hot

B. Write the correct form of each modifier in parentheses.

1. Apparently Daniel purposed in his heart (firmly) than did many of his fellow Jewish youth.
2. Certainly his life was (holy) than those who compromised to please the king.
3. God blessed Daniel so that he became the (good) of the king's wise men.
4. Even in the (grim) circumstances of all, Daniel prayed faithfully to his God.
5. Christ came as one of the (lowly) of men so that all could be saved.
6. It is (bad) to never try than to try and fail.
7. Worldly pleasures should have (little) appeal to us than do the glories of heaven.
8. Unless we are (zealous) for truth than for self-satisfaction, we will not make wise decisions.
9. Even with the medication, Bossy is (thin) than she was last week.
10. She is breathing (weakly) this morning than she did last evening.
11. Our goal of weeding this corn before noon seems (attainable) now than it did a while ago.
12. Of all the ones in Father's family, we live the (far) from Grandpa Seibel's farm.

C. Write 1–3 words to show how to correct the mistake in each sentence.

1. In 1990, both Illinois and Iowa produced over one million bushels of grain corn, but Iowa's production was highest.
2. Texas has more farms than any state in the United States.
3. This is the most loveliest mock orange bush I have seen in a long time!
4. We sang the third verse of the song softer than the other verses.
5. Eleanor's test score was more perfect than mine.
6. Sister Elizabeth is one of the most saintliest persons I know.
7. The kitchen corner beside the wood stove is warmer than any spot in the house.
8. Of the two boys' plans, I think Wilmer's will prove most workable.
9. The second half of the school term often seems to go fastest.
10. We succeeded in making the second flower bed rounder than the first.

Lesson 95 Answers
Applying the Lesson

A.
1. littler, littlest
2. farther, farthest
3. worse, worst
4. less, least
5. more carefully, most carefully
6. lowlier, lowliest
7. slimmer, slimmest
8. more masterful, most masterful
9. happier, happiest
10. hotter, hottest

B.
1. more firmly
2. holier
3. best
4. grimmest
5. lowliest
6. worse
7. less
8. more zealous
9. thinner
10. more weakly
11. more attainable
12. farthest

C.
1. higher
2. any other state
3. the loveliest
4. more softly
5. more nearly perfect
6. the saintliest
7. any other spot
8. more workable
9. faster
10. more nearly round

11. I have been trying to write neater for my school assignments.
12. Aunt Miriam has given me two of her painted mottoes, and I like this one best.

Review Exercises

A. Write whether the underlined sentence part is a nominative absolute (*NA*) or a participial phrase (*PP*). [24]
1. Satan's purposes having been defeated at Calvary, we know that his ultimate defeat is sure.
2. Our faith resting firmly in Christ Jesus, the storms of life cannot unsettle us.
3. Clinging firmly to God's Word, we are well fortified against the wiles of the devil.
4. The Christian stands justified by faith, his sins having been purged by the blood of Christ.
5. The Christian should refuse to waste time in foolishness, knowing that life is short.

B. Rewrite each sentence, changing the underlined subordinate clause to a nominative absolute. [24]
1. After the bell sounded, we gathered up our books to go home.
2. Because the radiator had sprung a leak, the engine soon overheated.
3. Since the temperature was falling rapidly, we prepared for a killing frost.

---

96. Chapter 11 Review

A. Copy each underlined adjective. First label it *L* (limiting) or *D* (descriptive); then label it *AT* (attributive), *AP* (appositive), or *PR* (predicate).
1. What specific goals, high yet attainable, have you set for your character development?
2. Every honest person intent on pleasing God admits that he has numerous important areas to improve.
3. If you truly seek that improvement, you must possess lowly attitudes, godly zeal, and living faith in the Lord.
4. Those old German tools outside are worn but usable because the Germans made their products to last for many years.
5. With plentiful rainfall throughout the growing season, we are now enjoying a fall harvest bountiful beyond our expectations.

B. Copy each adjective phrase or clause. If a phrase is part of a longer phrase or clause, include it with the longer item and also copy it separately. Label each item *prep.* (prepositional phrase), *part.* (participial phrase), *inf.* (infinitive phrase), or *cl.* (clause).
1. Artesian wells, found rather commonly in western North America, overflow because of the pressure of underground water.

Lesson 96

Purpose: To review the concepts taught in Chapter 11.

---

11. more neatly
12. better

Review Exercises
A. 1. NA
2. NA
3. PP
4. NA
5. PP

B. 1. The bell having sounded, we gathered up our books to go home.
2. The radiator having sprung a leak, the engine soon overheated.
3. The temperature falling rapidly, we prepared for a killing frost.

Lesson 96 Answers
A. 1. What—L, AT; specific—D, AT; high—D, AP; attainable—D, AP; your—L, AT; character—D, AT
2. Every—L, AT; honest—D, AT; intent—D, AP; numerous—L, AT; important—D, AT; to improve—D, AP
3. that—L, AT; lowly—D, AT; godly—D, AT; living—D, AT; the—L, AT
4. Those—L, AT; old—D, AT; German—D, AT; outside—L, AP; worn—D, PR; usable—D, PR; the—L, AT; their—L, AT; many—L, AT
5. plentiful—D, AT; the—L, AT; growing—D, AT; a—L, AT; fall—D, AT; bountiful—D, AP; our—L, AT

B. 1. found rather commonly in western North America—part.; of underground water—prep.

2. Can you describe the factors that cause artesian wells?
3. An area where artesian wells can occur must have water-filled subsoil trapped between two rock layers, and that subsoil must slope away from an opening that absorbs the water.
4. Gravity, pulling the water down the slope, causes a buildup of pressure in the water.
5. A well drilled into subsoil of that kind will have the pressure to overflow as an artesian well if all the conditions are right.

C. Copy the correct participle for each sentence.
1. Grandmother Horst, (memorizing, having memorized) many Scripture verses, can meditate on the Word even though she is blind.
2. (Roasting, Roasted) slowly since late last night, the turkey should be well done by noon.
3. (Breaking, Broken) above the knee, John's leg is causing him a great deal of pain.
4. (Soaring, Having soared) at a high altitude, the hawk swept the valley below with his keen eyes.

D. Label each underlined phrase or clause R (restrictive) or N (nonrestrictive). Also copy each word that should be followed by a comma, and add the comma.
1. Solomon ᵃblessed with many advantages began his reign as a king ᵇwho loved the Lord.
2. His father, David ᵃwho was a man after God's own heart surely inspired him to a faith ᵇthat should have remained intact.
3. Yet the course ᵃpursued by Solomon led him to the place ᵇwhere he actually turned from God to idolatry.

E. Copy the single-word adverbs, including infinitives, and the word or word group that each one modifies. Write *sentence* if it modifies the whole sentence.
1. Where can we always find wisdom for the dangerously perplexing temptations we face?
2. Certainly, we need to pray daily to the Lord, who understands our needs perfectly.
3. Quite often, zealously seeking God's wisdom is easy to neglect; however, prayer is a definitely needed response for those who would be wise.
4. Though problems may bring us almost to desperation, they will never baffle the Lord.
5. Indeed, He perfectly understands every answer long before man can even recognize his need.

F. Copy each adverb phrase or clause, including any that occurs within another phrase or clause. Also write the word or word group that the adverb modifies.
1. The banyan tree, growing natively in India, is classified by scientists as a fig tree.
2. To gain its needed external support, the banyan often begins its life as an epiphyte.

2. that cause artesian wells—cl.
3. where artesian wells can occur—cl.; trapped between two rock layers—part.; that absorbs the water—cl.
4. pulling the water down the slope—part.; of pressure—prep.
5. drilled into subsoil of that kind—part.; of that kind—prep.; to overflow as an artesian well—inf.

C. 1. having memorized
2. Roasting
3. Broken
4. Soaring

D. 1. a. N—Solomon, advantages,   b. R
2. a. N—David, heart,   b. R
3. a. R   b. R

E. 1. Where—can find; always—can find; dangerously—perplexing
2. Certainly—sentence; daily—to pray; perfectly—understands
3. Quite—often; often—is; zealously—seeking; to neglect—easy; however—is; definitely—needed
4. almost—to; never—will baffle
5. Indeed—sentence; perfectly—understands; long—before; even—can recognize

F. 1. in India—growing; by scientists—is classified; as a fig tree—is classified
2. To gain its needed external support— begins; as an epiphyte—begins

3. An epiphyte grows on some other object until it develops its own support.
4. As the tree develops, aerial roots grow from its branches to support and nourish the tree.
5. When a banyan tree is full grown, its main trunk may have a diameter of thirteen feet, and its secondary trunks, grown from its aerial roots, may have an almost equal diameter.
6. A long-standing legend states that Alexander the Great used a single banyan tree—a forest in itself—to provide shelter for his entire army.

G. Copy each word that should be followed by a comma, and add the missing comma. If no comma is needed, write *correct*.
1. To live in true contentment we must remove all selfishness from our hearts.
2. Because man is carnal by nature he is far more prone to covetousness than to contentment.
3. We must consciously develop contentment if we would possess this rare virtue.
4. As we recognize God's great provisions our hearts will overflow with joy and thanksgiving.
5. To enrich our lives as God intends contentment must be our daily companion.

H. Write the correct form of each modifier in parentheses.
1. All these mottoes are painted well, but I think this one is (good).
2. Myron must like his food (salty) than I do.
3. We should be (tolerant) of others' faults than of our own.

3. on some other object—grows;
   until it develops its own support—grows
4. As the tree develops—grow;
   from its branches—grow;
   to support and nourish the tree—grow
5. When a banyan tree is full grown—may have;
   from its aerial roots—grown
6. to provide shelter for his entire army—used

G. 1. contentment,
   2. nature,
   3. correct
   4. provisions,
   5. intends,

H. 1. best
   2. saltier
   3. more tolerant

4. If you oversleep, you will probably take (little) time for your devotions than you should.
5. To remain faithful, we need to be (determined) than Samson was to avoid temptation.

I. Write 1–3 words to show how to correct the mistake in each sentence.
   1. The Book of Psalms is longer than any book of the Bible.
   2. Psalm 23 is one of the most loveliest of all the psalms.
   3. Linford cut the corners of his motto more square than I cut the corners of mine.
   4. Time seems to be going more rapid this year than it did last year.
   5. Whose eyesight is worst, Mark's or Matthew's?

J. Write whether each statement is *true* or *false*.
   1. Both poetry and prose have rhythm, but the rhythm of prose is less regular.
   2. Reading a sentence aloud helps to reveal phrases that lack rhythm.
   3. Repetition of the same sounds or syllables should be avoided as much as possible.
   4. Placing the longest phrase of a series last often contributes to smooth sentence rhythm.

K. Rewrite the following sentences, improving the rhythm.
   1. Although he was not downright forthright, he was too upright to be outright dishonest.
   2. Many people are totally selfishly pursuing their own way today.
   3. I am enjoying looking at this mountain scenery, but the many turns turn my stomach.
   4. All day the tempestuous, cold wind blew across the wide-open, flat prairie.

---

4. less
5. more determined

I. 1. any other book
   2. the loveliest
   3. more nearly square
   4. more rapidly
   5. worse

J. 1. true
   2. true
   3. false
   4. true

K. (Sample sentences.)
   1. Although he was not completely straightforward, he was too upright to be altogether dishonest.
   2. Many people today are pursuing their own way in complete selfishness.
   3. I enjoy looking at this mountain scenery, but the many turns upset my stomach.
   4. All day the cold, tempestuous wind blew across the flat, wide-open prairie.

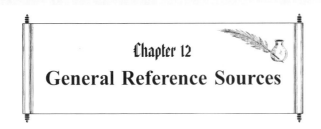

Chapter 12
General Reference Sources

97. Using a Dictionary

The dictionary ranks among the most useful reference books you will ever open. It puts at your fingertips a wealth of information about the English language. It may also contain one or more of the following: a history of the English language, a section listing information about famous persons, a section listing major place names and their pronunciations, a list of common abbreviations, tables of measures, and lists of rhyming words.

In your studies, you may use a variety of dictionaries. All these dictionaries are similar in certain ways, yet each one is also unique. Therefore, you should read the explanatory notes at the beginning of a dictionary that you use frequently. In fact, you should become familiar with your dictionary from beginning to end so that you can use all its features effectively.

Guide Words

Guide words help you to locate words in a dictionary quickly. Printed at the top of the page, these guide words show the first and last entries on a page. Any word coming between them in alphabetical order will be on that page.

Entry Words

Each word defined in a dictionary has an entry that begins with the entry word. An entry word shows two basic things about a word.

1. *Correct spelling.* If a word has more than one correct spelling, the dictionary shows both. If the two spellings are alphabetically close together (such as *neighbor* and *neighbour*), the dictionary lists them together with the more common spelling as the entry word. Otherwise, each spelling is entered separately (such as *gage* and *gauge*). The entry for the less common spelling (like *gage*) refers to the more common spelling, which has a complete entry. The entry for the more common spelling (like *gauge*) shows the alternate spelling. In many dictionaries, the word *also* precedes a spelling that is definitely less common.

> **neigh·bor** or **neigh·bour** (nā′·bər) *n.* **1.** A person who lives near another. **2.** A person, place, or thing located near another. **3.** A fellow human being.
> **gage** (gāj) *n. & v.* Var. of **gauge.**
> **gauge** *n.* **1.** A standard or scale of measurement. **2.** A standard dimension, quantity, or capacity. **3.** An instrument for measuring or testing. **4.** A means of estimating or judging; a test. Also **gage.**

Lesson 97

Purpose: To review the types of information found in dictionaries.

Teaching Suggestions:

Be sure to check your school's supply of the following reference books studied in this chapter: dictionary, thesaurus, encyclopedia, world atlas, road atlas, and statistical almanac. Ideally, you should have enough copies of each type of reference book for comfortable student use in class and in doing their assignments.

Your students should be quite familiar with the use of the dictionary. Many students, however, do not use this valuable tool to its greatest advantage. Your enthusiasm as you learn correct pronunciations, new definitions, and other interesting information will greatly affect your students' use (or disuse) of the dictionary.

You may wish to comment on the order of dictionary definitions. Some dictionaries give definitions in historical order, with the oldest meanings first and the newest ones last. Others start with the most common meanings and then give the least common ones. Just because a certain definition comes first does not mean it is the most important one or the one best suited to a given setting (such as a Bible verse). The context is the best clue for determining the most appropriate definition.

Correct capitalization is an element of spelling. If a word is always capitalized, the entry word shows it that way. If a word is capitalized only for certain definitions, the dictionary either lists two separate entries or specifies the definitions that require capitalization.

> **phar·i·see** (far′·i·sē) *n.* **1. Pharisee.** A member of an ancient Jewish sect that emphasized strict observance of the Mosaic Law. **2.** A self-righteous or hypocritical person.

2. *Correct syllabication.* A space or raised dot shows each syllable division, where a hyphen may be used to divide a word at the end of a line of writing. Because you should not divide a word so that a single letter is left at the beginning or end of a line, some dictionaries do not show such syllable divisions in the entry word.

Word Information

Information given after an entry word includes much more than the meaning of the word. Notice the different kinds of information given.

1. *Correct pronunciation.* A complete pronunciation key is printed near the front of the dictionary. Most dictionaries also print a short key at the bottom of each right-hand page. Pronunciation symbols vary considerably, so you must familiarize yourself with the key of the dictionary you are using.

Dictionaries show variant pronunciations in different ways, so check the explanatory notes in the front of your dictionary. For some dictionaries, the first option is the preferred or most common pronunciation; in others, that is not necessarily so. If only part of the word has varied pronunciation, only those syllables with variations may be shown. Sometimes a regional label shows where the variation is commonly heard. Any pronunciation following the word *also* is definitely less common.

> **tran·sient** (tran′·shənt, -zhənt, -zē·ənt)
> **clerk** (klėrk; *British* klärk)
> **scourge** (skėrj *also* skōrj)

2. *Parts of speech and definitions.* An abbreviation before the definition indicates the part of speech. Verbs include a label for transitive or intransitive. Definitions for different parts of speech are usually listed either in one grouping in an entry or under separate, numbered entries.

Dictionary A:

> **barb** (bärb) *n.* **1.** A sharp point projecting backward from the main point of a weapon or tool, as on an arrow or a fishhook. **2.** A cutting remark. **3.** *Zoology.* One of the parallel spines projecting from the main shaft of a feather. **4.** *Botany.* A short, sharply hooked bristle or hairlike projection. —**barb** *tr.v.* **barbed, barb·ing, barbs.** To provide or furnish with a barb.

Dictionary B:

> **barb**[1] (bärb) *n.* **1.** A sharp point projecting backward from the main point of a weapon or tool, as on an arrow or a fishhook. **2.** A cutting remark. **3.** *Zoology.* One of the parallel spines projecting from the main shaft of a feather. **4.** *Botany.* A short, sharply hooked bristle or hairlike projection.
> **barb**[2] *tr.v.* **barbed, barb·ing, barbs.** To provide or furnish with a barb.

Separate, numbered entries are used for words with the same spelling but different meanings and etymologies.

> **let**[1] (lĕt) *v.* **let, let·ting, lets.** —*tr.* **1.** To give permission to; allow. **2.** To cause to; make. **3.** Used as an auxiliary in the imperative to express a command, request, or proposal, or to give a warning or threat. **4.** To rent or lease: *let rooms.* —*intr.* **1.** To become rented or leased. **2.** To be or become assigned, as to a contractor. [Middle English *leten,* from Old English *lǣtan.*]
>
> **let**[2] (lĕt) *n.* **1.** Something that hinders; an obstacle. **2.** *Sports.* An invalid stroke that must be repeated, as in tennis and other net games. —**let** *tr.v.* **let·ted** or **let, let·ting, lets.** *Archaic.* To hinder or obstruct. [Middle English *lette,* from *letten,* to hinder, from Old English *lettan.*]

3. *Inflections.* These are changes in a word to show things like number and tense. The inflections most commonly shown are irregular plural forms of nouns, irregular principal parts of verbs, and irregular forms of comparison for adjectives and adverbs. Do not confuse inflections with derivatives (see point 6 below).

> **ver·tex** (vûr′·tĕks′) *n., pl.* **ver·tex·es** or **ver·ti·ces** (-tĭ·sēz′).
> **fly** (flī) *v.* **flew** (flü), **flown** (flōn).
> **love·ly** (lŭv′·lē) *adj.* **love·li·er, love·li·est.**

4. *Usage labels.* Not all words are proper to use in every context. Words labeled *nonstandard, substandard,* or *illiterate* should be avoided because they represent poor English. The label *vulgar* indicates that a word should be avoided altogether because of its association with evil. The label *slang* indicates words coined by people trying to say things in unique ways. Because many of these expressions come from the "street language" of immoral people, we should avoid the new, catchy expressions that are constantly showing up. Our speech should rather complement our entire lifestyle as the simple, modest, and holy people of God.

A number of labels limit the proper use of words. *Informal* words are acceptable in everyday speaking and in everyday writing, such as notes to yourself or friendly letters. However, they should not occur in formal speech (giving a topic or preaching a sermon) or in formal writing (schoolwork, articles for publication, or legal papers). Informal words include *barrel* for "a great quantity" and *grill* for "to question relentlessly."

The labels *regional* and *dialectal* mark words used in relatively small areas or by a limited group of people. Some dictionaries even specify regions where people use certain words. The labels *archaic* and *obsolete* designate words that are no longer in general use. Some dictionaries also use other descriptive labels, such as *poetic, technical, mathematics,* and *botany.*

5. *Etymology.* This information about the origin of a word usually appears within brackets either before the definitions or at the end of the entry. Etymologies are valuable for comparing words of similar origin. Study the explanatory notes of your dictionary to learn what the various abbreviations and symbols mean. Here is a typical etymology with an explanation of its meaning.

evade [< Fr *évader* < L *ēvādere* : *ē-, ex-,* out + *vādere,* to go.]
   Meaning: *Evade* comes from the French word *évader,* which came from the Latin word *ēvādere,* which consists of the word elements *ē-* (from *ex-,* meaning "out") and *vādere* (meaning "to go").

6. *Derivatives.* These are related words, usually of different parts of speech, that are made by adding various suffixes to the entry word.

   crisp (krisp) *adj.* —**crisp′·ly** *adv.* —**crisp′·ness** *n.* —**crisp′·y** *adj.*

7. *Synonyms and antonyms.* These are found mainly in advanced dictionaries and only for selected words. Along with the synonyms, some dictionaries give helpful pointers on their proper use. The next lesson deals more specifically with synonyms and antonyms in a thesaurus.

8. *Other information.* Some advanced dictionaries give biographical and geographical information, abbreviations, and foreign words and phrases. These types of information are found either in the main body of the dictionary (under the appropriate entry words) or in separate sections of the dictionary.

Applying the Lesson

A. Write another spelling for each word. If it follows the word *also,* underline it.
1. caldron
2. carousel
3. vise
4. likable
5. softy
6. programmer

B. Copy all the pronunciations for each word. If a pronunciation follows the word *also* or any label that limits the acceptability of the pronunciation, underline it.
1. learned (adj.)
2. nausea
3. financier
4. niche
5. thither
6. pastoral

C. Write a dictionary definition or a synonym that gives the meaning of each underlined word.
1. Though much of the world's art does not appeal to the Christian, he is no <u>Philistine</u>; he does enjoy noble, worthwhile art.
2. This field, having a slight <u>declivity</u> toward the south, yields excellent crops.
3. Mr. Tilley wears a <u>gauntlet</u> when he works at the rotary oven, where the metal handles are heated before they receive a plastic coating.
4. I hardly understand this article well enough to <u>abstract</u> it clearly.
5. For an interesting project, we will <u>found</u> some lead in science class today.
6. As I was smoothing out a mortise, the <u>tang</u> of my chisel cracked.
7. A few <u>pigs</u> remained at the site of the abandoned iron furnace.
8. The group of refugees slowly wended through the dangerous <u>defile</u>.
9. For many years, those who lived in the <u>marches</u> between France and Germany found their governance alternating between the two powers.
10. By late afternoon, our energies were seriously <u>flagging</u> in the intense heat.
11. Some of the photo albums have rich, thick <u>flock</u> on the covers.
12. Can we <u>prize</u> the door with a crowbar?

Lesson 97 Answers
Teacher: Answers are based on *The American Heritage Dictionary, Third Edition.* Other dictionaries may vary considerably. Check your school's dictionaries in order to properly credit your students' work.

Applying the Lesson
A. 1. <u>cauldron</u>
   2. carrousel
   3. <u>vice</u>
   4. <u>likeable</u>
   5. softie
   6. programer

B. 1. (lėr′·nid)
   2. (nô′·zē·ə, -zhə, -sē·ə, -shə)
   3. (fin′·ən·sir′, fə·nan′-, fi′·nən-)
   4. (nich, nēsh)
   5. (thith′·ər, thith′-)
   6. (pas′·tər·əl)

C. 1. one who is indifferent or antagonistic to artistic or cultural values
   2. downward slope
   3. protective glove
   4. summarize
   5. melt and pour into a mold
   6. projection by which a tool is attached to its handle
   7. crude blocks of metal (*or* molds in which metal is cast)
   8. narrow gorge or pass
   9. border regions
   10. declining in vigor and strength
   11. pulverized fibers applied to paper or cloth to produce a texture or pattern
   12. pry

D. Copy the inflected forms that your dictionary gives for these words.
   1. espy   4. bad   7. glad
   2. evanesce   5. far   8. lasso
   3. bacillus   6. moldy

E. Copy any usage labels your dictionary gives for these words.
   1. argent   3. nohow   5. gangway
   2. cheesy   4. leasing   6. typo

F. Write out the etymology of each word, using no abbreviations.
   1. orient   3. hieroglyphic
   2. alligator   4. circumference

Review Exercises

Label each underlined verb *TA* (transitive, active voice), *TP* (transitive, passive voice), *IC* (intransitive complete), or *IL* (intransitive linking). [76]
   1. Joseph Funk, a prominent Mennonite of Virginia, greatly <u>influenced</u> the music of the Mennonite Church.
   2. His introduction of shaped notes has <u>proved</u> especially helpful.
   3. An eight-tone scale with seven different syllable names <u>was promoted</u> by this outstanding music teacher.
   4. Although the scale then in use (do, re, mi, fa, sol, la, si, do) <u>differed</u> slightly from the modern scale, it is easily recognizable.
   5. In the fifth edition of his *Harmonia Sacra,* Funk <u>used</u> the seven note shapes that are common today.

---

98. Using a Thesaurus

In writing, do you sometimes find it hard to think of exactly the right word to express an idea? Suppose you have related an incident to illustrate how a misspelled word may cause a serious misunderstanding. Then you write, "This illustration (gives prominence to) the importance of always checking your spelling." But you do not like the phrase in parentheses. What is the best word to use as a replacement? You think of *shows, emphasizes,* and *stresses,* but none of those words says exactly what you mean. What can you do?

The thesaurus (thi·sôr′·əs) is a book designed for the very purpose of solving such a problem. Derived from the Greek word for *treasury,* this name refers to a book that is indeed a treasury of related words. Each entry word is followed by one or more groups of synonyms and, in many cases, of antonyms. By using the thesaurus, you should be able to find exactly the word you want.

In the case above, you may look up *emphasize* and find the synonyms *stress, accent, highlight,* and *underscore.* Ah, there it is! You choose the word *highlight* because it fits your sentence exactly.

Lesson 98

Purpose: To review the use of the thesaurus, and to encourage its use in choosing effective words.

Teaching Suggestions:

Since Part B contains paired sentences, you should not divide it in the normal odd–even manner. If you wish to do some in class, do the first half and assign the rest.

D. 1. espied, espying, espies
   2. evanesced, evanescing, evanesces
   3. bacilli
   4. worse, worst
   5. farther, farthest, further, furthest
   6. moldier, moldiest
   7. gladder, gladdest
   8. lassos, lassoes

E. 1. heraldry, archaic
   2. informal
   3. nonstandard
   4. archaic
   5. nautical, chiefly British
   6. informal

F. 1. Middle English, from Old French, from Latin *oriēns, orient-,* rising sun, east, from present participle of *orīrī,* to arise, be born.
   2. Alteration of Spanish *el lagarto,* the lizard : *el,* the (from Latin *ille,* that) + *lagarto,* lizard (from Latin *lacertus*).
   3. French *hiéroglyphique,* from Late Latin *hieroglyphicus,* from Greek *hiero-gluphikos* : *hieros,* holy + *gluphē,* carving (from *gluphein,* to carve).
   4. Middle English, from Old French *circonference,* from Latin *circumferentia,* from *circumferēns, circumferent-,* present participle of *circumferre,* to carry around : *circum-,* circum- + *ferre,* to carry.

Review Exercises

   1. TA   4. IC
   2. IL   5. TA
   3. TP

Understanding the Arrangement of a Thesaurus

Many modern thesauruses follow an easy-to-use alphabetical order. Using an alphabetical thesaurus is a simple matter of looking up the word you want to replace and searching the lists of synonyms for a suitable word. Some alphabetical thesauruses have cross-references at the end of many entries, directing the user to other entries with related words. However, if the word you look up is not a main entry, you will need to find a synonym that is a main entry.

Some thesauruses follow the original classification of words established by Peter Mark Roget (rō·zhā′), a British physician (1779–1869) who developed the first known English thesaurus. Over a period of fifty years, Roget collected thousands of words and classified them into six main categories: abstract relations, space, matter, intellect, volition, and affections. He further divided each of these categories into sections as shown below.

Class I. Abstract Relations
Section I. Existence (1–8)
    II. Relation (9–24)
   III. Quantity (25–57)
   IV. Order (58–83)
    V. Number (84–105)
   VI. Time (106–139)
  VII. Change (140–152)
 VIII. Causation (153–179)

Class II. Space
Section I. Generally (180–191)
    II. Dimensions (192–239)
   III. Form (240–263)
   IV. Motion (264–315)

Class III. Matter
Section I. Generally (316–320)
    II. Inorganic (321–356)
   III. Organic (357–449)

Class IV. Intellect
Section I. Formation of Ideas (450–515)
    II. Communication of Ideas (516–599)

Class V. Volition
Section I. Individual (600–736)
    II. Intersocial (737–819)

Class VI. Affections
Section I. Generally (820–826)
    II. Personal (827–887)
   III. Sympathetic (888–921)
   IV. Moral (922–975)
    V. Religious (976–1000)

Under these sections, Roget listed his words in one thousand numbered entries. The numbers in parentheses above show the range of numbered entries in each section. Of course, in a modern *Roget's Thesaurus,* many new words have been added and many outdated words removed. The numbering has also been changed somewhat. However, a thesaurus that bears Roget's name still uses a classification system based on the one devised by Peter Mark Roget.

Without an index, you would have great difficulty in finding treasures in Roget's thesaurus—unless you were to memorize its basic structure. A thorough index, therefore, is a standard part of the thesaurus. In fact, in many thesauruses the index covers nearly as many pages as does the body. To use a thesaurus of this kind, find a word in the index, turn to the numbered entry or entries that are given, and look through the lists of synonyms there.

A fully alphabetized thesaurus is convenient because you can go directly to synonym lists without needing to use an index first. But Roget's numbering system also has some advantages. The main advantage is that at most entries, you can find other words with related or opposite meanings in the entries before and after the one you looked up.

Choosing Synonyms Effectively

The thesaurus is a valuable aid in communicating expressively. As you dig into this treasury, you will find exact words that will add clarity and sparkle to your writing and speaking. By using the thesaurus regularly, you will enrich the treasury of your personal vocabulary. However, you must always use the thesaurus with discernment. Very few English synonyms are interchangeable in every context. So when you look at the list of synonyms, you must carefully choose a word that means precisely what you want to say. The following points will help you use a thesaurus effectively.

1. *Consider both the denotation and the connotation of the words.* The words *joy, delight, glee, bliss, ecstasy, mirth,* and *gaiety* are all synonyms of *happiness.* Study the definitions of these seven synonyms.

> **joy,** (1) Intense and especially ecstatic or exultant happiness. (2) The expression or manifestation of such feeling. (3) A source or an object of pleasure or satisfaction.
> **delight,** (1) Great pleasure; joy. (2) Something that gives great pleasure or enjoyment.
> **glee,** Jubilant delight; joy.
> **bliss,** (1) Extreme happiness; ecstasy. (2) The ecstasy of salvation; spiritual joy.
> **ecstasy,** (1) Intense joy or delight. (2) A state of emotion so intense that one is carried beyond rational thought and self-control.
> **mirth,** Gladness and gaiety, especially when expressed by laughter.
> **gaiety,** (1) A state of joyful exuberance or merriment; vivacity. (2) Merry or joyful activity; festivity.

A thesaurus will likely list these seven words as synonyms, yet you can see that each word is different from the rest. Part of that distinction results from differences in the denotation—the strict, exact meanings of words. Notice that the first three words above have relatively general meanings of strong happiness. The last four, however, incorporate other specific ideas within the definitions. *Bliss* denotes spiritual joy; *ecstasy,* an irrational or uncontrolled happiness; *mirth,* a happiness expressed by laughter; and *gaiety,* vivacious and festive happiness.

In addition to denotation, each word has its unique connotation—the "personality" of the word or the feeling it conveys. Consider the three synonyms above with similar denotations: *joy, delight,* and *glee.* Do they have the same connotation? If you are not sure, read the following sentence, using a different one of these words each time.

> Imagine our ——— when Grandfather Stoner's said they were coming to visit for a week.

Either *joy* or *delight* fits well, but *glee* definitely does not have the right connotation. Although by definition, it means "jubilant delight" or "joy," its connotation is too lighthearted for this sentence. Notice how that connotation makes it fit well in the following sentence.

> The little children laughed with <u>glee</u> as the puppies tumbled about on the lawn.

This means that you must be well familiar with the words you choose, lest you say or write an absurd statement. Suppose, for example, that a writer wants to replace the word *regularity* in one of his sentences, and in a thesaurus he finds the following synonyms: *rhythm, alternation, pulsation, routine, steadiness.* He chooses *pulsation* and writes the following sentence.

> We have always appreciated Todd's <u>pulsation</u> in performing his duties on the farm.

To avoid using wrong words, be sure to study all the definitions in a reliable dictionary. If the entry includes phrases or sentences showing how to use the word, study them carefully. Checking several dictionaries often proves helpful in developing a full-fledged understanding of a word. If possible, use an unabridged dictionary, which gives a complete listing of possible shades of meanings for each word.

2. *Consider the level of formality of the words.* Words labeled *informal* in the dictionary are acceptable only in everyday speaking and writing. However, some words not labeled *informal* may still have a more informal tone than other words with similar meanings. For example, one definition of *gush* is "to make an excessive display of sentiment or enthusiasm." Because of the relatively informal tone of this word, it would fit all right in the following sentences from a friendly letter.

> Marta, our little fresh-air girl, arrived last week. You should have heard her <u>gush</u> over the little calves!

But if you wrote a sentence about a Christian rejoicing over the blessing of God in his life, the word *gush* would definitely be unsuitable.

3. *Consider the range of application of the words.* The words *remuneration, salary,* and *earnings* are synonyms of *wages,* but each word has its own specific range of use. *Remuneration* covers a broad range of payments for goods provided, services rendered, or losses incurred. It may well include nonmonetary payments. *Earnings* also covers a broad range, referring not only to payments to an employee but also to profits from a business or an investment. *Wages,* on the other hand, generally refers to monetary payments to an employee. *Salary* refers to a regular, fixed payment to an employee.

> As a carpenter during the Great Depression, Grandfather often accepted food as <u>remuneration</u> for his services.
> Father's <u>wages</u> include both a <u>salary</u> and <u>earnings</u> based on the total sales in his department.

Do not be content with stale or mediocre words. Examine the gems in your treasury of English words, and choose fresh, precise words that will make your writing attractive and effective.

Applying the Lesson

A. Using a thesaurus, write at least five synonyms for each of these words.

1. painful	3. obstruction	5. atone
2. think	4. mixture	6. tidy

B. Write the synonym with the best denotation and connotation for each sentence.
1. The passengers and crew (abandoned, relinquished, renounced) the sinking ship.
2. During the war, several men (abandoned, relinquished, renounced) their citizenship and joined the ranks of the enemy.
3. King Solomon built a (gaudy, magnificent, pretentious) temple for the Lord.
4. Balaam grew (furious, peeved, pugnacious) when his donkey repeatedly went against his wishes.
5. Jesus rebuked His disciples for their (arguments, conversations, discussions) about which of them would be the greatest.
6. After a lengthy (argument, conversation, discussion), the brethren agreed to vote on the matter.
7. Grandma was (ecstatic, glad, satisfied) when she finally found her lost eyeglasses.
8. Hebrews 3 clearly (declines, refuses, repudiates) the idea that Moses was superior to Christ.
9. Many slaves had a life that was full of (effort, strain, toil) from sunrise until sunset.
10. Our science book explains that by applying (effort, strain, toil) to a lever, we can raise a heavy object.
11. Those who begin smoking usually find it an extremely difficult (custom, habit, routine) to break.
12. Bowing is a traditional (custom, habit, routine) in Oriental countries.

Lesson 98 Answers

Applying the Lesson

A. (Sample answers.)
1. hurtful, bitter, grievous, woeful, sore, racking, excruciating, torturous
2. reflect, cogitate, consider, deliberate, contemplate, meditate, ponder, muse
3. hindrance, stoppage, interception, interference, impediment, obstacle, blockage
4. alloy, miscellany, medley, patchwork, compound, composite, blend, assortment
5. expiate, propitiate, redeem, absolve, purge, compensate
6. neat, trim, clean, spotless, unspotted, unsoiled, spruce

B. (Allow slight variation if students can give logical reasons for their choices. Class discussion would be profitable.)

1. abandoned		7. glad
2. renounced		8. repudiates
3. magnificent		9. toil
4. furious		10. effort
5. arguments		11. habit
6. discussion		12. custom

C. Replace each underlined item with a synonym appropriate for formal writing.
1. You can easily see that this fossil is not confined to one <u>layer</u> of rock.
2. Obviously, the fossil did not form over long <u>eras</u> as evolutionists claim.
3. The intense forces present in the Flood offer a <u>reasonable</u> explanation for such fossils.
4. Diligence in everyday work helps to develop the <u>perseverance</u> needed for spiritual victory.
5. One who loves God does not find Biblical discipleship <u>burdensome</u>.
6. A <u>prudent</u> person will flee those situations that bring temptation.
7. We should never <u>overlook</u> the seriousness of trying to hide wrongdoing from those in authority over us.
8. As we hold to the unchanging Word, the <u>uncertainty</u> of life will never overwhelm us.
9. Only the power of God's grace can <u>free</u> sinful man from bondage to sin.
10. We need a <u>perceptive</u> view of life, or we will be sidetracked by the world's allurements.

Review Exercises

A. Copy the correct participle for each sentence. [90]
1. The hay, (drying, dried) rapidly in this heat, should be ready to bale before noon.
2. These huge drifts, (forming, formed) by yesterday's blizzard, will keep us snowed in for several days.
3. (Working, Having worked) at Grandfather's mill long ago, Matt Findley has remained a family friend.
4. Ye Olde Gristmill, (standing, having stood) at the edge of town, offers stone-ground wheat and rye flour as well as a variety of bulk foods.

B. Copy each word that should be followed by a comma, and add the comma. If the sentence needs no comma, write *correct*. [90, 93]
1. Forming as raindrops refract sunlight a rainbow consists of concentric arcs of red, orange, yellow, green, blue, and violet.
2. If the raindrops are quite small the rainbow will be pale.
3. A rainbow formed by large raindrops will be more vivid and may be accompanied by a secondary rainbow.
4. This secondary rainbow which results from refraction and reflection within the raindrops always has the colors reversed from the primary rainbow.
5. If a person stands at ground level he will never see more than a semicircle of a rainbow.
6. You might see the complete circle of a rainbow when you are flying in an airplane.

C. Write enough words to show how to correct the mistake in each sentence. [95]
1. We have had pleasanter weather today than we have had for a while.
2. My sister Elaine is better at math than anyone in our family.

C. (Sample answers. Check students' answers for connotation, formality, and range of application.)
1. stratum, substratum
2. eons, epochs, millennia
3. well-founded, credible, rational
4. determination, steadfastness, stamina, endurance
5. onerous, oppressive, grievous
6. circumspect, discreet, cautious, wary, careful
7. disregard, ignore, dismiss
8. insecurity, instability, changeableness, capriciousness, irregularity
9. liberate, deliver, release, unfetter, emancipate
10. discerning, astute, perspicacious

Review Exercises

A. 1. drying
2. formed
3. Having worked
4. standing

B. 1. sunlight,
2. small,
3. correct
4. rainbow, raindrops,
5. level,
6. correct

C. 1. more pleasant
2. anyone else

3. These strawberry plants are deader than I expected them to be.
4. Which of these two mottoes do you like best?
5. The rain has been falling more steady for the last hour than it had been earlier.
6. Duke is one of the most friendliest dogs I have ever known.

3. more nearly dead
4. better
5. more steadily
6. the friendliest

---

99. Using Reference Books of General Information

Dictionaries and thesauruses are among the most valuable reference books, for they help you to use words properly and effectively. Sometimes you need other kinds of information. What are the land and the climate of Andorra like? When did Vasco Núñez de Balboa live? What lands did he explore? How far apart are San Francisco and New York City? In what nation does nuclear power account for the highest percentage of the total electricity produced? For these and countless other questions, you will probably turn to reference books of general information. These books include encyclopedias, atlases, and statistical almanacs.

Encyclopedias

An encyclopedia contains articles on a wide range of subjects. In fact, the word *encyclopedia* comes from two Greek words: *enkyklios,* meaning "general," and *paideia,* meaning "education." And certainly that is a fitting name for these sets of volumes: they contain a general summary of much of the knowledge that man has gained.

1. *A useful tool for research.* A number of features make the encyclopedia valuable for research on a subject. First, cross-references at the end of some entries give titles of other articles in the set that contain related information. For example, the article about rubber may end with the following cross-references.

Elasticity	Indonesia (picture)
Faraday, Michael	Latex
Firestone, Harvey S.	Plastics
Goodrich, Benjamin F.	Polymerization
Goodyear, Charles	Tire

Second, some encyclopedia articles may include a bibliography, which refers you to books that give more detailed information on the subject. The article about rubber may have the following bibliography.

Gait, A. J., and Hancock, E. G. *Plastics and Synthetic Rubbers.* Pergamon, 1970.
Le Bras, Jean. *Introduction to Rubber.* Rev. ed. Hart Publishing Co., 1969.
Morton, Maurice, ed. *Rubber Technology.* 2nd ed. Van Nostrand, 1973.

A third valuable feature for research is the index. Usually the last volume of an encyclopedia is a comprehensive index, which lists all the information that the encyclopedia contains on a certain subject. The index is much more thorough than the

Lesson 99

Purpose: To review the use of encyclopedias and atlases, and
*to teach the use of statistical almanacs.

cross-references because it lists not only titles of articles that focus on related information but also titles of articles that may contain only a few sentences dealing with the subject.

The index will also help you to find information about a topic on which the encyclopedia has no specific article. For example, an encyclopedia may have no article about chloroprene. However, the index entry may look like this:

Chloroprene [chemical]
    Acetylene (Other Uses) **A:22**
    Rubber (The Chemistry of Synthetic Rubber) **R:469**

A fourth aid in research that you will find in encyclopedia sets is the annual yearbooks. Because new events and new discoveries constantly change man's knowledge, most encyclopedia publishers offer yearbooks to update their encyclopedias.

2. *A tool to be used with caution.* Although encyclopedias are a valuable resource, you must use them with discretion. First of all, learn to detect the errors commonly found in encyclopedias. The writers of these volumes generally hold a secular, humanistic philosophy of life. Therefore, the articles reflect a point of view that glorifies man and his achievements. They will laud warfare and ungodly movements. They will present as fact the erroneous teachings of philosophies like evolution, environmentalism, and humanism. Conspicuously absent is any acknowledgment of God and of the principles in His Word.

How important that you learn to compare all that you read with the standards of the Bible! Only in God's eternal Word do we find the principles by which we can know what is truth and what is error. Your parents and teachers will help you to identify false teachings as well as theories that are unproven.

A second important caution is to remember that an encyclopedia article does not provide an exhaustive coverage of a particular subject. This is a "general education" reference source—general both because it covers a wide range of information and because it does not thoroughly cover the precise details of the subject. Do not miss the bountiful fruits of broad research by limiting yourself to the encyclopedia. By reading any one of the books listed in the bibliography above, you will learn much more about rubber than by reading the encyclopedia article.

Atlases

An atlas is a book of maps. A world atlas has detailed maps showing all the regions of the world geographically and politically. Geographical maps portray such things as topography, vegetation, land use, rainfall, climate patterns, and population density. Political maps show the boundaries of nations, states, and provinces. But political changes occur frequently, and man is constantly building new roads, dams, and canals. Therefore, an atlas becomes outdated rather quickly.

A road atlas is a guide for traveling and an aid for learning many geographical facts. Such an atlas shows roads, airports, national parks, and similar items of interest to travelers. The atlas may also have information about climate, topography, and history for places that travelers may want to visit.

An atlas usually has an index, listing place names shown on the maps. Each index entry indicates which maps show that place, along with a key to locate the place on the maps.

Statistical Almanacs

Statistical almanacs provide factual information about the world today. The *World Almanac and Book of Facts* and the *Information Please Almanac* are two of the most popular ones. Published annually, these volumes contain a wide variety of information. They provide current statistics and information about things like agriculture, science, industry, and astronomy. They include historical and current political, geographical, and social information about nations, states, and provinces. And they contain articles on significant happenings and issues of the previous year.

Applying the Lesson

A. Using the index of an encyclopedia, list all the volumes and page numbers where you could find information on the following subjects.

1. Muscle
2. Waldenses
3. Hudson River
4. Millard Fillmore
5. Atmospheric pressure
6. Solomon Islands
7. John C. Calhoun
8. Kalahari Desert

B. Answer these questions by using one of the reference books described in this lesson. Give the source of information for each answer.
1. What were the lowest and the highest temperatures ever recorded in Hawaii?
2. Which state in the United States produces the most wheat?
3. Where do marsh deer live?
4. Which is farther north: Portland, Oregon, or Toronto, Ontario?
5. If both the President and the Vice President of the United States were removed from office in any way, what official is next in line to succeed to the Presidency?
6. What is the highest elevation in Tuvalu?
7. What is the most populous city in West Virginia?
8. How long is the Congo River?
9. What are three things for which gutta-percha is used?
10. What is one thing for which David Rittenhouse was well known?
11. What are the chief agricultural crops in Kansas?
12. What north–south interstate highway could a traveler use to reach Des Moines, Iowa? What east–west interstate highway?
13. What interstate highway connects New York City to San Francisco?
14. What three major roads would you use to travel from Greenville, South Carolina, to Florence, South Carolina?

Review Exercises

A. Name the five steps in the SQ3R study method. After each one, briefly explain how to apply that step in studying a lesson. [10]

Lesson 99 Answers

A. (Answers depend on the encyclopedia used.)

B. (Be sure the sources of information are included.)
1. *lowest:* 14°F (-10°C); *highest:* 100°F (38°C)
2. Kansas
3. in swampy areas and palm thickets in Brazil, Uruguay, Paraguay, and northern Argentina
4. Portland, Oregon (about 45° N, whereas Toronto is about 43° N)
5. the Speaker of the House of Representatives
6. 15 feet above sea level
7. Charleston
8. 2,900 miles (4,670 km)
9. (Any three.) electrical insulation, golf balls, surgical bandages, castings, machine belts, tooth fillings, chewing gum, soles for shoes, containers for acids
10. for building what was probably the first telescope made in America; for building a mechanical planetarium
11. wheat, sorghum grain, corn, hay, soybeans
12. *north–south:* Interstate 35; *east–west:* Interstate 80
13. Interstate 80
14. Interstates 385, 26, and 20

Review Exercises

A. Survey—Look over the lesson, noticing the headings and any pictures or diagrams.
Question—Ask questions for which you expect to find answers in the lesson.
Read—Carefully read the lesson, making sure you understand what it teaches.
Recite—Answer the questions you had asked; do the written assignment.
Review—Mentally recall the main points of the lesson.

B. Write whether each statement about studying is *true* or *false*. [9–12]

1. The rate at which you forget material that you have studied increases as time passes.
2. Surveying a lesson before reading it gives you a helpful overview of the material.
3. In a study period, it is generally best to do the hardest and least enjoyable assignments first.
4. Slouching tends to subconsciously tell your mind to relax.
5. Skillful skimming of a lesson can be a good substitute for the SQ3R method.
6. When you skim a book, you should first look over the table of contents.
7. Taking notes helps promote logical thinking.
8. When summarizing, you should try to preserve the original wording as much as possible.
9. Asking questions before reading a lesson helps to prepare you to read effectively.
10. Reading to find specific answers is the heart of meaningful study.

B. 1. false
    2. true
    3. true
    4. true
    5. false
    6. true
    7. true
    8. false
    9. true
    10. true

---

100. Improving Your Speaking Style, Part 3: Enthusiasm

What do you need to remember for effective public speaking? Good eye contact with your audience, for one thing. You should establish eye contact early in your discourse and maintain it throughout your talk. Good voice control is also important. Pronounce your words clearly, use a comfortable volume, and speak at a pitch and speed appropriate to what you are saying.

Conveying a sense of enthusiasm is another important part of an effective speaking style. Your enthusiasm definitely affects both the quality of your speech and the attention of your audience. On the one hand, a proper sense of enthusiasm helps you to put your best efforts into the speech. On the other hand, it will help to stimulate in your audience an enthusiasm that enables them to listen and understand you more easily. It may even make it easier for them to agree with you.

Developing Enthusiasm

Enthusiasm should not be something that you just put on for the need of the moment; rather, it should grow and develop within you. How can you cause it to grow? Can everyone attain this? You should be able to develop an enthusiasm for communicating with others if you do the following things.

1. *Choose a subject that interests you.* This is of utmost importance. How could you talk with enthusiasm about selling produce if you despise waiting on customers and counting out the correct change? By contrast, someone who thoroughly enjoys selling produce will be in an excellent position to give a talk about his family's vegetable stand.

Lesson 100

Purpose: To give students practice in speaking before a group, and to teach *enthusiasm as an element of effective speaking style.

Teaching Suggestions:

For Part A of the lesson exercises, you might ask the students for a suggestion; but you should also be ready with an idea of your own. For Part B, hold the students to subjects with which they are personally familiar to avoid the need for time-consuming research and to allow easier talking about the subjects.

Sometimes you will easily think of a good subject for your speech. You may know just what you want to talk about as soon as you receive the assignment. At other times you must explore numerous possibilities before you find something that appeals to you. Beware lest you throw out every idea you encounter, just because it fails to strike you with great force. Students often find that after a bit of study, a subject is much more interesting than they had thought it would be.

2. *Become thoroughly familiar with your subject.* You can hardly speak with enthusiasm about a subject that you do not know well. You become familiar with a subject by personal experience, by discussing it with others, and by reading about it. Do not cheat yourself. Study your subject until you know it well, until you find an enthusiasm for it growing within you.

3. *Organize your material.* It is essential that you plan your talk carefully. How will you begin? What main points will you present, and in what order will they come? How will you close? Few things dampen enthusiasm more effectively than standing before a group with only a vague idea of what you will say and how you plan to say it.

Make your plans carefully, and then practice giving your talk. As you do this, you will feel a growing confidence about your talk, and your enthusiasm will grow with it. You will actually begin looking forward—though perhaps still with apprehension—to sharing your information with the group. But if you still feel absolutely no spark of enthusiasm, you are doing something wrong! You must make a change somewhere, either in your subject or in your preparation. For as long as a subject fails to stir your own enthusiasm, it has no chance of stirring the enthusiastic attention of your listeners.

Expressing Enthusiasm

Having gained a genuine enthusiasm for your subject, you next face the challenge of communicating it to your listeners. To some degree this will happen automatically because enthusiasm in your heart will show on your face and in your actions. However, you as a speaker should pay deliberate attention to the following things, which help to add life and force to your words.

1. *Eye contact.* You will find it easier to look your listeners in the eye if you have an enthusiastic interest in your subject. This is true because you will be thinking more about your subject than about yourself. You will be confident that your subject is worthwhile and that your audience will also find it interesting. Meeting your listeners eye to eye will help you to communicate effectively as you move through the talk.

2. *Voice inflection.* What you feel will show in your voice. Remember the little boy who has just come home after receiving a lollipop from the doctor. You can hear his voice even now as he exclaims excitedly, "Father, look! A lollipop!" Contrast that with the same boy when he finds a not-so-cherished food on his plate. You now hear the same voice in quite a different tone saying, "Mother, must I eat all this?"

Be assured that your own enthusiasm or lack of it shows through just as clearly when you give a talk. Seek to develop a strong enthusiasm, and then let your voice naturally convey that feeling to your audience.

3. *Facial expression.* You need to show your enthusiasm by looking enthusiastic. Again, this is not a matter of putting something on, but of showing on the outside what you feel on the inside. Gain an enthusiastic interest in your subject, and then let it show on your face.

4. *Gestures.* The gestures you use help to express your enthusiasm. If you are not interested, you probably will use few if any gestures. If you are too self-conscious, you may use some gestures but they will not reinforce the points you make. But if you are truly interested in your speech, your gestures will take on life and meaning. They may indicate size, shape, or direction. They may help to emphasize a major point. Or they may simply reinforce what you are saying.

Of course, gestures can be overdone. You do not need to act out a story in order to tell it effectively. But appropriate gestures, used with reserve and discretion, will definitely add appeal to your presentation.

5. *Posture.* Enthusiasm will motivate you to stand up straight as you speak before the class. It will keep you from shuffling your feet and slouching your body. It will prompt you throughout your speech to maintain the dignity of standing with your weight evenly balanced on both feet and your shoulders straight. Your posture definitely communicates the degree of your enthusiasm.

Your assignment in this lesson will be to describe something of interest to you, such as an animal, a plant, or a place that you have seen. In order to do this in a fresh, appealing way, you must do more than talk about the item in a humdrum manner. You will need to think of specific reasons why the item is interesting to you. If it is an animal, are you impressed by its size? its appearance? its actions? Exactly what makes it impressive and interesting? You may need to do a little research to find exactly how tall, how long, or how heavy it is, or what purpose is served by its spots or other unusual features.

After you have considered the details themselves, you must decide how you will present them. Think of appealing ways to portray the thing you are describing. Was the building so tall that your neck hurt as you tried to see the top? Were you impressed by the hollow, echoing sounds or the damp, chilly feeling of the interior? Remembering exactly what you saw, heard, and felt will help you to describe your subject with interest and enthusiasm.

Applying the Lesson

A. Choose an interesting animal, plant, or place that is familiar to your class. On the board, list specific details that would be included in a description of it. Then work together at thinking of ways to present those details in fresh, creative ways.

B. Think of something interesting to describe, and prepare to give a talk of four to six minutes about it. Your talk should be based mainly on your personal knowledge, though you may use reference sources to obtain specific facts. The following ideas may stimulate your thinking.
1. An interesting animal
2. An unusual plant
3. A place your family has visited

Lesson 100 Answers
Applying the Lesson
A. (Class work.)

B. (Individual work.)

4. A hobby
5. A family project
6. A summer project of your own

Try to develop and show a genuine enthusiasm for your topic. Also remember to practice eye contact and voice control, as you studied in earlier lessons.

---

101. Using the Public Library

"Of making many books there is no end" (Ecclesiastes 12:12). Indeed, many thousands of books come off printing presses in a year's time. Public libraries provide the general public with access to a wide selection of books at little or no cost.

Value of the Public Library

A public library is a valuable source of information. On its shelves you will find numerous books of fiction and nonfiction. Fiction books contain stories made up by their authors. Even if a story is based on historical facts, it is fiction if the writer put it together by using his imagination. Nonfiction books are based on fact. They include biographies, reference books, and books on topics such as science, history, and language.

The library also contains a wide variety of magazines, newspapers, language records, and other literary materials. For a small fee, many libraries offer interlibrary services, giving you access to materials from other area libraries. Furthermore, the librarians are generally willing and able to help you locate hard-to-find information.

You should use a library only when you have a good purpose. It is not wise to browse at length through the materials in a public library—especially not through the books of fiction. However, there are occasions when a public library can offer you worthwhile services. You might need more information for a specific school assignment such as an English composition, a science report, or a history project. Or you might need further information for personal use on practical subjects, such as quilting, caring for a pet, building a doghouse, or starting plants in a cold frame. You might wish to research some local history or some points of interest in an area you plan to visit. Even a small public library contains information on any of these subjects.

Courteous Use of the Public Library

A public library has rules so that it can effectively serve everyone who uses it. You should show your appreciation for its services by obeying the rules courteously. In a library you should be quiet. You will probably not be the only one using the library. The others who have come to read or study need quietness for their concentration. Show respect for them and for the library by walking softly and talking quietly.

Be careful with the books. Remember that you are handling other people's property, so you should be even more careful than you would be with your own books. Turn the pages without creasing or tearing them. Lay the books down gently; never

---

Lesson 101

Purpose: To review the proper use of the public library as a reference source.

Teaching Suggestions:

The public library offers valuable services that we as Christian people can use to our benefit. Because of the unwholesome materials found there, however, we need to use great caution. Young people should never have free access to the library without the supervision of a mature, stable Christian. Although these lessons are designed to prepare students to use the library effectively, they are not intended to promote frequent use of the public library.

Teach the lesson in a matter-of-fact manner, emphasizing the caution that we must exercise when using the services of a public library.

toss them or let them drop. When you remove a book from the shelf, remember where it was so that you can replace it correctly.

Be punctual. If you borrow a book, note carefully the return date and have it back to the library on time. If you discover that a book is overdue or that you have lost one, make the required payment promptly and courteously. Showing appreciation for the library by quietness, carefulness, and punctuality is a small fee to pay for all the privileges the library offers to you.

Prudent Use of the Public Library

Use a library prudently. Go to a public library only with your parents' supervision, and be sure you have your parents' approval before you read a book from a public library. Christians have little or no use for the vast majority of books in a public library. Many books of fiction reflect a lifestyle and value system that is contrary to godliness. Although they may have a limited value in helping you to understand people of other times and cultures, the unwholesome influences often outweigh any benefit. Even nonfiction books pose certain danger to our minds. As noted in Lesson 99, many reference books glorify man's achievements while ignoring God, and many teach false ideas, such as evolution.

Only a full knowledge of God and His Word can keep you from being harmed by finding untruths in the books you read. God's Word is the most important and the only perfectly safe "library" in the world. Although it does not contain every detail of information, it does reveal basic principles that relate to every aspect of human knowledge. Fill your mind with the truth of the Bible, and you will have a standard with which to compare all other books. With this perspective, you will know which books to reject as having a harmful effect and which to accept as providing helpful information.

Applying the Lesson

A. Answer these questions.
1. What is the difference between fiction and nonfiction?
2. How might you as a school student make good use of a public library?
3. How might you or others in your family make good use of a public library for interests other than school matters?
4. What are three rules for using a library courteously?
5. Why is it important to be quiet in the library?
6. What are some guidelines for handling library books carefully?
7. Why must you use a public library prudently?
8. Why is it important to compare all books from a public library with the library of God's Word?

B. Write *fiction* or *nonfiction* for each book title.
1. *Glimpses of Mennonite History and Doctrine* (history of the Mennonite Church and a survey of her important teachings)
2. *Hyenas* (descriptions of various species of hyenas)
3. *The Chronicles of Mansoul* (allegory depicting the spiritual conflict for man's soul)

Lesson 101 Answers
Applying the Lesson

A. 1. Fiction books are stories that are made up, including stories based on facts but not strictly factual.

Nonfiction books include factual material, such as biographies, reference books, and books of general information.

2. for a specific school assignment, such as an English composition, a science report, or a history project

3. for information on practical subjects such as taking care of a pet, building a doghouse, starting plants in a cold frame, quilting, or first aid; for research on local history or points of interest in an area you plan to visit

4. Be quiet.
Be careful with the books.
Be punctual in returning books or in paying for overdue or lost books.

5. Others may be reading or studying and need quietness for concentration.

6. Turn the pages without creasing or tearing them.
Lay the books down gently.
Return books at the right places on the shelves.

7. Many books in a public library are unwholesome because they contain ungodly stories, they glorify man rather than God, or they promote false teachings.

8. to discern which books to reject as having a harmful effect and which to accept as providing helpful information

B. 1. nonfiction
2. nonfiction
3. fiction

4. *Faithfully, George R.* (story of a prominent Mennonite Church leader)
5. *The True Christian* (practical teaching on the Sermon on the Mount)
6. *Carmi of Judea* (story of a Jewish lad in the time just before Jesus' birth)
7. *War-Torn Valley* (realistic story about Mennonites in Virginia during the Civil War)
8. *A Sower Went Forth* (story of Ralph Palmer's service for the Lord)
9. *The Mighty Whirlwind* (account of tornadoes in several states on Palm Sunday, 1965)
10. *"Whom Shall I Fear?"* (portrays in story form the severe tests that the Anabaptists faced)

Review Exercises

Write whether each underlined adverb modifies a *verb,* a *verbal,* an *adjective,* an *adverb,* a *preposition,* a *conjunction,* or an entire *sentence.* [91, 92]

1. God created some plants to survive <u>indefinitely</u> <u>even</u> in dry environments.
2. <u>Generally,</u> such plants are called succulents because they store <u>amazingly</u> large amounts of water in their leaves or in their stems.
3. The word *succulent* <u>actually</u> comes from a Latin root meaning "juice."
4. <u>Obviously,</u> God created the succulents so that they retain water <u>quite</u> effectively.
5. Some succulents, like the cacti, look <u>almost</u> as though they were <u>fully</u> armored water barrels.
6. <u>Why</u> do <u>so</u> many people ignore this plain evidence of the Creator's skill?

4. nonfiction
5. nonfiction
6. fiction
7. fiction
8. nonfiction
9. nonfiction
10. fiction

Review Exercises

1. verbal; preposition
2. sentence; adjective
3. verb
4. sentence; adverb
5. conjunction; verbal (*or* adjective)
6. verb; adjective

---

102. Understanding the Library Filing System

If your school has a small library, the books may be arranged in alphabetical order by title. But a public library, with its thousands of books, needs a more detailed system of arrangement than that. Although libraries use various methods for arranging books, the one you are most likely to encounter is the Dewey decimal system.

The Dewey Decimal System

The Dewey decimal system is named after Melvil Dewey (1851–1931), the man who organized it. From his childhood, mathematics fascinated young Melvil. It was said that while still in the lower grades, Melvil could solve an arithmetic problem in his head more quickly than others could on paper. Another of his delights was arranging things according to a system. He organized his mother's pantry, classifying all its contents.

At twelve years of age, Melvil walked eleven miles to purchase a Webster's unabridged dictionary. The cost was ten dollars, a large sum for a boy in 1863. The book was so heavy that he needed help to carry it home! Melvil's interest in books led him to visit libraries frequently. But he was disturbed by the lack of organization that he saw. In some libraries the books were placed in alphabetical order. In others

Lesson 102

Purpose: To review the Dewey decimal system and the arrangement of three large groups of books: reference, fiction, and biography.

they were numbered in a "fixed location" system according to the room, tier, and shelf where the books chanced to stand on the day they were numbered!

At twenty-one years of age, Melvil Dewey devised the classification system that bears his name. This system arranges all books into ten main categories of subjects. Study the basic outline of the Dewey decimal system below. The number and subject name of each classification are shown in boldface, followed by several examples of the types of books in that category.

000–099 General Works

| Encyclopedias | Periodicals | Book lists |

100–199 Philosophy

| Nature of truth | Psychology | Logic |

200–299 Religion

| Bible | Science and the Bible |
| Church history | Non-Christian religions |

300–399 Social Sciences

Statistics	Government	Economics
Customs	Political science	Education
— Holidays	— International relations	— Curriculum
— Etiquette	— Parliamentary practice	— Instructional methods

400–499 Language

Nature of language	Sign language
English language	Romance languages
— Dictionaries	— Latin
— Grammar	— Spanish (and others)

500–599 Pure Sciences

| Astronomy | Biology | Chemistry |
| Geology | Mathematics | Zoology |

600–699 Applied Sciences

Home economics	Business	Manufacturing
— Cooking	Engineering	Medical science
— Sewing	Agriculture	— Medicine
Construction	— Field crops	— Health and hygiene
— Carpentry	— Fruit culture	— First aid
— Masonry	— Domestic animals	

700–799 Arts and Recreation

Architecture	Photography
Painting	Sculpture
Music	Recreation and hobbies
Drawing and lettering	— Hunting and fishing
Landscaping	— Indoor and outdoor games

800–899 Literature

Study and criticism of literature	English literature
— Prose and poetry	American literature
— Drama (and other literary types)	

900–999 Geography and History

Geography	Ancient history
— Atlases	World history
— Travel information	European history
Biography	American history

In the Dewey decimal system, each of these ten categories can be broken down indefinitely into ever more precise divisions and subdivisions. The following outline illustrates how this system works.

200–299 Religion

210–219—Natural religion
220–229—Bible
   220.00–220.99—General
   221.00–224.99—Old Testament
   225.00–229.99—New Testament
      226.00–226.99—Gospels and Acts
         226.10–226.19—Harmonies
         226.20–226.29—Matthew
         226.30–226.39—Mark
         226.40–226.49—Luke
         226.50–226.59—John
         226.60–226.69—Acts
         226.70–226.79—Miracles
         226.80–226.89—Parables
         226.90–226.99—Lord's Prayer
      227.00–227.99—Epistles
      228.00–228.99—Revelation
      229.00–229.99—Apocrypha

How does this classification system help to find one book among many? Each book in the library is given a specific *call number* based on this system. You know, for example, that the 700s relate to arts and recreation. The division 720 is assigned to architecture. In the library you may find a book titled *The Dome People,* which describes how a group of teenagers built a geodesic dome building. This book may be assigned the call number 721.042.

Since the Dewey decimal system has a call number for each book, and since each call number is recorded in the library computer used for finding books, you do not need to memorize each small part of the system. You should, however, remember the ten main classes.

Special Arrangements

Using the Dewey decimal system, librarians can classify every book in the library. But three groups of books—reference, fiction, and biography—are so large that they have special locations in the library, separate from the other books in the Dewey decimal system.

1. *Reference books.* Some books are not to be read from cover to cover; rather, we refer to them for specific bits of information. These reference books include any book in the 000–099 group. (Some are included in other groups, such as dictionaries and handbooks in the 400–499 group.) Reference books usually have a three-line spine tag. The first line is simply *R* for *reference,* and the second line is the Dewey decimal call number. The third line has a capital letter indicating the author's last name, a *Cutter number,* which is a number that libraries assign to a particular author or compiler, and a small letter for the first important word in the title. The following illustration shows the spine tag that may appear on the book *How to Organize and Operate a Small Library,* by Genore H. Bernhard.

```
R←——————— for Reference
025←——————— Dewey decimal number
B745h←——————— for How to Organize and Operate a Small Library
  ↑ ↑ ———————— Cutter number (745)
  └——————— for Genore H. Bernard
```

2. *Fiction.* Books of fiction are part of the 800–899 group in the Dewey decimal system. They usually have only a two-line spine tag. The first line is *F* for *fiction,* and the second line follows the same pattern as the third line on a reference book. No Dewey decimal system number is shown. Fiction books are arranged on the shelves alphabetically by the last name of the author. If an author has more than one book, those books are arranged alphabetically by title. *The Pilgrim's Progress,* by John Bunyan, might have the spine tag shown below.

F
B259p (*B* stands for Bunyan, the author; 259 is the Cutter number; *p* is the first letter in the first important word in the title.)

3. *Biography.* The 920–929 group of the Dewey decimal system consists of biographies. Like fiction books, they have a two-line spine tag. The first line is *B* for *biography* or the number 92, representing the Dewey decimal group for biographies. These books are arranged on the shelves in alphabetical order according to the name of the person they are written about. Books about the same person are grouped together and arranged alphabetically by the authors' last names. The book *David Livingstone,* by Mrs. J. H. Worcester, Jr., might have the following spine tag.

B
L4962w (*L* stands for Livingstone; 4962 is the Cutter number; *w* stands for Worcester, the author.)

In addition to the reference, fiction, and biography sections, many libraries have a special section with books written for younger readers. Books in this section may have simple call numbers that include the letter *J* (for *juvenile*). Below is the spine tag that may appear on *The Rainbow Book of American History,* by Earl Schenck Miers.

J
973 (Dewey decimal number)
Mie (for Earl Schenck Miers)

Applying the Lesson

A. Write the Dewey decimal number and subject name for the category in which each book belongs, such as *000–099 General Works* or *100–199 Philosophy.*

1. *The British Empire and Commonwealth of Nations* (history from the fifteenth century through the late twentieth century)
2. *Pets* (handbook on the care and understanding of all kinds of pets)
3. *Smiles, Nods, and Pauses* (activities for enriching children's communication skills)
4. *A History of the German Baptist Brethren in Europe and America* (history of German Baptists from their beginning through the late nineteenth century)
5. *The Art of Fine Baking* (general information on baking and a collection of recipes)
6. *Come Along to Saudi Arabia* (history of the kingdom of Saudi Arabia)
7. *Endeavor of Faith* (account of a conservative Mennonite provision for voluntary service during the time of a military draft)
8. *Echoes From My Heart* (collection of poetry)
9. *Why We Believe in Creation, Not in Evolution* (detailed illustrations from nature that cannot be explained by evolution)
10. *An Introduction to Music* (elementary and intermediate instructions in music rudiments)
11. *Century Readings in English Literature* (collection of English literary works grouped chronologically)
12. *Beyond Instinct* (debate between a Christian Russian peasant and an educated, atheistic Communist on creation versus evolution)

B. Tell whether each item speaks of *reference, fiction,* or *biography.*

1. Books arranged alphabetically by the name of the person written about.
2. Books arranged alphabetically by the last name of the author.
3. Books that may be placed in more than one category of the Dewey decimal system.
4. Belong to the 920–929 group of the Dewey decimal system.
5. Mostly belong to the 000–099 group of the Dewey decimal system.
6. Belong to the 800–899 group of the Dewey decimal system.
7. May include a few books from the 400–499 group of the Dewey decimal system.
8. Imaginary stories.
9. Books of general information.
10. Stories about the personal lives of individuals.
11. Books used for looking up facts.
12. May have the number 92 instead of a Dewey decimal number.

Review Exercises

A. Write the correct term to match each description. [49–53]

antagonist	conflict	protagonist
characterization	plot	setting
climax	point of view	theme

Lesson 102 Answers

Applying the Lesson

A. (Allow reasonable variation.)
1. 900–999 Geography and History
2. 600–699 Applied Sciences
3. 300–399 Social Sciences (*or* 400–499 Language)
4. 200–299 Religion
5. 600–699 Applied Sciences
6. 900–999 Geography and History
7. 200–299 Religion
8. 800–899 Literature
9. 200–299 Religion
10. 700–799 Arts and Recreation
11. 800–899 Literature
12. 200–299 Religion

B.
1. biography
2. fiction
3. reference
4. biography
5. reference
6. fiction
7. reference
8. fiction
9. reference
10. biography
11. reference
12. biography

Teacher: In the time since this book was originally published, libraries have switched from card catalogs to computer databases. Since knowing about the card catalog may no longer be useful, you may want to omit Lesson 103. In its place, tell the students that today library books and magazines are found by doing a computer search either by author name, by title, by subject keyword, or by a combination of search entries. Also make the following changes.

Lesson 104: Omit numbers 4–5 in Part D on pages 402 and 403. Also omit Part E on page 403.

Lesson 118: Omit number 5 in Part H on page 456.

Chapter 12 Test: Omit number 21.

1. The main character in a story.
2. The overall development of the story conflict.
3. The time, place, and atmosphere of a story.
4. The lesson that a story teaches.
5. The struggle or problem that the main character faces.
6. The process of portraying story characters.
7. The point where the main character's response brings either victory or defeat.
8. The perspective from which an author writes a story.

B. Write *true* if the statement is true, or *false* if it is false. [48–53]
1. The most effective stories are written about unusual, outstanding events.
2. An effective short story must develop only one main theme.
3. The opening paragraph of a story should give a detailed picture of the setting.
4. If the main character struggles to overcome a bad habit, the conflict is between the main character and his circumstances.
5. The story conflict should increase as the story progresses.
6. The major story characters should be characterized fully.
7. The minor story characters should not even be named.
8. Most stories portray the main characters by their speech and their actions.
9. In the omniscient point of view, the author poses as the main character.
10. When the author writes objectively, he reveals the thoughts of the main character.

Review Exercises

A. 1. protagonist
2. plot
3. setting
4. theme
5. conflict
6. characterization
7. climax
8. point of view

B. 1. false
2. true
3. false
4. false
5. true
6. true
7. false
8. true
9. false
10. false

---

103. Using the Indexes of a Library

Even a small public library contains thousands of books, magazines, newspapers, and other materials. Although these are arranged logically, very few people memorize all the major subdivisions of the Dewey decimal system, let alone all the further subdivisions. Without a good system of indexes to the locations of the books and other materials, the usefulness of a library would be greatly limited.

The Card Catalog

The card catalog, which is often located near the librarian's desk, is a special cabinet with many small drawers. Each drawer is labeled with one or more letters, and it contains hundreds of index cards. You will find three kinds of cards in this index system: title cards, author cards, and subject cards. These cards are arranged alphabetically so that you can easily find books of any title, by any author, or about any subject.

1. *Title cards.* Sometimes you might go to the card catalog to find a specific title. A title card shows the title, centered on the first line. Look for the first word of the title (except *a, an,* or *the*) in alphabetical order. Study the following title card for the book *Patent Laws and Legislation.*

Lesson 103

Purpose: To review how to use the card catalog, and *to teach how to use the *Readers' Guide to Periodical Literature.*

Teaching Suggestions:

For effective classwork on the cards in a card catalog, select several books from your school library and make cards for them. You can at least assign the books Dewey decimal numbers within the correct main group. If possible, find a more detailed index of the Dewey decimal system in a public library.

The last section of the lesson should receive little more than passing mention. Students are not mature enough to sort through much of the magazine material that is available. But they should know that this index exists for the time when they may have use for it.

Patent Laws and Legislation—United States
346.7304
    Rosenbaum, David G. 1956–
        Patent Laws and Legislation—United States
            Chelsea House Pub., Philadelphia, 1997
        115p.

            Patents, trademarks, and copyrights: prac-
        tical strategies for protecting your ideas.

Notice the information that the card provides.
1. The title. Since this is a title card, the title is centered in the first line.
2. The call number. This is the Dewey decimal number, which tells you exactly where to find the book.
3. The author. The dates of his birth and death may be shown after his name. (If there is more than one author, the following form is used: Jones, Harold and Smith, Carl.)
4. The title, the publisher, and the place and date of publication.
5. Number of pages. If the book contains illustrations, the label *illustrated* or *illus.* indicates that.
6. A brief description.
Any other information at the bottom of the card is for library personnel.

   2. *Author cards.* Perhaps you do not know the title of the book. You only know that someone had referred to a book about patents, written by David G. Rosenbaum. So you would go to the card catalog and look for an author card. You know that people's names are alphabetized according to the last name, so you look in the drawer that includes words beginning with *Ro.* Every library book that David G. Rosenbaum wrote will have an author card with the book title beneath his name. This card gives the same information as the title card, but the heading of the card is the author's name instead of the book title.

Rosenbaum, David G. 1956–
346.7304
    Patent Laws and Legislation—United States
        Chelsea House Pub., Philadelphia, 1997
    115p.

        Patents, trademarks, and copyrights: practical
    strategies for protecting your ideas.

---

3. *Subject cards.* Perhaps most often you will go to the card catalog, not looking for a specific book title or author's name, but for information on a particular subject. Then you look for subject cards. Most subject cards look just like the title and author cards, except that the subject heads the card. Some subject cards are cross-references, directing you to more specific or otherwise related subjects. A book of fiction, however, has no subject card.

Patent Laws

346.7304
    Rosenbaum, David G. 1956–
       Patent Laws and Legislation—United States
         Chelsea House Pub., Philadelphia, 1997
    115p.

       Patents, trademarks, and copyrights: practical strategies for protecting your ideas.

Most modern libraries no longer have card catalogs. They use microfilm or computer systems instead, but the information is basically the same. If you know how to use the card catalog, you will be able to use the other systems as well.

The *Readers' Guide to Periodical Literature*

A public library has magazines as well as books. Since the world's magazines contain much ungodly material, we generally have little use for them. But sometimes a writer needs up-to-date facts, which he may be able to find in one of the informational magazines available. Then he can use the *Readers' Guide to Periodical Literature,* an index to the contents of more than 150 magazines.

The *Readers' Guide* formerly consisted of booklets published throughout the year, but modern libraries have this index on computer. To use it, a person types in the subject on which he wants information, and the available articles on that subject will appear on the screen.

Remember that you must be prudent in using a public library. Many of the books are unsuitable for godly people, and some will do lasting harm. But if you have parental supervision and a mind filled with Bible truth, you can receive benefit by using a public library.

Applying the Lesson

A. Do the following exercises for each of the catalog cards shown.
    a. Name which kind of card this is.
    b. Write the subject of the main class in the Dewey decimal system to which this book belongs.
    c. Write the author's full name in normal order. If there is more than one author, list each.

d. Write how many pages the book contains.

e. Write whether the book is *illustrated* or *not illustrated.*

1.

Sign Language

419.045

Humphries, Tom

Sign Language—Study and Teaching

      T. J. Pub., Silver Spring, Md., 1989, c.1980

280p. illus.

      A basic course in American sign language.

2.

Grow, Lawrence

728.3

Cottages—Designs and Plans

      Main Street Press, Pittstown, N.J., 1987

127p. illus.

      The old house book of cottages and bungalows.

3.

Man Against Germs

614.4

Baron, A. L., Ph.D.

Man Against Germs

      E. P. Dutton & Co., Inc., New York, 1957

320p.

      The dramatic story of man's war against cholera, tuberculosis, leprosy, bubonic plague, syphilis, typhoid, dysentery, poliomyelitis, smallpox, yellow fever, influenza, typhus, rickettsia.

B. Draw three rectangles on your paper to represent catalog cards. Make one each of the three kinds of cards for the following book.

    Title: *The House of Saud*   Other: 569 pages; illustrated

    Call number: 953.8   Subject: Asian History

    Authors: David Holden and Richard Johns

    Publisher and date: Holt, Rinehart and Winston, New York, 1981

    Description: The rise and rule of the most powerful dynasty in the Arab world.

Lesson 103 Answers
Applying the Lesson

A. 1. a. subject card

    b. Language

    c. Tom Humphries

    d. 280

    e. illustrated

  2. a. author card

    b. Arts and Recreation

    c. Lawrence Grow

    d. 127

    e. illustrated

  3. a. title card

    b. Applied Sciences

    c. A. L. Baron, Ph.D.

    d. 320

    e. not illustrated

B. **Title card:**

      The House of Saud

953.8

Holden, David and Johns, Richard

   The House of Saud

      Holt, Rinehart and Winston, New York, 1981

   569p. illus.

      The rise and rule of the most powerful dynasty in the Arab world.

Author card:

   Holden, David and Johns, Richard

953.8

   The House of Saud

      Holt, Rinehart and Winston, New York, 1981

   569p. illus.

      The rise and rule of the most powerful dynasty in the Arab world.

Subject card:

      Asian History

953.8

Holden, David and Johns, Richard

   The House of Saud

      Holt, Rinehart and Winston, New York, 1981

   569p. illus.

      The rise and rule of the most powerful dynasty in the Arab world.

Review Exercises

Write *true* if the statement is true, or *false* if it is false. [81–85]

1. Careful research in reference books provides the necessary details for effective description.
2. A well-rounded description emphasizes several different impressions.
3. A description of an event usually follows chronological order.
4. Showing the details of a scene of action, rather than telling about them, produces the most effective description.
5. An effective description should give a general, overall view of a scene or an event.
6. The descriptive writer should use exact nouns, expressive verbs, and picturesque modifiers.
7. Descriptive writing is often woven into other kinds of essays.
8. By appealing to the senses, the descriptive writer helps the reader to experience what the author has described.
9. Imagery contributes to description both by making meaningful comparisons and by adding rich color.
10. A descriptive essay is different from other compositions in that it has no introduction or conclusion.

---

104.   Chapter 12 Review

A. Write the correct term for each description.
1. Words with similar meanings.
2. A brief history of a word.
3. The "personality" of a word.
4. The changes in a word to show number, tense, and so forth.
5. Words formed from root words by adding suffixes.
6. The strict, exact meaning of a word.
7. A system of classification for arranging books in a library.
8. The number that a library assigns to a book, based on the Dewey decimal system.
9. Words with opposite meanings.

B. Do these exercises on dictionary use.
1. Why does a word like *die* have more than one numbered entry?
2. What three types of inflections do most dictionaries show?
3. Name the usage labels that fit these descriptions. If more than one label fits, a number in parentheses indicates how many you should have.
   a. Words to avoid because of their association with evil.
   b. Words no longer in general use. (2)
   c. Words coined by people trying to say things in unique ways.
   d. Words to avoid because they represent poor English. (3)
   e. Words used in relatively small areas or by a limited group of people. (2)
   f. Words acceptable only in everyday speaking and everyday writing.

Review Exercises

1. false
2. false
3. true
4. true
5. false
6. true
7. true
8. true
9. true
10. false

Lesson 104 Answers

A. 1. synonyms   6. denotation
   2. etymology   7. Dewey decimal system
   3. connotation   8. call number
   4. inflections   9. antonyms
   5. derivatives

B. (Answers are based on *The American Heritage Dictionary, Third Edition.* Other dictionaries may vary.)
   1. Several words of different origins and meanings have the same spelling. Some dictionaries include a different entry for each part of speech that a word may be.
   2. irregular plural forms of nouns, irregular principal parts of verbs, and irregular forms of comparison for adjectives and adverbs
   3. a. vulgar
      b. archaic, obsolete
      c. slang
      d. nonstandard, substandard, illiterate
      e. regional, dialectal
      f. informal

Lesson 104

Purpose: To review the concepts taught in Chapter 12.

4. Find *league* in the dictionary.
   a. Give the meaning of the original Latin word for the *league* that means "a unit of measure."
   b. Give the meaning of the original Latin word for the *league* that means "an association or alliance."
5. Find the entry for the word *excise* with the meaning "a tax on the production, sale, or consumption of a commodity within a country."
   a. Write the phonetic spelling of this word.
   b. What part of speech is it?
   c. From what language does this word come?
6. Find the entry for the word *excise* with the meaning "to remove by or as if by cutting."
   a. Write the phonetic spelling of this word.
   b. What part of speech is it?
   c. From what language does this word come?
   d. What inflections are shown for this word?
7. What usage labels are given in the entries for these words?
   a. even   c. snag
   b. poke   d. irregardless

C. Do these exercises on using reference books.
   1. What three things should you consider when choosing a synonym from a thesaurus?
   2. What advantage does a Roget's thesaurus have over an alphabetical thesaurus?
   3. Name four research aids found in many encyclopedias.
   4. What two important cautions should you remember about using encyclopedias?
   5. What is the difference between a geographical and a political map?
   6. Using the index, list all the volumes and page numbers where you could find information on the following subjects in the school encyclopedia set.
      a. moon
      b. Alexander Graham Bell
   7. Using an encyclopedia or a statistical almanac, write answers to these questions.
      a. What nation has the largest number of nuclear power plants for electricity?
      b. What is another nation that produces much electricity with nuclear power?
      c. What type of livestock is most important in Oklahoma agriculture?
      d. Where is Niihau Island located?
      e. Where is the day lily a native flower?

D. Do these exercises about libraries.
   1. What are the three important rules for using a library courteously?
   2. Why must you use a library prudently?
   3. List the numbers and the subjects of the ten main groupings in the Dewey decimal system.
   4. What are the two main indexes of a library?

4. a. a measure of distance
   b. to bind
5. a. (ek′•sīz′)
   b. noun
   c. Middle Dutch
6. a. (ik•sīz′)
   b. verb
   c. Latin
   d. excised, excising, excises
7. a. archaic
   b. regional, slang
   c. informal, regional
   d. nonstandard

C. 1. the denotation and connotation, the level of formality, and the range of application
   2. You can often find other words with related or opposite meanings in the entries before and after the one you look up.
   3. cross-references, bibliographies, index, yearbooks
   4. Encyclopedias contain secular and humanistic ideas.
      They provide only general information about a particular subject.
   5. A geographical map shows such things as topography, vegetation, land use, rainfall, climate patterns, and population density.
      A political map shows the boundaries of nations, states, and provinces.
   6. (Answers depend on the encyclopedia used.)
   7. (Answers may vary according to sources used.)
      a. the United States
      b. (Any one.) Canada, France, Great Britain, Japan, Russia, Sweden, West Germany
      c. beef cattle
      d. Hawaii
      e. Europe and Asia

D. 1. Be quiet. Be careful. Be punctual.
   2. Many books in a public library are unwholesome to read.
   3. 000–099 General Works
      100–199 Philosophy
      200–299 Religion
      300–399 Social Sciences
      400–499 Language
      500–599 Pure Sciences
      600–699 Applied Sciences
      700–799 Arts and Recreation
      800–899 Literature
      900–999 Geography and History
   4. card catalog, *Readers' Guide to Periodical Literature*

5. What three types of cards will you find in a card catalog?
6. Classify each item as *reference, fiction,* or *biography.*
   a. Books arranged alphabetically according to the name of the person written about.
   b. Belong mostly to the 000–099 group of the Dewey decimal system.
   c. Imaginary stories.
   d. Books that may be placed in more than one category of the Dewey decimal system.
   e. Includes some books from the 400–499 group of the Dewey decimal system.
   f. Stories about the personal lives of individuals.
   g. Belong to the 800–899 group of the Dewey decimal system.
   h. Books used for looking up facts.
   i. May have the number 92 instead of a Dewey decimal number.
   j. Belong to the 920–929 group of the Dewey decimal system.
   k. Books of general information.
   l. Books arranged alphabetically by the last name of the author.
   m. Have no subject cards.

E. Draw a rectangle to represent an index card. Make a title card for the following book.

   Title: *Fishes and Their Young*
   Call number: 597.14
   Author: Alan Mark Fletcher
   Other: 47 pages, illustrated
   Publisher and date: Addison-Wesley Publishing Company, Inc., Reading, Mass.; 1974
   Description: Describes fascinating ways in which several kinds of fish care for their young.

F. Answer these questions about speaking style.
   1. What are three ways to develop enthusiasm before you speak to a group?
   2. What is one thing that can greatly dampen your enthusiasm?
   3. What are five things that will demonstrate your enthusiasm as you speak to a group?

---

5. title cards, author cards, subject cards
6. a. biography   h. reference
   b. reference   i. biography
   c. fiction   j. biography
   d. reference   k. reference
   e. reference   l. fiction
   f. biography   m. fiction
   g. fiction

E.

Fishes and Their Young
597.14
Fletcher, Alan Mark
Fishes and Their Young
Addison-Wesley Publishing Co., Inc., Reading, Mass., 1974
47p. illus.
Describes fascinating ways in which several kinds of fish care for their young.

F. 1. Choose a subject that interests you. Become thoroughly familiar with your subject.
      Organize your material.
   2. not having your material well organized (*or* not being well prepared to speak)
   3. eye contact, voice inflection, facial expression, gestures, posture

Chapter 13
Connecting Words, Interjections, and Idioms

105. Prepositions and Prepositional Phrases

We use many prepositions to show relationships between substantives and other words in sentences. Prepositions express relationships so precisely that changing a preposition can completely change the meaning of a sentence. Working *with* someone is quite different from working *against* someone. And falling *on* the ice is quite different from falling *through* the ice! A study of these simple but useful words will help you to express your ideas in a clear and meaningful way.

1. *A preposition is a word that shows the relationship between its object and some other word in the sentence.* The following tables show the prepositions used most commonly.

Common Prepositions

aboard	at	by	inside	outside	under
about	before	concerning	into	over	underneath
above	behind	despite	like	past	until
across	below	down	near	since	unto
after	beneath	during	of	through	up
against	beside	except	off	throughout	upon
along	besides	for	on	till	with
among	between	from	onto	to	within
around	beyond	in	out	toward	without
as	but				

Common Compound Prepositions

according to	by means of	in spite of	out of
along with	due to	instead of	owing to
aside from	in addition to	next to	prior to
as of	in front of	on account of	with regard to
because of	in place of		

2. *A prepositional phrase includes the preposition, its object, and any modifiers of the object.* The object of a preposition is the substantive that the preposition relates to another word. You can find it by saying the preposition and then asking *whom* or *what.* If two substantives answer the question, the preposition has a compound object.

Lesson 105

Purpose: To review common prepositions and their uses.

Teaching Suggestions:

This lesson reviews what the students have learned in previous books of this series. Be sure to give sufficient explanation of point 3 (prepositions not coming before their objects) and point 5 (prepositional phrases used as nouns).

In this chapter, the exercises are again divided in the normal odd–even pattern.

The following sentence contains three underlined prepositional phrases. The second one has a compound object, and the third has a compound preposition.

> If the well <u>of our heart</u> is filled <u>with pure thoughts and desires,</u> only pure words will come <u>out of our mouth</u>.

3. *A preposition normally precedes its object, except when the object is an interrogative or a relative pronoun or is modified by one of these.*

> The trust <u>which</u> the poet wrote <u>about</u> is the key to true peace.
> (*About which* modifies *wrote.*)
> <u>What key</u> is this song written <u>in</u>? (*In what key* modifies *is written.*)

4. *The object of a preposition is usually a noun or pronoun, but it may also be a verbal, a verbal phrase, or a noun clause.*

> <u>After picking five bushels of peas,</u> we were quite ready for a break.
> (The object of the preposition *After* is the verbal phrase *picking five bushels of peas.*)
> We must show respect <u>to whomever God grants authority</u>.
> (The object of the preposition *to* is the noun clause *whomever God grants authority.*)

5. *Prepositional phrases can function as adjectives, adverbs, or nouns.* An adjective prepositional phrase usually comes right after the substantive it modifies.

> A brother <u>from our church</u> operates the garage <u>next to Grandfather Bergey's farm</u>.

When an adverb prepositional phrase modifies a verb, it can often be placed at different locations without changing the meaning of the sentence. A phrase that modifies an adjective, an adverb, or a verbal usually comes right after the word it modifies.

> <u>Before breakfast</u> we have our family worship <u>in the living room</u>.
> (The underlined phrases can be moved to other positions.)
> By trusting <u>in God</u>, the martyrs could be courageous <u>beyond their enemies' comprehension</u>. (The underlined phrases cannot be moved to other positions.)

A noun prepositional phrase names a place or a thing and is usually the subject of a sentence with a linking verb.

> <u>In the kitchen</u> is not a good place for those muddy boots!
> (*In the kitchen* names a place for muddy boots not to be; it is the subject of the sentence.)
> <u>After seven o'clock</u> will be a good time to arrive.
> (*After seven o'clock* names the time for arriving; it is the subject of the sentence.)

6. *Several prepositional phrases in succession can be either a series of independent phrases or one unit of phrases.* In a series of independent phrases, each phrase modifies the same word. In a unit of phrases, each successive phrase is actually part of the first phrase, modifying the object in the previous prepositional phrase. Study the following examples.

The chickens are scratching <u>in the dirt</u> <u>for food</u>.
  (*In the dirt* and *for food* are independent modifiers of *are scratching*.)

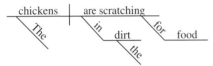

We ate our lunch <u>in the shade of a huge willow beside the river</u>.
  (*In the shade of a huge willow beside the river* is a unit modifying *ate;*
  of a huge willow modifies *shade; beside the river* modifies *willow*.)

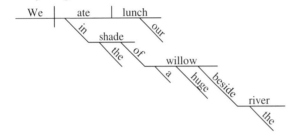

7. *Do not confuse prepositions with adverbs.* If the word is used alone to tell *when* or *where,* it is an adverb. It can be a preposition only if it has an object.

Adverbs:
  We should get <u>off</u> at the next station.
  We looked <u>inside,</u> but we could not find Timothy.
Prepositions:
  We should get <u>off the train</u> at the next station.
  We looked <u>inside the garage,</u> but we could not find Timothy.

8. *Do not confuse prepositional phrases beginning with* to *with infinitives. To* is part of an infinitive when a verb form follows it. *To* is a preposition when a substantive follows it.

Sharon hurried <u>to</u> the kitchen <u>to</u> prepare a quick lunch.
  (*To the kitchen* is a prepositional phrase; *to prepare a quick lunch* is an
  infinitive phrase.)

Applying the Lesson

A. Copy each prepositional phrase. If a phrase is part of a longer phrase, include it with the longer phrase, and also copy it separately. Label each phrase *adj., adv.,* or *n.*

1. Throughout human history, men have sought by various means to ignore their accountability to the Creator.
2. Deceived by the devil, many have vainly tried to cast God down from His throne.
3. Under God's blessing is the only place of true safety and satisfaction.
4. Whom shall we look to in difficult times when we face problems beyond our ability to solve?
5. The narrow valley between these two mountain ridges includes several farms with fertile fields.
6. Before sunrise is my favorite time to get up.
7. William H. Prescott, the son of a wealthy judge in Massachusetts, became a historian worthy of admiration.
8. In the middle 1800s, Prescott published four major histories in spite of being nearly blind.
9. Because of his handicap, his secretary read for him the resource materials that he used.
10. To write his notes in somewhat legible form, Prescott used a noctograph—a frame with guide wires across its width.
11. After taking his notes, Prescott had his secretary recopy them in large letters.
12. At some times, he was able to read those notes; but usually his secretary read them repeatedly until Prescott had them fixed in his memory.
13. The remarkable power of his memory is also evident in his writing method; he wrote each paragraph mentally until an entire chapter had taken shape within his mind.
14. On his noctograph, Prescott swiftly wrote the chapter; then his secretary read the copy, corrected it according to Prescott's directions, and recopied it in its final form.

B. Copy each underlined word, and label it *adv.* or *prep.*
1. We climbed <u>aboard</u> the train, and soon after leaving the station <u>behind</u>, we were speeding <u>across</u> the prairie.
2. A bitter wind blew <u>down</u> from the mountains, driving cold air <u>through</u> the thin walls of the cabin and bringing snowflakes <u>inside</u>.
3. The beautiful weather <u>outside</u> matches the joy <u>inside</u> my heart.
4. The Bible verse <u>over</u> the clock helps to lift our thoughts <u>above</u> to the eternal realities.

Review Exercises

A. Copy each underlined verb or verb phrase, and write whether its mood is indicative (*ind.*), imperative (*imp.*), or subjunctive (*sub.*). [75]
1. Brother Leland <u>requested</u> that each of us <u>pray</u> for his elderly mother.
2. <u>Will</u> you please <u>clean</u> up the water that you <u>spilled</u>.
3. If I <u>were</u> to give you too much help, <u>consider</u> how little you would actually learn.
4. Even if a man <u>live</u> to be a thousand years old, he <u>can</u> never <u>learn</u> all there is to learn.

Lesson 105 Answers
Applying the Lesson

A. 1. Throughout human history—adv.;
      by various means—adv.;
      to the Creator—adj.
   2. by the devil—adv.;
      from His throne—adv.
   3. Under God's blessing—n.;
      of true safety and satisfaction—adj.
   4. to Whom—adv.;
      in difficult times—adv.;
      beyond our ability to solve—adj.
   5. between these two mountain
         ridges—adj.;
      with fertile fields—adj.
   6. Before sunrise—n.
   7. of a wealthy judge in
         Massachusetts—adj.;
      in Massachusetts—adj.;
      of admiration—adv.
   8. In the middle 1800s—adv.;
      in spite of being nearly blind—adv.
   9. Because of his handicap—adv.;
      for him—adv.
  10. in somewhat legible form—adv.;
      with guide wires across its width—adj.;
      across its width—adj.
  11. After taking his notes—adv.;
      in large letters—adv.
  12. At some times—adv.;
      in his memory—adv.
  13. of his memory—adj.;
      in his writing method—adv.;
      within his mind—adv.
  14. On his noctograph—adv.;
      according to Prescott's directions—adv.;
      in its final form—adv.

B. 1. aboard—prep.; behind—adv.;
      across—prep.
   2. down—adv.; through—prep.;
      inside—adv.
   3. outside—adv.; inside—prep.
   4. over—prep.; above—adv.

Review Exercises

A. 1. requested—ind.; pray—sub.
   2. Will clean—imp.; spilled—ind.
   3. were—sub.; consider—imp.
   4. live—sub.; can learn—ind.

B. Write the words that are correct for the subjunctive mood. [75]
1. Biblical discipleship requires that the Christian (keep, keeps) himself free from worldliness.
2. We would be completely snowed in if this rain (was, were) all snow.
3. When Father was a boy, Grandfather required that his hired hand (go, went) to church.
4. If this cat (is, be) truly the queen of the barn, let her keep the mice under control.

C. Write a subjunctive verb or verb phrase to replace each underlined *would* phrase. [75]
1. The whole family would attend cousin Lucinda's wedding if that <u>would be</u> possible.
2. I move that a committee <u>would be appointed</u> to investigate the possibility of purchasing land to enlarge our parking lot.
3. Grandmother would appreciate if Sharon <u>would be</u> available to help her with housecleaning on Saturday.
4. Mrs. Williams would have come to the meeting if we <u>would have told</u> her about it.

B. 1. keep
   2. were
   3. go
   4. be

C. 1. were
   2. be appointed
   3. were
   4. had told

---

106. Coordinating Conjunctions

Coordinating conjunctions usually are small words, but they may join major sentence parts together. The joined parts are *coordinate;* that is, they have a definite equality. Coordinating conjunctions join sentence parts so that they can work unitedly together.

1. *Coordinating conjunctions join sentence parts and show the relationships between those parts.* The common coordinating conjunctions are *and, but, or, for, nor, yet,* and *so. And* shows addition or continuing thought; *but* and *yet* show contrast or unexpected outcome; *or* and *nor* show choice or option; *for* and *so* show cause and effect.

2. *Coordinating conjunctions join sentence parts of parallel structure and function.* Parallel structure means that the joined parts are both words, prepositional phrases, gerund phrases, dependent clauses, and so forth. Parallel function means that the joined parts both function as subjects, verbs, predicate nominatives, adverbs, and so forth.

> *Faith <u>and</u> works* complement each other in true Biblical obedience.
>   (*And* joins single words used as subjects.)
> People *trusting themselves <u>or</u> ignoring Bible teaching* cannot be saved.
>   (*Or* joins participial phrases used as adjectives.)
> *The obedience of faith is a concept easy to grasp,* <u>yet</u> *many stumble at its simplicity.* (*Yet* joins independent clauses.)

Lesson 106

Purpose: To review the use of common coordinating conjunctions, correlative conjunctions, and conjunctive adverbs.

Sometimes writers or speakers use a coordinating conjunction to join a word to a phrase or a phrase to a clause. This is improper because the structure of the two parts is different. Correct the mistake either by making the joined parts parallel or by rewriting the sentence.

Incorrect:
> The wind, *bitterly cold* <u>and</u> *showing furious strength,* piled the snow into deep drifts. (word joined to phrase)

Correct:
> The wind, *bitterly cold* <u>and</u> *furiously strong,* piled the snow into deep drifts.
> Showing furious strength, the bitterly cold wind piled the snow into deep drifts.

3. *When a coordinating conjunction joins the clauses in a compound sentence, a comma is usually needed before the conjunction.* If the two clauses are very short and closely related, you may omit the comma. If one or both of the clauses already have several commas, you may need to use a semicolon to show clearly the division between the clauses. Study the following sentences.

> Our words should be wholesome, and our tone of voice should be gracious.
> (normal compound sentence)
> Kind words bring cheer but harsh words bring grief.
> (short clauses; no comma needed)
> If we frequently let idle or thoughtless words slip from our tongue, we should examine our heart; for when the heart is well guarded, the tongue does not slip. (other commas; semicolon used)

4. *Correlative conjunctions are coordinating conjunctions that work in pairs.* Like the common coordinating conjunctions, correlative conjunctions show how the joined items are related. *Both—and* shows addition or continuing thought; *not only—but also* shows addition, with greater emphasis on the second item; *either—or, neither—nor,* and *whether—or* show choice or option.

5. *Be careful to place correlative conjunctions just before the sentence parts that they join.* If you put them in the wrong place, they will appear to join unparallel parts.

Incorrect:
> This finishing job <u>both</u> *requires* sandpaper <u>and</u> *steel wool.*
> <u>Either</u> *you* pushed down too hard <u>or</u> *sanded* across the grain on this piece.

Correct:
> This finishing job requires <u>both</u> *sandpaper* <u>and</u> *steel wool.*
> You <u>either</u> *pushed* down too hard <u>or</u> *sanded* across the grain on this piece.

6. *When using* not only—but also, *be careful not to omit the word* also.

Incorrect: This cake is <u>not only</u> *moist* <u>but</u> *tasty.*
Correct: This cake is <u>not only</u> *moist* <u>but also</u> *tasty.*

7. *With the correlative conjunction* whether—or, *the second item is often elliptical.* Because of the missing words, the joined sentence parts may appear to have unequal structure when in fact they are parallel.

> Margaret is not sure <u>whether</u> *to make spice cake* <u>or</u> *pound cake.*
> (Meaning: <u>whether</u> to make spice cake <u>or</u> to make pound cake)
> <u>Whether</u> *the service begins at 7:00* <u>or</u> *7:30,* we should start chores early.
> (Meaning: <u>whether</u> the service begins at 7:00 <u>or</u> the service begins at 7:30)

8. *Conjunctive adverbs function as both conjunctions and adverbs.* The following words are often used as conjunctive adverbs.

accordingly	henceforth	namely
afterward	however	nevertheless
also	indeed	otherwise
anyway	instead	still
besides	likewise	then
consequently	meanwhile	therefore
furthermore	moreover	thus
hence		

Conjunctive adverbs join independent clauses and show specific relationships between the clauses. A semicolon always precedes the conjunctive adverb, and a comma often follows it. If the sentence reads smoothly without a pause after the conjunctive adverb, you may omit the comma.

> Our carnal nature pulls us toward the world; <u>nevertheless</u>, we can choose to surrender our will to God's will.
> When we trust in the Lord, we receive power to overcome sin; <u>then</u> we can be more than conquerors.

Conjunctive adverbs are not considered true conjunctions, for they can be moved to different positions in a sentence. (True conjunctions must come between the sentence parts they join.) In one sense, a sentence with a conjunctive adverb simply has two clauses joined by a semicolon, with the conjunctive adverb modifying the verb in the second clause. Consider the following examples.

> The day was quite warm, yet a light breeze brought us welcome relief.
> (*Yet* cannot be moved; it is a true conjunction.)
> The day was quite warm; however, a light breeze brought us welcome relief.
> The day was quite warm; a light breeze, however, brought us welcome relief.
> (*However* can be moved; it is not a true conjunction. It modifies *brought.*)

Applying the Lesson

A. Copy the conjunctions, and label them *CC* (common coordinating conjunction), *Cor* (correlative conjunction), or *CA* (conjunctive adverb).
   1. A mirage is an illusion that can occur either on land or on water.

Lesson 106 Answers
Applying the Lesson
A. 1. either—or—Cor

2. The most common mirage is the deceptive appearance of water; indeed, many a weary desert traveler has been fooled by a mirage.
3. When the atmosphere is clear, calm, and dry, the heat of the earth warms a layer of air near the earth; however, the air at a person's eye level remains a bit cooler.
4. These layers of air have both differing temperatures and differing optical densities, so the light rays are refracted as they pass from one layer to another.
5. The mirage is actually light rays from the sky, but those rays appear to originate on the ground because of the way they are refracted.
6. Another kind of mirage can occur over cold water and is called a looming.
7. The air next to the water is colder than the air higher up; consequently, refraction causes a reversing of the image that results.
8. A ship beyond the horizon not only becomes visible but also appears in the sky, upside down!

B. Write enough of each sentence to show how to correct the mistake in it.
1. We should trust the Lord simply and without reserve.
2. We cannot direct our own steps but God will direct us if we trust Him.
3. If we truly trust the Lord, we will neither fear the threats nor the power of the enemy.
4. The Lord is well able to direct our steps in our youth and as we grow older.
5. God is well able to meet all our needs, moreover, He delights to do us good.
6. We either allow God to provide for us, or our deepest needs remain unmet.
7. The little children played quietly and without fighting.
8. Uncle Curvin sent me not only a birthday card but an interesting letter.
9. This story both illustrates a good plot and effective characterization.
10. If it does not rain tomorrow, we shall plant corn, otherwise we shall need to wait.
11. Glenda has gone to prepare lunch so Gordon and I will have to finish picking these beans.
12. This afternoon, the boys should either hoe the corn or the lima beans.
13. Uncle Brandon writes both poems and composes music.
14. The boys not only washed the outside of the car but cleaned the inside.

Review Exercises

Write whether each underlined adverb modifies a *verb*, a *verbal*, an *adjective*, an *adverb*, a *preposition*, a *conjunction*, or an entire *sentence*. [91, 92]
1. The muskellunge is an <u>unusually</u> large freshwater fish <u>often</u> sought by anglers.
2. <u>Perhaps</u> you are more familiar with the term *muskie,* a nickname used <u>quite</u> commonly.
3. Muskellunge live <u>only</u> in three North American watersheds: the Great Lakes–St. Lawrence, the upper Mississippi River, and the Ohio River.
4. A <u>fully</u> mature muskie may weigh sixty pounds and grow <u>nearly</u> to a length of six feet.

2. indeed—CA
3. and—CC; however—CA
4. both—and—Cor; so—CC
5. but—CC
6. and—CC
7. consequently—CA
8. not only—but also—Cor

B. (Corrections are underlined.)
1. and <u>unreservedly</u>
2. steps, but
3. will fear <u>neither</u> the threats nor the power
4. <u>when we are young</u> (*or* and <u>in our old age</u>)
5. needs;
6. <u>Either</u> we
7. and <u>peaceably</u> (*or* played <u>with little noise</u>)
8. but <u>also</u>
9. illustrates <u>both</u>
10. corn; otherwise, (Comma is optional.)
11. lunch,
12. hoe <u>either</u>
13. <u>both</u> writes
14. but <u>also</u>

Review Exercises
1. adjective; verbal (*or* adjective)
2. verb; adverb
3. preposition
4. adjective; preposition

5. <u>Obviously</u>, hooking this fish is not something to take <u>lightly</u>!
6. Muskellunge feed freely on <u>almost</u> any food they can swallow; <u>indeed</u>, they have been known to swallow muskrats.
7. <u>How</u> does this large fish catch its prey?
8. A muskellunge will lie quietly in a shaded spot; then <u>almost</u> before you can see what is happening, the muskie rushes out, snapping <u>up</u> the unsuspecting prey.

5. sentence; verbal
6. adjective; verb
7. verb
8. conjunction; verbal

107. Subordinating Conjunctions and Interjections

A subordinating conjunction joins clauses of unequal rank. The clause it introduces is *subordinate* to the rest of the sentence; that is, its function is less important than that of the main clause. The clause that a subordinating conjunction introduces cannot stand alone but has meaning only in relation to the rest of the sentence.

Subordinating Conjunctions

1. *A subordinating conjunction joins a dependent adverb clause to the independent clause in a complex sentence.* The following list shows a number of the most common subordinating conjunctions. Many of these words may also be used as adverbs or prepositions. They are subordinating conjunctions only when they introduce dependent clauses.

after	even if	so that	when
although	even though	than	whenever
as	how	that	where
as if	if	though	wherever
as though	in order that	till	whether
because	provided	unless	while
before	since	until	

2. *A subordinating conjunction shows a specific relationship between the dependent clause and the independent clause.* These relationships include *when, where, how, why, under what condition, in spite of what,* and *to what degree.*

We should treat others <u>*as* we want them to treat us.</u>
  (*As* links the dependent clause to the independent clause by telling *how* about *should treat.*)
Even though others mistreat us, we should return good for evil.
  (*Even though* links the dependent clause to the independent clause by telling *under what condition* about *should return.*)
The Lord Jesus suffered more intensely <u>*than* we ever have.</u>
  (*Than* links the dependent clause to the independent clause by telling *to what degree* about *more intensely.*)

Lesson 107

Purpose: To review the use of subordinating conjunctions and interjections.

Teaching Suggestions:

This lesson consists entirely of review. In teaching against the improper use of interjections, you might mention specific ones that you hear used by your students or in the local church community.

3. *A subordinating conjunction often provides a more effective link between clauses than does the coordinating conjunction* and. The word *and* provides a quick and handy way to join words and word groups. But *and* merely indicates one idea added to another, whereas subordinating conjunctions allow you to express a great variety of more specific relationships.

> **Vague:** Merely adds one idea to another
>> Douglas will fetch the ax, and Dennis will start stacking the smaller pieces of wood.
>
> **Specific:** Shows exact time relationship
>> While Douglas fetches the ax, Dennis will start stacking the smaller pieces of wood.

4. *When a dependent clause comes at the beginning of a complex sentence, a comma separates it from the independent clause.* Two commas are used if the dependent clause comes in the middle. But if the clause comes at the end of the sentence, no comma is needed.

> If we can remember, we should call Grandmother and tell her the news.
> We should call Grandmother, if we can remember, and tell her the news.
> We should call Grandmother and tell her the news if we can remember.

Interjections

1. *An interjection is a word that expresses strong feeling.* The cry or exclamation of an interjection may express pleasure, admiration, adoration, surprise, pain, or any other feeling. The following list shows some common interjections.

ah	good	lo	well
aha	ha	oh	what
alas	hallelujah	ouch	whew
amen	ho	say	why
behold	hurrah		

> Lo, our tender Shepherd guides us faithfully.
> Ah, what a privilege to trust His all-wise care!
> Alas! How often we tend to take our own way!

Words that represent sounds also frequently serve as interjections. Such a word is followed by an exclamation point or a period, depending on the intensity of the sound. Also, the word is italicized because it is "quoting" a sound. No italics are needed when such a word simply names a sound, as in the fourth example below.

> *Crack!* A large branch suddenly gave way under its heavy load of ice.
> *Knock, knock.* Who would be at the door this early in the morning?
> *Ring! Ring!* The telephone interrupted my thoughts.
> The loud ring of the telephone startled me.
>> (a noun that names a sound; no italics needed)

Actually, almost any word can function as an interjection if it is used as an independent exclamation. But if a verb gives a one-word request or command, it is a complete sentence, not an interjection.

<u>Salt</u>! No, I do not want salt on my watermelon. (interjection)
<u>Run</u>! I was so frightened that I could not even move! (interjection)
<u>Run</u>! A rainstorm is coming! (one-word command; a complete sentence)

2. *The use of commas and exclamation points with interjections depends on the degree of emotion intended by the writer.* Exclamation points mark strong interjections. The words *amen, hallelujah, hurrah, ouch, what,* and *whew* are usually strong exclamations, and so are words that represent sounds. If you use an exclamation point, capitalize the next word. Commas mark mild interjections. Many interjections can be used either way.

<u>Well</u>, this job might take you boys a half hour of hard work.
<u>Well</u>! You boys must have worked really hard if the job is finished already.

If the whole sentence shows strong feeling, you may use a comma after the interjection and an exclamation point at the end of the sentence. You may also use two exclamation points as in the second example below. But you must not overdo this in writing, for exclamation points should be used sparingly.

Oh<u>,</u> if only we had not been so careless<u>!</u>
Oh<u>!</u> If only we had not been so careless<u>!</u>

If an interjection comes in the middle of a compound sentence, set it off with commas.

In the darkest hour, we can look to the Lord; and<u>,</u> lo<u>,</u> He is there.

3. *Use interjections cautiously and sparingly.* They can easily become idle words of which we must give an account, and they can even fall into the category of profanity. Avoid the following kinds of interjections:
   a. The name of God or any alteration of it.
   b. Words that refer to characteristics of God.
   c. Words that refer to hell, Satan, or any part of his kingdom.
   d. Common words used as interjections that have nothing to do with their normal meanings. Words such as *boy, man,* and *rats* are sometimes used in that way.

Even interjections that are proper in themselves can be used in a wrong way. For example, it is improper to use *amen* and *hallelujah* in a light or carnal way. Also, the Bible commands us to control our emotions and our words. We need to avoid any exclamation of anger or disgust, no matter how acceptable the word itself may be.

Applying the Lesson
A. Copy each dependent clause, and underline the subordinating conjunction.
   1. Although godly children have always honored their mothers, the idea of a nationally recognized Mother's Day is more recent than you might suppose.

Lesson 107 Answers
Applying the Lesson
A. 1. <u>Although</u> godly children have always honored their mothers;
        <u>than</u> you might suppose

2. Anna Jarvis was born in 1864 at Grafton, West Virginia; however, when her father died in 1902, her mother moved the family to Philadelphia to live with relatives.

3. After her mother died in 1905, Anna was grief stricken.

4. Though she was apparently an exemplary daughter, Anna felt as if she had not honored her mother sufficiently.

5. She pondered those feelings for two years until they bore fruit in the first public call for a national Mother's Day.

6. Because the second Sunday of May marked the anniversary of her mother's death, Miss Jarvis chose that day for a meeting with her friends so that she could introduce her proposal.

7. If she harbored any doubts about her plan, they were dispelled as her friends enthusiastically supported the idea.

8. As Miss Jarvis desired, her church held a large Mother's Day service one year later in Grafton, West Virginia.

9. The idea of an annual Mother's Day became popular more quickly than some other proposed holidays have.

10. Because it gained such strong support, in 1914 President Wilson signed legislation designating the second Sunday of May as Mother's Day.

B. Rewrite each sentence, joining the clauses with a suitable subordinating conjunction instead of with *and.* Be sure to use commas correctly. You may change the order of the clauses if you wish.

1. We need to catch a glimpse of God's holiness, and we can live before Him in righteousness.

2. We truly love God, and we do not hanker after the things of the world.

3. God is love, and He will judge all wickedness.

4. Jesus Christ lived as a man upon earth, and He manifested the Father.

5. Brother Clyde's had left, and we discovered that they had left Sister Bonnie's purse behind.

6. We are remodeling our house, and Grandfather will come to live with us.

7. The new song was a little hard to learn, and we sang the melody several times.

8. We climbed the high hill behind Uncle Arlen's place, and we could see the whole valley.

C. Copy each interjection, the word before it (if there is one), and the word after it. Use correct capitalization and punctuation, and underline any word that should be italicized.

1. Lo our heavenly Father tenderly cares for us in every experience of life.

2. When we hardly know what to do, we can turn to God; and behold He will always be there.

3. Hallelujah our God will never fail us!

4. What shall we doubt a promise of the Lord God?

5. Though the enemy oppose God's children, he cannot prevail; and lo God always makes a way for them.

2. <u>when</u> her father died in 1902

3. <u>After</u> her mother died in 1905

4. <u>Though</u> she was apparently an exemplary daughter;

   <u>as if</u> she had not honored her mother sufficiently

5. <u>until</u> they bore fruit in the first public call for a national Mother's Day

6. <u>Because</u> the second Sunday of May marked the anniversary of her mother's death;

   <u>so that</u> she could introduce her proposal

7. <u>If</u> she harbored any doubts about her plan;

   <u>as</u> her friends enthusiastically supported the idea

8. <u>As</u> Miss Jarvis desired

9. <u>than</u> some other proposed holidays have

10. <u>Because</u> it gained such strong support

B. (Sample answers. It would be good to discuss the varying effects of the conjunctions chosen by the students.)

1. We need to catch a glimpse of God's holiness so that we can live before Him in righteousness.

2. If we truly love God, we do not hanker after the things of the world.

3. Although God is love, He will judge all wickedness.

4. While Jesus Christ lived as a man upon earth, He manifested the Father.

5. After Brother Clyde's had left, we discovered that they had left Sister Bonnie's purse behind.

6. Because Grandfather will come to live with us, we are remodeling our house.

7. Because the new song was a little hard to learn, we sang the melody several times.

8. We climbed the high hill behind Uncle Arlen's place so that we could see the whole valley.

C. 1. Lo, our

2. and, behold, He

3. Hallelujah! Our

4. What! Shall

5. and, lo, God

6. Astronomy this field of science has impressed me in a new way with God's infinite greatness.
7. Whoosh the snow sliding off the roof startled the entire family.
8. Ouch that low-hanging pipe gave my head quite a blow!
9. Wonderful we are planning a trip to Alberta this summer!
10. Caw the startled crow complained noisily about my intrusion.

6. Astronomy! This
7. <u>Whoosh</u>! The
8. Ouch! That
9. Wonderful! We
10. <u>Caw</u>! The

Review Exercises

Label each underlined verb *TA* (transitive, active voice), *TP* (transitive, passive voice), *IC* (intransitive complete), or *IL* (intransitive linking). [76]

1. A new day <u>has dawned</u> to God's glory.
2. God has graciously <u>tended</u> our restful hours, giving us peaceful sleep.
3. The eastern sky <u>grows</u> brighter as the moment of daybreak <u>nears</u>.
4. The clouds in the east <u>are being painted</u> in brilliant shades of pink, magenta, and purple.
5. Every sunrise <u>is</u> a testimony to God's faithfulness.

Review Exercises
1. IC
2. TA
3. IL; IC
4. TP
5. IL

---

108. Idioms

Have you ever said, "I am going to stay at home"? What did you mean? Where are you *going* if you intend to *stay*? This expression is quite familiar to any fluent speaker of the English language, and it is a perfectly acceptable English construction. Yet if you analyze it word by word, you will find that it makes no sense. Welcome to the fascinating study of idioms.

An **idiom** is an expression that cannot be explained grammatically or logically, yet it is an established part of a language. We learned English idioms naturally as we learned to speak the language. In fact, if a person makes errors in the use of common idioms, it is a sign that he does not know the language well.

Many idioms contain common words like *come, put, up,* and *down.* These words provide a handy way to communicate ideas that may require clumsy or unnatural wording to express in any other way. Read the examples below, with special attention to the natural, everyday tone of the sentences in the first group.

Sentences With Idioms:
How did you <u>come up with</u> that idea?
Wilma <u>came down with</u> a severe cold.
One boy fainted but soon <u>came to</u>.
Yesterday's work really <u>put us to it</u>.
Who <u>put</u> your little brother <u>up</u> to say that?

Sentences Without Idioms:
How did you devise that idea?
Wilma became sick with a severe cold.
One boy fainted but soon regained consciousness.
Yesterday's work really taxed us.
Who prompted your little brother to say that?

Lesson 108

Purpose: To introduce *idioms and to teach the recognition of some common idioms.

Teaching Suggestions:

The word *idiom* comes from a Greek word that means "peculiar to oneself." *Idiom* has two distinct but related meanings. An *idiom,* as defined in the lesson, is an expression that cannot be explained grammatically or logically. Some idioms are difficult if not impossible to diagram. For example, how would you diagram the following expressions?

all of a sudden   came in handy
left it up to Father   going to ask

Many idioms make no sense if one analyzes them according to the literal definitions of each word. For example, what do you visualize when you attempt to read the following as literal statements?

I can't lay my eyes on it now.
Did you catch a cold?
A hammer would come in handy.
The paper caught fire.

The second meaning of *idiom* refers to the characteristic structure of a particular language. With this usage, we refer not to *an idiom* but to *the idiom* of a language. The characteristic structure of one language differs from that of another language. For example, according to Spanish idiom, most

The stress was <u>bearing down on</u> Mr. Neal.	The stress was heavily burdening Mr. Neal.
Still, he <u>turned down</u> our offer to help.	Still, he refused our offer to help.
We stayed inside until the rain <u>let up</u>.	We stayed inside until the rain ceased.
Do not get <u>worked up</u> over such a trifle.	Do not get agitated over such a trifle.
Father <u>cut up</u> the tree to make firewood.	Father cut the tree in pieces to make firewood.

The illogical nature of many idioms is illustrated especially well by the last sentence. When we turn a tree into firewood, we first *cut it down* and then we *cut it up*! There are dozens of other idioms that are no more logical than these. Here are just a few of the many that you use in your everyday speaking and writing.

Other Idiomatic Expressions:
Mother asked me to <u>keep an eye on</u> the younger children. (watch carefully)
<u>By the way</u>, who was that lady on the back bench? (incidentally)
The clerk seemed to be <u>out of sorts</u> for some reason. (irritable)
Daniel <u>made up his mind</u> to be faithful at any cost. (determined)

Idiomatic Usage

The proper use of prepositions is often a matter of correct idioms. In other words, certain prepositions are "correct" or "incorrect" not because of their meanings but simply because of what is established as proper usage. This is the basis for a number of rules in the "Glossary of Usage" (Chapter 5). Here are three examples.

A person may be angry <u>with</u> another person, angry <u>about</u> a situation or an event, and angry <u>at</u> an animal or an inanimate object.
When observing literal similarities or differences, we compare one thing <u>with</u> another. When making figurative comparisons, we compare one thing <u>to</u> another.
One thing may differ <u>from</u> another. One person may differ <u>with</u> another.

Use the dictionary when you are not sure about an expression. Many advanced dictionaries have run-in entries that show established idioms. For example, the entry for *line* may include the following run-in entries at the end.

— **line up,** (1) To form a line. (2) To organize: *line up some people to help.*
— **down the line,** (1) Throughout. (2) In the future: *expect a harvest down the line.*
— **in line for,** Next in order for: *in line for spending the weekend with Grandfather.*
— **on the line,** (1) Ready for immediate payment. (2) In jeopardy: *put his life on the line.*

adjectives follow the nouns they modify; but according to English idiom, adjectives usually precede nouns. In this sense, the term *idiom* has much in common with *syntax.*

Applying the Lesson

A. Each of these sentences contains an expression that is not in natural, everyday language. Copy that phrase, and after it write an idiom with a form of *fall*, which could replace it.

1. The heavy snow caused many roofs to collapse toward the inside.
2. During a power outage, we can resort to using our coal furnace.
3. Because of a dispute over land, the neighbors ceased being friendly with each other.
4. Do not be deceived by that salesman's glowing promises.
5. If you miss many days of school, you will fail to keep current in your work.
6. We had hoped that all the cousins could travel together, but our plans met with failure.

B. Write the meaning of each underlined expression. You may use a dictionary.

1. Father has reminded us <u>time and again</u> to be careful with fire.
2. The secretary <u>summed up</u> the discussion in the minutes of the meeting.
3. Do not <u>pick holes in</u> your brother's ideas just because he is younger than you.
4. The second blizzard came <u>right on the heels of</u> the previous one.
5. This new bypass should <u>do away with</u> much of the congestion in the city.
6. The hunter stayed <u>on his guard</u> for wolves and panthers.
7. The teacher pointed out my mistake without <u>beating around the bush</u>.
8. Though the church building is not finished, it is well <u>under way</u>.

C. Rewrite each sentence so that it expresses the same thought without an idiom.

1. We could hardly make out what the sign said.
2. The rescue workers had to pick their way through the rubble.
3. It seemed like a hopeless situation, but the leader's suggestion carried the day.
4. Aunt Tina's remark made us wonder what plans she had up her sleeve.
5. If we all dig in right away, doing these dishes will not take long.
6. Every Christian should live up to his profession.
7. When our car engine blew a head gasket, we were out on a limb because we still had two hundred miles to go.
8. When planning any trip, you should take into account the possibility of unexpected delays.
9. I only lent you my special pocketknife; I did not give it to you for keeps.
10. When Brother Stephen became sick, Brother Dale filled his shoes very well.

Review Exercises

A. Copy the correct participle for each sentence. [90]

1. (Running, Having run) smoothly hour after hour, the generator is providing us electricity while the blizzard rages.
2. (Spending, Having spent) over an hour searching for Betsy's lost kitten, we finally gave up.
3. These pancakes, (frying, fried) to perfection, are delicious.
4. The bacon, (sizzling, sizzled) in the pan, is filling the house with an appetizing aroma.

Lesson 108 Answers
Applying the Lesson

A. 1. collapse toward the inside—fall in
   2. resort to using—fall back on
   3. ceased being friendly—fell out
   4. be deceived by—fall for
   5. fail to keep current—fall behind
   6. met with failure—fell through

B. 1. many times; repeatedly
   2. summarized
   3. find fault with
   4. directly behind; immediately after
   5. eliminate
   6. alert; watchful
   7. speaking indirectly
   8. in progress

C. (Sample answers. Rewritten expressions are underlined.)

1. We could hardly <u>read (decipher)</u> what the sign said.
2. The rescue workers had to <u>walk carefully</u> through the rubble. (An expression like "make their way" is still an idiom.)
3. It seemed like a hopeless situation, but the leader's suggestion <u>brought success</u>.
4. Aunt Tina's remark made us wonder what <u>hidden</u> plans she had.
5. If we all <u>work hard</u> right away, doing these dishes will not take long.
6. Every Christian should <u>live a life that matches</u> his profession.
7. When our car engine blew a head gasket, we were <u>in a difficult position (helpless)</u> because we still had two hundred miles to go.
8. When planning any trip, you should <u>consider</u> the possibility of unexpected delays.
9. I only lent you my special pocketknife; I did not give it to you <u>permanently</u>.
10. When Brother Stephen became sick, Brother Dale <u>replaced him</u> very well.

Review Exercises

A. 1. Running
   2. Having spent
   3. fried
   4. sizzling

B. Copy each word that should be followed by a comma, and add the comma. If the sentence needs no comma, write *correct*. [90, 93]

1. Clinging thickly to everything the hoarfrost turned the countryside into a dazzling wonderland.

2. Our visitors from the South were especially impressed when they saw the lovely scene.

3. All the students who failed this test must do some remedial work.

4. After they have completed those exercises they will take another test on this material.

5. This old farmhouse built by Great-grandfather Lutz has some huge stones in the walls.

6. Leon Wagner whose farm borders ours on the west is a kind, helpful neighbor.

C. Write enough words to show how to correct the mistakes in adjective and adverb comparisons. [95]

1. Most things are more cheaper at Springway Grocery Outlet than at other area stores.

2. Theodore is doing his work more careful now than he did when he first worked here.

3. James is the oldest of the two tenth grade boys in our school.

4. With a score of 98%, Lisa had the most perfect grade of all us students.

5. Canada is larger than any nation in North America.

6. The weather is delightfuller today than it has been all week.

B. 1. everything,
2. correct
3. correct
4. exercises,
5. farmhouse, Lutz,
6. Wagner, west,

C. 1. are cheaper
2. more carefully
3. older
4. most nearly perfect
5. any other nation
6. more delightful

---

109. Improving Your Writing Style, Part 6: Review

Originality
Active Verbs
Active Voice
Poetic Devices
Rhythm

In your previous writing style lessons, you have studied five elements of an effective writing style. This lesson reviews those elements.

1. Originality

You should not always use the first wording that comes to your mind. Rather, look for fresh, creative ways of expressing yourself—ways deliberately designed to add appeal. Sprinkle your creativity like salt throughout your writing, always remembering to keep your imagination within proper bounds. The added life in your compositions will be well worth the extra time and effort.

In your pursuit of originality, beware that you do not merely use clichés—expressions that once were clever but that now have lost their sparkle through too much use. Surely you do not want your writing to be *as dead as a doornail* because you have written everything *off the top of your head*!

Lesson 109

Purpose: To review the elements of an effective writing style.

2. Active Verbs

Remember to examine your use of the verb *be*. Whenever practical, reword sentences containing *there is, there are, there was,* and *there were,* as well as sentences with *be* as a main verb. Every time you replace *be* with an action verb, you add more life to your writing. If the verb in a sentence must *be* a linking verb, it will *grow* more appealing if you replace it with a linking verb that suggests action (*sound, look, remain,* and so forth).

3. Active Voice

Deliberately use verbs in the active voice. Passive verbs produce dull writing because they turn a scene of activity into a place where things happen but nobody makes them happen. Verbs in the passive voice *can be replaced* in almost every sentence—but that will happen only if *you replace* such verbs.

4. Poetic Devices

A sprinkling of alliteration, rhyme, and onomatopoeia can add a melodious appeal to your sentences. You have *surely seen* the *rich rewards* that these literary devices offer a writer.

5. Rhythm

Read your sentences aloud to judge whether they have a pleasant, smooth-flowing rhythm. Avoid the careless repetition of similar or identical syllables or words. *Un*planned repetition will *un*doubtedly produce *un*rhythmic, *un*pleasant sentences that will *un*settle your readers. If a sentence contains a compound part, place the shorter part first. Doing these things will give your sentences a smoothness that adds to the rhythmic appeal of your writing.

Work hard to incorporate these devices as you write. They will help you to produce compositions that others find enjoyable and impressive. As you read the following essay, notice how the writer has used the elements of effective style to make his composition appealing.

Mountain Musings

Man has a <u>love</u> for the mountains, but most of that

Repeated words — <u>love</u> is mere spectator <u>love</u>. He enjoys watching the west-

Figurative language — ern mountains <u>extinguish the fires of the day</u>. He thrills

Picturesque language — at the heart-stopping splendor of the snowcapped peaks.

Balanced sentence — But as long as a mountain does not hinder a man, the man usually does not bother the mountain.

Life contains <u>mountains</u> other than those <u>massive</u>

Alliteration — <u>mounds</u> of rocks and ice. It contains peaks of <u>danger</u>, <u>difficulty</u>, and <u>discouragement</u>. These are the real mountains of life; and though they are less <u>charming</u>, they are

Repeated syllables — just as <u>challenging</u>. God intends these mountains as <u>tests</u> and <u>contests</u> to make us mountaineers for Him.

Repeated syllables	Mountains have the ability to <u>prove</u> and <u>improve</u> our
Alliteration	strength. God does not intend us to <u>skirt</u> them but to <u>scale</u>
	them. He expects us to face life's challenges as "more
	than conquerors." He has promised that no <u>mountain</u>
Repeated syllables	will ever be <u>insurmountable</u>. With that <u>assurance</u> and
Rhyme	with firm <u>endurance</u>, we shall conquer any peak.

From a mountain summit, we have a clearer perspective of life. We can better <u>place</u> where we are and <u>plot</u> our course for the future. It is a <u>time</u> of <u>triumph</u> over <u>trials</u> and <u>delight</u> over <u>defeat</u>—a <u>foretaste</u> of the <u>future</u>. We often speak of these as our mountaintop experiences. But remember, it is only the <u>mountaineer</u> who stands at the <u>mountaintop</u>. We shall never <u>gain</u> the summit by <u>gazing</u> at it from the valley.

<u>Mountains</u> <u>make</u> us <u>more</u> like our <u>Maker</u>. The <u>trifles</u> of <u>life</u> will grow <u>dim</u> in the <u>distance</u> as we <u>rise</u> to <u>higher</u> ground. The upward trail is <u>rough</u> and <u>rugged</u>, but it leads ever homeward to God. When we finally stand on that holy hill of Zion and look back on the <u>heights</u> we have <u>climbed</u>, we shall surely sing, "It has been worth it all."

—Selected and adapted

(left margin notes for above paragraphs:)
- Alliteration and assonance
- Repeated syllables
- Alliteration and assonance
- Alliteration and assonance

Applying the Lesson

Write a composition of 150–200 words, using one of the following titles. Put special effort into applying the five elements of effective writing style that you have studied.

1. Voices of the Valley (Show parallels between valleys and the humiliating experiences of life.)
2. Drawn by the Dawn (Show parallels between the dawn and our forward look.)
3. Secrets of the Snow (Draw spiritual lessons from the snow.)
4. Lessons From Man's Best Friend (Show parallels for developing friendships. The following proverb may stimulate your thinking: "A dog is man's best friend because he wags his tail and not his tongue.")
5. Taught by the Trees (Draw lessons from trees, such as their standing upright in spite of storms.)
6. Leaf Lessons (Show parallels between our own lives and the life of a leaf. For example, a small leaf works with many others to accomplish great good.)

Lesson 109 Answers
(Individual work.)

110.   Chapter 13 Review

A. Copy each prepositional phrase. If a phrase is part of a longer phrase, include it with the longer phrase and also copy it separately. Label each phrase *adj.*, *adv.*, or *n.*

1. Through the power of Christ, we can overcome the world and the forces that work within our own lives.
2. In addition to personal zeal, the power to resist evil requires a full surrender to whatever God's Word teaches.
3. Through God's enabling grace, we can live in complete victory over evil.
4. Below zero degrees is bitterly cold for working in this high wind!
5. Throughout the day, cold drafts came in around the rattly windows of the old house.

B. Copy the conjunctions, and label them *CC* (common coordinating conjunction), *Cor* (correlative conjunction), *SC* (subordinating conjunction), or *CA* (conjunctive adverb).

1. When James Smith moved his family from Quebec and opened a restaurant in Poughkeepsie, New York, he probably had no thought of marketing the first cough drops in America.
2. The following winter, both coughs and sore throats were quite common, so Smith recognized the need for a cold medication.
3. Smith, a candymaker before he moved, was offered a recipe for a good cough remedy; therefore, he paid five dollars for the formula.
4. Before the winter had passed, news of his cough lozenges had spread not only throughout Poughkeepsie but also to neighboring towns.
5. James's sons, Andrew and William, became the famous Smith brothers, whose faces have appeared either on glass jars or on cardboard boxes for nearly 150 years.
6. Various competitors produced cough drops similar both in formula and in name; nevertheless, the Smith brothers saw their production soar from five pounds a day to five tons a day.

C. Write enough of each sentence to show how to correct the mistake in it.

1. Mocking another person is evil for that reproaches the Creator.
2. We must avoid not only the profane words but the seemingly innocent idle words.
3. Our carnal nature gives rise to selfish thoughts and words, however we must choose by God's grace to cultivate noble thoughts that will produce noble words.
4. Our speech reveals much about our attitudes and what we consciously think.
5. Our words either reveal a godly character or a carnal character.

D. Rewrite each sentence, joining the clauses with a suitable subordinating conjunction instead of with *and.* You may change the order of the clauses if you wish.

1. Peter has been complaining about his meals so often, and he shall have only water and a piece of dry bread for lunch today.

Lesson 110

Purpose: To review the concepts taught in Chapter 13.

Lesson 110 Answers

A. 1. Through the power of Christ—adv.;
   of Christ—adj.;
   within our own lives—adv.
2. In addition to personal zeal—adv.;
   to whatever God's Word teaches—adj.
3. Through God's enabling grace—adv.;
   in complete victory over evil—adv.;
   over evil—adj.
4. Below zero degrees—n.;
   for working in this high wind—adv.;
   in this high wind—adv.
5. Throughout the day—adv.;
   around the rattly windows of the old house—adv.;
   of the old house—adj.

B. 1. When—SC; and—CC
2. both—and—Cor; so—CC
3. before—SC; therefore—CA
4. Before—SC; not only—but also—Cor
5. and—CC; either—or—Cor
6. both—and—Cor; nevertheless—CA

C. 1. evil,
2. but also the
3. words; however,
4. and our conscious thoughts
5. reveal either

D. 1. Because Peter has been complaining about his meals so often, he shall have only water and a piece of dry bread for lunch today.

2. He is eating his meager lunch, and he should think about the many who would be glad to have the foods he complained about.
3. This dog is very friendly, and he likes to jump up on people.
4. My sister Vera teaches school at Glendale, and she will board with Uncle Lewis's.
5. Father must leave to teach at Bible school, and we hope to have the unloader fixed.

E. Copy each interjection, the word before it (if there is one), and the word after it. Use correct capitalization and punctuation, and underline any word that should be italicized.
   1. Hallelujah the Lord has answered our prayers.
   2. Before this week, we hardly knew what to do; but lo God has clearly shown us the answer.
   3. What you have not heard the perplexing predicament that Father is facing?
   4. Strange the accusations he faced made no sense at all.
   5. Well after a little investigation, the authorities recognized that the accusations were false.
   6. Bang the door slammed in my face.

F. Rewrite each sentence so that it communicates the same idea without an idiom.
   1. That peacock likes to show off his bright colors.
   2. I was tempted to give a sharp reply, but I held my tongue.
   3. Father walked ahead, and the children brought up the rear.
   4. It is usually best to take your time in making a major decision.
   5. Your kitten looks for all the world like a baby leopard.
   6. This cold lemonade really hits the spot.
   7. For some reason, the newcomer seemed to have it in for me.
   8. If your expenses exceed your income, you will soon be in the hole.

---

2. While he is eating his meager lunch, he should think about the many who would be glad to have the foods he complained about.
3. Although this dog is very friendly, he likes to jump up on people.
4. While my sister Vera teaches school at Glendale, she will board with Uncle Lewis's.
5. Before Father must leave to teach at Bible school, we hope to have the unloader fixed.

E. 1. Hallelujah! The   4. Strange! The
   2. but, lo, God   5. Well, after
   3. What! You   6. Bang! The

F. (Allow reasonable variation.)
   1. That peacock likes to make a flashy display of his bright colors.
   2. I was tempted to give a sharp reply, but I refrained from speaking.
   3. Father walked ahead, and the children were the last ones in line.
   4. It is usually best to avoid being hasty in making a major decision.
   5. Your kitten looks in every way like a baby leopard.
   6. This cold lemonade is really satisfying.
   7. For some reason, the newcomer seemed to have a grudge against me.
   8. If your expenses exceed your income, you will soon be in debt.

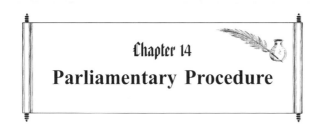

Chapter 14
Parliamentary Procedure

111.   Introduction to Parliamentary Procedure

Any group, committee, board, or congregation needs an orderly way to conduct business and make decisions. This order gives them an efficient method for planning and discussing matters to determine the will of the group on any given issue. *Parliamentary procedure* is a set of rules providing an orderly way to transact group business. Parliamentary procedure serves four basic purposes.

1. To determine the true intent of the assembly.
2. To allow full, free, and frank discussion.
3. To give a fair hearing to the minority.
4. To assure that the will of the majority is done.

Parliamentary procedure is a courteous, democratic way to accomplish business and to make decisions, but it is *not* the means of determining principles of truth. The Bible is the final authority for sound doctrine. Parliamentary procedure can be used to decide policies or practices that harmonize with Scriptural principles, but it can in no way establish, change, or abolish divine truth.

In this chapter, you will learn some of the basic things involved in parliamentary procedure. These lessons present the proceedings as followed in standard, formal practice. In our church committees and boards, however, we use a less formal version of parliamentary procedure.

Conducting a Meeting With Parliamentary Procedure

A formal meeting begins when the chairman stands before the group and calls the meeting to order. The following example portrays the upper grade students at Yorktown Mennonite School using parliamentary procedure to conduct a business meeting. For the sake of practice, they are imagining that they are responsible for the operation of the school. The teacher is the chairman; and rather than addressing him with the formal *Mr. Chairman,* the students call him *Brother Clyde.*

CHAIRMAN: The meeting will now come to order. Darwin Eberly will lead us in an opening prayer. [Darwin leads in prayer.]

CHAIRMAN: The secretary will now read the minutes of the last meeting.

SECRETARY: The upper grade class of Yorktown Mennonite School held a meeting in the classroom on Friday, March 3, 20—, at 2:00 P.M. Brother Clyde, our teacher, presided.

Lesson 111

Purpose: To introduce the concept of *parliamentary procedure.

Teaching Suggestions:

Parliamentary procedure has its name because it is based on the rules used by the British Parliament. A number of your students may have been present at a church business meeting where some degree of parliamentary procedure was followed. Perhaps some of your students have never observed parliamentary procedure in practice at all. So you will need to gauge your teaching somewhat according to your students' level of familiarity with the subject.

Emphasize the four purposes of parliamentary procedure.

We follow these patterns in many of our meetings because they allow us to fulfill these important purposes. Also point out that we are not strictly bound to these forms; we modify them as needed to fit our situation.

Unless you have a very small class, you should plan to practice parliamentary procedure with your students. These lessons will remain mere abstractions if they are not put into practice. Be sure to plan ahead to allow time in your schedule.

For your personal benefit and for class enrichment, it would be well for you to purchase or check out at a public library a copy of *Robert's Rules of Order.*

The minutes of the previous meeting were read. Richard Steiner noted that the secretary had recorded the date of the last meeting incorrectly. The minutes were approved as corrected.

Dean Martin moved that we purchase more stones for our parking area. Ronald Heath proposed an amendment to specify fine stones. The amendment carried. The motion carried as amended.

Kenneth Bucher moved that the meeting be adjourned. The motion carried.

Respectfully submitted,
Brian Hostetter, Secretary

CHAIRMAN: Are there any additions or corrections to the reading of the minutes? [Pause.] The minutes stand approved as read.

Brian Hostetter has been serving as our secretary. His term expired on the last day of March, so our first item of business today is to elect a new secretary. Nominations for secretary are now in order.

KENNETH: [rising] Brother Clyde.
CHAIRMAN: Kenneth.
KENNETH: I nominate Gary Lehman.
DEAN: [rising] Brother Clyde.
CHAIRMAN: Dean.
DEAN: I nominate Lynn Shank.
NEVIN AND MARCUS: [rising] Brother Clyde.
CHAIRMAN: Nevin. [The chairman called on Nevin because he recognized him first.]
NEVIN: I nominate Dean Martin.
CHAIRMAN: Marcus. [Marcus had remained standing.]
MARCUS: I move that nominations cease.
KENNETH: [remaining seated] I second the motion.
CHAIRMAN: It has been moved and seconded that nominations cease. All those in favor, raise your right hands. [Pause.] Those opposed, raise your right hands. [Pause.] The motion is carried. Richard and Kenneth will hand out the ballots and serve as tellers. The nominees for secretary are Gary Lehman, Lynn Shank, and Dean Martin. Write the name of one of these on your ballot. Then turn your ballot over and pass it to the front. [The tellers collect and count the votes.]

Lynn Shank has been elected as secretary.

There is no old business to dispose of. Is there any new business?
ARNOLD: [rising] Brother Clyde.
CHAIRMAN: Arnold.
ARNOLD: I move that we patch the cracked plaster on our classroom walls, and that we repaint the walls a light green.
BRIAN: I second the motion.

CHAIRMAN: It has been moved and seconded that we patch the cracked plaster on our classroom walls, and that we repaint the walls a light green. Is there any discussion?

DEAN: [rising] Brother Clyde.

CHAIRMAN: Dean.

DEAN: It seems to me that the plaster is in rather poor shape. That corner beside the bookshelves is not merely cracked; a piece of plaster is missing. I wonder if just patching the plaster will be satisfactory.

RICHARD: [rising] Brother Clyde.

CHAIRMAN: Richard.

RICHARD: I agree with Dean. After all, this plaster has been on the walls for a long time. I move that we replace the aging plaster on our classroom walls, and that we paint the walls a light green.

CHAIRMAN: Your motion is out of order, Richard, because a main motion is pending.

KENNETH: [rising] Brother Clyde.

CHAIRMAN: Kenneth.

KENNETH: I move that the motion be amended to say that the plaster be replaced instead of being patched.

RICHARD: I second the motion.

CHAIRMAN: It has been moved and seconded that the motion be amended to say that the plaster be replaced instead of being patched. Is there any discussion?

NEVIN: [rising] Brother Clyde.

CHAIRMAN: Nevin.

NEVIN: Are we sure we want to remove and replace all that old plaster? That could become quite expensive.

DEAN: [rising] Brother Clyde.

CHAIRMAN: Dean.

DEAN: I hadn't considered the expense. We should perhaps check some prices.

WAYNE: [rising] Brother Clyde.

CHAIRMAN: Wayne.

WAYNE: I really don't think most of the plaster is in such bad shape. Those few places where it is chipped out can be repaired quite easily. [A number of students nod their heads. The chairman waits a bit for more discussion.]

CHAIRMAN: Since there is no more discussion, we are now ready to vote. It has been moved and seconded that the motion be amended to say that the plaster would be replaced instead of patched. Those in favor, say "Aye." [A few say, "Aye."] Those opposed, say "Nay." [An obvious majority says, "Nay."] The motion is defeated.

The original motion is again on the floor, that we patch the cracked plaster on our classroom walls, and that we repaint the walls a light green. Is there any further discussion?

RONALD:	[rising] Brother Clyde.
CHAIRMAN:	Ronald.
RONALD:	I move that we refer the question to the Maintenance Committee to investigate and report back with specific plans and cost estimates at our regular May meeting.
LYNN:	I second the motion.
CHAIRMAN:	It has been moved and seconded that we refer the question to the Maintenance Committee to investigate and report back with specific plans and cost estimates at our regular May meeting. Is there any discussion? [Pause.] Those in favor of the motion, raise your right hands. [Pause.] Those opposed, raise your right hands. [Pause.] The motion carries.
MARCUS:	[rising] Brother Clyde.
CHAIRMAN:	Marcus.
MARCUS:	I move that the meeting be adjourned.
KENNETH:	I second the motion.
CHAIRMAN:	It has been moved and seconded that the meeting be adjourned. Those in favor, say "Aye." [Pause.] Those opposed, say "Nay." [Pause.] The motion carries, and the meeting is adjourned.

The Basic Order of Business

A meeting should follow a basic order of business. This will vary somewhat according to the nature of the meeting and the level of formality required. Here is a typical order of business.

1. *The chairman calls the meeting to order.* Depending on the nature of the meeting, the chairman will call on a member to have a devotional meditation, to lead in an opening prayer, or to lead the group in singing. A good chairman tries to call the meeting to order promptly at the announced time, for this helps to establish a businesslike atmosphere that contributes to order and efficiency throughout the meeting.

2. *The chairman asks for the reading of the minutes.* After they are read, the chairman gives an opportunity for additions or corrections. Then he should rule that "The minutes stand approved as read" or that "The minutes stand approved as corrected."

3. *The chairman calls for the treasurer's report.* After the report, he should ask if anyone has any questions about it. The group is not asked to approve the treasurer's report, for the members would probably not have any way of knowing whether it was accurate.

4. *The chairman calls for any committee reports.* A standing, or permanent, committee has an ongoing work; its report often takes the form of a progress report. A special committee may be formed to investigate or make plans relating to a given matter. Its report is a summary of the recommendations they have prepared.

5. *The chairman brings any old business to the floor.* Old business includes any matters unresolved at the adjournment of the previous meeting and any business that had been postponed to the current meeting. Usually, these items are mentioned in the minutes of the previous meeting.

6. *The chairman opens the meeting for new business.* This is the time for members to introduce matters that the group has not considered previously.

7. *The chairman adjourns the meeting.* Adjournment may occur after a motion to adjourn has passed. Or, if all items on the agenda have been properly disposed of and no member presents any more new business, the chairman may simply declare the meeting adjourned.

Applying the Lesson

A. Write the answers.
1. What is parliamentary procedure?
2. Why is order important when a group makes decisions?
3. List the four basic purposes of parliamentary procedure.
4. Why is parliamentary procedure not a safe way to determine truth?
5. How should the members address the chairman of the meeting according to strict parliamentary law? in a Christian assembly?
6. When may a member properly speak without rising?
7. Why should the chairman call the meeting to order at the scheduled time?
8. Why does the chairman not request approval for the treasurer's report as for the minutes?
9. What is old business? new business?

B. Write the seven points in the basic order of business, and memorize them.

C. Study the procedure that was used to elect a secretary in the sample meeting. Be prepared to participate in a meeting for the election of a vice-chairman, a secretary, and a treasurer.

Review Exercises

A. Write the correct term to match each description. [28–32]

| bibliography | footnote | theme |
| exposition | plagiarism | |

1. A comment about a detail in an expository essay.
2. The main point of an essay.
3. Copying another's writing and passing it off as your own.
4. A list of the sources used in preparing an essay.

B. Write *true* if the statement is true, or *false* if it is false. [28–35]
1. The purpose of expository writing is to define, clarify, or explain something.
2. The introduction to an exposition should begin with a statement of the theme.
3. Both the introduction and the conclusion should resemble a funnel—starting out with general ideas and ending with specific ideas.
4. You should avoid controversial topics for expositions.
5. After you have done thorough research for your exposition, you should write a statement of purpose to guide your writing.
6. Using at least two sources of information helps to make an essay more complete and more accurate.
7. The abbreviation *ibid.* means "from an anonymous source."

Lesson 111 Answers
Applying the Lesson

A. 1. A set of rules providing an orderly way to transact group business.
2. Order is important for efficient planning and discussion to determine the will of the group.
3. (1) To determine the true intent of the assembly.
(2) To allow full, free, and frank discussion.
(3) To give a fair hearing to the minority.
(4) To assure that the will of the majority is done.
4. Truth is based upon the unchanging Word of God.
5. Mr. Chairman;
Brother ———
6. when seconding a motion
7. Promptness helps to establish a businesslike atmosphere that contributes to order and efficiency.
8. The members have no way of checking its accuracy.
9. Old business is any matter unresolved at the adjournment of the previous meeting and any business that had been postponed to the current meeting.
New business is any matter that the group has not considered previously.

B. (Memorization is individual work.)
1. The chairman calls the meeting to order.
2. The chairman asks for the reading of the minutes.
3. The chairman calls for the treasurer's report.
4. The chairman calls for any committee reports.
5. The chairman brings any old business to the floor.
6. The chairman opens the meeting for new business.
7. The chairman adjourns the meeting.

C. (Class activity.)

Review Exercises

A. 1. footnote   3. plagiarism
2. theme   4. bibliography

B. 1. true
2. false
3. false
4. true
5. false
6. true
7. false

8. You should list the entries in a bibliography in alphabetical order.
9. You should write a footnote for every detail that you draw directly from your notes.
10. You should include in the bibliography every source from which you obtained information, even if you did not directly quote from it.

8. true
9. false
10. true

112. Fundamentals of Parliamentary Procedure

Realizing the value of decency and order, men have set up the system known as parliamentary procedure to aid group decision making. For parliamentary procedure to be an efficient process, each participant must understand well his role in the meeting. An orderly meeting illustrates the Scriptural command, "Let all things be done decently and in order" (1 Corinthians 14:40).

The Various Offices

If a meeting is to function smoothly, the group must have qualified persons in the various offices. The four most common offices are chairman, vice-chairman, secretary, and treasurer. The *chairman,* often called simply *the chair,* bears the primary responsibility for the overall progress of a meeting. He calls the meeting to order and asks for reports from the secretary, the treasurer, and any committee with business to report.

The most important part of the chairman's responsibility is presiding over the actual business of the meeting. He guides the discussion by giving members **the floor** (the right to address the assembly); he conducts the voting and announces the outcome; and he adjourns the meeting. Generally, the chairman reserves his right to vote for those occasions when he wishes to make or break a tie vote. In all these responsibilities, the chairman must make sure that the group observes the rules of parliamentary procedure as well as the constitution and bylaws of the specific organization.

The *vice-chairman* is the chairman's assistant. He presides over the meeting when the chairman is absent or when an action involves the chairman, as when he is nominated to serve on a committee.

The *secretary* handles the records and correspondence of the group. At the chairman's direction, the secretary writes and answers letters that pertain to the business of the group. His main responsibility, however, is to write the **minutes** of each meeting. (They are called minutes because they summarize the small details of the business transacted.)

The minutes stand as the official record of the meeting. Since the secretary does not have time to write everything in full during the meeting, he must learn to take good notes. He should write the complete minutes as soon after the meeting as practical, while the details are still fresh in his mind.

Although the form of the minutes may vary from one organization to another, the minutes should be a brief summary of the actual proceedings of the meeting. The secretary should strive for conciseness and clarity in writing the minutes.

Lesson 112

Purpose: To teach some of the *basics involved in parliamentary procedure.

Teaching Suggestions:

Stress the important position that a chairman fills. He is responsible to direct a meeting and to keep business moving. A skilled chairman is a great asset to any group. A chairman can improve his effectiveness by becoming more familiar with the patterns of parliamentary procedure.

Again be sure to plan ahead to allow time in your schedule for a class meeting. If time allows, you will do well to have several class meetings. You could conduct meetings on several succeeding days, even after you have completed the study of this chapter. The more exercise your students have, the better they will be able to use the forms of parliamentary procedure. You may choose to serve as chairman for all meetings. But if you have students capable of filling this role, they will benefit greatly from practice with serving as chairman themselves.

Give thought to some subjects to discuss in your meetings. Here are several suggestions: putting gravel (or macadam) on the school drive; purchasing a new lawn mower; deciding on a place to go singing as a school; repairing or replacing songbooks.

The minutes should follow a consistent pattern so that members can easily find the information they want. The first paragraph should state the name of the organization; the kind of meeting (regular or special); the place, date, and time of the meeting; the person presiding; and a statement regarding the reading of the minutes.

Depending on the nature of the organization, the next several paragraphs may contain the treasurer's report and reports from various committees. Each report should be given in a separate paragraph.

The bulk of the minutes should record the various items of business transacted during the meeting. Each item of business should be recorded in a separate paragraph. These paragraphs should contain the name of each member who makes a motion, the wording of the motion, and the way in which the motion was disposed of (passed, defeated, or postponed). But they should not include any details of the discussion about the motion or any personal views of the secretary.

The minutes should tell how the meeting was adjourned, and should end with the secretary's signature. The following example shows the form of the minutes read at the meeting described in Lesson 111.

> The upper grade class of Yorktown Mennonite School held a meeting in the classroom on Friday, March 3, 20—, at 2:00 P.M. Brother Clyde, our teacher, presided.
>
> The minutes of the previous meeting were read. Richard Steiner noted that the secretary had recorded the date of the last meeting incorrectly. The minutes were approved as corrected.
>
> Dean Martin moved that we purchase more stones for our parking area. Ronald Heath proposed an amendment to specify fine stones. The amendment carried. The motion carried as amended.
>
> Kenneth Bucher moved that the meeting be adjourned. The motion carried.
>
> Respectfully submitted,
> *Brian Hostetter, Secretary*

The *treasurer* is responsible for the finances of the group. He receives any income and pays any bills associated with the function of the group. He keeps a careful record of all such transactions in an account book. An *audit* of these books is made at least once a year. In auditing the books, two or more members of the organization check the accuracy of the treasurer's work. Sometimes one person serves as both secretary and treasurer.

The Work of the Group

The chairman, vice-chairman, secretary, and treasurer fill important roles. The efficiency of a meeting, however, depends also upon the work of each member in the group. The group as a whole, not just the officers, makes the decisions. A *quorum* is the minimum number of members that must be present to transact business, as stated in the constitution of the organization. When a quorum is present, the group can conduct its business—make *motions* (formal proposals), discuss them, offer *amendments* (changes) to motions, and vote on them. The members of the group serve on committees and make nominations.

Whatever your responsibility in a business meeting, try to understand it and do your best to fulfill it. If you have been appointed to leadership, fill that place to the best of your ability. If your place is found with the majority of the group, do your part in thinking seriously about the decisions to be made. Participate in group discussions so that others know your feelings and preferences. And whether you agree or disagree with the decisions of the group, do your best in giving them your support.

Voting Procedures

The whole idea of making motions and discussing them is to prepare the group for a final decision about a matter. When the chairman thinks that the group has amply discussed an issue and knows what decision they intend to make, he calls for a vote to be taken. The chairman can use any one of several specific methods of voting.

1. *Vote by general consent.* The chairman may use this method of voting when he can sense the general agreement of the group, especially on a procedural matter. For example, after the secretary reads the minutes, the chairman asks, "Are there any additions or corrections to the reading of the minutes?" If there are additions or corrections, they should come from the assembly then. In essence, those who remain silent are giving their consent to the minutes as they were read, and those who offer additions or corrections will give their consent after the minutes are changed. Using this basis for general consent, the chairman simply rules, "The minutes stand approved as read" or "The minutes stand approved as corrected."

2. *Vote by acclamation.* Those in favor say "Aye" (pronounced like *eye*); then those opposed say "Nay." This method is used mainly when the chairman knows that the vote will be unanimous or nearly unanimous. It cannot show the will of the group if the vote is close (nearly a tie).

3. *Vote by a show of hands.* Those in favor raise their right hands; then those opposed raise their hands. This allows the chairman to make an exact count of the vote, which is important when the vote is close or when a member questions the ruling of the chairman. The show of hands is the most common method for taking an exact vote on general matters.

4. *Rising vote.* Those in favor rise to their feet; then those opposed rise to their feet. Like the show of hands, this allows the chairman to make an exact count of the vote.

5. *Vote by secret ballot.* The chairman either hands out ballots or appoints tellers to do so. Each member writes his vote on a ballot. In a large assembly, this is the simplest way to establish an accurate count of the votes. It is also appropriate for electing officers and voting on sensitive issues. In a vote by secret ballot, the chairman may vote during the balloting, but he may not vote after the ballots are counted.

Most motions require a simple majority to pass. A simple majority occurs when the ayes have at least one more vote than the nays. A few motions require a two-thirds majority vote to pass. In particular, a two-thirds majority vote is required to pass a motion that would limit the free discussion of the group. For example, after some discussion on a matter, a member may move that the discussion be closed and the matter be brought to a vote. His motion will pass only if a two-thirds majority votes in favor of it.

A motion does not pass if the vote is a tie. In the event of a tie, the chairman may cast a positive vote to break the tie, thus causing the motion to pass. Or if a motion were to pass by only one vote, the chairman may cast a negative vote to create a tie and defeat the motion. If ballots are used, however, the chairman may not cast a vote to change the outcome after the ballots are counted.

Main Motions

A motion is a proposal to discuss or act upon an item of business. Any member except the chairman may make motions. The person making a motion should state it clearly and specifically. A wide variety of motions is available for the members to use in pursuing the business of the assembly. The chart in Lesson 114 summarizes the motions used most often.

Main motions carry the primary business in a meeting. Look at the sample in Lesson 111 as you study the following steps in making and disposing of a main motion. Arnold's motion to patch the cracked plaster is an example of a main motion.

1. A member stands and addresses the chairman to get his attention. If more than one person stands at the same time, the chairman calls on the one he recognizes first.
2. The member states his motion and sits down. He should say, "I move that…" or "I move to…" He should not say, "I make a motion that…"
3. Another member must second the motion. Requiring a second ensures that more than just one person in the assembly supports the idea. If a motion receives no second, it dies for lack of support, and a new motion may come to the floor.
4. The chairman repeats the motion in its original wording.
5. The assembly discusses the motion. Members should express their opinions freely so that the group can reach a proper understanding before voting.
6. After the members have adequately discussed the motion, the chairman repeats the motion and puts it to the assembly for a vote.
7. The chairman announces the result of the voting.

Applying the Lesson

A. Write the correct term for each description.
   1. A formal proposal for the group to consider.
   2. A change in the wording of a proposal.
   3. The minimum number of members that must be present to transact business.
   4. The official record of the time and place of a meeting, and of the business transacted.
   5. A check of the accuracy of the treasurer's records.
   6. The right to address the assembly.
   7. A proposal of the kind used primarily to carry the business of an assembly.

Lesson 112 Answers
Applying the Lesson
A. 1. motion
   2. amendment
   3. quorum
   4. minutes
   5. audit
   6. the floor
   7. main motion

B. For each description, write *chairman, vice-chairman, secretary, treasurer,* or *group.*
  1. Keeps account of money matters of the group.
  2. Presents motions and makes up the main voting body.
  3. Calls the meeting to order.
  4. Keeps detailed records of the meetings.
  5. Takes the place of an absent chairman.
  6. Adjourns the meeting.
  7. Discusses motions and amendments.
  8. Designates who shall have the floor.
  9. Writes and answers letters pertaining to the business of the group.
  10. Is primarily responsible to see that the rules of parliamentary procedure and the constitution and bylaws are observed.
  11. Receives any income and pays any bills.

C. Write *general consent, acclamation, show of hands, rising,* or *secret ballot* for each description. Some require more than one answer.
  1. Is especially suited for elections and sensitive issues.
  2. Is used primarily for procedural matters, such as approving the minutes.
  3. Allows the chairman to take an exact count.
  4. Cannot show the will of the group if the vote is close.
  5. Is used when the chairman senses that the group is largely in agreement.

D. Do these exercises.
  1. Why must the chairman be well acquainted with the rules of parliamentary procedure?
  2. Write the letter of the statement that is *not* true about the minutes of a meeting.
    a. They should include the wording of each motion that was acted upon.
    b. They should express facts about the meeting, not opinions of the secretary.
    c. They should include details about the time and place of the meeting.
    d. They should include specific details about the discussion on each motion.
    e. They should have a separate paragraph for each item of business recorded.
  3. If you are a member of the group, how can you help to make the meeting a profitable one?
  4. What should you do if the group decision is different from the way you preferred?
  5. If twenty members vote on a motion, how many ayes are needed for it to pass by a simple majority?
  6. When is a two-thirds majority vote required for a motion to pass?
  7. Why would a chairman cast a vote to cause a tie vote?
  8. Why would he cast a vote to break a tie vote?

E. Conduct a parliamentary meeting, using the following imaginary situation. Your teacher will appoint specific students to fill the various roles. Each student should act as a secretary and write minutes for the meeting.
  CHAIRMAN: Calls the meeting to order, and calls for the reading of the minutes.

B. 1. treasurer
    2. group
    3. chairman
    4. secretary
    5. vice-chairman
    6. chairman
    7. group
    8. chairman
    9. secretary
    10. chairman
    11. treasurer

C. 1. secret ballot
    2. general consent
    3. show of hands, rising, secret ballot
    4. acclamation
    5. general consent, acclamation

D. 1. He must see that the meeting is conducted according to the rules.
    2. d
    3. Think seriously about the decisions to be made. Participate in group discussion so that others know your feelings and preferences.
    4. Do your best in supporting the decision.
    5. eleven
    6. when a motion would limit the free discussion of the group
    7. to defeat a motion
    8. to pass a motion

E. (Class activity.)

SECRETARY: Reads the following minutes:

> The monthly meeting of the Room 4 students at Brockton Valley Mennonite School was held in the classroom on January 5, 20—, at 2:15 P.M. Brother Bradley, our teacher, served as chairman.
>
> The minutes of the previous meeting were read and approved.
>
> Raymond Steffy moved that we ask Wadel's Woodshop to make a new Ping-Pong table. Noah Weber moved to amend the motion by specifying a new folding Ping-Pong table. The amendment carried. The motion carried as amended.
>
> Clarence Oberholtzer moved that we buy two new snow shovels for clearing the walks and steps outside. The motion carried.
>
> Since there was no further business, the meeting was adjourned.
>
>   Respectfully submitted,
>   Leonard Brubacher, Secretary

CHAIRMAN: Takes proper action on the reading of the minutes. Opens the meeting for new business.

STUDENT A: Following proper form, moves that the upper grade boys use a series of art periods to design and make two racks for holding Ping-Pong paddles and balls.

STUDENT B: Properly seconds the motion. [Open discussion follows.]

STUDENT C: Suggests that perhaps they should ask Wadel's Woodshop to make them.

STUDENT D: Replies that this project is small enough to be manageable for the students at school.

STUDENT A: States that this would make an interesting and worthwhile project for the boys.

CHAIRMAN: When discussion lags, calls for a vote by a show of hands; announces the result; asks for any other new business.

STUDENT E: Moves that while the boys work on their project, the girls have knitting lessons.

STUDENT D: Seconds the motion. [Open discussion follows.]

STUDENT F: Comments that Sister Matilda enjoys knitting and would probably be willing and able to come and teach the girls.

STUDENT B: States that it sounds like a good idea.

CHAIRMAN: Calls for a vote by acclamation; announces the result; asks for any other new business. When no other business comes to the floor, adjourns the meeting.

Review Exercises

A. Name the tense of the underlined verb in each sentence. [74]

1. In 1898, H. Cecil Booth <u>watched</u> a demonstration of a new machine that forced air down into a carpet, causing dirt to billow up into an attached box.

2. When he asked the operator about the possibility of sucking the dust up, the man replied, "You <u>may try</u> it, but no one has yet succeeded with the idea."

Review Exercises

A. 1. past
   2. present

3. After he <u>had thought</u> about the idea for several days, he experimented by sucking on the back of a plush seat in a restaurant.
4. Although he choked violently on the dust, he <u>was inspired</u> to try his idea.
5. He declared to himself, "I <u>shall experiment</u> with various fabrics to serve as dust collectors."
6. As he lay at home sucking at his carpet with various fabrics over his lips, he may have thought, "I shall choke to death before I <u>shall have found</u> a way to make a suction sweeper."
7. Before such a calamity, however, he discovered that a tightly woven cloth handkerchief <u>traps</u> dust well as it allows air to pass through it freely.
8. The world <u>has benefited</u> greatly from Mr. Booth's invention of the vacuum cleaner.

3. past perfect
4. past
5. future
6. future perfect
7. present
8. present perfect

B. Identify the form of each underlined verb as simple (*S*), progressive (*P*), or emphatic (*E*). [77]
1. The first vacuum cleaners that Mr. Booth <u>made</u> were huge machines the size of modern refrigerators, and soon they <u>were extracting</u> large amounts of dirt from numerous buildings.
2. When Booth <u>was cleaning</u> the Westminster Abbey for the 1901 coronation of Edward VII, his machine extracted so much dirt that he <u>did receive</u> stares of amazement from the cleaning staff.
3. During World War I, Booth's machine <u>received</u> even greater publicity at London's Crystal Palace, where naval reserve men <u>had been dying</u> at epidemic rates from spotted fever.
4. The doctors <u>did</u> not <u>know</u> how to stop the epidemic, but they <u>did express</u> their suspicion that dirt in the palace was harboring disease germs.
5. The epidemic <u>did come</u> to an end after fifteen of Booth's vacuum cleaners <u>were used</u> to clean the palace.
6. Workers <u>hauled</u> away twenty-six truckloads of dirt before the authorities <u>declared</u> the building clean.

B. 1. S, P
2. P, E
3. S, P
4. S, E
5. E, S
6. S, S

---

113. Improving Your Editing Skills, Part 10

"Among all this people [the soldiers of Benjamin] there were seven hundred chosen men lefthanded; every one could sling stones at an hair breadth, and not miss" (Judges 20:16). When we read this verse, we say, "What amazing skill!" These men did better with slings than many people do today with rifles having high-powered scopes! How did they develop that kind of skill? Certainly they did not attain it in one day or even one year. These men must have practiced constantly, day after day and month after month. As the familiar saying goes, "Practice makes perfect."

Lesson 113

Purpose: To provide proofreading practice.

You have worked through nine lessons on editing skills. You have practiced your proofreading skills on various composition lessons. Perhaps you have also used these skills on other occasions. Do you now qualify as an expert proofreader? Probably not. But like the Benjamites with their slings, you have practiced and your ability has improved. This editing lesson will be a final test of the skills you have developed.

Marks Used in Editing and Proofreading

⌄or∧ insert (caret)	℘ delete	.... stet (let it stand)	—————— use italics
¶ begin new paragraph	no ¶ no new paragraph	*lc* change to lowercase (small letter)	*uc* change to uppercase (capital letter)
# insert space	⌢ delete space	← move (arrow)	⌒⌒ transpose

Editing Practice

A. Use proofreading marks to correct the ten spelling or spacing errors in the following paragraph. Some lines have more than one error, and some have none.

1.   The praying mantis, a wellcome guest in any garden, can
2. destroy alarge number of harmful insect pests. While it
3. pateintly waits for a meal, the mantis holds its claws in a
4. position that resembles a person praying. The mantis flies
5.   occasionally, but it spends most of its time on geen
6. plants were it is nearly invisible. Standing motion lessly
7. for long periods of time, the mantis waits until an
8. unsuspecting insect comes to near. Suddenly the mantis's
9. fore legs snap out; and the next instant, the mantis is
10. holding a victem tightly in its grip.

B. Use proofreading marks to make these corrections in the paragraph below.
   a. Divide the selection into two paragraphs.
   b. Correct two errors in joining or separating clauses.
   c. Improve the word order in two places.

1.   A dormant twig is interesting to observe. Even though it
2. looks completely bare. One thing you can see is the signs
3. of present life. At the end of each healthy, undamaged

Lesson 113 Answers

Editing Practice
(Answers are on pages 478–479.)

4. twig is a terminal bud, which causes the twig to grow in

5. length. You will also along the sides see numerous lateral

6. buds, which will develop new stems, flowers, or leaves.

7. Another thing you can observe is the evidence of life in

8. previous growing seasons. Bud-scale scars form at irregular

9. intervals rings around the stem, showing where each year's

10. growth stopped. The age of any branch equals the number

11. of these bud-scale scars. As you look over the branch,

12. you should also see lighter patches, or nodes, on the

13. bark. Each node indicates a place where a leaf had grown,

14. each one has a rim of tiny scars that mark where the sap

15. flowed from the stem to the leaf and back again.

C. Use proofreading marks to correct all the errors in this essay. No line has more than one error. Move the word *only* in line 11 to a different place in the sentence. Also join the paragraph beginning in line 14 to the preceding paragraph.

1. Is there inteligent life somewhere in this vast universe

2. other than on the earth. This question intrigues many

3. astronomers as they investigate the broad expanse of outer

4. of space. Assuming that man came into being by chance, they

5. wonder if chance has produced life some where else too.

6. These men do more than wonder; they are busy searching.

7. They think that discovering life elsewhere would give man

8. kind a new purpose and a greater faith in the future.

9. One of their search methods, is to monitor the radio

10. waves from the heavens, watching for patterns that could

11. only be produced by intelligent beings somewhere beyond us.

12. The child of God has different thoughts as turns his

13. eyes heavenward.

14. He has no interest in receiving messages from unknown,

15. illusory Beings. He has already received a message from

16. the heavens—the inspired word of God!

17.   The Christian finds purpose in life by excepting and

18. submitting to this message he gains an unshakable faith

19. in the future by believing its promises. "Blessed the is

20. man that trusteth in the Lord, and whose hope the Lord is

21. (Jeremiah 17:7.

---

114. Parliamentary Motions

There are four categories of parliamentary motions. In Lesson 112 you studied the main motion, which is in a category by itself. But sometimes a question demands attention before the main motion is disposed of. Such a question may or may not be directly related to the motion under discussion. When such questions arise, the assembly uses motions from the other three categories: privileged motions, subsidiary (səb·sid′·ē·er′·ē) motions, and incidental motions.

The Precedence of Motions

The motions that may come to the floor must follow a definite order. This order is called the *precedence* of motions, and it is determined by the rank of motions in relation to each other—that is, the order in which they must come to discussion and vote. Only one main motion may be *pending* (on the floor) at any given time. Depending on circumstances, however, one or more motions of the other three categories may be brought to the floor while a main motion is pending.

Whenever a motion is pending, only a motion that ranks higher in precedence may be presented. On the chart on the next page, each motion has precedence over all the ones below it. For example, suppose a main motion (number 11 on the chart) is on the floor. It would be allowable for someone to move to refer the motion to a committee (number 9). At this point another member could move to take a recess (number 3). This places three motions on the floor for consideration.

These motions must now be disposed of according to their precedence, from highest to lowest rank—number 3 first, number 9 second, and number 11 third. This is exactly the reverse of the order in which they were presented.

The chart on pages 440–441 summarizes the main details about a number of parliamentary motions. The chart lists the motions in order from highest to lowest rank. The motions that are most likely to contribute to efficiency in church business meetings and other church-related work are shaded for ready reference. Additional comments about these selected motions are given below.

Further Comments on Selected Motions

1. *Question of privilege.* This motion generally deals with unfavorable conditions in the meeting room. For example, a member might rise to a question of privilege if he cannot hear a speaker, if there is some disturbance among the members, or if the

---

Lesson 114

Purpose: To introduce several common parliamentary motions.

Teaching Suggestions:

Be sure that you understand and present clearly the precedence of motions. Lesson 112 introduced the main motion, which has the lowest rank of precedence. This lesson introduces some of the most common privileged, subsidiary, and incidental motions. The privileged and subsidiary motions follow a definite order of precedence. The incidental motions, which rank as a class between the privileged and the subsidiary motions, have no rank among themselves. Therefore

they are not numbered on the chart in this lesson.

The motions presented in this lesson bring into focus two common misunderstandings. One is that when a member thinks the final decision on a matter should be put off until a later meeting, he moves to lay the question on the table (table the motion). The proper motion to use for this is to postpone it to a definite time. The other misunderstanding is that to move the previous question (or simply call out "question") forces an immediate vote on the pending motion. Actually, a two-thirds majority must agree to close the debate and bring the question to a vote.

If at all possible, have your class conduct the meeting suggested in Part C. Without this practice, parliamentary room needs better ventilation. If the matter requires immediate attention, a member may interrupt a speaker with this motion.

2. *Point of order.* A member rises to a point of order when he observes a violation of a rule of parliamentary procedure that the chairman does not correct. He would use this motion, for example, if the chairman allowed two main motions on the floor at the same time. The member should immediately rise to his feet, interrupting the meeting if necessary, and say, "Mr. Chairman, I rise to a point of order." The chair should say, "You may state your point." After the member explains his point and sits down, the chairman states his decision on the matter.

3. *Lay on the table.* This motion sets aside a pending motion until the assembly votes to bring it back to the floor. If a motion is laid on the table, all other motions attached to it are automatically laid on the table as well. A tabled motion cannot be brought back to the floor during the same meeting in which it was tabled unless at least one other item of business has been disposed of. If the tabled motion is not brought back to the floor by the end of the next meeting, the question dies. In that case, the subject must be reintroduced as an altogether new main motion before it can be considered again.

4. *Previous question.* The term *previous question* refers to the most recently stated motion, the motion that is presently on the floor. Many people misunderstand the proper order of events when someone moves the previous question. One member's calling for the previous question does not force the pending motion to an immediate vote. Rather, this motion requires a second and a two-thirds affirmative vote to pass (because it limits the discussion of the group). If the vote on the previous question passes, the chair must immediately call for a vote on the pending motion. If the vote on the previous question is defeated, the group may continue debate on the pending motion.

5. *Postpone to definite time.* This motion postpones the pending motion to a definite hour, day, or meeting. However, the motion cannot be postponed beyond the next session of the assembly. Unlike the motion to lay on the table, this motion means that the question must again be brought to the floor at a specified time and without a vote to do so. If it is postponed to the next meeting, it automatically comes up as unfinished business in the reading of the minutes then.

6. *Refer to committee.* This motion refers the pending motion to a committee for further investigation before the motion comes to a vote. When a motion is referred to a committee, the following questions need to be answered:

    a. Is the motion referred to a standing committee, a special committee, or the committee of the whole? (The committee of the whole is the same as the assembly, but it allows more informal rules of discussion than the assembly does.)

    b. If the motion is referred to a special committee, how many members shall the committee comprise, and how shall the members be selected? (Members of a committee may be appointed by the chairman, they may be chosen by nominations and voting of the assembly, or they may be named by the person making the motion.)

    c. What is the committee's specific assignment, and when shall it report back to the assembly?

procedure will be meaningless facts in your students' minds, and they will not really be prepared to participate in organized meetings. If you can go beyond the suggestions in the text and conduct meetings of your own, your students will benefit even more.

Parliamentary

	May Interrupt Speaker	Second Required	Debat-able	Amend-able	Vote Required	May Be Recon-sidered
Privileged Motions						
1. Adjourn to a certain time	No	Yes	No	Yes	Maj.	Yes
2. Adjourn	No	Yes	No	No	Maj.	No
3. Take a recess	No	Yes	No	Yes	Maj.	No
4. Question of privilege	Yes (1)	No	No	No	(2)	No
Incidental Motions (These motions have no rank among themselves.)						
Closing nominations	No	Yes	No	No	2/3	No
Withdrawal of a motion	No	No	No	No	(3)	Yes (4)
Point of order	Yes	No	No	No	None	No
Subsidiary Motions						
5. Lay on the table	No	Yes	No	No	Maj.	No
6. Previous question	No	Yes	No	No	2/3	Yes
7. Limit or extend debate	No	Yes	No	Yes	2/3	Yes
8. Postpone to definite time	No	Yes	Yes	Yes	Maj.	Yes
9. Refer to committee	No	Yes	Yes	Yes	Maj.	Yes (6)
10. Amend	No	Yes	Yes	Yes	Maj.	Yes
11. **Main Motion**	No	Yes	Yes	Yes	Maj.	Yes
Specific Main Motions						
Take from the table	No	Yes	No	No	Maj.	No
Reconsider	Yes	Yes	Yes	No	Maj.	No

(1) If it requires immediate attention.

(2) Chair usually decides; majority if put to a vote.

(3) If chair has stated the motion, a majority vote is required if another member objects to the withdrawal.

(4) Negative vote only.

Motions

Purpose	Acceptable Forms
Sets the time for the next meeting.	"I move that when we adjourn, we adjourn to [specific time]."
Ends a meeting.	"I move that we adjourn."
Provides an intermission during a pro-longed meeting.	"I move to take a recess for [specific time]."
Requests immediate action relating to comfort, rights, or privileges.	"I rise to a question of privilege."

Purpose	Acceptable Forms
Ends further nominations.	"I move that nominations cease."
Allows a member who stated a motion to withdraw it from the floor.	"I withdraw my motion." "I request permission to withdraw my motion." (5)
Calls attention to a violation of a rule.	"I rise to a point of order."

Purpose	Acceptable Forms
Postpones the pending question until the group votes to return it to the floor.	"I move to lay the question on the table."
Closes debate and brings the pending question to an immediate vote.	"I move the previous question." "I move to vote immediately on the motion."
Shortens or lengthens the time agreed upon for the debate of a motion.	"I move to limit [extend] debate until [specific time]." "I move to limit [extend] the speaker's time to [specific time]."
Postpones the pending question to a specified time.	"I move to postpone the question until [specific time]."
Sends a question to a committee for investigation before vote. (7)	"I move to refer the question to a committee." (7)
Changes the content of motion.	"I move to amend the motion by [specific change]."

Purpose	Acceptable Forms
Introduces new business.	"I move that [to] . . ."

Purpose	Acceptable Forms
Returns a tabled motion to the floor.	"I move to take from the table the motion to . . ."
Returns a motion that has been acted upon to the floor.	"I move to reconsider the vote on . . ."

(5) If chair has stated the motion, member says, "I request permission to withdraw . . ."

(6) If the committee has not begun its work.

(7) May specify a standing committee or assign the chair to appoint a committee.

A member may simply move to refer the question to a committee and allow the group to decide these other details. If he prefers, he may specify some or all of the details in his motion. Here is an example of a motion to refer to a committee.

> "I move that we refer the question to a committee of three members to be appointed by the chairman. They shall bring carpet samples and prices to our next meeting."

7. *Amend.* This motion to alter another motion is probably the most common one used after the main motion. There are two kinds of amendments: a primary amendment, which is attached to any amendable motion; and a secondary amendment, which is attached to a primary amendment. A secondary amendment cannot be further amended.

An amendment may change the original motion by adding words, removing words, or substituting words. A motion to amend may call for the replacement of an entire paragraph, an entire section, or the complete original motion.

Applying the Lesson
A. Write the name of the specific motion that fits each description.
  1. Closes debate and brings the assembly to a vote on a motion.
  2. Used if a member notices a violation of a rule that the chairman does not address.
  3. Sets a question aside until the assembly votes to bring it back to the floor.
  4. Is probably the most common motion other than the main motion.
  5. Used if a member cannot hear the speaker.
  6. Sets a question aside until a specific time.
  7. Alters the wording of a motion.
  8. Used if the assembly feels that a subject needs to be investigated further before voting on it.

B. Write the letter of the correct choice.
  1. If a motion is pending,
     a. it has been laid aside until later.
     b. it is currently under discussion by the assembly.
  2. If a member wishes to set a question aside for debate at the next meeting, he should move to
     a. table the question.
     b. postpone the question to a definite time.
  3. If a member moves the previous question, he wishes to
     a. bring the question on the floor to a vote.
     b. raise a question about the last speaker's comments.
  4. Suppose the previous question has been moved and seconded. According to the principle of precedence, another member may now move to
     a. amend the motion.   b. take a recess.
  5. Two motions are on the floor: a motion to take a recess and a motion to lay the question on the table. According to the principle of precedence, which motion must be acted on first?
     a. Take a recess   b. Lay on the table

Lesson 114 Answers
Applying the Lesson
A. 1. Previous question
   2. Point of order
   3. Lay on the table
   4. Amend
   5. Question of privilege
   6. Postpone to definite time
   7. Amend
   8. Refer to committee

B. 1. b
   2. b
   3. a
   4. b
   5. a

6. Which motion requires a higher percentage of votes to pass?
   a. Closing nominations
   b. Referring to a committee

C. Conduct a parliamentary meeting, using the following imaginary situation. Your teacher will appoint specific students to fill the various roles. Each student should act as a secretary and take minutes of the meeting. Each student should be free to rise to a point of order at any appropriate time. (There will be no reading of minutes from a previous meeting in this exercise.)

CHAIRMAN: Calls the meeting to order and opens the floor for new business.
STUDENT A: Moves to install an exhaust fan to help ventilate the school.
STUDENT B: Seconds the motion. [Open discussion follows.]
STUDENT C: Comments that some exhaust fans are quite noisy.
STUDENT D: States that squirrel-cage fans run more quietly and work more efficiently than many other kinds.
STUDENT E: Proposes amendment to change "an exhaust fan" to "a squirrel-cage exhaust fan"
STUDENT F: Seconds the motion. [Open discussion follows.]
STUDENT D: Questions whether anyone in the group has an idea of what it would cost to purchase and install such a fan.
STUDENT B: Says that he wondered about that too and thinks the group needs more information before making any decision.
STUDENT G: Moves to refer the question to a committee, appointed by the chairman, to investigate the costs of purchasing and installing a squirrel-cage exhaust fan. (Remember to specify how many shall be on the committee and when they shall report back to the group.)
STUDENT A: Seconds the motion. [No open discussion follows immediately.]
STUDENT C: Makes a motion of the previous question.
STUDENT E: Seconds the motion.
CHAIRMAN: Calls for a vote by show of hands, and rules on the vote.
CHAIRMAN: Calls for a vote on the main motion, and rules on the vote.
CHAIRMAN: Appoints proper number of students to the committee.
STUDENT F: Moves to adjourn.
STUDENT G: Seconds the motion.
CHAIRMAN: Calls for a vote and announces the result. Adjourns the meeting.

---

115. Chapter 14 Review

A. Give the parliamentary term that fits each description.
   1. Another term for the chairman.
   2. A set of rules providing an orderly way to conduct the business of a group.
   3. Items of business that remain unresolved or postponed from the previous meeting.

Lesson 115

Purpose: To review the concepts taught in Chapter 14.

Teacher: The test on Chapter 14 is to be given after this lesson, with the final test to follow Lesson 118.

6. a

C. (Class activity.)

Lesson 115 Answers
A. 1. chair
   2. parliamentary procedure
   3. old business

4. The principle that determines the order in which motions are disposed of.
5. A check of the accuracy of the treasurer's accounts.
6. A formal suggestion or proposal.
7. A change in the wording of a motion.
8. The minimum number of members that must be present to transact business.
9. One of the motions that carry the primary business in a meeting.
10. The state of a motion when it is on the floor.
11. The official record of the business of a meeting.
12. Items of business that have not previously come before the group.
13. The right to address the assembly.

4. precedence
5. audit
6. motion
7. amendment
8. quorum
9. main motion
10. pending
11. minutes
12. new business
13. the floor

B. Write the letter of the best answer.
1. Before stating a main motion, a member must
   a. rise to his feet.   c. wait for the chairman to call his name.
   b. address the chairman.   d. do all the things above.
2. A member may remain seated to
   a. call attention to a point of order.
   b. second a motion.
   c. nominate someone for election to an office.
   d. do any of the things above.
3. The minutes of a meeting should include all the following *except*
   a. details about the time and place of the meeting.
   b. separate paragraphs for each item of business.
   c. details about the discussion on each motion.
   d. the wording of each motion that was acted upon.
4. The principle of precedence means
   a. that a main motion is put on hold if a member moves to take a recess.
   b. that a member could move to adjourn while a motion to amend is on the floor.
   c. that a motion to lay on the table must come to a vote before a motion to refer to a committee.
   d. all the things above.
5. A motion to amend can
   a. add words to the original motion.
   b. remove words from the original motion.
   c. completely replace the wording of the original motion.
   d. do any of the things above.

B. 1. d
   2. b
   3. c
   4. d
   5. d

C. For each description, write *chairman, vice-chairman, secretary, treasurer,* or *group.*
1. Discusses motions and amendments.
2. Keeps detailed records of the meetings.
3. Receives any income and pays any bills.
4. Presents motions and makes up the main voting body.
5. Takes the place of an absent chairman.
6. Writes and answers letters that pertain to the business of the group.

C. 1. group
   2. secretary
   3. treasurer
   4. group
   5. vice-chairman
   6. secretary

7. Keeps account of money matters of the group.
8. Determines who may have the floor.

D. Write *general consent, acclamation, hands, rising,* or *secret ballot* for each description. Some require more than one answer.
1. Allows the chairman to take an exact count.
2. Is used when the chairman senses that the group is largely in agreement.
3. Cannot show the will of the group if the vote is close.
4. Is especially suited for elections and sensitive issues.
5. Is used primarily for procedural matters, such as approving the minutes.
6. Is one of the most common methods for taking an exact vote on general matters.

E. Name the motion to be used for each of these purposes.
1. To address a violation of a rule when the chairman does not address it.
2. To assign several members to investigate a question before the group votes on it.
3. To set a time for the next meeting.
4. To introduce new business.
5. To change the wording of a motion.
6. To give a question more or less time on the floor.
7. To put off further debate on a motion until a specific later time.
8. To close a meeting.
9. To keep additional names from being added to a list for an election.
10. To put off further debate on a motion until the group votes to return it to the floor.
11. To give the group a break during a long meeting.
12. To bring back to the floor a motion that had earlier been voted on.
13. To request action relating to a member's comfort, rights, or privileges.
14. To take a motion off the floor after you proposed it.
15. To bring a tabled motion back to the floor.
16. To end debate on a motion and bring it to a vote.

F. Do these exercises.
1. List the four basic purposes served by parliamentary procedure.
2. Why can we not use parliamentary procedure to determine what is truth?
3. Arrange the following steps in the basic order of a business meeting: treasurer's report, new business, call to order, adjournment, old business, reading of the minutes, committee reports.
4. List at least three things you should do to help make a meeting flow smoothly and profitably.
5. What kind of motions can pass only by a two-thirds majority vote?
6. Why would a chairman cast a vote to break a tie? to make a tie?
7. Most properly stated motions begin with what words?

————————————

7. treasurer
8. chairman

D. 1. hands, rising, secret ballot
2. general consent, acclamation
3. acclamation
4. secret ballot
5. general consent
6. hands, rising

E. 1. point of order
2. refer to committee
3. adjourn to a certain time
4. main motion
5. amend
6. limit or extend debate
7. postpone to definite time
8. adjourn
9. closing nominations
10. lay on the table
11. take a recess
12. reconsider
13. question of privilege
14. withdrawal of a motion
15. take from the table
16. previous question

F. 1. (1) To determine the true intent of the assembly.
(2) To allow full, free, and frank discussion.
(3) To give a fair hearing to the minority.
(4) To assure that the will of the majority is done.
2. Truth is founded upon the unchanging Word of God.
3. (1) call to order
(2) reading of the minutes
(3) treasurer's report
(4) committee reports
(5) old business
(6) new business
(7) adjournment
4. (Any three of these.)
Effectively fill any office you have.
Think seriously about the decisions to be made.
Participate in group discussions so that others know your feelings and preferences.
Do your best to support the decisions of the group.
5. motions that would limit the free discussion of the group
6. to cause a motion to pass;
to defeat a motion
7. "I move that [to]"

Year-end Reviews

116. Final Review 1 (Chapters 1–5)

A. Write correctly each word that has an error in capitalization. For errors in punctuation, write the word before the error and add or omit the mark involved. Each sentence contains three mistakes. (A set of commas or a title counts as one item.)

1. Jesus spoke the following promise to his disciples "But when the Comforter is come, he shall testify of me" (John 15:26).
2. When God called Saul to be an Apostle He promised to do great things through this man
3. Spread the truth of the gospel o Lord over all the world.
4. Jesus' best-known prayer the Lord's Prayer holds a special place in many people's minds nevertheless relatively few live by its principles.
5. Ah these principles to be sure make strong demands on our carnal selfish nature.
6. My Grandfather's house which is a commodious dwelling serves as home to Lily Hoverdale, a young Christian who had to leave her parental home; Sandra Smith, the lower grade teacher at our school, and Martha Boll, a volunteer helper at the Pineville Rest Home.
7. Our Geography books point out how natives in the arctic live quite differently from those who live farther South.
8. Our library here at Lincolnshire Mennonite school has the book *The Way Down is the Way up,* but i have not read it yet.
9. William F. Gockley Sr owns a small machine shop at Johnsonville Illinois.
10. How zealously he serves the lord in his personal affairs, in his business life and in the church
11. Trusting the Lord to watch over us Father drove cautiously on but the storm grew worse, and made driving even more perilous.
12. In the latter part of the eighteenth century many americans were becoming increasingly hostile toward King George's Rule.
13. At our church cleaning is done weekly by the church families Mr. Long rather than by a paid Janitor.
14. Was Ferne glad to have aunt Abigail teach her Sunday School class

B. Each sentence below contains three errors in the use of quotation marks (and related capitalization), italics, dashes, parentheses, brackets, apostrophes, or hyphens. Write enough of each sentence to show the corrections. (A set of marks counts as one item.)

Lesson 116 Answers

A. (Corrections in capitalization are underlined.)

1. His disciples: come,…
2. apostle, man.
3. Gospel, O Lord,
4. prayer, Prayer, minds; nevertheless,
5. Ah, principles, sure, carnal,
6. grandfather's
   house, dwelling, school;
7. geography Arctic south
8. School
   The Way Down Is the Way Up   I
9. Gockley, Sr., Johnsonville,
10. Lord life, church!
11. us, on; worse
12. century, Americans rule
13. church, families, Long, janitor.
14. Aunt school class?

B. (Underlining is for italics. Allow variation in the use of dashes and parentheses to set off parenthetical elements.)

Lesson 116

Purpose: To review the concepts taught in Chapters 1–5.

Teaching Suggestions:

The exercises in these final reviews are not divided into the odd–even pattern. In this lesson, you may want to copy Parts A and B and have the students use proofreading marks.

1. The Lord God alone there is no other true God is all powerful, declared Brother Jerry.
2. See then that ye walk circumspectly (accurately; carefully), not as fools, but as wise Ephesians 5:15.
3. "Great aunt Hattie Rutt will turn eighty nine years old this weekend," noted Father, "So I think we as a family should plan to sing for her on Sunday afternoon."
4. You should get the book Our Northern Neighbors and read the chapter The Seal Hunt; its sure to give you some good ideas for your report on seal hunting by the Eskimos.
5. The word anoint does not have two consecutive ns.
6. The soon to be completed highway it will connect Elkdale to Mooseville will certainly be better than the present traffic congested road.
7. In the summer of 97, we took a two week trip to the mission in Guatemala to visit Fathers cousin who is serving there.
8. As the Silver Spray moved slowly up the river, the passengers heard one and two-minute recordings about the pre Columbian ruins that they passed.
9. The rain washed flowers how theyve grown these warm days! are smiling brightly in the morning sunshine.
10. Do you think well get the timing right in the song In Heavenly Love Abiding? asked Keith.

C. Do these exercises on study skills.
1. Why is interest the most important attitude for effective studying?
2. Name three ways to develop self-discipline in your studying.
3. What three noble purposes should motivate your study?
4. Why is having a regular study time valuable?
5. What two types of assignments should you tackle first in a study period?
6. Name at least three qualities of a suitable study environment.
7. How does good posture relate to effective studying?
8. List the five points of the SQ3R study method.
9. What is meant by reviewing actively?
10. List four worthwhile purposes of skimming.
11. What types of information should you include when taking notes on a speaker's topic?
12. How does outlining a lesson force a student to analyze it thoroughly?

D. Copy this outline correctly. Each starred line has at least one mistake.

Magnifying Christ in Our Bodies (Philippians 1)
*I. Paul's Prayer for the Philippians
A. His personal exercise of prayer
    *1. constancy (vv. 3–5)
    *2. Confident prayer (v. 6)
    *3. Having compassion (vv. 7, 8)

D. (Corrections are underlined; allow reasonable variation.)
Magnifying Christ in Our Bodies (Philippians 1)
I. Paul's prayer for the Philippians
A. His personal exercise of prayer
    1. Constancy (vv. 3–5)
    2. Confidence (v. 6)
    3. Compassion (vv. 7, 8)

1. "The —there is no other true God— all-powerful,"
2. "See [accurately; carefully] wise" (Ephesians 5:15).
3. Great-aunt eighty-nine so
4. Our Northern Neighbors "The Seal Hunt"; it's
5. anoint n's
6. soon-to-be-completed (it will connect Elkdale to Mooseville) traffic-congested
7. '97 two-week Father's
8. Silver Spray one- and pre-Columbian
9. rain-washed —how they've grown these warm days!—
10. "Do we'll 'In Heavenly Love Abiding'?"

C. 1. Interest helps you apply yourself to work.
2. Start working immediately. Be prepared to work hard. Stick to your work.
3. to master the material; to develop your mind; to glorify God
4. It helps prevent forgetfulness. Your mind is conditioned to study at that regular time.
5. the hardest and the least enjoyable
6. (Any three.) It should be a regular place to study. It should be as quiet and free from distractions as practical. Your study tools should be near at hand. It should be organized.
7. Good posture enables you to breathe naturally. It also helps to keep you alert and ready to work hard at studying.
8. Survey. Question. Read. Recite. Review.
9. recalling as many details by memory as possible, rather than merely looking at the lesson and remembering the details
10. to gain a bird's-eye view of a book or an article; to find information; to evaluate a book or an article; to review something studied previously
11. main ideas; significant subpoints; points that the speaker emphasizes; important definitions, figures, dates, names, and so forth; information that is new
12. The student must identify the main ideas and judge how the details relate to each other.

*B. The pointed expressions he gave
   1. Abound in love (v. 9)
  *2. That they would approve what is excellent (v. 10)
   *3. Attain full maturity (vv. 10, 11)
*II. How Paul served Christ
 *A. He endured persecution
  *1. in bonds (v. 13)
  *2. Suffered afflictions (vv. 15, 16)
  *3. Jeopardy of death (v. 20)
 *B. The purpose
  1. Commitment to the Gospel (v. 17)
  *2. Desired that Christ be magnified (v. 20)
  *3. He was surrendered to Christ (vv. 21–26)
  *4. consistent in life (vv. 27–30)
 *C. The prize
  *1. exultation at the spread of the Gospel (vv. 12, 18)
  *2. He inspired others to speak out (vv. 13, 14)
  *3. Anticipated a victorious death (v. 21)

E. Label each numbered word group *S* (complete sentence), *F* (fragment), *R* (run-on error), or *E* (elliptical sentence).

[1]"It looks as if it might rain tonight or tomorrow," said Father. [2]"We should try hard to get the corn planted today. [3]If we expect to be selling sweet corn by the middle of July."

[4]"Right. [5]The ground should be in excellent condition now," agreed Timothy. [6]"With a good rain, the seeds should germinate quickly, things should be in good shape in July."

F. Label each underlined word, using the following abbreviations.

S—subject	IO—indirect object
V—verb	OC—objective complement
PA—predicate adjective	OP—object of preposition
PN—predicate nominative	AP—appositive
DO—direct object	DA—noun of direct address

1. [a]Young person, developing a fear of God is extremely [b]important.
2. Indeed, godly fear makes [a]life truly [b]meaningful.
3. True godly fear, the [a]combination of devotion and reverence, has always been an essential [b]foundation for a satisfying life.
4. Without this quality, no [a]man can truly give God His rightful [b]place.
5. When a person fails to give [a]God His rightful place, sin takes control of his [b]life.
6. Sin always [a]destroys peace and [b]satisfaction.

G. Label each underlined word group *prep.* (prepositional phrase), *vb.* (verbal phrase), *ps.* (phrase of a single part of speech), *D* (dependent clause), or *I* (independent clause). Also label the part of speech for each item (except independent clauses).

B. His pointed expressions
  1. Abound in love (v. 9)
  2. Approve what is excellent (v. 10)
  3. Attain full maturity (vv. 10, 11)
II. Paul's service for Christ
 A. The persecution
  1. In bonds (v. 13)
  2. In afflictions (vv. 15, 16)
  3. In jeopardy of death (v. 20)
 B. The purpose
  1. Commitment to the Gospel (v. 17)
  2. Desire that Christ be magnified (v. 20)
  3. Surrender to Christ (vv. 21–26)
  4. Consistency in life (vv. 27–30)
 C. The prize
  1. Exultation at the spread of the Gospel (vv. 12, 18)
  2. Inspiration to others to speak out (vv. 13, 14)
  3. Anticipation of a victorious death (v. 21)

E.			
1. S		4. E	
2. S		5. S	
3. F		6. R	

F.		
1.	a. DA	b. PA
2.	a. DO	b. OC
3.	a. AP	b. PN
4.	a. S	b. DO
5.	a. IO	b. OP
6.	a. V	b. DO

1. Many short, simple words ᵃin our English language hide amazing word histories ᵇthat a study of etymologies can uncover.
2. ᵃExamining the simple word *barn,* for example, reveals a term ᵇderiving from two Old English words.
3. ᵃThe Old English word *bere* meant "barley," and the word *ærn* meant "place"; therefore, ᵇin the *bere-ærn* was where an Old English farmer stored his barley.
4. By using a dictionary ᵃto examine the history of *about,* we can find the meaning of this word ᵇwhen it was first used.
5. ᵃIn Old English days, the word *about* ᵇhad been *onbūtan,* meaning "on outside."
6. ᵃWhat was "on the outside" was not far away; hence the word has come to mean "nearby," "nearly," or "around" ᵇin Modern English.

H. Label each sentence according to its use (*dec., int., imp., exc.*) and its structure (*S, CD, CX, CD-CX*). End punctuation has been omitted.
1. Will Mother come home from the hospital today, or must she stay for further observation
2. Her speedy recovery has surprised everyone, including her doctor
3. If only the doctor would recognize that the prayer of faith has been effective
4. When he heard about the anointing service, he said nothing; but the look on his face betrayed his skepticism
5. Pray for him, that this experience might lead him toward faith in God

I. Label the word order of each sentence *N* (natural), *I* (inverted,) or *M* (mixed).
1. By her commitment of faith, Ruth the Moabitess found rest among God's people.
2. Along with Ruth's decision to stay with Naomi went her commitment to Naomi's God and Naomi's people.
3. When she left Moab, she made a complete break with her heathen past.
4. The Lord, under whose wings Ruth came to trust, richly rewarded her faith.

J. Label the style of each sentence *L* (loose), *P* (periodic), or *B* (balanced).
1. Faith in prayer is good, but prayer in faith is better.
2. The prayer of faith can work miracles because it links a mortal man to the omnipotent God.
3. If a person truly believes in God's ability and willingness to bless, he will pray regularly.
4. The more we pray about circumstances, the less we will worry about them.

K. Do these exercises on expository essays.
1. What is the goal of all expository writing?
2. How should the introductory paragraph begin, and how should it end?
3. Name three types of concrete details that the writer of exposition should use in developing his paragraphs.

G. 1. a. prep., adj.   b. D, adj.
2. a. vb., n.   b. vb., adj.
3. a. I   b. prep., n.
4. a. vb., adv.   b. D, adv.
5. a. prep., adv.   b. ps., v.
6. a. D, n.   b. prep., adv.

H. 1. int., CD
2. dec., S
3. exc., CX
4. dec., CD-CX
5. imp., CX

I. 1. M
2. I
3. M
4. N

J. 1. B
2. L
3. P
4. B

K. 1. to explain something (*or* to lead the reader to say, "I understand")
2. It should begin with a broad, general opening sentence.
It should end with a sentence that directly states the theme of the essay.
3. specific facts that tell *what;* sound reasons that tell *why;* clear illustrations that show *how*

4. What are three good ways to conclude an expository essay?
5. Why should you state the purpose of your essay before you begin doing research?
6. List four reasons why it is wise to use more than one reference source in researching for an essay.
7. What is plagiarism?
8. When taking notes, what three things can you do to help avoid plagiarism?
9. For what three types of information should you write footnotes?
10. What are three important characteristics of an appropriate title?
11. What does the abbreviation *ibid.* mean?
12. What is a bibliography?

L. Choose the standard expressions in parentheses.
1. Abraham demonstrated his (noted, noteworthy, notorious) faith by (almost, most) (always, all ways) building an (altar, alter) when he stopped in his sojourning.
2. Abraham's failure to (raise, rise) such a place of worship during his sojourn in Egypt (implies, infers) that his faith was weaker (than, then) it should (have, of) been.
3. Father (proposed, purposed) a plan to (adapt, adopt) the machine to our needs by using this (ingenious, ingenuous) device, and it (maybe, may be) that his idea will work.
4. Uncle Lewis thinks that (its, it's) (alright, all right) to (precede, proceed) with the plan, but Father is (kind of, somewhat) afraid it will not work.
5. Sometimes one (looses, loses) much time (setting, sitting) in a traffic jam, but in (them, those) times we must be sure (and, to) maintain a patient manner.
6. Rather than (flaunting, flouting) (your, you're) supposed wisdom, you should be willing to (accept, except) the (advice, advise) of others.
7. The influence of one youth with (respectable, respective) behavior goes a long (way, ways) toward helping others to have a right (perspective, prospective) and to behave (good, well).
8. The (comprehensible, comprehensive) data in the (eminent, imminent, immanent) scientist's report (lets, leaves) little doubt (anymore, any more) about the dangers of using tobacco.
9. Although this book was (some, somewhat) better than the other one, Father had to (censor, censure) a small (amount, number) of words from it; now I (can, may) finally read it.
10. (How come, Why) was the bicycle (laying, lying) (behind, in back of) the car, where someone might back (straight, strait) over it without seeing it?

———————————

4. (Any three.)
by summarizing the steps or main points;
by emphasizing the importance or usefulness of what has been explained;
by using a contrast;
by using a quotation;
by calling for a response from the reader
5. Stating the purpose will help you to stay on track as you select the right information.
6. to help balance the essay by giving a wider scope of details;
to help you express your ideas in your own words;
to verify information;
to help you avoid misinterpreting facts
7. copying another person's writing and passing it off as your own
8. Use other's ideas, not their exact words.
Write short phrases rather than whole sentences.
Place direct quotations in quotation marks and credit them properly.
9. direct quotations;
details that the reader might question;
technical information
10. is short;
relates directly to the theme;
catches the reader's interest
11. "in the same place"
12. a complete listing of all the sources (except the Bible) that you consulted in writing your essay

L. 1. noteworthy, almost, always, altar
2. raise, implies, than, have
3. proposed, adapt, ingenious, may be
4. it's, all right, proceed, somewhat
5. loses, sitting, those, to
6. flaunting, your, accept, advice
7. respectable, way, perspective, well
8. comprehensive, eminent, leaves, anymore
9. somewhat, censor, number, may
10. Why, lying, behind, straight

117. Final Review 2 (Chapters 6–9)

A. Write the term that fits each description.
1. The lesson that a story teaches.
2. The struggle or problem that the main character faces.
3. The point of highest intensity in the main character's struggle.
4. The process of portraying story characters.
5. Another name for the main character.
6. A name for a person who opposes the main character.
7. The perspective from which an author writes a story.
8. A perspective in which the author poses as the main character and uses *I* and *me.*
9. A perspective in which the author writes as if he were able to see every character equally well.
10. A perspective in which the author follows one particular character through the story.

B. Answer these questions about short stories.
1. Why can stories often communicate truth more effectively than essays?
2. What three things does a story setting include?
3. What three types of conflict do short stories commonly develop?
4. What are five ways in which the story characters may be portrayed?
5. What is the difference between a subjective and an objective point of view?
6. What are three things that help to make titles appealing?

C. Copy each noun, and label it *concrete* or *abstract.* Also label its gender (*M, F, N, C*).
1. The ten boys and twelve girls in our classroom had the opportunity to sing for Brother Henry's aged grandfather.
2. Many neighbors offered their assistance when our barn burned.
3. These kittens are enjoying their new liberty as they explore the world beyond their nest.

D. Write the plural form of each noun. Use the foreign plural spellings for numbers 8–12.
1. proof-of-purchase
2. knife
3. chimney
4. sheep
5. bluff
6. trio
7. tooth
8. nebula
9. apex
10. oasis
11. criterion
12. cactus

E. Rewrite each expression, using possessive forms. If it is better not to use a possessive form, write *X* after the number.
1. the aprons of the girls
2. the doors of the shed
3. the betrayal of Judas
4. the rapid spread of the fungi
5. the kittens of Abigail and Sheryl (joint ownership)
6. the chores of Curtis and Olen (separate ownership)

Lesson 117

Purpose: To review the concepts taught in Chapters 6–9.

Lesson 117 Answers

A.
1. theme
2. conflict
3. climax
4. characterization
5. protagonist
6. antagonist
7. point of view
8. first person point of view
9. omniscient point of view
10. third person point of view

B.
1. Readers identify with the story characters (and their emotions become involved). A story shows how truth works in real life.
2. place, time, emotional or spiritual atmosphere
3. main character against another character; main character against his circumstances; main character against himself
4. actions; speech; thoughts; appearance; reputation
5. In a subjective point of view, the author can show the thoughts of one or more characters.
   In an objective point of view, the author cannot show any character's thoughts.
6. alliteration; rhyming words; unusual word combinations

C.
1. boys—concrete, M; girls—concrete, F; classroom—concrete, N; opportunity—abstract, N; grandfather—concrete, M
2. neighbors—concrete, C; assistance—abstract, N; barn—concrete, N
3. kittens—concrete, C; liberty—abstract, N; world—concrete, N; nest—concrete, N

D.
1. proofs-of-purchase
2. knives
3. chimneys
4. sheep
5. bluffs
6. trios
7. teeth
8. nebulae
9. apices
10. oases
11. criteria
12. cacti

E.
1. the girls' aprons
2. X
3. Judas's betrayal
4. X (*or* the fungi's rapid spread)
5. Abigail and Sheryl's kittens
6. Curtis's and Olen's chores

F. Copy all the pronouns, including possessive pronouns. Label each one *P* (personal), *CP* (compound personal), *D* (demonstrative), *ID* (indefinite), *IR* (interrogative), or *R* (relative).
1. Who watches over us daily and is well able to deal with anything that we may face?
2. God Himself watches over each of His children, and that is a comforting thought to everyone who trusts Him.
3. Every morning you should commit yourself anew to the Lord's care, which provides the only true security that is available in this world.

G. Copy each substantive in these sentences, and label it *N* (one-word or compound noun), *pron.* (pronoun), *G* (gerund or gerund phrase), *I* (infinitive or infinitive phrase), *prep.* (prepositional phrase), *C* (clause), *T* (title), or *S* (subject of discussion). If a substantive is within a substantive phrase or clause or within a title, do not list it separately.
1. At Bible school, my brother bought the book *The Swiss Anabaptists* for his class.
2. Studying those lessons gave him a renewed appreciation for our faithful heritage.
3. Above ninety degrees is what the weatherman predicts for today.
4. To understand the Biblical use of *mansion*, you need to find an archaic definition.

H. Write each underlined item correctly. If an item has no error, write *correct*.
1. The responsibility was not <u>our's</u>, and we did not know <u>who</u> we should tell.
2. I could not understand <u>that there</u> algebra problem, but Elmer figured it out <u>hisself</u>.
3. Sue Ellen and <u>myself</u> could not seem to work as efficiently as <u>she</u>.
4. This week is <u>Amos's and Alvin's turn</u> to milk the cows, so <u>me and Gerald</u> will do the feeding and take care of the hogs.
5. We should be friendly to the visitors <u>which</u> come to church even though we do not know <u>who</u> they are.
6. This <u>calf coughing</u> indicates a serious problem that <u>them</u> in the other hutches do not seem to have.

I. Answer these questions about the style of short stories.
1. What are three ways to keep story dialogue natural?
2. Why do words like *perhaps, seemed,* and *somewhat* tend to mar the style of a story?
3. What are clichés, and where might you properly use them in a story?
4. Why should a story appeal to the reader's five senses?
5. Why should a story contain more verbs in the active voice than linking verbs and verbs in the passive voice?
6. What is static description, and how should it be included in a story?
7. What is arrested action?
8. What three categories of words should you use to paint descriptive details in your stories?

F. 1. Who—IR; us—P; anything—ID; that—R; we—P
2. Himself—CP; each—ID; His—P; that—D; everyone—ID; who—R; Him—P
3. you—P; yourself—CP; which—R; that—R

G. 1. Bible school—N; brother—N; book—N; *The Swiss Anabaptists*—T; class—N
2. Studying those lessons—G; him—pron.; appreciation—N; heritage—N
3. Above ninety degrees—prep.; what the weatherman predicts for today—C
4. use—N; *mansion*—S; you—pron.; to find an archaic definition—I

H. 1. ours; whom
2. that; himself
3. I; correct
4. Amos and Alvin's turn; Gerald and I
5. who; correct
6. calf's coughing; those

I. 1. Keep the tone informal.
Change speakers frequently.
Use descriptive explanatory words.
2. They make a story weak and inexact.
3. A cliché is an expression which has been repeated so often that it no longer has its original force.
You may properly use clichés in dialogue.
4. Appealing to the five senses helps the reader to live with the story characters.
5. Verbs in the active voice keep the story moving more briskly and energetically than do linking verbs or verbs in the passive voice.
6. Static description is description that does not move the story forward.
It should be slipped into a phrase or clause within a sentence that does carry the story action.
7. Arrested action occurs when story characters merely *begin* or *start* to do things rather than actually doing them.
8. exact, descriptive words; simple, familiar words; imagery

J. Choose the correct expressions in parentheses.
1. The wickedness of Sodom had (rose, risen) to God.
2. Apparently one of Abraham's visitors (was, were) the Lord Himself.
3. (Don't, Doesn't) God's Word warn us to remember Lot's wife?
4. Ten righteous people (represent, represents) a small remnant, but Sodom had fewer than that.
5. Jesus certainly (did, done) more for us than we can ever repay.
6. Christian ethics (call, calls) us to complete honesty in our dealings with others.
7. All of these issues (demand, demands) careful forethought.
8. *Brethren* (is, are) an archaic plural form that we use commonly within the church.
9. The crew of workers (have, has) scattered to their specific assignments.
10. The crew of workers (have, has) finished its work for the day.
11. Grandfather Ebb's have (went, gone) to India to visit Uncle Fred's family.
12. The shears (cut, cuts) much better since Father sharpened the blades.
13. Neither my book nor my papers (is, are) where I thought I put them.
14. About four-fifths of the peach harvest (have, has) been lost in the late freeze.
15. Josephine, along with her younger sisters, (do, does) Sister Arlene's cleaning.
16. Jelly and peanut butter (is, are) a common sandwich.
17. The jelly and the peanut butter (have, has) been put on the table.
18. Obed is the only one of us children who (is, are) left-handed.
19. Has the cattle hauler (took, taken) Big Bill to the auction yet?
20. Either Connie or Jennifer (make, makes) these pillow tops.

K. Name the tense of each underlined verb. Also write whether the verb is *TA* (transitive, active voice), *TP* (transitive, passive voice), *IC* (intransitive complete), or *IL* (intransitive linking).
1. Little white lambs <u>are frisking</u> in the meadow.
2. Grazing contentedly on the lush grass, the ewes <u>watched</u> their offspring.
3. This year our peas <u>had been planted</u> before the first day of spring.
4. Before the last day of school, we <u>shall have picked</u> peas several times.
5. The rains <u>have been</u> quite adequate so far this spring.
6. Father <u>will look</u> for some extra help during the busiest part of the season.

L. Write the correct subjunctive verb for each sentence.
1. We desire that God (grant, grants) us wisdom to live consistently in a wicked world.
2. Praise (be, is) to the Name of Jesus forever.
3. The officials urge that everyone (take, takes) special precautions against the coming storm.
4. If we (would not have, had not) trusted God, we too would have panicked.
5. Suppose a devastating storm (was, were) to destroy our house!

J. 1. risen
2. was
3. Doesn't
4. represents
5. did
6. calls
7. demand
8. is
9. have
10. has
11. gone
12. cut
13. are
14. has
15. does
16. is
17. have
18. is
19. taken
20. makes

K. 1. present, IC
2. past, TA
3. past perfect, TP
4. future perfect, TA
5. present perfect, IL
6. future, IC

L. 1. grant
2. be
3. take
4. had not
5. were

118. Final Review 3 (Chapters 10–14)

A. Answer these questions about descriptive essays.
   1. What is the goal of descriptive writing?
   2. What three types of words contribute to vivid language in descriptive writing?
   3. What two important considerations must you remember as you select the details for a descriptive essay?
   4. What two orders of development are used in descriptive essays, and what type of essay uses each order?
   5. You do not usually find an entire essay of descriptive writing. Then where do you find most descriptive writing?
   6. Why must you choose a familiar subject when you plan a descriptive essay?
   7. What is the theme of a descriptive essay?

B. Copy each underlined adjective. First label it *L* (limiting), or *D* (descriptive); then label it *AT* (attributive), *AP* (appositive), or *PR* (predicate).
   1. Two fragrant lilac bushes grace the front yard.
   2. We listened to the mockingbird singing, and that song certainly was a beautiful one to hear.
   3. These German paintings, colorful and detailed, look lovely.

C. Copy each underlined adverb and the word or word group that it modifies. Write *sentence* if it modifies the whole sentence.
   1. Mother could not stop on the treacherously icy roads, and the car went almost over the bank, dangling dangerously on the edge.
   2. If the roads are nearly too slippery for a short drive, how will Father go to Greenville to preach?
   3. Understandably, the strangers entered the church somewhat hesitantly.
   4. After the service, the visitors became pleasantly relaxed.

D. Label each underlined word group *prep.* (prepositional phrase), *part.* (participial phrase), *inf.* (infinitive phrase), or *cl.* (clause). Also label each *adj.* or *adv.*
   1. Newton's third law of motion, ᵃwhich states that for every action there is an equal and opposite reaction, gives the scientific basis ᵇfor jet propulsion.
   2. You can use a balloon ᵃfilled with air ᵇto illustrate this principle.
   3. ᵃWhile the opening is held shut, there is no action and the balloon does not move ᵇin any direction.
   4. ᵃWhen you release the balloon, its rubber sides, ᵇstretched tightly, perform the action of forcing air rapidly out.
   5. This action in one direction causes a reaction that gives the balloon a tendency ᵇto move in the opposite direction.

E. Label each underlined phrase or clause *R* (restrictive) or *N* (nonrestrictive). Also copy each word that should be followed by a comma, and add the comma.
   1. Jet engines ᵃwhich propel many large airplanes operate on the same principle ᵇdescribed in the preceding sentences.

Lesson 118

Purpose: To review the concepts taught in Chapters 10–14.

Lesson 118 Answers

A. 1. to paint a clear picture in the reader's mind
   2. exact nouns, expressive verbs, picturesque modifiers
   3. Recognize important details. Choose details that match your theme (the specific impression you want to give).
   4. spatial order for scenes; chronological order for events
   5. Most descriptive writing is woven into narrative essays (stories), argumentative essays, and expository essays.
   6. because a descriptive essay gives personal impressions about a scene or an event
   7. the specific impression the author wants to give

B. 1. Two—L, AT; fragrant—D, AT; front—L or D, AT
   2. singing—D, AP; that—L, AT; beautiful—D, AT; to hear—D, AP
   3. German—D, AT; colorful—D, AP; detailed—D, AP; lovely—D, PR

C. 1. treacherously—icy; almost—over; dangerously—dangling
   2. nearly—too slippery; too—slippery; how—will go; to preach—will go
   3. Understandably—sentence; somewhat—hesitantly; hesitantly—entered
   4. pleasantly—relaxed

D. 1. a. cl., adj.   b. prep., adj.
   2. a. part., adj.   b. inf., adv.
   3. a. cl., adv.   b. prep., adv.
   4. a. cl., adv.   b. part., adj.
   5. a. prep., adj.   b. inf., adj.

E. 1. a. N; engines, airplanes,
      b. R

2. In the front part is a powerful compressor ªforcing air into the engine; in the back is the combustion chamber ᵇwhere rapid burning of the fuel creates tremendous pressure.

3. The pressure ªthat has been described is an action; it produces a reaction of equal force ᵇwhich moves the engine and the airplane through the air.

F. Write enough of each sentence to show how to correct the errors in using forms of comparison.
  1. Of my two brothers, Gordon has the curliest hair.
  2. The calf in the first hutch seemed sick yesterday, and today it is much worser.
  3. You can make a circle rounder by using a compass than by drawing it freehand.
  4. With modern technology, we can do many chores easier than our grandparents could.
  5. We spend far littler time doing the basic jobs than they did.
  6. Of the boomerangs we four boys made, Vernon's goes the fartherest.
  7. Today's weather is more pleasanter than we have had all week.
  8. The temperature will probably rise higher today than on any day of this week.

G. Do these exercises on using reference books.
  1. Why does a word like *post* have more than one numbered entry?
  2. What three types of inflections do most dictionaries show?
  3. Read these sample dictionary entries, and do the exercises that follow.

  sound¹ (sound) *n.* **1.** Vibrations transmitted through a solid, liquid, or gas, which usually can be heard with the ears. **2.** A distinctive noise. **3.** The distance over which something can be heard. —**sound** *v.* **sound·ed, sound·ing, sounds.** —*intr.* **1.a.** To make or give forth a sound. **b.** To be given forth as a sound. **2.** To give a particular impression. —*tr.* **1.** To cause to give forth or produce a sound. **2.** To summon, announce, or signal by a sound. [Middle English *soun,* from Old French *son,* from Latin *sonus.*]

  sound² (sound) *adj.* **sound·er, sound·est. 1.** Free from defect, decay, or injury; in good condition. **2.** Having a firm basis; unshakable. **3.** Financially secure or safe. **4.** Based on valid reasoning. —**sound** *adv.* Thoroughly; deeply: *sound asleep.* [Middle English, from Old English *gesund.*] —**sound·ly** *adv.* —**sound·ness** *n.*

  a. What two parts of speech is entry 1? entry 2?
  b. From what language does entry 1 come? entry 2?
  c. What inflections are given for each entry?
  d. What derivatives are given for entry 2?

  4. Name the usage labels that fit these descriptions. If more than one label fits, a number in parentheses tells how many you should have.
  a. Words acceptable only in everyday speaking and everyday writing.
  b. Words used in relatively small areas or by a limited group of people. (2)
  c. Words to avoid because they represent poor English. (3)
  d. Words invented by people trying to say things in unique ways.
  e. Words no longer in general use. (2)
  f. Words to avoid because of their association with evil.

2. a. N; compressor,
   b. N; chamber,
3. a. R
   b. N; force,

F. 1. curlier
   2. worse
   3. more nearly round
   4. more easily
   5. less
   6. farthest
   7. more pleasant
   8. any other day

G. (Answers are based on *The American Heritage Dictionary, Third Edition.* Other dictionaries may vary.)
  1. Several words of different origins and meanings have the same spelling. Some dictionaries include a different entry for each part of speech that a word may be.
  2. irregular plural forms of nouns; irregular principal parts of verbs; irregular forms of comparison for adjectives and adverbs
  3. a. *entry 1:* noun, verb;
       entry 2: adjective, adverb
     b. *entry 1:* Latin;
       entry 2: Old English
     c. *entry 1:* sounded, sounding, sounds;
       entry 2: sounder, soundest
     d. soundly, soundness
  4. a. informal
     b. regional, dialectal
     c. nonstandard, substandard, illiterate
     d. slang
     e. archaic, obsolete
     f. vulgar

5. What is the etymology of a word?
6. What are word inflections?
7. What is the difference between the denotation and the connotation of a word?
8. Why is it important to consider the connotations of words you might choose from a thesaurus?
9. What two important cautions should you remember about using encyclopedias?
10. What is the difference between a geographical and a political map?

H. Do these exercises about libraries.
1. What are the three important rules for using a library courteously?
2. Why must you use a library prudently?
3. What is a common system of classification for arranging books in a library?
4. What is the call number of a book?
5. Name the primary index for the books within a library.
6. Classify each item as *reference, fiction,* or *biography.*
   a. Imaginary stories.
   b. Stories about the personal lives of individuals.
   c. Books used for looking up facts.
   d. May have the number 92 instead of a Dewey decimal number.
   e. Books arranged alphabetically according to the name of the person written about.
   f. Books of general information.
   g. Books arranged alphabetically by the last name of the author.
   h. Some books in more than one category of the Dewey decimal system.

I. Label each underlined word *prep.* (preposition), *CC* (common coordinating conjunction), *Cor* (correlative conjunction), *SC* (subordinating conjunction), or *CA* (conjunctive adverb).
1. ᵃIf we have not quiet in our minds, outward comfort will do no more for us than a golden slipper ᵇon a gouty foot. (John Bunyan)
2. Thought and theory must precede all [wholesome] action, ᵃyet action is nobler in itself than ᵇeither thought or theory. (William Wadsworth)
3. A man can fail many times; ᵃhowever, he isn't a failure ᵇuntil he begins to blame somebody else. (John Burroughs)
4. ᵃIn this world, it is not what we take up, ᵇbut what we give up, that makes us rich. (Henry Ward Beecher)

J. Write enough of each sentence to show how to correct the errors in using conjunctions.
1. Every Christian must both pray for wisdom and for strength if he is to endure.
2. Saving faith involves not only believing with the mind but obeying in life.
3. Many believe that faith only will save, however, the Bible clearly teaches that faith must be accompanied by obedience.
4. He who trusts in God can relate to life's uncertainties calmly and without fear.
5. We know that God rules over all with benevolent care so we trust our lives to Him.

5. a brief history of the origin of a word
6. the changes in a word to show number, tense, and so forth
7. The denotation of a word is its strict, exact meaning;
   the connotation is its "personality."
8. The connotation of one word may not fit the context in which a synonym might fit.
9. Encyclopedias contain secular and humanistic ideas.
   They provide only general information about a particular subject.
10. A geographical map shows things such as topography, vegetation, and land use.
    A political map shows the boundaries of nations, states, and provinces.

H. 1. Be quiet.
      Be careful.
      Be punctual.
2. Many books in a public library are unwholesome to read.
3. the Dewey decimal system
4. the number that a library assigns to a book, based on the Dewey decimal system
5. card catalog
6. a. fiction   e. biography
   b. biography   f. reference
   c. reference   g. fiction
   d. biography   h. reference

I. 1. a. SC   b. prep.
   2. a. CC   b. Cor
   3. a. CA   b. SC
   4. a. prep.   b. CC

J. 1. pray both for
   2. but also obeying
   3. save;
   4. calmly and fearlessly (*or* with calmness and without fear)
   5. care,

K. Copy each interjection, the word before it (if there is one), and the word after it. Use correct capitalization and punctuation, and underline any word that should be italicized.

1. Alleluia the Lord our God reigns with sovereign power.
2. Oh how restful to commit our cares and perplexities to Him!
3. In every age, God calls men to simple faith in Him; and behold the very ability to believe is a gift of His love.
4. Salt we thought this was the sugar bowl.
5. Buzz the sound of those hornets put wings on my feet!

L. Rewrite each sentence so that it communicates the same idea without the underlined idiom.

1. Do not allow yourself to be <u>out of sorts</u> simply because something did not please you.
2. We failed to <u>take into account</u> how hard-packed the earth would be.
3. This scroll saw has surely <u>lived up to</u> its promised performance.
4. We have <u>turned down</u> many invitations to buy new products.

M. Do these exercises on parliamentary procedure.

1. What is parliamentary procedure?
2. List the four basic purposes of parliamentary procedure.
3. Why can we not use parliamentary procedure to determine what is truth?
4. What is meant by having the floor in a meeting?
5. What are the minutes of a meeting?
6. What is a quorum?
7. What method of voting is used for procedural matters, such as approving the minutes?
8. What is voting by acclamation?
9. When is a two-thirds majority vote required to pass a motion?
10. Why would a chairman cast a vote to break a tie? to make a tie?
11. What is the purpose of main motions in a parliamentary meeting?
12. Most properly stated motions begin with what words?
13. When several motions are properly presented at the same time, what principle determines the order in which the motions are disposed of?
14. Explain the expression "A motion is pending."

K. 1. Alleluia! The
   2. Oh, how
   3. and, behold, the
   4. Salt! We
   5. <u>Buzz</u>! The

L. (Sample answers.)
   1. Do not allow yourself to be irritable simply because something did not please you.
   2. We failed to consider how hard-packed the earth would be.
   3. This scroll saw has performed as well as it was promised to.
   4. We have refused many invitations to buy new products.

M. 1. a set of rules providing an orderly way to transact group business
   2. to determine the true intent of the assembly;
      to allow full, free, and frank discussion;
      to give a fair hearing to the minority;
      to assure that the will of the majority is done
   3. because the Bible is the final authority for sound doctrine
   4. having the right to address the assembly
   5. the official record of the meeting
   6. the minimum number of members that must be present to transact business
   7. voting by general consent
   8. voting by voice—saying "Aye" or "Nay"
   9. when the motion would limit free discussion on a matter
   10. to pass a motion;
       to defeat a motion
   11. to carry the primary business in a meeting
   12. "I move that…" or "I move to…"
   13. the principle of precedence
   14. A motion is before the group for discussion and eventually for a vote.

Lesson 7

A. Use the proper proofreading marks to correct the errors in the sentences below. Each sentence needs one insertion and one deletion or replacement.

1. The fear of the Lord is the begining of wisdome.

2. If you want to be wise, fear God, obey the Bible, and respect ~~the~~ your parents.

3. Who would ever regret, any effort put forth in developing noble Christian ideals?

4. When Josephs brothers sold him, they did not ~~no~~ know that they would meet him in Egypt many years later.

5. The many plants in Grandmothers house reveal her love for growing thengs.

6. "How many busshels of apples did you pick? asked Kevin.

B. Use the proper proofreading marks to correct the errors in capitalization. In each sentence, one letter should be changed to uppercase and one to lowercase.

1. The Lord chose Paul to be the Apostle to the gentiles.

2. How many Sufferings he would need to endure as a christian!

3. Paul traveled through Asia minor and Parts of Europe, spreading the Gospel.

4. Do you know how many Missionary journeys are recorded in the Book of acts?

5. Just as I finished reading "Dreams of no Value," my Mother called.

C. Now try your editing skills on the selection below. You will need to do the following things.
   a. Make five insertions.
   b. Make five deletions or replacements. (Be sure to read the note following the selection.)
   c. Make five corrections in capitalization.
   d. Mark two places where a new paragraph should begin.
   e. Show that one word already deleted should be retained.

This means that eighteen corrections are needed. Can you find them all?

1. Solar eclipses have long struck fear in the hearts of

2. men and have given rise too many myths and superstitions.

3. For example, the ancient chinese thought a dragon was

4. swallowing the sun. They held noisy ceremonies to make

5. the Dragon sick and cause him to spew the sun out again.

6. Chinese astronomers were responsible to to predict coming

7. eclipses so that the people would be ready to rescue the

8. sun. The same kind of ignorance still exists today. Before

9. a total eclipse occurred over south America on July 11

10. 1991, warnings were circulated that looking at any part of

11. the sky during the eclipse could cause the blindness.

12. Therefore, all people and livestock—especially horses—

13. were supposed to stay inside all during the whole event.

14. Another report indicated that rocks and dirt mite might fall

15. from the sky if the sun and the moon rubbed against

16. each other. How much better is knowledge than Ignorance!

17. When a solar eclipse occurs, those living in ignorance

18. prepare to protect themselves from imaginary dangers.

19. But those who know the truth can appreciate the event

20. as one of the most awesome examples of God's Handiwork.

Note: In the editing lessons, you will proofread a number of paragraphs on the subject of astronomy. You will not be expected to check the spelling of proper nouns or to verify technical information, such as the distance to a star.

Lesson 8

A. Use proofreading marks to correct the errors in capitalization and end punctuation.

1. the theme for our Bible school studies this summer is "Lessons from Bible youth"

2. "are you developing, o youth," asked brother Seth, "The qualities that god can use to build his kingdom"

3. in Math class we calculated the approximate distance that the israelites traveled from egypt to canaan.

4. What a surprise i had when grandfather invited me to go along to the writers' meeting at Glendale Mennonite church.

5. Although king Solomon gave much good advice in proverbs and ecclesiastes, he apparently did not follow it all himself.

B. Use proofreading marks to add the missing commas.

1. "Do we my brethren have the faith, fortitude and fidelity" asked Brother Amos "to face any persecution that may come?"

2. Knowing the perils of these end times we must stay close to God's Word which is our source of spiritual direction.

3. At our church services are held on the third Sunday evening of each month and we have a song service whenever there is a fifth Sunday.

4. Mr. Alton F. Young Jr. paid $450000 for a productive well-maintained farm near Harrisonburg Virginia.

5. In the vicinity of Clarkdale a cloudburst it is reported dumped over five inches of rain.

C. Use proofreading marks to correct the errors in the use of colons, semicolons, and ellipsis points. Place ellipsis points below the caret, and colons and semicolons above the caret.

1. "This wisdom descendeth not from above, but is earthly, sensual, devilish. But the wisdom that is from above is first pure ...." (James 3:15–17).

2. When we feel a lack of wisdom, we should remember one important fact God gives His wisdom freely to those who sincerely ask.

3. "Surely God is good to man, but how often" Grandfather sighed.

4. Since God has blessed us richly, we should serve Him faithfully but too many people, proud and selfish by nature, ignore God.

5. Examples of ingratitude in the Scriptures include; the children of Israel, who murmured frequently in the wilderness; Solomon, who turned to idolatry after God had enriched him supernaturally; and Jonah, who complained bitterly because God spared Nineveh.

D. Use proofreading marks to correct the errors in capitalization, punctuation, and italics.

1. Did you expect to hear Mother say, "We are having vanilla pie and ice cream for dessert"?

2. "Get the book The Christian Short Story, and read Chapter 4, entitled 'Style'," suggested Brother Weber.

3. Mr. Reed quoted the saying, "God helps them who help themselves"; however, Father pointed out that this statement does not apply to salvation.

4. "Uncle Ben wonders if we would like a ride on his sleigh, Queen of the Snow, which he has restored," announced Galen.

5. "Before you leave, would you folks sing 'Footprints of Jesus'?" asked Mrs. Lee.

E. Use proofreading marks to add the missing dashes, parentheses, and brackets.

1. "When tribulation or persecution ariseth because of the word, by and by [immediately] he is offended" (Matthew 13:21).

2. "I don't quite—oh, now I see what you mean!" exclaimed Donna.

3. Our strawberries—they surely produced abundantly this year!—have sold well. (give sharp emphasis)

4. Aunt Regina (she really isn't related to us) spends much time knitting. (minimize the importance)

5. "Well, I certainly would not—" Timothy gasped as a bolt of lightning struck the tree behind the barn.

Lesson 13

A. Use the proper proofreading marks to correct two spacing errors in each sentence.

1. The Sermon on the Mount is meant for to day, not just for some future age.

2. If every one followed Jesus' teachings, no one would knowingly mistreat others.

3. True Christians would rather suffer wrong than use physical force against an other person.

4. Using physical force in cludes taking some one to court.

5. Paul rebuked the Corinthians because of their law suits against each other.

B. Use the proper proofreading marks to indicate one use of italics and to correct one error of transposition in each sentence.

1. John Bunyan wrote The Pilgrim's Progress while was he in prison.

2. You haven't removed all the unnecessary and's from these paragraphs.

3. To spell accommodate, you write must two sets of double letters.

4. The book War-torn Valley tells a challenging story about nonresistance during the Civil War.

5. In 1927, Charles Lindbergh used the Spirit of St. Louis to the make first solo nonstop flight across the Atlantic Ocean.

C. Use the proper symbols to mark the changes indicated in parentheses.

1. The children asked if they might eat their lunches under the shade trees outside. (Move *outside* so that it follows *lunches*.)

2. Chastening is not pleasant; if we respond properly to it, however, we can benefit from the experience. (Move *however* and the comma after it to a position after the semicolon.)

3. Job remained faithful to God in spite of great loss and suffering. (Use an arrow and a vertical line to move the indented text to the left.)

D. Now try your editing skills on the selection below. You will need to do the following things.
   a. Make one correction in each full line. (You will use each proofreading mark at least once.)
   b. Show that one word already deleted should be retained.
   c. Make the third paragraph begin in line 13 rather than line 12.
   d. Show that the term *solar constant* is to be italicized.

Sixteen changes should be marked. Can you find them all?

1. Suppose man had to pay for all the solar#power that the

2. earth receives. At eight cents per kilowatt-hour, the Energy (lc)

3. reciÉved every second would cost $4 billion, or about two

4. dollars for every living person. Imagine! Each man, woman

5. and child wᵒuld have to pay $120 per minute, which comes to

6. $7,200 per hour or $172,800 per day. how (uc) long could your

7. family afford this? Yet God sends solar energy completely
   stet

8. free.

9. Remember too that the earth is but one tinny sphere

10. in the vast the solar system. The sun produces 2 billion

11. times as much energy as what the earth receives. no ¶

12. |←In fact, the sun produces in one second as much energy

13. as the earth receives in about sixty years. ¶ Scientists care-

14. fully measure the solₐr energy reaching the earth. They

15. find that the approximate rate is about 5 million Horse- (lc)

16. power per acre. This is called the solar constant, for it

17. has shown hardly any measur‿able change over the past

18. hundred years.

Lesson 26

A. Use proofreading marks to add the missing punctuation. In each sentence, one mark will go above the caret and one below.

1. "Boys have you finished digging the red beets" asked Mother.

2. John (the only cousin my age) will be visiting our farm this coming Saturday

3. "Then Jonah prayed unto the Lord out of the fish's belly" (Jonah 2 1).

4. You are welcome to eat lunch with us however we have only sandwiches and apples.

5. The fire chief had one main goal to determine, if possible the cause of the fire.

B. Use proofreading marks to insert one hyphen or dash and to make one deletion in each sentence. Make the loop curve down for at least two of your deletions.

1. I'll show you you how to prune this young peach tree it's a fairly simple procedure.

2. Be sure to use well-sharpened shears, for clean cuts heal more readdily than jagged ones.

3. A broken branches will be a long-term liability; remove it.

4. If branches are tangled together this does happen often—leave only the branch that is growing most directly from the trunk off the tree.

5. Now trimm off those high-reaching shoots.

6. Just a few more cuts, and we will but I see that it's time time to quit.

C. Use proofreading marks to correct the fourteen errors in these paragraphs. No line contains more than one error.

1.   The universe is so large that our mind's falter when

2. we consider its vast extent. To begin, consider the

3. number of of individual stars. We can see about 3,000

4. stars with the unaided eye; and by using a telescope,

5. we can see many, many more. But our galaxie (the Milky

6. Way) contains an estimated 200 billion stars—a number

7. that defies are comprehension. And scientists calculate

8. that there are than more 10 billion galaxies in the

9. observ able part of the universe!

10.   When we consider the distances involved in the universe,

11. our minds again stagger. Consider this. Even at the grate

12. speeds attained by space craft, it takes three days to reach

13. ←the moon. Traveling to Jupiter would take 2 years, and

14. going to Pluto would require 15 years. But these figures

15. pail when we compare the distance to the stars. Reaching

16. Alpha Centauri, the nearest star, would mean a trip almost

17. 100,000 years—and the spacecraft would still be deep

18. inside the Milky way!

19.   No Design is greater than its designer. As we consider

20. the mind-boggling size of the universe, we begin to grasp

21. the greatness and power of the God who created it.

Lesson 33

A. Correct the two errors of transposition in each sentence. Notes in parentheses give specific instructions for correcting some errors.

1. On our trip to the Midwest, we visited Colby, Wisconsin, place the where Colby cheese was first made.

2. Mr. Zeiger, *an old friend* who has just moved to a nursing home, ~~an old friend~~, requested that our family him visit often. (Use delete and insert symbols to make *an old friend* come immediately after *Mr. Zeiger.* Omit the comma after *friend.*)

3. The above two sentences are both declarative, not imperative. (Use the transpose symbol to make *above* follow *sentences.*)

4. The rich man was able to buy a new, large, expensive car every year. (Use the transpose symbol to make *new* come immediately before *car.* Delete the comma after *new.*)

5. "The secret of faithfulness under test really not is hard to understand," said Brother Arnold. (Use the transpose symbol to make *is* come before *really.*)

6. The three courageous Hebrews simply determined that they would do what was right regardless of the consequences.

B. Use the "delete space" symbol twice in each sentence. Some uses will be in connection with a letter that you should delete.

1. When Father returned from South America, he arrived at the air port late on Friday evenning.

2. Christians should be grateful for the priviledge to spread the Gospel with out government interference.

3. Every one was impressed by the extra ordinary abilities revealed by Pedro's work.

4. Our prayers should include petition, praise, confesssion, thanks giving, and intercession.

C. Use proofreading marks to correct the thirteen errors in the following paragraphs. No line has more than one error.

1. If our galaxy (the Milky Way) is so large that spacecraft

2. would require almost 100,000 years to reach the nearest

3. star, how large is the whole universe? Suppose we could

4. reduce the known universe one trilion times. This would

5. make the sun the size of a pinhead, and the entire solar

6. system would fit in side your classroom. How close would

7. the nearest star be now? It would be 26 miles (42 km)

8. away. And the Milky Way still be would about 600,000 miles

9. (970,000 km) in diameter!

10. Let us reduce everything again, this time until the

11. Milky Way is the size of a large pie pan. How big would that

12. make the known universe? The greatest dinstace that man

13. has peered into outer space would be 30 miles (48 km) away.

14. What a grate and mighty God we serve! "Thou art worthy,

15. O Lord, to recieve glory and honour and power: for thou

16. hast created all things, and for thy pleasure they are

17. and were created" (Revelation 4:11.)

Lesson 44

A. Use proofreading marks to correct the two capitalization or punctuation errors in each sentence.

1. In Math we learned that one acre contains 43560 square feet.

2. When an inch of rain falls 3,630 cubic feet of water is dumped on one Acre.

3. "I have read that the weight of water varies slightly," said Conrad.

4. One cubic foot of water weighs an average of 62.4 pounds, thus, one inch of

   rain on one acre weighs about 113 tons.

5. "Can you convert that figure to gallons," asked brother Henry.

6. The Total comes to more than 27000 gallons of water.

7. "What a tremendous amount of water falls in just a small Spring shower,"

   exclaimed Carol.

8. Water is precious to people of desert region's like the Sahara.

9. One Missionary in africa wrote that even the children knelt in gratitude when

   he gave them a drink of water.

10. "As cold waters to a thirsty soul, so is good news from a far country

    (Proverbs 25:25).

B. Use proofreading marks to correct the two usage errors in each sentence.

1. Whitcomb L. Judson was enthused about most any kind of new gadget.
   (iastic, almost)

2. He invented a considerable amount of useful every day items.
   (number)

3. One of his friends had a dilemma that would of been a trial for anyone.
   (problem, have)

4. Because of his stiff back, this friend all ways had a heap of trouble putting on his shoes.
   (always, serious)

5. The ingenuous inventor devised a slide fastener that differed with any fastener ever made before.
   (i, from)

6. This invention left a person fasten or lose his shoes by using just one hand.
   (o)

7. Judson's fastener alluded popular notice until an imminent manufacturer used it in a line of boots called Zippers.
   (e, e)

8. Be sure and notice that its the slide fasteners rather than the boots that are called zippers today.
   (to)

C. Use proofreading marks to correct the sixteen errors in the following paragraphs. No line has more than one error.

1. Early astronomers believed that the earth was at the

2. center of the universe. This fit ~~good~~ well with their view of man

3. and his importance. About A.D. 150, a Greek astronomer name_d_

4. Ptolemy produced a work of thirteen volumes ~~on~~ based on

5. this theory. He described a stationary earth with the sun,

6. the moon and the stars all revolving around it. For nearly

7. 1,500 years, people considered Ptolemy's theory to be fact.

8. In 1543, Nicolaus Copernicus propposed that the sun

9. rather than the earth was the center of the universe,

10. and that the ~~the~~ earth and other planets revolve around

11. the sun. His ideas still were not alright, but they

12. were closer to the truth than Ptolemy's were. This

13. new theory stirred up a storm of opposition. Men who

14. ~~ex~~cepted it were charged with heresy, and at least one

15. was burned (the at) stake. Galileo with his telescope

16. ←observed four moons of Jupiter revolving around that

17. Planet, which provided further support for the Copernican

18. theory. But in 1633, Roman catholic officials forced

19. Galileo to confess that he was in error!

20. Astronomers continued to study the haevens until they

21. proved beyond doubt that the planets in deed revolve

22. around the sun. Instead of being at the center, man and

23. his World are a mere speck in the grand universe that

24. God created.

Lesson 50

A. Use proofreading marks to correct the two errors of spelling or spacing in each sentence.

1. God has given sevʳal kinds of fish strange ways of caring for their young.

2. ~~Sum~~ *Some* African fish carry their eggs around in their mouths be-

    fore they hatch.

3. In some specᵉⁱs the male caʳies the eggs, and in others the female does.

4. The eggs haᵗch in a few days, and the young continue to live in the adult's

    mouth.

5. Oᶜassionally the parent fish spits out the young, and they swim near by.

6. When any danger threᵃtens, the young dart back into the adult's protectinᵍ mouth.

7. In a few weeks, howᵉver, the little fish grow toᵒ large for the parent to carry.

8. The young are thᵉan left to care for them selves.

9. During those weᵉaks of caring for their young, the adult fish eats no thing.

10. By the time the young are one their own, the poᵒur adult is quite thin and weak.

B. Use proofreading marks to correct the errors in word order in these sentences.

1. Monsoons are great convectional currents that [between winter and summer] reverse

    their direction.

2. During the [winter cool] months, the oceans remain warmer than the continents.

3. So the winds blow out to the ocean and keep the land [dry mostly].

4. When the continent becomes warmer [during the summer] than the ocean, the winds

    blow inland from the ocean.

5. These winds *being laden with moisture,* bring heavy rain to the land, ~~being laden with moisture~~.

6. *Probably* lc The best-known monsoons occur in India ~~probably~~.

7. From December through March, a typical dry winter monsoon [only brings] about

    five inches of rain to a given region.

8. In April, the winds change and [five inches of rain] approximately may fall in

    that month.

9. When the moist summer monsoon blows from May through October, the rainfall may

   exceed one hundred inches⌐actually⌐.

10. Then as the monsoon changes⌐during November⌐again⌐, another five inches may fall.

C. Use proofreading marks to correct all the errors in this essay. Your corrections should include one use of the stet symbol and one joining of two paragraphs. No line has more than one error.

   1.   God created the earth "to be inhabited" (Isaiah 45:18).

   2. This required that the earth have an atmosphere.

   3.   The atmosphere provides oxygen for breatheing. But

   4. that is only a small part of the picture. The atmosphere

   5. serves to ~~to~~ regulate the surface temperature of the

   6. earth. Like a huge blanket, it surrounds us, allowing

   7. sunlight to pass ~~through~~ but preventing heat from escaping
                                                        stet
   8. freely into Space.

   9.   By contrast, the atmosphere of Venus traps so much solar
                                         er
  10. heat that the surface tempature of that planet is scorching

  11. hot. And the moon, which has no atmosphere, endures blister-

  12. ing noontime temperatures and freezing nights.
                                      uc
  13.   But there is more. meteors burn up and disintegrate in

  14. the atmosphere. If this did not ~~really~~ happen, even a small

  15. meteoric particel no larger than a dust speck would strike

  16. the earth with the force of a shot from a revolver. no ¶

  17. ⌐Since billions of such particles strike the atmosphere
                #
  18. everyday, we surely need its protection!

  19.   In addition to⌐these⌐all⌐ services, the atmosphere is a

  20. shield against deadly radiation from space. Truely, our

  21. atmosphere is the handiwork of an all-knowing Creator.

Lesson 70

A. Use proofreading marks to correct the two capitalization or punctuation errors in each sentence.

1. A new commission for patents was established shortly before the thirteenth
   lc State signed the *uc* constitution.

2. The first commission consisted of; Thomas Jefferson, Henry Knox, and Edmund
   Randolph.

3. Opening for business on *uc* april 10, 1790, this commission required a working
   model with each application for a patent.

4. An unmanageable number of models had accumulated by 1807; therefore, a new *lc* Law
   specified that the commissioner would determine whether a model was needed.

5. It appears, however, that the commissioner felt inadequate to decide, for the
   accumulation of models didn't decline.

6. Because of the large number of models, the patent office had been moved to
   Blodgett's *uc* hotel in 1810.

7. When the British burned the capital city during the *uc* war of 1812, this was the
   only government building spared.

8. Dr. William Thornton headed the patent office at that time, and he deserves the
   credit for saving its treasures.

9. News of the danger to the office raised Thornton's ire so much that he ignored
   self-interest and raced to the city.

10. He dissuaded the British from burning the building—what a waste that would have
    been!—by comparing such an action to the Turks' destruction of the Alexandrian
    Library.

B. Use proofreading marks to correct the one or two usage errors in each sentence.

1. If we maintain a heavenly p*er*ospective, we will continue to ~~feel~~ *believe* that the Bible always applies to present-day living.

2. Read often in the Book of Proverbs, and ~~leave~~ *let* those practical precepts influence your life.

3. If *you're* ~~your~~ not enthus*iastic*ed about a job, do the best you can anyway.

4. For three days a station*a*ery front s*a*et over the region, producing heavy rains.

5. Loretta's answer implied that she is progressing ~~right along~~ *steadily* with her work.

6. Father is doing some *what* better, but the doctor said that he will be in bed for a while yet.

7. I wonder ~~how come~~ *why* Duchess wants *to get* out of her pen so much.

8. Our neighbor's dog is ~~notable~~ *notorious* for continually disturbing the neighborhood chickens, lambs, and other animals.

9. Milford's idea surely differed ~~with~~ *from* mine, but I know he is more familiar with those ~~there~~ tools than I am.

10. There is nothing ~~in back of~~ *behind* you, so you should back *straight* (gh) to the loading dock.

C. Use proofreading marks to correct all the errors in this essay. Your corrections should include one use of the stet symbol and one joining of two paragraphs. No line has more than one error.

1.   Our sun is an average-sized star. That is, in comparing

2. it ~~to~~ *with* most other stars in the universe, we find that it

3. is similar in size. But let's consider a star that is not

4. average—one that is much ~~more~~ larger than the sun.

5.   Scientists classify Betelgeuse (bēt′·əl·jüz′), a b*r*ight

6. star in the constellation Orion, as a red supergiant. The

7. star is red (rather than yellow like the sun) because its

8. surface temperature is [half only] as hot. This star goes

9. through cycles of expanding and shrinking. With an average

10. diameter 460 times that of the sun, it has an enorm~~ity~~ *ousness*

11. that we can hardly fathom. no ¶

12. ⌐→If this star could be placed in the center of our solar

13. system, it would ~~completely~~ engulf the orbits of Mercury,   stet

14. Venus, *lc* Earth, and Mars!

15.   The diameter of Betelgeuse, varies by about 100 million

16. miles, which is more than the distance from the earth to

17. the sun. If our sun were a variable # star like that, life

18. as we know it would~~n't~~ hardly be possible. Truly we can

19. be glad for the *lc* Sun as God made it—a steady star that

20. provides a constant, depend able supply of heat and light.

Lesson 79

A. Use proofreading marks to correct the ten spelling or spacing errors in this selection.

1. George R. Brunk was an influental Mennonite bishop in

2. Virginia. He served the church faithfully until his death

3. in 1938. In one of his sermons, he denouced the infidel-

4. ity of men like Robert G. Ingersoll, a promanent agnostic.

5. After the service, one of the brethern from the audience

6. came to Brother Brunk with an intresting question. He

7. |←asked if it was allright to buy an Ingersoll watch.

8. The quick-thinking bishop smiled and replied, "Certianly;

9. Ingersoll will do for time, but not for eternity."

B. Use proofreading marks to make these corrections in the paragraph below.
   a. Divide the selection into two paragraphs.
   b. Correct two errors in sentence division.
   c. Improve the word order in two places.

(In line 1, the phrase *one day* may be moved to some other position in the sentence.)

1. George Brunk was visiting one day a brother who was

2. lying in the hospital, after speaking to him words of

3. comfort, the minister turned to a man in a bed nearby

4. and asked him about the state of his soul. Revealing his

5. Calvinist outlook, the man replied gruffly, "If God wants

6. me, let Him come and get me!" "Listen," said Brother

7. Brunk. "If you don't concern yourself about your soul's

8. salvation and do something about it, somebody will come

9. and get you—and it won't be God either."

C. Use proofreading marks to correct all the errors in these paragraphs. No line has more than one error.

1.   Whereas some stars are much larger then the sun, others

2. are much ~~more~~ smaller. One of these is Sirius B, which is a

3. companion of the bright star called Sirius (the Dog Star).

4. Scientists classsify Sirius B as a white dwarf. Because

5. of its white color, they think its surface temperature is

6. hot*t*er than that of the sun.

7.   Though the diameter of Sirius B appears to be about

8. equal to that of the earth, Scientists believe its total

9. mass is equal to that of the sun. Compressing so much

10. mass into such a small sphere produces a*n* extremely great

11. density. According to one estimate, a brick made of

12. substance from Sirius B weigh would thirty tons. That

13. is the weight of six full-grown elephants!

14.   According to scientists, the reason for differences in

15. stars is that they are in different stages of developement.

16. White dwarfs, they say, are millions of years older than

17. "young stars" like the gaint Betelgeuse. The Bible teaches

18. that God made all the stars on the fo*u*rth day of Creation.

19. It also says, "One star differeth from another star in

20. glory" (1 Corinthians 15:41). The stars are different, not

21. because they are in variuos stages of evolution, but

22. because God made them that way.

Lesson 86

A. Use proofreading marks to correct the two errors of capitalization or punctuation in each sentence.

1. Leopards are large members, of the *lc* cat family. They

2. live throughout most of Africa, the *uc* middle East, southern

3. Asia and eastern Asia. When a leopard is born it weighs

4. only about one pound, and is quite helpless. A young

5. leopard generally stays with its *lc* Mother until it is two

6. years old; then it becomes self-supporting.

7. *uc* did you know that people are a greater danger to leop-

8. ards than leopards are to people? Actually these animals

9. seldom attack human beings. But after they discover that

10. people are easy victims; they may become a serious threat

11. to *lc* Man. Poachers, herdsmen and shepherds have ruthlessly

12. hunted leopards, however, the species is protected today.

B. Use proofreading marks to correct the fifteen usage errors in these paragraphs, according to the rules you studied in Chapter 5.

1. Have you ever considered the enorm~ity~ *ousness* of the assign-

2. ment that Noah *ac* excepted from God? Because the Flood was

3. imm~a~nent *i*, he needed to build an ark of ~fabulous~ *outstanding* size. Also,

4. he and his family had to stand all alone in a society that

5. fla~u~nted *ou* the principles of godliness. A quote *ation* from 2 Peter

6. ~infers~ *implies* that Noah warned his fellow men while he worked,

7. but they were ~dis~interested *un* in his message. Apparently

8. none of them wanted *to get* into the ark.

9. What are some not~orious~ *able* lessons that we can learn

10. from this ~here~ account? First, Noah ~felt~ *believed* that God's words

11. would surely come to pass. He did not lo~o~se his faith

12. even though many years passed before the Flood came.

13. Second, Noah committed himself to obeying God regardless

14. of what ~~transpired~~ *happened*. It is ~~all ways~~ *always* best to believe and

15. obey God, no matter what other people may do.

C. Use proofreading marks to correct all the errors in these paragraphs, including the ones that are specifically mentioned below. No line has more than one error.

    a. In the first sentence of paragraph 1, "more and more elaborate telescopes" could mean "a greater and greater number of elaborate telescopes." Make it clear that the telescopes are becoming more and more elaborate.

    b. In line 12, change the position of *only* so that its meaning is clear.

    c. In the first sentence of paragraph 3, it sounds as if the mirror was *hauled* at an altitude of 7,200 feet. Make it clear that *Cerro Tololo* is at that altitude.

1.   In their effort to learn more about the heavens, men

2. have built *telescopes that are* more and more elaborate ~~telescopes~~. The great

3. telescope at the Cerro Tololo Inter-American Observatory

4. in *C*hile is one outstanding example. This huge instrument

5. has a mirror with a diameter of 4 meters (158 inches)—more

6. th*a*n 13 feet!

7.   When the molten glass was poured for this mirror, its

8. total ~~wait~~ *weight* was 25 tons. The huge mass first had to be

9. cooled for many months—very gradually, to keep it from

10. cracking. Then work men began to grind the glass into a

11. concave shape. They labored for 2½ years, and they remove*d*

12. so much material that the finished mirror [only] [weighed]

13. 17 tons. In the perfecting process, technicians used a

14. laser so accurate that it detect ed irregularities as

15. slight as 5 millionths of an inch.

16.   The finished mirror was hauled to Cerro Tololo, *which has* ~~at~~ an

17. altitude of 7,200 feet (2,200 m). Scientists chose this

18. place because of its clear, stable air and because of its

19. location *S*outh of the equator. The site is ideal for

20. studying the central portions of the Milky Way galaxy,

21. which are best observed from the Southern Hemisphere.

Lesson 113

A. Use proofreading marks to correct the ten spelling or spacing errors in the following paragraph. Some lines have more than one error, and some have none.

1.　　The praying mantis, a wellcome guest in any garden, can

2. destroy alarge number of harmful insect pests. While it

3. pateintly waits for a meal, the mantis holds its claws in a

4. position that resembles a person praying. The mantis flies

5. ←occasionally, but it spends most of its time on geen

6. plants were it is nearly invisible. Standing motionlessly

7. for long periods of time, the mantis waits until an

8. unsuspecting insect comes to near. Suddenly the mantis's

9. fore legs snap out; and the next instant, the mantis is

10. holding a victem tightly in its grip.

B. Use proofreading marks to make these corrections in the paragraph below.
　　a. Divide the selection into two paragraphs.
　　b. Correct two errors in joining or separating clauses.
　　c. Improve the word order in two places.

1.　　A dormant twig is interesting to observe. Even though it

2. looks completely bare. One thing you can see is the signs

3. of present life. At the end of each healthy, undamaged

4. twig is a terminal bud, which causes the twig to grow in

5. length. You will also along the sides see numerous lateral

6. buds, which will develop new stems, flowers, or leaves.

7. Another thing you can observe is the evidence of life in

8. previous growing seasons. Bud-scale scars form at irregular

9. intervals rings around the stem, showing where each year's

10. growth stopped. The age of any branch equals the number

11. of these bud-scale scars. As you look over the branch,

12. you should also see lighter patches, or nodes, on the

13. bark. Each node indicates a place where a leaf had grown,

14. _and_ each one has a rim of tiny scars that mark where the sap

15. flowed from the stem to the leaf and back again.

C. Use proofreading marks to correct all the errors in this essay. No line has more than one error. Move the word *only* in line 11 to a different place in the sentence. Also join the paragraph beginning in line 14 to the preceding paragraph.

1.   Is there inteligent life somewhere in this vast universe

2. other than on the earth? This question intrigues many

3. astronomers as they investigate the broad expanse of outer

4. ~~of~~ space. Assuming that man came into being by chance, they

5. wonder if chance has produced life some where else too.

6.   These men do more than wonder; they are busy searching.

7. They think that discovering life elsewhere would give man-

8. kind a new purpose and a greater faith in the future.

9. One of their search methods, is to monitor the radio

10. waves from the heavens, watching for patterns that could

11. only be produced by intelligent beings somewhere beyond us.

12.   The child of God has different thoughts as _he_ turns his

13. eyes heavenward. no ¶

14. ⌐←He has no interest in receiving messages from unknown,

15. illusory Beings. He has already received a message from

16. the heavens—the inspired word of God!

17.   The Christian finds purpose in life by ~~ex~~cepting and

18. submitting to this message; he gains an unshakable faith

19. in the future by believing its promises. "Blessed the is

20. man that trusteth in the Lord, and whose hope the Lord is

21. (Jeremiah 17:7).

Lesson 11

(Applying the Lesson, Part D)

Thanksgiving Vows

Thanksgiving is the natural response of the child of God. Singing and spoken testimony, two of the most common expressions of thankfulness, are certainly comely and appropriate. However, saying "thank you" with the lips is easier than proving it with the life. "Offer unto God thanksgiving; and pay thy vows unto the most High" (Psalm 50:14).

Counting our blessings and reviewing the goodness of God to us should always move us to thanksgiving and commitment. Can you concur with the following expressions of thankfulness and the subsequent vows?

We offer thanksgiving for the bountiful harvest of this year's growing season. As we gather the crops into our garners, we will also remember to bring our tithes and offerings into God's storehouse. We consecrate our material resources for use in the great harvest of souls.

In a world fragmented by war and strife, we humbly acknowledge our stable government. We will pray for our civil rulers. Paying our taxes will not cause us to grumble. We will obey the law for conscience' sake and not because a policeman is nearby. In this land of tranquillity, we will strive to live "in all godliness and honesty."

Freedom of the press has been a closely guarded freedom since the founding of this country. We praise God for the impact that conservative Mennonite publishers have made in calling people to a Biblical faith and practice. Our response will be one of appreciation and support for these efforts. Any helpful criticism we may have will be given in a manner that is not degrading or mocking. We will assist in the work by making use of the publications and by putting to work the talents that have been given to us.

We thank God for the priceless blessing of our religious heritage and for the martyrs, whose blood was the seed of the church. The Anabaptist church was born at a time when most of the freedoms we take for granted were nonexistent.

As the church grew and faced new issues over the years, God always had a man to "stand in the gap." If we have a true appreciation for our heritage, we will not have a negative mindset toward tradition, but will strive to preserve those practices that have been an asset to the church. Our determination is to live so that succeeding generations will also be able to say, "I have a goodly heritage."

We are thankful for the care and correction given by our spiritual shepherds. In response, we will follow them as they follow Christ, and "esteem them very highly in love for their work's sake, and be at peace among [ourselves]."

The blessings of the church body are evident as we meet collectively and edify our brethren in other ways as well. Each one of us will accept his place cheerfully and will conscientiously perform his duty. Together, we will strive for unity and so love each other that all who see us will know we are Jesus' disciples.

We thank God for His written message to us and for the avenue of prayer through which we can talk to Him. We will avoid the pottage of the world so that our appetite for the manna will not become dulled. We will follow the example of our Saviour who spent whole nights in prayer.

All our thanksgivings would be futile if it were not for the greatest blessing of all. "But thanks be to God, which giveth us the victory through our Lord Jesus Christ" (1 Corinthians 15:57). As we meditate on all that Christ has done and is doing for us, our only logical response is (like Peter's): "Lo, we leave all to follow Thee."

As we feast on the cornucopia of life's spiritual and natural abundance, let each of us solemnly promise to be a faithful steward so that we can someday join the angels in eternal thanksgiving, "saying, Amen: Blessing, and glory, and wisdom, and thanksgiving, and honour, and power, and might, be unto our God for ever and ever" (Revelation 7:12).

Should We Enter Sweepstakes?

There is a growing number of giveaway offers and sweepstakes that promise big dividends to the person who has the lucky number or whose name is selected in a random drawing. The advertisements offer huge cash prizes, trips to distant resorts, sports cars, color TVs, and other items; you simply send in the entry form before the deadline. State laws that regulate gambling forbid the advertisers to require those entering to buy their products or send money.

At a local business place, you may be handed a ticket to fill out and drop into a box, giving you a chance to win a prize. The business may also offer you free coffee and doughnuts or a variety of free products as a business promotion.

How should Christians respond to these opportunities? May we take them if we put our winnings to good use as faithful stewards?

Persons who would not enter the state lottery or go to a casino, where gambling is legal, may feel that sweepstakes and chance giveaways are in a different category. Yet the appeal is the same. It is the lure of receiving something for nothing. The desire to obtain things without working for them is as old as human nature. The serpent suggested that something could be gotten for nothing when he told Eve that the fruit of the tree would make her as wise as a god. Satan offered Jesus all the kingdoms of the world (as if they were his to give) in exchange for His worship. It was the glitter of gold that attracted people to California in 1849. And the greed and covetousness of men has inspired many a war.

Is there anything necessarily wrong with getting something for nothing? Didn't our parents feed and clothe us in our early years free of charge? God freely sends us the sunshine and the rain. Has He ever sent a bill? Is not even salvation a free gift? If the company that sent the sweepstakes offer is willing to give away $50,000, why not take it?

There are a number of Scriptural principles that help us to see this matter in proper perspective. First of all, the Scriptures teach us to work to supply our own needs. "For even when we were with you, this we commanded you, that if any would not work, neither should he eat" (2 Thessalonians 3:10). We should not expect others to provide for us when we are able to provide for ourselves. The Scriptures commend labor and diligence, and they rebuke those who are idle or lazy. We should desire to help others who cannot earn and provide for themselves rather than expecting others to provide for our needs. "Let him that stole steal no more: but rather let him labour, working with his hands the thing which is good, that he may have to give to him that needeth" (Ephesians 4:28). "I have shewed you all things, how that so labouring ye ought to support the weak, and to

remember the words of the Lord Jesus, how he said, It is more blessed to give than to receive" (Acts 20:35).

Yes, our parents did provide for us when we were unable to provide for ourselves. But when we came to a responsible age, that changed and we gradually took on personal responsibility. God provides without charge the sun and the rain—and even the gift of salvation—because we are unable to provide them ourselves.

The Scriptures also admonish us to be content with the necessities of life. Sweepstakes prizes are often luxury items. We should not spend time daydreaming about what we would do with another hundred dollars. According to 1 Timothy 6:6–11, those who are content avoid the snares that entrap covetous individuals. Solomon attested to the fact that riches do not satisfy (Ecclesiastes 5:9–17).

Winners in a sweepstakes are few, often only one in a hundred thousand or more, and wealth is distributed in an inequitable manner. In contrast, God is just, and He rewards every man according to his works (Matthew 16:27). We are all able to "win big" if only we will set our eye on the "prize of the high calling of God in Christ Jesus" (Philippians 3:14). Sweepstakes offer fading treasures "where moth and rust doth corrupt" (Matthew 6:19).

The person who is awarded a large cash prize often wastes it in a short time. "Wealth gotten by vanity shall be diminished: but he that gathereth by labour shall increase" (Proverbs 13:11). Since he does not work for it, he does not value it as he would if he had earned it by his own toil and sweat. Sudden wealth warps one's sense of stewardship. Money that comes easily is often squandered just as easily.

The desire to get something for nothing has driven many to dishonesty. Gehazi had his eye on easy money and lied twice to get it. Elisha could have had the free goods Naaman offered him without lying, but he refused to use the power God gave him for his own financial advantage (2 Kings 5:16). The list of Bible characters who fell prey to this snare includes Achan, Judas Iscariot, Ananias and Sapphira, and others.

It may be appropriate to accept a gift such as a free pen or pencil, a calendar, a fly swatter, or some other small item given as an advertisement by a businessman. It is understood that this is his way of promoting his business and of saying, "Thank you for your patronage." There may be nothing wrong with accepting refreshments offered at a place of business we regularly patronize. However, going from place to place in search of free food and gifts indicates a problem with covetousness. We should rather seek opportunities to be on the giving end.

We need the outlook of Paul, who said, "I have coveted no man's silver, or gold, or apparel. Yea, ye yourselves know, that these hands have ministered unto my necessities, and to them that were with me" (Acts 20:33, 34).

Lesson 77

(Applying the Lesson, Part D)

Verb Forms

Active Voice

	Simple Form	*Progressive Form*	*Emphatic Form*
Present:	_____	_____	_____
Past:	_____	_____	_____
Future:	_____	_____	
Pr. perf.:	_____	_____	
Past perf.:	_____	_____	
Fut. perf.:	_____	_____	

Passive Voice

	Simple Form	*Progressive Form*	*Emphatic Form*
Present:	_____	_____	
Past:	_____	_____	
Future:	_____		
Pr. perf.:	_____		
Past perf.:	_____		
Fut. perf.:	_____		

Communicating Effectively—Book 2

Chapter 1 Test   Score _____

Name _____ Date _____

A. Use proofreading marks to correct each capitalization error.

1. Knowing that Jesus is our master will temper our loyalty to earthly Masters.

2. although the law of moses reveals much about god's holiness, only the gospel gives the power to have His holiness within.

3. Will aunt Jolene take some of her african violets to Market on saturday?

4. Here in the east, Hurricanes from the gulf of Mexico or the Atlantic ocean can cause great devastation.

5. During the revolutionary war, some mennonites suffered persecution from patriotic americans.

6. After English Class, we have biology and typing I.

7. Does mr. Michael Woodward, Jr., of zanesville still sell electrolux sweepers?

(28 points)

B. Use proofreading marks to add the missing commas, colons, semicolons, and end punctuation. Delete any unnecessary punctuation.

8. Well children if we love the Lord we can be assured of one thing everything will work out for our good

9. Can you sense the poetic quality of Job Psalms and Proverbs?

10. What a blessing it is to have the plain simple teachings of the Bible!

11. Sparkle our little puppy is very playful moreover he seems quite intelligent.

12. Mark I told Conrad and William to clean out the calf pens and when you finish your chores you shall help them.

13. After you read the book report briefly on the chief causes of fires and the common types of fire extinguishers.

14. **From our house on top of the hill we can see the dwellings of Joshua Troyer and his family, who attend our church. Marian Brown, an elderly widow, and Lloyd Little, Sr., a retired doctor.**

(22 points)

C. Add the missing dashes, parentheses, brackets, and ellipsis points, marking each insertion with a caret. Place ellipsis points below the caret, and dashes in the line above.

15. **"Our Father which art in heaven, Hallowed [holy] be thy name" (Matthew 6:9).**

16. **"Many people can quote this prayer taught by Jesus, but it seems" Brother Wilbur sighed.**

17. **Louise made six loaves of bread (she used Grandmother's favorite recipe) that look delicious.** (treat as somewhat beside the point)

18. **The sights and sounds of the ocean—a symbol of God's majesty—almost overwhelmed me.** (give sharp emphasis)

19. **"Norma, did you finish—oh, what a surprise this is!" declared Mother.**

(6 points)

D. Insert the missing quotation marks, using inverted carets. Also add the needed italics (underlining), and show any correction of capitalization.

20. **Have you experienced the reality of the verse that says, "Whatsoever a man soweth, that shall he also reap?**

21. **"Bradley is reading Year of Growth, so I must wait," said Lucinda.**

22. **"Were you surprised," wondered Ray, "to hear Brother Stover say, 'We'll have ten minutes of extra recess this afternoon?'"**

23. **"Has everyone finished reading the poem 'Then Do It'?" asked Brother Gehman.**

24. **"I heard Mr. Wharton say, 'what a pleasure to be here!'" stated Mahlon.**

(10 points)

E. Use proofreading marks to add italics (underlining), apostrophes, and hyphens.

25. **In giving a talk, exercise humble self-confidence but avoid trying to impress people with high-sounding oratory.**

26. **The canister of all-purpose flour is only one-third full.**

27. Vast areas of the flood‑damaged mid‑Arkansas region were declared disaster areas.

28. Do not use &s for ands in your formal writing.

29. Great‑grandmother Stauffer usually isnt out of bed before eight oclock.

30. We wont be able to have the service that was scheduled for 10:00 A.M. on Saturday, D.V. (<u>Deo volente</u>), because we have twenty‑three inches of snow.

31. My brother‑in‑law sells potting soil in five, ten, and fifty‑pound bags, and he also offers it in bulk amounts.

(18 points)

F. Circle *T* if the statement is true or *F* if it is false.

Ⓣ F 32. A sentence may lack originality even if it is clear and understandable.

T Ⓕ 33. A good way to improve originality is to write expressions that you would not normally use in speech.

Ⓣ F 34. Using slang is a poor way to gain originality in writing.

T Ⓕ 35. Clichés are helpful for improving the originality of your writing.

(4 points)

Total points: 88

Communicating Effectively—Book 2

Chapter 2 Test   Score _____

Name _____ **Date** _____

A. Name the five steps in the SQ3R study method. After each one, briefly explain how to apply that step in studying a lesson.

    1. _____ Survey _____ : <u>Look over the lesson, noticing the headings and any pictures or diagrams.</u>

                                         _____

    2. _____ Question _____ : <u>Ask questions for which you expect to find answers in the lesson.</u>

                                           _____

    3. _____ Read _____ : <u>Carefully read the lesson, making sure you understand what it teaches.</u>

                                           _____

    4. _____ Recite _____ : <u>Answer the questions you had asked; do the written assignment.</u>

                                           _____

    5. _____ Review _____ : <u>Mentally recall the main points of the lesson.</u>

                                           _____

(5 points)

B. Circle *T* if the statement is true or *F* if it is false.

    T **(F)** 6. For good eye contact, you should look at your audience but avoid meeting the eyes of individual listeners.

    (T) F 7. You should make eye contact with listeners in all parts of the audience.

    (T) F 8. Eye contact is important at the beginning and the end of your talk.

    T **(F)** 9. Eye contact can easily be more distracting than helpful when you emphasize a major point.

(4 points)

C. Write a brief answer to each question.

    10. For the most effective study, what attitude should you have toward the subject at hand? _____

       <u>an attitude of interest</u> _____

    11. When do you most rapidly forget something that you have studied? <u>immediately afterward</u>

    12. In a study period, which work should you do first? Which should you save for last? _____

       <u>Do first the hardest work (or work that is due first).</u>

       <u>Do last the easiest (most pleasant) work.</u>

13. What is a physical benefit of maintaining good posture as you study? _____

 It allows normal breathing to supply the brain with plenty of oxygen for clear thinking.

 _____

14. Why should you briefly look over a whole lesson before reading it? _____

 to see how the various parts fit together

15. How can you get ideas for asking good questions about a lesson? _____

 by looking at the headings

16. When skimming a book to find information for a report, which two parts should you look at first?

 table of contents, index

17. Where are the two best places to look for the main ideas in a paragraph or composition? _____

 beginning, ending

18. How many of the main points should be included in good notes? How many of the subpoints? _____

 all the main points, some of the subpoints

19. Should a summary be written mostly in the author's words or in your own words? _____

 in your own words

20. How long should a summary be? _____

 up to one-third as long as the original composition

21. What is meant by the points of an outline being parallel? _____

 They should begin with the same part of speech and be similar in structure.

(12 points)

D. Write an outline of this composition on the lines after it.

The Transfer of Heat

The transfer of heat energy from one place to another is an interesting study. Why does the handle of a skillet get hot? How does a stove in one corner of a room heat the whole room? How does the energy of the sun warm the earth? Each of these illustrates one of the three methods of heat transfer: conduction, convection, and radiation.

Heat transfer by conduction is simple to understand. First, a heat source causes one part of a solid to become hot. For example, you might put a cast-iron skillet on a hot stove. The iron in the lowest portion of the skillet becomes hot, and the heat in that part causes the surrounding part to also become hot. This process is repeated over and over until even the end of the skillet handle becomes too hot to touch.

Certain materials are good heat conductors; that is, they transfer heat especially well. Some of the best heat conductors are silver, copper, aluminum, and iron, in that order. Silver is too expensive for common use. Copper is often used for the outside bottoms of cookware, though not for the inner surfaces because some copper compounds are poisonous. Aluminum and alloys of iron (such as cast iron and stainless steel) are used frequently for cookware. Iron is also used commonly in stoves and radiators.

Heat transfer by convection begins when heat is applied to part of a liquid or gas. The molecules in the heated portion expand, causing that part of the liquid or gas to become less dense and to rise. Cooler molecules then move in to take the place of the warmer molecules that have risen. The process of heated molecules rising and cooler ones moving in is repeated over and over until the whole body of liquid or gas is heated.

You are familiar with several examples of convectional currents, as this cycle of heat transfer is called. When you heat water on a stove, the water at the bottom of the pan becomes hot; it expands and rises; cooler water moves down to take its place; and the process continues until all the water is hot. A room heated by a stove or by baseboard heaters also demonstrates heat transfer by convection.

Radiation is the least understood method of heat transfer. The process of radiation begins as rays of energy move out from a heat-producing source. These rays can pass through transparent and translucent solids, such as clear or frosted glass and many kinds of plastic. The rays can also travel through liquids, such as water, and through gases, such as air. Most amazing of all, radiant energy travels freely through a vacuum. The rays change into heat energy when they are absorbed by an object that they cannot penetrate.

The sun is the most important example of heat transfer by radiation. It sends forth rays that travel through 93 million miles of space, a near vacuum, to heat the earth. Perhaps you have used heat lamps in raising baby chicks. The rays from the lamp pass through the air and change into heat as the chicks absorb them. Although stoves heat an entire room by convection, they may heat you or some other object by radiation. When you stand close to a stove, the hot surface radiates heat and you feel the warmth as you absorb those rays.

In His infinite wisdom, God designed a world in which heat can be transferred from place to place in several different ways. Not one of these methods works efficiently in every case where heat transfer is needed. But together, they serve the world and its people very well.

(Sample outline; allow reasonable variation.) **The Transfer of Heat**

I. <u>By conduction</u>

    A. <u>Description of the process</u>

        1. <u>Heat source makes part of a solid hot</u>

        2. <u>Heated part makes surrounding parts hot</u>

        3. <u>Process repeated over and over</u>

    B. <u>Conductors of heat</u>

        1. <u>Silver—too expensive for common use</u>

        2. <u>Copper—used for outside bottoms of cookware</u>

        3. <u>Aluminum—used frequently for cookware</u>

        4. <u>Iron—used for cookware, stoves, and radiators</u>

II. By convection

   A. Description of the process

      1. Heat applied to part of liquid or gas

      2. Heated molecules expand and rise

      3. Cooler molecules take their place

      4. Process repeated over and over

   B. Examples of convection

      1. Heating water on a stove

      2. Heating air in a room

III. By radiation

   A. Description of the process

      1. Rays of energy move out from heat-producing source

      2. Rays pass through certain solids, liquids, and gases

      3. Rays pass through vacuums

      4. Rays change to heat energy when absorbed

   B. Examples of radiation

      1. Sun

      2. Heat lamps

      3. Stoves

(29 points)

Total points: 50

Communicating Effectively—Book 2

Chapter 3 Test

Score _____

Name _____ Date _____

A. Use proofreading marks to correct the fragments and run-on errors in these paragraphs of dialogue. Do not change elliptical sentences.   (Allow reasonable variation.)

1.   "The Lord's Day is a special day. That God has set aside for our spiritual and physical refreshment," stated Father. "Can you name some spiritual refreshments of the day?"

2.   "Hearing the Bible preached," replied Karen. "Of course, Sunday school is important too, we can discuss the Bible together."

3.   "Well said," added Kevin. "I also appreciate the opportunity to visit with friends. Many of whom I seldom see except at church."

4.   "That's right," said Father. "Christian fellowship is very important, that's one reason why we must be part of a Scriptural church."

(4 points)

B. Underline the simple subjects once and the simple predicates twice.

5. Honesty may not always pay the best material rewards.

6. However, honesty is always God's requirement and will bring eternal rewards.

7. In the honest heart abides the assurance of God's favor.

8. Both God and men will appreciate honesty in your life.

(10 points)

C. Underline each complement, and write one of the following labels above it: *PN* (predicate nominative), *PA* (predicate adjective), *DO* (direct object), *IO* (indirect object), or *OC* (objective complement).

9. This new tiller makes the soil [DO] quite fine [OC].

10. The weather has grown too hot [PA] and dry [PA] for gardening.

11. Mr. Luffton sold us [IO] a used irrigation pump [DO] and some pipes [DO].

12. An irrigation system might make the strawberry patch [DO] a profitable venture [OC].

13. Our largest plantings are Sparkle [PN] and Lateglow [PN].

(11 points)

D. Underline each retained object, and write *DO ret.* or *IO ret.* above it.

14. We were given a strong <u>incentive</u> to do our best.
    (above "incentive": DO ret.)

15. A good home was offered the lost <u>kitten</u> by Aunt Matilda.
    (above "kitten": IO ret.)

16. Larry was given a welcome <u>boost</u> by Father.
    (above "boost": DO ret.)

(3 points)

E. Underline the appositives and independent elements. Use proofreading marks to correct the punctuation and capitalization.

17. **Michael Henry <u>a young man from Locustdale</u> has been attending our services for six months I believe.**

18. **<u>There</u> must be many young people seeking for meaning in life.**

19. **We must be careful <u>my friends</u> that we consistently demonstrate a life that has true meaning.**

20. **<u>The world providing no true satisfaction</u> we should have little interest in its allurements.**

21. **<u>Allurements</u> the world dangles many allurements that appeal to our carnal nature.**

22. **<u>Yes</u> the song <u>"Take the World, but Give Me Jesus"</u> should express our desire.**

(8 points)

F. In the first blank, write *prep.* (prepositional phrase), *vb.* (verbal phrase), *ps.* (phrase of a single part of speech), *I* (independent clause), or *D* (dependent clause) to tell what kind of word group is underlined. In the second blank, write what part of speech it is, or write *X* if it is an independent clause.

prep.	adj.	23.	Prudence <u>in small things of life</u> prepares us for further usefulness.
vb.	n.	24.	<u>Taking a careless attitude toward life</u> is a bad habit to develop.
D	adv.	25.	<u>If we are careless in natural duties</u>, we will likely be careless in spiritual duties.
I	X	26.	<u>We should show kindness to others</u> even when they try our patience.
prep.	adv.	27.	The true church is <u>in the world</u> but not of the world.
D	n.	28.	We must recognize <u>that this world is an enemy to true faith</u>.
vb.	adv.	29.	Only a fool will show off <u>to gain the notice of others</u>.
ps.	v.	30.	Through eternal ages, the faithful <u>will be praising</u> the Lord.

_____vb._____   _____adj._____   31. The saints will worship the Lamb of God, <u>crowned with many crowns</u>.

_____D_____   _____adj._____   32. The saints, <u>who have received crowns of reward</u>, will cast them before Jesus.

(20 points)

G. In the first blank, label the sentence according to its use: *dec.* (declarative), *imp.* (imperative), *int.* (interrogative), or *exc.* (exclamatory). In the second blank, label the sentence according to its structure: *S* (simple), *CD* (compound), *CX* (complex), or *CD-CX* (compound-complex). End punctuation has been omitted.

_____int._____   _____S_____   33. Did Aunt Martha come home or stay for an operation

_____dec._____   _____CD_____   34. She came home, but an operation is scheduled for Thursday morning

_____imp._____   _____CX_____   35. Pray for God's will to be done as she faces this operation

_____exc._____   _____S_____   36. How comforting it is to trust in God

_____dec._____   _CD-CX_   37. Aunt Martha has committed all to the Lord, and she wants to accept God's will even if it means continued suffering.

(10 points)

H. Label the word order of each sentence *N* (natural), *I* (inverted), or *M* (mixed). Then rewrite the sentence in a different word order. Watch the punctuation.   (Allow reasonable variation in rewritten sentences.)

_I_ 38. From the lilac bushes is coming a sweet fragrance. _____

      A sweet fragrance is coming from the lilac bushes. _____

_N_ 39. Mother planted a row of mock orange bushes between the house and the road. _____

      Between the house and the road, Mother planted a row of mock orange bushes. _____

      _____

_M_ 40. When Aunt Leah lived with us, we girls had less work in the flower beds. _____

      We girls had less work in the flower beds when Aunt Leah lived with us. _____

_N_ 41. A sense of vigor comes with the arrival of spring. _____

      With the arrival of spring comes a sense of vigor. _____

(8 points)

I. Label the style of each sentence *L* (loose), *P* (periodic), or *B* (balanced).

_B_ 42. Learn from the experience of others, or you must experience what others have already learned.

_L_ 43. Good counsel is better than experience because you can learn many valuable lessons apart from tragic mistakes and bitter reaping.

_P_ 44. When you receive godly counsel from parents, teachers, or church leaders, give serious heed to their word.

_B_ 45. The more willingly we take advice from the right source, the more readily advice will take us to the right goal.

(4 points)

J. Rewrite or finish these sentences in the style indicated.   (Allow reasonable variation.)

46. Read good books for a sound frame of reference and for help in developing character. (periodic)

   For a sound frame of reference and for help in developing character, read good books.

47. You cannot study your lesson without reading it, but you can . . . (balanced)

   read your lesson without studying it.

48. When you dismiss an opportunity, you miss a potential success. (loose)

   You miss a potential success when you dismiss an opportunity.

(3 points)

K. Circle *T* if the statement is true or *F* if it is false.

T (F) 49. Linking verbs help to add life and action to your writing.

T (F) 50. You should usually change a linking verb like *appear* or *remain* to a form of *be*.

(T) F 51. You should rewrite most sentences that begin with *There is* or *There was.*

(T) F 52. A form of *be* may serve as the best main verb available for some sentences.

(4 points)

Total points: 85

Communicating Effectively—Book 2

Chapter 4 Test

Score _____

Name _____ Date _____

A. Circle *T* if the statement is true or *F* if it is false.

T (F)   1. One purpose of an expository essay is to convince the reader of your point of view.

T (F)   2. You should write your statement of purpose after you have taken notes for your topic.

(T) F   3. The introductory paragraph of an expository essay should begin with a broad statement and then narrow to the topic of the essay.

T (F)   4. With practice, you can learn to proofread your essay in a single reading.

(T) F   5. If you type the final draft of the essay, you should use double or 1½ line spacing.

(T) F   6. A direct quotation needs no footnote if you credit the source in the essay itself.

(6 points)

B. In each blank, write the correct word or phrase to complete the sentence.

_____plagiarism_____   7. Copying another person's writing and passing it off as your own is ———.

_____short phrases_____   8. Good notes consist primarily of ———, not sentences or paragraphs.

_____theme_____   9. You should end the introductory paragraph by stating the ——— of the essay.

_____summary_____   10. The conclusion to an expository essay should include a ——— of the main points.

_____footnote_____   11. The source of a specific quotation may be credited in a ——— at the bottom of the page or at the end of the essay.

_____bibliography_____   12. A complete listing of the reference sources cited in an essay is the ———.

_____ibid._____   13. When two consecutive footnotes credit the same reference source, the second one has the abbreviation ———, meaning "in the same place."

(7 points)

C. Answer these questions.

14. What are two things you can do to make sure you avoid plagiarism?   _(Any two.)_____

___Use others' ideas, not their exact words._____

___Write notes in short phrases rather than whole sentences or paragraphs._____

___Place direct quotations in quotation marks, and credit them properly._____

15. What are two types of information for which you should write footnotes?   (Any two.)

 direct quotations

 details that the reader might question

 technical information

16. What is one guideline for the order of reference sources in a bibliography?   (Any one.)

 List the sources in alphabetical order according to the last names of the authors.

 If more than one reference source from an author is used, list them alphabetically by title.

 If no author's name is given, list the source alphabetically according to the title.

(5 points)

Total points: 18

Note: In Lesson 35, the pupil was told that the score on his expository essay would make up a considerable part of his Chapter 4 test score. The essay and the test together contain a total of 66 points (48 on the essay and 18 on the test).

Communicating Effectively—Book 2

Chapter 5 Test

Score _____

Name _____   Date _____

A. Underline the standard expressions in parentheses.

1. God has made His Word easily (<u>comprehensible</u>, comprehensive) so that people can readily (precede, <u>proceed</u>) in the right way if they want to.

2. (<u>Its</u>, It's) message goes (<u>straight</u>, strait) to the heart of man, but a large (amount, <u>number</u>) of people refuse to heed it.

3. We (<u>believe</u>, feel) that no matter how much a person (<u>flaunts</u>, flouts) his might and wisdom, he can never (allude, <u>elude</u>) God's sovereignty.

4. It is much better to (let, <u>leave</u>) matters in God's hands (<u>than</u>, then) to think we should (persecute, <u>prosecute</u>) those who mistreat us.

5. The forest fire raged (continually, <u>continuously</u>) for (<u>almost</u>, most) a whole week; it (<u>always</u>, all ways) defeated the firefighters until rain came.

6. The dangerous lion (<u>burst</u>, bursted, busted) out of its cage, but the (<u>ingenious</u>, ingenuous) keepers soon captured it again.

7. This heavy fog will (raise, <u>rise</u>) after the sun has been up (<u>awhile</u>, a while).

8. If we (<u>propose</u>, purpose) our plan in a (<u>respectful</u>, respective) manner, Mr. Taylor may give his approval.

9. Although Mother is (some, <u>somewhat</u>) better, we were glad to (<u>accept</u>, except) the help that the sisters of the church offered us.

10. As heavy rains soaked the area, serious flooding seemed (eminent, <u>imminent</u>, immanent), and we anxiously watched the river (everyday, <u>every day</u>).

11. If our lives are on the (<u>altar</u>, alter) of Christian discipleship, our conduct will differ (<u>from</u>, with) that of general society.

12. If we are truly (disinterested, <u>uninterested</u>) in earthly pursuits, the luxuries of this world will (loose, <u>lose</u>) their appeal.

13. We will surely come to ruin if we (adapt, <u>adopt</u>) the (<u>perspective</u>, prospective) of the world.

14. Father said that we (can, <u>may</u>) read the book after he has (<u>censored</u>, censured) it.

15. Old age is often compared (<u>to</u>, with) a sunset because the time of labor is ending and a time of rest (lays, <u>lies</u>) ahead.

16. Has anyone (advised, <u>informed</u>) you that (<u>maybe</u>, may be) the amount of sugar in this (receipt, <u>recipe</u>) is incorrect?

17. Many of the neighbors were angry (about, at, <u>with</u>) the young men who committed the (<u>contemptible</u>, contemptuous) deed of desecrating a church building.

18. Within a week, the patient did not have (anymore, <u>any more</u>) pain, and he felt (good, <u>well</u>) enough to (set, <u>sit</u>) up in a chair.

19. What does (<u>your</u>, you're) father think is (<u>implied</u>, inferred) by the (above paragraph, <u>paragraph above</u>)?

20. The boys considered it a (<u>notable</u>, notorious) accomplishment when they had installed the (<u>stationary</u>, stationery) loudspeaker (<u>as</u>, like) Brother Lyle had requested.

21. We were quite anxious after the accident (transpired, <u>occurred</u>), but everyone seems (<u>all right</u>, alright) now.

22. Although our area was (impacted, <u>affected</u>) by the hurricane, we were shocked by the (enormity, <u>immensity</u>) of the damage along the coast.

(52 points)

B. Use proofreading marks to correct or improve the underlined expressions in these sentences. If an underlined item needs no improvement, label it *C* for *correct.*   (Allow reasonable variation.)

23. What <u>for</u> *kind of* efforts do you need to make if you want your grades to improve <s>right along</s> *steadily*?

24. You must simply <u>try to do</u> *C* your best; then you can be satisfied even though your grades <s>ain't</s> *aren't* perfect.

25. <s>Hopefully,</s> *It is hoped that* we shall <s>momentarily</s> *soon* know <s>how come</s> *why* the engine stopped running.

26. <s>Them</s> *Those* calves seem <s>poorly</s> *in poor health*, but we are <s>sort of</s> *rather* helpless since the antibiotics are <u>all</u> *gone*.

27. You must <u>be sure</u> <s>and</s> *to* call the veterinarian, for we need his help <s>in the worst way</s> *very much*.

28. When the harvest was <u>over</u> <s>with</s>, the farmers were <u>enthused</u> *iastic* about the <s>fabulous</s> *abundant* crops that they had brought in.

29. We <u>want</u> <s>off</s> *to get* the bus at the next stop, but we still have a <s>ways</s> *distance* to go on foot to Martino's village.

30. We <u>should</u> <s>of</s> *have* checked <s>in back of</s> *behind* the truck before moving it.

31. This report <s>hasn't</s> *has* but one <u>quote</u> *ation* taken from the encyclopedia.

32. One of the <s>dilemmas</s> *difficulties* that a businessman faces is deciding when it is <s>okay</s> *all right* to expand his business.

33. The men shown in <u>this</u> <s>here</s> picture belonged to a medieval <u>counsel</u> *cil* of church leaders.

34. We have <s>heaps of</s> *much* applesauce to make, so it is <s>nice</s> *pleasant* to have Grandmother Showalter here to help.

(28 points)

C. Circle *T* if the statement is true or *F* if it is false.

T (F) 35. In the active voice, the subject receives the action of the verb; and in the passive voice, the subject performs the action of the verb.

(T) F 36. It is usually better to use verbs like *heard* than verbs like *was heard* in your writing.

(T) F 37. The passive voice is suitable for a sentence in which the doer of the action is unknown.

T (F) 38. In your writing, about half of the verbs should be active and half should be passive.

(4 points)

Total points: 84

Communicating Effectively—Book 2

Chapter 6 Test

Score _____

Name _____   Date _____

A. Circle *T* if the statement is true or *F* if it is false.

T (F)   1. The best short stories are about unusual or dramatic happenings.

(T) F   2. A good short story develops one basic theme.

T (F)   3. The beginning paragraphs should describe the setting in detail.

T (F)   4. A short story needs no conclusion after the climax.

T (F)   5. A story should use as much direct characterization of the main character as practical.

(T) F   6. In the omniscient point of view, the author can describe what happens to any character.

T (F)   7. The third person point of view tends to give the strongest impression of reality.

(T) F   8. If a story reveals any character's thoughts, it is written subjectively.

(T) F   9. Proper voice control includes articulation, volume, pitch, and speed.

T (F) 10. You should use variety in all the elements of voice control.

(10 points)

B. Write the word or words that fit each description.

_____conflict_____ 11. The struggle or problem that the main character faces.

_____characterization_____ 12. The process of portraying the traits of characters.

_____theme_____ 13. The lesson that a story teaches.

_____setting_____ 14. Information about the place, time, and atmosphere of the story.

_____plot_____ 15. The overall development of a story conflict.

_____point of view (*or* viewpoint)_____ 16. The perspective from which a story is written.

(6 points)

Use the following samples for Parts C–G.

a.   "Here comes the goody-goody," sneered Donald under his breath.
        "Yeah," added Curtis, brushing his long hair out of his eyes. "He must be Preacher Caleb." His loud
    whisper was gauged to let me hear without Father or Uncle Leroy hearing.
        "Good morning," I replied pleasantly, ignoring their comments.

I had just arrived with my family at Grandfather's farm, where most of the Schrock relatives had gathered for a workday. Father's earlier words, however, encouraged me: "I'll see to it that you don't need to work alone with Uncle Leroy's boys today. If they try anything on the sly, just excuse yourself and find me."

b.   Freda stared out the window. The merry shouts of her brothers and sisters filtered into the cozy living room. "If only I could be out there sledding on that perfectly crusted snow!" she said bitterly to no one in particular. "By the time this cast is off my leg, the snow will be gone. We haven't had such a perfect snow ever since we moved here to Maryland. And I'll miss all the fun."

Freda sighed. She blinked. She swallowed hard. And suddenly she burst into wrenching sobs.

Mother was at her side in a moment. "Why, what's wrong, dear?" she asked in a sweet, gentle voice.

c.   "Oh, why did I ever say such a thing?" Roland asked himself for the fifth time as he walked along. "Of course, I didn't make three home runs yesterday."

"Confess it to Daryl," prompted his conscience.

"But whatever will he think?" Roland's mind was a troubled sea. "He'll think I'm a liar."

"You did tell a lie, didn't you? What are you if not a liar?" his conscience accused him again.

Walking beside him, Daryl was mulling over questions of his own. "Wonder what got into Roland?" he wondered. "Why is he suddenly so quiet?"

d.   *R-i-i-ing!* The telephone demanded an answer.

"Oh, no! Telephone again!" Faye quickly wiped the bread dough off her hands. "So many interruptions! I'll barely finish this baking before noon at this rate," she thought as she dashed to the telephone.

"Hello; Zimmermans', Faye speaking," Faye answered cheerfully.

"Hello; this is Ferne Weber calling. I'm sorry to bother you, but I wondered if you'd perhaps have time to help us can peaches this afternoon," came Ferne's weary voice over the line. "We still have five bushels to finish, and baby Rhoda has been so fussy that I can hardly help the girls."

"Well," Faye began slowly, "I'm in the middle of baking bread right now. But I should be finished with it by noon. Yes, I think that will work out all right."

C. In each blank, write the letter of the story which most likely develops that theme.

____c____ 17. Confessing sin is essential to Christian victory.

____a____ 18. "Yea, and all that will live godly in Christ Jesus shall suffer persecution."

____d____ 19. Helping others is a valuable service to the Lord.

____b____ 20. Even in dark circumstances, there are hidden blessings.

(4 points)

D. In each blank, give a brief description of the requested setting information.

21. The atmosphere of sample *a*. __in a rather worldly or inconsistent setting__

22. The time of sample *b*. _____in winter_____

23. The place of sample *b*. _____in Maryland_____

(3 points)

E. For each sample, write whether the conflict is with another person (*P*), with circumstances (*C*), or with the main character himself (*S*).

  _P_   24. Sample *a*.   _S_ 26. Sample *c*.

  _C_   25. Sample *b*.   _C_ 27. Sample *d*.

(4 points)

F. In each blank, write the character trait that is portrayed by the method indicated.   (Sample answers.)

  28. Caleb, by reputation. _conscientiousness, good behavior_

  29. Curtis, by appearance. _worldliness, carelessness_

  30. Freda, by actions.   _self-pity, discouragement_

  31. Faye, by thoughts.   _impatience, excitableness_

  32. Faye, by words.   _helpfulness, thoughtfulness_

(5 points)

G. In each blank, write the point of view that is used. Also write whether it is subjective (*S*) or objective (*O*), unless it is first person.

  33. Sample *a*. _first person_

  34. Sample *b*. _third person, O_

  35. Sample *c*. _omniscient, S_

  36. Sample *d*. _third person, S_

(4 points)

Total points: 36

Communicating Effectively—Book 2

Chapter 7 Test   **Score** _____

Name _____ **Date** _____

A. In the first blank, write *C* or *A* to tell whether the noun is concrete or abstract. In the second blank, write *M, F, N,* or *C* to tell whether its gender is masculine, feminine, neuter, or common.

_C_ _N_	1. sweater	_C_ _C_ 5. audience
_A_ _N_	2. joy	_C_ _F_ 6. queen
_C_ _C_	3. companion	_A_ _N_ 7. gentleness
_C_ _M_	4. rooster	_C_ _M_ 8. nephew

(8 points)

B. Write the plural form of each noun. For numbers 16–20, use the foreign spellings.

major generals	9. major general	mice	15. mouse
thieves	10. thief	larvae	16. larva
berries	11. berry	apices	17. apex
salmon	12. salmon	analyses	18. analysis
gulfs	13. gulf	millennia	19. millennium
altos	14. alto	gladioli	20. gladiolus

(12 points)

C. Rewrite these expressions, using possessive forms. If changing to the possessive form should not be done, write *X* in the blank.

Judas's treachery	21. the treachery of Judas
X	22. the writer of the book
the boss's directions	23. the directions of the boss
the prophets' messages	24. the messages of the prophets
Carl and Cindy's parents	25. the parents of Carl and Cindy (joint ownership)
Andrew's and Daryl's shoes	26. the shoes of Andrew and Daryl (separate ownership)

(6 points)

D. Underline the pronoun in each sentence, and label it *P* (personal), *CP* (compound personal), *D* (demonstrative), *ID* (indefinite), *IR* (interrogative), or *R* (relative).

  <u>ID</u> 27. A distinguishing mark of Christianity is love for <u>others</u>.

  <u>P</u> 28. How often does inner compassion move <u>us</u> to action?

  <u>IR</u> 29. <u>What</u> is the proper response to personal insults?

  <u>R</u> 30. James and John, <u>whom</u> Jesus restrained, wanted to call fire from heaven.

  <u>ID</u> 31. <u>None</u> of this world's forces can quench true love.

  <u>CP</u> 32. To have friends, a man must show <u>himself</u> friendly.

  <u>D</u> 33. <u>This</u> is stated clearly in the Book of Proverbs.

  <u>R</u> 34. Jesus said <u>what</u> a person should do if he is smitten on the cheek.

(8 points)

E. Underline the three substantives in each sentence; do not mark separately the substantives within substantive phrases or clauses. Above each item you underline, write *N* (one-word or compound noun), *Pron.* (pronoun), *G* (gerund phrase), *I* (infinitive phrase), *Prep.* (prepositional phrase), *C* (clause), *T* (title), or *S* (subject of discussion).

35. <u>Raking the leaves</u> [G] will be a good <u>job</u> [N] for <u>us</u> [Pron.].

36. After the <u>fire</u> [N] was extinguished, the <u>firemen</u> [N] said <u>that they suspected arson</u> [C].

37. <u>Below thirty degrees</u> [Prep.] can bring <u>disaster</u> [N] in a <u>greenhouse</u> [N].

38. This <u>article</u> [N], <u>"The Test of Thanksgiving,"</u> [T] should help <u>us to appreciate our blessings</u> [I].

39. <u>Most</u> [Pron.] of your <u>sentences</u> [N] begin with <u>*Then*</u> [S]!

(15 points)

F. Use proofreading marks to correct the errors in these sentences.

40. ~~Me and my~~ [uc] my brother ∧and I found an interesting story about a little girl whom~~ who~~ was given two quarters.

41. Her father said, "This quarter is for ~~yourself~~you, and that ~~there~~that is for the offering on Sunday."

42. Because she liked sweets as much as ~~us~~we, she hurried to buy some candy from the lady ~~which~~who owned a nearby store.

43. ~~Them~~Those who know little children can well imagine how tightly each of the quarters ~~were~~was held in her hand.

44. Suddenly the little girl's running was interrupted as she tripped over the ~~street's~~ of the street curb and lost one of the quarters.

45. When most of her tears ~~was~~ were dried, she decided that the coin in her hand was her's and the lost one was for the offering.

46. This can be a lesson for you and I me when we are tempted to put ourself ves and our interests ahead of the Lord.

(14 points)

G. Identify the poetic device in each sentence as alliteration (*A*), rhyme (*R*), or onomatopoeia (*O*).

__R__ 47. Procrastination is the thief of time, and this thief will bring grief to the soul.

__O__ 48. A procrastinator wastes much time as he goes muttering and grumbling from one dreaded task to another.

__R__ 49. Putting things off will not make them any more pleasurable or treasurable.

__A__ 50. We must learn to do things promptly, patiently, and pleasantly.

(4 points)

Total points: 67

Communicating Effectively—Book 2

Chapter 8 Test   **Score** _____

Name _____   **Date** _____

A. Write the correct words to complete these sentences.

_____explanatory words_____   1. In an extended conversation, you may omit the ——— ———.

_____short_____   2. In natural dialogue, most quotations are (long, short).

_____active_____   3. Verbs in the ——— voice help to give life and vigor to the story action.

_____metaphor_____   4. A ——— uses literal terms to describe something that happens only in a figurative sense.

_____personification_____   5. Imagery that pictures a thing or quality as having the characteristics of a living creature is ———.

_____hyperbole_____   6. A figurative, artistic exaggeration is a ———.

_____simile_____   7. A figurative comparison that uses *like* or *as* is a ———.

_____cliché_____   8. A once-vivid expression that has become stale through overuse is a ———.

_____arrested action_____   9. With ——— ———, story characters *begin* or *start* to do something but apparently do not finish.

(9 points)

B. Underline the correct choices in parentheses.

10. For an informal tone in dialogue, it is proper to use all the following things *except* (interruptions, <u>poor grammar</u>, contractions, elliptical sentences).

11. To make a story lively and forceful, all the following methods are helpful *except* (<u>using clichés</u>, avoiding expressions like *perhaps* and *probably,* appealing to the five senses).

12. Static description includes all the following things *except* (details about the setting, explanations of a character's appearance, <u>portrayals of a character's actions</u>).

(3 points)

C. Circle the capital letter before the better sample in each pair. In the blank, write the letter of the quality below that makes it the better choice.

    a. appeal to the five senses   d. imagery   g. simple, familiar words
    b. exact, descriptive words   e. lively action verbs   h. straightforward language
    c. fresh, original language   f. natural dialogue

_e_ 13. A.   "Charles, the pasture gate was left unlatched again." Father's words were stern. "Too many such things have been done recently. This habit must be broken."

       (B)   "Charles, you left the pasture gate unlatched again." Father spoke sternly. "You have done too many such things recently. You must break this habit."

_f_   14.   A.   "Well, girls, we will need to hurry this morning," Mother said as she rose from the breakfast table. "Why must we hurry, Mother?" asked Nora.

"We must hurry because Grandfather's are coming for dinner. I want all the Saturday cleaning and baking done by noon," Mother said.

Ⓑ   "Well, girls, we'll need to hurry this morning," Mother said as she rose from the breakfast table. "Why, Mother?" asked Nora.

"Because Grandfather's are coming for supper. I want—"

_a_   15.   Ⓐ   "M-m-m. My favorite breakfast," Brian murmured as he entered the kitchen. Potatoes sputtered in the cast-iron skillet, saturating the air with their hearty aroma. Lifting the lid of a kettle, Brian saw the steaming, rich-brown hot chocolate.

B.   "M-m-m. My favorite breakfast," Brian murmured as he entered the kitchen. Potatoes were frying in the cast-iron skillet. Lifting the lid of a kettle, Brian saw the hot chocolate.

_d_   16.   Ⓐ   All morning those words weighed on Orpha's heart like a heavy chain. Everywhere she turned, she saw Mark's hurt eyes. "If only I could control my tongue! But that's just it. I can't control it, and I failed to let God control it."

Quietly, Orpha slipped off to her bedroom and poured it all out before the Lord. A few minutes later, she rose with a heart as light as a summer cloud. "Now, before I do anything else, I must apologize to Mark."

B.   All morning those words bothered Orpha. She could not forget Mark's hurt look. "If only I could control my tongue! But that's just it. I can't control it, and I failed to let God control it."

Quietly, Orpha slipped off to her bedroom and prayed. A few minutes later, she rose with a light heart. "Now, before I do anything else, I must apologize to Mark."

_b_   17.   A.   "Any homework this evening?" Father asked.

"A little," his son answered. "I must finish one lesson and study for a test."

"Very well. As soon as you are ready, come outside and help me."

Ⓑ   "Any homework this evening?" Father asked.

"A little," Laverne answered. "I must finish my algebra lesson and study for a history test."

"Very well. As soon as you've changed your clothes, come out to the implement shed and help me grease the combine."

_h_   18.   A.   It was perhaps Tuesday afternoon when the whole problem started. At least that's about the first time I noticed that Laura was acting rather cool toward me.

"Whatever could I have said or done," I wondered for maybe the hundredth time, "that might possibly have offended her?"

Ⓑ   The whole problem must have started on Tuesday afternoon. At least that's when I first noticed that Laura was acting cool toward me.

"Whatever could I have said or done," I wondered for the hundredth time, "that might have offended her?"

_g_   19.   A.   The obscurity of the night gave a measure of asylum to the believers' rendezvous at their clandestine place of worship. "God bless you," Brother Hans softly saluted Brother Leonhart. "Will you expound the message tonight?"

Ⓑ   The darkness of the night gave a measure of safety to the believers' meeting at their secret place of worship. "God bless you," Brother Hans softly greeted Brother Leonhart. "Will you preach the message tonight?"

_c_ 20. (A)   William gazed in horror at the pale form lying on the ground. Then he rushed at top speed to the barn. "Father," gasped William, "Vincent fell out of the tree. Come quick!"

Father raced to the yard. By the time he arrived, Vincent was sitting up. After checking him carefully, Father said, "Thank God, you don't seem to have any broken bones. The Lord was surely taking care of you."

Vincent was as stiff as an arthritic horse for a few days, but before long he was back to his normal self.

B.   William gazed in horror at Vincent as he lay on the ground, as white as a sheet. Then he hurried to the barn as fast as his legs could carry him. "Father," gasped William, "Vincent fell out of the tree. Come quick!"

Father ran like the wind to the yard. By the time he arrived, Vincent was sitting up. After checking him carefully, Father said, "Thank God, you don't seem to have any broken bones. The Lord was surely taking care of you."

Vincent was as stiff as a board for a few days, but before long he was as good as new.

(8 points)

Total points: 20

Note: In Lesson 67, the pupil was told that the score on his original story would make up a considerable part of his Chapter 8 test score. The story and the test together contain a total of 78 points (58 on the story and 20 on the test).

Communicating Effectively—Book 2

Chapter 9 Test

Score _____

Name _____ Date _____

A. If an underlined verb is incorrect, write the correct form in the blank. If the verb is correct, write *correct*.

_____seen_____ 1. After the women had <u>saw</u> Jesus' tomb, they returned home.

_____risen_____ 2. Today we rejoice that our Lord has <u>rose</u> from the grave.

_____correct_____ 3. Many Anabaptists were <u>dragged</u> to prison for their faith.

_____gone_____ 4. They have <u>went</u> willingly to their death at the stake.

_____correct_____ 5. We <u>bade</u> our friends farewell and left for home.

_____ridden_____ 6. After we had <u>rode</u> in silence for several minutes, Mother started to sing.

_____burst_____ 7. Sunshine suddenly <u>bursted</u> through a break in the clouds.

_____swung_____ 8. Albert <u>swang</u> the hammer but missed the nail.

(8 points)

B. Underline each verb or verb phrase. In the first blank, write the lowercase letter showing the tense of the verb. In the second blank, write the capital letter showing the form of the verb.

Tenses		Forms
a. present	d. present perfect	S—simple
b. past	e. past perfect	P—progressive
c. future	f. future perfect	E—emphatic

_e_ _P_ 9. Before his heart attack, Grandfather <u>had been speaking</u> of chest pains.

_b_ _S_ 10. In addition, he <u>complained</u> about shortness of breath.

_a_ _S_ 11. <u>Do</u> you <u>understand</u> the cause of a heart attack?

_a_ _P_ 12. Due to a blocked artery, the heart <u>is</u> not <u>receiving</u> enough blood.

_c_ _S_ 13. The heart muscle <u>will be damaged</u> from lack of blood.

_b_ _E_ 14. Grandfather <u>did receive</u> numerous visitors during his hospital stay.

(18 points)

C. Write *ind.* (indicative), *imp.* (imperative), or *sub.* (subjunctive) to identify the mood of each underlined verb or verb phrase.

imp. 15. <u>Will</u> you please <u>pass</u> your papers forward.

ind. 16. Your new assignment <u>begins</u> on page 273.

ind. 17. <u>Do</u> you <u>see</u> the questions at the bottom of this sheet?

sub. 18. If the assignment <u>were</u> any shorter, you would not have much written work.

(4 points)

D. Underline the words that are correct for the subjunctive mood.

19. Jethro recommended that Moses (<u>have</u>, had) more help.

20. If your ankle (was, <u>were</u>) healed, we could go for a hike.

21. Though a man (<u>be</u>, is) rich, he can never save himself.

(3 points)

E. Underline each verb or verb phrase, and label it *TA* (transitive, active voice), *TP* (transitive, passive voice), *IC* (intransitive complete), or *IL* (intransitive linking).

<u>TA</u> 22. Last year we <u>took</u> a trip to British Columbia.

<u>TP</u> 23. Many of the people there <u>are engaged</u> in the lumber industry.

<u>IL</u> 24. Our trip into the bush <u>was</u> an educational experience.

<u>IC</u> 25. Tall spruce trees <u>fell</u> like mere boards before the buncher.

<u>TP</u> 26. Large piles of trees <u>were dragged</u> by a skidder to a nearby clearing or landing.

<u>TA</u> 27. A processor <u>stripped</u> the branches from the tree trunks.

<u>IL</u> 28. The machine loading the timber <u>looked</u> immense.

<u>IC</u> 29. The lumber trucks <u>roared</u> away to the sawmill.

(8 points)

F. Underline the correct words in parentheses.

30. Each of the suggestions (offer, <u>offers</u>) some significant benefits.

31. A large flock of blackbirds often (land, <u>lands</u>) in this tree.

32. *Crises* (<u>is</u>, are) the plural of *crisis.*

33. (<u>Have</u>, Has) the new windows reduced your fuel bill?

34. The pretzels or the orange juice (come, <u>comes</u>) from Aunt Martha.

35. Sandra is the only one of the artists who (enjoy, <u>enjoys</u>) drawing people.

36. Electronics (<u>is</u>, are) becoming an important field in today's world.

37. Three-fourths of the tree (appear, <u>appears</u>) to be dead.

38. Biscuits and gravy (<u>is</u>, are) a common breakfast in the South.

39. The scissors (was, <u>were</u>) sharpened only last week.

40. We all agreed that fifteen pounds (<u>was</u>, were) how much sugar we needed.

41. "Angry Words" (challenge, <u>challenges</u>) us to restrain ourselves from speaking harshly.

42. Some of the arguments that (<u>have</u>, has) been presented are almost absurd.

43. All of the corn (taste, <u>tastes</u>) burnt.

44. Neither a jot nor a tittle of God's Word (have, <u>has</u>) been written in vain.

(15 points)

Total points: 56

Communicating Effectively—Book 2

Chapter 10 Test

Score _____

Name _____   Date _____

A. Circle *T* if the statement is true or *F* if it is false.

T (F)   1. You can write your best description of a place by doing careful research in reference books.

(T) F   2. An effective description emphasizes only one outstanding impression.

T (F)   3. A description of a scene usually follows chronological order.

T (F)   4. Descriptive writing usually consists of a whole essay that portrays a scene or an event.

(T) F   5. By appealing to the senses, the descriptive writer helps the reader to live what the author has described.

T (F)   6. The descriptive writer should use exact nouns and expressive verbs but try to avoid modifiers.

T (F)   7. A descriptive essay is different from other compositions in that it has no introduction or conclusion.

(T) F   8. Imagery contributes to description both by making meaningful comparisons and by adding rich color.

(8 points)

B. Circle the capital letter before the better sample in each pair. In the blank, write the letter of the quality below that makes it the better choice.

    a. appeal to the five senses   d. one specific impression
    b. imagery   e. rich detail
    c. logical order of development   f. vivid, concrete words

_f_ 9. A.   The animal looked cautiously out of his hole. Noticing no danger, he came out into the evening air. Gaining confidence by another quick look, he went to some grass at the edge of the garden. He took a few nibbles and then stood on his hind feet. Silently, almost motionlessly, he looked around. Soon he was on all four feet, moving toward the garden plants.

        (B.)   The fat woodchuck peered cautiously out of his hole. Seeing and smelling no danger, he crawled out into the evening air. Reassured by another glance, he waddled to a patch of tender grass at the edge of the garden. He took five nibbles and then stood erect. Silently, almost motionlessly, he surveyed his surroundings. A minute later he dropped on all fours and headed for the tender young lima beans.

_b_ 10. (A)   "Let's rest here a bit," announced Father.

        I sank wearily to the ground beside the merry mountain stream. Its clear, cold water laughed to itself as it bounded over and around the rocks on its race to the valley below.

        B.   "Let's rest here a bit," announced Father.

        I sank wearily to the ground beside the swift mountain stream. Its clear, cold water made a pleasant sound as it ran over and around the rocks on its way to the valley below.

_c_ 11. (A)   We called him Mr. Haughty, and everything about his appearance made it a suitable name. On broad feet and long legs, he towered four inches higher than any other rooster on our farm. A magnificent plume of brown, mahogany, and tan tail feathers arched boldly into the air. His powerful wings, whenever he stretched them out, measured nearly three feet from tip to tip. Whether surveying his domain or strutting around in it, he thrust his chest as far out as possible. Mr. Haughty always held his head high in the air, as if trying to make himself even taller than he was. Dominating his whole haughty appearance were his eyes. What a look those beady eyes held as he glared coldly upon the world about him!

      B.   We called him Mr. Haughty, and everything about his appearance made it a suitable name. On broad feet and long legs, he towered four inches higher than any other rooster on our farm. His powerful wings, whenever he stretched them out, measured nearly three feet from tip to tip. Mr. Haughty always held his head high in the air, as if trying to make himself even taller than he was. A magnificent plume of brown, mahogany, and tan tail feathers arched boldly into the air. Whether surveying his domain or strutting around in it, he thrust his chest as far out as possible. Dominating his whole haughty appearance were his eyes. What a look those beady eyes held as he glared coldly upon the world about him!

_a_ 12. A.   For a few moments, I sat back and surveyed the scene. In the center stood the wood fire, now a mass of embers. Even from my distance of five feet, I could feel its heat. A large cast-iron spider stood over the center of the fire. On its left simmered a kettle of baked beans, suspended by a cast-iron hook. On its right hung a pot of coffee, just beginning to percolate.

      (B.)   For a few moments, I sat back and surveyed the scene. In the center stood the wood fire, now a mass of red-hot embers. Even from my distance of five feet, its glow flushed my face and heated my hands. A large cast-iron spider stood over the center of the fire. On its left, a kettle of simmering baked beans, suspended by a cast-iron hook, sent its sweet, hearty aroma over the picnic area. On its right hung a pot of coffee, its steady *glug-GLUG* just beginning to produce a rich, bracing aroma.

_d_ 13. (A)   Sister Lena's cottage is always the picture of cheerfulness. A wide variety of geraniums, African violets, ferns, and other plants brighten each room. The sofa, the stuffed chair, and the recliner wear attractively patterned afghans that she has crocheted. And each wall holds at least one motto that beams a message of faith, hope, or love.

      B.   Sister Lena's cottage is always the picture of cheerfulness. A wide variety of geraniums, African violets, ferns, and other plants grow in each tiny room. The sofa, the stuffed chair, and the recliner provide comfortable resting places for the weary. And each wall holds at least one motto that reminds us of God, who sees all things.

_e_ 14. A.   There before us stood the old cabin. It had obviously been abandoned many years before. Grasses and weeds grew on the inside, and vines clung to the outside. Indeed, it looked as if it would fall into a heap at any moment.

      (B)   There before us stood the old cabin, obviously abandoned many years before. We could see tall grass and weeds growing inside, well-nurtured by the rain and sunshine that entered through the gaping hole in the roof. Vines of poison ivy and morning glory clung to the outside. The remains of a sagging door hung from a single rusted hinge. The walls, leaning precariously, threatened to fall into a heap with the next puff of wind.

(12 points)

Note: In Lesson 87, the pupil was told that the score on his descriptive essay would make up a considerable part of his Chapter 10 test score. The essay and the test together contain a total of 71 points (51 on the essay *Total points: 20* and 20 on the test).

Communicating Effectively—Book 2

Chapter 11 Test

Score _____

Name _____ Date _____

A. Above each underlined adjective, write *D* for descriptive or *L* for limiting. Also write *AT* for attributive, *AP* for appositive, or *PR* for predicate.

              D, AT   D, AP   L, AT
1. Because we have <u>Bible</u> teaching <u>to follow</u>, we need not stumble in darkness as do those who seek <u>their</u> direction

   L, AT   L, AP
  from <u>this</u> world <u>below</u>.

  L, AT   D, PR   D, PR   L, AT D, AT
2. <u>God's</u> authority is <u>absolute</u> yet <u>gracious</u>, for He loves man with <u>a</u> <u>perfect</u> love.

  L, AT   D, PR   L, AT
3. <u>What</u> blessings can be more <u>valuable</u> than <u>those</u> blessings that God gives?

                                                                  (13 points)

B. Underline the adjective phrases and clauses. Above each, write *prep.* for prepositional, *part.* for participial, *inf.* for infinitive, or *cl.* for clause. If a phrase is part of a longer phrase or clause, do not underline it separately.

                          cl.
4. Menno Simons, <u>who spent twelve years as a priest in the Roman Catholic Church</u>, became a prominent Anabaptist

                part.
  leader, <u>serving faithfully for twenty-five years</u>.

         part.   cl.
5. <u>Reflecting on his life years later</u>, Menno admitted that he had lived carelessly during those years <u>when he was a priest</u>.

                                  prep.
6. Menno's awareness <u>of serious doctrinal error in the Roman Catholic Church</u> produced a growing readiness

        inf.
  <u>to commit his life to truth</u>.

                                                                                 (6 points)

C. Above each underlined phrase or clause, write *R* for restrictive or *N* for nonrestrictive. Use proofreading marks to add any missing commas.

                      N   R
7. Brother Kuhns <u>who has taught school for thirty years</u> has the ability <u>to explain difficult things clearly</u>.

                                   N
8. We watched Arnold Stauffer <u>working painstakingly with his crippled hands</u> as he carved the picture frame

      R
  <u>that would replace the old frame brought in by a customer</u>.

                  N   R
9. Sister Anita <u>afflicted with rheumatoid arthritis</u> appreciates the many friends <u>whose visits brighten her days</u>.

                                                                       (6 points)

D. Underline the correct participle in each sentence.

10. (Growing, <u>Having grown</u>) up during the Great Depression, Grandfather deplores the wastefulness that is common

  today.

11. This snow, (drifting, <u>drifted</u>) into huge piles by yesterday's high winds, has us well isolated.

12. Tippy, (<u>gnawing</u>, having gnawed) on the big ham bone, was too busy to play fetch with us.

                                                                        (3 points)

E. Underline each single-word adverb, including any infinitive used as an adverb. Put parentheses around the word or word group that the adverb modifies, and draw an arrow from each underlined modifier to the item it modifies.

13. <u>Clearly</u>, (the travelers misinterpreted our intentions).

14. <u>Finally</u> they (understood) that we were (eager) <u>to help</u>.

15. (Helping) others <u>graciously</u> is a <u>definitely</u> (meaningful) way to show our love to God and others.

16. If we <u>always</u> (seek) our own interests <u>first</u>, we <u>actually</u> (are saying) that we consider ourselves <u>more</u> (important) than

others.

(9 points)

F. Underline each adverb phrase or clause, and use proofreading marks to add any missing commas.

17. <u>If others entice you</u>̂ remember that a clear conscience is more valuable <u>than anything else is</u>.

18. <u>To maintain a clear conscience</u>̂ we must resist temptation <u>at all times</u>.

19. A faithful person, strengthened <u>through the fortitude of godly fear</u>, will rise <u>above temptation</u>.

(6 points)

G. Use proofreading marks to correct the mistakes in using the forms of comparison for adjectives and adverbs.

20. We had ~~littler~~ less snow this winter than we did last winter.

21. Randall plays with his new dump truck more than with any ^other^ toy that he has.

22. By explaining something to another person, you may understand it ^more^ ~~clearer~~ yourself.

23. Father plans to make Mother's new flower bed ^more nearly^ ~~rounder~~.

24. I have been feeling ~~more~~ better since early this morning.

25. The girls have been ^more^ ~~carefuller~~ in their baking since Mother talked to them about

their wastefulness.

26. Although both of my grandfathers are becoming bald, Grandfather Showalter's

hair is thinne~~s~~t.

(7 points)

H. Circle *T* if the statement is true or *F* if it is false.

T (F) 27. Placing two words that end with -*ly* together contributes to good sentence rhythm.

(T) F 28. The repetition of similar sounds can mar sentence rhythm.

T (F) 29. For the best rhythm, place the longer item in a compound first and the shorter item second.

(3 points)

Total points: 53

Communicating Effectively—Book 2

Chapter 12 Test

Score _____

Name _____   Date _____

A. Circle *T* if the statement is true or *F* if it is false.

T F   1. The label *informal* indicates a word that is acceptable only in everyday speech and everyday writing.

T **F**   2. The label *archaic* indicates a word that is spoken by a limited group of people.

T **F**   3. Dictionaries usually show the forms of comparison for all adjectives and adverbs.

T F   4. A Roget's thesaurus can help you find related words in entries near the word you have looked up.

T **F**   5. An encyclopedia is one of the best sources for finding detailed information about a subject.

T F   6. For the most complete list of articles with information on a subject, you should use the index of an encyclopedia rather than the cross-references at the end of an article.

T F   7. To contribute to effective speaking style, enthusiasm must grow within the speaker.

T **F**   8. Eye contact tends to hinder the enthusiasm that a speaker should convey to the audience.

(8 points)

B. Write the letter of the correct term for each description. Not all the letters will be used.

__c__   9. The "personality" of a word.

__j__   10. Words that are similar in meaning.

__h__   11. A brief history of a word.

__b__   12. A label telling where a book is located in the library.

__e__   13. The strict, exact meaning of a word.

__f__   14. Words formed from root words by adding suffixes.

__i__   15. Changes in a word to show number, tense, and so forth.

__g__   16. A method for classifying books into ten main groupings.

a. antonyms
b. call number
c. connotation
d. Cutter number
e. denotation
f. derivatives
g. Dewey decimal system
h. etymology
i. inflections
j. synonyms

(8 points)

C. Match these letters and descriptions. You will use the letters several times each.

_b_ 17. Imaginary stories.

_a_ 18. Belong to the 920–929 group of the Dewey decimal system.

_c_ 19. May be placed in more than one category of the Dewey decimal system.

_b_ 20. Belong to the 800–899 group of the Dewey decimal system.

_b_ 21. Class of books without subject cards in the card catalog.

_c_ 22. Books used to look up information.

_b_ 23. Books arranged alphabetically by author.

_a_ 24. Stories about specific individuals.

_c_ 25. Mostly belong to the 000–099 group of the Dewey decimal system.

_a_ 26. Books arranged alphabetically according to the name of the person written about.

a. biography
b. fiction
c. reference

(10 points)

D. Read these sample dictionary entries, and do the exercises that follow.

grate[1] (grāt) *v.* **grat·ed, grat·ing, grates.** —*tr.* **1.** To grind into small pieces by rubbing against an abrasive surface. **2.** To cause to make a harsh grinding or rasping sound through friction. **3.** To irritate or annoy persistently. —*intr.* **1.** To make a harsh rasping sound by or as if by grinding. **2.** To cause irritation or annoyance. —**grate** *n.* A harsh rasping sound made by scraping or rubbing. [ME *graten* < OFr. *grater,* to scrape, of Ger. orig.] —**grat·er** *n.*

grate[2] (grāt) *n.* **1.** A framework of parallel or latticed bars placed over an opening. **2.** A framework of metal bars for holding fuel or food in a stove, furnace, or fireplace. **3.** A fireplace. [ME < Med.Lat. *grāta,* alteration of Lat. *crātis,* wickerwork.] —**grat·ed** *adj.*

27. Why are there two numbered entries for *grate*? _____

   <u>There are two words from different origins.</u>_____

28. Write *1* or *2* to tell which entry fits each description.

   _2_ a. Comes from a Latin word.

   _1_ b. Can be used as a noun or a verb.

   _1_ c. Shows inflections.

   _2_ d. Shows a derivative used as an adjective.

(5 points)

Total points: 31

Communicating Effectively—Book 2

Chapter 13 Test

Score _____

Name _____   Date _____

A. Underline each prepositional phrase, and above it write whether it functions as an adjective (*adj.*), an adverb (*adv.*), or a noun (*n.*). If a phrase is part of a longer phrase, underline it twice, and label both phrases clearly.

           adv.   adj.   adv.
  1. Because of our position as stewards, we must use our possessions to God's glory.

           adv.   adj.   adv.   adv.
  2. By the light of divine knowledge, we can live as God's people through whatever life brings our way.

             n.   adj.   adv.
  3. Under God's blessing is the only station in this life that offers to humanity an eternal hope.

(10 points)

B. Underline the conjunctions, and label them as follows: *CC* (common coordinating conjunction), *Cor* (correlative conjunction), *SC* (subordinating conjunction), or *CA* (conjunctive adverb). Be sure to include all the parts of correlative conjunctions.

                      SC   CA
  4. In 1948, George de Mestral grew frustrated when burs clung to his clothing during an Alpine hike; however, the burs

     also inspired him to make a fastener that would work on the same basis.

      SC
  5. Although most textile experts scoffed at his idea, a weaver in Lyons, France, soon produced one strip of cotton with

               CC
     tiny hooks and another with tiny eyes that interlocked quite well.

                            CC   Cor
  6. The cotton fibers wore out too quickly; so George experimented with nylon, which proved to be both more pliable

  Cor
  and more durable than cotton.

                                                                      CA
  7. By the late 1950s, manufacturers were producing sixty million yards of this new Velcro yearly; nevertheless, Velcro

                         SC
     has not replaced the zipper as its inventor had predicted.

(8 points)

C. Write *I* above each interjection. Use proofreading marks to show corrections in punctuation, capitalization, and italics.

                                                          I
  8. With two tires flat, I'm not sure what to do; but well the Lord will surely

     provide for us.

      I   lc
  9. Cold! it was bitterly cold all day.

       I   lc
 10. Honk! the blaring horn jolted me fully awake.

(6 points)

D. Use proofreading marks to correct the errors in using coordinating conjunctions.

 11. I both enjoyed the words and the music of that song.

12. **The words of the hymn contain many inspiring thoughts; moreover, the music**

complements those thoughts beautifully.

13. **We must concentrate not only on singing the notes correctly but** also **on comprehending**

the words properly.

14. **I thought that I understood the lesson but these exercises have me confused.**

15. **That dog ⌐neither¬ ⌊looks⌋ well fed nor healthy.**

16. **The mockingbird sings** ~~energetically~~ with energy **and with great variety.**

(6 points)

E. Use proofreading marks to remove *and* from each sentence and insert a subordinating conjunction that shows a more specific relationship between the clauses.

17. Because lc **Man has willfully rejected the knowledge of God, ~~and~~ his foolish heart is**

darkened with superstition and wickedness.

18. **The sinner vainly imagines that he is master of his own life,** when ~~and~~ **he is ac-**

tually a slave to Satan.

19. If lc **A man sincerely searches God's Word, ~~and~~ the light of truth will illuminate**

his soul.

20. **Man must be willing to surrender to the lordship of Jesus Christ,** before ~~and~~ **he can**

know the truth.

(4 points)

F. Underline each idiom, and write its meaning in the blank. (Sample answers.)

21. The car picked up speed as it rolled down the hill. gained; increased

22. Most of the children quickly caught on to the idea. understood; grasped

23. Some of the younger ones were at a loss. puzzled; perplexed

24. We were able to put out the fire by ourselves. extinguish

25. To his surprise, Arnold's great plans fell through. failed; were unsuccessful

26. He was compelled to eat his words. take back an earlier statement

(6 points)

Total points: 40

Communicating Effectively—Book 2

Chapter 14 Test

Score _____

Name _____ Date _____

A. Circle *T* if the statement is true, or *F* if it is false.

T(F) 1. Parliamentary procedure is an effective way to determine what the Bible teaches.

(T)F 2. Parliamentary procedure helps to promote fairness for both the majority and the minority.

T(F) 3. Motions must be voted on in the same order in which they are presented.

(T)F 4. To present most motions, a member must rise, address the chairman, and wait for the chairman to recognize him.

(T)F 5. A member may remain seated to second a motion.

T(F) 6. The proper wording to begin most motions is, "I make a motion to . . ."

T(F) 7. An amendment may change the wording of part of a motion, but it may not change the entire motion.

T(F) 8. The minutes should clearly record the discussions and decisions of the group.

T(F) 9. If a motion is pending, it will be disposed of at the next meeting.

(T)F 10. Old business includes any matters carried over from a previous meeting.

(T)F 11. According to the principle of precedence, only a motion of higher rank can be presented when another motion is on the floor.

(T)F 12. Parliamentary procedure helps to ensure that all members of a group can discuss an issue openly and completely.

T(F) 13. The reading of the minutes should follow all other reports and business.

(T)F 14. When a motion affects the group's freedom of discussion, a two-thirds majority is required for the motion to pass.

T(F) 15. If a vote results in 8 ayes and 9 nays, the chairman can cause the motion to pass by voting aye.

(15 points)

B. Write the letter of the correct term to match each description. Some letters may be used more than once, and some not at all.

Parliamentary Terms

__f__ 16. The order of discussion and vote.

__g__ 17. The minimum number of members needed to conduct business.

__b__ 18. A check of the accuracy of the treasurer's records.

__a__ 19. A change in the wording of a motion.

__c__ 20. The right to address the assembly.

__d__ 21. The official record of the business of a meeting.

a. amendment
b. audit
c. floor
d. minutes
e. motion
f. precedence
g. quorum

Offices

_j_ 22. Keeps detailed records of the meetings.

_h_ 23. Has charge of who may address the assembly.

_i_ 24. Discusses motions and votes.

_l_ 25. Takes the place of an absent chairman.

_k_ 26. Receives any income and pays any bills.

_j_ 27. Writes and answers letters pertaining to group business.

_i_ 28. Makes up the main voting body.

h. chairman
i. group
j. secretary
k. treasurer
l. vice-chairman

Voting Methods

_n_ 29. Is used for procedural matters, such as approving minutes.

_o_ 30. Is commonly used to take an exact vote on general matters.
_or p_

_q_ 31. Is used especially for elections and sensitive issues.

_m_ 32. Cannot show the will of the group if the vote is close.

m. acclamation
n. general consent
o. show of hands
p. rising
q. secret ballot

(17 points)

C. For each situation described, write the letter of the motion that should be made.

a. amend
b. point of order
c. previous question
d. question of privilege
e. refer to committee
f. take a recess

_e_ 33. It seems that the group is not ready to make a decision, but that several individuals should study the matter and report back to the group.

_d_ 34. You cannot hear what is being said.

_b_ 35. While a motion is pending, the chairman allows someone to introduce another main motion.

_a_ 36. You would like to change several words in a motion.

_f_ 37. The meeting has become extended, and the members would profit from a short break.

_c_ 38. A question has been thoroughly discussed and should be voted upon.

(6 points)

D. Number the following in the order they would occur in a normal business meeting.

_2_ The chairman asks for the reading of the minutes.

_7_ The chairman adjourns the meeting.

_4_ The chairman calls for any committee reports.

_6_ The chairman opens the meeting for new business.

_1_ The chairman calls the meeting to order.

_3_ The chairman calls for the treasurer's report.

_5_ The chairman brings old business to the floor.

(4 points)

Total points: 42

Communicating Effectively—Book 2

Final Test   Score _____

Name _____ **Date** _____

Part I: Mechanics, Grammar, and Usage (197 points)

A. Use proofreading marks to correct the mistakes in capitalization, quotation marks, italics, and end punctuation. Each sentence has three errors. (A pair of marks or a title is one item.)

1. "The gospel of christ provides power to live above sin," declared brother Walter.

2. Our theme song this month is When on quiet seas I Sail, from Life Songs.

3. "Can you tell me," asked mother, "Which song has the line, Never a burden that He doth not bear?"

4. "When saying the word picture, observed Paula, don't forget to pronounce the c."

5. Janette said with a chuckle, "On our trip across the great plains, one of the boys exclaimed, 'what a huge tractor.'"

6. Since we moved to a small church in the south last summer, we have adjusted to much smaller Sunday School classes.

(18 points)

B. Use proofreading marks to correct the mistakes in commas, colons, and semicolons. Each sentence has three errors. (A pair of commas is one item.)

7. From her chair near the wood stove Grandmother enjoys listening to the family conversations often she has wise practical counsel to offer.

8. Ah for every need of our hearts Mr. Baker there is one sure answer God.

9. Mother has brothers and sisters who live in the following areas Lewis County, New York Holmes County, Ohio and Lancaster County, Pennsylvania.

10. Gordon Snavely Sr. one of Father's childhood friends makes cheese, ice cream and yogurt from goat's milk.

11. "David was gazing into the starry sky it seems when he said the words in Psalm 8 3" commented Bonita.

(15 points)

C. Use proofreading marks to correct the mistakes in ellipsis points, dashes, parentheses, brackets, apostrophes, and hyphens. Each sentence has three errors. (A pair of marks or a title is one item.)

12. **"And every man that striveth for the mastery is temperate [self-controlled]**

    in all things" (1 Corinthians 9:25).

13. **"We've had some all-time high temperatures already in May. What do you suppose"**

    Mary's voice trailed away.

14. **Christine is working in her flower beds she surely enjoys flowers! while the**

    rest of the girl's are neglecting their's. (Give sharp emphasis.)

15. **At the ripe age of eighty-nine, Great-uncle Levi has a store of time-honored**

    maxims and proverbs.

16. **"If all the girls chores are finished, we should oh, is it really ten oclock**

    already?" gasped Mother.

(15 points)

D. Write the parts of speech that the underlined words are. Use these abbreviations.

n.—noun	adj.—adjective	conj.—conjunction
pron.—pronoun	adv.—adverb	interj.—interjection
v.—verb	prep.—preposition	

(a) __adj.__ (b) __n.__   17. God's peace, ᵃabiding in our hearts, is a ᵇguard against sin.

(a) __v.__ (b) __conj.__   18. We must ᵃguard our thoughts carefully ᵇbefore they produce evil actions.

(a) __adv.__ (b) __pron.__   19. The peaceful soul has a ᵃmore valuable treasure than ᵇanyone else has.

(a) __adj.__ (b) __adv.__   20. ᵃMore people should consider this treasure worthwhile ᵇto seek.

(a) __prep.__ (b) __pron.__   21. ᵃBefore the beginning of each day's work, ᵇwe should seek God's grace.

(a) __interj.__ (b) __conj.__   22. ᵃBehold, God is our sure help, ᵇfor He knows all and has all power.

(12 points)

E. Label each numbered word group S (complete sentence), F (fragment), R (run-on error), or E (elliptical sentence).

__S__ 23.   ²³"God certainly is good to us." ²⁴Brother Laban looked down at the frail form of his bedfast wife, his wrinkled face shone with joy.

__R__ 24.   ²⁵"Yes, indeed. ²⁶His grace makes all the difference," she agreed in a trembling voice. ²⁷Which nevertheless carried a tone of unwavering faith.

__E__ 25.

__S__ 26.

__F__ 27.

(5 points)

F. Name the sentence part that each underlined word is. Use these abbreviations.
    S—subject   IO—indirect object   PA—predicate adjective
    V—verb   DA—noun of direct address   OC—objective complement
    DO—direct object   PN—predicate nominative   AP—appositive

(a)__S__ (b)__DO__ 28. In six days, ªGod created the ᵇworld.

(a)__DA__ (b)__OC__ 29. Yes, ªMr. Ervin, I consider Genesis an accurate ᵇaccount of history.

(a)__V__ (b)__IO__ 30. Indeed, God Himself ªgave ᵇus these facts.

(a)__AP__ (b)__PA__ 31. Man, a mere ªcreature of dust, is ᵇprone to exalt himself above God.

(a)__V__ (b)__PN__ 32. Through faith we ªcan become the ᵇmen that God wants us to be.

(10 points)

G. Label each sentence *S* (simple), *CD* (compound), *CX* (complex), or *CD-CX* (compound-complex).

___S___ 33. A number of words in the English language can be used with nearly opposite meanings.

__CD-CX__ 34. For example, if a person seeds an alfalfa field, he puts the seeds into the field; but if he seeds raisins, he removes the seeds from the raisins.

___CD___ 35. A fast horse runs rapidly, but a fast color does not run at all!

___CX___ 36. While dusted furniture has the dust removed, dusted crops have chemical dust applied.

___CD___ 37. We understand these words quite well, but to someone learning English as a second language, they can be quite confusing.

(5 points)

H. In the first blank, write *dec.* (declarative), *int.* (interrogative), *imp.* (imperative), or *exc.* (exclamatory) to identify the sentence type. In the second blank, write *N* (natural), *I* (inverted), or *M* (mixed) to identify the word order. End punctuation has been omitted.

__exc.__ ___M___ 38. How thoughtful Aunt Sarah was to send us this casserole

__dec.__ ___I___ 39. Across the floor crept a tiny mouse

__int.__ ___M___ 40. After last evening's thunderstorm, did you see the double rainbow

__imp.__ ___N___ 41. Read these Bible promises often for your encouragement

(4 points)

I. In the blank, write *L* (loose), *P* (periodic), or *B* (balanced) to identify the sentence style.

_B_ 42. The greater our trust in the Lord, the greater our sense of contentment will be.

_P_ 43. Although a Biblical lifestyle may be unpopular or even dangerous, the Christian obeys the Bible.

_L_ 44. We must respect all earthly authority if we expect to live under the blessing of God, the ultimate authority.

_B_ 45. A fool often speaks without thinking, but a wise man often thinks without speaking.

(4 points)

J. Underline the correct or preferred expressions in parentheses.

46. Do not (flaunt, <u>flout</u>) the good (<u>advice</u>, advise) of older people, for their experience and (<u>perspective</u>, prospective) are valuable indeed.

47. Since we (<u>believe</u>, feel) that God will judge us as we judge others, we must (<u>always</u>, all ways) be careful about (censoring, <u>censuring</u>) our fellow men.

48. I (implied, <u>inferred</u>) from Mr. Winnick's words that business has prospered fairly (good, <u>well</u>) as the demand for his small sheds keeps (raising, <u>rising</u>).

49. Grandmother's vision is (some, <u>somewhat</u>) better (<u>than</u>, then) she had expected it to be after having (them, <u>those</u>) cataracts removed.

50. In his machine shop, Father receives quite a large (amount, <u>number</u>) of orders to (<u>adapt</u>, adopt) tools and machinery in (<u>ingenious</u>, ingenuous) ways.

51. The dishes are (<u>almost</u>, most) finished, so you girls (can, <u>may</u>) be excused to take (<u>your</u>, you're) walk.

52. If you (<u>let</u>, leave) the boys pick at those cupcakes, there soon will be nothing left (<u>anymore</u>, any more) (accept, <u>except</u>) a few crumbs.

53. The (<u>eminent</u>, imminent, immanent) scientist made a (comprehensible, <u>comprehensive</u>) study of the subject before he (preceded, <u>proceeded</u>) to write his report.

54. When (setting, <u>sitting</u>) in church, you should be sure (and, <u>to</u>) maintain a posture that shows you are (respectable, <u>respectful</u>, respective) toward sacred things.

55. Since it (maybe, <u>may be</u>) that we shall (loose, <u>lose</u>) our way through this dark forest, I (<u>propose</u>, purpose) that we go around by the road.

(30 points)

K. Label each underlined phrase or clause by writing *prep.* (prepositional phrase), *vb.* (verbal phrase), *ps.* (phrase of a single part of speech), *D* (dependent clause), or *I* (independent clause) in the first blank. If it is a phrase or a dependent clause, write the abbreviation for its part of speech in the second blank.

<u>vb.</u> <u>adj.</u> 56. *Coleus,* a three-syllable word <u>accented on the first syllable</u>, names a genus of plants.

<u>prep.</u> <u>adv.</u> 57. This genus of plants is <u>in the mint family</u>.

<u>I</u> _____ 58. Although these plants are native to tropical Africa and Asia, <u>they are commonly grown in the United States</u>.

<u>vb.</u> <u>n.</u> 59. <u>To grow them in the temperate zone</u> requires protection from the cold.

<u>D</u> <u>adj.</u> 60. Many *Coleus* plants <u>that are grown in the United States</u> are sold for summer bedding plants.

<u>ps.</u> <u>n.</u> 61. <u>Coleus thyrsoideus</u> is one of the few flowering species in this genus.

(6 points)

L. Write the plural form of each noun. For numbers 69–73, use the foreign spellings.

___brothers-in-law___ 62. brother-in-law   ___loaves___ 68. loaf

___chairmen___ 63. chairman   ___fungi___ 69. fungus

___patios___ 64. patio   ___vertebrae___ 70. vertebra

___enemies___ 65. enemy   ___memoranda___ 71. memorandum

___trout___ 66. trout   ___vertices___ 72. vertex

___giraffes___ 67. giraffe   ___diagnoses___ 73. diagnosis

(12 points)

M. Rewrite these expressions, using possessive forms. If no possessive form should be used, write *X* in the blank.

___Jesus' teachings___ 74. the teachings of Jesus

___the apostles' writings___ 75. the writings of the apostles

___X___ 76. the door of the shed

___the women's work___ 77. the work of the women

___Lee's and Wilmer's essays___ 78. the essays of Lee and Wilmer (separate ownership)

___Ann and Sue's flower beds___ 79. the flower beds of Ann and Sue (joint ownership)

(6 points)

N. Underline the pronoun in each sentence, and label it *P* (personal), *CP* (compound personal), *D* (demonstrative), *ID* (indefinite), *IR* (interrogative), or *R* (relative).

_R_ 80. The person <u>who</u> fears the Lord enjoys a blessed security.

_P_ 81. To truly fear the Lord is to obey <u>His</u> holy Word.

_IR_ 82. <u>Whom</u> does the man of this world fear more than God?

_ID_ 83. The ungodly fear <u>anything</u> threatening to earthly securities.

_D_ 84. <u>That</u> is foolish indeed, for earthly securities are temporal.

_R_ 85. The only life <u>that</u> truly satisfies is a life of godly fear and obedience.

_CP_ 86. The godly person gives <u>himself</u> in dedication to God's purposes.

_ID_ 87. <u>Everyone</u> enduring faithfully to the end will receive an eternal reward.

(8 points)

O. Write the underlined expressions correctly. If the item is correct, write *correct*.

_____who_____ 88. The men <u>which</u> have been fighting that fire must be growing exhausted.

_____himself_____ 89. One man put <u>hisself</u> in grave danger to rescue a child.

_____whom_____ 90. We enjoyed visiting with the family <u>who</u> Father invited home for dinner.

_____I_____ 91. Lamar and <u>myself</u> have cleaned the inside of the van.

_____that_____ 92. Can you identify <u>that there</u> bird sitting on the bush beside the barn?

_____correct_____ 93. My oldest cousin is nearly thirty years older than <u>I</u>.

_____those_____ 94. The strawberries in this patch are Earliglow, but <u>them</u> are Surecrop.

(7 points)

P. Underline the correct words in parentheses.

95. The (mockingbird, <u>mockingbird's</u>) singing has such variety that it never becomes boring.

96. The large glass pitcher has (broke, <u>broken</u>) into myriad pieces.

97. This broom (don't, <u>doesn't</u>) work very well for sweeping up glass.

98. The gallows built for Mordecai (<u>was</u>, were) used for Haman instead.

99. Dorothy is the only one of my sisters who (have, <u>has</u>) red hair.

100. Arlen McVey has (went, <u>gone</u>) to Honduras for a term of service at the mission there.

101. We do not know who (<u>did</u>, done) this work while we were gone, but we are surely thankful.

102. "Wolves in the Flock" (<u>is</u>, are) a narrative poem.

103. Either of these colors (blend, <u>blends</u>) well with the background of your picture.

104. Two weeks (<u>is</u>, are) a long time to be snowed in.

105. Neither the river nor the smaller streams (was, <u>were</u>) frozen over this winter.

106. More than two-fifths of the class (was, <u>were</u>) absent because of the flu epidemic.

107. The pliers I am using (<u>need</u>, needs) to be adjusted.

108. The congregation (<u>have</u>, has) expressed their opinions on the matter.

109. The congregation (have, <u>has</u>) voted to buy new hymnals.

(15 points)

Q. In the first blank, write the tense of the underlined verb. In the second blank, write whether the verb is *TA* (transitive, active voice), *TP* (transitive, passive voice), *IC* (intransitive complete), or *IL* (intransitive linking).

_____present_____ _IC_ 110. The apricot tree is blooming beautifully.

_____future_____ _TA_ 111. The blossoms will fill the air with a wonderfully sweet fragrance.

present perfect _IL_ 112. The tea in these beds surely has grown tall and thick.

future perfect _TA_ 113. Before the summer is past, we shall have gathered enough tea leaves to freeze for our winter use.

_____past_____ _TP_ 114. The snake in the cellar was captured before Mother knew it was there.

past perfect _IL_ 115. These woods had been much thicker when Father was a boy.

(6 points)

R. If the underlined sentence part contains an error in using a form of comparison, write the correct form. If it is correct, write *correct*.

most beautiful 116. Mrs. Garver's tulips were the most beautifullest of all.

correct 117. Of the three containers, this one holds the least.

more nearly dead 118. The plants in this flat look more dead than those.

better 119. Both Olympia and Green Arrow are good varieties of peas, but we like Olympia best.

any other person 120. Uncle Stanley is taller than any person I know.

worst 121. All the rooms need repairs, but this one is worst.

less brightly 122. This lamp is shining less bright than I had expected it to.

prettier 123. Which of Nanny's twins has the prettiest markings?

(8 points)

S. Label the underlined words by writing *prep.* (preposition), *CC* (common coordinating conjunction), *Cor* (correlative conjunction), *SC* (subordinating conjunction), or *CA* (conjunctive adverb) in the blanks.

_SC_ 124. Since the Martin Nolt family moved, there are four boys in my grade at school.

Cor 125. The weatherman is predicting either rain or snow for tonight.

prep. 126. I have felt rather sick since early this morning.

_CA_ 127. I studied hard all year; nevertheless, the final test was demanding.

_CC_ 128. Most of the sections were not difficult, but the test did take a long time to complete.

(5 points)

T. Use proofreading marks to correct the errors in using conjunctions.

129. The three boys should both hoe the beans and the peppers.

130. After much practice, the younger students could sing the song both correctly and ~~with~~ enthusias~~m~~ _tically_.

131. The heifers not only broke through the fence but also trampled the garden.

(3 points)

U. Write *I* above each interjection. Use proofreading marks to show corrections in punctuation, capitalization, and italics.

132. _I_
   Ah that is just what I had expected.

133. _I_ _uc_
   Plop a large walnut landed on the leafy carpet of the woods.

134. _I_ _uc_
   Pain the pain was so severe that I hardly knew what to do.

(3 points)

Part II. Composition (83 points)

A. Circle *T* if the statement is true or *F* if it is false.

T **(F)** 1. You should save the least enjoyable assignments to do at the end of a study period.

(T) F 2. Good posture helps you to remain alert during a study period.

(T) F 3. Having a regular time to study helps to prepare your mind for study.

T **(F)** 4. To review actively, you need only to skim the material and see how much you remember.

T **(F)** 5. Skimming can become a useful method of mastering your school lessons without reading them closely.

T **(F)** 6. A good rule for taking notes on a sermon is "The more, the better."

T **(F)** 7. The main points of a topical outline should be capitalized as titles are.

(T) F 8. An item on an outline must never have only one subordinate point.

(T) F 9. Outlining is a good study aid because it forces a student to identify both the main ideas and the lesser ideas.

(T) F 10. The introductory paragraph of an expository essay should begin with a general statement and then narrow to the theme of the essay.

T **(F)** 11. You should write the statement of purpose for an expository essay after taking notes.

(T) F 12. Taking notes in short phrases, rather than in whole sentences, will help you to write your essay in your own words.

T **(F)** 13. Another name for the main character is *antagonist*.

T **(F)** 14. In the first person point of view, the author writes as if he were able to see every character equally well.

(T) F 15. In the third person point of view, the author follows one particular character through the story.

T **(F)** 16. If an author writes objectively, he reveals the thoughts of one or more story characters.

T **(F)** 17. Clichés are acceptable in the narrative parts of a story, but not in the dialogue.

(T) F 18. Any static description included in a story should be woven into a paragraph that carries the story action.

(T) F 19. To write that a story character began or started to do something is often poor because it unnecessarily arrests the character's action.

T **(F)** 20. To write the most effective description of a place, you should carefully research it in reference books.

(T) F 21. An effective description emphasizes only one main impression.

T **(F)** 22. A descriptive writer should use exact nouns and expressive verbs but try to avoid modifiers.

(T) F 23. Most descriptive writing is woven into other types of compositions, rather than standing alone as a descriptive essay.

T **(F)** 24. The label *informal* indicates a word that is spoken by a limited group of people.

(T) F 25. The label *archaic* indicates a word that is no longer in general use.

(T)F 26. For procedural matters such as approving the minutes, voting is often done by general consent.

T(F) 27. In a vote by acclamation, the chairman calls for the members to raise their right hands.

T(F) 28. Most properly worded motions begin with the words, "I make a motion."

(T)F 29. A chairman may defeat a motion by casting a vote that results in a tie.

T(F) 30. If a motion is pending, it has been put aside for further discussion later.

T(F) 31. If a motion is before the group, only a motion of lower rank may be presented.

T(F) 32. Motions must come to a vote in the same order in which they came before the group.

(32 points)

B. Write the correct term for each description.

__exposition (expository essay)__ 33. Type of composition that explains and leads the reader to say, "I understand."

__description (descriptive essay)__ 34. Type of composition that paints word pictures.

__plagiarism__ 35. Copying another person's writing and passing it off as your own.

__footnote__ 36. A credit for a source of a specific quotation, found at the bottom of the page or at the end of the essay.

__bibliography__ 37. A complete listing of the reference sources cited in an essay.

__ibid.__ 38. An abbreviation meaning "in the same place."

__theme__ 39. The lesson that a story teaches.

__conflict__ 40. The struggle or problem that the main character faces.

__chronological__ 41. The order usually followed in a description of an event.

__connotation__ 42. The "personality" of a word.

__etymology__ 43. A brief history of the origin of a word.

__inflection__ 44. A change in a word to show number or tense.

__Dewey decimal system__ 45. A method for classifying books into ten main categories.

__fiction__ 46. An imaginary story.

__biography__ 47. The life story of a specific individual.

__reference__ 48. Kind of book not read from cover to cover, but used to look up information.

__thesaurus__ 49. A book of synonyms (and sometimes of antonyms).

__political map__ 50. A map that shows boundaries of nations, states, and so forth.

__geographical map__ 51. A map that shows topography, land use, rainfall, and so forth.

_____the floor_____ 52. The right to address the assembly in a parliamentary meeting.

_____minutes_____ 53. The official record of a business meeting.

_____quorum_____ 54. The minimum number of members that must be present to transact business.

(22 points)

C. Do these exercises.

55. List the five points of the SQ3R study method. _____

   __Survey, Question, Read, Recite, Review.__

56. Give at least two reasons why it is wise to use more than one reference source in researching for an essay. (Any two reasons.)
   __(1) It helps to balance the essay by giving a wider scope of details.__

   __(2) It helps you to express your ideas in your own words.__

   __(3) It helps you to verify information.__

   __(4) It helps you to avoid misinterpreting facts.__

57. Name at least two types of information that you should credit at the bottom of the page or at the end of the essay. (Any two.)
   __(1) direct quotations;__

   __(2) details that the reader might question;__

   __(3) technical information__

58. What three things does a story setting include? _____

   __place, time, atmosphere__

59. Name five ways in which the author may portray his story characters. _____

   __actions; speech; thoughts; appearance; reputation__

60. What are three ways to keep story dialogue natural? _____

   __Keep the tone informal.__

   __Change speakers frequently.__

   __Use descriptive explanatory words.__

61. What two important cautions should you remember about using encyclopedias? _____

    Encyclopedias contain secular and humanistic ideas.

    They provide only general information about a particular subject.

    _____

62. Why must you use a library prudently? _____

    Many books in a public library are unwholesome to read.

63. List the four basic purposes of parliamentary procedure. _____

    to determine the true intent of the assembly;

    to allow full, free, and frank discussion;

    to give a fair hearing to the minority;

    to assure that the will of the majority is done

64. Why can we not use parliamentary procedure to determine what is truth? _____

    The Bible is the unchanging source of truth.

65. When is a two-thirds majority vote required to pass a motion? _____

    when the motion would limit free discussion on a matter

(29 points)

Total points: 280

Index

A

Abbreviations, 12, 33
Above, 144
Absolute possessive pronouns, 248
Absolute qualities, 368
Abstract nouns, 232
Accept, except, 144
Active verbs, 92–95, 420
Active voice, 152–153, 308–310
Adapt, adopt, 144–145
Addresses, 16–17
Adjectives
    appositive, 344
    articles, 342
    attributive, 344
    clauses, 347–348
    comparative degree, 367–369
    definition, 342
    demonstrative pronouns, 342
    descriptive, 343–344
    indefinite pronouns, 342
    infinitive phrases, 347
    infinitives, 343
    interrogative pronouns, 343
    limiting, 342–343
    needing commas, 344
    nouns used as, 343
    number words, 342
    objective complements, 85–86, 89–90
    participial phrases, 346–347
    participles, 343, 346–347
    position in sentences, 344
    positive degree, 367
    possessive nouns and pronouns, 343
    predicate, 344
    prepositional phrases, 346
    suffixes, 343
    superlative degree, 367–369
Adverbs
    clauses, 361–362
    comparative degree, 367–369
    conjunctive, 410
    definition, 351
    of degree, 351
    distinguishing between adverbs and prepositions, 406
    infinitive phrases, 360
    infinitives, 353–354
    introductory words, 355–357
    positive degree, 367
    prepositional phrases, 359–361
    relative, 347
    superlative degree, 367–369
    with verbals, 352
Advice, advise, 145
Agreement of pronouns and antecedents, 249
Agreement of subjects and verbs, 312–315
Ain't, 145
All, 145
All-, 33
Alliteration, 257–258
All right, 145
Allude, elude, refer, 145–146
Almanacs, 386
Almost, most, 146
Altar, alter, 146
Always, all ways, 148
Amendments, 431
Amount, number, 148
Angry about, at, with, 148–149
Antonyms, 377
Anymore, any more, 149
Apostrophes, 33
Appositive adjectives, 344
Appositives, 100
Archaic words, 247–249
Arguments, 329–330
Arrested action, 274–275
Articles, 342
As (if), like, 149
Atlases, 385–386
Attributive adjectives, 344
Audits, 430
Awhile, a while, 149

B

Balanced sentences, 105–106
Be, **forms of,** 92–95, 306
Believe, feel, 149

Be sure and, 150
Bibliographies, 136–139
Biographies, 395
Brackets, 32–33
Burst, bursted, busted, 150

C

Can, may, 150
Capitalization
    abbreviations, 10–12
    direct quotations, 10
    first word in sentence, 10
    I, 11–12
    initials, 10
    after interjections, 414
    in letters, 12
    O, 11–12
    outlines, 65
    personal pronouns for God, 10
    poetry, 10
    proper adjectives, 11
    proper nouns, 10–11
    seasons, 11
    titles, 11
    trademarks, 11
Card catalogs, 397–399
Cardinal numbers, 342
Case of pronouns, 246–250
Censor, censure, 155
Characterization, 206–209, 221–223
Charts
    compound personal pronouns, 249
    conjunctive adverbs, 410
    Dewey decimal system, 393–394
    evaluation of
        descriptive essays, 340
        expository essays, 140
        speaking style, 77
        stories, 286
        writing style, 21
    foreign plurals, 243
    interjections, 413
    parliamentary motions, 440–441
    point of view, 213
    prepositions, 404
    proofreading an essay, 133–134
    proofreading symbols, 108
    Roget's thesaurus, 379
    subordinating conjunctions, 412
    verb forms, 291, 310, T–482
    word usage list, Book 1, 142
    word usage list, Book 2, 143
Chronological order, 327

Clauses
    adjective, 347–348
    adverb, 361–362
    definition, 98
    dependent, 98
    elliptical, 290, 361
    independent, 98
    nonrestrictive, 348
    noun, 238–239
    relative, 347
    restrictive, 348
Clichés, 20, 269
Collective nouns, 314
Colons
    in business letters, 23
    to introduce, 23
    with numbers, 23
    with quotation marks, 28
Commas
    in addresses, 16–17
    with adjectives, 15, 344
    with appositives, 16
    in compound sentences, 14–15
    after conjunctive adverbs, 410
    in dates, 16–17
    with direct address, 16
    with direct quotations, 17
    after interjections, 15
    after introductory words, 15
    in letters, 17
    with nonrestrictive elements, 15–16
    in numbers, 17
    with parenthetical expressions, 15–16
    to prevent misunderstanding, 17
    with quotation marks, 28
    in series, 15
    with *yes* or *no,* 15
Common gender, 232, 249
Common nouns, 232
Comparative degree, 367–369
Compare to, with, 155
Comparison, forms of, 367–369
Complements
    object, 84–85
    objective, 85–86
    retained object, 88–89
    retained objective, 89–90
    subjective, 84–85
Complete predicates, 80
Complete sentences, 80–81
Complete subjects, 80
Complex sentences, 104
Complication plots, 213

Composition examples
Asa—Revival and Failure, 73–75
"He Rides Upon the Storm," 192–194
How Nevin Helped, 154–155
Room for Sixteen Children, 334–335
Should We Enter Sweepstakes? T–481
A Summary of "Modern Times," 58–59
Swiss Mennonite Encounters With Indians, 66–67
Terry's Temper, 190–192
Thanksgiving Vows, T–480
The Beautiful Nuisance, 114–116
The Pool of Siloam, 331
The Transfer of Heat, T–487, T–488
Twenty Pounds, 215–218
Who Were the Pharisees? 137–139
Compound-complex sentences, 104
Compound personal pronouns, 249–250
Compound relative pronouns, 254
Compound sentences, 104
Compound verbs, 290
Compound words, 33–34
Comprehensible, comprehensive, 155
Conclusion of a composition, 117–118
Concrete nouns, 232
Conflict in stories, 203–204, 222, 224–225
Conjugations, 296
Conjunctions
coordinating, 408–410
correlative, 409–410
subordinating, 412–413
Conjunctive adverbs, 410
Connotation, 380–381
Contemptible, contemptuous, 155
Continual, continuous, 156
Contractions, 33, 312
Coordinating conjunctions, 408–410
Correlative conjunctions, 409–410
Could (should, would) of, 156
Council, counsel, 156
Courtesy, 250, 390–391

D

Dashes
for interruptions, 31
with other punctuation marks, 32
with quotation marks, 28
Dates, 16–17
Declarative sentences, 10–12, 104
Definitions, 375–376
Degrees of comparison, 367–369
Demonstrative pronouns, 252–253
Denotation, 380–381

Derivatives, 377
Descriptive adjectives, 343–344
Descriptive writing, 322–324, 325–327, 328–330, 331–333, 334–335, 339
Dewey decimal system, 392–395
Diagraming
adverbs, 351–353, 356
gerunds and gerund phrases, 236–237
infinitives and infinitive phrases, 237–238
noun clauses, 238–239
objective complements, 85
prepositional phrases, 238, 406
subjects of infinitives, 247–248
verbs, 306
Dialectal words, 376
Dialogue, 266–268
Dictionaries, 374–377
Differ from, with, 156
Dilemma, 156
Direct address, 100
Direct objects, 84
Direct quotations, 27–28
Disinterested, uninterested, 156–157
Distinguishing parts of speech, 101–102, 236, 238, 406
Double comparisons, 368

E

Editing skills, 36–37, 61–62, 108–109, 131, 172–173, 198, 282, 317–318, 336, 435–436
Ellipsis points, 24–25
Elliptical clauses, 290, 361
Elliptical sentences, 81
Elude, allude, refer, 145–146
Eminent, imminent, immanent, 159
Emphasis in sentences, 105–106
Emphatic verb forms, 309–310
Encyclopedias, 384–385
Ending of a story, 223, 225
End punctuation, 12
Enormity, 160
Enthused, 160
Enthusiasm, 387–389
Entry words, 374–375
Etymologies, 376–377
Evaluation charts, 21, 77, 140, 286, 340
Everyday, every day, 160
Except, accept, 144
Exclamation points
after exclamatory sentences, 12
after interjections, 12
with quotation marks, 28

Exclamations, 101
Exclamatory sentences, 12, 104
Expletives, 100–101
Expositions, 328–329
Expository essays
   bibliographies, 136–139
   definition, 114
   finding information, 122–123
   footnotes, 135–139
   form of, 116–118, 134–139
   limiting the topic, 120
   organizing main points, 125
   proofreading, 133–134
   purpose of, 114
   reference sources, 122–123
   standard layout, 134–135
   structure of, 116–118
   taking notes, 122–124
   titles, 129
   writing, 126–130
Eye contact, 76–77

F
Fabulous, 160
Feel, believe, 149
Feminine gender, 232, 249
Fiction, 390
First person point of view, 210–213
Flashbacks, 204, 222, 225
Flaunt, flout, 160
Floor, the, 429
Footnotes, 135–139
Foreign plural endings, 243
Foreign words, 29
Formal quotations, 23
Formal writing
   abbreviations, 12
   contractions, 33
   like, as, 149
   shall, will, 294
Fractions, 33
Fragments, sentence, 80–81
Friendly letters, 17
Future perfect tense, 295
Future tense, 294

G
Gender of nouns, 232
Gender of pronouns, 249
Gerund phrases, 96
Gerunds, 235–237
Good, well, 160–161

Great-, 33
Guide words, 374

H
Haven't but, only, 161
Heap, heaps, 161
Hopefully, 161
How come, 164
Hyperboles, 280–281, 323–324
Hyphens, 33–34

I
I, 11–12
Ibid., 136
Idioms, 416–417
Illiterate words, 376
Imagery, 323–324
Imminent, eminent, immanent, 159
Impact, 164
Imperative mood, 299
Imperative sentences, 104
Imply, infer, 164
In back of, 164
Indefinite pronouns
   as adjectives, 342
     possessive forms, 255
     singular and plural, 254–255
Independent elements, 100–102
Indicative mood, 299
Indirect objects, 85
Indirect questions, 12
Infer, imply, 164
Infinitive phrases, 97
Infinitives, 237–238, 343, 353–354
Inflections, 376
Informal tone, 266–267, 381
Informal usage, 144
Informal words, 376
Ingenious, ingenuous, 165
Initials, 10–12
-In-law, 33
Intensive pronouns, 249
Interjections, 413–414
Interrogative pronouns, 254
Interrogative sentences, 104
Intransitive verbs, 305–306
Introduction of a composition, 116–118
Inverted word order, 105
It, 100
Italics, 29
Its, it's, 165

K

Kind (sort) of, 165

L

Lay, lie, 165
Let, leave, 165
Libraries, 390–391, 392–395, 397–399
Like, 149
Limiting adjectives, 342–343
Linking verbs, 305–306
Loose, lose, 166
Loose plots, 213
Loose sentences, 105
-Ly endings, 352–353

M

Main motions, 432
Masculine gender, 232, 249
Maybe, may be, 168
May, can, 150
Metaphors, 280
Mild interjections, 414
Minutes of meetings, 429–430
Mixed word order, 105
Modifiers, 342–344, 351–354
Momentarily, 168–169
Moods of verbs, 298–302
Motions, 431–432
My, mine, 249

N

Narration, 328
Natural word order, 105
Neuter gender, 232, 249
Nice, 169
Nominative absolutes, 101, 102
Nominative case pronouns, 247
Nonfiction, 390
Nonrestrictive appositives, 100
Nonrestrictive elements, 15–16
Nonrestrictive modifiers, 348
Nonstandard words, 376
Notable, noted, noteworthy, notorious, 169
Notes, taking, 56–58, 122–124
Not only, but also, 409
Nouns
    abstract, 232
    as adjectives, 343
    appositives, 100
    clauses, 238–239
    collective, 314
    common, 232
    concrete, 232
    definition, 232
    direct address, 100
    gender, 232
    plural forms, 241–243
    possessive, 243–245
    proper, 232
    suffixes, 233
    verbals, 235–238
Number, amount, 148
Number of pronouns, 246
Numbers, 17
Number words, 33, 342

O

O, 11–12
Object complements, 84–85, 88–89
Objective case pronouns, 247–248
Objective complements, 85–86, 89–90
Objective viewpoint, 212–213
Objects
    direct, 84
    indirect, 85
    retained, 88–89
Obsolete words, 376
Officers of business meetings, 429–430
Of, used with verbs, 156
OK, okay, 169
Omissions, 24–25
Omniscient point of view, 211–213
Onomatopoeia, 258, 323–324
Opening of a story, 222, 224
Ordinal numbers, 342
Organizing notes, 125–126
Originality, 19–22
Outlines
    chronological, 72, 73–74
    for compositions, 125–126
    content of, 64–66
    definition, 64
    form of, 64–65
    headings, 65–66
    logical order, 125–126
    main topics, 121, 125
    parallel structure, 65–66
    topical, 74–76
    writing, 65–68, 71–73, 125–126
Over with, 169

P

Parentheses, 31–32
Parenthetical expressions, 31–32

Parliamentary motions, 438–442

Parliamentary procedure, 424–428, 429–432, 438–442

Participial phrases, 346–347

Participles, 346–347

Parts of speech. *See individual parts of speech.*

Passive voice, 305–306, 309–310

Past forms of verbs, 291

Past participles, 291

Past perfect tense, 294–295

Past tense, 293

Pending, 438

Perfect verb tenses, 294–296

Periodic sentences, 105

Periods

    with abbreviations, 12

    at ends of sentences, 12

    after initials, 12

    in outlines, 65

    with quotation marks, 28

Persecute, prosecute, 169

Personal pronouns, 246–250

Personification, 280, 323–324

Person of pronouns, 246

Perspective, prospective, 169

Phrases

    adjective, 346–348

    adverb, 359–361

    definition, 96

    gerund, 96

    infinitive, 97, 347, 360

    participial, 97, 346–347

    prepositional, 96, 346, 359–360

    single part of speech, 97

    verb, 290

    verbal, 96–97

Plagiarism, 123

Plots, 213

Plural nouns

    abbreviations, 33

    archaic endings, 243

    compound nouns, 242–243

    foreign endings, 243

    irregular forms, 243

    letters and figures, 33

    numbers with several digits, 33

    regular forms, 241–243

    words as words, 33

Poetic devices, 257–259

Point of view, 210–213, 327

Poorly, 170

Positive degree, 367

Possessive nouns, 243–245

Possessive pronouns

    indefinite, 255

    personal, 248–249

    relative, 254

Precedence of motions, 438–441

Precede, proceed, 170

Predicate adjectives, 344

Predicate nominatives, 84

Prepositional phrases, 404–406

Prepositions, 404–406

Present forms of verbs, 291

Present participles, 292

Present perfect tense, 294

Present tense, 293

President, 10

Principal parts of verbs, 291

Progressive verb forms, 308–310

Pronouns, 246–250, 252–255

Pronunciations, 375

Proofreading, 133–134, 285, 339

Proofreading marks, 36–37, 61–62

Proper nouns, 232

Propose, purpose, 175

Punctuation

    apostrophes, 33

    brackets, 32–33

    colons, 23

    commas, 14–17

    dashes, 31

    ellipsis points, 24–25

    exclamation points, 12

    hyphens, 33–34

    italics, 29

    parentheses, 31–32

    periods, 12

    question marks, 12

    quotation marks, 27–29

    semicolons, 23–24

Q

Question marks

    after interrogative sentences, 12

    within parentheses, 12

    with quotation marks, 28–29

Quorum, 430–431

Quotation marks, 27–29

Quotations, 24–25, 27–29, 32

Quote, 175

R

Raise, rise, 175–176

Readers' Guide to Periodical Literature, 399

Receipt, recipe, 176
Refer, allude, elude, 145–146
Reference books
    almanacs, 386
    atlases, 385–386
    dictionaries, 374–377
    encyclopedias, 384–385
    library classification, 393–395
    thesauruses, 378–380
References following quotations, 28
Reflexive pronouns, 249
Regional words, 376
Relative adverbs, 347
Relative clauses, 347
Relative pronouns, 253–254
Repeated words, 102
Repetition of similar syllables, 364–365
Respectable, respectful, respective, 176
Restrictive appositives, 100
Restrictive modifiers, 348
Retained object complements, 88–89
Retained objective complements, 89–90
Review exercises
    adverbs, 392, 411–412
    capitalization, 18, 30–31, 83
    classes of sentences, 189, 234–235
    colons, semicolons, and ellipsis points, 35, 55, 91, 358
    commas, 27, 46, 87–88, 241, 383, 419
    complements, 99, 246, 350
    descriptions, 401
    expository essays, 205–206, 272, 428–429
    modifiers that compare, 383-384, 419
    moods of verbs, 317, 363, 407–408
    nominative absolutes, 108, 148, 197–198, 311–312, 370
    participial phrases, 108, 148, 197–198, 311, 370, 383, 418
    parts of speech, 14
    plural nouns, 252, 293
    possessive nouns, 256–257, 293, 297–298
    pronouns, 262–263, 304, 345–346
    punctuation, 27, 35, 46, 55–56, 87–88, 91–92, 241, 358–359, 383, 419
    retained complements, 99, 246, 350
    stories, 278, 396–397
    study skills, 70–71, 103, 122, 387–388
    subjunctive mood, 317, 363, 407–408
    tenses of verbs, 307–308, 434–435
    transitive and intransitive verbs, 378, 416
    verb forms, 355, 435
    word usage, 152, 159, 163–164, 168, 172, 179, 183
    writing style, 259, 366

Rhyme, 258
Rhythm, 364–365
Right along, 176
Run-in entries, 417
Run-on errors, 81

S

Scripture references, 23, 32–34
Self-, 33
Semicolons, 23–24, 28
Sentence rhythm, 364–365
Sentences
    balanced, 105–106
    complements, 83–86
    complete, 80–81
    complex, 104
    compound, 104
    compound-complex, 104
    declarative, 104
    definition, 80
    elliptical, 81
    exclamatory, 104
    first word, 10
    fragments, 80–81
    imperative, 104
    interrogative, 104
    loose, 105
    periodic, 105
    simple, 104
    skeletons, 80
    types, 105–106
    word order, 105
Sentence styles, 104–106
Series
    adjective–noun combinations, 34
    connected numbers, 34
    items with commas, 24
    words, phrases, or clauses, 15
Set, sit, 176
Setting of stories, 201–202
-S **forms of verbs,** 292
Shall, will, 294
Similes, 280, 323
Simple predicates, 80
Simple sentences, 104
Simple subjects, 80
Simple verb forms, 308–310
Simple verb tenses, 293–294
Single quotation marks, 27–28
Skeletons of sentences, 80
Skimming, 52–54

Slang words, 376
So-called, 28
Some, somewhat, 177, 268–270
Spatial order, 327
Speaking style
    enthusiasm, 387–389
    eye contact, 76–77
    facial expression, 389
    gestures, 389
    posture, 389
    voice control, 226–227
Spellings, 374–375
SQ3R method, 47–49
Standard word usage, 144
Static description, 273–274
Stationary, stationery, 177
Statistical almanacs, 386
Stories
    action verbs, 272–276
    arrested action, 274–275
    characterization, 206–209, 221–223
    conflict, 203–204, 222, 224–225
    descriptive words, 279–281
    dialogue, 266–268
    ending of, 223, 225
    fiction, 196
    flashbacks, 204, 225
    imagery, 280–281
    informal tone, 266–267
    main characters, 202–203, 206–209
    message of, 189–196
    opening of, 222, 224
    planning, 219–221, 221–223
    plot, 213
    point of view, 210–213
    proofreading, 285
    purpose of, 186, 194–195
    secondary characters, 206–207
    setting, 201–202
    static description, 273–274
    structure of, 201–204
    style, 266–270
    theme, 195–196
    titles, 225
    word choice, 279–280
    writer, 186–188
    writing, 224–225
Storywriters, 186–188
Straight, strait, 177
Study skills
    attitudes, 42–43
    environment, 44–45
    interest, 42–43
    outlining, 64–68
    posture, 45
    self-discipline, 43
    skimming, 52–54
    SQ3R method, 47–49
    summarizing, 56–59
    taking notes, 56–58
    time schedules, 43–44
Subjective complements, 84–85
Subjective viewpoint, 212–213
Subjects of infinitives, 247–248
Subject–verb agreement, 312–315
Subjunctive mood, 299–302
Subordinating conjunctions, 412–413
Substandard words, 376
Substantives, 260–261
Suffixes
    adjective, 343
    noun, 233
Summarizing, 56–59
Superlative degree, 367–369
Syllable divisions, 34, 375
Synonyms, 377, 378–382

T
Taking notes, 56–58, 122–124
Tenses of verbs, 293–296
Than, then, 179
That, 252–253
The floor, 429
Them, 180
There is (are, was, were), 92–93
Thesauruses, 378–380
Third person point of view, 210–213
This (these) here, that (those) there, 180
Thy, thine, 249
Titles
    appealing, 129
    capitalization, 11
    punctuation, 27–29
    with singular verbs, 314
    of stories, 225
Topical outlines, 72–73, 74–76
Trademarks, 11
Transitional words, 16
Transitive verbs, 304–306
Transpire, 180
Try and, 180
Type of, 165

U

Underlining, 29
Uninterested, disinterested, 156–157
Usage labels, 144, 376
Usage of words. *See individual words.*

V

Vehicle names, 29
Verbal phrases, 96–97
Verbals, 235–238, 343, 353–354
Verbs
    active, 92–95, 420
    active voice, 152–153, 308–310
    agreement with subjects, 312–315
    chart, 291, 310
    compound, 290
    conjugations, 296
    definition, 290
    emphatic forms, 309–310
    first principal part, 291
    future perfect tense, 295
    future tense, 294
    imperative mood, 299
    indicative mood, 299
    intransitive, 305–306
    linking, 305–306
    passive voice, 305–306, 309–310
    past forms, 291
    past participles, 291
    past perfect tense, 294–295
    past tense, 293
    perfect tenses, 294–296
    phrases, 290
    present forms, 291
    present participles, 292
    present perfect tense, 294
    present tense, 293
    principal parts, 291
    progressive forms, 308–310
    second principal part, 291
    -s forms, 292
    simple forms, 308–310
    simple tenses, 293–294
    subjunctive mood, 299–302
    third principal part, 291
    transitive, 304–306
Viewpoints, 210–213
Voice control, 226–227
Voice of verbs, 308–310
Voting procedures, 431–432
Vulgar words, 376

W

Want in, off, out, through, 180
Way, ways, 180
Well, good, 160–161
What for, 181
Whether, or, 409–410
Who, whom, whose, which, 253–254
Words
    antonyms, 377
    archaic, 247–249
    compound, 33–34
    descriptive, 322–324, 343
    dialectal, 376
    entry, 374–375
    exact, 323
    foreign, 29
    guide, 374
    illiterate, 376
    informal, 376
    interjections, 413–414
    metaphors, 280
    nonstandard, 376
    obsolete, 376
    onomatopoeia, 258, 323–324
    regional, 376
    similes, 280, 323
    slang, 376
    substandard, 376
    synonyms, 377, 378–382
    transitional, 16
    vulgar, 376
    as words, 29
Word usage. *See individual words.*
Worst kind, sort, way, 181
Would **phrases,** 302
Writing style, 19–22, 92–95, 152–153, 257–259, 364–365, 419–421
Writing
    descriptions, 322–324, 325–327, 328–330, 331–333, 334–335, 339
    dialogue, 266–268
    expositions, 119–121, 122–124, 125–126, 126–130, 133–134, 134–139
    outlines, 64–68, 125–126
    stories, 219–221, 221–223, 224–225, 266–270, 272–276, 279–281, 285
    summaries, 56–59

Y

Your, you're, 181